湖北统计年鉴

HUBEI STATISTICAL YEARBOOK

2014

（总第30期）

湖 北 省 统 计 局
国家统计局湖北调查总队 编

中国统计出版社
China Statistics Press

图书在版编目（CIP）数据

湖北统计年鉴.2014 / 湖北省统计局，国家统计局湖北调查总队编
- 北京：中国统计出版社，2014.8
ISBN 978-7-5037-7197-2

Ⅰ. ①湖…
Ⅱ. ①湖…②国…
Ⅲ. ①统计资料-湖北省-2014-年鉴-汉-英
Ⅳ. ①C832.63-54

中国版本图书馆CIP数据核字（2014）第182571号

湖北统计年鉴—2014

作　　者 / 湖北省统计局　国家统计局湖北调查总队
责任编辑 / 佘竞雄　邓有成　周家庆　王　道
封面设计 / 刘亚非
出版发行 / 中国统计出版社
地　　址 / 北京市丰台区西三环南路甲6号
邮　　编 / 100073
电　　话 / 邮购（010）63376909　书店（010）68786171
网　　址 / http://csp.stats.gov.cn
印　　刷 / 湖北省统计局印刷厂
经　　销 / 新华书店
开　　本 / 890×1240毫米 1/16
字　　数 / 1240千字
印　　张 / 39
印　　数 / 2000册
版　　别 / 2014年8月第1版
版　　次 / 2014年8月第1次印刷
定　　价 / 380元

编 辑 说 明

一、《湖北统计年鉴—2014》是一本信息密集的资料工具书。通过大量数据，全面地分析、记载和反映了湖北省2013年经济、社会、科技、文化等方面的发展情况。具有信息量大、权威性强、适用性广等特点。

二、本年鉴包括综合、人口、从业人员和职工工资、固定资产投资、能源生产和消费、物价指数、人民生活、资源和环境、城市概况、农业、工业、建筑业、运输和邮电、国内贸易、对外经济和旅游、财政、金融和保险业、教育、科技和文化、体育、卫生、社会福利、湖北省开发区主要经济指标、武汉城市圈、鄂西生态文化旅游圈、县市概况、附录等23个部分。

三、2014年的湖北统计年鉴，篇章结构与《中国统计年鉴》保持一致，参照执行了国家统计局《省级统计年鉴指标体系目录》，采用了最新的国民经济行业分类标准和指标口径，并对英文注释和指标解释进行了全面修订。

四、本年鉴对过去发表的统计资料重新予以审核，凡与本年鉴资料有出入的，均以本年鉴为准。本年鉴中统计公报的数据为初步数，若与年鉴正文数据不一致，请以正文数据为准。涉及经济普查的核算、建筑、工业、贸易等部分数据为快报数。

五、年鉴中指标的使用要结合文中的指标解释，以及注解合理使用，以免发生错误。

六、《湖北统计年鉴》公开出版以来，受到国内外读者的爱护与支持，对本年鉴的内容和编辑工作提出了许多宝贵意见，为此，我们特表谢意。由于水平有限，编辑工作中难免有疏误之处，竭诚欢迎读者批评指正。

COMPLIERS NOTES

I. *Statistical Yearbook of Hubei* 2014 is an information-intensive data reference book. Through a large amount of data, comprehensive analysis, records and reflects the Hubei province 2013 economy, society, science and technology, culture and other aspects of development. With a large amount of information, authoritative, wide applicability and so on.

II. The Yearbook includes comprehensive, population, practitioners and staff salaries, fixed assets investment, energy production and consumption, price index, the life of people and natural resources and the environment, city situation, agriculture, industry, construction, transportation, post and telecommunications, domestic trade, foreign economy and tourism, finance, banking and insurance, education, science and culture, sports, public health, social welfare, Hubei Province Development Zone of main economic norms, Wuhan city circle, ecological cultural tourism circle of Western Hubei, county profiles, Appendix 23 departments, city of part of the Department of city information, not including the city administer county.

III. In the 2014 statistical yearbook of Hubei, discourse structure and "China Statistical Yearbook" remain the same, with reference to the implementation of the "provincial statistics index system directory". The statistic of yearbook adopted the lastest standard and diameter range. And the English version and the interpretation of indicators were revised thoroughy.

IV. The Yearbook of the past published statistical data to examine every and the almanac data discrepancies, refer to this yearbook prevail. The Yearbook of statistics data for the initial count, if the Yearbook text data are not consistent, please refer to the text data is accurate.

V. In the annals of indicators are used to combine the interpretation of indicators, as well as annotations and reasonable use, so as to avoid mistakes.

VI. *Statistical Yearbook of Hubei* published since, by domestic and foreign readers to care and support, the Yearbook content and editorial work put forward a lot of valuable advice, for this, we express our gratitude. Because the level is limited, in the editing work of unavoidable errors, we welcome suggestions and criticisms.

《湖北统计年鉴-2014》

编委会和编辑出版人员

一、编委会

二、编辑工作人员

Hubei Statistical Yearbook – 2014

EDITORIAL BOARD AND STAFF

目　　录

CONTENTS

2 人 口

POPULATION

3 就业人员和职工工资

EMPLOYMENT AND WAGES

4　固定资产投资

INVESTMENT IN FIXED ASSETS

5 对外经济贸易和旅游

FOREIGN ECONOMIC，TRADE AND TOURISM

6 能 源

ENERGY

7 财政、金融、保险

GOVERNMENT FINANCE， BANKING AND INSURANCE

8 价 格

PRICE

9 居民生活

PEPOLE'S LIVELIHOOD

10　城市概况

CITY OVERVIEW

11 资源和环境

RESOURCES AND ENVIRONMENT

12 农　业

AGRICULTURE

13 工业

INDUSTRY

14 建筑业

CONSTRUCTION

15 交通运输、邮电

TRANSPORTATION, POSTAL AND TELECOMMUNICATIONS SERVICES

16 国内贸易

DOMESTIC TRADE

17　科技和教育

SCIENCE，TECHNOLOGY AND EDUCATION

18 卫生和社会服务

HEALTH AND SOCIAL SERVICES

19 文化和体育

CULTURE AND SPORTS

20　公共管理及其他

PUBLIC ADMINISTRATION AND OTHER

2013年湖北省国民经济和社会发展统计公报

湖　北　省　统　计　局

国家统计局湖北调查总队

2013年是全面落实党的十八大和省第十次党代会精神的第一年，是扎实推进“五个湖北”建设的起步之年。面对国际经济形势环境复杂多变，国内经济下行压力加大，我省经济较长时间低于发展预期的严峻形势，全省人民在省委、省政府的坚强领导下，坚持以党的十八大和习近平总书记考察湖北重要讲话精神为指导，始终坚持“竞进提质、效速兼取”不动摇，凝神聚力，沉着应对，攻坚克难，砥砺奋进，经济社会发展呈现“总体平稳、稳中有进、进中向好”的良好态势，为全面建成小康社会奠定了扎实基础。

一、综 合

2013年，全省完成生产总值24668.49亿元，按可比价格计算，比上年增长10.1%。其中：第一产业完成增加值3098.16亿元，增长4.7%；第二产业完成增加值12171.56亿元，增长11.3%；第三产业完成增加值9398.77亿元，增长10.0%。三次产业结构由2012年的12.8：50.3：36.9 调整为12.6 :49.3:38.1 。在第三产业中交通运输仓储和邮政业、批发

2013年，全省完成生产总值24668.49亿元，按可比价格计算，比上年增长10.1%。其中：第一产业完成增加值3098.16亿元，增长4.7%；第二产业完成增加值12171.56亿元，增长11.3%；第三产业完成增加值9398.77亿元，增长10.0%。三次产业结构由2012年的12.8：50.3：36.9 调整为12.6 :49.3:38.1 。在第三产业中交通运输仓储和邮政业、批发和零售业、住宿和餐饮业、金融业、房地产业、营利性服务业及非营利性服务业增加值分别增长10.5%、7.9%、4.9%、15.6%、10.2%、11.8%和8.9%。

全省居民消费价格总指数（CPI）为102.8，价格水平上涨2.8%，其中：城市上涨2.7%，农村上涨3.0%。分类别看，食品上涨4.9%，烟酒及用品上涨0.5%，衣着上涨2.2%，家庭设备用品及维修服务上涨1.9%，医疗保健及个人用品上涨2.1%，交通和通信下跌0.6%，娱乐教育文化用品及服务上涨1.5%，居住上涨3.1%。全年农业生产资料价格上涨3.1%。工业生产者出厂价格下降0.8%，工业生产者购进价格下降1.8%。

市场主体发展加快。2013年，全省新登记市场主体109.04万户，增长73.5%，其中：新登记私营企业13.13万户，增长90.8%；新登记个体工商户93.54万户，增长73.8%。

据省人力资源和社会保障部门统计，年末全省城镇登记失业率为3.49%，比上年末下降0.34个百分点。

二、农业

全年全省农林牧渔业增加值按可比价格计算，比上年增长4.7%。粮食种植面积425.84万公顷，比上年增加7.83万公顷；棉花种植面积41.56万公顷，减少5.73万公顷；油料种植面积151.7万公顷，增加1.54万公顷。粮食总产量2501.3万吨，

比上年增产 59.49 万吨，增长 2.4%；棉花总产量 45.97 万吨，减产 8.56 万吨，下降 15.7%；油料产量 333.17 万吨，增产 13.51 万吨，增长 4.2%（主要农产品产量见表 1）。

2013 年全省主要农产品产量

表 1　　单位：万吨

产品名称	产　量	比上年增长%
粮　食	2501.30	2.4
棉　花	45.97	−15.7
油　料	333.17	4.2
#花　生	68.11	−8.4
油菜籽	250.47	8. 9
茶　叶	22.20	7.2
水　果(不含果用瓜)	569.42	5.1
蔬　菜	3578.31	2.1

畜牧、水产业稳步增长。全年全省生猪出栏 4356.43 万头，增长 4.2%；水产品产量达到 410.38 万吨，增长 5.5%。

三、工业和建筑业

工业生产保持稳定增长。2013 年年末，全省规模以上工业企业达到 13441 家，比上年净增 2107 家，增长 18.6%。完成工业增加值按可比价格计算，比上年增长 11.8%。其中：国有及国有控股企业增长 8.0%；集体企业增长 11.1%；股份合作企业增加值 38.87 亿元，增长 11.9%；外商及港澳台投资企业增长 7.4%；其他经济类型企业增长 11.2%。轻工业增长 11.7%；重工业增长 11.8%（主要工业产品产量见表 2）。

2013 年主要工业产品产量

表 2

产品名称	单位	产　量	比上年增长%
纱	万　吨	302.00	7. 9
布	亿　米	79.25	12.6
化　纤	万　吨	21.67	20.1
卷　烟	亿　支	1397.99	2.2
家用电冰箱	万　台	226.07	11.7
房间空调器	万　台	1189.37	46.7
原　油	万　吨	80.08	1.5
发电量	亿千瓦小时	2118.82	−2.3
#水电	亿千瓦小时	1153.51	−14.1
钢	万　吨	3000.98	1.1
钢　材	万　吨	3344.92	−5.8
十种有色金属	万　吨	107.82	11.3
其中：精炼铜	万　吨	50.25	36.5
水　泥	万　吨	11056.52	5.3
硫　酸	万　吨	680.11	4.6
纯　碱	万　吨	132.22	−3.9
烧　碱	万　吨	99.23	23.0
化　肥（折 100%）	万　吨	1186.69	10.0
发电设备	万千瓦	145.70	−37.5
汽　车	万　辆	158.70	9.6
#轿　车	万　辆	66.59	8.3
移动通信手持机	万　台	714.76	70.6

工业产品结构改善，高新技术制造业增长较快，全年完成增加值 3267.06 亿元，比上年增长 16.5%，占规模以上工业增加值的比重达 29.3%。

工业产销衔接较好，经济效益继续提高。全年全省工业完成销售产值 37078.1 亿元，比上年增长 17.5%，其中：农副食品加工业、饮料和精制茶制造业、纺织、化学原料和化学制品制造业、建材、钢铁、有色、金属制造业、通用设备制造业、汽车、电气机械制造业、电子设备制造业、电力等重点行业实现销售产值超千亿元。工业产品销售率为 97.3%。全年全省工业企业实现利润 2080.66 亿元，增长 26.4%；其中国有控股工业实现利润 695.34 亿元，增长 19.9%。

建筑业发展步伐加快。全年全省资质以内建筑企业完成施工产值 8343.40 亿元，比上年增长 18.5%；实现利润 335.19 亿元，增长 20.5%；税金 299.50 亿元，增长 17.7%。新开工房屋建筑施工面积 26552.71 万平方米，增长 18.6%。

四、固定资产投资

2013 年全省完成固定资产投资(不含农户) 20177.45 亿元，比上年增长 25.8% ，其中房地产开发投资完成 3286.02 亿元，增长 29.4%，商品房销售面积 5298.54 万平方米，增长 31.2 %，实现商品房销售额 2790.32 亿元，增长 37.0%。按产业划分，全省一、二、三次产业投资分别为 404.63 亿元、 9187.25 亿元和 10585.57 亿元，分别增长 3.5 %、26.2%、26.4 %。全省 589 个在建重点建设项目全年完成投资 3199.51 亿元，占全社会固定资产投资的比重为 15.4 %。

五、国内贸易

全年全省实现社会消费品零售总额 10465.94 亿元，比上年增长 13.8%。分城乡看，城镇实现零售额 8851.85 亿元，增长 13.5 %；乡村实现零售额 1614.10 亿元，增长 15.2%。其中，限额以上企业（单位）实现消费品零售额 5096.49 亿元，增长 16.6%。

六、对外经济

全年全省实现外贸进出口总额 363.90 亿美元，比上年增长 13.8%，其中：出口 228.38 亿美元，增长 17.7 %；进口 135.52 亿美元，增长 7.9%。新批外商直接投资项目 297 个。全年外商直接投资 68.88 亿美元，增长 21.6%。

七、交通运输、邮电通信和旅游

全年全省完成货物周转量 4883.01 亿吨公里，比上年增长 12.2 %；旅客周转量 1761.10 亿人公里，增长 11.7%。

全省邮电业务总量 547.34 亿元，增长 11.4 %。长途光缆线路总长度达到 2.81 万公里；局用交换机达到 1482.60 万门；固定电话用户 984.00 万户；移动电话用户达到 4416.80 万户；全省电话普及率为 93 部／百人；计算机宽带互联网用户 813.30 万户。

全年全省国内旅游人数 40621.04 万人次，比上年增长 18.7%；国内旅游收入 3130.13 亿元，增长 22.6%。入境旅游人数 267.96 万人次，增长 1.2%。国际旅游外汇收入 12.19 亿美元，增长 1.3%。

八、财政、金融和保险

全年全省完成财政总收入 3565.10 亿元，比上年增长 15.4%，其中地方公共财政预算收入 2189.98 亿元，增长 20.1%。在地方公共财政预算收入中，税收收入 1603.69 亿元，增长 21.1%。全年财政支出 4330.63 亿元，增长 15.2%。

年末全省金融机构各项存款余额32902.83亿元，比年初增加4641.89亿元。其中：个人存款15972.15亿元，增加2363.03亿元。金融机构各项贷款余额21902.55亿元，比年初增加3001.96亿元。其中：短期贷款7857.28亿元，增加1519.00亿元；中长期贷款13127.20亿元，增加1431.54亿元。

全年保费收入712.12亿元，增长19.6%。其中，财产险公司实现保费收入181.86亿元，增长27.7%；人身险公司保费收入530.27亿元，增长17.1%。支付各类赔款及给付191.47亿元，增长40.8%，其中，财产险公司赔款90.99亿元，增长27.7%；人身险公司赔付100.49亿元，增长55.1%。

九、教育和科学技术

2013年末，全省普通高等教育招生40.39万人，在校生142.14万人，毕业生36.16万人；研究生招生3.9万人，在校研究生11.27万人，毕业生3.46万人；各类中等职业教育招生17.01万人，在校生51.56万人，毕业生23.61万人；普通高中招生31.65万人，在校生98.82万人，毕业生39.12万人；普通初中在校生148.37万人，小学在校生328.26万人，幼儿园在园幼儿147.34万人。

科学研究和技术开发取得新的成果。全年全省共取得省部级以上科技成果1621项。其中，基础理论成果22项，应用技术成果1570项，软科学成果29项。全年共签订技术合同14909项，技术合同成交金额418.74亿元，增长78.5%。

全省科学研究与实验发展(R&D)经费支出450亿元，增长17%，占全省生产总值的1.8%。全年安排“973”计划项目169项（课题），经费1.9亿元，“863”计划项目102项(课题)，经费1.9亿元。争取国家高技术产业发展项目28个，项目总投资57.6亿元，安排国家资金11.4亿元。

全省具备向社会出具检测报告的产品质量监督检验机构有135个，其中国家产品质量监督检验中心20个。全省通过CNAL认可的检测/校准实验室135家。累计有7832家企业通过ISO9000体系认证；企业获得强制性认证证书8550张。法定计量技术机构有138个，强制检定计量器具181万台件。

全省天气雷达观测站点有11个，卫星云图接受站点17个。数字测震台网2个，地震台站48个。

十、文化、卫生和体育

2013年末，全省共有国有艺术表演团体96个，群艺馆、文化馆120个，公共图书馆112个，博物馆136个。电影放映管理机构88个，放映单位1460个。广播电台6座，电视台7座，有线电视用户1040.05万户。全年出版全国性和省级报纸20.86亿份，各类期刊3.35亿册，图书2.61亿册。

全省共有卫生机构34645个(含村卫生室)，卫生人员30.5万人，病床床位28.4万张；专科疾病防治机构76家，疾病预防控制中心113个。

全年全省运动健儿在国际比赛中共获得冠军25项次、亚军 9项次、季军17项次，其中奥运会项目最高水平比赛冠军3项次、季军4项次；在各类全国比赛中，获冠军57项次、亚军72项次、第三名82项次，其中，全运会项目全国最高水平比赛中冠军13项次、亚军32项次、第三名32项次。全年销售体育彩票35亿元。

十一、人口、人民生活和社会保障

2013 年末，全省常住人口 5799 万人（指常住本省半年以上人口），其中：城镇 3161.03 万人，乡村 2637.97 万人。城镇化率达到 54.51%。全年出生人口 64.14 万人，出生率为 11.08‰；死亡人口 35.60 万人，死亡率为 6.15‰，人口自然增长率为 4.93‰。

城乡居民收入继续增加。全年全省城镇居民人均可支配收入 22906 元，增长 9.9%；农民人均纯收入 8867 元，增长 12.9%。

社会保障进一步加强。年末全省参加基本养老保险人数 1219.1 万人，比上年增加 49 万人，其中：在职职工 823.3 万人，离退休人员 395.8 万人；参加失业保险人数 511.3 万人；参加医疗保险人数 1960.6 万人；参加工伤保险 556.9 万人；参加生育保险 465.3 万人。年末全省企业参加基本养老保险离退休人员 377.5 万人，100%实现了养老金按时足额发放；全年累计领取失业保险金人数 11.2 万人。

全年全省城镇居民最低生活保障对象 126 万人，农村居民最低生活保障人数 235 万人，国家抚恤、补助各类优抚对象 55 万人。社会福利事业不断发展。年末全省各类社会福利收养床位 24 万张，收养 19 万人，城镇社区服务中心、站共计 4700 个。全年销售社会福利彩票 73.8 亿元。

十二、节能降耗、资源环境

全省继续大力推进节能降耗工作，单位 GDP 能耗继续保持下降态势，可望完成年初确定下降 3%的目标。

长江干流总体水质状况为优。监测的 7 个断面水质符合Ⅱ～Ⅲ类的比例为 100%。

全省累计已发现矿种 149 种，累计已查明资源储量的矿种 92 种。2013 年国土资源调查及地质勘查新增查明矿产地大型 2 处，中小型 27 处。

全省自然保护区达到 67 个，其中国家级自然保护区 15 个；省级自然保护区 24 个，自然保护区面积 104.45 万公顷。

注：本公报所列数据为初步统计数。

STATISTICAL COMMUNIQUE OF HUBEI PROVINCE ON THE 2013 NATIONAL ECONOMIC AND SOCIAL DEVELOPMENT

PROVINCIAL STATISTICAL BUREAU OF HUBEI
HUBEI INVESTIGATION TEAM OF NATIONAL STATISTICAL BUREAU

(1st July 2013)

The 2013 year is the first year to implementation the spirit of the 18th Party Congress and the 10th Party Congress of Hubei, is also the start year of promoting "five Hubei" construction. Facing the complex changeable environment of international economic, and the increasing downward pressure of domestic economic, the economic development of our province is lower than expected level for a long time, people of the whole province in the strong leadership of the provincial Party committee and government, adhere the spirit of the18th Party Congress and Xi Jinping's important speech in Hubei as a guide, adhere "quality, speed and efficiency" simultaneous development, improving calmly, overcoming difficulties. As a result of these, the overall situation of our economic and social development is good, laying a solid foundation for building a well-off society.

I. General Outlook

In 2013, the whole province achieves a gross domestic product of 2466.849 billion yuan. In comparable prices, it is an increase 10.1% over the previous year. Among which, the primary industry completes 309.816 billion yuan, grows by 4.7%; the secondary industry completes 1217.156 billion yuan, grows by 11.3%; the tertiary industry completes 939.877 billion yuan, grows by 10.0%. The proportion of three industries adjust from 12.8:50.3:36.9 in 2012 to12.6:49.3:38.1. In the tertiary industry, transport and storage and postal services, wholesale and retail, accommodation and catering, finance, real estate, profit and nonprofit services grow by 10.5%, 7.9%, 4.9%, 15.6%, 10.2%, 11.8% and 8.9%, respectively.

The consumer price index is 102.8, a 2.8% increase in the price level. Among which, in city it rises 2.7% and in rural area 3.0%. On details, food rises 4.9%; cigarette and wine rises 0.5%; clothing rises 2.2%; household appliances and services rises 1.9%; medical care and personal items rises 2.1%; transportation and communication falls 0.6%; entertainment and education services rises 1.5%; residence rises 3.1. The price for agricultural production rises 3.1%. The producer price for industrial products falls 0.8%, the purchasing price for industrial producers falls 0.8%.

Market main body development accelerates. In 2013, the number of provincial new registered market players is 1090.4 thousand, grows 73.5%. Among which, the number of new registered private enterprise is 131.3thousand, grows 90.8%; the number of new registered individual businessman is 935.4 thousand, grows 73.8%.

According to statistics from human resources and social security departments, till the end of 2013, the provincial registered urban unemployment rate is 3.49%, which is 0.34% less than the previous year.

II. Agriculture

The value-added of agriculture, forestry, animal husbandry and fishery is a 4.7% growth than previous year. Grain acreage is 4.26 million hectares, grows 78.3 thousand hectares; cotton planting area is of 415.6 thousand hectares, reduces 57.3 thousand hectares; Oilseed acreage is 1.52 million hectares, grows 15.4 thousand hectares. The total grain output is 25.01 million tons, which is 594.9 thousand tons greater than the previous year, increasing 2.4%; total cotton output is 459.7 thousand tons, reduces 85.6 thousand tons, falls 15.7%; total oilseed output is 3.33 million tons, increases 135.1 thousand tons, grows 4.2%. (Table 1: Major Agricultural Products)

Table 1: Output of Major Agricultural Products, 2013

Item	Output(10,000 tons)	Increased over 2012(%)
Grain	2501.30	2.4
Cotton	45.97	-15.7
Oil-bearing Crops	333.17	4.2
Peanuts	68.11	-8.4
Rapeseed	250.47	8.9
Tea	22.20	7.2
Fruits (do not contain melon as fruit)	569.42	5.1
Vegetables	3578.31	2.1

Livestock breeding and aquaculture are growing steadily. In this year, live pig output is 43.56 million, grows 4.2%; aquatic product output reaches 4.10 million tons, grows 5.5%.

III. Industry and Construction

Industrial production maintains a steady growth. The number of provincial industrial enterprises above designated size reaches 13441, which is 2107 greater than the previous year, grows 18.6%. The industrial added value grows 11.8% in comparable prices. Among which, the state-owned and state-holding enterprises grows 8.0%; collective enterprises increases 11.1%; joint-stock cooperative enterprises increases 11.9%; foreign, Hong Kong and Macao investment enterprises increases 7.4%; other economic enterprises grows 11.2%. Light industrial added value grows 11.7%; heavy industrial added value grows 11.8%. (Table 2: Output of Major Industrial Products)

Table2: Output of Major Industrial Products, 2013

Product	Unit	Output	Increase over 2012(%)
Yarn	10000 tons	302.00	7.90
Cloth	100 million meters	79.25	12.6
Chemical Fiber	10000 tons	21.67	20.1
Cigarettes	100 million units	1397.99	2.2
Household Refrigerators	10000 units	226.07	11.7
Air Conditioner	10000 units	1189.37	46.7
Raw Coal	10000 tons	80.08	1.5
Crude Oil	10000 tons	2118.82	-2.3
Electricity	100 million kilowatt-hours	1153.51	-14.1
Hydropower	100 million kilowatt-hours	3000.98	1.1
Crude Steel	10000 tons	3344.92	-5.8
Rolled Steel	10000 tons	107.82	11.3
Ten Kinds of Nonferrous Metal	10000 tons	50.25	36.5
Copper	10000 tons	11056.52	5.3
Cement	10000 tons	680.11	4.6
Sulfuric Acid	10000 tons	132.22	-3.9
Sodium Carbonate	10000 tons	99.23	23.0
Caustic Soda	10000 tons	1186.69	10.0
Chemical Fertilizer（100% equivalent）	10000 tons	145.70	-37.5
Electricity Generation Equipments	10000 kilowatt-hours	158.70	9.6
Motor Vehicles	10000 units	66.59	8.3
Automobile	10000 units	714.76	70.6
Mobile Phones	10000 units	302.00	7.9

The structure of total industrial products improves and high-tech industry is growing rapidly. The province completes high-tech industry added value 326.706 billion yuan, grows 16.5%, which makes 29.3% of the whole added value of industrial enterprises above designated size.

Industrial production and marketing link well and economic benefit continues to rise. The provincial industrial sales value is 3707.81 billion yuan, grows 17.5%. Among which, processing of food from agricultural products, manufacture of beverages, manufacture of textile, steel, automobile, petrochemical, electricity, food, electronic information, textile, equipment manufacturing, building materials industry achieve sales value exceeding 100 billion yuan. Industrial product sales rate is 97.3%. The provincial industrial enterprises realizes profits of 208.066 billion yuan, increases 26.4%. Among which, the state-holding industrial enterprises realized profits of 69.534 billion yuan, grows 19.9%.

Development of construction industry accelerates. Qualified construction enterprises together achieve a production value of 834.34 billion yuan, grows 18.5%; realize profits 33.519 billion yuan, grows 20.5%; pay taxes 29.95 billion yuan, grows 17.7%. New construction area is 265.527 million square meters, grows 18.6%.

IV. Investment in Fixed Assets

The investment in fixed assets(excluding rural households) is 2017.745 billion yuan, increases 25.8%. Among which, real estate investment makes 328.602 billion yuan, grows 29.4%. The total saleable area of commodity house is 52.995 million square meters, grows 31.2%%. The total sales value of commodity house is 279.032 billion yuan, grows 37.0%. Divided by industry, the provincial investment in primary, secondary and tertiary industries are 40.463, 918.725 and 1058.557 billion yuan, respectively; accordingly grow by 3.5%, 26.2% and 26.4%.

The 547 key provincial construction projects complete investment value 319.951 billion yuan, accounting for 15.4% of the total investment in fixed assets.

V. Domestic Trade

The total retail sales of social consumer goods is 1046.594 billion yuan, grows 13.8%. In terms of urban and rural differences, cities and towns achieve retail sales 885.185 billion yuan, increases 13.5%; the retail sales in rural areas is 161.41 billion yuan, grows 15.2%. In particular, the retail sales by businesses above designated size reaches 509.649 billion yuan, up by 16.6%.

VI. Foreign Economy

Hubei Province achieves a total foreign trade value of 36.39 billion dollars, grows 13.8% than the previous year. Among them, the amount of export is 22.838 billion dollars, grows 17.7%; import amount is 13.552 billion dollars, grows 7.9%. 297 projects of foreign direct investment are approved, and the total amount of FDI is 6.888 billion dollars, grows 21.6%.

VII. Transportation, Post and Telecommunications and Tourism

The provincial annual tonnage mileage is 488.301 billion ton kilometers, grows 12.2%; the volume of passenger transport is 176.110 billion passenger kilometers, grows 11.7%.

The annual income of post and telecommunications industries is 54.734 billion yuan, grows 11.4%. Long distance optical cable lines reach a total length of 28.1 thousand kilometers; the capacity of office telephone exchanges reaches 14.826 million lines. There are 9.84 million fixed phone users and 44.168 million mobile phone users, which are 167 thousand less and 6004 thousand more, respectively. The provincial telephone penetration rate is 93 units/100 people. Broadband Internet users reach 8.133 million.

The number of domestic tourists is 406.21 million person-times, grows 18.7% than last year; domestic tourism income reaches 313.013 billion yuan, grows 22.6%. The number of inbound tourism is 2.68 million person-times, grows 1.2%. International tourism foreign exchange income reaches 1.219 billion dollars, grows 1.3%.

VIII. Finance, Banking and Insurance

The provincial annual general finance revenue is 356.51 billion yuan, a growth of 15.4% over last year. In particular, the local public finance budget revenue is 218.998 billion yuan, grows 20.1%. In local public finance budget revenue, tax income accounts for 160.369 billion yuan, grows 21.1%. The annual expenditure is 433.063 billion yuan, grows 15.2%.

At the end of 2013, the savings deposit in all items of financial institutions totaled 3290.283 billion yuan, increases 464.189 billion yuan over last year. Among which, personal deposit is 1597.215 billion yuan, an increase of 236.303 billion yuan. Loans in all items of financial institutions reach 2190.255 billion yuan, up 300.196 billion yuan. In particular, short-term loan is 785.728 billion yuan, an increase of 151.90 billion yuan; long-term loan is 1312.72 billion yuan, increases 143.154 billion yuan.

The annual premium income reaches 71.212 billion yuan, grows 19.3%. Among which, property insurance companies achieve a premium income of 18.186 billion yuan, increases 27.7%; personal insurance companies achieve a premium income of 53.027 billion yuan, grows 17.1%. Payment of various claims is 19.147 billion yuan, grows 40.8%. In particular, property insurance companies pay 9.099 billion yuan, increases 27.7%; personal insurance companies pay 10.049 billion yuan, grows 55.1%.

IX. Education, Science and Technology

At the end of 2013, the total number of regular higher education enrollment is 403.9 thousand, the number of students at school is 1.42 million, and the number of graduated students is 361.6 thousand. Postgraduate enrollment number is 39 thousand, in-school graduate students number is 112.7 thousand, and 34.6 thousand graduated. The number of enrollment for vocational education is 170.1 thousand, the number at school is 515.6 thousand, and the number graduated is 236.1 thousand. For regular high school the number of enrollment is 316.5 thousand, the number at school is 0.988 million, and the number graduated is 391.2 thousand. There are 1.484 million middle school students, 3.282 million primary school students and 1.473 million kindergarten pupils.

Scientific research and technology development make new achievements. There are 1621 achievements meet or surpass provincial level. In particular, 22 are about basic theory, 1570 are about application and 29 are about soft science. 14909 technological contracts are signed, which makes an amount of 41.874 billion yuan, grows 78.5%.

The scientific research and experimental development (R&D) expenditure achieves 45.0 billion yuan, grows 17.0%, occupying 1.8% of provincial gross domestic product. The arrangement of '973' projects are 169 tasks, with 190 million yuan of funds; '863' projects make 102 tasks, with 190 million yuan of funds. There are 28 national high technology industry development projects with a total investment of 5.76 billion yuan and 1.14 billion of it is from state found.

There are 135 inspection institutions that are capable of issuing quality test report and 20 of them are of national level. 135 detection and calibration laboratories are certified by CNAL. 7832 enterprise receive ISO9000 certification and 8550 China Compulsory Certifications are issued. The number of legal technical institution of metrology is 138 and they complete 1.81 million pieces of compulsory verification.

The number of weather radar observatories is 11. The number of satellite image receiving stations is 17. There are together 2 seismic network and 48 seismic stations.

X. Culture, Public Health and Sports

The province has 96 state-owned art troupes, 120 mass art/culture galleries, 112 public libraries and 136 museums. There are 88 film censorship institutions and 1460 showing units. There are 6 broadcasting stations, 7 television stations and 10.40 million cable television subscribers. 2.086 billion national and provincial newspapers copies, 335 million journals and 261 million books are issued.

There are 34645 health institutions (including village clinic), 305 thousand health personnel, and 284 thousand hospital beds. There are 88 specialized disease prevention and control institutions and 112 Centers for Disease Control and Prevention.

In international sports competitions, our athletes win the first, second and third place for 25, 9 and 17 times, respectively. In particular, in Olympic Games it is 3, 0 and 4 times respectively. In all types of nationwide competitions, it is 57, 72 and 82 times respectively, among which, the highest level Championship Games project ,is 13,32 and 32 times respectively. Annual sales value of sports lottery tickets is 3.5 billion yuan,.

XI. Population, Living Conditions and Social Security

At the end of 2013, the provincial resident population is 57.99 million (refers to the number of people living for more than half a year). In particular, 31.61 million people live in town and 26.38 million people live in the country, reaching a 54.51% urbanization rate. The newly-born population is 641.4 thousand, a birth rate of 11.08‰. The death population is 3560 thousand, a death rate of 6.15‰. The natural population growth rate is 4.93‰.

The income of urban and rural residents continues to increase. The disposable income of urban residents is 22906 yuan a year, increases 9.9%; the disposable income of rural residents is 8867 yuan a year, increases 12.9%.

Social security is further strengthened. At the end of the year, the number of basic pension insurance contributors is 12.191 million, grows 490 thousand. In particular, 8.233 million are on-the-job and 3.958 million are retired; There are 5.113 million unemployment insurance contributors; there are 19.606 million medicare contributors; there are 5.569 million work injury insurance contributors; there are 4.653 million maternity insurance contributors. The number of provincial enterprise retirees who attend basic pension insurance is 3.775 million, achieving a 100% on time and in full distribution. The number of person receiving unemployment insurance is 112 thousand.

There are 1.26 million urban lowest social security objects and 2.35 million rural lowest social security objects. 550 thousand people are comforted and compensated by the government. Social welfare continues to develop. At the end of the year, social welfare institutions of various types provided 240 thousand beds for 190 thousand people. There are together 4700 social service center in urban area. The sales value of welfare lottery is 7.38 billion yuan.

XII. Energy-saving and Environment

The province continues to propel energy saving. The energy consumption per GDP maintains a trend of decline, expecting to achieve the goal of a 3% decrease settled at the beginning of this year.

Water quality of the main stream of Yangtze River is generally good. 7 water quality monitoring sections show that 100% achieves grade II~III.

Inside the province, 149 types of mineral have been found. 92 kinds are with proven reserves. 2013 land resource survey and geological exploration discover 2 large orefields and 27 medium and small orefields.

The province has 67 natural protection areas. In particular, there are 15 national nature reserves and 24 provincial nature reserves. The total area is 1044.5 thousand hectares

Note: All figures in the Communiqué are preliminary statistics.

1 综　合

General Survey

资料整理：黄　文　舒　猛
朱　江　闵胜男

综 合

General Survey

从数字看2013年的湖北

Statistic about Hubei in 2013

湖北的地位

Position of Hubei in the Country

地区生产总值24668.49亿元	Gross Domestic Production: billion yuan	占全国4.34 %
#第三产业9398.77亿元	Tertiary Industry: billion yuan	占全国3.58 %
人均地区生产总值42613元	Per Capita Regional GDP: yuan	相当于全国101.7 %
全社会固定资产投资总额20753.9亿元	TotaL Investment in Fixed Assets: billion yuan	占全国4.64%
社会消费品零售总额10885.9亿元	Total Retail Sales of Social Consumption: billion yuan	占全国4.58%
进出口总额363.9亿美元	Total Imports and Exports: billion yuan	占全国0.87%
#出口总额228.38亿美元	Total Exports: billion yuan	占全国1.03%
实际外商直接投资68.88亿美元	Actual Foreign Direct Investment: billion dollars	占全国5.86%
粮食产量2501.3万吨	Grain: million tons	占全国4.16%
钢产量3383.32万吨	Rolled Steel: 28.07 milliom tons	占全国3.17%
发电量2118.82亿千瓦小时	Electricity: (100 billion kwh)	占全国3.93%
城镇居民人均可支配收入22906元	Per Capita Disposable Income of Urban Residents: yuan	相当于全国85.0 %
农村居民人均纯收入8867元	Per Capita Net Incomes of Rural Residents:yuan	相当于全国99.7%

湖北的人口

Population of Hubei

常住人口	Population of Permanent Residents	5799万人
从业人员	Employment	3692万人
#在岗职工人数	Staff and Workers	939.88万人
出生人口	Birth Population	64.14万人
死亡人口	Death Population	35.60万人
城镇人口	Urban Population	3161.03万人
乡村人口	Rural Population	2637.97万人
人口密度	Density of Population	312人/平方公里

湖北的经济发展

Economic Development of Hubei

		1979-2013年平均增长(%)
地区生产总值	Regional Gross Production	10.8
第一产业	Primary Industry	4.7
第二产业	Second Industry	12.9
第三产业	Tertiary Industry	12.7
全社会固定资产投资	Investment in Fixed Assets	19.4
财政收入	Government Revenue	12.9
货物运输量	Cargo Transport Volume	7.8
社会消费品零售总额	Total Retail Sales of Social Consumption	13.8
出口总额	Total Exports	15.2

湖北的一天

One Day in Hubei

地区生产总值	Gross Domestic Product	67.58亿元
第一产业	First Industry	8.49亿元
第二产业	Second Industry	33.35亿元
第三产业	Tertiary Industry	25.75亿元
地方公共财政收入	Local Government Public Finance Income	6.00亿元
货物运输量	Freight Traffic	382.85万吨
竣工房屋面积	Floor Space of Building Completed	62.39万平方米
社会消费品零售总额	Total Retail Sales of Social Consumption	29.82亿元
出口总额	Total Exports	6256.99万美元
出版报纸	Newspapers Published	543.01万份
邮寄函件	Letters and Correspondents Delivered	28.77万件

1-1 土地面积与行政区划
LAND AREA AND ADMINISTRATIVE DIVISION

项 目	单 位	Item	unit	1990	2000	2005	2011	2012	2013
常住人口	(万人)	Population of the Whole Province	(10 000 persons)	5439	5960	5710	5758	5779	5799
土地面积	(万平方公里)	Land Area	(10 000 sq.km)	18.59	18.59	18.59	18.59	18.59	18.59
耕地面积	(千公顷)	Cultivated Area	(1000 hectares)	3476.77	3282.96	3161.17	3361.86	3390.06	3409.91
行政区划		Adinimisrtative Division							
省辖市	(个)	Municipality	(unit)	8	12	12	12	12	12
自治州	(个)	Autonomous	(unit)	1	1	1	1	1	1
林区	(个)	Forest Zone	(unit)	1	1	1	1	1	1
县级市	(个)	City	(unit)	22	24	24	24	24	24
省辖行政单位	(个)	Adinimistrative Units under the Jurisdiction of Province	(unit)		3	3	3	3	3
县	(个)	County	(unit)	48	41	39	40	40	40
乡政府	(个)	Local Government	(unit)	1121	476	217	194	188	175
镇政府	(个)	Township Government	(unit)	844	853	737	742	746	757
办事处	(个)	Office	(unit)		145	163	297	298	300
村民委员会	(个)	Village Community	(unit)	32765	32400	26678	26025	25991	25955
村民小组	(个)	Village Groups	(unit)	260847	259250	212587	206848	210432	210108

1-2　市、州行政区划

ADMINISTRATIVE DIVISION OF MUNICIPALITIES AND PREFECTURE

单位：个　　(2013年底)(by the End of 2013)　　(unit)

地 区	Region	县级市 Cities	县 Counties	区 Districts	乡政府 Village Government	镇政府 Township Government	村民委员会 Village Community	村民小组 Village Groups
全　省	Total	24	40	38	175	757	25955	210108
武汉市	Wuhan Municipality			13	3	5	1988	17777
黄石市	Huangshi Municipality	1	1	4	1	27	773	7710
十堰市	Shiyan Municipality	1	5	2	35	71	1857	10545
荆州市	Jingzhou Municipality	3	3	2	13	89	2457	20464
宜昌市	Yichang Municipality	3	5	5	20	67	1379	8150
襄阳市	Xiangyang Municipality	3	3	3	4	74	2391	14910
鄂州市	Ezhou Municipality			3	3	18	316	4027
荆门市	Jingmen Municipality	1	2	2	2	50	1394	9940
孝感市	Xiaogan Municipality	3	3	1	23	72	2945	23553
黄冈市	Huanggang Municipality	2	7	1	16	99	4303	37074
咸宁市	Xianning Municipality	1	4	1	12	52	909	10068
恩施自治州	Enshi Prefecture	2	6		36	47	2532	22962
随州市	Suizhou Municipality	1	1	1	4	34	852	8360
仙桃市	Xiantao Municipality	1				15	625	4537
天门市	Tianmen Municipality	1			1	21	778	6735
潜江市	Qianjiang Municipality	1				10	389	2973
神农架林区	Shennongjia Forest Zone				2	6	67	323

注：乡政府、镇政府、村民委员会、村民小组数只涉及农村生产经营单位数

Note:The number of village government, township government, village community and village groups only refers to the number of units run by village production operation.

1-3 全省法人、产业活动单位数(2013年)

指 标 名 称	Item	合 计 Total
总 计	Total	458136
一、按登记注册类型分组	**Grouped by Type of Registration**	
内资企业	Inner Funded Enterprises	455323
国有企业	State-owned Enterprises	57790
集体企业	Collective-owned Enterprises	13331
股份合作企业	Share Holding Cooperative Enterprises	2839
联营企业	Joint Funded Enterprises	1064
国有联营企业	State Joint owned Enterprises	162
集体联营企业	Collective Joint-owned Enterprises	452
国有与集体联营企业	State - owned and Collective Joint-owned Enterprises	110
其他联营企业	Other Joint-owned Enterprises	340
有限责任公司	Co. Ltd	76664
国有独资公司	State-owned Solely Funded Co.	404
其他有限责任公司	Other Co. Ltd	76260
股份有限公司	Share Holding Co.Ltd.	6665
私营企业	Private - owned Enterprises	212999
私营独资企业	Private Solely Funded Enterprises	72476
私营合伙企业	Private Partnership Enterprises	15425
私营有限责任公司	Private Co. Ltd	117523
私营股份有限公司	Private Share Holding Co.Ltd.	7575
其他内资企业	Others	83971
港、澳、台商投资企业	Hongkong, Macao and Taiwan Funded Enterprises	1331
合资经营企业(港或澳、台资)	Joint Venture with Hongkong, Macao and Taiwan	510
合作经营企业(港或澳、台资)	Cooperate with Hongkong, Macao and Taiwan Funded	41
港、澳、台商独资经营企业	Enterprises Solely Funded by Hongkong, Macao and Taiwan	680
港、澳、台商投资股份有限公司	Share Holding Co.Ltd. with Hongkong, Macao and Taiwan Investment	86
其他港、澳、台商投资企业	Other Hongkong, Macao and Taiwan Investment	14
外商投资企业	Foreign Funded Enterprises	1482
中外合资经营企业	Sino - Foreign Joint Funded Enterprises	671
中外合作经营企业	Sino - Foreign Cooperative Funded Enterprises	34
外资企业	Foreign Solely Funded Enterprises	673
外商投资股份有限公司	Foreign Funded Share Holding Co.Ltd.	78
其他外商投资企业	Other Foreign Investment	26
二、按国民经济行业门类分组	**Grouped by Sector**	
农、林、牧、渔业	Farming, Forestry, Animal husbandary and Fishery	19168
采矿业	Mining	5505
制造业	Manufacturing	74919
电力、燃气及水的生产和供应业	Power, Gas and Water Production and Supply	3297
建筑业	Construction	23629
交通运输、仓储和邮政业	Transportaation, Storage and Post	12779
信息传输、计算机服务和软件业	Information Transmission, Computer Service and software	9472
批发和零售业	Wholesale and Retail Sale	111317
住宿和餐饮业	Hotel and Catering	8840
金融业	Banking	3520
房地产业	Real Estate	18600
租赁和商务服务业	Leasing and Commerical Service	35647
科学研究、技术服务和地质勘查业	Scietific Research, Polytechnical Service and Geological Prospecting	15757
水利、环境和公共设施管理业	Water Conservancy, Environment and Public Facility Management	4791
居民服务和其他服务业	Resident Service and Others	9802
教育	Education	18020
卫生、社会保障和社会福利业	Health Care, Social Security and Social Welfare	11361
文化、体育和娱乐业	Culture, Sports and Recreation	6143
公共管理和社会组织	Public Management and Social Organization	65569
国际组织	International Organization	

注：数据截至2013年6月份.
Note：The data is as of June.

NUMBER OF CORPORATIONS, INDUSTRIAL ACTIVITIES UNITS(2013)

法人单位数(个) Corporation Units		产业活动单位数(个) Number of Economic Activities Units	
单产业法人单位 Single-Industry Corperation Units	多产业法人单位 Multi-Industry Corperation Units	合 计 Total	其中：多产业法人所属的产业活动单位 Economic Activities Units under Multi-Industry Corperation Units
438310	19826	536256	97946
435675	19648	531708	96033
51033	6757	88456	37423
12700	631	22767	10067
2707	132	4008	1301
1030	34	1761	731
158	4	262	104
435	17	902	467
106	4	145	39
331	9	452	121
75154	1510	81961	6807
345	59	741	396
74809	1451	81220	6411
6156	509	12987	6831
210763	2236	222251	11488
72028	448	75986	3958
15281	144	16063	782
116002	1521	122207	6205
7452	123	7995	543
76132	7839	97517	21385
1246	85	2265	1019
478	32	844	366
41		60	19
634	46	1132	498
79	7	200	121
14		29	15
1389	93	2283	894
629	42	825	196
32	2	42	10
634	39	1231	597
69	9	149	80
25	1	36	11
19099	69	20508	1409
5425	80	5788	363
73994	925	76820	2826
3132	165	4481	1349
23094	535	24956	1862
12435	344	15639	3204
9335	137	12326	2991
109313	2004	129070	19757
8630	210	11951	3321
3065	455	10800	7735
18131	469	19531	1400
35236	411	37400	2164
15385	372	17096	1711
4621	170	5665	1044
9692	110	10295	603
15975	2045	22001	6026
10346	1015	27436	17090
6001	142	6706	705
55401	10168	77787	22386

1-4 国民经济和社会发展总量与速度指标

指 标		Item		总 量 指 标		
				1978	1990	2000
人口与就业		**Population and Employment**				
人口	（万人）	**Population**	**(10 000 persons)**			
年末人口		Population at Year-end		4574.91	5439.29	5950.89
城镇人口		Urban		690.23	1551.51	2408.49
乡村人口		Rural		3884.68	3887.78	3542.40
就业	（万人）	**Employment**	**(10 000 persons)**			
就业人数		Employment		1910.37	3040.40	3384.90
职工人数		Staff and Workers		457.34	698.55	677.96
#国有单位		State-owned Units		371.56	524.12	501.11
宏观经济		**Marcoeconomy**				
国民核算	（亿元）	**National Accounting**	**(100 million yuan)**			
地区生产总值		Gross Domestic Products		151.00	824.38	3545.39
第一产业		First Industry		61.11	289.45	662.30
第二产业		Second Industry		63.71	313.39	1437.38
第三产业		Tertiary Industry		26.18	221.54	1445.71
支出法地区生产总值		Gross Domestic Expenditures				
#最终消费		Final Consumption Expenditures		81.70	535.49	2030.07
居民消费		Resident Consumption		74.70	434.62	1594.08
政府消费		Government Consumption Expenditures		7.00	100.87	436.00
资本形成总额		Gross Capital Formation		43.11	261.95	1882.47
固定资本形成		Fixed Capital Formation		31.40	147.13	1451.85
存货增加		Changes in Stock		11.71	114.82	430.62
固定资产投资	（亿元）	**Investment in Fixed Assets**	**(100 million yuan)**			
全社会固定资产投资总额		Total Investment in Fixed Assets		33.58	144.44	1421.55
#国有单位		State-Owned Units		33.19	100.35	857.01
集体单位		Collective-owned Units		0.39	15.59	128.32
#房地产开发		Real Estate Development			5.94	134.63
财政	（亿元）	**Public Finance**	**(100 million yuan)**			
地方公共财政收入		Local Public Financial Revenue		31.38	77.85	214.35
地方公共财政支出		Local Public Financial Expenditures		29.98	84.82	368.77
物价(上年= 100)		**Price (preceding year = 100)**				
商品零售价格总指数		General Retail Price Index		100.50	102.90	97.80
居民消费价格指数		General Consumer Price Index		100.30	104.20	99.00
工业品出厂价格指数		Ex-factory Price Index of Industrial products			109.00	101.70
利用外资	（亿美元）	**Utilization of Foreign Capital**	**(100 million dollars)**			
实际外商直接投资		Actual Foreign Direct Investment			0.29	9.44
产 业		**Industry**				
农业		**Agriculture**				
乡村从业人员	（万人）	Rural Employment	(10 000 persons)	1525.14	1791.30	1781.70
农林牧渔业总产值	（亿元）	Gross Output Value of Farming, Forestry, Animal Husbandry and Fishery	(100 million yuan)	84.46	402.23	1125.64
主要农产品产量	（万吨）	Output of Major Farm Products	(10 000 tons)			
粮食		Grain		1725.63	2475.03	2218.49
棉花		Cotton		36.67	51.73	30.43
油料		Oil-Bearing Crops		23.71	95.75	269.98
糖料		Sugar Crops		8.73	34.66	101.66
蚕茧		Silkworm Cocoons		0.47	0.79	1.22
肉类产量		Output of Meat		64.00	146.85	271.19
水产品		Aquatic Products		11.00	70.98	234.34

注：1.人口数除1982年、1990年、2000年、2010年是以人口普查为基数推算外，1982年及以后为人口抽样调查推算数。
2.2000年以前数据是总人口数，2001年以后数据为常住人口数。

AGGREGATE INDICATORS OF NATIONAL ECNONOMIC AND SOCIAL DEVELOPMENT，THEIR INDICES AND GROWTH RATES

Aggregate Data			速度指标 Indices and Growth Rates								
			2013年比下列各年增长(%) Increases					年平均增长(%) Average Annual Growth Rate			
2005	2012	2013	1978	1990	2000	2005	2012	1979~2013	1991~2013	2001~2013	2006~2013
5710.00	5779.00	5799.00	26.8	6.6	-2.6	1.6	0.3	0.7	0.3	-0.2	0.2
2466.70	3091.77	3161.03	358.0	103.7	31.2	28.1	2.2	4.4	3.1	2.1	3.1
3243.30	2687.23	2637.97	-32.1	-32.1	-25.5	-18.7	-1.8	-1.1	-1.7	-2.2	-2.5
3537.00	3687.00	3692.00	93.3	21.4	9.1	4.4	0.1	1.9	0.8	0.7	0.5
563.93	823.76	939.88	105.5	34.5	38.6	66.7	14.1	2.1	1.3	2.5	6.6
349.99	275.77	251.97	-32.2	-51.9	-49.7	-28.0	-8.6	-1.1	-3.1	-5.2	-4.0
6590.19	22250.45	24668.49	3507.6	1121.0	334.8	167.4	10.1	10.8	11.5	12.0	13.1
1082.13	2848.77	3098.16	405.0	164.5	79.9	46.9	4.7	4.7	4.3	4.6	4.9
2852.12	11193.10	12171.56	6959.0	1961.0	474.6	229.1	11.3	12.9	14.1	14.4	16.1
2655.94	8208.58	9398.77	6379.2	1359.6	326.1	152.2	10.0	12.7	12.4	11.8	12.3
3645.71	9982.79	11161.21	2658.8	761.1	282.8	132.2	9.1	9.9	9.8	10.9	11.1
2785.42	7085.46	8053.82	2006.3	625.1	251.3	118.6	11.0	9.1	9.0	10.1	10.3
860.29	2897.33	3107.39	9350.9	1413.0	394.7	175.4	4.5	13.9	12.5	13.1	13.5
2943.58	12554.67	14245.35	6798.9	2158.6	417.7	270.0	13.1	12.9	14.5	13.5	17.8
2804.01	12064.75	13701.86	3601.1	1393.7	162.3	51.8	13.2	10.9	12.5	7.7	5.4
139.57	489.92	543.49	601.1	52.4	-42.5	94.8	11.6	5.7	1.9	-4.2	8.7
2834.75	16504.17	20753.91	49048.8	14268.5	1359.9	632.1	25.7	19.4	23.8	21.6	28.7
1095.71	4265.95	5068.42	12753.1	4950.7	491.4	362.6	18.8	15.3	19.3	13.6	23.6
79.47	733.92	826.51	188084.6	5201.5	544.1	940.0	12.6	24.8	18.8	12.8	39.6
447.95	2539.46	3286.02		55220.2	2340.8	633.6	29.4		32.2	27.7	28.3
375.52	1823.05	2191.22	6882.9	2714.7	922.3	483.5	20.2	12.9	15.6	19.6	24.7
778.72	3759.79	4371.65	14481.9	5054.0	1085.5	461.4	16.3	15.3	18.7	21.0	24.1
102.10	102.60	101.80	367.9	138.6	30.1	25.2	1.8	4.5	3.8	2.0	2.9
102.90	102.90	102.80	576.0	227.2	43.3	29.9	2.8	5.6	5.2	2.8	3.3
104.50	100.30	99.20							-0.4	-0.2	-0.6
21.85	56.66	68.88		23651.7	629.7	215.2	21.6		26.9	16.5	15.4
1931.15	2259.91	2280.14	49.5	27.3	28.0	18.1	0.9	1.2	1.1	1.9	2.1
1775.58	4732.10	5161.00	6010.6	1183.1	358.5	190.7	9.1	12.5	11.7	12.4	14.3
2177.38	2441.81	2501.30	45.0	1.1	12.7	14.9	2.4	1.1	0.0	0.9	1.7
37.50	53.15	45.97	25.4	-11.1	51.1	22.6	-13.5	0.6	-0.5	3.2	2.6
293.90	319.70	333.17	1305.2	248.0	23.4	13.4	4.2	7.8	5.6	1.6	1.6
42.90	31.08	28.72	229.0	-17.1	-71.7	-33.1	-7.6	3.5	-0.8	-9.3	-4.9
1.07	0.82	0.77	63.8	-2.5	-36.9	-28.0	-6.1	1.4	-0.1	-3.5	-4.0
342.63	412.30	430.08	572.0	192.9	58.6	25.5	4.3	5.6	4.8	3.6	2.9
318.21	388.94	410.97	3636.1	479.0	75.4	29.2	5.7	10.9	7.9	4.4	3.2

Note：a)Data of 1982,1990,2000.and 2010 are based on population census Data of other years are based on sampling survey
b)Data before 2000 refer to total population. Data after 2001 refer to permanent residents

1-4 续表 1 continued

指 标	单位	Item	unit	总量指标 1978	1990	2000
工业		**Industry**				
工业增加值	(亿元)	Added value of Industries	(100 million yuan)		313.24	1011.78
主要工业产品产量	(万吨)	Output of Major Industrial Products	(10000 tons)			
钢		Steel		307.97	629.25	895.92
成品钢材		Rolled-Steel		184.63	533.07	811.10
发电量	(亿千瓦小时)	Electricity	(100 million kWh)	91.64	340.39	538.11
原煤		Coal		644.01	924.26	389.34
农用化肥(折100%)		Chemical Furtilizers		27.62	132.07	221.11
化学农药		Chemical Pesicide		2.97	1.07	5.18
水泥		Cement		328.65	987.00	2460.92
化学纤维		Chemical Fiber		0.48	2.48	9.82
布	(亿米)	Cloth	(100 million meter)	6.70	14.09	17.15
汽车	(万辆)	Automobile	(10000 Units)	0.80	11.38	19.57
建筑业		**Construction**				
建筑业企业职工平均人数	(万人)	Average Number of Employed Persons	(10000 persons)	25.94	41.88	82.76
建筑业总产值	(亿元)	Gross Output Value	(100 million yuan)	11.11	49.30	454.35
施工房屋面积	(万平方米)	Floor Space of Building Under Construction	(10 000 sq.m)	596.00	1684.90	6256.50
竣工房屋面积	(万平方米)	Floor Space of Building Completed	(10 000 sq.m)	297.40	785.90	3150.10
交通运输		**Transportation**				
货运量	(万吨)	Freight Traffic	(10 000 tons)	10199.08	10916.10	9345.19
#铁路		Railway		3342.00	3901.00	3857.00
公路		Highway		3382.00	2941.00	2228.00
水运		Waterway		3096.00	3784.00	3255.00
客运量	(万人)	Passenger Capacity	(10000 persons)	12009.20	32145.93	31593.00
#铁路		Railway		2854.00	2107.00	3469.00
公路		Highway		7429.00	27333.00	27184.00
水运		Waterway		1722.00	2693.00	679.00
港口货物吞吐量	(万吨)	Volume of Freight Handled at Seaports	(10 000 tons)			4113.46
邮电通信业		**Postal Telecommunication Services**				
邮电业务总量	(亿元)	Total Business Revenue	(100 million yuan)	0.56	4.80	116.60
函件	(亿件)	Number of Letters Delivered	(100 million pieces)	1.18	2.39	3.62
年末移动电话用户	(万户)	Number of Local Telephone Users	(10 000 units)			
国际互联网用户	(万户)	Internet Users	(10 000 units)			
农村电话用户	(万户)	Rural Telephone Users	(10 000 units)	4.13	7.07	180.00
国内商业		**Domestic Commerce**				
社会消费品零售总额	(亿元)	Total Retail Sales of Consumer Goods	(100 million yuan)	59.84	326.36	1789.35
对外经济贸易和旅游		**Foreign Trade and Tourism**				
进出口总额	(亿美元)	Total Imports and Exports	(100 million dollars)	1.73	11.90	32.10
进口		Imports		0.14	1.18	12.79
出口		Exports		1.59	10.72	19.31
入境旅游人数	(万人次)	Number of Tourists Received	(10 000 persons)	1.01	15.57	45.08
金融保险	**(亿元)**	**Banking and Insurance**	**(100 million yuan)**			
金融机构存款		Deposits of Banking System		42.16	406.56	3037.22
金融机构贷款		Loans of Banking System		96.78	732.77	3147.77
国内保险保费收入		Domestic Premium			6.19	60.53

Aggregate Data			速　度　指　标 Indices and Growth Rates								
			2013年比下列各年增长(%) Increases					年平均增长(%) Average Annual Growth Rate			
2005	2012	2013	1978	1990	2000	2005	2012	1979~ 2013	1991~ 2013	2001~ 2013	2006~ 2013
1847.90	9552.35	10531.37	8010.0	1997.2	482.7	231.5	11.2	13.4	14.1	14.5	16.1
1571.41	2806.65	2687.81	772.8	327.1	200.0	71.0	-4.2	6.4	6.5	8.8	6.9
1585.85	3558.42	3383.32	1732.5	534.7	317.1	113.3	-4.9	8.7	8.4	11.6	9.9
1257.19	2174.07	2118.82	2212.1	522.5	293.8	68.5	-2.5	9.4	8.3	11.1	6.7
478.07	1171.83	855.88	32.9	-7.4	119.8	79.0	-27.0	0.8	-0.3	6.2	7.6
375.50	1164.26	1043.95	3679.7	690.5	372.1	178.0	-10.3	10.9	9.4	12.7	13.6
5.03	29.58	27.83	837.0	2500.9	437.3	453.3	-5.9	6.6	15.2	13.8	23.8
4512.53	10255.53	11187.84	3304.2	1033.5	354.6	147.9	9.1	10.6	11.1	12.4	12.0
11.74	17.94	28.90	5920.8	1065.3	194.3	146.2	61.1	12.4	11.3	8.7	11.9
20.89	69.16	79.45	1085.8	463.9	363.3	280.3	14.9	7.3	7.8	12.5	18.2
46.38	154.81	170.79	21248.8	1400.8	772.7	268.2	10.3	16.6	12.5	18.1	17.7
110.09	169.33	174.20	571.5	316.0	110.5	58.2	2.9	5.6	6.4	5.9	5.9
1349.32	7040.65	8465.50	76097.1	17071.4	1763.2	527.4	20.2	20.9	25.1	25.2	25.8
12091.20	39112.19	48937.96	8111.1	2804.5	682.2	304.7	25.1	13.4	15.8	17.1	19.1
6896.90	20395.16	22773.70	7557.6	2797.8	623.0	230.2	11.7	13.2	15.8	16.4	16.1
49923.52	126194.57	139740.26	1270.1	1180.1	1395.3	179.9	10.7	7.8	11.7	23.1	13.7
8491.00	9177.40	9010.40	169.6	131.0	133.6	6.1	-1.8	2.9	3.7	6.7	0.7
33481.00	97136.00	108824.21	3117.7	3600.2	4784.4	225.0	12.0	10.4	17.0	34.9	15.9
7944.00	19872.60	21897.00	607.3	478.7	572.7	175.6	10.2	5.7	7.9	15.8	13.5
71399.00	129510.90	143100.28	1091.6	345.2	352.9	100.4	10.5	7.3	6.7	12.3	9.1
4615.00	9764.90	9010.40	215.7	327.6	159.7	95.2	-7.7	3.3	6.5	7.6	8.7
66183.00	118369.00	129533.75	1643.6	373.9	376.5	95.7	9.4	8.5	7.0	12.8	8.8
601.00	443.50	528.00	-69.3	-80.4	-22.2	-12.1	19.1	-3.3	-6.8	-1.9	-1.6
13992.51	23518.12	26219.00			537.4	87.4	11.5			15.3	8.2
373.63	491.46	547.62	97689.3	11308.8	369.7	46.6	11.4	21.7	22.9	12.6	4.9
1.52	1.31	1.05	-11.0	-56.1	-71.0	-30.9	-19.8	-0.3	-3.5	-9.1	-4.5
1401.00	4554.10	4416.80				215.3	-3.0				15.4
128.00	708.00	813.30				535.4	14.9				26.0
336.00	337.40	321.10				-4.4	-4.8	13.2	18.0	4.6	-0.6
2964.58	9562.50	10885.90	18091.7	3235.5	508.4	267.2	13.8	16.0	16.5	14.9	17.7
90.92	319.59	363.89	20934.1	2957.9	1033.6	300.2	-4.8	16.5	16.0	20.5	18.9
46.42	125.59	135.52	96700.0	11384.7	959.6	191.9	-10.6	21.7	22.9	19.9	14.3
44.50	194.01	228.38	14263.5	2030.4	1082.7	413.2	-0.6	15.2	14.2	20.9	22.7
82.57	264.71	267.96	26430.7	1621.0	494.4	224.5	1.2	17.3	13.2	14.7	15.9
8184.96	28006.36	32636.15	77310.2	7927.4	974.5	298.7	16.5	20.9	21.0	20.0	18.9
5649.67	18004.54	20796.86	21388.8	2738.1	560.7	268.1	15.5	16.6	15.7	15.6	17.7
145.08	533.31	587.40		9389.5	870.4	304.9	10.1		21.9	19.1	19.1

1-4 续表 2 continued

指 标	单位	Item	unit	1978	1990
教育、科技、文化		**Education, Science and Technology,Culture and**			
教育		**Education**			
高等学校本专科在校学生	(万人)	Students Enrollment in Institutions of Higher Eduction	(10 000persons)	4.94	13.04
中等专业学校在校学生	(万人)	Students Enrollment in Specialized Secondary Schools	(10 000persons)	5.36	1458.00
普通中学在校学生	(万人)	Students Enrollment in Regular Secondary Schools	(10 000persons)	372.38	211.56
小学在校学生	(万人)	Students Enrollment in Primary Schools	(10 000persons)	765.73	623.06
科技		**Science and Technology**			
国有企事业单位各类专业技术人员	(万人)	Scietific and Technological Personels	(10 000persons)	22.00	56.10
#工程技术人员		Engineering Personels		7.50	24.40
文化		**Culture**			
图书出版量	(亿册)	Books Published	(100 million copies)	1.62	4.02
杂志出版量	(亿册)	Magazines Issued	(100 million copies)	0.09	0.73
报纸出版量	(亿份)	Newspaper Issued	(100 million copies)	1.97	6.24
家庭、生活、环境		**Family, People's Livelihood and Environment**			
家庭		**Family**			
城镇居民平均每户家庭人口	(人)	Average Household size in Urban Areas	(person)	4.32	3.47
农村居民平均每户家庭人口	(人)	Average Household size in Rural Areas	(person)	6.02	4.67
居住		**Housing**			
城镇居民人均住房建筑面积	(平方米)	Per Capita Net Floor Space of Urban Residents	(sq.m)		9.80
农村居民人均住房面积	(平方米)	Per Capita Net Floor Space of Rural Residents	(sq.m)		25.73
生活		**People's Livelihood**			
城镇居民人均可支配收入	(元)	Per Capita Annual Disposbale Income of Urban Residents	(yuan)	325.00	1427.20
农村居民人均纯收入	(元)	Per Capita Annual Disposbale Income of Rural Residents	(yuan)	110.52	670.80
居民储蓄存款余额	(亿元)	Saving Deposit	(100 million yuan)	6.96	244.38
工资		**Wages**			
工资总额	(亿元)	Total Wages of Staff and Workers	(100 million yuan)	25.89	131.24
职工平均工资	(元)	Average Wages of Staff and Workers	(yuan)	581.00	1903.00
卫生		**Health Care**			
卫生机构数	(个)	Number of Health Care Organizations	(unit)	5940	10472
#医院		Hospitals		1817	2024
床位数	(万张)	Number of Hospital Beds	(10 000 units)	11.52	16.34
#医院		Hospitals		10.34	13.16
卫生技术人员数	(万人)	Number of Medical Technical Personels	(10 000 persons)	14.06	20.92
#医生		Doctors		5.82	8.68
环境		**Environment**			
污染治理项目本年完成投资	(亿元)	Investment for the Pollusion Treatment projects Completed	(100 million yuan)		1.81
本年施工污染治理项目数	(个)	Number of Pullution Treatment Project Under Construction	(unit)		1545
工业废水排放量	(亿吨)	Volume of Industrial Waste Water Discharged	(100 million tons)		16.23

总量指标 Aggregate Data				速度指标 Indices and Growth Rates								
				2013年比下列各年增长(%) increases					年平均增长(%) Average Annual Growth Rate			
2000	2005	2012	2013	1978	1990	2000	2005	2012	1979~ 2013	1991~ 2013	2001~ 2013	2006~ 2013
34.66	101.27	138.61	142.14	2777.3	990.0	310.1	40.4	2.5	10.1	10.9	11.5	4.3
27.86	60.60	50.05	41.12	667.2	-97.2	47.6	-32.1	-17.8	6.0	-14.4	3.0	-4.7
350.93	446.69	265.22	247.19	-33.6	16.8	-29.6	-44.7	-6.8	-1.2	0.7	-2.7	-7.1
667.74	429.19	326.75	328.26	-57.1	-47.3	-50.8	-23.5	0.5	-2.4	-2.7	-5.3	-3.3
89.27	82.75	82.26		273.9	46.6	-7.9	-0.6					
16.50	9.14	8.22		9.6	-66.3	-50.2	-10.1					
2.88	3.46	2.60	2.63	62.3	-34.6	-8.7	-24.0	1.2	1.4	-1.8	-0.7	-3.4
2.20	1.97	3.41	3.09	3333.3	323.3	40.5	56.9	-9.4	10.6	6.5	2.6	5.8
13.42	19.57	20.61	19.82	906.1	217.6	47.7	1.3	-3.8	6.8	5.2	3.0	0.2
3.14	2.98	2.89	2.77	-35.9	-20.2	-11.8	-7.0	-4.2	-1.3	-1.0	-1.0	-0.9
4.11	4.01	3.98	3.09	-48.7	-33.8	-24.8	-22.9	-22.4	-1.9	-1.8	-2.2	-3.2
13.90	29.92	35.79	38.80		295.9	179.1	29.7	8.4		6.2	8.2	3.3
30.11	36.05	44.98	41.84		62.6	39.0	16.1	-7.0		2.1	2.6	1.9
5524.50	8786.00	20839.59	22906.42	6948.1	1505.0	314.6	160.7	9.9	12.9	12.8	11.6	12.7
2268.50	3099.20	7851.71	8866.95	7922.9	1221.8	290.9	186.1	12.9	13.3	11.9	11.1	14.0
1908.80	4465.79	13607.35	15972.15	229384.9	6435.8	736.8	257.7	17.4	24.7	19.9	17.8	17.3
405.34	653.81	2786.67	3588.71	13761.4	2634.5	785.4	448.9	28.8	15.1	15.5	18.3	23.7
7565.00	13330.00	35179.00	38720.00	6564.4	1934.7	411.8	190.5	10.1	12.7	14.0	13.4	14.3
11065	10152	35423	35633	499.9	240.3	222.0	251.0	0.6	5.3	5.5	9.4	17.0
2041	574	650	713	-60.8	-64.8	-65.1	24.2	9.7	-2.6	-4.4	-7.8	2.7
14.96	13.96	25.30	28.85	150.4	76.6	92.8	106.7	14.0	2.7	2.5	5.2	9.5
12.99	9.67	17.38	20.05	93.9	52.4	54.3	107.3	15.4	1.9	1.8	3.4	9.5
23.88	21.50	28.85	31.16	121.6	48.9	30.5	44.9	8.0	2.3	1.7	2.1	4.7
10.30	8.98	10.91	11.94	105.2	37.6	15.9	33.0	9.4	2.1	1.4	1.1	3.6
8.52	14.81	15.45	25.17		1290.6	195.4	70.0	62.9		12.1	8.7	6.9
851	473	136	113		-92.7	-86.7	-76.1	-16.9		-10.7	-14.4	-16.4
10.67	9.24	9.16	8.50		-47.6	-20.3	-8.0	-7.2		-2.8	-1.7	-1.0

1-5 国民经济和社会发展结构指标
STRUCTURAL INDICATORS ON NATIONAL ECONOMIC AND SOCIAL DEVELOPMENT

单位：%　　(%)

指　标	Item	1978	2000	2005	2010	2011	2012	2013
人口与就业	**Population and Employment**							
人　口	**Population**							
城乡结构	Urban and Rural Structure							
城镇	Urban	14.6	40.2	43.2	49.7	51.8	53.5	54.5
乡村	Rural	85.4	59.8	56.8	50.3	48.2	46.5	45.5
性别结构	Sexual Structure							
男	Male	51.3	52.1	51.8	51.4	51.3	51.3	51.3
女	Female	48.7	47.9	48.2	48.6	48.7	48.7	48.7
就　业	**Employment**							
产业结构	Industrial Structure							
第一产业	First Industry	77.0	48.0	47.7	46.4	45.7	44.5	42.8
第二产业	Second Industry	14.1	20.8	20.5	20.7	21.0	21.2	21.5
第三产业	Tertiary Industry	8.9	31.2	31.8	32.9	33.3	34.3	35.7
经济类型结构	Structrues by Ownership							
城镇单位从业人员	Staff and Workers Employed in Urban Units							
国有单位	State-Owned	81.2	74.7	62.1	40.4	36.0	34.6	26.8
城镇集体单位	Collective-Owned	18.8	14.3	8.0	3.1	2.2	2.3	1.5
其他单位	Others		11.0	29.9	56.5	61.8	63.1	71.7
宏观经济	**Macroeconomy**							
国民核算	**National Accounting**							
地区生产总值产业结构	Industrial Structure							
第一产业	First Industry	40.5	18.7	16.4	13.4	13.1	12.8	12.6
第二产业	Second Industry	42.2	40.5	43.3	48.7	50.0	50.3	49.3
第三产业	Tertiary Industry	17.3	40.8	40.3	37.9	36.9	36.9	38.1
地区生产总值支出结构	Domestic Expenditures							
最终消费	Total Consumption	54.0	54.0	55.9	45.7	44.3	44.1	43.9
居民消费	Residents Consumption	49.4	42.4	42.7	31.7	31.0	31.3	31.7
政府消费	Government Consumption Expenditures	4.6	11.6	13.2	13.9	13.3	12.8	12.2
资本形成总额	Gross Capital Formation	28.5	50.0	45.1	52.6	54.7	55.4	56.0
固定资本	Fixed Capital Formation	20.8	38.6	43.0	50.7	52.5	53.2	53.9
存货增加	Changes in Stock	7.7	11.4	2.1	1.9	2.1	2.2	2.1
净出口	Net Exports	17.4	-4.0	-1.0	1.7	1.0	0.5	0.1
投　资	**Investment**							
经济类型结构	Structrues by Ownership							
国有经济	State-Owned	98.8	60.3	38.7	34.9	29.1	25.8	24.4
集体经济	Collective-Owned	1.2	9.0	2.8	5.6	5.1	4.4	4.0
其他	Others		30.7	58.5	59.5	65.8	69.8	71.6
资金来源结构	Structure of Funded Sources							
国家预算资金	State Budget	77.2	10.0	9.0	8.0	5.1	4.8	4.3
国内贷款	Domestic Loans	0.4	17.2	16.7	16.4	13.2	11.9	13.1
利用外资	Foreign Investment		2.0	2.5	1.4	1.5	0.8	0.3
自筹资金	Fundraising	18.0	54.9	52.7	62.1	68.0	71.6	71.4
其他投资	Others	4.3	15.9	19.1	12.2	12.2	11.0	10.9

1-5 续表 1 continued

指 标	Item	1978	2000	2005	2010	2011	2012	2013
财 政	**Finance**							
地方公共支出结构	Local Public Financial Expenditure Structure							
#一般公共服务	#General Public Service				12.6	12.3	12.4	12.5
教育	Education				14.7	15.2	19.5	15.8
社会保障和就业	Social Security and Employment				14.7	14.0	13.3	13.9
利用外资	**Foreign Investment**							
实际外商直接投资结构	Actual Foreign Direct Investment							
合资经营企业	Joint Venture		63.4	40.8	35.3	62.7	45.5	32.5
合作经营企业	Cooperation		3.0	4.8	1.6	5.7	0.1	0.5
独资经营企业	Sole Proprietorship Business		33.6	34.5	63.1	30.0	52.7	64.2
外商投资股份制企业	Joint-stock Enterprises with Foreign Investment			0.9			1.7	2.8
产业经济	**Industrial Economy**							
农 业	**Agriculture**							
农林牧渔业产值结构	Agricultural Output Value Structure							
农业	Agriculture	77.3	54.7	52.5	54.9	54.1	52.6	51.9
林业	Forestry	4.9	3.6	2.1	1.9	2.0	2.1	2.4
牧业	Animal Husbandry	12.8	30.1	30.7	26.4	28.4	28.2	27.0
渔业	Fishery	0.8	11.6	13.3	13.1	12.0	13.2	14.5
农林牧渔服务业	Agriculture,Animal Husbandry and Fishery service			1.4	3.8	3.6	3.9	4.2
工 业	**Industry**							
工业产值按经济类型分	Industrial Output by Type							
#国有企业	#State-owned Enterprises	77.3	35.3	25.3	21.0	18.1	15.1	9.3
集体企业	Collective Enterprises	22.7	18.4	1.8	0.9	0.8	0.8	0.4
港澳台商投资企业	Hong Kong, Macao And Taiwan Invested Enterprises		4.2	4.3	5.1	6.2	5.7	5.1
外商投资企业	Foreign-invested Enterprises		6.8	18.3	15.0	12.7	11.0	11.3
工业产值按轻重分	Industrial Output Divided by Weight							
轻工业	Light Industry	47.1	38.4	24.8	27.5	29.8	32.7	34.2
重工业	Heavy Industry	52.9	61.6	75.2	72.5	70.2	67.3	65.8
建筑业	**Building Industry**							
建筑业总产值结构	Gross Output Value Structure							
国有经济	State-owned Economy	88.6	58.6	57.6	52.6	52.5	48.7	46.5
地方	Local	42.8	23.5	19.9	9.5	9.0	8.9	8.9
中央	Central	45.6	35.1	37.7	43.1	43.6	39.8	37.5
城镇集体经济	Urban Collective Economy	11.4	27.2	5.2	1.4	1.5	1.9	0.8
其它经济	Other Economic		14.3	37.3	45.9	45.9	49.4	52.7
运输业	**Transport**							
货运量结构	Cargo Structures							
铁路	Railway	32.8	41.3	17.0	10.5	9.1	7.3	6.4
公路	Highway	33.2	23.8	67.1	73.2	75.1	77.0	77.9
水运	Water Transport	30.3	34.8	15.9	16.3	15.8	15.7	15.7

1-5 续表 2 continued

指 标	Item	1978	2000	2005	2010	2011	2012	2013
国内商业	**Domestic Trade**							
社会消费品零售总额结构	Total Retail Sales of Consumer Goods							
#批发零售贸易业	Wholesale and Retail Sale	85.1	61.9	81.5	85.3	85.1	84.1	84.1
住宿及餐饮业	Hotel and Catering	2.8	10.8	13.1	10.5	12.5	12.1	12.0
其他	Others	12.1	27.3	5.4	4.2	3.4	3.8	3.9
对外经济贸易和国际旅游	**Foreign Trade and Tourism**							
进出口总额	Total Imports and Exports							
#出口	Exports	8.1	39.8	51.1	55.7	58.3	60.7	62.8
进口	Imports	91.9	60.2	48.9	44.3	41.7	39.3	37.2
海外旅游人数结构	Structure of Tourists							
外国人	Foreigners	47.3	79.3	75.9	76.2	75.0	72.9	76.4
港澳台同胞	Compatriots from Hongkong, Macao and Taiwan	52.7	20.7	24.1	23.8	25.0	27.1	23.6
教育、科技、文化	**Education,Science and Culture**							
教 育	**Education**							
在校学生结构	Structure of Students Enrollment							
大学生	College and University Students	0.4	3.3	10.4	15.1	16.1	19.0	19.8
中学生	Secondary School Students	32.6	33.3	45.7	40.6	38.6	36.3	34.4
小学生	Primary School Students	67.0	63.4	43.9	44.3	45.3	44.7	45.7
专任教师结构	Full-Time Teacher by Type							
大学	College and Universities	2.9	11.9	17.5	18.2	15.8	16.6	16.9
中学	Secondary Schools	39.6	38.9	44.5	40.3	45.2	43.8	42.4
小学	Primary Schools	57.5	49.2	38.0	41.5	39.0	39.6	40.6
科 技	**Science and Technology**							
各类专业技术人员结构	Structure of Scientific and Technical Personel							
工程技术人员	Engineering Personel	34.2	18.5	11.1	10.5	10.3	10.0	
农业技术人员	Agriculture	5.5	3.4	3.2	2.2	2.2	2.1	
科学研究人员	Scientific Research	6.7	0.6	0.8	0.5	0.5	0.5	
卫生技术人员	Health Care	32.1	20.9	22.8	24.1	21.6	22.3	
教学人员	Teaching	21.5	56.6	62.2	62.6	56.8	55.9	
生活、环境	**People's Livelihood and Environment**							
生 活	**People's Livelihood**							
城镇居民消费结构	Consumption Structutre of Urban Residents							
食品	Food		38.3	39.0	38.7	40.7	40.3	39.7
衣着	Clothing		11.4	12.0	12.4	12.7	12.3	11.9
居住	Residence		14.1	10.2	10.4	8.9	9.5	9.2
其他	Others		36.2	38.8	38.5	37.6	38.0	39.1
农村居民消费结构	Consumption Structutre of Rural Residents							
食品	Food	70.8	53.2	49.1	43.1	39.0	37.6	36.8
衣着	Clothing	12.0	4.8	5.1	5.3	5.4	5.5	5.5
居住	Residence	8.9	11.5	12.8	20.0	21.7	21.1	22.5
其他	Others	8.3	30.5	33.0	31.6	33.9	35.8	35.2

1-6 湖北国民经济占全国的比重(2013)
PERCENTAGE OF HUBEI'S NATIONAL ECONOMY IN THE COUNTRY(2013)

指　　标	单位	Item	unit	全　国 Country	湖北 Hubei	湖北占全国的比重(%) Percentage to the Country
土地面积	(万平方公里)	Ground space	(10 000 sq.km.)	960.00	18.59	1.94
年末常住人口	(万人)	Population	(Year-end)	136072	5799	4.26
地区生产总值	(亿元)	Local Gross Production	(100 million yuan)	568845.21	24668.49	4.34
第一产业		First Industry		56957.00	3098.16	5.44
第二产业		Second Industry		249684.42	12171.56	4.87
第三产业		Tertiary Industry		262203.79	9398.77	3.58
人均地区生产总值	(元)	Local Gross Production Per Capita	(yuan)	41908	42613	相当于全国101.7%
全社会固定资产投资	(亿元)	Total Investment in Fixed Assets	(100 million yuan)	447074.36	20753.91	4.64
#固定资产投资		Investment in Fixed Assets		436527.70	20177.45	4.62
#房地产开发		Development of Real Estate		86013.38	3286.02	3.82
地方公共财政收入	(亿元)	Local Public Financial Revenue		129142.90	2191.22	1.70
社会消费品零售总额	(亿元)	Total Retail Sales of Social Consumption	(100 million yuan)	237809.91	10885.90	4.58
进出口总额	(亿美元)	Total Imports and Exports	(100 million dollars)	41596.93	363.90	0.87
#出口		Exports		22093.72	228.38	1.03
实际外商直接投资	(亿美元)	Actual Foreign Direct Investment	(100 million dollars)	1175.86	68.88	5.86
普通高等学校本专科在校生	(万人)	Students Enrollment in Institutions of Higher Eductioan	(10 000 persons)	2468.07	142.14	5.76
医院卫生院床位数	(万张)	Number of Hospital Beds	(10 000 units)	457.86	28.85	6.30
卫生技术人员	(万人)	Number of Medical Technical Personnels	(10 000 persons)	721.06	31.16	4.32
#执业(助理)医师		Professional (assistant) Doctors		279.48	11.94	4.27
在岗职工平均工资	(元)	Average Wages of Employee		51474	38720	相当于全国75.2%
城镇居民人均可支配收入	(元)	Per Capita Disposable Income of Urban Residents	(yuan)	26955	22906	相当于全国85.0%
农村居民人均纯收入	(元)	Per Capita Net Incomes of Rural Residents	(yuan)	8896	8867	相当于全国99.7%
居民人均储蓄存款余额	(元)	Deposit Balance Per Capita	(yuan)	32894	27591	相当于全国83.9%
工农业主要产品产量	(万吨)	Output of Major Products in Argriculture and Industry				
粮食		Grain		60193.84	2501.30	4.16
棉花		Cotton		629.90	45.97	7.30
油料		Oil-Bearing Crops		3516.99	333.17	9.47
粗钢		Crude steel		77904.10	2687.81	3.45
钢材		Steel		106762.20	3383.32	3.17
发电量	(亿千瓦小时)	Electricity	(100 million kWh)	53975.86	2118.82	3.93
原煤		Coal		368000.00	855.88	0.23
农用化肥(折100%)		Chemical Furtilizer		7036.96	1043.95	14.84
水泥		Cement		241613.60	11187.84	4.63
化学纤维		Chemical Fiber		4121.94	28.90	0.70
布	(亿米)	Cloth	(100 million meter)	882.70	79.45	9.00
汽车	(万辆)	Moter Vehicles	(10 000 units)	2211.72	170.79	7.72

1−7 全省人均国民经济主要指标

指 标	单位	Item	unit	1990
地区生产总值	(元)	Gross Domestic Product	(yuan)	1541.00
第一产业		First Industry		541.00
第二产业		Second Industry		586.00
第三产业		Tertiary Industry		414.00
地方公共财政预算收入	(元)	Government Revenue	(yuan)	145.54
地方财政支出	(元)	Government Expenditure	(yuan)	158.57
全社会固定资产投资额	(元)	TotaL Investment in Fixed Assets	(yuan)	270.00
社会消费品零售额	(元)	Total Retail Sales of Consumer Goods	(yuan)	610.00
进出口总额	(美元)	Total Imports and Exports	(US.dollars)	22.24
#出口		Exports	(US.dollars)	20.04
农村居民纯收入	(元)	Net Income of Rural Residents	(yuan)	671.00
城镇居民可支配收入	(元)	Disposable Income of Urban Residents	(yuan)	1427.00
居民储蓄存款	(元)	Outstanding Amount of Saving Deposits of Urabn And Rural Residents	(yuan)	455.00
在校大学生数	(人/万人)	Number of Students Enrollment in Institutions of Higher Education	(person/10 000 persons)	24.38
医院病床数	(张/万人)	Hospital Beds	(bed/10000 persons)	24.50
卫生技术人员数	(人/万人)	Number of Medical Technical Personnels	(person/10000 persons)	39.11
#医 生		Doctors		16.22
主要工农业产品产量	(千克)	Output of Major Industrial and Agricultural Products	(kg)	
粮 食		Grain		467.10
棉 花		Cotton		9.76
油 料		Oil-Bearing Crops		18.07
钢 材		Steel		100.60
原 煤		Coal		174.43
发电量	(千瓦小时)	Electricity	(kWh)	639.62

MAJOR PER CAPITA INDICATORS OF HUBEI'S NATIONAL ECONOMY

2000	2005	2008	2009	2010	2011	2012	2013
6293.00	11554.00	19858.00	22677.00	27906.00	34197.27	38572.33	42613.00
1164.00	1897.00	3120.07	3139.69	3766.67	4475.44	4938.49	5351.81
2525.00	4926.00	8700.46	10556.08	13626.74	17098.30	19403.83	21025.32
2540.00	4607.00	8039.91	8963.50	10619.95	12623.52	14230.01	16235.57
376.61	658.36	1244.94	1424.60	1767.30	2560.79	3160.35	3785.14
1647.93	1368.21	2871.22	3655.45	4371.64	5503.96	6517.79	7551.65
2498.00	4970.00	10163.99	14356.38	18879.60	22525.71	28610.85	35850.60
3144.00	5197.00	8704.33	10364.35	11743.40	14414.00	16577.10	18804.46
56.40	159.40	360.51	301.21	452.77	583.87	554.03	628.61
33.93	78.02	203.19	174.44	252.40	340.28	336.33	394.51
2268.00	3099.00	4656.38	5035.00	5832.27	6898.00	7851.71	8866.95
5524.00	8786.00	13153.00	14367.00	16058.37	18374.00	20839.59	22906.42
3209.00	7929.00	11920.00	14388.00	17211.00	19879.00	23589.00	27591.00
60.89	177.54	207.70	218.37	226.66	233.00	240.29	245.53
21.80	23.10	27.50	32.73	35.08	26.41	43.86	49.84
41.96	37.69	41.23	42.49	43.97	45.31	50.01	53.83
17.40	14.90	15.20	13.97	16.93	17.40	18.91	20.63
372.92	382.00	390.40	403.69	404.73	416.00	423.30	432.08
5.12	6.26	9.00	8.40	8.30	9.20	9.21	7.94
45.38	51.50	50.09	54.90	54.50	53.10	55.42	57.55
136.34	278.04	519.27	379.77	505.90	626.02	616.87	464.30
64.45	83.80	140.25	185.89	225.75	165.93	203.14	147.85
904.54	2204.00	3145.00	3114.95	3545.46	3574.00	3768.87	3660.08

1-8 湖 北 的 一 天
ONE DAY IN HUBEI

指 标	单位	Item	unit	2000	2005	2010	2011	2012	2013
每天创造的财富		**Daily Production**							
地区生产总值	(亿元)	Gross Domestic Products	(100 million yuan)	9.71	17.86	43.75	53.79	60.96	67.58
第一产业		First Industry		1.81	2.96	5.88	7.04	7.80	8.49
第二产业		Second Industry		3.94	7.70	21.28	26.89	30.67	33.35
第三产业		Tertiary Industry		3.96	7.20	16.58	19.85	22.49	25.75
地方公共财政预算收入	(亿元)	Government Revenue	(100 million yuan)	0.59	1.03	2.77	4.03	4.99	6.00
粮食	(万吨)	Grain	(10 000 tons)	6.08	5.97	6.34	6.54	6.69	6.85
肉类产量	(吨)	Meat	(tons)	7430.00	9387.00	10395.07	10462.19	11295.89	11783.01
水产品	(吨)	Aquatic Products	(tons)	6420.00	8718.00	9673.70	10008.77	10654.79	11259.45
钢	(万吨)	Steel	(10 000 tons)	2.45	4.31	6.85	7.54	7.69	7.36
成品钢材	(万吨)	Rolled-Steel	(10 000 tons)	2.22	4.34	7.93	9.85	9.75	9.27
发电量	(亿千瓦小时)	Electricity	(100 million kWh)	1.47	3.44	5.56	5.62	5.96	5.80
水泥	(万吨)	Cement	(10 000 tons)	6.74	12.36	24.61	25.60	28.10	30.65
布	(万米)	Cloth	(10 000 meters)	470.00	573.00	1270.69	1705.75	1894.79	2176.71
每天消费量		**Daily Consumption**							
最终消费	(亿元)	Final Consumption	(100 million yuan)	5.56	9.99	20.25	24.47	27.35	30.58
居民消费	(亿元)	Resident Consumption	(100 million yuan)	4.37	7.63	14.07	17.10	19.41	22.07
城镇居民每人消费性支出	(元)	Per Capita Living Expenditure of Urban Residents	(yuan)	12.72	18.46	31.37	36.07	39.71	43.15
#食品消费		Food Consumption		4.88	7.19	12.14	14.70	15.99	17.15
农村居民每人生活消费支出	(元)	Per Capita Living Expenditure of Rural Residents	(yuan)	4.26	6.66	11.21	13.73	15.69	17.20
#食品消费		Food Consumption		2.27	3.27	4.83	5.36	5.90	6.32
政府消费	(亿元)	Government Consumption Expenditure	(100 million yuan)	1.19	2.36	6.17	7.37	7.94	8.51
社会消费品零售总额	(亿元)	Total Retail Sales of Consumer Goods	(100 million yuan)	4.90	8.12	18.41	22.67	26.20	29.82
每天其他经济活动		**Other Daily Economic Acitivities**							
货物运输量	(万吨)	Freight Traffic	(10 000 tons)	25.60	136.78	265.77	301.83	345.74	382.85
旅客运输量	(万人)	Passenger Traffic	(10 000 persons)	86.56	195.61	288.81	314.35	354.82	392.06
竣工房屋面积	(万平方米)	Floor Space of Housing Completed	(10 000 sq.m)	8.63	18.90	35.11	39.96	55.88	62.39
出版报纸	(万份)	Newspapers Published	(10 000 pieces)	367.67	536.16	497.80	548.98	564.66	543.01
函件	(万件)	Letters Delivered	(10 000 pieces)	99.00	41.64	27.40	28.76	35.89	28.77
进出口总额	(万美元)	Total Imports and Exports	(10 000 USD)	879.45	2490.96	7097.81	9183.29	8755.89	9969.86
#出口		Exports		529.04	1219.18	3956.71	5352.05	5315.34	6256.99
实际外商直接投资	(万美元)	Actual Foreign Direct Investment	(10 000 USD)	258.63	598.63	1109.59	1275.35	1552.33	1887.12
每天人口变动和婚姻		**Daily Population Changes and Marriages**							
出生人数	(人)	Birth	(persons)	1582	1441	1625	1635	1738	1757
死亡人数	(人)	Death	(persons)	979	940	944	946	967	975
结婚对数	(对)	Marriage	(couple)	969	1080	1564	1718	1687	1769
离婚对数	(对)	Divorce	(couple)	58	146	244	271	301	350

1-9 地区生产总值

GROSS DOMESTIC PRODUCT

本表按当年价格计算 (At current price)

年 份 Year	地区生产总值 (亿元) Total Output (100 million yuan)	第一产业 Primary Industry	第二产业 Secondary Industry	工业 Industry	建筑业 Contruction	第三产业 Tertiary Industry	#金融业 Banking	#房地产业 Real Estate	人均地区生产总值 (元) Per Capita GDP (yuan)	人均地区生产总值 (美元) Per Capita GDP (USD)
1952	24.51	13.90	3.83	3.17	0.66	6.78			90.13	34.44
1955	34.05	18.14	7.45	6.25	1.20	8.46			117.88	47.88
1957	48.86	24.33	11.59	9.03	2.56	12.94			162.17	65.87
1962	52.13	29.30	10.63	9.10	1.53	12.20			161.47	65.59
1965	72.43	37.74	21.16	17.36	3.80	13.53			209.26	85.00
1970	88.15	44.41	26.90	21.79	5.11	16.84			221.78	90.09
1975	120.10	53.71	45.48	32.68	12.80	20.91			274.30	139.50
1978	151.00	61.11	63.71	52.17	11.54	26.18	4.54	1.42	332.03	210.53
1979	188.46	85.15	73.03	58.98	14.05	30.28	5.26	1.62	409.35	273.60
1980	199.38	71.22	91.67	75.63	16.04	36.49	5.51	2.83	427.98	279.67
1981	219.75	87.00	92.85	78.73	14.12	39.90	6.02	3.19	466.32	273.49
1982	241.55	101.73	94.97	82.69	12.28	44.85	6.50	3.10	506.33	267.53
1983	262.58	105.40	106.50	92.19	14.31	50.68	7.09	2.53	543.27	274.98
1984	328.22	126.36	136.50	120.32	16.18	65.36	9.04	3.89	670.97	288.34
1985	396.26	144.44	174.35	152.88	21.47	77.47	10.71	4.61	800.69	272.66
1986	442.04	163.61	187.96	164.93	23.03	90.47	13.68	5.97	881.61	255.33
1987	517.77	183.99	224.53	197.66	26.87	109.25	17.09	7.39	1018.42	273.61
1988	626.52	214.66	271.25	244.17	27.08	140.61	20.82	8.88	1215.93	326.68
1989	717.08	239.07	300.46	276.47	23.99	177.55	28.14	9.18	1373.22	364.72
1990	824.38	289.45	313.39	284.15	29.24	221.54	33.77	11.36	1541.17	322.20
1991	913.38	279.30	359.86	327.50	32.36	274.22	40.30	13.61	1668.03	313.34
1992	1088.39	303.00	444.61	402.59	42.02	340.78	48.07	17.22	1962.45	355.86
1993	1325.83	346.39	537.60	475.44	62.16	441.84	52.22	25.63	2360.53	409.67
1994	1700.92	501.44	657.63	580.80	76.83	541.85	56.83	37.85	2991.33	347.07
1995	2109.38	619.77	780.18	680.92	99.26	709.43	60.86	42.07	3671.41	439.64
1996	2499.77	716.34	923.68	805.53	118.15	859.75	65.37	62.23	4310.98	811.22
1997	2856.47	767.92	1071.86	929.91	141.95	1016.69	69.68	69.65	4883.80	589.13
1998	3114.02	778.22	1199.08	1041.20	157.88	1136.72	74.14	81.78	5287.03	638.60
1999	3229.29	653.99	1314.44	1139.52	174.92	1260.86	78.81	85.01	5452.46	658.65
2000	3545.39	662.30	1437.38	1243.24	194.14	1445.71	81.49	99.40	6293.41	760.22
2001	3880.53	692.17	1574.39	1360.10	214.29	1613.97	88.48	122.49	6866.99	829.65
2002	4212.82	707.00	1709.89	1473.00	236.89	1795.93	96.95	145.17	7436.58	898.46
2003	4757.45	798.35	1956.02	1682.16	273.86	2003.08	107.31	176.80	8378.01	1012.20
2004	5633.24	1020.09	2320.60	1987.50	333.10	2292.55	118.85	204.80	9897.64	1195.83
2005	6590.19	1082.13	2852.12	2478.66	373.46	2655.94	127.32	217.17	11554.00	1410.45
2006	7617.47	1140.41	3365.08	2929.19	435.89	3111.98	174.99	294.73	13360.00	1710.91
2007	9333.40	1378.00	4143.06	3588.00	555.06	3812.34	337.27	409.65	16386.00	2178.55
2008	11328.92	1780.00	5082.07	4391.23	690.84	4466.85	393.05	526.88	19858.00	2859.57
2009	12961.10	1795.90	6038.08	5183.68	854.40	5127.12	479.11	546.11	22677.00	3317.24
2010	15967.61	2147.00	7767.24	6726.53	1040.71	6053.37	561.27	564.41	27906.00	4122.31
2011	19632.26	2569.30	9815.94	8538.04	1277.90	7247.02	674.57	634.67	34197.27	5294.68
2012	22250.45	2848.77	11193.10	9735.15	1457.95	8208.58	870.36	692.82	38572.33	6110.47
2013	24668.49	3098.16	12171.56	10531.37	1640.19	9398.77	1073.89	797.19	42612.70	6880.56

1-10 地区生产总值指数

INDICES OF GROSS DOMESTIC PRODUCT

按可比价计算，上年=100 (In comparable price, preceding year=100)

年 份 Year	地区生产总值(%) Total Output (%)	第一产业 Primary Industry	第二产业 Secondary Industry	工业 Industry	建筑业 Contruction	第三产业 Tertiary Industry	#金融业 Banking	#房地产业 Real Estate	人均地区生产总值(%) Per Capita GDP (%)
1953	114.0	107.4	129.4	141.0	93.3	122.7			111.6
1955	127.1	135.5	104.9	100.2	139.2	127.1			124.8
1957	107.4	106.4	115.3	109.5	146.0	102.6			104.8
1962	100.9	112.3	84.0	92.7	50.5	94.0			99.0
1965	118.1	111.5	132.5	124.5	196.4	114.9			115.4
1970	126.9	112.2	161.2	151.2	222.0	111.3			123.4
1975	111.4	94.5	139.0	135.2	152.5	116.0			110.0
1978	113.5	103.4	128.4	131.9	112.2	107.4			112.2
1979	115.6	118.9	113.1	112.1	118.4	114.4	114.5	112.7	114.2
1980	106.4	86.9	123.5	126.7	107.0	111.0	96.3	160.6	105.1
1981	106.5	113.3	101.5	104.3	87.1	104.9	104.8	108.2	105.3
1982	111.9	115.7	104.7	107.3	88.6	121.6	116.9	105.2	110.6
1983	105.9	99.6	109.9	109.2	115.9	111.5	107.5	80.3	104.6
1984	120.9	114.4	125.0	127.6	106.1	125.2	123.8	149.6	119.5
1985	116.2	108.3	124.7	124.7	124.3	112.4	112.4	112.3	114.8
1986	105.5	103.3	105.2	103.9	116.8	110.2	120.5	122.2	104.1
1987	108.4	103.1	111.3	112.9	99.0	110.7	114.5	113.4	106.9
1988	107.8	94.9	113.7	115.1	101.5	114.3	107.0	105.6	106.4
1989	104.5	105.2	102.1	104.2	81.3	109.3	121.8	93.2	103.1
1990	105.0	107.5	99.0	99.5	92.8	114.8	108.9	109.7	102.5
1991	106.6	95.1	111.1	111.6	106.1	115.4	114.4	114.7	104.2
1992	114.1	108.2	116.6	117.5	107.5	116.9	111.5	117.8	112.6
1993	113.0	105.8	116.7	116.1	123.3	115.2	112.0	119.4	111.6
1994	113.7	107.1	118.8	118.9	117.6	112.4	107.7	127.3	112.3
1995	113.2	108.9	116.1	115.9	118.5	112.5	107.3	121.0	112.0
1996	111.6	104.5	115.5	115.4	116.6	111.3	107.3	116.5	110.5
1997	111.9	106.9	113.4	113.5	112.3	113.5	103.4	110.3	110.9
1998	108.6	99.4	111.2	110.9	113.9	111.5	107.0	117.9	107.9
1999	107.8	101.9	108.2	108.2	107.5	111.0	103.7	106.1	107.2
2000	108.6	102.5	109.1	109.0	110.7	111.5	105.6	116.8	114.2
2001	108.9	102.5	109.9	110.1	108.5	110.8	107.4	122.1	108.5
2002	109.2	102.0	110.1	110.1	110.5	111.4	108.4	114.5	108.9
2003	109.7	105.8	110.2	110.2	110.6	110.8	110.1	119.0	109.5
2004	111.2	106.5	113.6	113.5	114.4	110.6	106.3	114.4	111.0
2005	112.1	104.0	115.2	116.0	109.9	111.8	104.4	103.5	111.8
2006	113.2	105.1	116.0	116.3	115.3	113.5	135.0	129.4	113.2
2007	114.6	104.7	116.7	115.7	123.3	115.9	167.3	132.0	114.7
2008	113.4	106.0	116.6	116.9	114.8	112.4	110.8	115.1	113.2
2009	113.5	105.2	116.8	115.7	123.7	112.3	122.8	111.1	113.3
2010	114.8	104.6	120.2	121.3	112.9	111.3	110.3	103.1	114.7
2011	113.8	104.4	117.9	119.1	110.1	112.0	112.8	104.4	113.5
2012	111.3	104.7	113.2	113.4	111.5	110.8	126.1	105.0	110.7
2013	110.1	104.7	111.3	111.2	111.9	110.0	115.6	110.2	109.7

1－11　地区生产总值指数

INDICES OF GROSS DOMESTIC PRODUCT

按可比价计算，1952=100 (In comparable price, 1952 = 100)

年　份 Year	地区生产总值(%) Total Output (%)	第一产业 Primary Industry	第二产业 Secondary Industry	工业 Industry	建筑业 Contruction	第三产业 Tertiary Industry	#金融业 Banking	#房地产业 Real Estate	人均地区生产总值(%) Per Capita GDP (%)
1953	114.0	107.4	129.4	141.0	93.3	122.7			111.6
1955	121.5	115.8	152.4	168.5	102.2	118.3			114.4
1957	169.6	143.9	280.1	295.3	233.2	172.1			153.0
1962	141.7	130.2	223.9	258.0	116.1	124.2			119.3
1965	205.6	161.5	490.4	538.5	338.9	161.1			161.5
1970	242.6	158.7	705.6	745.9	580.5	202.3			166.0
1975	320.2	185.3	1126.3	1165.1	995.9	259.1			198.9
1978	399.0	204.6	1616.5	1857.1	926.0	314.2			238.6
1979	461.3	243.2	1828.2	2082.1	1096.8	359.5	114.5	112.7	272.5
1980	490.8	211.4	2257.6	2637.6	1173.5	398.9	110.3	181.0	286.5
1981	523.0	239.5	2292.0	2751.0	1021.9	418.4	115.6	195.8	301.8
1982	585.4	277.2	2399.3	2950.6	905.2	508.6	135.1	206.0	333.7
1983	620.1	276.1	2637.8	3220.9	1048.9	567.0	145.2	165.4	348.9
1984	749.7	315.9	3297.0	4111.0	1113.2	709.9	179.8	247.5	416.8
1985	871.1	342.0	4111.1	5128.2	1383.1	797.9	202.1	277.9	478.7
1986	919.1	353.1	4326.3	5327.6	1615.8	879.3	243.5	339.6	498.5
1987	996.7	364.1	4816.5	6017.4	1599.1	973.3	278.8	385.1	533.1
1988	1074.3	345.4	5475.9	6925.0	1623.7	1112.1	298.3	406.7	567.0
1989	1122.7	363.3	5592.5	7218.5	1319.6	1215.1	363.4	379.1	584.7
1990	1178.9	390.6	5536.7	7181.9	1224.3	1394.6	395.7	415.8	599.3
1991	1257.2	371.2	6151.9	8018.2	1298.9	1609.6	452.7	477.0	624.3
1992	1434.3	401.6	7175.3	9419.0	1396.0	1881.8	504.7	561.8	703.3
1993	1621.2	424.7	8372.8	10939.2	1720.9	2166.9	565.3	670.8	784.9
1994	1843.3	454.7	9948.0	13008.9	2024.1	2435.8	608.7	854.0	881.6
1995	2086.5	495.2	11547.9	15073.3	2398.9	2740.9	653.4	1033.2	987.5
1996	2327.5	517.4	13342.9	17402.1	2796.6	3050.0	701.2	1204.1	1091.5
1997	2604.6	553.0	15131.7	19753.3	3139.6	3461.5	725.3	1328.7	1211.0
1998	2829.4	549.4	16822.5	21912.2	3576.3	3858.8	776.3	1566.2	1306.3
1999	3048.8	560.1	18195.4	23713.5	3845.1	4285.0	805.2	1661.6	1399.9
2000	3310.6	574.1	19858.1	25847.7	4254.6	4777.6	850.3	1941.2	1598.1
2001	3604.0	588.5	21828.1	28458.3	4618.0	5291.6	913.2	2370.0	1734.3
2002	3936.2	600.2	24038.5	31332.6	5104.3	5892.2	990.1	2713.0	1889.5
2003	4318.6	634.9	26494.8	34517.7	5643.2	6525.7	1090.1	3229.7	2068.1
2004	4802.5	676.2	30099.5	39171.3	6456.0	7218.6	1158.5	3696.0	2294.6
2005	5383.6	703.2	34674.7	45438.7	7095.2	8070.4	1209.5	3825.4	2565.4
2006	6094.2	739.1	40222.6	52845.2	8180.7	9159.9	1632.8	4948.5	2904.0
2007	6984.0	773.8	46939.8	61141.9	10086.8	10616.3	2731.6	6532.1	3330.9
2008	7919.8	820.3	54731.8	71474.9	11579.7	11932.8	3026.7	7518.4	3770.6
2009	8989.0	862.9	63926.7	82696.4	14324.1	13400.5	3716.7	8353.0	4272.1
2010	10319.4	902.6	76839.9	100310.7	16171.9	14914.8	4099.5	8611.9	4900.1
2011	11746.5	942.3	90571.2	119440.0	17810.1	16701.5	4623.8	8994.3	5561.6
2012	13073.9	986.6	102526.6	135444.9	19858.3	18505.3	5830.7	9444.0	6156.7
2013	14394.4	1032.9	114112.1	150614.8	22221.4	20355.8	6740.3	10407.3	6753.8

注：金融业、房地产业指数以1978年为100。
Note:The indices of banking and real estate are 1978=100

1-12 地区生产总值构成
COMPOSITION OF GROSS DOMESTIC PRODUCT

本表按当年价格计算 (At current prices)

年 份 Year	地区生产总值(%) Total Output (%)	第一产业 Primary Industry	第二产业 Secondary Industry	工业 Industry	建筑业 Contruction	第三产业 Tertiary Industry	#金融业 Banking	#房地产业 Real Estate
1952	100	56.7	15.6	12.9	2.7	27.7		
1955	100	53.3	21.9	18.4	3.5	24.8		
1957	100	49.8	23.7	18.5	5.2	26.5		
1962	100	56.2	20.4	17.5	2.9	23.4		
1965	100	52.1	29.2	24.0	5.2	18.7		
1970	100	50.4	30.5	24.7	5.8	19.1		
1975	100	44.7	37.9	27.2	10.7	17.4		
1978	100	40.5	42.2	34.5	7.6	17.3	3.0	0.9
1979	100	45.2	38.8	31.3	7.5	16.1	2.8	0.9
1980	100	35.7	46.0	37.9	8.0	18.3	2.8	1.4
1981	100	39.6	42.3	35.8	6.4	18.2	2.7	1.5
1982	100	42.1	39.3	34.2	5.1	18.6	2.7	1.3
1983	100	40.1	40.6	35.1	5.4	19.3	2.7	1.0
1984	100	38.5	41.6	36.7	4.9	19.9	2.8	1.2
1985	100	36.5	44.0	38.6	5.4	19.6	2.7	1.2
1986	100	37.0	42.5	37.3	5.2	20.5	3.1	1.4
1987	100	35.5	43.4	38.2	5.2	21.1	3.3	1.4
1988	100	34.3	43.3	39.0	4.3	22.4	3.3	1.4
1989	100	33.3	41.9	38.6	3.3	24.8	3.9	1.3
1990	100	35.1	38.0	34.5	3.5	26.9	4.1	1.4
1991	100	30.6	39.4	35.9	3.5	30.0	4.4	1.5
1992	100	27.8	40.9	37.0	3.9	31.3	4.4	1.6
1993	100	26.1	40.5	35.9	4.7	33.3	3.9	1.9
1994	100	29.5	38.7	34.1	4.5	31.9	3.3	2.2
1995	100	29.4	37.0	32.3	4.7	33.6	2.9	2.0
1996	100	28.7	37.0	32.2	4.7	34.4	2.6	2.5
1997	100	26.9	37.5	32.6	5.0	35.6	2.4	2.4
1998	100	25.0	38.5	33.4	5.1	36.5	2.4	2.6
1999	100	20.3	40.7	35.3	5.4	39.0	2.4	2.6
2000	100	18.7	40.5	35.1	5.5	40.8	2.3	2.8
2001	100	17.8	40.6	35.0	5.5	41.6	2.3	3.2
2002	100	16.8	40.6	35.0	5.6	42.6	2.3	3.4
2003	100	16.8	41.1	35.4	5.8	42.1	2.3	3.7
2004	100	18.1	41.2	35.3	5.9	40.7	2.1	3.6
2005	100	16.4	43.3	37.6	5.7	40.3	1.9	3.3
2006	100	15.0	44.2	38.5	5.7	40.8	2.3	3.9
2007	100	14.8	44.4	38.4	6.0	40.8	3.6	4.4
2008	100	15.7	44.9	38.8	6.1	39.4	3.5	4.7
2009	100	13.8	46.6	40.0	6.6	39.6	3.7	4.2
2010	100	13.5	48.6	42.1	6.5	37.9	3.5	3.5
2011	100	13.1	50.0	43.5	6.5	36.9	3.4	3.2
2012	100	12.8	50.3	43.8	6.5	36.9	3.9	3.1
2013	100	12.6	49.3	42.7	6.6	38.1	4.4	3.2

1-13　按支出法计算的地区生产总值
GROSS DOMESTIC PRODUCT BY EXPENDITURE APPROACH

本表按当年价格计算 (At current prices)

年　份 Year	地区生产总值 (亿元) Gross Domestic Product (100 million yuan)	最终消费 Final Consumption Expenditure	居民消费 Residents Consumption Expenditure	政府消费 Government Consumption Expenditure	资本形成总额 Gross Capital Formation	固定资本形成 Fixed Capital Formation	存货增加 Changes in Inventories	货物和服务净流出 Net Export of Goods and Services
1978	151.20	81.70	74.70	7.00	43.12	31.40	11.72	26.38
1980	200.19	107.79	93.51	14.28	40.10	33.19	6.91	52.30
1985	386.76	240.02	203.23	36.79	135.43	96.71	38.72	11.31
1989	718.07	478.66	398.09	80.57	201.39	115.50	85.89	38.02
1990	818.89	535.49	434.62	100.87	261.95	147.13	114.82	21.45
1991	913.22	597.42	475.85	121.57	281.92	176.32	105.60	33.88
1992	1089.68	689.93	546.61	143.32	355.46	235.63	119.83	44.29
1993	1423.92	876.16	694.49	181.67	512.31	377.95	134.36	35.45
1994	1858.89	1043.25	845.14	198.10	740.13	571.68	168.45	75.51
1995	2364.45	1305.21	1095.97	209.20	973.63	778.25	195.38	85.61
1996	2720.28	1599.74	1346.76	253.00	1191.75	985.03	206.72	-71.21
1997	3107.91	1720.23	1438.12	282.10	1466.81	1102.10	364.71	-79.13
1998	3344.45	1859.97	1518.92	341.10	1614.60	1238.90	375.70	-130.12
1999	3504.01	1887.86	1507.12	380.70	1754.79	1320.10	434.69	-138.64
2000	3760.48	2030.07	1594.08	436.00	1882.47	1451.85	430.62	-152.06
2001	4102.08	2262.67	1767.38	495.30	1884.57	1610.93	273.64	-45.16
2002	4416.88	2499.95	1951.54	548.41	1905.92	1699.78	206.14	11.01
2003	4910.53	2819.24	2188.05	631.20	2037.19	1875.78	161.41	54.10
2004	5633.30	3174.18	2452.62	721.56	2538.77	2325.87	212.90	-79.65
2005	6520.14	3645.71	2785.42	860.29	2943.58	2804.01	139.57	-69.15
2006	7972.33	4245.68	3124.37	1121.31	3634.13	3555.21	78.92	92.52
2007	9550.04	4999.66	3709.69	1289.97	4450.25	4371.14	79.11	100.13
2008	11728.64	5892.03	4225.38	1666.65	5716.36	5368.99	347.37	120.25
2009	13240.42	6325.15	4456.31	1868.84	6827.00	6612.85	214.15	88.27
2010	16182.27	7389.80	5136.78	2253.02	8511.17	8200.40	310.77	281.30
2011	20167.28	8931.48	6241.95	2689.53	11027.27	10597.82	429.45	208.53
2012	22659.38	9982.79	7085.46	2897.33	12554.67	12064.75	489.92	121.92
2013	25431.66	11161.21	8053.82	3107.39	14245.35	13701.86	543.49	25.10

1-14 按支出法计算的地区生产总值指数

INDICES OF GROSS DOMESTIC PRODUCT BY EXPENDITURE APPROACH

按可比价计算 1952=100 (In comparable price, 1952=100)

年份 Year	地区生产总值 (%) Gross Domestic Product (%)	最终消费 Final Consumption Expenditure	居民消费 Residents Consumption Expenditure	政府消费 Government Consumption Expenditure	资本形成总额 Gross Capital Formation	固定资本形成 Fixed Capital Formation	存货增加 Changes in Inventories
1952	100.0	100.0	100.0	100.0	100.0	100.0	100.0
1978	488.3	313.7	308.9	369.3	820.0	1396.6	388.5
1980	605.4	388.8	363.4	706.7	663.9	1270.1	209.7
1985	1007.5	736.7	674.8	1492.5	1962.9	3155.5	1067.1
1990	1337.5	1004.9	897.4	2307.0	2504.8	3460.7	1786.7
1991	1344.2	970.7	850.8	2403.9	2595.0	3955.5	1604.4
1992	1471.9	1023.1	870.3	2819.7	2979.1	4806.0	1670.2
1993	1764.8	1242.1	1045.3	3550.0	3598.7	6218.9	1747.0
1994	2075.4	1379.9	1174.9	3802.1	4530.8	8246.3	1920.0
1995	2339.0	1508.3	1302.9	3950.4	5432.4	9945.0	2261.8
1996	2619.7	1702.8	1467.1	4507.4	6475.4	12520.8	2257.2
1997	2902.6	1776.1	1541.9	4584.0	8120.2	14486.6	3634.1
1998	3140.6	1985.6	1697.7	5418.3	9257.0	16775.4	3961.2
1999	3357.3	2130.6	1765.6	6431.5	10099.4	17966.5	4543.5
2000	3629.3	2260.5	1852.1	7055.4	10927.6	19709.2	4738.9
2001	3930.5	2513.7	2042.9	8057.2	10807.4	21542.2	3028.2
2002	4276.4	2795.3	2281.9	8814.6	11099.2	23093.2	2313.5
2003	4618.5	3072.0	2494.1	9890.0	11443.2	24594.3	1753.6
2004	5052.7	3336.2	2683.6	11086.7	13422.9	28775.3	2121.9
2005	5709.6	3726.5	2976.1	12672.1	15288.7	34041.2	1398.3
2006	6531.8	4326.5	3318.4	16600.0	18315.8	42245.1	465.6
2007	7446.3	4785.1	3680.1	18226.8	21667.6	20102.7	450.2
2008	8399.4	5282.8	3952.4	21653.4	25026.1	22575.3	1848.5
2009	9356.9	5689.6	4177.7	24381.7	30606.9	28151.4	1144.2
2010	11014.0	6423.5	4658.1	28307.2	36758.9	33669.1	1660.3
2011	12886.4	7310.0	5319.6	31902.2	44662.1	40806.9	2148.4
2012	14162.2	7931.3	5862.2	33401.6	50021.5	45662.9	2440.6
2013	15705.9	8653.1	6507.0	34904.7	56574.4	51690.5	2723.7

1-15　三次产业贡献率

CONTRIBUTING RATE OF THE THREE INDUSTRIES

单位：%　　本表按可比价格计算 (In comparable price)　　(%)

年 份 Year	地区生产总值 Gross Domestic Product	第一产业 Primary Industry	第二产业 Second Industry	#工 业 Industry	第三产业 Tertiary Industry
1990	100	42.68	-9.84	-4.64	67.16
1991	100	-25.9	65.6	62.7	60.3
1992	100	18.0	48.2	46.4	33.8
1993	100	13.0	53.5	47.7	33.5
1994	100	14.2	59.2	54.7	26.6
1995	100	17.5	54.9	49.8	27.6
1996	100	9.6	62.2	56.7	28.2
1997	100	13.5	53.9	49.8	32.6
1998	100	-1.6	62.8	56.4	38.8
1999	100	5.1	52.2	48.2	42.7
2000	100	5.6	53.0	47.9	41.3
2001	100	5.3	45.2	40.0	49.5
2002	100	3.8	45.1	38.9	51.1
2003	100	9.8	43.4	37.4	46.8
2004	100	9.2	50.4	43.2	40.5
2005	100	6.5	53.5	48.8	40.0
2006	100	6.3	52.4	46.6	41.3
2007	100	4.9	50.9	41.8	44.2
2008	100	6.2	56.0	49.2	37.8
2009	100	5.1	57.9	47.0	37.0
2010	100	3.7	66.1	60.3	30.2
2011	100	4.3	62.9	58.1	32.8
2012	100	5.1	59.1	52.6	35.8
2013	100	5.4	57.6	50.1	37.0

注：产业贡献率指各产业增加值增量与GDP增量之比。

Note:Contribution share of the three components to the increase of the GDP refers to the proportion of the increment of the each component of GDP expenditure approach to the increment of GDP.

1–16　三次产业拉动率
CONTRIBUTION OF THE THREE STRATA OF INDUSTRY TO GDP GROWTH

单位：百分点　　本表按可比价格计算(In comparable price)　　(percentage point)

年　份 Year	地区生产总值 Gross Domestic Product	第一产业 Primary Industry	第二产业 Second Industry	#工　业 Industry	第三产业 Tertiary Industry
1990	5.00	2.1	-0.5	-0.2	3.4
1991	6.6	-1.7	4.3	4.1	4.0
1992	14.1	2.5	6.8	6.5	4.8
1993	13.0	1.7	7.0	6.2	4.4
1994	13.7	1.9	8.1	7.5	3.6
1995	13.2	2.3	7.3	6.6	3.6
1996	11.6	1.1	7.2	6.6	3.3
1997	11.9	1.6	6.4	5.9	3.9
1998	8.6	-0.1	5.4	4.8	3.3
1999	7.8	0.4	4.1	3.8	3.3
2000	8.6	0.5	4.6	4.1	3.6
2001	8.6	0.5	3.9	3.4	4.3
2002	9.2	0.4	4.1	3.6	4.7
2003	9.7	0.9	4.2	3.6	4.5
2004	11.2	1.0	5.6	4.8	4.5
2005	12.1	0.8	6.5	5.9	4.8
2006	13.2	0.8	6.9	6.1	5.5
2007	14.6	0.7	7.4	6.1	6.5
2008	13.4	0.8	7.5	6.6	5.1
2009	13.5	0.7	7.8	6.3	5.0
2010	14.8	0.5	9.8	8.9	4.5
2011	13.8	0.6	8.7	8.0	4.5
2012	11.3	0.6	6.7	5.9	4.0
2013	10.1	0.6	5.8	5.1	3.7

注：三次产业对生产总值增长的拉动指GDP增长速度与各产业贡献率之乘积。

Note:Contribution of the three components to GDP growth refers to the growth rate of GDP multiplied by the contribution share of the three components.

1-17 三大需求贡献率

CONTRIBUTING RATE OF THE THREE REQUIREMENTS

单位：% 本表按可比价格计算 (In comparable price) (%)

年 份 Year	地区生产总值 Gross Domestic Product	最终消费支出 Final Consumption Expenditure	资本形成总额 Gross Capital Formation	货物和服务净流出 Net Outflow of Goods and Services
1990	100.0	59.4	111.8	-71.3
1991	100.0	-464.2	238.4	325.8
1992	100.0	35.7	51.8	12.5
1993	100.0	65.2	36.3	-1.5
1994	100.0	38.8	51.3	10.0
1995	100.0	42.5	58.3	-0.8
1996	100.0	60.2	63.5	-23.7
1997	100.0	22.7	99.2	-21.8
1998	100.0	76.6	81.1	-57.6
1999	100.0	58.2	65.9	-24.1
2000	100.0	41.6	51.7	6.8
2001	100.0	72.3	-6.4	34.1
2002	100.0	70.3	13.9	15.8
2003	100.0	70.5	17.0	12.5
2004	100.0	52.6	76.1	-28.6
2005	100.0	50.7	49.0	0.3
2006	100.0	44.3	43.9	11.9
2007	100.0	40.8	58.7	0.5
2008	100.0	35.5	64.4	0.1
2009	100.0	27.4	74.0	-1.4
2010	100.0	27.8	61.6	10.6
2011	100.0	36.9	66.3	-3.2
2012	100.0	38.2	66.2	-4.4
2013	100.0	36.7	67.2	-3.9

注：贡献率指三大需求增量与支出法地区生产总值增量之比。

Note:Contribution share of the three components to the increase of the GDP refers to the proportion of the increment of the each component of GDP expenditure approach to the increment of GDP.

1-18 三大需求拉动率
CONTRIBUTION OF THE THREE COMPONENTS OF GDP TO THE GROWTH OF GDP

单位：百分点　　本表按可比价格计算 (In comparable price)　　(percentage point)

年 份 Year	地区生产总值 Gross Domestic Product	最终消费支出 Final Consumption Expenditure	资本形成总额 Gross Capital Formation	货物和服务净流出 Net Outflow of Goods and Services
1990	5.0	3.0	5.6	-3.6
1991	6.6	-30.6	15.7	21.5
1992	14.1	5.0	7.3	1.8
1993	13.0	8.5	4.7	-0.2
1994	13.7	5.3	7.0	1.4
1995	13.2	5.6	7.7	-0.1
1996	11.6	7.0	7.4	-2.7
1997	11.9	2.7	11.8	-2.6
1998	8.6	6.6	7.0	-5.0
1999	7.8	4.5	5.1	-1.9
2000	8.6	3.6	4.4	0.6
2001	8.9	6.4	-0.6	3.0
2002	9.2	6.5	1.3	1.5
2003	9.7	6.8	1.6	1.2
2004	11.2	5.9	8.5	-3.2
2005	12.1	6.1	5.9	0.1
2006	13.2	5.8	5.8	1.6
2007	14.6	6.0	8.6	0.1
2008	13.4	4.8	8.6	
2009	13.5	3.7	10.0	-0.2
2010	14.8	4.1	9.1	1.6
2011	13.8	5.1	9.1	-0.4
2012	11.3	4.3	7.5	-0.5
2013	10.1	3.7	6.8	-0.4

注：1.三大需求指支出法地区生产总值的三大构成项目，即最终消费支出、资本形成总额、货物和服务净流出。
2.三大需求对国内生产总值增长的拉动指地区生产总值增长速度与三大需求贡献率的乘积。

Notes: a)Three components of GDP by exoenditure approach are final consumption expenditure, gross capital formation and net exports of goods and services.
b)Contribution of the three components to GDP growth refers to the growth refers to the growth rate of GDP multiplied by the contribution share of the three components.

1-19　市、州生产总值(2013)

GROSS DOMESTIC PRODUCT OF CITIES AND PREFECTURES(2013)

单位:亿元　　(100 million yuan)

地　区	Regions	地区生产总值 Gross Domestic Product	第一产业 Primary Industry	第二产业 Secondary Industry	第三产业 Tertiary Industry
武　汉	Wuhan	9051.27	335.40	4396.17	4319.70
黄　石	Huangshi	1142.03	95.21	699.20	347.62
十　堰	Shiyan	1080.59	143.03	547.01	390.55
宜　昌	Yichang	2818.07	335.95	1693.77	788.35
襄　阳	Xiangyang	2814.02	386.45	1611.41	816.16
鄂　州	Ezhou	630.94	78.51	375.08	177.35
荆　门	Jingmen	1202.61	190.30	651.93	360.38
孝　感	Xiaogan	1238.93	243.13	602.31	393.49
荆　州	Jingzhou	1334.93	319.09	596.20	419.64
黄　冈	Huanggang	1332.55	356.79	521.28	454.48
咸　宁	Xianning	872.11	162.90	423.09	286.12
随　州	Suizhou	661.94	124.79	320.26	216.89
恩 施 州	Enshi	552.48	133.28	197.75	221.45
仙　桃	Xiantao	504.28	80.17	268.77	155.34
潜　江	Qianjiang	492.70	65.00	290.97	136.73
天　门	Tianmen	365.19	74.30	190.04	100.85
神 农 架	Shennongjia	18.57	1.77	7.67	9.14

1-20　市、州生产总值指数(2013)

INDICES OF GROSS DOMESTIC PRODUCT OF CITIES AND PREFECTURES(2013)

(上年=100,单位:%)　　(preceding year = 100,%)

地　区	Regions	地区生产总值 Gross Domestic Product	第一产业 Primary Industry	第二产业 Secondary Industry	第三产业 Tertiary Industry
武　汉	Wuhan	110.0	104.5	110.3	110.0
黄　石	Huangshi	109.8	104.8	110.2	110.1
十　堰	Shiyan	110.4	105.0	112.2	109.2
宜　昌	Yichang	111.5	104.8	112.6	111.6
襄　阳	Xiangyang	111.4	104.8	113.3	110.7
鄂　州	Ezhou	110.5	104.9	112.2	109.0
荆　门	Jingmen	110.5	104.8	112.4	110.5
孝　感	Xiaogan	110.8	104.8	114.0	109.6
荆　州	Jingzhou	110.4	104.9	113.5	110.2
黄　冈	Huanggang	110.5	104.8	112.7	111.9
咸　宁	Xianning	110.6	104.8	113.6	109.0
随　州	Suizhou	110.6	104.8	112.8	110.5
恩 施 州	Enshi	109.9	105.1	112.1	111.3
仙　桃	Xiantao	111.3	104.9	113.8	110.5
潜　江	Qianjiang	110.9	104.8	112.8	110.1
天　门	Tianmen	110.9	104.8	113.4	111.2
神 农 架	Shennongjia	109.8	105.0	109.7	110.9

1-21 市、州支出法生产总值(2013)
GROSS DOMESTIC PRODUCT BY EXPENDITURE APPROACH OF CITIES AND PREFECTURES(2013)

单位:亿元 (100 million yuan)

地 区	Regions	Total Gross Domestic Product by Expenditure	最终消费支出 Final Consumption Expenditure	资本形成总额 Gross Capital Formation	货物和服务净流出 Net Export of Goods and Services
武 汉	Wuhan	9051.27	4067.42	5979.49	-995.64
黄 石	Huangshi	1142.00	457.59	647.46	36.95
十 堰	Shiyan	1014.20	448.70	494.80	70.70
宜 昌	Yichang	2818.07	1170.43	1564.14	83.50
襄 阳	Xiangyang	2814.40	1288.70	1490.70	35.00
鄂 州	Ezhou	630.94	186.63	419.00	25.31
荆 门	Jingmen	1202.61	501.94	685.67	15.00
孝 感	Xiaogan	1241.35	517.24	712.48	11.63
荆 州	Jingzhou	1334.93	630.75	1184.13	-479.95
黄 冈	Huanggang	1332.55	681.21	671.71	-20.37
咸 宁	Xianning	1108.35	327.83	766.53	13.99
随 州	Suizhou	659.74	292.83	335.86	31.05
恩施州	Enshi	552.48	409.12	480.03	-336.67
仙 桃	Xiantao	504.28	124.05	314.17	66.06
潜 江	Qianjiang	495.20	148.70	338.27	8.23
天 门	Tianmen	355.70	182.49	157.93	15.28
神农架	Shennongjia	18.57	9.35	11.85	-2.63

1-22 市、州民营经济增加值(2013)
VALUE ADDED OF PRIVATE ECONOMY(2013)

地 区	Regions	增加值(亿元) Value-Added (100 million yuan)		占GDP比重(%) Percentage(%)	
		2012	2013	2012	2013
全 省	**Total**	**11805.95**	**13321.71**	**53.1**	**54.0**
武 汉	Wuhan	3131.88	3508.87	39.1	38.8
黄 石	Huangshi	565.42	628.34	54.3	55.0
十 堰	Shiyan	454.10	476.00	47.5	44.1
宜 昌	Yichang	1481.12	1671.75	59.0	59.3
襄 阳	Xiangyang	1290.00	1458.00	51.6	51.8
鄂 州	Ezhou	337.24	391.26	60.2	62.0
荆 门	Jingmen	591.25	679.15	54.5	56.5
孝 感	Xiaogan	689.56	781.65	62.4	63.1
荆 州	Jingzhou	544.19	616.23	45.5	46.2
黄 冈	Huanggang	734.36	833.84	61.6	62.6
咸 宁	Xianning	559.52	637.68	73.5	73.1
随 州	Suizhou	400.14	456.94	67.8	69.0
恩施州	Enshi	192.30	231.31	39.9	41.9
仙 桃	Xiantao	312.23	358.57	70.3	71.1
潜 江	Qianjiang	299.10	336.37	67.7	68.3
天 门	Tianmen	216.86	248.26	67.5	68.0
神农架	Shennongjia	6.67	7.49	39.7	40.3

主要统计指标解释

平均增长速度　计算平均增长速度有两种方法：一种是习惯上经常使用的“水平法”，又称几何平均法，是以间隔期最后一年的水平同基期水平对比来计算平均每年增长(或下降)速度；另一种是“累计法”，又称代数平均法或方程法，是以间隔期内各年水平的总和同基期水平对比来计算平均每年增长(或下降)速度。在一般正常情况下，两种方法计算的平均每年增长速度比较接近；但在经济发展不平衡、出现大起大落时，两种方法计算的结果差别较大。

国民经济行业分类　自2003年定期报表开始使用新的《国民经济行业分类》（GB/T4754-2002）该分类是由国家统计局组织修订，经国家质量监督检验检疫总局批准，于2002年5月10日发布实施。这次修订是在1994年分类标准的基础上，参照联合国《全部经济活动的国际标准产业分类》（ISIC/Rev.3）进行的。修订后的《国民经济行业分类》（GB/T4754-2002）共有门类20个，大类95个，中类396个，小类913个。新增门类4个，大类增加3个，中类增加28个，小类增加67个。

企业(单位)登记注册类型　是以在工商行政管理机关登记注册的各类企业为划分对象，以工商行政管理部门对企业登记注册的类型为依据，将企业登记注册类型分为内资企业、港澳台商投资企业和外商投资企业三大类。内资企业包括国有企业、集体企业、股份合作企业、联营企业、有限责任公司、股份有限公司、私营公司和其他企业；港澳台商投资企业和外商投资企业分别包括合资经营企业、合作经营企业、独资经营企业和股份有限公司。对不在工商行政管理部门进行登记注册的行政机关、事业单位和社会团体，主要按其经费来源和管理方式进行划分。

国有企业　指企业全部资产归国家所有，并按《中华人民共和国企业法人登记管理条例》规定登记注册的非公司制的经济组织。不包括有限责任公司中的国有独资公司。

集体企业　指企业资产归集体所有，并按《中华人民共和国企业法人登记管理条例》规定登记注册的经济组织。

股份合作企业　指以合作制为基础，由企业职工共同出资入股，吸收一定比例的社会资产投资组建，实行自主经营，自负盈亏，共同劳动，民主管理，按劳分配与按股分红相结合的一种集体经济组织。

联营企业　指两个及两个以上相同或不同所有制性质的企业法人或事业单位法人，按自愿、平等、互利的原则，共同投资组成的经济组织。联营企业包括国有联营企业、集体联营企业、国有与集体联营企业和其他联营企业。

有限责任公司　指根据《中华人民共和国公司登记管理条例》规定登记注册，由两个以上、五十个以下的股东共同出资，每个股东以其所认缴的出资额对公司承担有限责任，公司以其全部资产对其债务承担责任的经济组织。有限责任公司包括国有独资公司以及其他有限责任公司。

股份有限公司　指根据《中华人民共和国公司登记管理条例》规定登记注册，其全部注册资本由等额股份构成并通过发行股票筹集资本，股东以其认购的股份对公司承担有限责任，公司以其全部资产对其债务承担责任的经济组织。

私营企业　指由自然人投资设立或由自然人控股，以雇佣劳动为基础的营利性经济组织。包括按照《公司法》、《合伙企业法》、《私营企业暂行条例》规定登记注册的私营有限责任公司、私营股份有限公司、私营合伙企业和私营独资企业。

其他企业　指上述企业之外的其他内资经济组织。

与港澳台商合资经营企业　指港澳台地区投资者与内地企业依照《中华人民共和国中外合资经营企业法》及有关法律的规定，按合同规定的比例投资设立、分享利润和分担风险的企业。

与港澳台商合作经营企业　指港澳台地区投资者与内地企业依照《中华人民共和国中外合作经营企业法》及有关法律的规定，依照合作合同的约定进行投资或提供条件设立、分配利润和分担风险的企业。

港澳台商独资经营企业　指依照《中华人民共和国外资企业法》及有关法律的规定，在内地由港澳台地区投资者全额投资设立的企业。

港澳台商投资股份有限公司　指根据国家有关规定，经原外经贸部依法批准设立，其中港、澳、台商的股本占公司注册资本的比例达 25% 以上的股份有限公司。凡其中港、澳、台商的股本占公司注册资本的比例小于 25%的，属于内资企业中的股份有限公司。

中外合资经营企业 指外国企业或外国人与中国内地企业依照《中华人民共和国中外合资经营企业法》及有关法律的规定，按合同规定的比例投资设立、分享利润和分担风险的企业。

中外合作经营企业 指外国企业或外国人与中国内地企业依照《中华人民共和国中外合作经营企业法》及有关法律的规定，依照合作合同的约定进行投资或提供条件设立、分配利润和分担风险的企业。

外资企业 指依照《中华人民共和国外资企业法》及有关法律的规定，在中国内地由外国投资者全额投资设立的企业。

外商投资股份有限公司 指根据国家有关规定，经原外经贸部依法批准设立，其中外资的股本占公司注册资本的比例达 25% 以上的股份有限公司。凡其中外资股本占公司注册资本的比例小于 25%的，属于内资企业中的股份有限公司。

行政机关、事业单位和社会团体 参照企业登记注册类型，主要按其经费来源和管理方式划分。具体规定如下：

⑴行政机关：包括国家机关和政党机关，原则上均列为“国有”。但有特殊规定的，如供销社等，则列为“集体”。

⑵事业单位：包括经国家机构编制部门和有关业务主管部门批准成立的各类事业单位，不包括实行企业化管理的事业单位。事业单位的划分办法如下：

①由国家财政预算拨款或列入财政预算外资金管理以及经费主要来源于国有主管部门或国有上级单位的事业单位，列为“国有”。

②经费主要来源于集体单位的事业单位，列为“集体”。

③公民个人(或个人合伙)开办的事业单位，列为“私营”。

④上述以外的其他事业单位，如果其经费来源不明确，按管理方式进行归类。

⑶社会团体：包括经民政部门批准成立以及未纳入社会团体管理条例范围的工会、妇联等各类社会团体。社会团体的划分办法如下：

①未纳入民政部社会团体管理条例范围的工会、妇联、共青团、青联、工商联、科协、侨联等社会团体，国家拨款设立的基金会或基金管理组织以及经费主要来源于国有业务主管部门或国有上级单位的社会团体，列为“国有”。

②经费主要来源于集体单位的社会团体，列为“集体”。

③公民个人(或个人合伙)开办的社会团体，划为“私营”。

④上述以外的其他社会团体，如果其经费来源不明确，改按管理方式进行归类。

地区生产总值(GDP) 指按市场价格计算的一个地区所有常住单位在一定时期内生产活动的最终成果。地区生产总值有三种表现形态，即价值形态、收入形态和产品形态。从价值形态看，它是所有常住单位在一定时期内生产的全部货物和服务价值超过同期投入的全部非固定资产货物和服务价值的差额，即所有常住单位的增加值之和；从收入形态看，它是所有常住单位在一定时期内创造并分配给常住单位和非常住单位的初次收入之和；从产品形态看，它是所有常住单位在一定时期内最终使用的货物和服务价值减去货物和服务流进价值。在实际核算中，地区生产总值有三种计算方法，即生产法、收入法和支出法。三种方法分别从不同的方面反映地区生产总值及其构成。

国民总收入（GNI） 即国民生产总值，指一个国家(或地区)所有常住单位在一定时期内收入初次分配的最终结果。一国常住单位从事生产活动所创造的增加值在初次分配中主要分配给该国的常住单位，但也有一部分以生产税及进口税(扣除生产和进口补贴)、劳动者报酬和财产收入等形式分配给非常住单位；同时，国外生产所创造的增加值也有一部分以生产税及进口税(扣除生产和进口补贴)、劳动者报酬和财产收入等形式分配给该国的常住单位，从而产生了国民总收入的概念。它等于国内生产总值加上来自国外的净要素收入。与国内生产总值不同，国民总收入是个收入概念，而国内生产总值是个生产概念。

三次产业 三产业的划分是世界上较为常用的产业结构分类，但各国的划分不尽一致。我国的三次产业划分是：

第一产业是指农、林、牧、渔业。

第二产业是指采矿业，制造业，电力、煤气及水的生产和供应业，建筑业。

第三产业是指除第一、二产业以外的其他行业。

劳动者报酬　指劳动者因从事生产活动所获得的全部报酬。包括劳动者获得的各种形式的工资、奖金和津贴，既包括货币形式的，也包括实物形式的，还包括劳动者所享受的公费医疗和医药卫生费、上下班交通补贴、单位支付的社会保险费、住房公积金等。对于个体经济来说，其所有者所获得的劳动报酬和经营利润不易区分，这两部分统一作为劳动者报酬处理。

生产税净额　指生产税减生产补贴后的余额。生产税指政府对生产单位从事生产、销售和经营活动以及因从事生产活动使用某些生产要素(如固定资产、土地、劳动力)所征收的各种税、附加费和规费。生产补贴与生产税相反，指政府对生产单位的单方面转移支出，因此视为负生产税，包括政策亏损补贴、价格补贴等。

固定资产折旧　指一定时期内为弥补固定资产损耗按照规定的固定资产折旧率提取的固定资产折旧，或按国民经济核算统一规定的折旧率虚拟计算的固定资产折旧。它反映了固定资产在当期生产中的转移价值。各类企业和企业化管理的事业单位的固定资产折旧是指实际计提的折旧费；不计提折旧的政府机关、非企业化管理的事业单位和居民住房的固定资产折旧是按照统一规定的折旧率和固定资产原值计算的虚拟折旧。原则上，固定资产折旧应按固定资产当期的重置价值计算，但是目前我国尚不具备对全社会固定资产进行重估价的基础，所以暂时只能采用上述办法。

营业盈余　指常住单位创造的增加值扣除劳动者报酬、生产税净额和固定资产折旧后的余额。它相当于企业的营业利润加上生产补贴，但要扣除从利润中开支的工资和福利等。

支出法地区生产总值　是从最终使用的角度反映一个地区一定时期内生产活动最终成果的一种方法，包括最终消费支出、资本形成总额及货物和服务净流出三部分。计算公式为：

支出法国内生产总值=最终消费支出+资本形成总额+货物和服务净流出

最终消费支出　指常住单位为满足物质、文化和精神生活的需要，从本国经济领土和国外购买的货物和服务的支出。它不包括非常住单位在本国经济领土内的消费支出。最终消费支出分为居民消费支出和政府消费支出。

居民消费支出　指常住住户在一定时期内对于货物和服务的全部最终消费支出。居民消费支出除了直接以货币形式购买的货物和服务的消费支出外，还包括以其他方式获得的货物和服务的消费支出，即所谓的虚拟消费支出。居民虚拟消费支出包括如下几种类型：单位以实物报酬及实物转移的形式提供给劳动者的货物和服务；住户生产并由本住户消费了的货物和服务，其中的服务仅指住户的自有住房服务和付酬的家庭雇员提供的家庭和个人服务；金融机构提供的金融媒介服务；保险公司提供的保险服务。

政府消费支出　指政府部门为全社会提供的公共服务的消费支出和免费或以较低的价格向居民住户提供的货物和服务的净支出，前者等于政府服务的产出价值减去政府单位所获得的经营收入的价值，后者等于政府部门免费或以较低价格向居民住户提供的货物和服务的市场价值减去向住户收取的价值。

资本形成总额　指常住单位在一定时期内获得减去处置的固定资产和存货的净额，包括固定资本形成总额和存货增加两部分。

固定资本形成总额　指生产者在一定时期内获得的固定资产减处置的固定资产的价值总额。固定资产是通过生产活动生产出来的，且其使用年限在一年以上、单位价值在规定标准以上的资产，不包括自然资产。可分为有形固定资本形成总额和无形固定资本形成总额。有形固定资本形成总额包括一定时期内完成的建筑工程、安装工程和设备工器具购置(减处置)价值，以及土地改良、新增役、种、奶、毛、娱乐用牲畜和新增经济林木价值。无形固定资本形成总额包括矿藏的勘探、计算机软件等获得减处置。

存货增加　指常住单位在一定时期内存货实物量变动的市场价值，即期末价值减期初价值的差额，再扣除当期由于价格变动而产生的持有收益。存货增加可以是正值，也可以是负值，正值表示存货上升，负值表示存货下降。存货包括生产单位购进的原材料、燃料和储备物资等存货，以及生产单位生产的产成品、在制品和半成品等存货。

货物和服务净流出　指货物和服务流出减货物和服务流进的差额。流出包括常住单位向非常住单位出售或无偿转让的各种货物和服务的价值；流进包括常住单位从非常住单位购买或无偿得到的各种货物和服务的价值。由于服务活动的提供与使用同时发生，一般把常住单位从非常住单位得到的服务作为流进，非常住单位从常住单位得到的服务作为流出。

Explanatory Notes on Main Statistical Indicators

Average Annual Growth Rate Two methods for calculating average annual growth rate are applied, one is often called level approach, or the method of calculating geometric average, which is derived by comparing the level of the last year of the interval with that of the beginning year; the other is called accumulative approach or algebraic average or equation method, which is derived by the summation of the actual figure of each year in the interval divided by the figure in the base year. Usually the results calculated by the two methods are fairly close, but they differed sharply when uneven economic development occurred with striking fluctuations in growth.

Industrial Classification of the National Economy The new Industrial Classification of the National Economy (GB/T 4754-2002) is introduced starting from the compilation of 2003 annual statistics. The new revision was based on the 1994 classification and organized by the National Bureau of Statistics taking into consideration of the International Standards of the Industrial Classification of All Economic Activities (ISIC/Rev.3) of the United Nations, and the new Classification was promulgated by the National Administration of Quality Supervision, Inspection and Quarantine on May 10, 2002. The revised version of the Industrial Classification of the National Economy (GB/T 4754-2002) is composed of 20 major divisions, 95 divisions, 396 major groups and 913 groups, including 4 new major divisions, 3 new divisions, 28 major groups and 67 groups.

Registration Status of Enterprises Enterprises are classified into 3 categories, namely domestic-funded enterprises, enterprises with investment from Hong Kong, Macau and Taiwan, and enterprises with foreign investment, in the light of the registration status of an enterprise in industrial and commercial administration agencies. Domestic-funded enterprises include state-owned enterprises, collective-owned enterprises, cooperative enterprises, joint ownership enterprises, limited liability corporations, share-holding corporations Ltd., private enterprises and other enterprises. Included in the enterprises with investment from Hong Kong, Macau and Taiwan and enterprises with foreign investment are joint-venture enterprises, cooperative enterprises, sole investment enterprises and share-holding corporations Ltd. For government agencies, institutions and social organizations which are not requested to be registered in industrial and commercial administration agencies, they are classified mainly by their sources of funds and way of management.

State-owned Enterprises refer to non-corporation economic units where the entire assets are owned by the state and which have registered in accordance with the Regulation of the People's Republic of China on the Management of Registration of Corporate Enterprises. Excluded from this category are sole state-funded corporations in the limited liability corporations.

Collective-owned Enterprises refer to economic units where the assets are owned collectively and which have registered in accordance with the Regulation of the People's Republic of China on the Management of Registration of Corporate Enterprises.

Cooperative Enterprises refer to a form of collective economic units (enterprises) where capitals come mainly from employees as their shares, with certain proportion of capital from the outside, where production is organized on the basis of independent operation, independent accounting for profits and losses, joint work, democratic management, and a distribution system that integrates remuneration according to work with dividend according to capital share.

Joint Ownership Enterprises refer to economic units established by two or more corporate enterprises or corporate institutions of the same or different ownership, through joint investment on the basis of equality, voluntary participation and mutual benefits. They include state joint ownership enterprises, collective joint ownership enterprises, joint state-collective enterprises, other joint ownership enterprises.

Limited Liability Corporations refer to economic units established with investment from 2-50 investors and registered in accordance with the Regulation of the People's Republic of China on the Management of Registration of Corporations, each investor bearing limited liability to the corporation depending on its share of investment, and the corporation bearing liability to its debt to the maximum of its total assets. Limited liability corporations include exclusive state-funded limited liability corporations and other limited liability corporations.

Share-holding Corporations Ltd. refer to economic units registered in accordance with the Regulation of the People's Republic of China on the Management of Registration of Corporations, with total registered capitals divided into equal shares and raised through issuing stocks. Each investor bears limited liability to the corporation depending on the holding of shares, and the corporation bears liability to its debt to the maximum of its total assets.

Private Enterprises refer to profit-making economic units invested and established by natural persons, or controlled by natural persons using employed labour. Included in this category are private limited liability corporations, private share-holding corporations Ltd., private partnership enterprises and private-funded enterprises registered in accordance with the Corporation Law, Partnership Enterprises Law and Interim Regulations on Private Enterprises .

Other Domestic-funded Enterprises refer to domestic-funded economic units other than those mentioned above.

Cooperative Enterprises with Funds from Hong Kong Macau and Taiwan established by investors from Hong Kong, Macau and Taiwan with enterprises in the mainland of China in accordance with the Law of the People's Republic of China on Sino-foreign Cooperative Enterprises and other relevant laws, where the investment or provision of facilities, and the share of profits and risks is stipulated in the cooperative contract.

Enterprises with Sole (exclusive) Investment from Hong Kong, Macau and Taiwan refer to enterprises established in the mainland of China with exclusive investment from investors from Hong Kong, Macau and Taiwan in accordance with the Law of the People's Republic of China on Foreign-Funded Enterprises and other relevant laws.

Share-holding Corporations Ltd. with Investment from Hong Kong, Macau and Taiwan refer to share-holding corporations Ltd. established with the approval from the former Ministry of Foreign Trade and Economic Relations in line with relevant state regulations, where the share of investment from Hong Kong, Macau or Taiwan businessmen exceeds 25% of the total registered capital of the corporation. In case the share of investment from Hong Kong, Macau or Taiwan is less than 25% of the total registered capital, the enterprise is to be classified as domestic-funded share-holding corporation Ltd.

Joint-venture Enterprises with Foreign Investment refer to enterprises jointly established by foreign enterprises or foreigners with enterprises in the mainland of China in accordance with the Law of the People's Republic of China on Sino-foreign Joint Venture Enterprises and other relevant laws, where the share of investment, profits and risks is stipulated in the contract.

Cooperation Enterprises with Foreign Investment refer to enterprises jointly established by foreign enterprises or foreigners with enterprises in the mainland of China in accordance with the Law of the People's Republic of China on Sino-foreign Cooperative Enterprises and other relevant laws, where the investment or provision of facilities, and the share of profits and risks is stipulated in the cooperative contract.

Enterprises with Sole (exclusive) Foreign Investment refer to enterprises established in the mainland of China with exclusive investment from foreign investors in accordance with the Law of the People's Republic of China on Foreign-Funded Enterprises and other relevant laws.

Share-holding Corporations Ltd. with Foreign Investment refer to share-holding corporations Ltd. established with the approval from the Ministry of Foreign Trade and Economic Relations in line with relevant state regulations, where the share of investment from foreign investors exceeds 25% of the total registered capital of the corporation. In case the share of foreign investment is less than 25% of the total registered capital, the enterprise is to be classified as domestic-funded share-holding corporation Ltd.

Government Agencies, Institutions and Social Organizations are classified into following categories by source of funds and way of management taking reference of the registration status of enterprises:

(1) Government agencies: include state and party agencies, classified in principle as state-owned. There are exceptions, such as supply and marketing cooperatives which are classified as collective-owned.

(2) Institutions: include institutions of various types established with the approval by organization and staffing departments of the government, but exclude institutions where enterprise management system is introduced. Institutions are further classified as follows:

(a) Institutions whose main budget is listed in the government budget appropriations or extra-budget funds, or allocated from the budget of their competent government agencies. Such institutions are classified as state-owned.

(b) Institutions whose budget mainly comes from collective units. Such institutions are classified as collective-owned.

(c) Institutions other than those mentioned above whose source of budget is not clear. Such institutions are classified by way of management.

(3) Social organizations: include social organizations established with the approval from the Ministry of Civil Affairs, and organizations that are not covered by social organization management regulations such as trade unions, womens federations etc.. Social organizations are further classified as follows:

(a) Social organizations that are not covered by social organization management regulations of the Ministry of Civil Affairs such as trade unions, womens federations, communist youth leagues, youth associations, industrial and commerce associations, scientists associations, overseas Chinese associations, etc., foundations and fund management organizations established with funds from the state, and social organizations whose funds mainly come from the budget of their competent government agencies. Such institutions are classified as state-owned.

(b) Social organizations whose budget mainly comes from collective units. Such institutions are classified as collective-owned.

(c) Social organizations established by individual or a group of citizens, which are classified as private.

(d) Social organizations other than those mentioned above whose source of budget is not clear. Such organizations are classified by way of management.

Gross Domestic Product (GDP) refers to the final products at market prices produced by all resident units in a country (or a region) during a certain period of time. Gross domestic product is expressed in three different forms, i.e. value, income, and products respectively. GDP in its value form refers to the total value of all goods and services produced by all resident units during a certain period of time, minus the total value of input of goods and services of the nature of non-fixed assets; in other term, it is the sum of the value-added of all resident units. GDP in the form of income includes the income created by all resident units and distributed to resident and non-resident units. GDP in the form of products refers to the value of all goods and services for final consumption by all resident units minus the net exports of goods and services during a given period of time. In the practice of national accounting, gross domestic product is calculated with three approaches, i.e. production approach, income approach and expenditure approach, which reflect gross domestic product and its composition from different aspects.

Gross National Income (GNI) also known as gross national product, refers to the final result of the primary distribution of the income created by all the resident units of a country (or a region) during a certain period of time. The value-added created by the resident units of a country engaged in production activities is distributed, during the primary distribution, mainly to the resident units of that country, while part of it is distributed to the non-resident units in the form of production tax and import duties (minus subsidies to production and import), remuneration for the labourers and property income. At the meantime, a part of the value-added created abroad is distributed to the resident units of the country in the form of production tax and import duties (minus subsidies to production and import), remuneration for the labourers and property income. The concept of gross national income is thus developed, which equals to the gross domestic product plus the net factor income from abroad. Unlike the gross domestic product which is a concept of production, the gross national income is a concept of income.

Three Industries Classification of economic activities into three branches of industries is a common practice in the world, although the grouping varies to some extent form country to country. In China economic activities are categorized into following industries:

Primary industry: refers to agriculture, forestry, animal husbandry and fishery.

Secondary industry: refers to mining and quarrying, manufacturing, production and supply of electricity, water and gas, and construction.

Tertiary industry: refers to all other economic activities not included in primary or secondary industry.

Labourers Remuneration refers to the whole payment of various forms earned by the labourers from the productive activities they are engaged in. It includes wages, bonuses and allowances the labourers earned in monetary form and in kind. It also includes the free medical services provided to the labourers and the medicine expenses, traffic subsidies and social insurance, housing fund paid by the employers. As the individual economy is concerned, since the labourers remuneration is not easily distinguished from the operating profit, both are treated as labourers remuneration.

Net Taxes on Production refers to the difference of the taxes on production minus the subsidies on production. The taxes on production refers to the various taxes, extra charges and fees levied on the production units on their production, sale and business activities as well as on the use of some factors of production, such as fixed assets, land and labour force in the production activities they are engaged in. In contrast to the taxes on production, the subsidies on production refer to the unilateral government transfer to the production units and are therefore regarded as negative taxes on production. They include subsidies on the loss due to implementation of government policies, price subsidies, etc.

Depreciation of Fixed Assets refers to the depreciation of fixed assets of a given period, drawn in accordance with the stipulated depreciation rate for the purpose of compensating the wear loss of the fixed assets or the depreciation of fixed assets calculated in a fictitious way in accordance with the stipulated unified depreciation rate in the national economic accounting system. It reflects the value of transfer of the fixed assets in the production of the current period. The depreciation of fixed assets in various enterprises and institutions managed as enterprises refers to the depreciation expenses actually drawn. In government agencies and institutions not managed as enterprises which do not draw the depreciation expenses, as well as for the houses of residents, the depreciation of fixed assets is the imputed depreciation, which is calculated in accordance with the stipulated unified depreciation rate. In principle, the depreciation of fixed assets should be calculated on the basis of the re-purchased value of the fixed assets. However, there is no actual condition to re-evaluate all the fixed assets in China. Therefore, the above-mentioned methods are temporarily adopted at present.

Operating Surplus refers to the balance of the value added created by the resident units deducting the labourers remuneration, net taxes on production and the depreciation of fixed assets. It is equivalent to the business profit of the enterprises plus subsidies on production, but the wages and welfare expenses paid from the profits should be deducted.

GDP by Expenditure Approach refers to the method of measuring the final results of production activities of a country (region) during a given period from the perspective of final use. It includes final consumption expenditure, total capital formation and net export of goods and services, i.e.:

GDP by expenditure approach = final consumption expenditure + total capital formation + net export of goods and services

Final Consumption Expenditure refers to the total expenditure of resident units for purchases of goods and services from domestic economic territory and abroad to meet the requirements of material, cultural and spiritual life. It excludes the expenditure of non-resident units on consumption in the economic territory of the country. The final consumption expenditure is broken down into household consumption expenditure and government consumption expenditure.

Households Consumption Expenditure refers to the total expenditure of resident households on the final consumption of goods and services. In addition to the consumption of goods and services bought by the households directly with money, the households consumption expenditure also includes expenditure on goods and services obtained by the households in other ways, i.e. the so-called imputed consumption expenditure, which includes the following: (a) the goods and services provided to the households by the employer in the form of payment in kind and transfer in kind; (b) goods and services produced and consumed by the households themselves, in which the services refer only to the owner-occupied housing and domestic and individual services provided by the paid household workers; (c) financial intermediate services provided by financial institutions; (d) insurance services provided by insurance companies.

Government Consumption Expenditure refers to the expenditure on the consumption of the public services provided by the government to the whole society and the net expenditure on the goods and services provided by the government to the households free of charge or at low prices. The former equals to the output value of the government services minus the value of operating income obtained by the government departments. The latter equals to the market value of the goods and services provided by the government free of charge or at low prices to the households minus the value received by the government from the households.

Total Capital Formation refers to the fixed assets acquired minus those disposed of and the net value of inventory, including the total fixed capital formation and the increase in inventory.

Total Fixed Capital Formation refers to the value of fixed assets acquired minus those disposed of during a given period. Fixed assets are the assets produced through production activities with specified unit value which could be used for over one year, excluding natural assets. Total fixed capital formation can be categorized into total tangible capital formation and total intangible capital formation. The total tangible capital formation include the value of the construction projects, installation projects completed and the equipment, apparatus and instruments purchased as well as the value of land improved, the value of draught animals, breeding stock, animals for milk, wool and for recreational purpose, and the newly increased forest with economic value during a given period. The total intangible capital formation includes the prospecting of minerals, the acquisition of computer software minus the disposal of them.

Increase in Inventory refers to the market value of the change in inventory of resident units during a given period, i.e. the difference of value between the beginning and the end of the period minus the current gains due to the change in prices. The increase in inventory can be positive or negative. A positive value indicates the increase in inventory while a negative value indicates the decrease in stock. The inventory includes the raw materials, fuels and reserve materials purchased by the production units as well as the inventory of finished products, semi-finished products, work-in-progress, etc.

Outflow of Goods and Services refers to the difference of the exports of goods and services minus the imports of goods and services. The imports include the value of various goods and services sold or gratuitously transferred by the resident units to the non-resident units. The imports include the value of various goods and services purchased or gratuitously acquired by the resident units from the non-resident units. Because the provision of services and the use of them happen simultaneously, the acquisition of services by the resident units from abroad is usually treated as import while the acquisition of services by non-resident units in this country is usually treated as export. The export and import of goods are calculated at FOB.

2 人 口

Population

资料整理：陆小红

2-1 总 人 口
POPULATION

单位：万人　　(年底数)(number at year-end)　　(10 000 persons)

年份 Year	总人口 Total Population	男 Male	女 Female
1952	2745.0	1414.6	1330.4
1957	3062.4	1579.7	1482.7
1965	3504.5	1793.4	1711.2
1975	4408.2	2261.6	2146.5
1979	4632.8	2376.6	2256.2
1980	4684.5	2401.7	2282.7
1981	4740.3	2430.9	2309.4
1982	4800.9	2464.3	2336.6
1983	4835.3	2485.6	2349.8
1984	4876.1	2510.9	2365.2
1985	4931.0	2540.0	2391.0
1986	4989.0	2573.4	2415.6
1987	5058.1	2608.7	2449.4
1988	5144.2	2652.1	2492.1
1989	5223.9	2694.6	2529.3
1990	5373.5	2771.5	2602.0
1991	5446.8	2805.4	2641.4
1992	5513.6	2841.3	2672.4
1993	5590.5	2880.8	2709.6
1994	5656.8	2915.6	2741.2
1995	5727.1	2952.2	2775.0
1996	5776.3	2979.6	2796.8
1997	5838.8	3014.1	2824.8
1998	5890.6	3039.9	2850.7
1999	5942.5	3061.8	2880.7
2000	5936.0	3066.1	2869.9
2001	5956.6	3073.2	2883.4
2002	5978.2	3086.2	2892.0
2003	6000.5	3109.9	2890.6
2004	6001.3	3107.8	2893.5
2005	5984.1	3102.4	2881.7
2006	6038.3	3129.7	2908.7
2007	6084.9	3154.0	2930.9
2008	6110.8	3167.5	2943.3
2009	6141.9	3185.5	2956.4
2010	6176.0	3202.0	2974.0
2011	6164.1	3194.0	2970.1
2012	6165.4	3193.9	2971.4
2013	6170.6	3199.5	2971.1

注：总人口为户籍总人口，2010年为人口普查户籍人口数。

Note: The total population of the total household population in 2010 census household population.

2-2 人口城乡构成

COMPOSITION OF URBAN AND RURAL POPULATION

单位：万人　　(年底数) (number at year-end)　　(10 000 persons)

年份 Year	Total Population	城镇人口 Urban Population	乡村人口 Rural Population
1952	2687.58	271.41	2416.17
1957	3062.41	411.69	2650.72
1965	3504.54	485.06	3019.48
1975	4408.15	626.22	3781.93
1979	4632.78	747.92	3884.86
1980	4684.45	786.49	3897.96
1981	4740.35	815.60	3924.75
1982	4800.92	848.76	3952.16
1983	4835.34	873.91	3961.43
1984	4876.07	877.41	3998.66
1985	4930.97	1120.50	3810.47
1986	5047.83	1187.23	3860.60
1987	5120.27	1288.61	3831.66
1988	5184.94	1389.99	3794.95
1989	5258.83	1491.37	3767.46
1990	5439.29	1551.51	3887.78
1991	5512.33	1433.06	4079.27
1992	5579.85	1637.68	3942.17
1993	5653.48	1731.66	3921.82
1994	5718.81	1604.13	4114.68
1995	5772.07	1800.89	3971.18
1996	5825.13	1965.40	3859.73
1997	5872.60	1834.60	4038.00
1998	5907.23	1884.41	4022.82
1999	5938.03	1990.17	3947.86
2000	5646.00	2285.11	3360.89
2001	5658.00	2308.50	3349.50
2002	5672.00	2348.20	3323.80
2003	5685.00	2387.70	3297.30
2004	5698.00	2427.30	2466.70
2005	5710.00	2466.70	3243.30
2006	5693.00	2493.50	3199.50
2007	5699.00	2524.70	3174.30
2008	5711.00	2581.40	3129.60
2009	5720.00	2631.20	3088.80
2010	5723.77	2844.51	2879.26
2011	5758.00	2984.32	2773.68
2012	5779.00	3091.77	2687.23
2013	5799.00	3161.03	2637.97

注：1.人口数除1982年、1990年、2000年是以人口普查为基数推算外，1982年及以后为人口抽样调查推算数。
2.2000年以前数据是总人口数，2010年以后数据为常住人口数,2010年为第六次人口普查数据。

Notes:a) Population than in 1982，1990，2000 census as the base is projected, the population in 1982 and beyond as the number of sample projections.
b)2000 before the data on total population, since 2010 data for the resident population.

2-3　全省人口自然变动
NATURAL CHANGE OF POLULATION

年　份 Year	人口变动数(万人) Number of Population Changed (10 000 persons)			变动系数(‰) Growth Rates		
	出生数 Number of Birth	死亡数 Number of Death	自然增长数 Number of Nature Growth	出生率 Birth Rate	死亡率 Death Rate	自然增长率 Natural Growth Rate
1965	121.48	34.75	86.73	35.10	10.04	25.06
1975	90.80	34.52	56.28	20.74	7.88	12.86
1980	94.84	32.59	62.25	20.36	7.00	13.36
1985	97.83	37.37	60.46	19.95	7.62	12.33
1986	107.09	39.45	67.64	21.01	7.74	13.27
1987	108.56	36.12	72.44	21.43	7.13	14.30
1988	97.62	32.95	64.67	19.08	6.44	12.64
1989	110.13	36.24	73.89	21.09	6.94	14.15
1990	114.40	38.66	75.74	21.60	7.30	14.30
1991	113.34	40.30	73.04	20.70	7.36	13.34
1992	105.60	38.08	67.52	19.05	6.87	12.18
1993	112.55	38.92	73.63	20.04	6.93	13.11
1994	103.31	37.98	65.33	18.17	6.68	11.49
1995	92.96	39.70	53.26	16.18	6.91	9.27
1996	93.24	40.18	53.06	16.08	6.93	9.15
1997	86.62	39.13	47.49	14.81	6.69	8.12
1998	74.09	39.46	34.63	12.58	6.70	5.88
1999	68.52	37.73	30.79	11.57	6.37	5.20
2000	57.76	35.75	22.01	9.71	6.01	3.70
2001	50.84	36.27	14.57	8.51	6.07	2.44
2002	50.10	36.90	13.20	8.38	6.17	2.21
2003	49.50	35.60	13.90	8.26	5.94	2.32
2004	50.66	36.23	14.43	8.43	6.03	2.40
2005	52.60	34.30	18.30	8.74	5.69	3.05
2006	54.80	35.90	18.90	9.08	5.95	3.13
2007	55.69	36.12	19.57	9.19	5.96	3.23
2008	55.98	39.51	16.47	9.21	6.50	2.71
2009	57.80	36.58	21.22	9.48	6.00	3.48
2010	59.30	34.46	24.84	10.36	6.02	4.34
2011	59.67	34.52	25.15	10.39	6.01	4.38
2012	63.45	35.30	28.15	11.00	6.12	4.88
2013	64.14	35.60	28.54	11.08	6.15	4.93

注：1985年以后人口变动系数为人口抽样调查数，其余为公安年报数。

Note: the data of change of population after 1985 was based on census, the rest were from public security annual report.

2-4 全省市、州、县年底人口数(2013)
POPULATION OF CITIES, TOWNS, AND COUNTIES OF HUBEI AT YEAR-END(2013)

单位:万人 (10 000 persons)

地区	Region	户籍人口(万人) Total Population	常住人口(万人) Population of Permnant Residents
全省	**Province**	**6170.58**	**5799.00**
武汉市	**Wuhan City**	**822.04**	**1022.00**
江岸区	Jiang'an District	70.01	92.68
江汉区	Jianghan District	47.63	71.31
硚口区	Qiaokou District	53.78	84.83
汉阳区	Hanyang District	53.81	61.67
武昌区	Wuchang District	112.00	124.68
青山区	Qingshan District	44.23	51.26
洪山区	Hongshan District	78.76	147.74
东西湖区	Dongxihu District	27.64	50.06
汉南区	Hannan District	11.15	12.68
蔡甸区	Caidian District	47.81	66.34
江夏区	Jiangxia District	68.96	83.40
黄陂区	Huangpi District	111.25	89.78
新洲区	Xinzhou District	94.95	85.57
黄石市	**Huangshi City**	**262.27**	**244.50**
黄石港区	Huangshigang district	20.36	23.70
西塞山区	Xisai mountainous area	21.65	24.64
下陆区	Xialu District	15.27	18.21
铁山区	Tieshan District	5.49	5.82
大冶市	Daye City	96.23	89.96
阳新县	Yangxin County	103.25	82.17
十堰市	**Shiyan City**	**346.69**	**336.70**
张湾区	Zhangwan District	26.22	37.96
茅箭区	Maojian District	28.11	41.15
丹江口市	Danjiangkou City	46.06	44.69
郧县	Yun County	62.57	56.17
郧西县	Yunxi County	51.53	45.06
竹山县	Zhushan County	46.35	41.26
竹溪县	Zhuxi County	37.43	31.02
房县	Famg County	48.40	39.39
宜昌市	**Yichang City**	**400.07**	**409.83**
西陵区	Xilin District	43.68	53.57
伍家岗区	Wujiagang District	16.02	22.46
点军区	Dianjun District	10.47	10.44
猇亭区	Huting District	5.09	6.33
夷陵区	yiling District	52.13	52.24
远安县	Yuan'an District	19.38	18.64
兴山县	xingshan District	17.31	17.05
秭归县	Zigui District	37.98	36.11
长阳县	Changyang District	40.22	38.58
五峰县	Wufeng District	20.54	18.74
宜都市	Yidu City	39.68	38.85
当阳市	Dangyang City	48.42	46.76
枝江市	Zhijiang City	49.11	50.06
襄阳市	**Xiangyang City**	**595.09**	**559.12**
襄城区	Xiangcheng District	46.37	48.78
樊城区	Fancheng District	78.15	88.71
襄州区	Xiangzhou District	102.20	91.49
南漳县	Nanzhang County	58.83	53.99
谷城县	Gucheng County	59.65	52.01
保康县	Baokang County	27.23	25.28
老河口市	Laohekou City	53.21	48.36
枣阳市	Zaoyang City	112.59	98.68
宜城市	Yicheng City	56.82	51.82
鄂州市	**Ezhou City**	**109.78**	**105.70**
梁子湖区	Liangzihu District	18.65	14.39
华容区	Huarong District	25.94	23.94
鄂城区	Ercheng District	65.19	67.37

注：以上数据为第六次人口普查数，常住人口是指常住本地半年以上人口。
Note:The permanent resident population is more than half the local population.

2-4 续表 Continued

单位:万人 (10 000 persons)

地　区	Regions	户籍人口 Total Population	常住人口 Permnant Population	地　区	Regions	户籍人口 Total Population	常住人口 Permnant Population
荆门市	**Jingmen Municipality**	**300.78**	**288.72**	蕲春县	Hanchun County	102.23	77.02
掇刀区	Duodao District	33.48	37.12	黄梅县	Huangmei County	106.13	86.35
东宝区	Dongbao District	37.29	30.07	麻城市	Macheng City	117.83	87.02
京山县	Jingshan County	64.71	62.67	武穴市	Wuxue City	80.77	65.12
沙洋县	Shayang District	59.02	57.38	**咸宁市**	**Xianning City**	**300.51**	**248.5**
钟祥市	Zhongxiang City	106.27	101.48	咸安区	Xian'an District	62.35	51.65
孝感市	**Xiaogan City**	**527.43**	**485.3**	嘉鱼县	Jiayu county	37.07	31.62
孝南区	Xiaonan District	96.43	91.61	通城县	Tongcheng County	51.07	40.85
孝昌县	Xiaochang County	67.10	59.35	崇阳县	Congyang County	49.23	39.74
大悟县	Dawu County	63.88	61.8	通山县	Tongshan county	47.95	36.34
云梦县	Yunmeng County	57.78	52.75	赤壁市	Chibi City	52.82	48.30
应城市	Yingcheng City	67.20	59.71	**随州市**	**Suizhou City**	**257.58**	**218.01**
安陆市	Anlu City	62.76	57.62	曾都区	Zengdu City	65.27	62.37
汉川市	Hanchuan City	112.25	102.46	随县	Sui County	97.57	79.42
荆州市	**Jingzhou City**	**661.00**	**573.94**	广水市	Guangshui City	94.73	76.22
沙市区	Shashi District	54.80	64.79	**恩施州**	**Enshi Prefecture**	**405.41**	**331.20**
荆州区	Jingzhou District	57.09	56.92	恩施市	Enshi City	81.43	76.45
公安县	Gong'an County	105.40	89.62	利川市	Jianli City	92.38	65.84
监利县	Jianli County	157.94	109.84	建始县	Jianshi County	51.39	41.47
江陵县	Jianglin County	40.90	33.97	巴东县	Badong County	49.77	42.37
石首市	Shishou City	66.55	56.56	宣恩县	Xuan'en County	36.17	30.14
洪湖市	Honghu City	93.45	84.89	咸丰县	Xianfeng County	38.86	30.37
松滋市	Songzi City	84.84	77.35	来凤县	Laifeng County	33.03	24.45
黄冈市	**Huanggang City**	**750.15**	**625.19**	鹤峰县	Hefeng County	22.35	20.12
黄州区	Huangzhou City	35.58	36.91	**省直管单位**	**Jurisdictional Area**	**431.71**	**350.29**
团风县	Tuanfeng County	38.47	34.15	仙桃市	Xiantao City	156.12	118.49
红安县	Hong'an County	65.76	60.38	潜江市	Qianjiang City	103.78	95.24
罗田县	Luotian County	59.37	54.68	天门市	Tianmen City	163.84	128.90
英山县	Yingshan County	40.28	35.91	神农架林区	Shennongjian Forest Area	7.96	7.66
浠水县	Xishui County	103.62	87.65				

主要统计指标解释

人口数 指一定时点、一定地区范围内有生命的个人总和。

年度统计的年末人口数指每年12月31日24时的人口数。

城镇人口和乡村人口 城镇人口是指居住在城镇范围内的全部常住人口；乡村人口是除上述人口以外的全部人口。

出生率(又称粗出生率) 指在一定时期内(通常为一年)一定地区的出生人数与同期内平均人数(或期中人数)之比，用千分率表示。本资料中的出生率指年出生率，其计算公式为：

$$\text{出生率}=\frac{\text{年出生人数}}{\text{年平均人数}}\times 1000‰$$

式中：出生人数指活产婴儿，即胎儿脱离母体时(不管怀孕月数)，有过呼吸或其他生命现象。年平均人数指年初、年底人口数的平均数，也可用年中人口数代替。

死亡率(又称粗死亡率) 指在一定时期内(通常为一年)一定地区的死亡人数与同期内平均人数(或期中人数)之比，用千分率表示。本资料中的死亡率指年死亡率，其计算公式为：

$$\text{死亡率}=\frac{\text{年死亡人数}}{\text{年平均人数}}\times 1000‰$$

人口自然增长率 指在一定时期内(通常为一年)人口自然增加数(出生人数减死亡人数)与该时期内平均人数(或期中人数)之比，用千分率表示。计算公式为：

$$\text{人口自然增长率}=\frac{\text{本年出生人数}-\text{本年死亡人数}}{\text{年平均人数}}\times 1000‰$$
$$=\text{人口出生率}-\text{人口死亡率}$$

Explanatory Notes on Main Statistical Indicators

Total Population refers to the total number of people alive at a certain point of time within a given area.

The annual statistics on total population is taken at midnight, the 3lst of December.

Urban Population and Rural Population Urban population refer to all people residing in cities and towns, while rural population refer to population other than urban population.

Birth Rate (or Crude Birth Rate) refers to the ratio of the number of births to the average population (or mid-period population) during a certain period of time (usually a year), expressed in ‰. Birth rate in the chapter refers to annual birth rate. The following formula is used:

Birth Rate = (Number of Births/Average Number of Population)×1000‰

Number of births in the formula refers to live births, i.e. when a baby has breathed or showed any vital phenomena regardless of the length of pregnancy.

Annual average number of population is the average of the number of population at the beginning of the year and that at the end of the year. Sometimes it is substituted by the mid-year population.

Death Rate (or Crude Death Rate) refers to the ratio of the number of deaths to the average population (or mid-period population) during a certain period of time (usually a year), expressed in ‰. Death rate in the chapter refers to annual death rate. The following formula is used:

Death Rate= (Number of Deaths/Annual Average Number of Population)×1000‰

Natural Growth Rate of Population refers to the ratio of natural increase in population (number of births minus number of deaths) in a certain period of time (usually a year) to the average population (or mid-period population) of the same period, expressed in ‰. The following formula is applied:

Natural Growth Rate of Population = [(Number of Births-Number of Deaths)/Average Number of Population]×1000‰

Natural Growth Rate of Population = Birth Rate-Death Rate

3 就业人员和职工工资

Employment and Wages

资料整理：张　蔚　陆小红

3-1　全社会从业人员

NUMBER OF EMPLOYED PERSONS

单位：万人　　(10 000 person)

年份 Year	合计 Total	按城乡分 Grouped by Areas		按产业分 Grouped by Industries		
		城镇 Urban	乡村 Rural	第一产业 Primary Industry	第二产业 Secondary Industry	第三产业 Tertiary Industry
1952	1020.30	141.60	878.70			
1965	1404.20	222.70	1181.60			
1970	1618.50	278.00	1340.80			
1975	1802.50	381.70	1420.80			
1978	1910.40	458.00	1452.30	1470.60	269.00	170.80
1980	1986.90	507.20	1479.70	1453.70	286.30	247.00
1985	2238.10	637.60	1600.50	1383.30	485.40	369.50
1990	3040.40	890.80	2149.60	1859.80	628.50	552.10
1991	3082.70	909.40	2173.30	1897.40	623.00	562.30
1992	3118.60	923.10	2195.50	1869.00	650.90	598.70
1993	3157.60	940.90	2216.70	1818.80	684.60	654.20
1994	3196.90	980.10	2216.80	1760.50	717.10	719.30
1995	3232.50	1015.00	2217.50	1697.00	743.50	792.00
1996	3275.50	1050.80	2224.70	1677.10	746.80	851.60
1997	3311.20	1070.50	2240.70	1663.20	752.00	896.00
1998	3328.20	1093.60	2234.60	1612.50	705.60	1010.10
1999	3358.10	1110.50	2247.60	1612.60	697.80	1047.70
2000	3384.90	1123.80	2261.10	1625.10	702.40	1057.40
2001	3414.50	1148.70	2265.80	1639.00	706.80	1068.70
2002	3443.00	1177.00	2266.00	1652.60	704.10	1086.30
2003	3476.00	1211.00	2265.00	1661.50	712.60	1101.90
2004	3507.00	1245.00	2262.00	1672.90	720.30	1113.80
2005	3537.00	1271.00	2266.00	1687.30	725.00	1124.70
2006	3564.00	1297.00	2267.00	1694.70	732.40	1136.90
2007	3584.00	1322.00	2262.00	1697.00	740.10	1146.90
2008	3607.00	1337.00	2270.00	1707.91	730.42	1168.67
2009	3622.00	1357.00	2265.00	1702.30	736.60	1183.10
2010	3645.00	1382.60	2262.40	1691.10	754.70	1199.20
2011	3672.00	1413.00	2259.00	1678.10	771.12	1222.78
2012	3687.00	1430.60	2256.40	1638.90	781.60	1266.50
2013	3692.00	1438.00	2254.00	1582.00	793.80	1316.20

3–2 分行业城镇单位从业人员数(2013)
NUMBER OF EMPLOYEES IN URBAN UNITS BY SECTOR (2013)

单位：人 (person)

行业	Sector	城镇全部单位 All the Units In Urban Area	国有经济单位 State Owned Units	城镇集体单位 Urban Collective Owned Units	其他经济单位 Other Units	城镇私营单位 Urban Private Units
总计	**Total**	**9928987**	**2686091**	**152522**	**4126508**	**2963866**
农、林、牧、渔业	Farming, Forest, Herd, Fishery	116166	89996	586	381	25203
采矿业	Mining and Quarrying	189391	11928	8112	69456	99895
制造业	Manufacturing	3299733	204305	21303	1682987	1391138
电力、燃气及水的生产和供应业	Power, Gas and water production and supply	200248	131100	1418	48805	18925
建筑业	Construction	1958227	93747	45353	1264852	554275
批发和零售业	Wholesale and Retail sale	779569	44817	17741	354608	362403
交通运输、仓储和邮政业	Transportation, storage and post	408357	198004	5912	127998	76443
住宿和餐饮业	Hotel and Catering	274100	11012	2074	108821	152193
信息传输、软件和信息技术服务业	Information Transmission, Software and Computer Services	119747	16880	105	73984	28778
金融业	Banking	177776	70660	12781	89759	4576
房地产业	Real Estate	201808	10252	1349	108094	82113
租赁和商务服务业	Leasing and Commerical Services	143972	37276	2794	49848	54054
科学研究、技术服务业	Scietific Research, polytechnical	169243	85565	1229	64373	18076
水利、环境和公共设施管理业	Water Conservance, Environment and Public Facilities Management	99842	77333	6455	9589	6465
居民服务、修理和其他服务业	Resident Service and Others	52309	5780	1808	9086	35635
教育	Education	708633	640978	3085	37391	27179
卫生和社会工作	Health, Social Security and	379113	335175	19758	17269	6911
文化、体育和娱乐业	Culture, Sports and Entertainment	74015	46034	615	9037	18329
公共管理、社会保障和社会组织	Public management, social security and social organization	576738	575249	44	170	1275

注：城镇全部单位统计范围含城镇私营单位。(后表未经特别注明均同此口径)

Note: All Statistics of Units in Urban Areas of 2010 including all the private run unit.

(The following tables if without specific notes are considered the same standard with this one.)

3-3 分行业在岗职工人数(2013)

NUMBER OF STAFF AND WORKERS BY SECTOR(2013)

单位：人 (person)

行业	Sector	城镇全部单位 All the Units In Urban Area	国有经济单位 State Owned Units	城镇集体单位 Urban Collective Owned Units	其他经济单位 Other Units	城镇私营单位 Urban Private Units
总计	**Total**	**9398807**	**2519722**	**140115**	**3775104**	**2963866**
农、林、牧、渔业	Farming, Forest, Herd, Fishery	102142	76008	552	379	25203
采矿业	Mining and Quarrying	182389	9389	7887	65218	99895
制造业	Manufacturing	3262905	196496	20313	1654958	1391138
电力、燃气及水的生产和供应业	Power, Gas and water production and supply	196996	129002	1413	47656	18925
建筑业	Construction	1684049	77012	40424	1012338	554275
批发和零售业	Wholesale and Retail sale	763250	42550	15623	342674	362403
交通运输、仓储和邮政业	Transportation, storage and post	395096	189873	5644	123136	76443
住宿和餐饮业	Hotel and Catering	270851	9960	1994	106704	152193
信息传输、软件和信息技术服务业	Information Transmission, Software and Computer Services	114746	16187	104	69677	28778
金融业	Banking	148945	65563	12454	66352	4576
房地产业	Real Estate	193673	9171	1230	101159	82113
租赁和商务服务业	Leasing and Commerical Services	139729	36479	2666	46530	54054
科学研究、技术服务业	Scietific Research, polytechnical	159095	80993	1083	58943	18076
水利、环境和公共设施管理业	Water Conservance, Environment and Public Facilities Management	83596	63587	4406	9138	6465
居民服务、修理和其他服务业	Resident Service and Others	51135	4986	1664	8850	35635
教育	Education	674930	609517	2736	35498	27179
卫生和社会工作	Health, Social Security and	359718	316603	19275	16929	6911
文化、体育和娱乐业	Culture, Sports and Entertainment	71386	43626	605	8826	18329
公共管理、社会保障和社会组织	Public management, social security and social organization	544176	542720	42	139	1275

3-4 分行业在岗女职工人数(2013)

NUMBER OF FEMALE STAFF AND WORKERS BY SECTOR(2013)

单位：人 (person)

行业	Sector	城镇全部单位(不含私营单位) All the Units In Urban Area	国有经济单位 State Owned Units	城镇集体单位 Urban Collective Owned Units	其他经济单位 Urban Private Units
总计	**Total**	**2279379**	**973922**	**49293**	**1256164**
农、林、牧、渔业	Farming, Forest, Herd, Fishery	37791	37568	130	93
采矿业	Mining and Quarrying	18782	4211	1012	13559
制造业	Manufacturing	664752	35327	8609	620816
电力、燃气及水的生产和供应业	Power, Gas and water production and supply	56446	39787	615	16044
建筑业	Construction	144163	14539	6903	122721
批发和零售业	Wholesale and Retail sale	218090	15302	10150	192638
交通运输、仓储和邮政业	Transportation, storage and post	97860	60731	1576	35553
住宿和餐饮业	Hotel and Catering	72496	6498	1344	64654
信息传输、软件和信息技术服务业	Information Transmission, Software and Computer Services	35129	6157	52	28920
金融业	Banking	87905	34156	5644	48105
房地产业	Real Estate	42605	3592	563	38450
租赁和商务服务业	Leasing and Commerical Services	29771	12073	734	16964
科学研究、技术服务业	Scietific Research, polytechnical	40829	24080	324	16425
水利、环境和公共设施管理业	Water Conservance, Environment and Public Facilities Management	35765	28732	2933	4100
居民服务、修理和其他服务业	Resident Service and Others	7617	2600	516	4501
教育	Education	296953	278579	1745	16629
卫生和社会工作	Health, Social Security and	211679	193559	6228	11892
文化、体育和娱乐业	Culture, Sports and Entertainment	23244	19028	200	4016
公共管理、社会保障和社会组织	Public Management、social security and Social Organization	157502	157403	15	84

注：统计范围为城镇非私营单位在岗女职工.

3-5 城镇登记失业人数及失业率

NUMBER OF URBAN UNEMPLOYED PERSONS AND UNEMPLOYMENT RATE

单位：万人 (10 000 person)

年份 Year	年末城镇登记失业人数 The Number of Unemployeed in Urban Areas by the End of Year	年末城镇登记失业率(%) Year End Unemployment registered Rate %
1978	20.03	4.19
1980	15.54	2.97
1990	12.66	1.72
1991	14.20	1.88
1992	16.89	2.17
1993	17.96	2.20
1994	21.06	2.90
1995	24.45	3.10
1996	28.25	3.50
1997	29.83	3.50
1998	31.33	3.30
1999	33.10	3.30
2000	36.64	3.50
2001	42.15	4.00
2002	44.66	4.30
2003	49.34	4.30
2004	49.37	4.20
2005	52.60	4.33
2006	52.56	4.22
2007	46.72	4.21
2008	55.07	4.20
2009	55.25	4.21
2010	55.65	4.18
2011	55.11	4.10
2012	42.26	3.83
2013	40.26	3.49

3-6 职工平均工资及指数

年份 Year	平均货币工资(元) Average Money Wages (yuan)					指数(上年=100) Indices(preceding year=100)	
	合计 Total	国有经济单位 State Owned Units	城镇集体经济单位 Urban Collective Owned	其他经济单位 Other Units	城镇私营单位 Urban private units	货币工资 Money Wages	国有经济单位 State Owned Units
1978	581	592	532			104.5	104.5
1980	719	744	619			116.0	115.9
1990	1903	2045	1467	2259		111.7	107.6
1991	2081	2213	1662	2363		109.4	108.2
1992	2370	2532	1837	2575		113.9	114.4
1993	2933	3141	2183	3248		123.8	124.1
1994	4050	4348	2845	4352		138.1	138.4
1995	4685	4991	3308	5093		115.7	114.8
1996	5099	5411	3590	5754		108.8	108.4
1997	5401	5741	3731	5740		105.9	106.1
1998	6436	6783	4748	6166		108.7	109.1
1999	6991	7381	5001	6681		108.6	108.8
2000	7565	7989	5090	7327		108.2	108.2
2001	8619	9133	5677	8035		113.9	114.3
2002	9611	10403	6534	8180		111.5	113.9
2003	10692	11806	7137	8698		111.2	113.5
2004	11855	13096	7608	10270		110.9	110.9
2005	13330	14774	8663	11572		112.4	112.8
2006	15172	17078	9848	13098		113.8	115.6
2007	17397	21971	12921	16829		114.7	128.7
2008	19597	24756	14840	20293		112.6	112.7
2009	23709	30032	19181	23528	15615	121.0	121.3
2010	28092	35981	24429	28799	18626	118.5	119.8
2011	32050	40345	26988	34354	20788	114.1	112.1
2012	35179	43438	33551	38675	23037	109.8	107.7
2013	38720	46126	34181	43975	25898	110.1	106.2

注：1998年以后为在岗职工平均工资。2007年以后统计范围含城镇全部私营单位。

AVERAGE WAGES AND INDICES OF STAFF AND WORKERS

指数(上年=100) Indices(preceding year=100)							
城镇集体经济单位 Urban Collective Owned	其他经济单位 OtherUnits	城镇私营单位 Urban private units	实际工资 Real Wages	国有经济单位 State Owned Units	城镇集体经济单位 Urban Collective Owned	其他经济单位 OtherUnits	城镇私营单位 Urban private units
106.4			104.2	103.9	106.1		
116.4			108.6	108.5	109.0		
107.1	107.1		107.8	108.3	104.4	103.9	
113.3	104.6		103.0	101.9	106.7	98.5	
110.5	109.0		103.1	103.5	100.0	98.7	
118.8	126.1		106.6	106.8	102.3	108.6	
130.3	134.0		108.7	109.0	102.6	105.5	
116.3	117.0		96.3	95.6	96.8	97.4	
108.5	113.0		95.1	94.0	95.3	99.9	
103.9	99.8		97.6	96.6	95.9	96.6	
109.2	99.1		110.2	110.2	110.8	100.5	
105.3	108.4		110.0	111.0	107.4	110.6	
101.8	109.7		109.3	109.3	102.7	110.8	
111.5	109.7		113.6	114.0	111.2	109.3	
115.1	101.8		112.0	114.4	115.6	102.2	
109.2	106.3		108.8	111.1	106.8	104.0	
106.6	118.1		105.7	105.7	101.6	112.6	
113.9	112.7		109.2	109.6	110.7	109.5	
113.7	113.2		112.0	113.8	111.9	111.4	
131.2	128.5		109.4	122.8	125.2	122.6	
114.9	120.6		106.0	106.0	108.0	113.4	
129.3	115.9		121.8	122.2	130.2	116.8	
127.4	122.4	119.3	115.1	116.4	123.8	119.0	115.9
110.5	119.3	111.6	107.8	106.0	104.4	112.8	105.5
124.3	112.6	110.8	106.7	104.6	120.8	109.4	107.7
101.9	113.7	112.4	107.1	103.3	99.1	110.6	109.4

Notes:Data after 1998 refers to average wages and indices of employed staff and workers.Statistics of 2007 involves all the private run units in urban areas.

3-7 分行业在岗职工平均工资(2013)

AVERAGE WAGES OF STAFF AND WORKER BY SECTOR(2013)

单位：元 (yuan)

行业	Sector	城镇全部单位 All the Units In Urban Area	国有经济单位 State Owned Units	城镇集体单位 Urban Collective Owned Units	其他经济单位 Other Units	城镇私营单位 Urban Private Units
总计	**Total**	**38720**	**46126**	**34181**	**43975**	**25898**
农、林、牧、渔业	Farming, Forest, Herd, Fishery	23693	25654	18780	26039	17742
采矿业	Mining and Quarrying	36091	47343	36119	43454	29872
制造业	Manufacturing	35750	58016	31230	41509	25696
电力、燃气及水的生产和供应业	Power, Gas and water production and supply	53693	58492	28513	52166	26030
建筑业	Construction	38766	39304	30528	45379	27611
批发和零售业	Wholesale and Retail sale	30599	49874	24308	37786	23028
交通运输、仓储和邮政业	Transportation, storage and post	45470	55912	25605	43832	23379
住宿和餐饮业	Hotel and Catering	26282	32019	31951	29349	23694
信息传输、软件和信息技术服务业	Information Transmission, Software and Computer Services	51791	39493	17567	62426	33526
金融业	Banking	73564	74336	57197	78169	37203
房地产业	Real Estate	39146	36303	32606	44218	33762
租赁和商务服务业	Leasing and Commerical Services	34514	32266	29656	48430	24110
科学研究、技术服务业	Scietific Research, polytechnical	59060	48140	30342	84023	29828
水利、环境和公共设施管理业	Water Conservance, Environment and Public Facilities Management	32428	32131	28781	43761	21578
居民服务、修理和其他服务业	Resident Service and Others	26008	30411	32675	33772	23151
教育	Education	41480	42312	37249	39747	25519
卫生和社会工作	Health, Social Security and	49217	50242	43298	45451	26457
文化、体育和娱乐业	Culture, Sports and Entertainment	40728	44737	38126	52800	23887
公共管理、社会保障和 社会组织	Public Management、social security and Social Organization	40523	40572	25512	25050	19994

主要统计指标解释

经济活动人口　指在16周岁及以上，有劳动能力，参加或要求参加社会经济活动的人口。包括就业人员和失业人员。

就业人员　指在16周岁及以上，从事一定社会劳动并取得劳动报酬或经营收入的人员。这一指标反映了一定时期内全部劳动力资源的实际利用情况，是研究我国基本国情国力的重要指标。

单位就业人员　指报告期末最后一日24时在各类单位工作，并取得工资或其他形式劳动报酬的人员数。该指标为时点指标，不包括最后一日当天及以前已经与单位解除劳动合同关系的人员，是在岗职工、劳务派遣人员及其他从业人员之和。从业人员不包括：

1.离开本单位仍保留劳动关系，并定期领取生活费的人员；

2.利用课余时间打工的学生及在本单位实习的各类在校学生；

3.本单位因劳务外包而使用的人员。

在岗职工　指在本单位工作且与本单位签订劳动合同，并由单位支付各项工资和社会保险、住房公积金的人员，以及上述人员中由于学习、病伤、产假等原因暂未工作仍由单位支付工资的人员。在岗职工还包括：

1.应订立劳动合同而未订立劳动合同人员（如使用的农村户籍人员）；

2.处于试用期人员；

3.编制外招用的人员，如临时人员；

4.派往外单位工作，但工资仍由本单位发放的人员（如挂职锻炼、外派工作等情况）。

在岗职工平均工资　指单位在岗职工在一定时期内平均每人所得的货币工资。它表明一定时期在岗职工工资收入的高低程度，是反映在岗职工工资水平的主要指标。计算公式为：

$$平均工资=\frac{报告期实际支付的全部在岗职工工资总额}{报告期全部在岗职工平均人数}$$

平均工资指数　指报告期在岗职工平均工资与基期平均工资的比率，是反映不同时期在岗职工货币工资水平变动情况的相对数。计算公式为：

$$平均工资指数=\frac{报告期在岗职工平均工资}{基期在岗职工平均工资}\times 100\%$$

平均实际工资指数　在岗职工平均实际工资指扣除物价变动因素后的在岗职工平均工资。在岗职工平均实际工资指数是反映实际工资变动情况的相对数，表明职工实际工资水平提高或降低的程度。计算公式为：

$$平均实际工资指数=\frac{报告期职工平均工资指数}{报告期城镇居民消费价格指数}\times 100\%$$

城镇登记失业人员　指有非农业户口，在一定的劳动年龄内(16周岁至退休年龄)，有劳动能力，无业而要求就业，并在当地就业服务机构进行求职登记的人员。

城镇登记失业率　城镇登记失业人员与城镇单位就业人员(扣除使用的农村劳动力、聘用的离退休人员、港澳台及外方人员）、城镇单位中的不在岗职工、城镇私营业主、个体户主、城镇私营企业和个体就业人员、城镇登记失业人员之和的比。

$$城镇登记失业率=\frac{城镇登记失业人数}{（城镇单位就业人员-使用的农村劳动力-聘用的离退休人员-聘用的港澳台及外方人员）}\times 100\%$$

Explanatory Notes on Main Statistical Indicators

Economically Active Population refers to the population aged 16 and over who are capable to work, are participating in or willing to participate in economic activities, including employed persons and unemployed persons.

Employed Persons refer to the persons aged 16 and over who are engaged in social working and receive remuneration payment or earn business income. This indicator reflects the actual utilization of total labour force during a certain period of time and is often used for the research on China's economic situation and national power.

Persons Employed in Various Units refer to all the persons working in government agencies of various levels, political and party organizations, social organizations, enterprises and institutions, and receiving wages or other forms of payment. They include fully-employed staff and workers, re-employed retirees, teachers in schools run by the local people, foreigners and Chinese compatriots from Hong Kong, Macao, and Taiwan working in various units, part-time employees, employees of other units working temporarily at current posts, and employees holding the second job, but exclude staff and workers who have left their working units while keeping their labour contract (employment relation) unchanged. This indicator reflects the total number of laborers actually engaged in production or other operations in various units.

Persons Employed in Private Enterprises and Self-Employed Individuals in Urban Areas Persons employed in private enterprises refer to the persons employed in the private enterprises which have been registered at the departments of industrial and commercial administration and are situated at a county town (i.e. a town where the county government is located) for business operation or at urban areas with the level higher than a county town. The self-employed individuals in urban areas refer to persons who hold the certificates of residence in urban areas or have resided in the urban areas for a long time and have been registered at the departments of industrial and commercial administration and approved to be engaged in individual industrial or commercial business, including self-employed persons as well as helpers and hired labourers who work in the individual households engaged in industrial or commercial business.

Registered Urban Unemployed Persons refer to the persons with non-agricultural household registration at certain working ages (16-50 years for male and 16-45 years for females), who are capable of work, unemployed and willing to work, and have been registered at the local employment service agencies to apply for a job.

Registered Urban Unemployment Rate refers to the ratio of the number of the registered unemployed persons to the sum of the number of persons employed in various units (minus the rural labour force, retirees, and Hong Kong, Macao, Taiwan or foreign employees they employ) laid-off workers in urban units, owners and employees in urban private enterprises, urban self-employed individuals and the registered urban unemployed persons. The formula is as follows:

Registered urban unemployment rate = number of registered urban unemployed persons÷(number of persons employed in urban units - rural labour force employed retirees employed - Hong Kong, Macao, Taiwan or foreign employees employ + laid-off workers + owners and employees in urban private enterprises + self-employed individuals in urban areas + registered urban unemployed persons) × 100%.

Staff and Workers refer to persons working in, and receive payment from units of state ownership, collective ownership, joint ownership, share holding ownership, foreign ownership, and ownership by entrepreneurs from Hong Kong, Macao, and Taiwan, and other types of ownership and their affiliated units. They do not include 1) persons employed in township enterprises, 2) persons employed in private enterprises, 3) urban self-employed persons, 4) retirees, 5) re-employed retirees, 6) teachers in the schools run by the local people, 7) foreigners and persons from Hong Kong, Macao and Taiwan who work in urban units, and 8) other persons not to be included by relevant regulations. (Data of 1998 and afterward refer to fully employed staff and workers. Other related statistics such as total wage bill and average wage are adjusted since 1998 accordingly).

State-owned Units refer to economic units whose assets are owned by the state. Included are non-corporation units registered according to Regulation of the People Republic of China on the Registration of Enterprises and Corporations, state organs, institutions and social organizations at the central and local levels.

Collective-Owned Units refer to economic units registered according to Regulation of the People抯 Republic of China on the Registration of Enterprises and Corporations where the means of production are collectively owned.

Units of Other Types of Ownership refer to units registered with other types of ownership, including cooperative units, joint ownership units, limited companies, share holding corporations, units invested by entrepreneurs from Hong Kong, Macao, and Taiwan, and foreign-invested units.

Fully Employed Staff and Workers refer to persons who work in, and receive wages from their working units, as well as persons who have their work posts, but are temporarily absent from work for reasons of study or on sick, injury or maternal leave and still receive wages from their working units.

Total Wages Bill refer to the total remuneration payment to staff and workers in various units during a certain period of time. The calculation of total wages is based on the total remuneration payment to the staff and workers. Therefore, all the wages and salaries and other payments to staff and workers are included in the total wages regardless of their sources, category, and forms (in kind or cash). (Total wages of staff and workers in this yearbook include only total wages of fully employed staff and workers, excluding the living allowances distributed to those who have left their working units while keeping their labour contract/employment relation unchanged).

Average Wage refers to the average wage in money terms per person during a certain period of time for staff and workers in enterprises, institutions, and government agencies, which reflects the general level of wage income during a certain period of time and is calculated as follows:

Average Wage = Total Wages of Staff and Workers at Reference Time /Average Number of Staff and Workers at Reference Time.

Average Wage Indices refers to the ratio of average wage of staff and workers in the report period to that in the base period, which reflects the change of wage of staff and workers at the different period. It is calculated as follows:

Average Wage Indices = Average Wage of Staff and Workers at Reference Time / Average Wage of Staff and Workers at Base Period x 100%

Average Real Wage Indices average real wage of staff and workers refers to the average wage of staff and workers after removing the effects of the price changes and average real wage indices of staff and workers refers to the change of real wage, which reflects the relative increasing or decreasing level of real wage of staff and workers, which is calculated as follows:

Average Real Wage Indices = Average Wage Indices of Staff and Workers at the Reference Time / Urban Consumer Price Indices at Reference Time × 100%

4 固定资产投资

Investment In Fixed Assets

资料整理：柯　超

固 定 资 产 投 资

INVESTMENT IN FIXED ASSETS

2013

全社会固定资产投资完成额	Total Completed Investment in Fixed Assets	20753.91	亿元
固定资产投资	Urban Investment	20177.45	亿元
#房地产开发	Real Estate Development	3286.02	亿元
#国有经济	State-Owned	5068.42	亿元
集体经济	Collective-Owned	826.51	亿元
房屋施工面积	Floor Space of Building Under Construction	51939.51	万平方米
房屋竣工面积	Floor Space of Building Completed	18828.87	万平方米

全社会固定资产投资完成额构成（%）

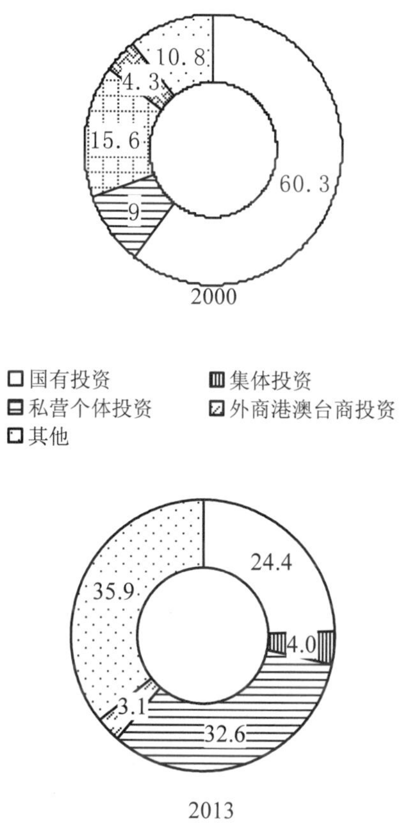

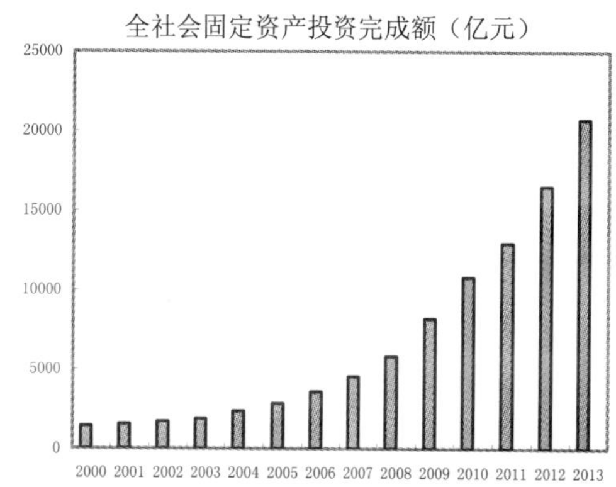

附：全社会固定资产投资完成额构成(%)

		2000	2003	2004	2005	2006	2007	2009	2010	2011	2012	2013
国有投资	State-Owned	60.3	47.2	40.4	38.7	41.2	39.9	38.1	34.9	29.1	25.8	24.4
集体投资	Collective-Owned	9.0	5.8	4.5	2.8	3.1	3.4	5.0	5.6	5.1	4.4	4.0
私营个体投资	Individuals	15.6	16.1	18.5	19.6	17.8	19.9	21.6	23.2	25.6	28.6	32.6
外商港澳台商投资	Foreign, HK, Macao and Taiwan	4.3	6.0	6.8	7.4	6.9	6.8	4.9	4.2	4.5	4.1	3.1
其他	Others	10.8	24.9	29.8	31.5	31.0	30.0	30.4	32.1	35.7	37.1	35.9

注：从2011年起固定资产投资统计口径调整为计划总投资500万元及以上项目，取消城镇农村公布口径，其他年份未做相应调整。

Note:Since 2011, the fixed assets investment accounts for investment over 5 million yuan, canceling town and countryside. Other years' statistics do not correspond to this adjustment.

4-1 全社会固定资产投资主要指标

指 标	Item	1990	2000	2005
投资总额(亿元)	**Total Investment (100 million yuan)**	**144.44**	**1421.55**	**2834.75**
按经济类型分	**Grouped by Ownership**			
国有经济	State-owned Units	100.35	857.01	1095.71
集体经济	Collective-owned Units	15.59	128.32	79.47
#农村	Rural Area	9.59	98.95	26.55
私营个体经济	Individuals	28.50	221.43	554.27
#农村	Rural Area	23.62	106.65	135.95
联营经济	Joint-ownership Economic Units		3.94	19.56
股份制经济	Share Holding Co.Ltd.		86.29	232.34
有限责任公司	Limited Liability Corporations		53.33	557.21
港澳台投资经济	Economic Units Funded by Hongkong, Macao and Taiwan		36.57	92.68
外商投资经济	Foreign Funded Enterprise Units		23.90	116.23
其他经济	Others		10.76	87.28
按资金来源分	**Grouped by Source of Finance**			
国家预算内资金	State Budgetary Apporpriations	11.38	141.48	255.76
国内贷款	Domestic Loans	22.22	243.90	474.21
利用外资	Foreign Investment	4.79	28.28	71.34
自筹资金	Fund Raising	92.96	781.50	1492.66
其他资金来源	Others	13.09	226.39	540.78
按构成分	**Grouped by Usage of Funds**			
建筑安装工程	Construction Installation	92.64	814.66	1696.80
设备工器具购置	Purchase of Equipments and Instruments	41.02	371.56	642.86
其他费用	Others	10.78	235.33	495.09
按产业分	**Grouped by Industry**			
#住宅	Residential Housing	39.61	290.24	510.04
第一产业	Primary Industry	12.16	103.05	92.88
第二产业	Second Industry	67.41	521.58	1086.34
第三产业	Tertiary Industry	64.87	796.92	1655.53
房屋建筑面积(万平方米)	**Floor Space of Building (10000 sq.m)**			
施工面积	Floor Space under Construction	5103.48	9920.42	12572.00
#住宅	Residential Housing	3507.53	6831.02	8401.20
竣工面积	Floor Space Completed	4169.12	7508.96	7863.85
#住宅	Residential Housing	3058.40	5417.38	5627.67
商品房销售面积(万平方米)	**Floor Space of Commercial House (sq.m)**	130.53	612.05	1708.02

注：2006年全社会投资(城镇投资)不含城镇工矿区私人建房投资(下同)。由于方法制度调整，按可比口径计算，2005年扣除城镇工矿区私人建房投资基数应为2788.92亿元；从2011年起固定资产投资统计口径调整为计划总投资500万元及以上项目，取消城镇农村公布口径，其他年份未做相应调整。从2012年起，三次产业采用新的划分标准。

MAJOR INDICATORS OF TOTAL INVESTMENT IN FIXED ASSETS

2006	2007	2008	2009	2010	2011	2012	2013
3572.69	**4534.14**	**5798.56**	**8211.85**	**10802.69**	**12935.02**	**16504.17**	**20753.91**
1473.70	1808.61	2273.83	3124.90	3768.95	3764.22	4265.95	5068.42
110.67	155.66	253.32	411.18	602.80	660.59	733.92	826.51
31.68	44.10	65.02	77.50	99.23	137.69	118.29	137.45
636.25	900.48	1201.53	1771.61	2510.61	3307.47	4712.60	6763.68
176.87	186.65	190.19	240.48	301.05	365.51	459.30	576.46
19.42	26.59	15.05	11.32	19.89	22.49	47.70	38.96
245.27	344.51	462.81	659.79	896.87	987.66	1319.31	1487.62
716.16	872.80	1109.43	1648.26	2221.99	3056.98	3805.18	4692.14
119.85	145.53	160.62	202.38	207.81	253.89	302.69	245.87
127.71	164.84	178.60	200.79	245.92	328.55	367.76	397.02
123.66	115.12	143.37	181.62	327.85	553.17	949.06	1233.69
378.79	472.98	570.17	711.98	868.46	663.18	784.27	886.58
708.39	790.84	894.57	1432.98	1768.79	1707.46	1964.14	2720.19
79.32	88.37	57.02	68.33	147.03	189.26	131.64	66.82
1902.71	2470.28	3677.00	4956.65	6703.61	8800.61	11812.15	14823.15
503.48	711.66	599.80	1041.91	1314.80	1574.51	1811.96	2257.17
2252.72	2857.31	3568.96	5025.62	6701.91	8056.53	11054.16	14312.25
717.10	896.36	1245.73	1753.28	2308.73	2812.91	3162.99	3856.68
602.87	780.47	983.87	1432.95	1792.05	2065.58	2287.02	2584.98
572.50	709.63	901.26	1127.28	1417.95	1750.16	2198.86	2907.29
107.43	149.40	231.25	321.59	393.00	440.91	525.45	590.61
1317.12	1710.59	2344.36	3097.68	4169.92	5526.40	7281.04	9187.25
2148.23	2674.15	3222.95	4792.58	6239.77	6967.71	8697.68	10976.04
12346.48	13686.34	16417.07	20142.81	25284.83	31388.88	40103.56	51939.51
8039.75	8910.75	9896.66	11762.06	14486.90	16337.96	19154.75	23443.19
7126.64	7557.62	7551.82	9772.28	11802.18	14585.68	16576.18	18828.87
4812.39	5036.19	4679.96	5556.71	6785.61	7375.38	7890.08	8006.06
2038.46	2538.90	1941.62	2718.30	3508.61	4187.62	4037.85	5298.54

Note: In 2006 the social investment (town investment) does not contain town private house industrial investment.(same below) Because of method adjustment, according to comparable caliber, 2005's investment base should be 278.892 billion yuan deducting industrial town private house. Since 2011, the fixed assets investment accounts for investment over 5 million yuan, canceling town and countryside. Other years' statistics do not correspond to this adjustment. Since 2012, the division of three industries emploies a new standard.

4-2 全社会固定资产投资额
TOTAL INVESTMENT IN FIXED ASSETS

单位：亿元 (100 million yuan)

年 份 Year	投资额 Investment	#房地产开发 Real Estate Development	#国有经济 State Owned Units	#集体经济 Collective Owned Units	#私营个体 Individuals
"六五" 时期 Period of the Six-Year Plan	**315.82**		**207.57**	**49.41**	**58.84**
1981	33.48		29.51	3.69	0.28
1982	48.83		34.46	8.45	5.92
1983	56.13		36.69	8.84	10.60
1984	74.47		45.25	10.99	18.23
1985	102.91		61.66	17.44	23.81
"七五" 时期 Peroid of the Seven-Year Plan	**680.12**	**5.94**	**435.32**	**94.17**	**150.64**
1986	111.44		66.42	15.89	29.13
1987	140.08		85.32	22.31	32.46
1988	160.46		102.21	24.60	33.64
1989	123.70		81.02	15.78	26.91
1990	144.44	5.94	100.35	15.59	28.50
"八五" 时期 Peroid of the Eight-Year Plan	**2211.67**	**253.77**	**1467.69**	**190.04**	**261.87**
1991	168.19	7.88	119.07	19.49	29.63
1992	240.73	12.55	182.86	22.52	35.35
1993	383.18	37.01	275.84	30.62	40.37
1994	593.07	76.20	401.16	44.83	56.62
1995	826.50	121.13	518.76	72.58	99.90
"九五" 时期 Peroid of the Nine-Year Plan	**6022.80**	**334.60**	**3425.23**	**573.74**	**943.77**
1996	984.38	118.40	593.32	96.50	124.78
1997	1083.60	126.47	567.60	107.12	160.56
1998	1231.10	131.23	661.94	116.92	194.52
1999	1302.17	123.87	745.36	124.88	242.48
2000	1421.55	134.63	857.01	128.32	221.43
"十五" 时期 Peroid of the Ten-Year Plan	**10321.69**	**1354.15**	**4817.55**	**541.41**	**1806.78**
2001	1551.75	151.24	918.21	126.41	249.59
2002	1695.22	178.64	963.18	121.42	263.00
2003	1883.59	239.04	888.72	109.05	303.90
2004	2356.38	337.28	951.73	105.06	436.02
2005	2834.75	447.95	1095.71	79.47	554.27
"十一五" 时期 Peroid of the Eleven-Year Plan	**32919.93**	**4999.84**	**12449.99**	**1533.63**	**7020.48**
2006	3572.69	564.76	1473.70	110.67	636.25
2007	4534.14	723.73	1808.61	155.66	900.48
2008	5798.56	892.67	2273.83	253.32	1201.53
2009	8211.85	1200.44	3124.90	411.18	1771.61
2010	10802.69	1618.24	3768.95	602.80	2510.61
"十二五" 时期 Peroid of the Twelve-Year Plan					
2011	12935.02	2066.48	3764.22	660.59	3307.47
2012	16504.17	2539.46	4265.95	733.92	4712.60
2013	20753.91	3286.02	5068.42	826.51	6763.68

注：房地产开发投资统计制度从1990年开始建立。从2011年起固定资产投资统计口径调整为计划总投资500万元及以上项目，取消城镇农村公布口径，其他年份未做相应调整。

Note: The statistical system of real estate development investment is established in 1990. Since 2011, the fixed assets investment accounts for investment over 5 million yuan, canceling town and countryside. Other years' statistics do not correspond to this adjustment.

4-3 按登记注册类型分全社会固定资产投资

TOTAL INVESTMENT IN FIXED ASSETS BY TYPE OF REGISTRATION

单位：亿元

指　　标	Itcm	2010	2011	2012	2013
总　计	**Total**	**10802.69**	**12935.02**	**16504.17**	**20753.91**
内资企业	Domestic Funded Enterprises	9969.16	11922.24	15315.74	19497.88
国有企业	State-owned Enterprises	3531.40	3576.83	4117.99	4871.98
集体企业	Collective-owned Enterprises	507.68	554.48	651.70	677.53
股份合作企业	Share Holding Cooperative Enterprises	79.11	97.38	73.43	131.21
联营企业	Joint Owned Enterprise	56.52	47.30	68.75	78.13
国有联营	State Joint ownership	20.62	16.07	12.27	21.40
集体联营	Collective Joint Ownership	16.01	8.73	8.79	17.77
国有与集体联营	Joint State-Collective	6.12	5.70	12.16	21.23
其他联营企业	Other Joint Owned Enterprise	13.77	16.79	35.54	17.73
有限责任公司	Co. Ltd	2438.92	3228.30	3940.87	4867.18
国有独资公司	Solely State Funded Co.	216.93	171.32	135.69	175.04
其他有限责任公司	Other Co. Ltd	2221.99	3056.98	3805.18	4692.14
股份有限公司	Share Holding Co.Ltd.	896.89	987.66	1319.31	1487.62
私营企业	Private - owned enterprises	2130.81	2877.12	4194.63	6150.55
其他企业	Others	327.85	553.18	949.05	1233.69
港、澳、台商投资企业	Hongkong, Macao and Taiwan Funded	207.81	253.89	302.69	245.87
合资经营企业	Joint Funded Enterprises	66.96	138.56	121.23	63.81
合作经营企业	Cooperative Operation Enterprises	3.94	3.50	1.54	1.12
股份有限公司	Share Holding Co.Ltd.	116.96	87.57	147.23	142.00
独资经营企业	Solely Funded Enterprises	19.96	24.26	29.64	35.62
外商投资企业	Foreign Invested Enterprises	245.92	328.55	367.76	397.02
合资经营企业	Joint Funded Enterprises	114.17	156.38	195.14	227.87
合作经营企业	Cooperative Operation Enterprises	16.60	9.74	11.67	8.06
独资企业	Solely Funded Enterprises	83.96	132.90	124.48	116.11
股份有限公司	Share Holding Co.Ltd.	31.19	29.53	14.09	34.38
个体经营	Individual Investment	379.80	430.35	517.97	613.13
个体户	Individual Self-Employed	345.36	406.54	487.04	595.47
个人合伙	Individual Pattenership	34.44	23.81	30.94	17.66

注：从2011年起固定资产投资统计口径调整为计划总投资500万元及以上项目，取消城镇农村公布口径，其他年份未做相应调整。

Note:Since 2011, the fixed assets investment accounts for investment over 5 million yuan, canceling town and countryside. Other years' statistics do not correspond to this adjustment.

4-4 按构成分城镇固定资产投资（2013）
URBAN INVESTMENT IN FIXED ASSETS BY USAGE OF FUNDS(2013)

单位：亿元 (100 million yuan)

行业	Sector	投资额 Investment	建筑工程 Construction	安装工程 Installation	设备工器具购置 Purchases of Equipments and Instruments	其他 Others
总 计	**Total**	**20177.45**	**12161.77**	**1760.01**	**3670.69**	**2584.98**
农、林、牧、渔业	Farming, Forestry, Animal Husbandry and Fishery	562.54	344.93	47.37	92.72	77.51
农业	Farming	159.87	92.82	12.25	27.04	27.75
林业	Forestry	50.14	25.91	3.79	7.47	12.97
畜牧业	Animal Husbandry	155.48	96.12	14.42	27.55	17.38
渔业	Fishery	39.14	22.77	3.87	7.82	4.69
农、林、牧、渔服务业	Farming, Forestry, Animal Husbandry and Fishery Services	157.92	107.31	13.05	22.85	14.71
采矿业	Mining	369.67	192.99	37.77	107.34	31.58
制造业	Manufacturing	8219.26	4153.76	834.05	2456.36	775.09
农副食品加工业	Food Processing	684.86	348.64	71.22	199.03	65.97
食品制造业	Food Production	243.04	126.97	23.42	67.10	25.55
酒、饮料和精制茶制造业	Beverage Production	244.96	129.55	22.00	67.42	25.98
烟草制品业	Tobacco Processing	11.51	5.54	1.33	4.40	0.24
纺织业	Textile Industry	329.08	161.67	35.19	105.87	26.36
纺织服装、服饰业	Textile Wearing Apparel and Accessaries	194.71	100.56	19.25	58.02	16.89
皮革、毛皮、羽毛及其制品和制鞋业	Leather, Fur, Feather and Related Products	69.10	31.37	7.60	25.41	4.71
木材加工和木、竹、藤、棕、草制品业	Timber Processing and Wood, Bamboo, Rattan, Palm and Straw Products	99.89	49.97	8.73	32.60	8.59
家具制造业	Furniture Manufacturing	132.09	70.56	15.65	34.03	11.85
造纸和纸制品业	Papermaking and Paper Products	149.27	79.41	14.66	42.43	12.78
印刷和记录媒介复制业	Printing and Record Processing	80.75	40.50	8.13	26.35	5.77
文教、工美、体育和娱乐用品制造业	Stationery, Education, Art, Sport and Entertainment Products	64.75	35.68	6.33	17.82	4.92
石油加工、炼焦和核燃料加工业	Petroleum Processing, Coking Products and Nuclear Fuel Processing	58.36	22.08	6.49	16.14	13.65
化学原料和化学制品制造业	Raw Chemical Material and Chemical Products	605.09	263.38	61.78	235.58	44.34
医药制造业	Medical and Pharmaceutical Products	267.54	145.74	21.07	74.26	26.47
化学纤维制造业	Chemical Fibres	15.22	5.86	0.72	5.37	3.27
橡胶和塑料制品业	Rubber Products and Plastic Products	250.32	124.77	23.87	81.30	20.37
非金属矿物制品业	Non-metal Material Products	818.85	373.53	82.81	288.31	74.20
黑色金属冶炼和压延加工业	Smelting and Processing of Ferrous Metals	192.16	80.44	26.50	68.55	16.67
有色金属冶炼和压延加工业	Smelting and Processing of Non-ferrous Metals	126.18	58.90	9.63	48.85	8.80
金属制品业	Metal Products	323.24	158.87	35.05	95.83	33.49
通用设备制造业	General Machinery Manufacturing	386.23	183.52	45.77	127.15	29.78
专用设备制造业	Special Purpose Equipment Manufacturing	550.85	294.34	73.78	132.19	50.54
汽车制造业	Automobile Manufacturing	1017.94	559.63	74.43	290.60	93.28
铁路、船舶、航空航天和其他运输设备制造业	Realway, Ship, Aircraft and Other Transport Equipment Manufacturing	151.88	86.61	19.13	31.78	14.35
电气机械和器材制造业	Electric Machinery and Equipment	522.99	302.08	51.53	123.61	45.76
计算机、通信和其他电子设备制造业	Computers, Communication Equipment and Other Electronic Equipment Manufacturing	401.94	201.75	44.30	98.00	57.88
仪器仪表制造业	Measuring Instruments Manufacturing	94.39	40.33	10.84	25.39	17.84
其他制造业	Other Equipment	48.13	35.14	3.33	5.79	3.87
废弃资源综合利用业	Recycling and Disposal of Waste	69.24	29.96	7.42	23.20	8.65
金属制品、机械和设备修理业	Repairing of Metal and Mechanical Equipment	14.71	6.39	2.09	3.96	2.27
电力、热力、燃气及水生产和供应业	Electric Power, Gas and Water Production and Supply	531.71	239.38	65.48	176.49	50.35
电力、热力生产和供应业	Electric Power and and Heat Power Production and Supply	343.14	130.61	39.64	139.76	33.13
燃气生产和供应业	Gas Production and Supply	51.25	27.63	6.64	12.05	4.94
水的生产和供应业	Water Production and Supply	137.31	81.15	19.20	24.68	12.28

注：从2011年起固定资产投资统计口径调整为计划总投资500万元及以上项目，取消城镇农村公布口径，其他年份未做相应调整。从2012年起执行新的国民经济行业代码（GB/T4754-2011）

Note:Since 2011, the fixed assets investment accounts for investment over 5 million yuan, canceling town and countryside. Other years' statistics do not correspond to this adjustment.Since 2012,a new national economy industry code(GB/T4754-2011)is implemented.

4-4 续表 continued

单位：亿元 (100 million yuan)

行业	Sector	投资额 Investment	建筑工程 Construction	安装工程 Installation	设备工器具购置 Purchases of Equipments and Instruments	其他 Others
建筑业	Construction	104.63	71.37	10.01	15.14	8.11
交通运输、仓储和邮政业	Transportation, Storage and Post	1733.95	1255.61	80.22	143.01	255.11
铁路运输业	Railway Transportation	70.08	58.86	3.95	1.13	6.13
道路运输业	Road Transportation	1205.69	892.85	39.94	77.82	195.08
水上运输业	Waterway Transportation	94.11	65.69	4.27	11.33	12.83
航空运输业	Air Transportation	48.43	41.21	0.59	5.52	1.11
管道运输业	Pipeline Transportation	2.96	1.03	0.34	0.86	0.74
装卸搬运和运输代理业	Load, Unload, and Agency	46.98	24.40	2.09	7.41	13.08
仓储业	Transportation Storage	260.50	168.20	28.77	37.86	25.67
邮政业	Post	5.20	3.37	0.28	1.07	0.48
信息传输、软件和信息技术服务业	Information Transmission, Software and Information Technology Service	114.95	33.32	14.60	59.20	7.84
电信、广播电视和卫星传输服务	Telecom, Radio Tv and Satellite	70.34	14.20	6.07	47.93	2.14
互联网和相关服务	Internet and Related	14.77	2.78	3.05	8.58	0.37
软件和信息技术服务业	Software and Information Technology	29.84	16.34	5.48	2.68	5.33
批发和零售业	Wholesale and Retail	520.65	341.18	39.20	71.75	68.52
住宿和餐饮业	Hotel and Catering Service	270.24	169.19	25.09	45.25	30.71
金融业	Finance	81.53	49.92	9.68	13.93	8.00
货币金融服务	Monetary Financial Service	48.52	26.40	6.49	10.59	5.04
资本市场服务	Monetary Financial Service	14.61	10.58	2.11	0.85	1.08
保险业	Insurance	2.11	1.34	0.07	0.56	0.15
其他金融业	Other Financial Acitivities	16.29	11.60	1.02	1.94	1.73
房地产业	Real Estate	4317.35	2925.89	351.44	142.15	897.86
租赁和商务服务业	Leasing and Commercial Service	307.23	209.52	25.19	32.51	40.00
租赁业	Leasing Service	7.20	3.11	0.45	2.91	0.73
商务服务业	Commercial Service	300.03	206.41	24.74	29.61	39.27
科学研究和技术服务业	Scientific Research and Technical Services	93.62	49.57	9.91	23.61	10.53
水利、环境和公共设施管理业	Water Conservancy, Environment and Public Facility Management	1853.06	1367.81	121.99	142.99	220.27
水利管理业	Water Conservancy Management	247.98	192.29	17.95	20.92	16.83
生态保护和环境治理业	Environment Management	72.58	44.13	4.65	13.50	10.30
公共设施管理业	Public Facility Management	1532.49	1131.39	99.39	108.57	193.14
居民服务、修理和其他服务业	Resident Service and Others	108.69	81.25	9.46	9.93	8.06
教育	Education	203.36	139.26	12.92	33.32	17.85
卫生和社会工作	Health Care and Social Work	177.35	109.64	12.01	44.09	11.60
卫生	Health Care	142.44	84.98	9.31	39.83	8.31
社会工作	Social Work	34.91	24.66	2.70	4.26	3.29
文化、体育和娱乐业	Culture, Sports and Recreation	194.01	127.01	22.07	26.44	18.50
新闻和出版业	News and Publication	4.01	3.27		0.27	0.47
广播、电视、电影和影视录音制作业	Radio, Television, Film and Recordin	7.47	2.91	1.55	2.53	0.48
文化艺术业	Culture and Arts	69.96	52.72	5.83	5.69	5.72
体育	Sports	34.04	23.49	3.45	4.10	3.01
娱乐业	Receation	78.54	44.63	11.25	13.84	8.82
公共管理、社会保障和社会组织	Public Management and Social Organizations	413.64	300.16	31.54	34.47	47.48

4−5 按建设性质分固定资产投资（2013）
URBAN INVESTMENT IN FIXED ASSETS BY TYPE OF CONSTRUCTION(2013)

单位：亿元 (100 million yuan)

行业	Sector	投资额 Investment	#新建 New Construction	#扩建 Expension	#改建 Replacement
总计	Total	**20177.45**	**14725.89**	**1907.02**	**3094.83**
农、林、牧、渔业	Farming, Forestry, Animal Husbandry and Fishery	562.54	420.72	77.71	51.48
农业	Farming	159.87	119.20	25.71	13.29
林业	Forestry	50.14	40.17	6.00	3.05
畜牧业	Animal Husbandry	155.48	131.03	19.39	2.46
渔业	Fishery	39.14	30.88	6.39	1.87
农、林、牧、渔服务业	Farming, Forestry, Animal Husbandry and Fishery Services	157.92	99.44	20.23	30.80
采矿业	Mining and Qarrying	369.67	131.13	54.72	182.51
制造业	Manufacturing	8219.26	5234.58	858.97	1978.34
农副食品加工业	Food Processing	684.86	403.56	87.30	182.53
食品制造业	Food Production	243.04	161.24	28.27	51.38
酒、饮料和精制茶制造业	Beverage Production	244.96	150.46	25.57	64.05
烟草制品业	Tobacco Processing	11.51	4.24	0.18	6.76
纺织业	Textile Industry	329.08	165.58	47.65	110.23
纺织服装、服饰业	Textile Wearing Apparel and Accessaries	194.71	127.49	24.13	39.34
皮革、毛皮、羽毛及其制品和制鞋业	Leather, Fur, Feather and Related Products	69.10	52.85	6.17	9.21
木材加工和木、竹、藤、棕、草制品业	Timber Processing and Wood, Bamboo, Rattan, Palm and Sraw Works	99.89	49.00	27.92	20.35
家具制造业	Furniture Manufacturing	132.09	112.65	4.93	14.01
造纸和纸制品业	Papermaking and Paper Products	149.27	91.49	21.92	29.06
印刷和记录媒介复制业	Printing and Record Processing	80.75	47.97	7.20	19.84
文教、工美、体育和娱乐用品制造业	Stationery, Education, Art, Sport and Entertainment Products	64.75	53.29	3.89	7.03
石油加工、炼焦和核燃料加工业	Petroleum Processing,Coking products and Nuclear Fuel Processing	58.36	18.28	4.63	34.29
化学原料和化学制品制造业	Raw Chemical Material and Chemical Products	605.09	264.38	68.64	258.98
医药制造业	Medical and pharmaceutical Products	267.54	180.01	20.95	62.51
化学纤维制造业	Chemical Fibers	15.22	9.11	1.84	4.27
橡胶和塑料制品业	Rubber Products and Plastic Products	250.32	155.06	27.91	63.69
非金属矿物制品业	Nonmetal Material Products	818.85	431.35	108.14	261.78
黑色金属冶炼和压延加工业	Smelting and Processing of ferrous Metals	192.16	101.64	8.08	79.69
有色金属冶炼和压延加工业	Smelting and Processing of Nonferrous Metals	126.18	64.46	27.87	33.10
金属制品业	Metal Products	323.24	188.90	44.37	86.35
通用设备制造业	Ordinaryly Machinery Manufacturing	386.23	245.49	38.49	91.90
专用设备制造业	Special Purpose Equipment Manufacturing	550.85	434.03	35.12	76.02
汽车制造业	Automobile Manufacturing	1017.94	746.73	74.91	178.67
铁路、船舶、航空航天和其他运输设备制造业	Realway, Ship, Aircraft and Other Transport Equipment Manufacturing	151.88	93.18	11.37	41.32
电气机械和器材制造业	Electric Machinery and Equipment	522.99	400.68	52.73	62.24
计算机、通信和其他电子设备制造业	Computers, Communication Equipment and Other Electronic Equipment Manufacturing	401.94	307.61	29.47	62.34
仪器仪表制造业	Measuring Instruments Manufacturing	94.39	66.12	15.17	12.25
其他制造业	Other Equipment	48.13	41.94	1.64	4.55
废弃资源综合利用业	Recycling and Disposal of Waste	69.24	59.30	2.09	4.54
金属制品、机械和设备修理业	Repairing of Metal and Mechanical Equipment	14.71	6.50	0.42	6.08
电力、热力、燃气及水生产和供应业	Electric Power, Gas and Water Production and Supply	531.71	282.88	47.02	189.52
电力、热力生产和供应业	Electric Power, Steam and Hot Water Production and Supply	343.14	174.56	17.85	142.02
燃气生产和供应业	Gas Production and Supply	51.25	35.98	5.93	7.41
水的生产和供应业	Tap Water Production and Supply	137.31	72.34	23.24	40.10

注：从2011年起固定资产投资统计口径调整为计划总投资500万元及以上项目，取消城镇农村公布口径，其他年份未做相应调整。从2012年起执行新的国民经济行业代码（GB/T4754−2011）

Note:Since 2011, the fixed assets investment accounts for investment over 5 million yuan, canceling town and countryside. Other years' statistics do not correspond to this adjustment.Since 2012,a new national econmy industry code(GB/T4754-2011) is implemanted.

4-5 续表 continued

单位：亿元 (100 million yuan)

行 业	Sector	投资额 Investment	#新 建 New Construction	#扩 建 Expension	#改 建 Replacement
建筑业	Construction	104.63	85.09	3.72	8.47
交通运输、仓储和邮政业	Transportation, storage and Post	1733.95	1203.16	277.45	214.88
铁路运输业	Railway Transportation	70.08	53.41	13.10	3.56
道路运输业	Road Transportation	1205.69	820.06	177.57	182.95
水上运输业	Waterway Transportation	94.11	80.51	7.76	1.45
航空运输业	Air Transportation	48.43	41.34	2.50	0.05
管道运输业	Pipeline Transportation	2.96	2.43	0.29	0.24
装卸搬运和运输代理业	Load, Unload, and Agency	46.98	29.79	12.78	1.81
仓储业	Transportation Storage	260.50	172.25	62.47	24.50
邮政业	Post	5.20	3.37	0.96	0.31
信息传输、软件和信息技术服务业	Information Transmission, Software and Information Technology Service	114.95	55.72	3.21	21.85
电信、广播电视和卫星传输服务	Telecom, Radio Tv and Satellite	70.34	24.45	1.71	17.23
互联网和相关服务	Internet and Related	14.77	5.37		2.18
软件和信息技术服务业	Software and Information Technology	29.84	25.90	1.50	2.44
批发和零售业	Wholesale and Retail Trade	520.65	422.25	46.02	34.88
住宿和餐饮业	Hotel and Catering Services	270.24	216.38	26.66	11.50
金融业	Finance	81.53	58.86	7.89	8.30
货币金融服务	Monetary Financial Service	48.52	26.98	7.27	7.79
资本市场服务	Capital Markets Service	14.61	13.93	0.62	0.06
保险业	Insurance	2.11	1.66		0.46
其他金融业	Other Financial Acitivities	16.29	16.29		
房地产业	Real Estate Trade	4317.35	4144.41	88.56	49.14
租赁和商务服务业	Leasing and Commercial Service	307.23	266.04	25.84	7.21
租赁业	Leasing Service	7.20	3.82	1.58	
商务服务业	Commercial Service	300.03	262.22	24.25	7.21
科学研究和技术服务业	Scientific Research, Polytechnical Services	93.62	73.81	3.81	7.70
水利、环境和公共设施管理业	Water Conservancy, Environment and Public Facility Management	1853.06	1365.24	215.45	248.19
水利管理业	Water Conservancy Management	247.98	123.59	47.57	72.41
生态保护和环境治理业	Environment Management	72.58	47.94	5.50	16.82
公共设施管理业	Public Facility Management	1532.49	1193.71	162.37	158.95
居民服务、修理和其他服务业	Resident Service and Others	108.69	86.53	17.12	2.88
教育	Education	203.36	138.87	27.30	17.89
卫生和社会工作	Health Care and Social Work	177.35	111.41	24.17	13.99
卫生	Health Care	142.44	83.31	19.51	12.25
社会工作	Social Work	34.91	28.10	4.66	1.74
文化、体育和娱乐业	Culture, Sports and Recreation	194.01	153.38	17.83	17.45
新闻和出版业	News and Publication	4.01	4.01		
广播、电视、电影和影视录音制作业	Radio, Television, Film and Recording	7.47	2.45	1.48	3.29
文化艺术业	Culture and Arts	69.96	57.10	7.01	3.84
体育	Sports	34.04	28.93	1.55	3.56
娱乐业	Receation	78.54	60.89	7.79	6.75
公共管理、社会保障和社会组织	Public Management and Social Organizations	413.64	275.43	83.57	28.65

4-6 按控股情况分固定资产投资(2013)
URBAN INVESTMENT IN FIXED ASSETS BY THE SITUATION OF CONTROLLING SHARE HOLDING(2013)

单位：亿元 (100 million yuan)

行业	Sector	投资额 Investment	国有控股 State Share Holding	集体控股 Collective Share Holding	私人控股 Private Share Holding	港澳台商控股 Hongkong, Macao and Taiwan Share Holding	外商控股 Foreign Sgare Holding
总计	Total	**20177.45**	**5906.47**	**1272.94**	**11021.54**	**244.49**	**287.63**
农、林、牧、渔业	Farming, Forestry, Animal Husbandry and Fishery	562.54	116.25	37.31	367.83	2.68	
农业	Farming	159.87	21.19	19.79	105.82	0.08	
林业	Forestry	50.14	11.77	0.69	33.13		
畜牧业	Animal Husbandry	155.48	4.62	5.54	137.42	0.10	
渔业	Fishery	39.14	4.17	1.10	29.70		
农、林、牧、渔服务业	Farming, Forestry, Animal Husbandry and Fishery Services	157.92	74.49	10.19	61.75	2.50	
采矿业	Mining and Qarrying	369.67	94.68	16.88	241.08		
制造业	Manufacturing	8219.26	885.00	299.42	6245.82	91.26	158.80
农副食品加工业	Food Processing	684.86	12.44	25.47	605.19	9.88	2.97
食品制造业	Food Production	243.04	12.60	3.41	210.23	5.54	4.06
酒、饮料和精制茶制造业	Beverage Production	244.96	10.24	8.10	189.91	9.96	1.58
烟草制品业	Tobacco Processing	11.51	5.82		3.85		
纺织业	Textile Industry	329.08	2.56	9.49	294.66	1.50	0.15
纺织服装、服饰业	Textile Wearing Apparel and Accessarie	194.71		4.75	173.60	2.35	4.40
皮革、毛皮、羽毛及其制品和制鞋业	Leather, Fur, Feather and Related Products	69.10		0.24	66.60	1.46	
木材加工和木、竹、藤、棕、草制品业	Timber Processing and Wwood, Bamboo,Rattan, Palm and Sraw Works	99.89	1.22	0.71	90.73	0.09	
家具制造业	Furniture Manufacturing	132.09	0.23	2.56	116.17	1.70	
造纸和纸制品业	Papermaking and Paper Products	149.27	14.54	1.43	121.71	1.26	1.84
印刷和记录媒介复制业	Printing and Record Processing	80.75	2.10	1.50	64.96	0.57	1.09
文教、工美、体育和娱乐用品制造业	Stationery, Education, Art, Sport and Entertainment Products	64.75	1.41	1.87	55.41	5.35	
石油加工、炼焦和核燃料加工业	Petroleum Processing, Coking Products and Nuclear Fuel Processing	58.36	28.74	0.17	26.84		
化学原料和化学制品制造业	Raw Chemical Material and Chemical Products	605.09	102.10	27.65	450.02	1.21	5.14
医药制造业	Medical and pharmaceutical Products	267.54	28.93	19.44	181.23	11.61	0.51
化学纤维制造业	Chemical Fibers	15.22			15.22		
橡胶和塑料制品业	Rubber Products and Plastic Products	250.32	10.88	6.19	217.52	0.22	3.69
非金属矿物制品业	Nonmetal Material Products	818.85	28.35	29.84	695.58	0.51	8.89
黑色金属冶炼和压延加工业	Smelting and Processing of ferrous Metals	192.16	59.47	7.89	99.50		7.49
有色金属冶炼和压延加工业	Smelting and Processing of Nonferrous Metals	126.18	3.08	3.15	102.29		
金属制品业	Metal Products	323.24	15.43	9.02	260.06	8.28	10.29
通用设备制造业	Ordinaryly Machinery Manufacturing	386.23	29.86	14.08	296.61		8.65
专用设备制造业	Special Purpose Equipment Manufacturing	550.85	51.09	18.68	422.58	1.36	9.08
汽车制造业	Automobile Manufacturing	1017.94	236.88	44.12	593.90	3.15	74.22
铁路、船舶、航空航天和其他运输设备制造业	Realway, Ship, Aircraft and Other Transport Equipment Manufacturing	151.88	56.77	0.82	89.28		0.48
电气机械和器材制造业	Electric Machinery and Equipment	522.99	51.93	22.42	404.75	0.57	8.14
计算机、通信和其他电子设备制造业	Computers, Communication Equipment Other Electronic Equipment Manufacturing	401.94	78.13	10.45	261.12	22.20	5.89
仪器仪表制造业	Measuring Instruments Manufacturing	94.39	14.02	20.67	50.62	2.41	0.24
其他制造业	Other Equipment	48.13	12.40	1.38	32.69	0.08	
废弃资源综合利用业	Recycling and Disposal of Waste	69.24	12.48	3.38	49.93		
金属制品、机械和设备修理业	Repairing of Metal and Mechanical Equipment	14.71	1.30	0.54	3.07		
电力、热力、燃气及水生产和供应业	Electric Power, Gas and Water Production and Supply	531.71	364.32	39.12	110.77	3.07	1.56
电力、热力生产和供应业	Electric Power, Steam and Hot Water Production and Supply	343.14	265.56	3.92	66.22	1.21	0.73
燃气生产和供应业	Gas Production and Supply	51.25	18.74	4.23	23.57	1.86	0.41
水的生产和供应业	Tap Water Production and Supply	137.31	80.02	30.98	20.97		0.43

注：从2011年起固定资产投资统计口径调整为计划总投资500万元及以上项目，取消城镇农村公布口径，其他年份未做相应调整。从2012年起执行新的国民经济行业代码（GB/T4754—2011）

Note:Since 2011, the fixed assets investment accounts for investment over 5 million yuan, canceling town and countryside. Other years' statistics do not correspond to this adjustment.Since 2012,a new national econmy industry code(GB/T4754-2011) is implemanted.

4–6 续表 continued

单位：亿元 (100 million yuan)

行业	Sector	投资额 Investment	国有控股 State Share Holding	集体控股 Collective Share Holding	私人控股 Private Share Holding	港澳台商控股 Hongkong, Macao and Taiwan Share Holding	外商控股 Foreign Sgare Holding
建筑业	Construction	104.63	61.75	15.13	25.57		
交通运输、仓储和邮政业	Transportation, storage and Post	1733.95	1262.21	62.09	342.82	8.89	18.61
铁路运输业	Railway Transportation	70.08	67.93	0.23	1.92		
道路运输业	Road Transportation	1205.69	1048.08	40.51	71.45	3.41	15.01
水上运输业	Waterway Transportation	94.11	57.48	3.32	25.38	3.26	3.60
航空运输业	Air Transportation	48.43	41.12		2.78		
管道运输业	Pipeline Transportation	2.96	2.58	0.09			
装卸搬运和运输代理业	Load, Unload, and Agency	46.98	4.09	0.22	40.91		
仓储业	Transportation Storage	260.50	37.01	17.72	199.51	2.21	
邮政业	Post	5.20	3.93		0.88		
信息传输、软件和信息技术服务业	Information Transmission, Software and Information Technology Service	114.95	62.09	8.45	18.67	0.93	0.88
电信、广播电视和卫星传输服务	Telecom, Radio Tv and Satellite	70.34	58.91	2.45	0.97	0.93	0.78
互联网和相关服务	Internet and Related	14.77	2.92		5.57		
软件和信息技术服务业	Software and Information Technolog	29.84	0.27	6.00	12.13		0.10
批发和零售业	Wholesale and Retail Trade	520.65	74.10	51.53	336.33	9.44	11.11
住宿和餐饮业	Hotel and Catering Services	270.24	18.09	8.80	214.76	0.31	14.92
金融业	Finance	81.53	20.29	15.46	34.63		
货币金融服务	Monetary Financial Service	48.52	16.73	15.24	6.37		
资本市场服务	Capital Markets Service	14.61	1.42	0.08	12.15		
保险业	Insurance	2.11	1.97	0.14			
其他金融业	Other Financial Acitivities	16.29	0.18		16.11		
房地产业	Real Estate Trade	4317.35	864.45	387.23	2340.43	123.28	78.05
租赁和商务服务业	Leasing and Commercial Service	307.23	76.49	25.58	188.75	0.72	
租赁业	Leasing Service	7.20	3.30		3.61		
商务服务业	Commercial Service	300.03	73.19	25.58	185.15	0.72	
科学研究和技术服务业	Scientific Research, Polytechnical Services	93.62	36.71	11.94	37.06		2.44
水利、环境和公共设施管理业	Water Conservancy, Environment and Public Facility Management	1853.06	1288.93	174.17	313.77	3.81	0.06
水利管理业	Water Conservancy Management	247.98	206.32	23.56	10.56		
生态保护和环境治理业	Environment Management	72.58	48.30	3.74	18.72		
公共设施管理业	Public Facility Management	1532.49	1034.31	146.87	284.49	3.81	0.06
居民服务、修理和其他服务业	Resident Service and Others	108.69	31.81	17.55	35.93		
教育	Education	203.36	151.46	9.72	31.59		
卫生和社会工作	Health Care and Social Work	177.35	128.34	13.04	27.54		
卫生	Health Care	142.44	106.97	8.78	20.34		
社会工作	Social Work	34.91	21.36	4.25	7.20		
文化、体育和娱乐业	Culture, Sports and Recreation	194.01	87.37	10.90	79.95	0.11	1.20
新闻和出版业	News and Publication	4.01	3.31		0.70		
广播、电视、电影和影视录音制作业	Radio, Television, Film and Recording	7.47	5.41		1.46	0.05	
文化艺术业	Culture and Arts	69.96	41.73	7.27	17.29	0.06	
体育	Sports	34.04	20.41	1.42	10.59		
娱乐业	Receation	78.54	16.51	2.20	49.91		1.20
公共管理、社会保障和社会组织	Public Management and Social Organizations	413.64	282.14	68.61	28.24		

4-7 按行业分施工投产项目个数(2013)
NUMBER OF URBAN PROJECTS UNDER CONSTRUCTION AND PUT INTO PRODUCTION BY SECTOR(2013)

行业	Sector	施工项目(个) Number of Projects under Construction (unit)	#新开工 Newly Started	全部建成投产项目(个) Completion and Put into Production of All Projects (unit)	项目建成投产率(%) Rate of Completion and Put into Production (%)
总　计	Total	**26228**	**19245**	**17308**	**66.0**
农、林、牧、渔业	Farming, Forestry, Animal Husbandry and Fishery	1635	1250	1179	72.1
农业	Farming	439	324	306	69.7
林业	Forestry	132	94	78	59.1
畜牧业	Animal Husbandry	475	367	341	71.8
渔业	Fishery	124	101	89	71.8
农、林、牧、渔服务业	Farming, Forestry, Animal Husbandry and Fishery Services	465	364	365	78.5
采矿业	Mining and Qarrying	638	477	445	69.7
制造业	Manufacturing	10477	7674	6874	65.6
农副食品加工业	Food Processing	1216	935	832	68.4
食品制造业	Food Production	356	266	232	65.2
酒、饮料和精制茶制造业	Beverage Production	341	261	203	59.5
烟草制品业	Tobacco Processing	12	7	9	75.0
纺织业	Textile Industry	498	375	351	70.5
纺织服装、服饰业	Textile Wearing Apparel and Accessaries	346	253	253	73.1
皮革、毛皮、羽毛及其制品和制鞋业	Leather, Fur, Feather and Related Products	104	81	66	63.5
木材加工和木、竹、藤、棕、草制品业	Timber Processing and Wwood, Bamboo, Rattan, Palm and Sraw Works	200	155	141	70.5
家具制造业	Furniture Manufacturing	175	126	106	60.6
造纸和纸制品业	Papermaking and Paper Products	169	117	121	71.6
印刷和记录媒介复制业	Printing and Record Processing	125	95	89	71.2
文教、工美、体育和娱乐用品制造业	Stationery, Education, Art, Sport and Entertainment Products	87	62	62	71.3
石油加工、炼焦和核燃料加工业	Petroleum Processing, Coking Products and Nuclear Fuel Processing	41	24	20	48.8
化学原料和化学制品制造业	Raw Chemical Material and Chemical Products	778	579	562	72.2
医药制造业	Medical and pharmaceutical Products	308	218	169	54.9
化学纤维制造业	Chemical Fibers	20	13	15	75.0
橡胶和塑料制品业	Rubber Products and Plastic Products	361	261	261	72.3
非金属矿物制品业	Nonmetal Material Products	1516	1162	1091	72.0
黑色金属冶炼和压延加工业	Smelting and Processing of ferrous Metals	167	125	108	64.7
有色金属冶炼和压延加工业	Smelting and Processing of Nonferrous Metals	119	82	70	58.8
金属制品业	Metal Products	414	296	264	63.8
通用设备制造业	Ordinaryly Machinery Manufacturing	511	383	358	70.1
专用设备制造业	Special Purpose Equipment Manufacturing	582	416	361	62.0
汽车制造业	Automobile Manufacturing	920	636	559	60.8
铁路、船舶、航空航天和其他运输设备制造业	Realway, Ship, Aircraft and Other Transport Equipment Manufacturing	100	60	49	49.0
电气机械和器材制造业	Electric Machinery and Equipment	476	348	267	56.1
计算机、通信和其他电子设备制造业	Computers, Communication Equipment and Other Electronic Equipment Manufacturing	296	189	121	40.9
仪器仪表制造业	Measuring Instruments Manufacturing	100	63	52	52.0
其他制造业	Other Equipment	58	28	33	56.9
废弃资源综合利用业	Recycling and Disposal of Waste	62	45	33	53.2
金属制品、机械和设备修理业	Repairing of Metal and Mechanical Equipment	19	13	16	84.2
电力、热力、燃气及水生产和供应业	Electric Power, Gas and Water Production and Supply	1032	732	659	63.9
电力、热力生产和供应业	Electric Power, Steam and Hot Water Production and Supply	538	358	329	61.2
燃气生产和供应业	Gas Production and Supply	112	80	73	65.2
水的生产和供应业	Tap Water Production and Supply	382	294	257	67.3

注：从2011年起固定资产投资统计口径调整为计划总投资500万元及以上项目，取消城镇农村公布口径，其他年份未做相应调整。从2012年起执行新的国民经济行业代码（GB/T4754-2011）

Note:Since 2011, the fixed assets investment accounts for investment over 5 million yuan, canceling town and countryside. Other years' statistics do not correspond to this adjustment.Since 2012,a new national econmy industry code(GB/T4754-2011) is implemanted.

4-7 续表 continued

行　　业	Sector	施工项目(个) Number of Projects under Construction (unit)	#新开工 Newly Started	全部建成投产项目(个) Completion and Put into Production of All Projects (unit)	项目建成投产率(%) Rate of Completion and Put into Production (%)
建筑业	Construction	200	160	153	76.5
交通运输、仓储和邮政业	Transportation, storage and Post	2217	1623	1409	63.6
铁路运输业	Railway Transportation	25	9	7	28.0
道路运输业	Road Transportation	1800	1376	1192	66.2
水上运输业	Waterway Transportation	82	49	27	32.9
航空运输业	Air Transportation	7	3	2	28.6
管道运输业	Pipeline Transportation	9	7	5	55.6
装卸搬运和运输代理业	Load, Unload, and Agency	53	34	36	67.9
仓储业	Transportation Storage	223	129	125	56.1
邮政业	Post	18	16	15	83.3
信息传输、软件和信息技术服务业	Information Transmission, Software and Information Technology Service	143	106	106	74.1
电信、广播电视和卫星传输服务	Telecom, Radio Tv and Satellite	104	87	88	84.6
互联网和相关服务	Internet and Related	13	6	9	69.2
软件和信息技术服务业	Software and Information Technology	26	13	9	34.6
批发和零售业	Wholesale and Retail Trade	1004	790	651	64.8
住宿和餐饮业	Hotel and Catering Services	547	420	358	65.4
金融业	Finance	103	76	68	66.0
货币金融服务	Monetary Financial Service	81	62	53	65.4
资本市场服务	Capital Markets Service	13	9	7	53.8
保险业	Insurance	7	4	6	85.7
其他金融业	Other Financial Acitivities	2	1	2	100.0
房地产业	Real Estate Trade	1324	884	841	63.5
租赁和商务服务业	Leasing and Commercial Service	361	227	184	51.0
租赁业	Leasing Service	10	7	5	50.0
商务服务业	Commercial Service	351	220	179	51.0
科学研究和技术服务业	Scientific Research, Polytechnical Services	170	124	116	68.2
水利、环境和公共设施管理业	Water Conservancy, Environment and Public Facility Management	3143	2337	1972	62.7
水利管理业	Water Conservancy Management	826	681	642	77.7
生态保护和环境治理业	Environment Management	162	117	105	64.8
公共设施管理业	Public Facility Management	2155	1539	1225	56.8
居民服务、修理和其他服务业	Resident Service and Others	242	199	161	66.5
教育	Education	876	681	693	79.1
卫生和社会工作	Health Care and Social Work	547	374	390	71.3
卫生	Health Care	383	258	267	69.7
社会工作	Social Work	164	116	123	75.0
文化、体育和娱乐业	Culture, Sports and Recreation	400	283	259	64.8
新闻和出版业	News and Publication	4	1	2	50.0
广播、电视、电影和影视录音制作业	Radio, Television, Film and Recording	35	27	29	82.9
文化艺术业	Culture and Arts	190	135	123	64.7
体育	Sports	55	36	29	52.7
娱乐业	Receation	116	84	76	65.5
公共管理、社会保障和社会组织	Public Management and Social Organizations	1169	828	790	67.6

4-8 按资金来源和构成分全社会固定资产投资
TOTAL INVESTMENT IN FIXED ASSETS BY SOURCE OF FUNDS AND USE OF FUNDS

年 份 Year	按资金来源分 Grouped by Source of Finance					按构成分 Grouped by Use of Funds		
	国家预算内资金 State Budgetary Appropriations	国内贷款 Domestic Loans	利用外资 Foreign Investment	自筹资金 Fund Raising	其他资金来源 Others	建筑安装工程 Construction Installation	设备工器具购置 Purchases of Equipment and Instruments	其他费用 Others
投资额(亿元) Investment(100 million yuan)								
1985	10.99	24.86	0.23	62.28	4.56	67.53	28.67	6.71
1990	11.38	22.22	4.79	92.96	13.09	92.64	41.02	10.78
1995	58.40	173.47	88.71	422.92	83.00	454.40	248.51	123.59
1996	72.53	206.15	74.86	537.31	93.53	510.52	307.89	165.97
1997	68.08	172.05	51.24	651.08	141.15	600.04	264.16	219.40
1998	85.18	225.95	33.86	703.44	182.66	695.55	323.47	212.08
1999	108.18	207.61	36.57	730.92	218.89	771.24	329.26	201.67
2000	141.48	243.90	28.28	781.50	226.39	814.66	371.56	235.33
2001	174.03	241.96	29.89	874.60	231.27	890.60	419.20	241.95
2002	200.95	280.11	63.22	717.24	433.69	974.73	418.55	301.94
2003	150.20	291.60	57.41	786.40	597.98	1059.98	463.23	360.38
2004	197.03	383.78	64.74	1182.36	528.47	1409.25	537.25	409.88
2005	255.76	474.21	71.34	1492.66	540.78	1696.80	642.86	495.09
2006	378.79	708.39	79.32	1902.71	503.48	2252.72	717.10	602.87
2007	472.98	790.84	88.37	2470.28	711.66	2857.31	896.36	780.47
2008	570.17	894.57	57.02	3677.00	599.80	3568.96	1245.73	983.87
2009	711.93	1432.89	68.32	4956.88	1041.83	5025.62	1753.28	1432.95
2010	868.46	1768.79	147.03	6703.61	1314.80	6701.91	2308.73	1792.05
2011	663.18	1707.46	189.26	8800.61	1574.51	8056.52	2812.91	2065.59
2012	784.27	1964.14	131.64	11812.15	1811.96	11054.16	3162.99	2287.02
2013	886.58	2720.19	66.82	14823.15	2257.17	14312.25	3856.68	2584.98
构成(%) Composition (%)								
1985	10.7	24.2	0.2	60.5	4.4	65.6	27.8	6.6
1990	7.9	15.4	3.3	64.4	9.0	64.1	28.4	7.5
1995	7.1	21.0	10.7	51.2	10.0	58.6	30.3	11.1
1996	7.4	20.9	7.6	54.6	9.5	62.1	25.9	12.0
1997	6.3	15.9	4.7	60.1	13.0	67.7	22.1	10.2
1998	6.9	18.4	2.8	57.1	14.8	70.2	18.4	11.4
1999	8.3	15.9	2.8	56.1	16.9	63.4	26.5	10.1
2000	10.0	17.2	2.0	55.0	15.8	64.3	23.9	11.8
2001	11.2	15.6	1.9	56.4	14.9	64.8	24.3	10.9
2002	11.9	16.5	3.7	42.3	25.6	64.4	23.6	12.1
2003	8.0	15.5	3.0	41.8	31.7	60.9	23.4	15.7
2004	8.4	16.3	2.7	50.2	22.4	63.9	20.8	15.3
2005	9.0	16.7	2.5	52.7	19.1	59.9	22.7	17.4
2006	10.6	19.8	2.2	53.3	14.1	63.1	20.1	16.8
2007	12.6	19.7	1.3	81.1	13.2	78.7	27.5	21.7
2008	9.8	15.4	1.0	63.4	10.4	61.5	21.5	17.0
2009	8.7	17.4	0.8	60.4	12.7	61.2	21.4	17.4
2010	8.1	16.4	1.4	62.1	12.0	62.0	21.4	16.6
2011	5.1	13.2	1.5	68.0	12.2	62.3	21.7	16.0
2012	4.8	11.9	0.8	71.6	11.0	67.0	19.2	13.9
2013	4.3	13.1	0.3	71.4	10.9	69.0	18.6	12.4

注：从2011年起固定资产投资统计口径调整为计划总投资500万元及以上项目，取消城镇农村公布口径，其他年份未做相应调整。

Note:Since 2011,the fixed assets investment statistical adjustment plan for a total investment of 5 million yuan RMB and the above project, cancel the town and countryside,other years did not do corresponding adjustment.

4-9 国有单位固定资产投资

INVESTMENT IN FIXED ASSETS BY STATE OWNED UNITS

指 标	Item	2010		2011		2012		2013	
		合计 Total	#房地产开发 Real Estate Development	合计 Total	#房地产开发 Real Estate Development	合计 Total	#房地产开发 Real Estate Development	合计 Total	#房地产开发 Real Estate Development
建设项目	Number of Construction Projects								
施工项目(个)	Projects under Construction (unit)	9619		7889		8311		8861	
全部建成投产项目(个)	Total Projects Completed Put into Operation	7258		5687		5380		5663	
建成项目投产率(%)	Rate of Projects Completed Put into Operation %	75.5		72.1		64.7		63.9	
建设周期(年)	Construction Cycle (year)	1.33		1.39		1.54		1.56	
资金来源(亿元)	**Tatal Financial Allocation and Loans(100 million yuan)**	**3937.35**	**251.59**	**3875.10**	**291.90**	**4577.28**	**460.92**	**5248.89**	**467.81**
国家预算内资金	State Appropriation	855.71		591.77		722.06		782.29	
国内贷款	Domestic Loans	974.69	56.27	832.92	37.25	761.68	98.62	855.37	111.51
利用外资	Foreign Investment	7.03	4.00	4.66		9.73		16.47	
自筹资金	Fund Raising	1741.46	62.92	2078.05	126.48	2679.28	126.97	3082.45	123.30
其他资金	Others	358.46	128.40	367.70	128.17	463.47	235.43	512.32	233.00
投资总额(亿元)	**Total Value of Investment (100 million yuan)**	**3768.95**	**193.80**	**3764.22**	**213.55**	**4265.95**	**203.98**	**5068.42**	**243.23**
按构成分	Grouped by Use of Funds								
#建筑工程	Construction Projects	2369.87	108.58	2306.57	105.51	2799.58	150.21	3481.50	164.77
安装工程	Installation Projects	223.30	5.60	193.12	3.26	269.83	11.87	318.10	15.15
设备工具器具购置	Purchase of Equipment, Tools and Instruments	549.00	1.62	569.86	0.71	577.74	4.55	606.81	8.41
按产业分	Grouped by Industry								
第一产业	Primary Industry	129.19		103.21		52.51		41.40	
第二产业	Second Industry	764.92		891.80		916.20		1083.13	
第三产业	Tertiary Industry	2874.84	193.80	2769.21	213.55	3297.24	203.98	3943.88	243.23
#住宅	Residential Housing	233.82	156.16	213.99	150.67	239.63	157.97	266.36	171.32
按建设性质分	Grouped by Type of Construction								
#新建	New Construction		193.80	1963.88	213.55	2425.78	203.98	3168.09	243.23
扩建	Expension	590.86		578.63		567.03		613.32	
改建	Replacement	739.92		824.77		860.22		862.82	
房屋建筑面积(万平方米)	**Floor Space of Building (10000 sq.m)**								
施工面积	Floor Space Under Construction	3860.49	1188.68	3807.60	1042.20	5132.23	1087.36	6695.15	1485.48
#住宅	Residential Buildings	2056.16	1092.00	1671.01	940.83	1868.05	935.84	2457.39	1231.75
竣工面积	Floor Spaace Completed	1871.64	355.39	1544.76	247.28	2042.82	285.45	2344.15	276.69
#住宅	Residential Buildings	994.18	338.31	622.90	232.34	658.05	268.43	757.20	246.64

注：建设周期按项目个数计算；本表资金来源均为资金到位数。从2012年起，三次产业采用新的划分标准。

Note: The constructive period is counted by the numbers of project.The sources of capital in this table are the number of achieved funds.Since 2012, the division of three industries emploies a new standard.

4-10 房地产开发投资主要指标

指　　标	Item	1990	1995	2000
企业个数(个)	**Number of Enterprises (unit)**	**129**	**571**	**1052**
内资	Inner Funded	129	404	848
#国有	State - owned	129	292	380
集体	Collective-owned		51	105
港澳台投资	Funded by Enterprises from Hongkong, Macao and Taiwan		68	149
外商投资	Foreign Funded		99	55
投资完成额(亿元)	**Investment Completed This Year**	**5.94**	**121.13**	**134.63**
按构成分	Grouped by Use of Funds			
#建筑安装工程	Construction Projects	5.45	89.56	99.59
设备工器具购置	Installation Projects		4.47	2.83
按工程用途分	Grouped by Use of Projects			
#住宅	Residential Houses	4.70	61.78	93.15
#经济适用房屋	Economical Houses		7.44	23.53
资金来源	Grouped by Source of Finance	5.94	138.88	117.88
国内贷款	Domestic Loans	1.21	39.01	18.08
利用外资	Foreign Investments		16.35	1.15
自筹投资	Fund Raising	3.72	41.26	47.27
其他投资	Others	1.01	42.26	51.38
房屋建筑面积(万平方米)	**Floor Space of Building (10000 sq.m)**			
施工面积	Floor Space Under Construction	390.11	2049.30	2102.86
#住宅	Residential Buildings	325.82	1299.03	1673.84
竣工面积	Floor Spaace Completed	183.91	518.88	843.55
#住宅	Residential Buildings	156.77	427.19	733.27
土地开发及购置(万平方米)	**Land Development and Purchase (10000sq.m)**			
本年土地开发面积	Area of Land development This Year		903.00	469.28
本年土地购置面积	Area of Land Purchased This Year		719.00	838.12
商品房销售情况	**Selling of Commercial Houses**			
房屋销售面积(万平方米)	Floor Psace of Selling Houses (10000sq.m)	130.53	240.00	612.05
#住宅	Residential Buildings	112.67	211.00	571.04
#经济适用房	Economic Houses		40.00	172.99
商品房销售额(亿元)	Sales Value of Commercial House	6.93	31.00	83.74
#住宅				

注：本表资金来源均为资金到位数；从2010年起本年土地开发面积指标取消；从2011年起经济适用房分组指标取消。

MAJOR INDICATORS OF INVESTMENT IN REAL ESTATE DEVELOPMENT

2005	2008	2009	2010	2011	2012	2013
1990	**3410**	**3460**	**3556**	**3648**	**3785**	**4267**
1782	3245	3299	3395	3505	3654	4140
228	166	191	187	189	184	194
74	53	75	66	66	59	57
129	109	109	106	96	90	87
79	56	52	55	47	41	40
447.95	**892.67**	**1200.44**	**1618.24**	**2066.48**	**2539.46**	**3286.02**
315.15	668.18	828.62	1059.26	1407.17	1902.65	2426.17
4.68	11.92	18.51	29.07	36.29	56.16	75.79
317.65	660.48	804.16	1040.25	1334.42	1698.38	2251.56
13.49	68.87	74.37	40.33			
513.44	1042.33	1714.76	2219.50	2864.05	3363.83	4224.48
100.41	227.37	388.45	415.43	462.25	512.05	796.57
1.82	10.37	15.83	97.29	39.03	1.27	
186.95	448.99	577.76	784.39	1195.28	1425.31	1735.33
224.26	355.60	732.71	922.40	1167.49	1425.20	1692.58
4804.35	7800.50	9536.03	11589.44	13922.07	16819.71	21865.81
4012.13	6659.53	7727.09	9172.43	11013.30	13013.01	16640.27
1627.03	2057.88	2312.11	2541.21	3221.05	3273.71	3040.84
1411.67	1795.76	2007.34	2129.33	2728.39	2795.21	2547.39
941.26	954.48	1361.67				
1530.64	1006.16	1000.08	1422.06	1582.27	1303.19	1894.68
1708.02	1941.62	2718.30	3508.61	4187.62	4037.85	5298.54
1549.19	1821.31	2576.32	3236.88	3788.68	3620.10	4765.68
111.31	225.38	176.99	99.48			
386.57	582.61	959.88	1313.20	1878.73	2036.20	2790.32
335.19	525.89	879.33	1134.94	1569.32	1689.86	2310.04

Note: The source of capital in this table are the number of achieved funds; From 2010 the land development indicators of this year had been canceled.From 2011 the group index of affordable housing had been canceled.

4-11 按登记注册类型分房地产开发投资(2013)

单位：亿元

项目	Item	总计 Total	内资 Inner Funded	国有 State - owned	集体 Collective -owned	股份合作 Share Holding Cooperation	联营 Joint- Owned	国有独资公司 Solely co.	其他有限责任公司 Responsibility Co. Ltd
企业个数(个)	**Number of Enterprises (unit)**	**4267**	**4140**	**165**	**31**	**26**	**3**	**29**	**1542**
#亏损企业个数	Loss- Making Enterprises	1190	1150	35	4			17	497
本年完成投资	**Investment Completed This Year**	**3286.02**	**3110.54**	**176.12**	**21.56**	**11.43**	**0.84**	**67.10**	**1385.09**
按构成分	Grouped by Use of Funds								
建筑工程	Construction Projects	2166.09	2053.79	140.00	12.93	7.17	0.14	24.77	905.32
安装工程	Installation Projects	260.08	246.79	10.17	0.92	1.48	0.62	4.98	88.50
设备工器具购置	Purchase of Equipment, Tools and Instruments	75.79	75.16	7.81	0.21	0.31	0.08	0.60	21.87
其他费用	Other Funds	784.07	734.80	18.14	7.50	2.47		36.75	369.40
#土地购置费	Purchase of Land	441.01	400.91	7.34	3.35	1.47		16.50	197.33
按构成用途分	Grouped by Use of Projects								
住宅	Residential Buildings	2251.56	2154.65	123.92	13.51	6.76	0.84	47.40	1027.49
#经济适用房	Economical Houses								
别墅、高档公寓	Villa, Top Grade Flat	63.80	48.51	0.95				0.03	29.08
办公楼	Office Building	147.44	139.11	16.76	0.05	1.81		8.87	33.61
商业营业用房	Business Buildings	496.70	468.31	11.06	2.09	1.97		3.02	185.48
其他	Others	390.33	348.47	24.38	5.91	0.89		7.81	138.51
本年新增固定资产	**Newly Increased Fixed Assets This Year**	**1134.31**	**1119.77**	**60.61**	**13.37**	**7.52**		**8.47**	**504.29**
资金来源	**Finance Sources**	**4224.48**	**4017.06**	**394.24**	**22.31**	**13.04**	**0.84**	**73.56**	**1870.79**
国内贷款	Domestic Loans	796.57	772.55	106.39	1.28	2.01		5.12	365.90
利用外资	Foreign Investments								
自筹资金	Fund Raising	1735.33	1653.87	85.59	11.25	5.42	0.84	37.71	769.17
#自有资金	Self Owned	756.69	712.66	40.77	8.02	0.20		7.94	290.54
其他资金来源	Others	1692.58	1590.64	202.26	9.78	5.61		30.73	735.72
#定金及预收款	Funds Ordered and Pre-received	928.17	855.44	57.73	4.44	1.15		15.69	431.42
土地开发(万平方米)	**Land Development (10000 sq.m)**								
待开发土地面积	Area of Land to be Developed	1618.21	1462.00	36.55				68.97	646.07
本年购置土地面积	Area of Land Purchased This Year	1894.68	1828.17	26.93	4.92	3.57		20.51	887.98
本年土地成交价款	Value of Land Transaction	391.80	373.20	5.60	4.34	0.54		4.70	227.14

注：本表资金来源均为资金到位数，从2010年起土地开发投资额和本年土地开发面积指标取消。

INVESTMENT IN REAL ESTATE DEVELOPMENT BY TYPE OF REGISTRATION(2013)

(100 million yuan)

股份有限公司 Share Holding Co.Ltd.	私营 Private	其他 Others	港澳台商投资 Hongkong, Macao and Taiwan Funded	合资经营 Joint Venture Corperation	合作经营 Cooperative Corperation	独资 Solely Funded	股份有限公司 Share Holding Co.Ltd.	外商投资 Foreign Investment	合资经营 Joint Venture Corperation	合作经营 Cooperative Corperation	独资 Solely Funded	股份有限公司 Share Holding Co.Ltd.
231	**2045**	**68**	**87**	**42**	**2**	**41**	**2**	**40**	**20**	**1**	**16**	**1**
57	539	1	31	10		21		12	6		5	
280.32	**1094.17**	**73.90**	**117.83**	**17.74**	**0.50**	**97.76**	**1.82**	**57.66**	**24.76**	**5.61**	**26.30**	**0.99**
158.06	750.41	55.01	78.93	16.56	0.35	60.32	1.71	33.36	18.71	3.26	10.54	0.85
29.66	98.75	11.71	6.90	0.92	0.05	5.81	0.12	6.40	3.79		2.48	0.13
8.62	33.76	1.90	0.42		0.05	0.37		0.21	0.15		0.05	0.01
83.97	211.26	5.29	31.57	0.26	0.05	31.26		17.70	2.12	2.35	13.23	
40.44	132.26	2.22	27.39			27.39		12.71	0.54		12.16	
158.88	729.53	46.34	64.58	15.99	0.35	46.42	1.82	32.33	10.01	3.93	17.40	0.99
2.80	11.31	4.34	13.99			13.99		1.30	0.08		1.22	
21.99	49.64	6..38	3.35	0.04		3.31		4.98	4.98			
62.81	194.14	7.73	15.83	0.89	0.10	14.84		12.56	5.62	0.99	5.95	
36.64	120.86	13.45	34.07	0.82	0.05	33.19	0.00	7.80	4.15	0.70	2.95	
70.95	**440.18**	**14.38**	**8.31**	**6.75**		**0.56**	**1.00**	**6.22**	**4.21**	**1.31**	**0.70**	
310.97	**1261.80**	**69.51**	**145.81**	**35.94**	**0.50**	**104.12**	**5.26**	**61.61**	**18.37**	**11.45**	**26.81**	**4.98**
90.11	193.29	8.45	15.67	1.51		14.16		8.35	5.33	1.50	1.52	
94.55	608.31	41.03	60.50	8.90	0.50	46.10	5.00	20.96	6.26		14.70	
29.72	320.18	15.29	40.11	8.05		32.03	0.02	3.93	3.93			
126.31	460.20	20.04	69.64	25.53		43.86	0.26	32.30	6.78	9.95	10.59	4.98
75.68	256.80	12.52	49.76	15.52		34.12	0.12	22.98	5.93	9.53	5.35	2.15
50.12	607.60	52.70	122.35	25.65		96.71		33.85	26.19		7.66	
43.68	828.62	11.97	7.55			7.55		58.96	32.25		26.71	
6.27	123.09	1.52	7.19			7.19		11.41	1.88		9.53	

Note: The sources of capital in this table are the number of achieved funds.From 2010,the indicators of investment and area of land development had been canceled.

4-12 市、州全社会固定资产投资

TOTAL INVESTMENT IN FIXED ASSETS IN CITIES AND PREFECTURES

单位：亿元 (100 million yuan)

市、州	Cities and Prefectures	2005	2006	2007	2008	2009	2010	2011	2012	2013
全省	**Total**	**2834.75**	**3572.69**	**4534.14**	**5798.56**	**8211.85**	**10802.69**	**12935.02**	**16504.17**	**20753.91**
武汉市	Wuhan Municipality	1055.18	1325.29	1732.79	2222.91	3001.10	3752.92	4263.24	5031.25	6001.96
黄石市	Huangshi Municipality	106.46	138.05	179.85	232.90	343.05	474.06	597.45	750.95	963.50
十堰市	Shiyan Municipality	103.63	116.61	141.66	185.44	278.35	406.31	522.37	702.72	904.32
宜昌市	Yichang Municipality	295.80	323.55	390.36	523.46	750.27	949.51	1189.92	1620.98	2106.96
襄阳市	Xiangyang Municipality	156.62	200.50	265.80	373.77	574.79	835.32	1134.74	1600.09	2086.64
鄂州市	Ezhou Municipality	55.17	72.05	105.01	150.01	220.60	298.64	336.85	450.01	571.69
荆门市	Jingmen Municipality	104.15	127.74	153.25	210.08	317.18	448.62	590.63	794.40	1014.64
孝感市	Xiaogan Municipality	121.71	144.82	195.93	270.83	397.26	570.70	729.24	980.82	1260.82
荆州市	Jingzhou Municipality	116.78	149.67	210.75	291.46	435.16	600.93	771.42	1042.89	1355.60
黄冈市	Huanggang Municipality	158.56	192.89	258.50	370.85	553.29	736.06	823.71	1102.94	1416.02
咸宁市	Xianning Municipality	83.09	103.83	138.38	200.83	301.58	436.29	563.08	756.45	971.84
随州市	Suizhou Municipality	55.79	70.96	101.92	147.07	208.70	291.18	384.48	514.73	654.60
恩施自治州	Enshi Prefecture	78.07	87.53	116.09	139.37	182.21	244.38	314.27	406.19	510.40
仙桃市	Xiantao Municipality	56.14	52.73	64.29	85.24	120.05	167.46	178.11	241.33	314.99
潜江市	Qianjiang Municipality	40.67	52.61	72.37	88.32	123.96	172.92	175.54	237.06	305.88
天门市	Tianmen Municipality	41.15	50.81	67.28	86.07	116.51	153.62	156.07	210.99	272.18
神农架林区	Shennongjia Forest Zone	4.89	5.63	5.63	7.50	10.65	14.15	15.77	20.02	25.56
不分地区		200.88	357.42	334.29	212.43	277.14	249.61	188.13	40.34	16.30

注：2006年全社会投资(城镇投资)不含城镇工矿区私人建房投资(下同)。由于方法制度调整，按可比口径计算，2005年扣除城镇工矿区私人建房投资基数应为2788.92亿元，各市、州全社会投资未做调整。
从2011年起固定资产投资统计口径调整为计划总投资500万元及以上项目，取消城镇农村公布口径，其他年份未做相应调整。

Note: in 2006 the social investment (town investment) does not contain town private house industrial investment (the same below). Because method system adjustment, the comparable caliber calculation, 2005 deduct industrial town private house should be 278.892 billion yuan investment base; Since 2011,the fixed assets investment statistical adjustment plan for a total investment of 5 million yuan RMB and the above project, cancel the town and countryside,other years did not corresponding adjustment.

4-13 市、州国有单位固定资产投资
INVESTMENT IN FIXED ASSETS BY STATE OWNED UNITS IN CITIES AND PREFECTURES

单位：亿元 (100 million yuan)

市、州	Cities and Prefectures	2005	2006	2007	2008	2009	2010	2011	2012	2013
全省	**Total**	**1095.71**	**1473.70**	**1808.61**	**2273.83**	**3124.16**	**3768.95**	**3764.22**	**4265.95**	**5068.42**
武汉市	Wuhan Municipality	427.68	556.09	748.71	1072.32	1312.11	1655.04	1703.62	1676.10	1717.62
黄石市	Huangshi Municipality	28.65	30.74	45.70	57.71	106.17	166.26	126.63	166.27	220.15
十堰市	Shiyan Municipality	51.35	55.42	71.51	76.53	136.88	176.18	226.42	344.22	454.68
宜昌市	Yichang Municipality	153.75	151.49	163.69	200.93	281.88	279.98	246.92	368.67	474.67
襄阳市	Xiangyang Municipality	44.45	58.19	63.70	96.61	111.61	144.10	202.59	300.18	323.20
鄂州市	Ezhou Municipality	19.41	28.87	36.40	62.67	112.80	107.33	63.70	102.35	76.26
荆门市	Jingmen Municipality	19.63	23.92	37.70	37.64	69.84	113.69	121.27	166.31	203.16
孝感市	Xiaogan Municipality	37.53	47.57	54.81	74.62	111.71	119.95	136.08	121.02	214.72
荆州市	Jingzhou Municipality	28.52	41.67	59.14	67.44	130.57	144.46	164.24	191.88	291.50
黄冈市	Huanggang Municipality	47.02	61.70	79.98	116.76	199.84	236.10	194.99	271.21	399.09
咸宁市	Xianning Municipality	27.41	39.15	44.53	59.27	103.42	129.30	155.54	184.16	238.80
随州市	Suizhou Municipality	14.32	21.17	25.71	37.99	70.68	77.94	77.30	73.57	124.28
恩施自治州	Enshi Prefecture	21.52	32.26	45.29	57.47	88.85	111.07	110.16	149.84	193.99
仙桃市	Xiantao Municipality	9.65	9.98	9.47	6.54	26.99	12.79	14.48	16.52	25.56
潜江市	Qianjiang Municipality	19.44	24.19	38.88	38.82	53.64	68.65	51.62	63.30	60.47
天门市	Tianmen Municipality	11.84	11.94	15.78	28.47	30.47	46.30	25.51	15.31	30.16
神农架林区	Shennongjia Forest Zone	1.90	2.61	3.18	4.89	8.69	10.20	13.36	14.79	17.69
不分地区	Azoanl	131.62	276.72	264.43	177.16	168.00	169.60	129.79	40.24	2.40

4-14 市、州按经济类型分的全社会固定资产投资(2013)
TOTAL INVESTMENT IN FIXED ASSETS BY OWNERSHIP IN CITIES AND PREFECTURES(2013)

单位：亿元 (100 million yuan)

市、州	Cities and Prefectures	合 计 Total	国有经济单位 State Owned Units	集体经济单位 Collective Owned Units	城乡私人 Private Owned Units	其他经济单位 Others
全省	**Total**	**20753.91**	**5068.42**	**826.51**	**6763.17**	**8095.80**
武汉市	Wuhan Municipality	6001.96	1717.62	229.76	988.39	3066.19
黄石市	Huangshi Municipality	963.50	220.15	55.75	431.15	256.46
十堰市	Shiyan Municipality	904.32	454.68	22.99	287.36	139.29
宜昌市	Yichang Municipality	2106.96	474.67	41.34	685.62	905.34
襄阳市	Xiangyang Municipality	2086.64	323.20	58.60	859.74	845.09
鄂州市	Ezhou Municipality	571.69	76.26	25.09	240.29	230.06
荆门市	Jingmen Municipality	1014.64	203.16	56.52	561.79	193.17
孝感市	Xiaogan Municipality	1260.82	214.72	66.36	605.22	374.52
荆州市	Jingzhou Municipality	1355.60	291.50	42.62	506.63	514.85
黄冈市	Huanggang Municipality	1416.02	399.09	118.59	476.13	422.21
咸宁市	Xianning Municipality	971.84	238.80	27.27	377.20	328.57
随州市	Suizhou Municipality	654.60	124.28	43.26	134.50	352.56
恩施自治州	Enshi Prefecture	510.40	193.99	2.77	182.26	131.37
仙桃市	Xiantao Municipality	314.99	25.56	14.44	145.12	129.87
潜江市	Qianjiang Municipality	305.88	60.47	10.24	163.07	72.10
天门市	Tianmen Municipality	272.18	30.16	10.92	115.02	116.08
神农架林区	Shennongjia Forest Zone	25.56	17.69		3.69	4.18
不分地区	Azoanl	16.30	2.40			13.90

4-15 市、州基本建设投资
INVESTMENT IN INFRASTRUCTION CONSTRUCTION IN CITIES AND PREFECTURES

单位：亿元 (100 million yuan)

市、州	Cities and Prefectures	2005	2006	2007	2008	2009	2010	2011	2012	2013
全省	**Total**	**1515.21**	**2059.18**	**2623.06**	**3393.06**	**4955.85**	**6504.20**	**8037.32**	**10715.01**	**13511.09**
武汉市	Wuhan Municipality	507.34	665.77	846.72	1132.30	1511.96	1873.82	2312.36	2851.17	3438.78
黄石市	Huangshi Municipality	61.42	80.31	107.58	135.11	214.79	295.51	368.95	550.46	718.40
十堰市	Shiyan Municipality	52.63	61.58	78.47	99.94	165.87	266.99	335.23	468.50	641.53
宜昌市	Yichang Municipality	219.36	226.79	275.39	371.91	547.86	680.30	854.05	1092.25	1527.28
襄阳市	Xiangyang Municipality	70.19	108.53	133.85	210.13	310.74	428.23	651.27	980.84	1287.08
鄂州市	Ezhou Municipality	34.93	46.04	66.35	84.44	125.34	200.98	266.48	369.63	484.67
荆门市	Jingmen Municipality	49.59	68.73	75.34	122.10	207.60	278.03	336.03	519.00	578.07
孝感市	Xiaogan Municipality	35.68	76.21	119.52	149.33	226.40	338.58	425.55	619.60	824.23
荆州市	Jingzhou Municipality	50.15	67.60	121.12	173.44	290.16	390.92	534.24	750.55	947.60
黄冈市	Huanggang Municipality	78.32	106.56	151.82	245.58	413.73	547.27	567.38	787.85	976.36
咸宁市	Xianning Municipality	38.88	56.29	72.63	117.42	175.98	287.62	395.79	526.46	601.17
随州市	Suizhou Municipality	28.88	38.96	65.07	96.23	152.87	206.41	257.42	406.04	466.65
恩施自治州	Enshi Prefecture	50.13	59.22	76.86	90.74	122.32	158.37	214.65	292.50	365.62
仙桃市	Xiantao Municipality	12.32	21.43	39.62	52.62	89.47	135.29	145.69	159.09	238.72
潜江市	Qianjiang Municipality	27.60	19.77	26.34	39.40	36.41	66.68	97.11	150.18	167.45
天门市	Tianmen Municipality	24.45	29.36	43.09	56.79	75.96	101.33	80.24	130.98	210.89
神农架林区	Shennongjia Forest Zone	4.19	5.13	5.47	7.25	10.40	13.80	15.37	19.56	22.71
不分地区	Azoanl	169.16	320.90	317.81	208.32	277.99	234.06	179.52	40.34	13.90

4-16 市、州技术改造投资
INVESTMENT IN TECHNOLOGY TRANFER IN CITES AND PREFECTURES

单位：亿元 (100 million yuan)

市、州	Cities and Prefectures	2005	2006	2007	2008	2009	2010	2011	2012	2013
全省	**Total**	**531.72**	**625.43**	**807.56**	**1033.28**	**1301.07**	**1609.33**	**1696.12**	**2032.15**	**2333.72**
武汉市	Wuhan Municipality	176.70	216.04	316.90	406.15	410.32	419.75	374.97	331.50	249.30
黄石市	Huangshi Municipality	22.92	27.19	38.75	48.91	64.46	83.45	128.33	93.12	119.49
十堰市	Shiyan Municipality	23.12	18.96	27.66	31.67	46.87	54.38	35.19	62.66	84.19
宜昌市	Yichang Municipality	32.78	46.91	47.67	65.62	86.65	105.96	114.68	257.85	235.32
襄阳市	Xiangyang Municipality	39.20	38.80	57.34	70.35	137.43	205.46	229.29	258.40	275.00
鄂州市	Ezhou Municipality	8.77	15.82	22.88	38.90	64.77	65.08	31.83	44.37	58.08
荆门市	Jingmen Municipality	31.13	32.42	46.26	52.92	60.57	100.51	159.65	165.63	221.70
孝感市	Xiaogan Municipality	50.85	35.12	31.16	55.47	79.35	105.82	158.31	190.66	255.04
荆州市	Jingzhou Municipality	25.54	41.72	42.15	61.98	75.23	121.84	113.04	131.57	129.36
黄冈市	Huanggang Municipality	21.18	31.01	53.16	56.74	61.45	68.45	96.79	142.12	213.75
咸宁市	Xianning Municipality	17.30	20.84	25.65	38.68	61.43	62.46	61.96	113.14	177.29
随州市	Suizhou Municipality	7.63	10.24	10.87	11.45	12.02	28.86	54.64	45.95	117.72
恩施自治州	Enshi Prefecture	11.38	10.65	11.33	17.30	21.62	31.96	29.72	37.42	35.71
仙桃市	Xiantao Municipality	14.68	8.62	7.99	8.82	4.75	9.10	4.80	54.92	28.60
潜江市	Qianjiang Municipality	10.34	29.43	34.02	43.17	81.01	94.07	59.74	73.14	107.68
天门市	Tianmen Municipality	6.31	14.53	17.26	21.00	29.68	36.60	34.57	29.69	22.96
神农架林区	Shennongjia Forest Zone	0.33	0.36	0.04	0.05	0.02	0.05			2.35
不分地区		31.55	26.77	16.48	4.11	3.43	15.56	8.60		0.18

4-17 市、州房地产开发投资
INVESTMENT IN REAL ESTATE DEVELOPMENT IN CITIES AND PREFECTURES

单位：亿元 (100 million yuan)

市、州	Cities and Prefectures	2005	2006	2007	2008	2009	2010	2011	2012	2013
全省	**Total**	**447.95**	**564.76**	**723.73**	**892.67**	**1200.44**	**1618.24**	**2066.48**	**2539.46**	**3286.02**
武汉市	Wuhan Municipality	297.99	366.15	459.75	560.36	778.59	1017.40	1282.25	1574.86	1905.60
黄石市	Huangshi Municipality	11.33	16.96	19.66	21.53	25.30	38.36	42.51	56.04	84.68
十堰市	Shiyan Municipality	20.95	25.18	26.05	28.99	35.73	41.08	52.00	76.64	101.11
宜昌市	Yichang Municipality	31.70	39.18	48.71	56.68	79.33	105.78	135.97	176.59	203.18
襄阳市	Xiangyang Municipality	22.09	29.67	36.87	46.21	55.39	106.52	144.97	186.19	301.94
鄂州市	Ezhou Municipality	6.06	7.84	9.39	10.79	8.11	11.49	18.82	11.65	22.78
荆门市	Jingmen Municipality	5.31	9.07	11.38	16.84	27.19	38.83	55.65	64.31	87.79
孝感市	Xiaogan Municipality	9.38	11.26	19.16	28.57	32.40	49.60	56.40	74.95	111.13
荆州市	Jingzhou Municipality	16.19	18.14	22.20	26.59	32.87	35.53	55.80	54.89	76.79
黄冈市	Huanggang Municipality	9.08	12.17	23.33	27.38	37.33	43.84	62.15	78.57	132.73
咸宁市	Xianning Municipality	3.80	7.88	14.60	25.35	39.55	59.57	65.46	84.96	112.06
随州市	Suizhou Municipality	4.53	6.83	9.11	15.96	17.05	21.66	24.68	19.79	29.23
恩施自治州	Enshi Prefecture	5.24	8.29	16.22	16.48	16.97	25.65	35.47	40.28	57.06
仙桃市	Xiantao Municipality	1.96	2.39	2.95	3.92	4.79	7.75	16.34	15.66	26.62
潜江市	Qianjiang Municipality	0.86	1.32	1.44	2.76	3.57	6.39	5.75	9.15	18.11
天门市	Tianmen Municipality	1.48	2.44	2.92	4.27	6.27	8.77	12.26	14.93	15.24
神农架林区	Shennongjia Forest Zone									

4−18 按国民经济行业分的基本建设投资
ACCORDING TO THE NATIONAL ECONOMIC CONSTRUCTION OF BASIC INDUSTRY INVESTMENT

单位：亿元 (100 million yuan)

行业	sector	全省 2012	全省 2013	#地方 2012	#地方 2013
总　计	**Total**	**10715.01**	**13511.09**	**10336.48**	**13220.43**
农、林、牧、渔业	Farming, Forestry, Animal Husbandry and Fishery	426.50	509.11	426.18	507.78
农业	Farming	129.10	146.09	128.78	144.76
林业	Forestry	26.80	47.09	26.80	47.09
畜牧业	Animal Husbandry	150.09	151.81	150.09	151.81
渔业	Fishery	24.00	37.27	24.00	37.27
农、林、牧、渔服务业	Farming, Forestry, Animal Husbandry and Fishery Services	96.51	126.85	96.51	126.85
采矿业	Mining and Qarrying	189.18	186.36	184.71	183.42
制造业	Manufacturing	4721.39	6140.72	4601.09	6049.71
农副食品加工业	Food Processing	342.24	497.73	341.41	497.50
食品制造业	Food Production	141.52	191.00	141.52	191.00
酒、饮料和精制茶制造业	Beverage Production	122.00	178.14	122.00	178.14
烟草制品业	Tobacco Processing	2.07	4.42	2.07	4.42
纺织业	Textile Industry	164.77	213.89	164.36	213.11
纺织服装、服饰业	Textile Wearing Apparel and Accessaries	127.84	152.69	127.84	152.69
皮革、毛皮、羽毛及其制品和制鞋业	Leather, Fur, Feather and Related Products	35.59	59.52	35.59	59.52
木材加工和木、竹、藤、棕、草制品业	Timber Processing and Wwood, Bamboo,Rattan, Palm and Saw Works	76.10	77.43	75.82	76.32
家具制造业	Furniture Manufacturing	85.71	117.90	85.71	117.90
造纸和纸制品业	Papermaking and Paper Products	84.44	117.71	84.44	117.71
印刷和记录媒介复制业	Printing and Record Processing	52.32	55.48	52.32	55.48
文教、工美、体育和娱乐用品制造业	Stationery, Education, Art, Sport and Entertainment Products	26.89	57.43	26.89	57.43
石油加工、炼焦和核燃料加工业	Petroleum Processing, Coking Products and Nuclear Fuel Processing	31.18	22.91	31.18	19.80
化学原料和化学制品制造业	Raw Chemical Material and Chemical Products	318.00	341.40	317.45	324.68
医药制造业	Medical and pharmaceutical Products	162.06	201.51	160.32	200.24
化学纤维制造业	Chemical Fibers	14.76	10.95	14.76	10.95
橡胶和塑料制品业	Rubber Products and Plastic Products	127.32	183.37	127.32	183.37
非金属矿物制品业	Nonmetal Material Products	475.27	545.62	475.10	545.62
黑色金属冶炼和压延加工业	Smelting and Processing of ferrous Metals	108.61	110.06	83.51	110.06
有色金属冶炼和压延加工业	Smelting and Processing of Nonferrous Metals	48.74	92.95	48.74	92.95
金属制品业	Metal Products	183.79	233.39	183.31	233.14
通用设备制造业	Ordinaryly Machinery Manufacturing	294.00	285.46	262.04	275.51
专用设备制造业	Special Purpose Equipment Manufacturing	393.85	469.34	374.10	452.64
汽车制造业	Automobile Manufacturing	583.50	825.36	562.37	808.09
铁路、船舶、航空航天和其他运输设备制造业	Realway, Ship, Aircraft and Other Transport Equipment Manufacturing	89.94	106.79	86.98	105.01
电气机械和器材制造业	Electric Machinery and Equipment	231.73	454.29	226.57	441.01
计算机、通信和其他电子设备制造业	Computers, Communication Equipment and Other Electronic Equipment Manufacturing	224.80	337.50	220.25	329.38
仪器仪表制造业	Measuring Instruments Manufacturing	61.62	81.28	60.93	80.95
其他制造业	Other Equipment	63.00	43.58	58.49	43.48
废弃资源综合利用业	Recycling and Disposal of Waste	32.41	64.70	32.41	64.70
金属制品、机械和设备修理业	Repairing of Metal and Mechanical Equipment	15.36	6.92	15.29	6.92
电力、热力、燃气及水生产和供应业	Electric Power, Gas and Water Production and Supply	328.52	335.57	276.15	298.50
电力、热力生产和供应业	Electric Power, Steam and Hot Water Production and Supply	233.92	194.88	182.52	158.80
燃气生产和供应业	Gas Production and Supply	24.66	43.48	23.95	42.49
水的生产和供应业	Tap Water Production and Supply	69.93	97.21	69.68	97.21

注：从2012年起执行新的国民经济行业代码（GB/T4754—2011）

4-18 续表 continued

单位：亿元 (100 million yuan)

行业	sector	全省		#地方	
		2012	2013	2012	2013
建筑业	Construction	39.26	89.75	38.05	89.75
交通运输、仓储和邮政业	Transportation, storage and Post	1192.79	1492.42	1142.01	1435.04
铁路运输业	Railway Transportation	63.28	66.51	16.54	16.27
道路运输业	Road Transportation	828.71	1007.73	828.21	1001.04
水上运输业	Waterway Transportation	67.14	88.37	66.32	88.37
航空运输业	Air Transportation	13.41	43.84	13.41	43.84
管道运输业	Pipeline Transportation	1.15	2.72	1.15	2.72
装卸搬运和运输代理业	Load, Unload, and Agency	24.79	43.30	24.79	43.30
仓储业	Transportation Storage	189.31	235.62	186.59	235.17
邮政业	Post	4.99	4.33	4.99	4.33
信息传输、软件和信息技术服务业	Information Transmission, Software and Information Technology Service	57.14	59.83	39.25	47.59
电信、广播电视和卫星传输服务	Telecom, Radio Tv and Satellite	25.75	27.01	7.92	14.77
互联网和相关服务	Internet and Related	7.48	5.42	7.43	5.42
软件和信息技术服务业	Software and Information Technology	23.90	27.40	23.90	27.40
批发和零售业	Wholesale and Retail Trade	386.27	472.61	366.58	450.97
住宿和餐饮业	Hotel and Catering Services	190.17	243.99	190.17	243.99
金融业	Finance	38.96	66.83	37.66	64.84
货币金融服务	Monetary Financial Service	30.52	34.33	29.39	32.34
资本市场服务	Capital Markets Service	5.13	14.55	5.13	14.55
保险业	Insurance	1.23	1.66	1.06	1.66
其他金融业	Other Financial Acitivities	2.09	16.29	2.09	16.29
房地产业	Real Estate Trade	613.36	979.12	597.65	971.12
租赁和商务服务业	Leasing and Commercial Service	210.63	291.88	210.63	291.88
租赁业	Leasing Service	3.64	5.40	3.64	5.40
商务服务业	Commercial Service	206.99	286.47	206.99	286.47
科学研究和技术服务业	Scientific Research, Polytechnical Services	76.05	78.08	72.00	75.16
水利、环境和公共设施管理业	Water Conservancy, Environment and Public Facility Management	1200.54	1594.42	1156.10	1567.35
水利管理业	Water Conservancy Management	165.92	175.29	141.82	155.57
生态保护和环境治理业	Environment Management	33.85	54.59	33.85	54.59
公共设施管理业	Public Facility Management	1000.77	1364.54	980.44	1357.19
居民服务、修理和其他服务业	Resident Service and Others	45.22	105.22	45.22	105.22
教育	Education	166.23	174.80	137.29	157.82
卫生和社会工作	Health Care and Social Work	133.62	139.06	126.75	135.36
卫生	Health Care	93.52	105.89	86.65	102.24
社会工作	Social Work	40.10	33.17	40.10	33.11
文化、体育和娱乐业	Culture, Sports and Recreation	153.50	173.43	153.50	170.51
新闻和出版业	News and Publication	2.65	4.01	2.65	4.01
广播、电视、电影和影视录音制作业	Radio, Television, Film and Recording	6.24	3.93	6.24	3.93
文化艺术业	Culture and Arts	66.06	66.12	66.06	66.10
体育	Sports	20.27	30.48	20.27	27.58
娱乐业	Receation	58.28	68.89	58.28	68.89
公共管理、社会保障和社会组织	Public Management and Social Organizations	545.69	377.91	535.48	374.45

4−19 按国民经济行业分的技术改造投资
ACCORDING TO THE NATIONAL ECONOMIC INDUSTRY TECHNICAL TRANSFORMATION INVESTMENT

单位：亿元 (100 million yuan)

行业	sector	全省		#地方	
		2012	2013	2012	2013
总　计	Total	**2032.15**	**2333.72**	**1806.07**	**2165.12**
农、林、牧、渔业	Farming, Forestry, Animal Husbandry and Fishery	46.82	29.34	46.82	29.34
农业	Farming	10.24	10.83	10.24	10.83
林业	Forestry	2.61	1.80	2.61	1.80
畜牧业	Animal Husbandry	5.84	0.68	5.84	0.68
渔业	Fishery	5.33	1.44	5.33	1.44
农、林、牧、渔服务业	Farming, Forestry, Animal Husbandry and Fishery Services	22.80	14.60	22.80	14.60
采矿业	Mining and Qarrying	128.13	171.36	89.55	124.99
制造业	Manufacturing	1495.87	1604.71	1357.02	1535.72
农副食品加工业	Food Processing	97.39	161.80	97.39	161.80
食品制造业	Food Production	43.86	46.61	43.86	46.61
酒、饮料和精制茶制造业	Beverage Production	23.37	52.00	23.37	52.00
烟草制品业	Tobacco Processing	6.52	6.76	6.52	6.76
纺织业	Textile Industry	96.79	102.35	96.79	102.35
纺织服装、服饰业	Textile Wearing Apparel and Accessaries	32.26	35.06	32.26	35.06
皮革、毛皮、羽毛及其制品和制鞋业	Leather, Fur, Feather and Related Products	11.29	9.07	11.29	9.07
木材加工和木、竹、藤、棕、草制品业	Timber Processing and Wwood, Bamboo,Rattan, Palm and Sraw Works	20.25	15.71	20.25	15.71
家具制造业	Furniture Manufacturing	11.29	8.83	11.29	8.83
造纸和纸制品业	Papermaking and Paper Products	23.54	25.43	23.54	25.43
印刷和记录媒介复制业	Printing and Record Processing	13.06	9.60	13.06	9.60
文教、工美、体育和娱乐用品制造业	Stationery, Education, Art, Sport and Entertainment Products	0.75	6.55	0.75	6.55
石油加工、炼焦和核燃料加工业	Petroleum Processing, Coking Products and Nuclear Fuel Processing	83.08	32.96	5.34	10.60
化学原料和化学制品制造业	Raw Chemical Material and Chemical Products	175.13	206.83	170.11	205.56
医药制造业	Medical and pharmaceutical Products	42.43	50.44	42.43	48.06
化学纤维制造业	Chemical Fibers		4.27		4.27
橡胶和塑料制品业	Rubber Products and Plastic Products	42.86	58.30	42.86	58.30
非金属矿物制品业	Nonmetal Material Products	183.40	218.53	181.29	218.31
黑色金属冶炼和压延加工业	Smelting and Processing of ferrous Metals	69.62	66.99	42.71	52.89
有色金属冶炼和压延加工业	Smelting and Processing of Nonferrous Metals	21.82	22.00	20.99	19.82
金属制品业	Metal Products	78.01	74.92	78.01	74.92
通用设备制造业	Ordinaryly Machinery Manufacturing	52.64	80.60	52.64	71.55
专用设备制造业	Special Purpose Equipment Manufacturing	42.03	53.74	41.99	49.92
汽车制造业	Automobile Manufacturing	164.37	116.55	155.42	114.85
铁路、船舶、航空航天和其他运输设备制造业	Realway, Ship, Aircraft and Other Transport Equipment Manufacturing	6.57	12.52	6.36	5.91
电气机械和器材制造业	Electric Machinery and Equipment	76.67	53.26	60.03	53.26
计算机、通信和其他电子设备制造业	Computers, Communication Equipment and Other Electronic Equipment Manufacturing	61.10	50.83	60.75	45.73
仪器仪表制造业	Measuring Instruments Manufacturing	9.36	10.81	9.31	10.61
其他制造业	Other Equipment	1.72	3.32	1.72	3.32
废弃资源综合利用业	Recycling and Disposal of Waste	3.72	3.14	3.72	3.14
金属制品、机械和设备修理业	Repairing of Metal and Mechanical Equipment	0.97	4.95	0.97	4.95
电力、热力、燃气及水生产和供应业	Electric Power, Gas and Water Production and Supply	87.09	154.93	67.22	110.30
电力、热力生产和供应业	Electric Power, Steam and Hot Water Production and Supply	70.12	124.35	50.24	79.72
燃气生产和供应业	Gas Production and Supply	6.27	2.36	6.27	2.36
水的生产和供应业	Tap Water Production and Supply	10.71	28.22	10.71	28.22

注：从2012年起执行新的国民经济行业代码（GB/T4754—2011）

Note:Since 2012,a new national economy industry code(GB/T4754-2011)is implemented.

4-19 续表 continued

单位：亿元 (100 million yuan)

行业	sector	全省		#地方	
		2012	2013	2012	2013
建筑业	Construction	4.00	6.68	3.86	6.68
交通运输、仓储和邮政业	Transportation, storage and Post	58.66	124.46	52.79	123.97
铁路运输业	Railway Transportation	5.74	0.89	0.82	0.64
道路运输业	Road Transportation	42.81	95.78	42.61	95.55
水上运输业	Waterway Transportation	2.53	1.37	2.53	1.37
航空运输业	Air Transportation	0.25		0.25	
管道运输业	Pipeline Transportation		0.24		0.24
装卸搬运和运输代理业	Load, Unload, and Agency	0.63	1.81	0.63	1.81
仓储业	Transportation Storage	5.96	24.17	5.96	24.17
邮政业	Post	0.75	0.20		0.20
信息传输、软件和信息技术服务业	Information Transmission, Software and Information Technology Service	34.29	20.65	12.56	14.64
电信、广播电视和卫星传输服务	Telecom, Radio Tv and Satellite	12.63	16.56	5.50	10.76
互联网和相关服务	Internet and Related	18.14	2.18	3.54	1.97
软件和信息技术服务业	Software and Information Technology	3.52	1.91	3.52	1.91
批发和零售业	Wholesale and Retail Trade	18.02	13.45	17.84	13.25
住宿和餐饮业	Hotel and Catering Services	11.07	6.60	11.07	6.60
金融业	Finance	2.96	2.83	2.60	1.81
货币金融服务	Monetary Financial Service	2.27	2.59	1.91	1.81
资本市场服务	Monetary Financial Service	0.59		0.59	
保险业	Insurance	0.10	0.24	0.10	
其他金融业	Other Financial Acitivities				
房地产业	Real Estate Trade	7.08	21.48	6.87	21.48
租赁和商务服务业	Leasing and Commercial Service	4.44	4.49	4.44	4.49
租赁业	Leasing Service	0.34		0.34	
商务服务业	Commercial Service	4.10	4.49	4.10	4.49
科学研究和技术服务业	Scientific Research, Polytechnical Services	5.13	6.40	5.13	6.40
水利、环境和公共设施管理业	Water Conservancy, Environment and Public Facility Management	82.79	121.53	82.79	120.73
水利管理业	Water Conservancy Management	46.63	46.07	46.63	46.07
生态保护和环境治理业	Environment Management	8.25	11.89	8.25	11.89
公共设施管理业	Public Facility Management	27.91	63.57	27.91	62.77
居民服务、修理和其他服务业	Resident Service and Others	3.90	0.49	3.90	0.49
教育	Education	9.29	10.93	9.29	10.93
卫生和社会工作	Health Care and Social Work	7.49	9.53	7.49	9.53
卫生	Health Care	6.94	8.77	6.94	8.77
社会工作	Social Work	0.55	0.75	0.55	0.75
文化、体育和娱乐业	Culture, Sports and Recreation	9.43	13.51	9.43	13.51
新闻和出版业	News and Publication				
广播、电视、电影和影视录音制作业	Radio, Television, Film and Recording	1.99	3.06	1.99	3.06
文化艺术业	Culture and Arts	2.76	1.34	2.76	1.34
体育	Sports		3.37		3.37
娱乐业	Receation	4.68	5.75	4.68	5.75
公共管理、社会保障和社会组织	Public Management and Social Organizations	15.66	10.35	15.37	10.25

4-20 全社会按构成分的投资额

ACCORDING TO THE COMPOSITION OF SOCIAL CAPITAL

单位:亿元 (100 million yuan)

年 份 In copies	全省			#地方		
	建筑安装工程 Building installation	设备工具器具购置 Equipment tools, equipment purchase	其他费用 Other expenses	建筑安装工程 Building installation	设备工具器具购置 Equipment tools, equipment purchase	其他费用 expenses Other
1978	20.30	9.98	3.30	9.89	4.51	0.48
1980	23.85	9.76	1.89	14.01	4.55	0.97
"六五"时期	**216.19**	**83.11**	**16.52**	**155.63**	**59.71**	**7.43**
1985	67.53	28.67	6.71	54.64	23.00	3.39
"七五"时期	**434.43**	**195.59**	**50.10**	**352.24**	**152.75**	**32.96**
1986	72.40	31.24	7.84	60.18	23.91	4.81
1987	86.83	40.54	12.71	71.79	32.83	7.83
1988	100.58	49.28	10.60	82.40	41.51	7.35
1989	81.98	33.51	8.21	64.30	25.19	5.86
1990	92.64	41.02	10.78	73.58	29.31	7.11
"八五"时期	**1300.95**	**606.68**	**304.04**	**972.09**	**429.78**	**178.69**
1991	108.07	45.11	15.01	86.74	33.68	10.64
1992	149.34	68.03	23.36	119.61	51.46	15.94
1993	227.25	98.91	57.02	174.02	74.17	39.83
1994	361.89	146.12	85.06	261.27	99.72	49.60
1995	454.40	248.51	123.59	330.45	170.75	62.68
"九五"时期	**3392.01**	**1596.34**	**1034.45**	**2593.68**	**1108.81**	**598.32**
1996	510.52	307.89	165.97	392.06	218.14	82.28
1997	600.04	264.16	219.40	405.69	171.97	201.38
1998	695.55	323.47	212.08	556.36	230.59	101.48
1999	771.24	329.26	201.67	594.41	248.78	94.54
2000	814.66	371.56	235.33	645.16	239.33	118.64
"十五"时期	**6031.36**	**2481.09**	**1809.24**	**5317.08**	**1883.69**	**1216.75**
2001	890.60	419.20	241.95	739.97	276.93	124.89
2002	974.73	418.55	301.94	829.11	303.57	155.49
2003	1059.98	463.23	360.38	945.58	363.78	243.47
2004	1409.25	537.25	409.88	1282.71	416.98	307.87
2005	1696.80	642.86	495.09	1519.71	522.43	385.03
"十一五"时期	**20406.53**	**6921.20**	**5592.20**	**18649.08**	**5890.61**	**4859.93**
2006	2252.72	717.10	602.87	1918.63	601.90	477.07
2007	2857.31	896.36	780.47	2492.24	756.58	660.27
2008	3568.97	1245.73	983.86	3226.13	971.37	819.50
2009	5025.62	1753.28	1432.95	4683.30	1472.52	1243.52
2010	6701.91	2308.73	1792.05	6328.78	2088.24	1659.57
"十二五"时期						
2011	8056.52	2812.91	2065.59	7626.28	2520.40	1950.61
2012	11054.16	3162.99	2287.02	10609.45	2942.10	2192.00
2013	14312.25	3856.68	2584.98	13934.73	3702.30	2508.97

4-21 全社会按国民经济行业分的固定资产投资
ACCORDING TO THE NATIONAL ECONOMY SOCIETY OF FIXED ASSETS INVESTMENT

单位：亿元 (100 million yuan)

行业	sector	全省		#地方	
		2012	2013	2012	2013
总　计	Total	**16504.17**	**20753.91**	**15743.55**	**20146.00**
农、林、牧、渔业	Farming, Forestry, Animal Husbandry and Fishery	654.89	748.53	654.57	747.19
农业	Farming	291.42	345.85	291.10	344.51
林业	Forestry	35.06	50.14	35.06	50.14
畜牧业	Animal Husbandry	167.35	155.48	167.35	155.48
渔业	Fishery	31.62	39.14	31.62	39.14
农、林、牧、渔服务业	Farming, Forestry, Animal Husbandry and Fishery	129.44	157.92	129.44	157.92
采矿业	Mining and Qarrying	339.72	369.67	296.66	320.36
制造业	Manufacturing	6485.08	8219.26	6218.75	8055.16
农副食品加工业	Food Processing	460.39	684.86	459.56	684.63
食品制造业	Food Production	194.62	243.04	194.62	243.04
酒、饮料和精制茶制造业	Beverage Production	154.39	244.96	154.39	244.96
烟草制品业	Tobacco Processing	11.70	11.51	11.70	11.51
纺织业	Textile Industry	272.61	329.08	272.20	328.30
纺织服装、服饰业	Textile Wearing Apparel and Accessaries	171.44	194.71	171.44	194.71
皮革、毛皮、羽毛及其制品和制鞋业	Leather, Fur, Feather and Related Products	47.56	69.10	47.56	69.10
木材加工和木、竹、藤、棕、草制品业	Timber Processing and Wwood, Bamboo,Rattan, P	97.58	99.89	97.30	98.78
家具制造业	Furniture Manufacturing	100.75	132.09	100.75	132.09
造纸和纸制品业	Papermaking and Paper Products	111.06	149.27	111.06	149.27
印刷和记录媒介复制业	Printing and Record Processing	66.70	80.75	66.70	80.75
文教、工美、体育和娱乐用品制造业	Stationery, Education, Art, Sport and Entertainment Products	29.56	64.75	29.56	64.75
石油加工、炼焦和核燃料加工业	Petroleum Processing, Coking Products and Nucle	116.02	58.36	38.29	32.90
化学原料和化学制品制造业	Raw Chemical Material and Chemical Products	508.40	605.09	502.83	587.09
医药制造业	Medical and pharmaceutical Products	213.66	267.54	211.92	263.89
化学纤维制造业	Chemical Fibers	16.36	15.22	16.36	15.22
橡胶和塑料制品业	Rubber Products and Plastic Products	180.98	250.32	180.98	250.32
非金属矿物制品业	Nonmetal Material Products	686.90	818.85	684.62	818.05
黑色金属冶炼和压延加工业	Smelting and Processing of ferrous Metals	192.27	192.16	140.22	177.96
有色金属冶炼和压延加工业	Smelting and Processing of Nonferrous Metals	71.44	126.18	70.61	124.00
金属制品业	Metal Products	277.77	323.24	277.30	322.99
通用设备制造业	Ordinaryly Machinery Manufacturing	356.23	386.23	324.28	367.23
专用设备制造业	Special Purpose Equipment Manufacturing	453.10	550.85	432.70	530.34
汽车制造业	Automobile Manufacturing	780.90	1017.94	750.82	998.97
铁路、船舶、航空航天和其他运输设备制造业	Realway, Ship, Aircraft and Other Transport Equipment Manufacturing	97.24	151.88	93.82	142.06
电气机械和器材制造业	Electric Machinery and Equipment	317.43	522.99	295.63	509.71
计算机、通信和其他电子设备制造业	Computers, Communication Equipment and Other Electronic Equipment Manufacturing	288.19	401.94	283.08	387.86
仪器仪表制造业	Measuring Instruments Manufacturing	80.68	94.39	79.95	93.86
其他制造业	Other Equipment	65.75	48.13	61.25	48.03
废弃资源综合利用业	Recycling and Disposal of Waste	39.97	69.24	39.97	69.24
金属制品、机械和设备修理业	Repairing of Metal and Mechanical Equipment	23.41	14.71	17.29	13.58
电力、热力、燃气及水生产和供应业	Electric Power, Gas and Water Production and Supply	443.34	531.71	362.83	444.99
电力、热力生产和供应业	Electric Power, Steam and Hot Water Production a	318.57	343.14	239.03	257.97
燃气生产和供应业	Gas Production and Supply	38.94	51.25	38.23	50.26
水的生产和供应业	Tap Water Production and Supply	85.83	137.31	85.57	136.76

注：从2012年起执行新的国民经济行业代码（GB/T4754—2011）

4-21 续表 continued

单位：亿元 (100 million yuan)

行业	sector	全省		#地方	
		2012	2013	2012	2013
建筑业	Construction	51.03	104.63	45.43	99.97
交通运输、仓储和邮政业	Transportation, storage and Post	1305.44	1733.95	1241.32	1671.03
铁路运输业	Railway Transportation	69.02	70.08	17.36	16.98
道路运输业	Road Transportation	897.95	1205.69	897.25	1198.77
水上运输业	Waterway Transportation	81.17	94.11	72.89	91.70
航空运输业	Air Transportation	13.66	48.43	13.66	48.38
管道运输业	Pipeline Transportation	1.15	2.96	1.15	2.96
装卸搬运和运输代理业	Load, Unload, and Agency	31.70	46.98	31.70	46.98
仓储业	Transportation Storage	204.80	260.50	202.07	260.05
邮政业	Post	5.99	5.20	5.25	5.20
信息传输、软件和信息技术服务业	Information Transmission, Software and Information Technology Service	94.29	114.95	54.67	90.48
电信、广播电视和卫星传输服务	Telecom, Radio Tv and Satellite	40.03	70.34	15.06	52.30
互联网和相关服务	Internet and Related	26.18	14.77	11.54	8.34
软件和信息技术服务业	Software and Information Technology	28.08	29.84	28.08	29.84
批发和零售业	Wholesale and Retail Trade	438.28	520.65	418.41	497.89
住宿和餐饮业	Hotel and Catering Services	213.56	270.24	213.56	270.24
金融业	Finance	48.12	81.53	46.11	73.71
货币金融服务	Monetary Financial Service	37.69	48.52	35.85	41.15
资本市场服务	Monetary Financial Service	6.28	14.61	6.28	14.61
保险业	Insurance	1.94	2.11	1.77	1.66
其他金融业	Other Financial Acitivities	2.21	16.29	2.21	16.29
房地产业	Real Estate Trade	3573.33	4708.01	3440.60	4592.16
租赁和商务服务业	Leasing and Commercial Service	231.76	307.23	231.76	307.23
租赁业	Leasing Service	3.98	7.20	3.98	7.20
商务服务业	Commercial Service	227.78	300.03	227.78	300.03
科学研究和技术服务业	Scientific Research, Polytechnical Services	85.64	93.62	81.36	90.30
水利、环境和公共设施管理业	Water Conservancy, Environment and Public Facility Management	1351.35	1853.06	1304.63	1824.38
水利管理业	Water Conservancy Management	232.40	247.98	206.55	228.26
生态保护和环境治理业	Environment Management	44.72	72.58	44.72	72.58
公共设施管理业	Public Facility Management	1074.23	1532.49	1053.36	1523.54
居民服务、修理和其他服务业	Resident Service and Others	55.40	108.69	54.83	108.69
教育	Education	188.95	203.36	153.70	177.85
卫生和社会工作	Health Care and Social Work	154.29	177.35	146.32	173.19
卫生	Health Care	112.93	142.44	104.96	138.33
社会工作	Social Work	41.36	34.91	41.36	34.85
文化、体育和娱乐业	Culture, Sports and Recreation	175.68	194.01	174.68	191.09
新闻和出版业	News and Publication	2.65	4.01	2.65	4.01
广播、电视、电影和影视录音制作业	Radio, Television, Film and Recording	10.43	7.47	10.43	7.47
文化艺术业	Culture and Arts	71.56	69.96	70.56	69.94
体育	Sports	22.09	34.04	22.09	31.14
娱乐业	Receation	68.96	78.54	68.96	78.54
公共管理、社会保障和社会组织	Public Management and Social Organizations	614.01	413.64	603.33	410.08

4－22　全社会按三次产业划分的投资额
ACCORDING TO THE THREE INDUSTRIES OF WHOLE SOCIETY OF INVESTMENT

单位：亿元　　(100 million yuan)

年　份 In copies	全省			#地方		
	第一产业 The first industry	第二产业 The second industry	第三产业 The third industry	第一产业 The first industry	第二产业 The second industry	第三产业 The third industry
1978	**2.24**	**25.28**	**6.06**	**2.24**	**8.80**	**3.85**
1980	2.11	22.75	10.64	2.03	9.98	7.52
"六五"时期	**24.77**	**155.02**	**136.03**	**24.05**	**83.83**	**114.89**
1985	8.37	47.42	47.12	8.09	31.48	41.46
"七五"时期	**49.76**	**335.53**	**294.83**	**47.24**	**245.00**	**245.71**
1986	7.89	50.33	53.22	7.40	34.88	46.62
1987	9.52	70.17	60.39	9.07	52.40	50.98
1988	11.11	85.76	63.59	10.53	67.14	53.59
1989	9.08	61.86	52.76	8.63	44.28	42.43
1990	12.16	67.41	64.87	11.61	46.30	52.09
"八五"时期	**78.98**	**1074.06**	**1058.63**	**73.97**	**674.84**	**831.75**
1991	12.48	77.95	77.76	12.12	55.25	63.69
1992	12.42	121.00	107.31	11.04	87.18	88.79
1993	11.89	170.93	200.36	10.10	114.05	163.87
1994	14.97	302.49	275.61	14.38	173.32	222.89
1995	27.22	401.69	397.59	26.11	220.95	316.82
"九五"时期	**272.08**	**2298.38**	**3452.34**	**271.69**	**1265.99**	**2763.13**
1996	29.76	451.28	503.34	29.73	272.79	389.96
1997	41.02	436.04	606.54	41.02	269.87	468.15
1998	59.48	450.16	721.46	59.48	234.94	594.01
1999	71.22	439.32	791.63	71.22	227.20	639.31
2000	70.60	521.58	829.37	70.24	261.19	671.70
"十五"时期	**416.79**	**3952.90**	**5969.82**	**414.74**	**2724.92**	**5277.86**
2001	77.48	590.01	902.08	77.33	323.55	740.91
2002	80.08	648.81	966.33	79.02	375.77	833.38
2003	88.80	714.81	1079.98	88.35	489.49	974.99
2004	77.55	912.93	1365.90	77.16	684.54	1245.86
2005	92.88	1086.34	1655.53	92.88	851.57	1482.72
"十一五"时期	**1202.88**	**12641.78**	**19075.27**	**1197.58**	**10748.83**	**17471.71**
2006	107.64	1317.12	2147.93	107.56	1044.17	1845.87
2007	149.40	1710.74	2674.00	148.72	1395.28	2365.09
2008	231.25	2346.32	3220.99	230.95	1859.42	2926.62
2009	321.59	3097.68	4792.58	319.58	2656.02	4442.25
2010	393.00	4169.92	6239.77	390.77	3793.94	5891.88
"十二五"时期						
2011	440.91	5526.40	6967.71	440.51	5032.88	6623.90
2012	525.45	7281.04	8697.68	525.13	6891.67	8326.75
2013	590.61	9187.25	10976.04	589.28	8883.83	10672.89

注：从2012年起，三次产业采用新的划分标准。

4-23 全社会竣工房屋建筑面积及竣工率

THE FLOOR SPACE OF BUILDINGS COMPLETED ALL SOCIAL AND COMPLETION RATE

年 份 In copies	施工面积(万平方米) Construction area (million square meters)	#住宅 # residential	竣工面积(万平方米) Completion of (million square meters)	#住宅 # residential	竣工率(%) Completion rate (%)	#住宅 # residential
1978	**1343.27**	**513.20**	**666.76**	**280.16**	**49.6**	**54.6**
1980	1951.16	1004.17	1024.51	586.27	52.5	58.4
"六五"时期			**25700.97**	**19626.87**		
1985	8079.90	5965.71	6899.59	5434.20	85.4	91.1
"七五"时期			**29202.17**	**22387.23**		
1986	8760.15	6686.78	7754.53	6308.96	88.5	94.3
1987	7922.23	5684.88	6803.61	5233.59	85.9	92.1
1988	7225.98	4892.04	6060.44	4484.69	83.9	91.7
1989	5250.24	3590.22	4414.47	3301.59	84.1	92.0
1990	5103.48	3507.53	4169.12	3058.40	81.7	87.2
"八五"时期			**23403.26**	**16559.28**		
1991	5300.98	3652.67	4211.39	3157.13	79.4	86.4
1992	5954.84	4066.51	4621.87	3383.72	77.6	83.2
1993	5807.24	3540.57	4050.56	2798.42	69.8	79.0
1994	7158.68	4476.46	4916.24	3482.20	68.7	77.8
1995	8294.84	5304.79	5603.20	3737.81	67.6	70.5
"九五"时期			**35861.86**	**26378.48**		
1996	8749.65	5581.32	6073.43	4485.82	69.4	80.4
1997	8963.28	5976.86	6430.48	4790.34	71.7	80.1
1998	10485.86	7179.25	7897.96	5792.97	75.3	80.7
1999	10228.93	7219.06	7951.03	5891.97	77.7	81.6
2000	9920.42	6831.02	7508.96	5417.38	75.7	79.3
"十五"时期			**40164.49**	**29588.06**		
2001	10040.11	7273.21	7716.37	5850.27	76.9	80.4
2002	10301.00	7019.76	7796.76	5583.27	75.7	79.5
2003	10667.78	7276.62	7469.17	5457.42	70.0	75.0
2004	13152.08	9285.64	9318.34	7069.45	70.6	75.9
2005	12572.00	8401.20	7863.85	5627.67	62.6	67.0
"十一五"时期			**43810.54**	**26870.86**		
2006	12346.48	8039.75	7126.64	4812.39	57.7	59.9
2007	13686.34	8910.75	7557.62	5036.19	55.2	56.5
2008	16417.07	9896.66	7551.82	4679.96	46.0	47.3
2009	20142.81	11762.06	9772.28	5556.71	48.5	47.2
2010	25284.83	14486.90	11802.18	6785.61	46.7	46.8
"十二五"时期						
2011	31388.88	16337.96	14585.68	7375.38	46.5	45.1
2012	40103.56	19154.75	16576.18	7890.08	41.3	41.2
2013	51939.51	23443.19	18828.87	8006.06	36.3	34.2

主要统计指标解释

全社会固定资产投资 是以货币形式表现的在一定时期内全社会建造和购置固定资产的工作量以及与此有关的费用的总称。该指标是反映固定资产投资规模、结构和发展速度的综合性指标，又是观察工程进度和考核投资效果的重要依据。全社会固定资产投资按登记注册类型可分为国有、集体、个体、联营、股份制、外商、港澳台商、其他等。

固定资产投资 指各种登记注册类型的企业、事业、行政单位及个体户进行的计划总投资500万元及500万元以上的建设项目投资、房地产开发投资、城镇和工矿区私人建房投资。

房地产开发投资 指各种登记注册类型的房地产开发公司、商品房建设公司及其他房地产开发法人单位和附属于其他法人单位实际从事房地产开发或经营活动的单位统一开发的包括统代建、拆迁还建的住宅、厂房、仓库、饭店、宾馆、度假村、写字楼、办公楼等房屋建筑物和配套的服务设施，土地开发工程（如道路、给水、排水、供电、供热、通讯、平整场地等基础设施工程）的投资；不包括单纯的土地交易活动。

城镇和工矿区私人建房投资 包括市、县城、城关镇、工矿区所辖范围内的全部私人建房，不论其房主是否系本地的常住户口均应包括。

农村投资 包括在农村区域范围内进行固定资产投资活动的企业、事业、行政单位及农村个人投资。

固定资产投资的资金来源 根据固定资产投资的资金来源不同，分为国家预算内资金、国内贷款、利用外资、自筹资金和其他资金。

(1)国家预算内资金：分为财政拨款和财政安排的贷款两部分。包括中央财政的基本建设基金(分经营性基金和非经营性基金两部分)、专项支出(如煤代油专项等)、收回再贷、贴息资金，财政安排的挖潜改造和新产品试制支出、城建支出、商业部门简易建筑支出、不发达地区发展基金等资金中用于固定资产投资的资金；地方财政中由国家统筹安排的资金等。

(2)国内贷款：指报告期固定资产投资单位向银行及非银行金融机构借入的用于固定资产投资的各种国内借款，包括银行利用自有资金及吸收的存款发放的贷款、上级主管部门拨入的国内贷款、国家专项贷款(包括煤代油贷款、劳改煤矿专项贷款等)、地方财政专项资金安排的贷款、国内储备贷款、周转贷款等。

(3)利用外资：指报告期收到的用于固定资产建造和购置的国外资金(包括设备、材料、技术在内)。包括对外借款(外国政府、国际金融组织贷款、出口信贷、外国银行商业贷款、对外发行债券和股票)、外商直接投资及外商其他投资。不包括我国自有外汇资金(国家外汇、地方外汇、留成外汇、调剂外汇和中国银行自有资金发行的外汇贷款等)。计算利用外资时，需要折算成人民币，折算中所使用的外汇汇率按现汇计算，即按使用外汇时的汇率计算。

(4)自筹资金：指固定资产投资单位报告期收到的，由各地区、各部门及企、事业单位筹集用于固定资产投资的预算外资金，包括中央各部门、各级地方和企、事业单位的自筹资金。

(5)其他资金：指在报告期收到的除以上各种资金之外其他用于固定资产投资的资金，包括企业或金融机构通过发行各种债券筹集到的资金、群众集资、个人资金、无偿捐赠的资金及其他单位拨入的资金等。

固定资产投资按国民经济行业分 根据建设项目建成投产后的主要产品或主要用途及社会经济活动性质来确定国民经济行业。一般情况下，一个建设项目或一个企业、事业单位只能属于一种国民经济行业。

固定资产投资按隶属关系分 是按建设单位或企业、事业、行政单位的主管上级机关确定的。

（1）中央：是指中共中央、人大常委会和国务院各部、委、局、总公司以及直属机构直接领导的建设项目和企业、事业、行政单位。这些单位的固定资产投资计划由国务院各部门直接编制和下达，建设中所需物资、主要设备以及建设中的问题都由中央有关部门安排和解决。

（2）地方：是由省（自治区、直辖市）、地区（州、盟、省辖市）、县（旗、县级市）三级政府及业务主管部门直接领导和管理的建设项目、企业、事业、行政单位。地方项目还包括不隶属以上各级政府及主管部门的建设项目和企业、事业单位，如外商投资企业和无主管部门的企业等。

固定资产投资按建设性质分 根据整个建设项目情况来确定。建设项目的性质一般分为新建、扩建、改建和技术改造、迁建、恢复。房地产开发单位、农村投资、城镇工矿区私人建房投资不划分建设性质。

(1)新建：一般指从无到有“平地起家”开始建设的企业、事业和行政单位或建设项目。现有企业、事业、行政单位一般不属于新建。但如有的单位原有基础很小，经过建设后新增的固定资产价值超过该企、事业、行政单位原有固定资产价值(原值)三倍以上的也应作为新建。

(2)扩建：指在厂内或其他地点，为扩大原有产品的生产能力(或效益)或增加新的产品生产能力，而增建主要的生产车间(或主要工程)、分厂、独立的生产线。行政、事业单位在原单位增建业务用房(如学校增建教学用房、医院增建门诊部、病房等)也作为扩建。

现有企、事业单位为扩大原有主要产品生产能力或增加新的产品生产能力，增建一个或几个主要生产车间(或主要工程)、分厂，同时进行一些更新改造工程的，也应作为扩建。

(3)改建和技术改造：指现有企业、事业单位，对原有设施进行技术改造或更新(包括相应配套的辅助性生产、生活福利设施) 的建设项目。现有企业、事业单位为适应市场变化的需要，而改变企业的主要产品种类(如军工企业转产民用品等) 的建设项目，应作为改建。原有产品生产作业线由于各工序(车间)之间能力不平衡，为填平补齐充分发挥原有生产能力而增建不增加本企业主要产品设计能力的车间，也应作为改建。技术改造是指企业、事业单位在现有基础上，用先进的技术代替落后的技术，用先进的工艺和装备代替落后的工艺和装备，以改变企业落后的技术经济面貌，实现以内涵为主的扩大再生产，达到提高产品质量、促进产品更新换代、节约能源、降低消耗、扩大生产规模、全面提高社会经济效益的目的。技术改造具体包括以下内容：机器设备和工具的更新改造；生产工艺改革、节约能源和原材料的改造；厂房建筑和公共设施的改造；劳动条件和生产环境的改造等。

固定资产投资按构成分 固定资产投资活动按其工作内容和实现方式分为建筑安装工程，设备、工具、器具购置，其他费用三个部分。

(1)建筑安装工程(建筑安装工作量)：指各种房屋、建筑物的建造工程和各种设备、装置的安装工程。包括各种房屋建造工程；各种用途设备基础和各种工业窑炉的砌筑工程及金属结构工程；为施工而进行的各种准备工作和临时工程以及完工后的清理工作等；铁路、道路的铺设，矿井的开凿及石油管道的架设等；水利工程；防空地下建筑等特殊工程；列入房屋工程预算内的暖气、卫生、通风、照明、煤气等设备的价值及装设油饰工程；列入建筑工程预算内的各种管道(蒸汽、压缩空气、石油、给排水等管道)、电力、电讯电缆导线等的敷设工程；以及各种机械设备的安装工程；为测定安装工程质量，对设备进行的试运工作；房地产开发单位进行的商品房屋开发建设工程、土地开发工程。

在安装工程中，不包括被安装设备本身的价值。

(2)设备、工具、器具购置：指建设单位或企、事业单位购置或自制的，达到固定资产标准的设备、工具、器具的价值。新建单位及扩建单位的新建车间，按照设计或计划要求购置或自制的全部设备、工具、器具，不论是否达到固定资产标准均计入“设备、工具、器具购置”中。

(3)其他费用：指在固定资产建造和购置过程中发生的，除上述几项内容以外的各种应分摊计入固定资产的费用。

施工项目 指报告期内进行过建筑或安装施工活动的项目。凡是报告期内施过工的建设项目，不论施工时间长短，均作为施工项目统计。施工项目个数可以反映一定时期固定资产投资的实际规模，与同期全部建成投产项目个数相比，可以从建设速度的角度反映固定资产投资的效果。根据建设项目施工活动的不同性质，施工项目又分为：本年正式施工项目、本年收尾项目和以前年度全部停缓建项目。

全部建成投产项目 工业项目指设计文件规定形成生产能力的主体工程及其相应配套的辅助设施全部建成，经负荷试运转，证明具备生产设计规定合格产品的条件，并经过验收鉴定合格或达到竣工验收标准，与生产性工程配套的生活福利设施可以满足近期正常生产的需要，正式移交生产的建设项目。非工业项目指设计文件规定的主体工程和相应的配套工程全部建成，能够发挥设计规定的全部效益，经验收鉴定合格或达到竣工验收标准，正式移交使用的建设项目。

新增生产能力(或工程效益) 指通过固定资产投资活动而增加的设计能力(或工程效益)，该指标是以实物形态表现的反映固定资产投资成果的指标，也是考核投资经济效果的重要依据之一。

房屋建筑面积 指房屋建筑物勒脚以上外墙外围的水平截面面积，包括房屋建筑物的有效面积和结构面积。该指标是从实物形态上反映建设规模和建设成果的重要指标之一，也是检查工程形象进度、计算工程造价、分析投资效果、研究施工任务和建筑材料之间平衡情况的重要依据。

住宅建筑面积 指施工和竣工房屋建筑面积中供居住用的房屋建筑面积。

施工面积 指报告期内施工的全部房屋建筑面积。包括本期新开工的面积和上期开工跨入本期继续施工的房屋面积，以及上期已停建在本期恢复施工的房屋面积。本期竣工和本期施工后又停缓建的房屋，其建筑面积仍计入本期房屋施工面积中。

竣工面积 指在报告期内房屋建筑按照设计要求已经全部完工，达到住人和使用条件，经验收鉴定合格(或达到竣工验收标准)，正式移交使用单位的各栋房屋建筑面积的总和。

房屋建筑面积竣工率 指一定时期内房屋竣工面积占同期房屋施工面积的比率。是从房屋建筑施工速度的角度反映投资效果的指标。

新增固定资产 指报告期内已经完成建造和购置过程，并已交付生产或使用单位的固定资产价值。该指标是表示固定资产投资成果的价值指标，也是反映建设进度，计算固定资产投资效果的重要指标。

项目建设投产率 指一定时期内全部建成投产项目个数与同期施工项目个数的比率。该指标是从建设单位建设速度的角度反映投资效果的指标。

固定资产交付使用率 指一定时期新增固定资产与同期完成投资额的比率。该指标是反映固定资产动用速度，衡量建设过程中宏观投资效果的综合指标。由于新增固定资产是较长时期内形成的结果，而投资额则是当年完成的，因此，该指标一般适宜于反映较长时期内固定资产的动用情况。

商品房销售面积 指报告期内出售商品房屋的合同总面积(即双方签署的正式买卖合同中所确定的建筑面积)。由现房销售建筑面积和期房销售建筑面积两部分组成。

商品房销售额 指报告期内出售商品房屋的合同总价款(即双方签署的正式买卖合同中所确定的合同总价)。该指标与商品房销售面积同口径，由现房销售额和期房销售额两部分组成。

经济适用房 指根据地方经济适用房计划安排建设的政策性住宅。经济是指房屋建筑造价和销售价格低于一般商品住宅；适用是指适合中低收入家庭购买使用。经济适用房主要是由国家统一下达投资计划，房地产公司开发，对外销售；用地一般采用行政划拨或招标投标方式，免收土地出让金；对各种经批准的收费减半征收，开发利润不超过3%；销售价格实行政府指导价。该指标可以分析房地产投资结构，反映中低收入家庭商品住宅的供求平衡情况。

Explanatory Notes on Main Statistical Indicators

Total Investment in Fixed Assets in the Whole Country refers to the volume of activities in construction and purchases of fixed assets and related fees, expressed in monetary terms. It is a comprehensive indicator which shows the size, structure and growth of the investment in fixed assets, providing basis for observing the progress of construction projects and evaluating results of investment. Total investment in fixed assets in the whole country includes, by type of ownership, the investment by the state-owned units, collective units, individuals, joint ownership units, share-holding units, as well as investment by businessmen from foreign countries and from Hong Kong, Macao and Taiwan, and by other units.

Investment in Fixed Assets refers to construction projects involving a total planned investment of 500,000 yuan and over by enterprises and institutions of various types of ownership, by administrative units and by individuals, investment in real estate development, and housing investment by individuals in urban areas and in industrial and mining areas.

Investment in Real Estate Development refers to the investment by the real estate development companies, commercial buildings construction companies and other real estate development units of various types of ownership in the construction of house buildings, such as residential buildings, factory buildings, warehouses, hotels, guesthouses, holiday villages, office buildings, and the complementary service facilities and land development projects, such as roads, water supply, water drainage, power supply, heating, telecommunications, land leveling and other projects of infrastructure. It excludes the activities in pure land transactions.

Investment in Housing Construction in Urban Areas and in Industrial and Mining Areas refers to all private housing construction under the jurisdiction of cities, county towns and industrial and mining areas, no matter whether the owner of the house is registered as the permanent resident in the locality or not.

Investment in Rural Areas refers to investment in fixed assets by enterprises, institutions and individuals in rural areas.

Sources of Funds for Investment in Fixed Assets include fund from state budget, domestic loans, foreign investment, self-raised funds, and others depending on the source of investment.

(1) Fund from state budget consists of budgetary appropriation and loans from state budget. More specifically, it includes, from the budget of the central government, capital construction fund (operation fund and non-operational fund), special expenses (e.g. expenses on substituting petroleum with coal), loans from repayment, discount fund, expenses on innovation and trial production of new products, expenses on urban construction, expenses on temporary construction by trade departments, development fund for less developed areas, as well as local budgetary fund transferred from the central budget.

(2) Domestic loans refer to loans of various forms borrowed by investing units from banks and non-bank financial institutions during the reference period for the purpose of investment in fixed assets, including loans issued by banks from their self-owned funds and deposit, loans appropriated by higher responsible authorities, special loans by government (including loan for substituting petroleum with coal, special loan for reform-through-labour coal mines), loans arranged by local government from special funds, domestic reserve loan, and working loan, etc..

(3) Foreign Investment refers to foreign funds received during the reference period for the construction and purchase of investment in fixed assets (covering equipment, materials and technology), including foreign borrowings (loans from foreign governments and international financial institutions, export credit, commercial loans from foreign banks, issue of bonds and stocks overseas), foreign direct investment and other foreign investment. Excluded in this category are capitals in foreign exchanges owned by China (foreign exchanges owned by the central and local governments, foreign exchanges retained by enterprises, foreign exchanges by enterprises through regulating mechanism, loans in foreign exchanges issued by the Bank of China with its own fund, etc.). In calculating the utilization of foreign capitals, foreign currencies are converted into Chinese Renminbi applying the current exchange rate when the foreign capitals are actually used.

(4) Self-raised funds refer to extra-budgetary funds for investment in fixed assets received by investing units from central government ministries, local governments, enterprises and institutions, including their self-raised funds.

(5) Others refer to funds for investment in fixed assets received from the sources other than those listed above, including capitals raised through issuing bonds by enterprises or financial institutions, funds raised from individuals and through donations, and funds transferred from other units.

Investment in Fixed Assets by Sector The classification of construction projects by sector is determined by the major products or the purpose of the projects when they are put into production or use, and by the nature of their social economic activities. In general, one project or one enterprise or institution can only be classified into one sector.

Investment in Fixed Assets by Jurisdiction of Management refers to the classification of investment by the competent authorities under which investment is made by construction units, enterprises, institutions or administrative units.

(1) Central investment refers to the investment in projects or by enterprises, institutions or administrative units which are under the direct leadership and management of the CPC Central Committee, the NPC Standing Committee, the State Council and of the national commissions, ministries, agencies and state-owned large corporations. Various ministries and departments of the State Council prepare and implement plans for investment in fixed assets by those departments, and arrange and ensure the supply of materials and key equipment required for the projects.

(2) Local investment refers to the investment in projects or by enterprises, institutions or administrative units which are under the direct leadership and management of departments under the provincial, prefecture and county governments. Also included are projects

by foreign-invested enterprises and enterprises without competent managing authorities.

Investment in Fixed Assets by Type of Construction The construction projects in general can be classified, by the type of construction, into new construction, expansion, reconstruction and technical transformation, moving and restoration. However, investment by type of construction is not applied to investment by real-estate development units, investment in rural areas and investment in housing by urban individuals.

(1) New construction in general refers to newly constructed enterprises, institutions, administrative agencies or independent projects from scratch. Construction in the existing enterprises, institutions or agencies is not considered as new construction. In case the assets of the existing unit is quite small, and the value of newly added fixed assets exceeds the original value of assets by three times, the expansion will be considered as new construction.

(2) Expansion refers to construction of new major production workshop, branch factory or independent production line within a factory or in other locations, for the purpose of increasing the production capacity (or improving efficiency) of the original products. Newly constructed houses for the operation of institutions and administrative organizations (such as the newly constructed buildings for teaching in schools, buildings for clinics or wards in hospitals, etc.) are also classified as expansion.

Also included in the expansion are investments by existing enterprises or institutions in building major production line(s) or branch factory(ies) along with some work on innovation, for the purpose of expending the production capacity of original products or producing new products.

(3) Reconstruction refers to construction projects by existing enterprises or institutions in innovation or technical transformation of the old facilities (including auxiliary production equipment and welfare facilities). Also considered as reconstruction is the construction of new workshops by the existing enterprises or institutions to change the variety of products to meet the market demand (such as the production of civil products by defence industries), or to bring the designed production capacity into full play through a more balanced production process on production lines. Technical transformation refers to replacement of old technology or equipment by new technology or equipment, in order to expand the reproduction through improvement of technology contents in production, to improve product quality, to promote new products, to save energy and reduce consumption and to improve overall social-economic efficiency. Contents of technical transformation include: updating of machinery, equipment and tools; reforming production process by using energy or materials saving technology; construction of factory workshops and transformation of public facilities; improvement of working conditions and environment, etc.

Investment in Fixed Assets by Structure By their contents, investment activities are classified into 3 categories, i.e. construction and installation, purchase of equipment and instrument, and other expenses.

(1) Construction and installation (work volume of construction and installation) refers to the construction of various houses and buildings and installation of various kinds of equipment and instruments. They include construction of various houses; equipment foundations, industrial kilns and stoves, and metal structure work; preparation works for project construction, and clearing up works post project construction; pavement of railways and roads, drilling of mines and putting up of oil pipes; construction of projects of water conservancy; construction of underground air-raid shelters and construction of other special projects; value of equipment for heating, sanitation, ventilation, lighting, gas, painting, etc. that are covered by the budget of housing projects; laying out of various pipelines (for steam, compressed air, petroleum, tap water and sewage) and lines for electric power and for communications; installation of various machinery equipment, testing operation for pre-testing the quality of installation projects, and land and other development work conducted by real estate developers for commercial housing. The value of equipment installed is not included in the value of installation projects.

(2) Purchase of equipment and instruments refers to the total value of equipment, tools, and instruments purchased or self-produced which come up to standards for fixed assets by the construction units or investing enterprises or institutions. Equipment, tools and instruments purchased or self-produced for new workshops by newly established or expanded units are categorized as "purchase of equipment and instruments" no matter whether they come up to the standards for fixed assets.

(3) Other expenses refer to expenses occurring during the construction or purchase of fixed assets other than those mentioned above.

Projects under Construction refer to projects with construction and installation activities undertaken in the reference period. All projects that have construction activities undertaken during the reference period are reported as projects under construction irrespective of the length of construction work. The number of projects under construction can reflect the actual size of investment in fixed assets during a given period, and when compared with the number of projects completed and put into use during the same period, it demonstrates the results of investment in fixed assets. Depending on the nature of construction activities, projects under construction can also be classified into projects under construction in current year, winding-up projects in current year and stopped or suspended projects in previous years (with preservation work in current year).

Projects Completed and Put into Use Industrial projects refer to the major projects and accessory facilities completed which result in forming production capacity and have been checked and accepted while the living and welfare facilities have been completed and can ensure normal production and formally put into production. Non-industrial projects refer to the major projects and accessory facilities completed which possess the designed capacity and have been checked, accepted and formally put into production.

Newly Increased Production Capacity (or Project Efficiency) refers to the increase of designed capacity (or project efficiency) through investment in fixed assets, which reflects the accomplishment of investment in fixed assets in kind and serves as important basis for evaluating the economic efficiency of investment.

Floor Space of Buildings under Construction refers to total floor space of the horizontal section of outer walls above the plinth of the building, including the effective area and the area occupied by the structure. This indicator is one of the important indicators in physical terms to reflect the scale and accomplishment of the construction industry, and important basis for monitoring the progress, calculating the cost, analyzing the efficiency and studying the supply of building materials in relation with the construction projects.

Floor Space of Residential Buildings refers to the floor space of the residential buildings among the total space of buildings under construction or completed.

Floor Space under Construction refers to total floor space of all buildings under construction during the reference period, including floor space of newly started buildings during the reference period, floor space of construction extended from the previous period to the current period, and floor space of construction suspended during the previous period and resumed in the current period. Floor space of construction completed in the current period, and floor space of construction started and then suspended in the current period are also included in the floor space under construction of the current year.

Floor Space of Buildings Completed refers to the floor space of all buildings completed in the reference period, which have been appraised and accepted (or come up to the designed standards) and have been transferred to the owners for use.

Completion Rate of Floor Space of Buildings refers to the ratio of the floor space of buildings completed in certain period of time to the floor space of buildings under construction in the same period. This indicator reflects the investment result from the perspective of the speed of construction.

Newly Increased Fixed Assets refer to the newly increased value of fixed assets, constructed or purchased, that have been transferred to the investors. This is an indicator that demonstrates the results of investment in fixed assets in monetary terms, and an important indicator to reflect the speed of construction and to calculate the efficiency of investment.

Rate of Construction Projects Completed and Put into Use refers to the ratio of the number of construction projects completed and put into use in certain period of time to the number of projects under construction in the same period. This reflects the investment efficiency from the perspective of the speed of projects construction.

Rate of Projects of Fixed Assets Completed and Put into Operation refers to the ratio of the newly increased fixed assets to the total investment made in the same period. This is a comprehensive indicator reflecting the speed of the employment of fixed assets and the investment efficiency at the macro-level. As the newly increase fixed assets is the result of a long period while the investment is completed in the current year, this indicator is expected to be used to reflect the employment of fixed assets over a long period of time.

Area of Commercial Housing Sold refers to total contracted area of commercial housing (i.e. area of floor space as designated in the formal contracts signed by both sides) during the reference time. It constitutes floor space of completed housing and floor space of future housing.

Value of Commercial Housing Sold refer to total value of contracts (i.e. value of sales/purchase for selling/purchase of commercial housing as designated in the contracts signed by both sides) during the reference time. It has the same coverage as the area of commercial housing sold, constituting completed housing and floor space of future housing

Economically Affordable Housing refers to housing constructed according to the state plan for economically affordable housing. Houses of this category featured in low cost in construction and low prices, and therefore are affordable to mid-income or low income households. Economically affordable housing projects are developed by real estate companies under the state investment plan, with the land provided through government allocation or tendering procedures. Developers are exempted from land utilization fees and enjoy another 50% exemption of all other legitimate fees, while their profits are limited to less than 3%, and the completed houses are sold under the government-guided prices. This indicator helps to analyze the investment structure of the real estate industry and the demand and supply of housing for mid or low income households.

5 对外经济贸易和旅游

Foreign Economic，Trade and Tourism

资料整理：陈彬彬

5−1 对外经济主要指标

MAJOR INDICATORS OF FOREIGN TRADE AND ECONOMIC COOPERATION

单位：万美元 (USD 10 000)

指 标	Item	1995	2000	2005	2008	2009	2010	2011	2012	2013
进出口总额	**Total Imports and Exports**	**340920**	**320249**	**905475**	**2070567**	**1725102**	**2593211**	**3358693**	**3196409**	**3638928**
进口总额	Total Imports	142484	127369	462607	899676	727222	1149031	1405233	1256525	1355160
出口总额	Total Exports	198435	192880	442868	1170891	997880	1444180	1953460	1939884	2283768
合同外商直接投资项目(个)	**Contracted Projets of Foreign Direct Investment (uint)**	**881**	**331**	**520**	**343**	**268**	**306**	**339**	**271**	**297**
合同外商直接投资	**Contracted Value of Foreign Direct Investment**	**108847**	**106583**	**211023**	**433742**	**204916**	**278627**	**497130**	**363927**	**485467**
实际外商直接投资	**Actual Value of Foreign Direct Investment**	**62253**	**94368**	**218475**	**324481**	**365766**	**405015**	**465503**	**566591**	**688847**
对外经济合作	**Economic and Technical Cooperation with Foreign Countries**									
合同金额	Contracted Value	7300	36706	35953	331419	532879	776945	639273	737945	1033540
#对外承包工程	#Contracted Projects			27952	318872	526671	765547	631308	726900	1021254
对外劳务合作	Labor Services			5568	6016	6208	11398	7965	11045	12286
完成营业额	Value of Business Fulfilled	4100	15815	31843	152116	263356	327164	415002	465863	538927
#对外承包工程	#Contracted Projects			28852	142456	256368	319979	406741	456194	520733
对外劳务合作	Labor Services			2601	6856	6988	7186	8261	9669	18194

5−2 对外贸易进出口总额

TOTAL IMPORTS AND EXPORTS

单位：万美元 (USD 10 000)

年 份 Year	合 计 Total	进 口 Imports	出 口 Exports
1990	121342	26852	94490
1991	152188	39185	113003
1992	174533	58696	115837
1993	222912	100170	122743
1994	274880	103035	171845
1995	340920	142484	198435
1996	286287	133684	152603
1997	320668	128583	192084
1998	283189	112478	170711
1999	268107	116729	151378
2000	320249	127369	192880
2001	357720	178041	179679
2002	395314	185488	209826
2003	510930	245393	265537
2004	676581	338361	338219
2005	905475	462607	442868
2006	1176219	550157	626063
2007	1489647	669593	820054
2008	2070567	899676	1170891
2009	1725102	727222	997880
2010	2593211	1149031	1444180
2011	3358693	1405233	1953460
2012	3196409	1256525	1939884
2013	3638928	1355160	2283768

注：根据海关统计有关文件规定2008年年终数据部分调整。

Note:According to the provisions of the relevant documents to customs statistics data portion of the 2008 year-end adjustments.

5-3 按贸易方式和经济类型分的进出口总额

单位：万美元

项 目	Item	2000		2005	
		进 口 Imports	出 口 Exports	进 口 Imports	出 口 Exports
总 计	**Total**	**127369**	**192880**	**462607**	**442868**
按贸易方式分	**Grouped by Type of Trade**				
一般贸易	General Trade	91576	138907	340768	350354
来料加工装配贸易	Processing and Assembling Trade	20136	13265	15428	22381
进料加工贸易	Raw Material Input Processing Trade	32803	14154	54328	71920
来料加工装配进口的设备	Processing and Assembling Import Equipment Provided With Material	6		18	
外商作为投资进口的设备	Goods as Invested for Import Equipments	8602		45087	
租赁贸易	Leasing Trade			114	
出料加工贸易	Raw Material Output Processing Trade				
易货贸易	Repalce Goods with Goods				
保税仓库进出境货物	Import and Export Goods of Protcetive Tariff Storage	105		8028	33
按经济类型分	**Grouped by Ownership**				
#国有企业	#State-Owned Enterprises	64805	140826	221963	213955
集体企业	Collective-Owned Enterprises	1255	9124	5719	20033
外商投资企业	Foreign-funded Enterprises	61691	42901	190170	130579
民营企业	Private-Owned Enterprises	111	240	45839	80397

(USD 10 000)

2009		2010		2011		2012		2013	
进 口 Imports	出 口 Exports	进 口 Imports	出 口 Exports	进 口 Imports	出 口 Exports	进 口 Imports	出 口 Exports	进 口 Imports	出 口 Exports
727222	**997880**	**1149031**	**1444180**	**1405233**	**1953460**	**1256525**	**1939884**	**1355160**	**2283768**
520937	604915	841306	829994	1029457	1104728	947733	1152839	1000601	1520152
25255	33081	28304	32269	27162	39859	21218	39039	18128	38854
124410	300408	210483	518911	261048	687508	208043	622969	281413	593316
173		348		37				230	
35285		43809		42713		24772		13487	
4930		5	144	5		7	92	5	150
245	95	320	212	568	319	187	322	729	532
12347	9382	20511	16794	33697	29981	50275	41619	32427	38794
292224	366163	513134	472230	633360	618532	500014	540497	452200	527257
2209	15168	4021	16161	4729	18140	3802	18511	2427	19933
363956	338730	534565	569501	647416	760098	618044	762022	665555	732420
64949	277567	93032	386177	108581	556609	130133	618934	190004	1002635

5-4 进出口商品主要国别和地区
IMPORTS AND EXPORTS VALUE BY COUNTRIES AND REGIONS

单位：万美元 (USD 10 000)

国家(地区)	Countries (Regions)	2012			2013		
		进出口 Imports and Exports	进口 Imports	出口 Exports	进出口 Imports and Exports	进口 Imports	出口 Exports
亚 洲	**Asia**	**1406241**	**571460**	**834781**	**1712629**	**577203**	**1135426**
#香港	#Hongkong	128911	3211	125700	253776	36060	217716
印度	India	105771	7799	97972	125416	10559	114858
日本	Japan	292798	208266	84531	252613	165265	87348
新加坡	Singapore	69208	9751	59457	78360	17076	61283
韩国	Korea, Rep.	129169	72577	56592	130304	65879	64425
台湾省	Taiwan Province	86485	56942	29542	98249	67967	30282
非 洲	**Afria**	**162063**	**54629**	**107434**	**184190**	**81650**	**102540**
#南非	#South Africa	52772	40026	12746	68052	53971	14082
欧 洲	**European**	**651147**	**211958**	**439188**	**719755**	**254663**	**465092**
#比利时	#Belgium	28000	5297	22703	33141	11789	21352
英国	United Kingdom	40284	8320	31964	64776	11375	53401
德国	Germany	105341	58129	47213	124615	60687	63927
法国	France	83867	66373	17494	121266	98233	23033
意大利	Italy	37657	13502	24155	43530	15861	27669
荷兰	Netherland	52019	7144	44875	53581	7260	46321
西班牙	Spanish	19104	3439	15666	26658	6045	20613
芬兰	Finland	29945	6528	23417	6655	3862	2792
拉丁美洲	**Latin America**	**298879**	**92841**	**206038**	**333673**	**116670**	**217003**
#巴西	#Brazil	77402	40373	37029	63730	25784	37946
智利	Chile	34331	20968	13362	54384	36128	18256
北美洲	**North America**	**453238**	**159459**	**293779**	**454298**	**150429**	**303870**
#加拿大	#Canada	90171	75375	14796	79062	62226	16836
美国	United States of America	363041	84084	278957	375226	88202	287024
大洋洲	**Occeania**	**224346**	**165505**	**58841**	**234351**	**174491**	**59861**
#澳大利亚	#Australia	197544	165103	32442	213046	173897	39149
附：东南亚国家联盟	**Association of Southeast-Asia Nations**	**364868**	**102100**	**262768**	**533251**	**123524**	**409727**
欧洲联盟	**European Union**	**575471**	**195930**	**379542**	**638111**	**242190**	**395921**
亚太经济合作组织	**Asia-Pacific Economic Cooperation**	**1911395**	**895871**	**1015524**	**2258220**	**954830**	**1303390**

5-5 合同外商直接投资项目

NUMBER OF CONTRACTED PROJECTS OF FOREIGN DIRECT INVESTMENT

单位：个 (unit)

指 标	Item	1990	1995	2000	2005	2008	2009	2010	2011	2012	2013
合 计	**Total**	**99**	**881**	**331**	**520**	**343**	**268**	**306**	**339**	**271**	**297**
合资经营企业	Joint Venture	17	577	156	203	131	86	108	138	102	116
合作经营企业	Cooperative Operation	75	44	16	29	15	16	5	8	5	8
独资经营企业	Foreign Solely Funded Enterprises	7	260	158	285	197	165	193	193	164	173
外商投资股份制企业	Share Holding Enterprises With Foreign Investment			1	3		1				

5-6 合同外商直接投资金额

VALUE OF CONTRACTED PROJECTS OF FOREIGN DIRECT INVESTMENT

单位：万美元 (USD 10 000)

指 标	Item	1990	1995	2000	2005	2008	2009	2010	2011	2012	2013
合 计	**Total**	**3947**	**108847**	**106583**	**211023**	**301964**	**204916**	**278627**	**497130**	**363927**	**485467**
合资经营企业	Joint Venture	1364	68923	27936	51010	150500	122227	132679	253542	93573	135618
合作经营企业	Cooperative Operation	2464	7899	48711	24480	26418	21117	3319	11217	7315	15924
独资经营企业	Foreign Solely Funded	119	32025	29936	132897	253900	198474	235498	224344	252964	334151
外商投资股份制企业	Share Holding Enterprises With Foreign Investment				2636	2924	23948	33519	8027	10075	-226

5-7 实际外商直接投资金额

ACTUAL VALUE OF FOREIGN DIRECT INVESTMENT

单位：万美元 (USD 10 000)

指　标	Item	1990	1995	2000	2003	2004	2005
合　计	**Total**	**2900**	**62253**	**94368**	**155702**	**207126**	**218475**
合资经营企业	Joint Venture	2492	40259	59879	104622	130048	65472
合作经营企业	Cooperative Operation	85	5012	2789	5513	11741	5089
独资经营企业	Foreign Solely Funded	323	16982	31700	45139	62155	75305
外商投资股份制企业	Share Holding With Foreign Investment						2739

5-7 续表 continued

单位：万美元 (USD 10 000)

指　标	Item	2007	2008	2009	2010	2011	2012	2013
合　计	**Total**	**276622**	**324481**	**365766**	**405015**	**465503**	**566591**	**688847**
合资经营企业	Joint Venture	43946	101474	122227	132679	202268	257765	223950
合作经营企业	Cooperative Operation	6077	16665	21117	3319	2992	647	3758
独资经营企业	Foreign Solely Funded	81762	180960	198474	235498	231847	298393	442107
外商投资股份制企业	Share Holding Enterprises With Foreign Investment	1650	25382	23948	33519	28396	9786	19032

5–8 按行业分外商直接投资(2013)
FOREIGN DIRECT INVESTMENT GROUPED BY SECTOR (2013)

行 业	Item	项目(个) Number of Projects (unit)	合同外资 (万美元) Contracted Foreign Capital (USD 10 000)	实际投资 (万美元) Actual Foreign Investment (USD 10 000)
总 计	**Total**	**297**	**485467**	**688847**
农、林、牧、渔业	Farming, Forestry, Animal Husbandry and Fishery	22	11050	6945
采矿业	Mining and Quarrying	2	2020	16071
制造业	Manufactruring	117	195041	353536
电力、燃气及水的生产和供应业	Power, Gas and Water Production and Supply	6	28162	38330
建筑业	Construction	8	9825	4896
交通运输、仓储和邮政业	Transportation, Storage and Post	12	14308	17326
信息传输、计算机服务和软件业	Information Transmmision, Computer Service and software	9	792	735
批发和零售业	Wholesale and Retail sale	41	38232	18456
住宿和餐饮业	Hotel and Catering	6	1416	4001
金融业	Finance	5	9919	10655
房地产业	Real Estate	11	125255	189318
租赁和商务服务业	Leasing and Commerical Service	35	29393	24349
科学研究、技术服务和地质勘查业	Scietific research, Polytechnical Service and Geological Prospecting	12	15053	2341
水利、环境和公共设施管理业	Water Conservancy, Environment and Public Facility Management	5	3406	388
居民服务和其他服务业	Resident Service and Others	5	1367	921
教育	Education			
卫生、社会保障和社会福利业	Health Care, Social Security and Social Welfare			
文化、体育和娱乐业	Culture, Sports and Recreation	1	228	579

5-9 年末登记外商投资企业行业分布情况(2013)
SECTOR DISTRIBUTION REGISTERED OF FOREIGN-FUNDED ENTERPRISES AT THE YEAR-END(2013)

单位：个 (unit)

行 业	Item	企业数 Number of Enterprises
总 计	**Total**	**297**
农、林、牧、渔业	Farming, Forestry, Animal Husbandry and Fishery	22
采矿业	Mining and Quarrying	2
制造业	Manufactruring	117
电力、燃气及水的生产和供应业	Power, Gas and Water Production and Supply	6
建筑业	Construction	8
交通运输、仓储和邮政业	Transportation, Storage and Post	12
信息传输、计算机服务和软件业	Information Transmmision, Computer Service and software	9
批发和零售业	Wholesale and Retail sale	41
住宿和餐饮业	Hotel and Catering	6
金融业	Finance	5
房地产业	Real Estate	11
租赁和商务服务业	Leasing and Commerical Service	35
科学研究、技术服务和地质勘查业	Scietific research, Polytechnical Service and Geological Prospecting	12
水利、环境和公共设施管理业	Water Conservancy, Environment and Public Facility Management	5
居民服务和其他服务业	Resident Service and Others	5
教育	Education	
卫生、社会保障和社会福利业	Health Care, Social Security and Social Welfare	
文化、体育和娱乐业	Culture, Sports and Recreation	1

5-10 对外承包工程和劳务合作
CONTRACTED PROJECTS AND LABOR SERVICES CO-OPERATION WITH FOREIGN COUNTRIES

年份 Year		合同金额（万美元） Contracted Value (USD 10 000)	实际完成营业额（万美元） Value of Business Fulfilled (USD 10 000)	年末在外人数(人) Number of Persons Working Abroad at Year-end (person)
1996		8800	5100	3919
1997		18100	6800	4338
1998		17400	9500	4933
1999		18100	12200	5718
2000		36706	15815	6584
2001		12019	14653	7058
2002		29469	15863	7102
2003		29882	20333	4923
2004		31141	27384	5854
2005		35953	31843	7599
2006		63704	41097	10363
2007		195692	62267	15115
2008		331419	152116	15406
2009		532879	263356	15148
2010		776945	327164	22372
2011		639273	415002	17386
2012		737945	465863	24662
2013		1033540	538927	29097
对外承包工程	**Contracted Projects**			
2002		12515	27295	1535
2003		17900	28552	1759
2004		28027	25334	2199
2005		27952	28852	2365
2006		56930	36266	2671
2007		183749	54416	5950
2008		318872	142456	9145
2009		526671	256368	10546
2010		765547	319978	17655
2011		631308	406741	13961
2012		726900	456194	16404
2013		1021254	520733	20801
对外劳务合作	**Labor Cooperation**			
2002		1633	3081	5525
2003		823	1783	3136
2004		1565	1597	3583
2005		5568	2601	5143
2006		6331	4379	7602
2007		6520	5340	8704
2008		6016	6856	6239
2009		6208	6988	4602
2010		11398	7186	4717
2011		7965	8261	3425
2012		11045	9669	8258
2013		12286	18194	8296
对外设计咨询	**Design Consulting**			
2002		541	267	42
2003		507	650	28
2004		475	1517	72
2005		390	2433	91
2006		983	452	90
2007		5423	2511	461
2008		6531	2804	22

注:2009年起“对外设计咨询”指标数并入“对外承包工程”中；“年末在外人数(人)”修订为“劳务外派人数(人)”

Note:From 2009, "design and consultation," index number into the "International Contractors" in; "at the end of outer (person)" to "manning (person)".

5-11 湖北旅游主要指标

MAJOR INDICATORS OF HUBEI TOURISM

年 份 Year	旅游总收入 (亿元) Total Earnings of Tourism (100 million yuan)	国内旅游收入 (亿元) Earnings from Domestic Tourism (100 million yuan)	国内旅游人数 (万人次) Number of Domestic Tourists (10 000 persons-time)	外汇收入 (万美元) Foreign Exchange Earnings (USD 10 000)	入境旅游人数 (万人次) Number of Tourists Received (10 000 persons-time)
1981				297.20	1.60
1982				299.60	2.00
1983				355.30	2.40
1984				731.30	5.40
1985				1008.60	8.50
1986	3.47	2.50	1262	1166.00	10.50
1987	3.67	2.40	1184	1545.00	12.20
1988	3.56	2.40	1208	1411.80	11.30
1989	3.99	3.10	1034	1085.50	8.20
1990	4.56	2.70	890	2263.20	15.60
1991	5.83	3.90	984	2350.00	17.00
1992	9.03	5.40	1071	4432.20	26.30
1993	13.26	9.50	1350	4588.90	23.10
1994	18.09	13.00	1500	6211.40	24.70
1995	24.00	18.00	1700	7316.90	27.10
1996	163.28	153.00	3152	12545.60	36.90
1997	193.92	180.00	3600	16977.50	58.00
1998	217.24	210.00	4044	8831.40	29.60
1999	247.11	238.50	4659	10498.50	30.50
2000	282.26	270.30	5478	14572.10	45.10
2001	353.66	337.20	6064	20075.20	66.80
2002	407.48	384.20	6670	28390.90	102.40
2003	342.77	331.60	5684	13626.90	40.50
2004	410.00	394.20	6849	19240.40	61.20
2005	473.15	450.80	7630	27636.30	82.60
2006	539.74	514.24	8459.78	32000.38	105.57
2007	640.87	609.40	10135.00	41264.00	131.81
2008	744.19	713.43	11678.00	44255.31	118.75
2009	1004.48	969.63	15065.18	51020.22	133.46
2010	1460.53	1409.48	20946.00	75116.49	181.74
2011	1992.89	1931.80	27154.87	94018.00	213.52
2012	2629.54	2553.55	34230.00	120296.72	264.72
2013	3205.61	3130.13	40621.04	121892.18	267.96

5-12 接待入境旅游人数

NUMBER OF ENTRANCE TOURISTS

单位:人次 (person-times)

年 份 Year	总计 Total	外国人 Foreigners	港澳台同胞 Compatroits from Hongkong, Maco and Taiwan	#港澳同胞 #Compatroits from Hongkong, Macao	#台湾同胞 #Compatroits from Taiwan
1981	16390	10916	5474		
1982	19775	15126	4649		
1983	24200	18903	5297		
1984	53800	40496	13304		
1985	84598	68103	16495		
1986	105300	83570	21730		
1987	122390	82029	40361		
1988	113051	78206	34845	19725	15120
1989	81781	49511	32270	13908	18362
1990	155734	36374	119360	11560	107800
1991	170121	53055	117066	12645	104421
1992	263401	72691	190323	14054	176269
1993	230883	84552	146331	28460	117871
1994	247212	133343	113869	56417	57452
1995	270890	172869	98021	42785	55236
1996	368877	243595	125282	58949	66333
1997	580223	359700	220523	64466	156057
1998	295643	209402	86241	30337	55904
1999	305408	224748	80660	30935	49725
2000	450805	357352	93453	42928	53162
2001	667818	542737	125081	48417	76664
2002	1024312	755718	268594	49113	219481
2003	405214	323151	82063	40294	41769
2004	611859	501873	109986	57086	52900
2005	825700	626805	198895	107141	91754
2006	1055752	857028	198724	110246	88478
2007	1318179	1077189	240990	140384	100606
2008	1187549	926625	260924	152631	108293
2009	1334634	1017620	317014	182616	134398
2010	1817416	1385457	431959	241430	190529
2011	2135247	1601129	534118	291487	242631
2012	2647163	1929571	717592	410921	306671
2013	2679623	2047316	632307	365184	267123

5-13 入境旅游外汇收入
FOREIGN EXCHANGE REVENUE OF ENTRANCE TOURISTS

年 份 Year	外汇收入(万美元) Foreign Exchange Earnings (USD 10 000)	发展指数(1978年为100) Development Index (year1978=100)	同比 Comparision Percentage (±%)	人均天花费(美元) Expenditures Per Capita (USD)	
				全国 The Whole Nation	湖北 Hubei
1981	297.20	128.80	34.48		
1982	299.64	129.85	82.00		
1983	355.30	153.98	18.58		
1984	731.30	316.92	105.83		
1985	1008.58	327.69	37.92		
1986	1166.00	505.31	15.61		
1987	1545.00	669.56	32.50		
1988	1411.75	611.81	-8.62		
1989	1085.45	470.40	-23.11		
1990	2263.18	980.79	108.50		
1991	2350.00	1018.42	3.84		
1992	4432.16	1920.76	88.60		
1993	4588.88	1988.68	3.54		
1994	6211.42	2691.84	35.36	125.10	125.10
1995	7316.86	3170.90	17.80	141.10	155.70
1996	12545.60	5436.88	71.46	131.16	167.04
1997	16977.51	7357.53	35.33	135.11	168.52
1998	8831.43	3827.27	-47.98	133.87	162.87
1999	10498.49	4549.72	18.88	135.00	166.31
2000	14572.13	6315.12	38.80	136.85	166.58
2001	20075.16	8699.96	37.76	138.76	164.25
2002	28390.95	12303.77	41.42	140.09	160.57
2003	13626.93	5905.50	-52.00	140.09	160.57
2004	19240.41	8338.21	51.00	156.84	169.92
2005	27636.30	11976.73	43.64	154.16	170.14
2006	32000.38	13867.99	15.79	164.29	177.16
2007	41264.00	17882.56	28.95	179.79	181.68
2008	44255.31	19178.90	7.25	186.18	197.56
2009	51020.22	22110.60	15.29	180.77	193.43
2010	75116.49	32553.20	47.23	184.01	192.84
2011	94018.00	40744.53	25.16	195.38	195.36
2012	120296.72	52132.92	27.95	195.53	193.04
2013	121892.18	52824.35	1.33	200.17	194.44

5-14 接待入境旅游者天数

NUMBER OF DAYS THE ENTRANCE TOURISTS STAYED IN HUBEI

单位：人天 (person/day)

年 份 Year	总计 Total	外国人 Foreigners	港澳台同胞 Compatroits from Hongkong, Maco and Taiwan	#港澳同胞 #Compatroits from Hongkong, Macao	#台湾同胞 #Compatroits from Taiwan
1980	20700	12130	8570		
1981	22946	15282	7664		
1982	29016	24188	4828		
1983	29830	25298	4532		
1984	107600	37806	69794		
1985	143815	115774	28041		
1986	186379	139677	46702		
1987	167035	115219	51816		
1988	190486	132301	58185	35505	22680
1989	127891	79217	48674	20862	27812
1990	178737	49487	129250	11960	117290
1991	235595	74913	160682	17450	143232
1992	351591	101878	249713	18973	230740
1993	324350	142240	182110	49959	132151
1994	472467	231716	240751	117889	122862
1995	501038	317246	183792	86910	96882
1996	729968	477152	252816	131993	120823
1997	949661	591127	358534	111291	247243
1998	513569	366348	147221	61491	85730
1999	622037	478486	143551	57765	85786
2000	852455	676130	176325	81432	94893
2001	1208938	891787	317151	93376	223775
2002	1712230	1232818	479412	86427	392985
2003	799824	603001	196823	98230	98593
2004	1069442	849071	220371	118234	102137
2005	1513678	1135995	377683	194122	183561
2006	1824387	1502277	322110	176901	145209
2007	2342786	1926484	416302	233946	182356
2008	2217172	1734211	482961	243638	239323
2009	2640362	2025972	614390	338898	275492
2010	3750746	2868024	882722	481484	401238
2011	4596252	3494098	1102154	581193	520961
2012	5934359	4424239	1510060	822210	687850
2013	6009111	4581165	1427946	802642	625304

注：2000年国家不再设“华侨”指标，“华侨”人数含在“外国人”中。
Note:The item of "overseas Chinese" is cancled by state since 2000, The number of "Overseas Chinese" is included in the number of "Foreigner".

5-15 湖北国内旅游接待人数及收入
TOATL NUMBER OF DOMESTIC TOURISTS AND EARNINGS FORM DOMESTIC TORUISM

年份 Year	接待人数(万人次) Number of Tourists Received (10 000person-times)	同比(±%) Comparision Percentage (±%)	旅游收入(亿元) Earnings (100 million yuan)	同比(±%) Comparision Percentage (±%)	人均天花费(元) Expenditures Per Capita a day (yuan) 全国 The Whole Nation	湖北 Hubei
1987	1184	-6.18	2.37	-6.0		
1988	1208	2.03	2.42	2.1		
1989	1034	-14.40	3.10	28.1		
1990	890	-13.92	2.67	-13.9		
1991	984	10.56	3.93	47.2		
1992	1071	8.84	5.36	36.4		
1993	1350	26.05	9.50	77.2		
1994	1500	11.11	13.00	36.8		
1995	1700	13.33	18.00	38.5		
1996	3152	85.41	152.95		256	485
1997	3600	14.21	180.00	17.7	328	500
1998	4044	12.33	210.03	16.7	344	519
1999	4659	15.21	238.50	13.6	394	511
2000	5478	17.58	270.31	13.3	427	493
2001	6064	10.70	337.18	24.7	450	556
2002	6670	9.99	384.24	14.0	441	576
2003	5684	-14.78	331.60	-13.7	395	583
2004	6849	20.50	394.22	18.9	550	576
2005	7630	11.40	450.76	14.3	436	591
2006	8460	10.88	514.24	14.1	447	607
2007	10135	19.80	609.40	18.5	482	601
2008	11678	15.2	713.43	17.1	511	610
2009	15065	29.0	969.63	35.9	535	644
2010	20946	39.0	1409.48	45.4	598	673
2011	27155	29.6	1931.80	37.1	731	711
2012	34230	26.1	2553.55	32.2	766	746
2013	40621	18.6	3130.13	22.6	806	771

注：表中所列是人均花费(元)。
Note: The table is a list of per capita spending ($).

5-16 湖北旅游总收入及占全省GDP比重
THE RATIO OF TOTAL EARNINGS OF HUBEI TOURISM IN PROVINCIAL GDP

年 份 Year	旅游总收入 Total Earnings of Tourism		占GDP及第三产业比重 Percentage in GDP and Three Industries	
	绝对额(亿元) (100 million yuan)	同比(±%) Comparision Percentage (±%)	占GDP比重(%) GDP(%)	占第三产业增加值比重(%) Proportion of total added value of tertiary industry (%)
1997	193.92	18.8	5.6	18.0
1998	217.27	12.0	5.9	18.1
1999	247.11	13.7	6.4	18.8
2000	282.26	14.2	6.6	18.9
2001	353.64	24.9	7.6	21.4
2002	407.52	15.2	8.2	22.4
2003	342.77	-15.9	6.4	17.0
2004	410.00	19.6	6.5	17.8
2005	473.15	15.5	7.3	20.6
2006	539.74	14.1	7.2	18.0
2007	640.87	18.7	7.0	17.6
2008	744.19	16.1	6.6	16.2
2009	1004.48	35.0	7.8	20.1
2010	1460.53	45.4	9.2	24.8
2011	1992.89	36.5	10.2	27.7
2012	2629.54	32.0	11.8	32.0
2013	3205.61	21.9	13.0	34.1

5-17 分地区接待国内旅游者人数

NUMBER OF DOMESTIC TOURISTS RECEIVED BY REGION

单位:万人次 (10 000 person-time)

地 区	Regions	2005	2006	2007	2008	2009	2010	2011	2012	2013
全 省	**Province**	**7630.00**	**8459.78**	**10134.53**	**11678.28**	**15065.18**	**20946.48**	**27154.87**	**34230.26**	**40621.04**
武 汉 市	Wuhan Municipality	2901.00	3283.05	3889.07	4612.79	6359.99	8852.34	11636.12	14067.70	17022.11
黄 石 市	Huangshi Municipality	140.00	198.22	312.47	426.84	517.60	788.69	981.29	1070.76	1254.21
十 堰 市	Shiyan Municipality	595.00	666.70	737.53	921.45	1123.71	1466.16	1850.87	2316.58	2853.42
宜 昌 市	Yichang Municipality	862.00	901.81	1000.05	970.00	1197.22	1519.00	1905.43	2606.44	3286.03
襄 阳 市	Xiangyang Municipality	626.00	690.22	750.10	820.05	993.51	1397.48	1804.55	2348.80	2824.20
鄂 州 市	Ezhou Municipality	115.00	125.99	140.26	161.98	212.43	284.54	376.66	395.37	482.62
荆 门 市	Jingmen Municipality	380.00	437.76	507.71	543.30	662.14	864.03	1100.63	1501.82	1804.96
孝 感 市	Xiaogan Municipality	310.00	312.14	429.13	508.07	643.46	822.86	995.18	1182.59	1485.95
荆 州 市	Jingzhou Municipality	387.00	434.05	512.56	564.02	649.78	916.24	1205.34	1570.46	1901.15
黄 冈 市	Huanggang Municipality	300.00	323.91	465.42	515.05	667.81	819.78	1015.32	1205.90	1500.44
咸 宁 市	Xianning Municipality	332.00	334.04	430.25	560.09	715.74	1155.95	1500.98	2101.48	2649.08
随 州 市	Suizhou Municipality	322.00	323.94	334.15	398.57	481.69	597.19	850.82	1203.85	1459.74
恩 施 州	Enshi Prefecture	200.00	225.73	429.55	450.10	505.53	1014.24	1400.48	1971.03	2441.74
仙 桃 市	Xiantao Municipality	41.00	47.62	49.13	49.24	88.19	105.00	133.70	165.62	179.54
潜 江 市	Qianjiang Municipality	36.00	36.57	29.21	29.31	38.09	41.62	46.77	51.40	52.22
天 门 市	Tianmen Municipality	30.00	30.95	28.27	29.31	41.87	48.76	53.70	62.44	65.77
神农架林区	Shennongjia Forest Zone	51.00	87.07	89.67	118.09	166.42	252.15	297.03	408.02	517.01

5-18 分地区接待国内旅游收入
EARNINGS FROM RECEIVING DOMESTIC TOURISTS BY REGION

单位:亿元 (100 million yuan)

地　区	Regions	2005	2006	2007	2008	2009	2010	2011	2012	2013
全　省	**Province**	**450.76**	**514.24**	**609.40**	**744.19**	**969.63**	**1409.48**	**1992.89**	**2553.55**	**3130.13**
武汉市	Wuhan Municipality	221.22	250.70	296.98	373.68	486.18	721.40	1054.10	1342.17	1633.40
黄石市	Huangshi Municipality	5.98	8.45	12.50	18.55	26.68	40.36	51.20	55.20	62.02
十堰市	Shiyan Municipality	24.40	28.02	29.12	43.10	62.32	87.05	119.28	157.62	198.51
宜昌市	Yichang Municipality	53.80	65.09	67.52	65.09	75.95	100.34	141.28	195.92	255.00
襄阳市	Xiangyang Municipality	28.70	34.54	39.51	47.82	60.94	85.91	117.80	148.85	179.01
鄂州市	Ezhou Municipality	7.10	7.86	8.85	10.56	12.98	17.96	24.73	33.60	41.37
荆门市	Jingmen Municipality	13.40	15.89	18.34	21.88	29.86	40.17	53.07	74.96	90.29
孝感市	Xiaogan Municipality	11.72	12.59	23.15	29.10	37.39	48.26	57.77	69.93	88.68
荆州市	Jingzhou Municipality	19.60	22.05	27.20	31.75	34.77	51.75	70.65	91.00	111.26
黄冈市	Huanggang Municipality	14.80	16.75	27.70	28.20	34.35	44.45	55.57	64.39	78.07
咸宁市	Xianning Municipality	8.40	9.55	15.06	20.46	33.90	59.05	77.52	107.70	130.11
随州市	Suizhou Municipality	12.80	13.22	14.30	18.62	26.54	38.45	52.48	69.50	84.67
恩施州	Enshi Prefecture	16.70	20.61	21.23	26.17	29.21	47.99	79.59	96.82	124.88
仙桃市	Xiantao Municipality	2.30	2.91	3.37	3.01	5.57	6.96	8.71	11.91	11.94
潜江市	Qianjiang Municipality	2.44	2.51	1.40	1.52	2.31	2.57	3.09	3.62	3.63
天门市	Tianmen Municipality	1.40	1.60	1.12	1.25	2.42	3.05	3.66	3.84	3.85
神农架林区	Shennongjia Forest Zone	6.00	1.94	2.05	3.43	8.25	13.75	22.39	26.52	33.44

主要统计指标解释

进出口总额 指实际进出我国国境的货物总金额。包括对外贸易实际进出口货物，来料加工装配进出口货物，国家间、联合国及国际组织无偿援助物资和赠送品，华侨、港澳台同胞和外籍华人捐赠品，租赁期满归承租人所有的租赁货物，进料加工进出口货物，边境地方贸易及边境地区小额贸易进出口货物(边民互市贸易除外)，中外合资企业、中外合作经营企业、外商独资经营企业进出口货物和公用物品，到、离岸价格在规定限额以上的进出口货样和广告品(无商业价值、无使用价值和免费提供出口的除外)，从保税仓库提取在中国境内销售的进口货物，以及其他进出口货物。该指标可以观察一个国家在对外贸易方面的总规模。我国规定出口货物按离岸价格统计，进口货物按到岸价格统计。

商品经营单位所在地进、出口额 指所在地海关注册登记的有进出口经营权的企业实际进、出口额。

商品目的地进口额和商品货源地出口额 目的地进口额指进口货物的消费、使用或最终抵运地的实际进口额；货源地出口额指出口货物的产地或原始发货地的实际出口额。

利用外资 指我国各级政府、部门、企业和其他经济组织通过对外借款、吸收外商直接投资以及用其他方式筹措的境外现汇、设备、技术等。

对外借款 指通过对外正式签订借款协议，从境外筹措的资金，包括外国政府贷款、国际金融组织贷款、外国银行商业贷款、出口信贷以及对外发行债券等。1996年及以前还包括对外发行股票。该指标是我国利用外资的重要部分。

外商直接投资 指外国企业和经济组织或个人(包括华侨、港澳台胞以及我国在境外注册的企业)按我国有关政策、法规，用现汇、实物、技术等在我国境内开办外商独资企业、与我国境内的企业或经济组织共同举办中外合资经营企业、合作经营企业或合作开发资源的投资(包括外商投资收益的再投资)，以及经政府有关部门批准的项目投资总额内企业从境外借入的资金。

外商其他投资 指除对外借款和外商直接投资以外的各种利用外资的形式。包括企业在境内外股票市场公开发行的以外币计价的股票（目前主要是在香港证券市场发行的H股和在境内证券市场发行的B股）发行价总额，国际租赁进口设备的应付款，补偿贸易中外商提供的进口设备、技术、物料的价款，加工装配贸易中外商提供的进口设备、物料的价款。

对外直接投资 指我国国内投资者以现金、实物、无形资产等方式在国外及港澳台地区设立、购买国（境）外企业，并以控制该企业的经营管理权为核心的经济活动。

对外承包工程 指各对外承包公司以招标议标承包方式承揽的下列业务：(1)承包国外工程建设项目；(2)承包我国对外经援项目；(3)承包我国驻外机构的工程建设项目；(4)承包我国境内利用外资进行建设的工程项目；(5)与外国承包公司合营或联合承包工程项目时我国公司分包部分；(6)对外承包兼营的房屋开发业务。对外承包工程的营业额是以货币表现的本期内完成的对外承包工程的工作量，包括以前年度签订的合同和本年度新签订的合同在报告期内完成的工作量。

对外劳务合作 指以收取工资的形式向业主或承包商提供技术和劳动服务的活动。我国对外承包公司在境外开办的合营企业，中国公司同时又提供劳务的，其劳务部分也纳入劳务合作统计。劳务合作营业额按报告期内向雇主提交的结算数(包括工资、加班费和奖金等)统计。

对外设计咨询 指以服务成果向业主收费的技术服务项目。包括承担地形地貌测绘，地质资源勘探与普查，建设区域规划，提供设计文件、图纸、生产工艺技术资料和工程技术经济咨询，工程项目的可行性考察、研究和评估，进行技术指导和培训人员等；也包括承担国(境)内利用外资建设工程项目中的设计咨询项目内收取外币部分。

旅游者人数

(1)入境国际旅游者人数：指来中国参观、访问、旅行、探亲、访友、休养、考察、参加会议和从事经济、科技、文化、教育、宗教等活动的外国人、华侨、港澳同胞和台湾同胞的人数。不包括外国在我国的常驻机构，如使领馆、通讯社、企业办事处的工作人员；来我国常住的外国专家、留学生以及在岸逗留不过夜人员。

(2)出境居民人数：指大陆居民因公务活动或私人事务短期出境的人数。公务活动出境居民人数包括在国际交通工具上的中国服务员工，因私出境居民人数不包括在国际交通工具上的中国服务员工。

(3)国内旅游者人数：指我国大陆居民和在我国常住1年以上的外国人、华侨、港澳台同胞离开常住地在境内其他地方的旅游设施内至少停留一夜，最长不超过6个月的人数。

国际旅游(外汇)收入　指入境旅游的外国人、华侨、港澳同胞和台湾同胞在中国大陆旅游过程中发生的一切旅游支出，其对于国家来说就是国际旅游(外汇)收入。

国际旅行社　指经营对外招徕并接待外国人、华侨、港澳同胞和台湾同胞来中国、归国或回内地旅游业务的旅行社。

国内旅行社　指负责经营招徕、组团、接待国内旅客的旅游业务，以及不对外招徕，负责经营接待国际旅行社或其它涉外部门组织的外国人、华侨、港澳同胞和台湾同胞来中国、归国或回内地的旅游业务的旅行社。

星级饭店　指已评定星级的饭店。

Explanatory Notes on Main Statistical Indicators

Total Imports and Exports at Customs refer to the real value of commodities imported into and exported from the boundary of China. They include the actual imports and exports through foreign trade, imported and exported goods under the processing and assembling trades and materials, supplies and gifts as aid given gratis between governments and by the United Nations and other international organizations, and contributions donated by overseas Chinese, compatriots in Hong Kong and Macao and Chinese with foreign citizenship, leasing commodities owned by tenant at the expiration of leasing period, the imported and exported commodities processed with imported materials, commodities trading in border areas (excluding mutual exchange goods), the imported and exported commodities and articles for public use of the Sino-foreign joint ventures, cooperative enterprises and ventures exclusively with foreign own investment. Also included are import or export of samples and advertising goods for whose CIF or FOB value are beyond the permitted ceiling (excluding goods of no trading or use value and free commodities for export), imported goods sold in China from bonded warehouses and other imported or exported goods. The indicator of the total imports and exports at customs can be used to observe the total size of external trade in a country. In accordance with the stipulation of the Chinese government, imports are calculated at CIF, while exports are calculated at FOB.

Import Export Value by Location of China' s Foreign Trade Managing Units refers to actual value of imports and exports carried out by corporations which have been registered by the local customhouse and are vested with right to run import export business.

Import Value of Commodities by the Places of their Destination and Export Value of Commodities by the Places of their Origin in China The former indicator refers to the value of import commodities of the places of their consumption, utilization or the places of their final destination. The latter indicator refers to the value of export commodities of the places of their origin or the places of the commodities dispatched.

Utilization of Foreign Capitals refers to remittance, equipment and technology financed from abroad, by loans, foreign direct investment and other forms undertaken by the Chinese governments at all levels, by various departments, enterprises and other economic units.

Foreign Borrowings refer to funds borrowed from abroad through formal signing of borrowing agreements with foreign institutions, including loans of foreign governments, loans of international financial institutions, commercial loans of foreign banks, export credit, and funds raised by Chinese bonds (and shares before 1996) issued abroad. It is an important part of China's utilization of foreign capitals.

Foreign Direct Investment refers to the investments inside China by foreign enterprises and economic organizations or individuals (including overseas Chinese, compatriots from Hong Kong, Macao and Taiwan, and Chinese enterprises registered abroad), following the relevant policies and laws of China, for the establishment of ventures exclusively with foreign own investment, Sino-foreign joint ventures and cooperative enterprises or for co-operative exploration of resources with enterprises or economic organizations in China. It includes the re investment of the foreign entrepreneurs with the profits gained from the investment and the funds that enterprises borrow from abroad in the total investment of projects which are approved by the relevant department of the government.

Overseas Direct Investment refers to enterprises set up or bought by domestic investors in foreign countries and in Hong Kong, Macao and Taiwan, and the economic activities centering on operation and management of those enterprises are under the control of domestic investors. The statistical scope covers various corporation type enterprises and non-corporation type enterprises receiving direct investment from domestic investment entities.

Other Investment by Foreign Entrepreneurs refers to all forms of utilization of foreign capitals other than foreign borrowings and foreign direct investment. It includes the total value of stock shares in foreign currencies issued by enterprises at domestic or foreign stock exchanges (now mainly consisting of H shares issued at Hong Kong Security Market and B shares issued at domestic security markets), rent payable for the imported equipment through international leasing arrangement, cost of imported equipment, technology and materials provided by foreign counterparts in compensation trade and processing and assembly trade.

Contracted Projects with Foreign Countries refer to projects undertaken by Chinese contractors (project contracting companies) through bidding process. They include: (1) overseas civil engineering construction projects financed by foreign investors; (2) overseas projects financed by the Chinese government through its foreign aid programs; (3) construction projects of Chinese diplomatic missions, trade offices and other institutions stationed abroad; (4) construction projects in China financed by foreign investment; (5) sub-contracted projects to be taken by Chinese contractors through a joint umbrella project with foreign contractor(s); (6) housing development projects. The business income from international contracted projects is the work volume of contracted projects completed during the reference period, expressed in monetary terms, including completed work on projects signed in previous years.

Service Cooperation with Foreign Countries refers to the activities of providing technology and labor services to employers or contractors in the forms of receiving salaries and wages. Labor services providing by contractual joint ventures of Chinese international contracting corporations should be included in the statistics of service co-operation with foreign countries. The business income of labor service cooperation is the income in the form of wages and salaries, overtime pay, bonuses and other remuneration received from the employers during the reference period.

Overseas Design and Consultation Service refers to projects with charges for technical services from overseas operators. It includes geographic and topographic mapping, geological resource prospecting and survey, planning of construction areas, provision of design documents, blueprints, materials on production process and techniques, as well as engineering, technical and economic consultation, and feasibility study, research and evaluation of projects. Also included under this category are the above-mentioned services of foreign-financed projects in China that are paid in foreign currencies.

Number of Tourists

(1) International tourists refer to foreigners, overseas Chinese, Chinese compatriots from Hong Kong, Macao and Taiwan coming to China for sight-seeing, visits, tours, family reunions, vacations, study tours, conferences and other activities of a business, scientific and technological, cultural, educational and religious nature. It does not include representatives and employees of resident institutions of foreign countries in China such as embassies, consulates, news agencies and offices of foreign companies and organizations, nor does it include long-term foreign experts or students residing in China, or persons in transition without spending a night in China.

(2) Chinese residents going abroad refer to Chinese residents going abroad for short terms for either public business or private purposes. Chinese employees working on international transport carriers are included in those going abroad for public business purpose, not in those for private purpose.

(3) Domestic tourists refer to residents of the mainland of China who stay for one night at least but no more than 6 months at tourist facilities in other places than their permanent residence within the territory of the mainland China, including foreigners, overseas Chinese and Chinese compatriots from Hong Kong, Macao and Taiwan who have resided in China for over one year.

Foreign Exchange Earnings from International Tourism refer to the total expenditures of foreigners, overseas Chinese, Chinese compatriots from Hong Kong, Macao and Taiwan during their stay in the mainland of China, which are earnings of foreign exchange from international tourism from the point of view from China.

International Travel Agencies refer to travel agencies engaged in the promotion, solicitation, organization and reception of tours to the mainland of China by foreigners, overseas Chinese, Chinese compatriots from Hong Kong, Macao and Taiwan.

Domestic Travel Agencies refer to travel agencies engaged in the promotion, solicitation, organization and reception of domestic tourists, and in the reception of foreigners, overseas Chinese, Chinese compatriots from Hong Kong, Macao and Taiwan organized by international travel agencies or other departments concerned, without their own promotion and solicitation programmes.

Star-Hotels refer to hotels rated with stars.

6 能　源

Energy

资料整理：李　川

6-1 规模以上工业能源生产量

OUTPUT OF ENERGY PRODUCTION OF INDUSTRY ABOVE DESGINATED SIZE

产品	单位	Item	Unit	2010	2011	2012	2013
一次能源生产量	（万吨标煤）	Primary Encrgy Output	10 000 tons standardized coal)	5330.51	4719.90	5582.98	5024.99
原煤	（万吨）	Coal	(10 000 ton)	1291.71	952.60	887.44	855.88
原油	（万吨）	Crude Oil	(10 000 ton)	86.50	88.00	78.90	80.08
天然气	（亿立方米）	Natural Gas	(100 million cu.m)	1.97	1.55	1.65	3.09
水电	（亿千瓦时）	Water and Electricity	(100 million KW/h)	1249.50	1166.72	1379.59	1175.30

注：水电采用等价值核算。

Note: The value of water use such as accounting.

6-2 规模以上工业能源消费量

ENERGY CONSUMPTION OF INDUSTRY ABOVE DESIGNATED SIZE

产品	计量单位	Item	Unit	2010	2011	2012	2013
能源消费量合计	（万吨标煤）	Total	10000 tons standardized coal）	11308.94	12328.80	12083.97	13310.45
原煤	（万吨）	Coal	（10000 ton）	7211.93	8077.16	7674.12	8270.13
洗精煤	（万吨）	Cleaned Coal	（10000 ton）	1355.22	1427.61	1340.05	1382.42
其他洗煤	（万吨）	Other Washed Coal	（10000 ton）	14.87	11.48	10.72	13.04
煤制品	（万吨）	Moulded Coal	（10000 ton）	12.65	6.88	8.69	11.35
焦炭	（万吨）	Coke	（10000 ton）	1120.83	1172.72	1113.90	1114.39
其他焦化产品	（万吨）	Other Coked Products	（10000 ton）	6.61	5.38	3.96	1.34
焦炉煤气	（亿立方米）	Coke-oven Gas	（100 million cu.m）	40.13	42.39	39.18	38.59
高炉煤气	（亿立方米）	Bblast Furnace Gas	（100 million cu.m）	334.43	360.83	344.72	345.87
其他煤气	（亿立方米）	Other Gases	（100 million cu.m）	26.38	24.47	22.80	24.04
天然气	（亿立方米）	Natural Gas	（100 million cu.m）	10.37	11.79	13.56	18.10
原油	（万吨）	Crude Oil	（10000 ton）	1022.26	1025.83	946.99	1176.30
汽油	（万吨）	Gasoline	（10000 ton）	18.36	11.65	14.62	13.48
煤油	（万吨）	Kerasene	（10000 ton）	1.49	1.02	0.93	1.08
柴油	（万吨）	Diesel Oil	（10000 ton）	47.72	45.49	48.30	49.72
燃料油	（万吨）	Fuel Oil	（10000 ton）	12.46	8.89	8.55	6.74
液化石油气	（万吨）	LPG	（10000 ton）	3.43	3.46	2.47	8.95
炼厂干气	（万吨）	Dry Gas	（10000 ton）	36.45	33.18	29.62	34.68
其他石油制品	（万吨）	Other Petroleum Products	（10000 ton）	126.13	120.50	110.13	176.62
热力	（万百万千焦）	Heat	（10 billion kilo-joule）	7053.41	7388.78	7916.47	7744.13
电力	（亿千瓦时）	Electricity	（100 million kW/h）	1032.58	1162.64	1215.06	1281.29
其他燃料	（万吨标准煤）	Other Fuels	10000 tons standardized coal）	43.09	23.52	18.20	22.97

注：能源消费量包括加工转换投入量，且为当量值。

Note: The conversion of energy consumption, including processing input, and when the money is.

6-3 规模以上工业分行业能源消费量（2013）

ENERGY CONSUMPTION OF INDUSTRY ABOVE DESGINATED SIZE(2013)

行业	Item	原煤消费量（万吨）Coal Consumption (10000 tons)	汽油消费量（万吨）Gasoline Consumption (10000tons)	柴油消费量（万吨）Diesel Consumption (10000tons)	电力消费量(亿千瓦小时) Electricity Consumption (100million
总消费量	**Total Consumption**	**8270.13**	**13.48**	**49.72**	**1281.29**
采矿业	**Mining**	**100.91**	**1.77**	**17.57**	**46.38**
煤炭开采和洗选业	Mining and Washing of Coal	41.64	0.07	0.23	3.39
石油和天然气开采业	Extraction of Petroleum and Natural Gas	13.38	0.20	1.11	9.48
黑色金属矿采选业	Mining and Processing of Ferrous Metal Ores	8.87	0.07	1.74	13.27
有色金属矿采选业	Mining and Processing of Non-Ferrous Metal Ore	0.54	0.04	0.10	3.83
非金属矿采选业	Mining and Processing of Non-metal Ores	25.23	1.12	4.47	15.33
开采辅助活动	Mining Auxiliary	11.24	0.28	9.92	1.06
其他采矿业	Mining of Other Ores	0.00	0.00	0.00	0.03
制造业	**Manufacturing**	**4289.01**	**11.46**	**31.07**	**1076.29**
农副食品加工业	Processing of Food from Agricultural Products	124.89	0.53	1.92	42.70
食品制造业	Manufacture of Foods	124.96	0.19	0.45	15.77
酒、饮料和精制茶制造业	Manufacture of Wine, Beverages and Tea	61.81	0.30	0.38	13.12
烟草制品业	Manufacture of Tobacco	1.73	0.01	0.03	1.43
纺织业	Manufacture of Textile	41.23	0.56	1.27	70.71
纺织服装、服饰业	Manufacture of Textile Wearing Apparel	8.78	0.37	0.83	7.02
皮革、毛皮、羽毛及其制品和制鞋业	Manufacture of Leather, Fur, Feather and Related and Footware	1.12	0.06	0.05	2.30
木材加工和木、竹、藤、棕、草制品业	Processing of Timber, Manufacture of Wood, Bamboo, Rattan, Palm, and Straw Products	7.60	0.08	0.46	11.67
家具制造业	Manufacture of Furniture	1.83	0.05	0.27	1.15
造纸和纸制品业	Manufacture of Paper and Paper Products	71.13	0.04	0.52	17.15
印刷和记录媒介复制业	Printing and Reproduction of Recording Media	0.74	0.22	0.07	3.04
文教、工美、体育和娱乐用品制造业	Manufacture of Articles for Culture, Education, Art, Sport and Entertainment	1.04	0.03	0.01	1.23
石油加工、炼焦和核燃料加工业	Processing of Petroleum, Coking and Nuclear Fuel	7.66	0.09	0.15	11.45
化学原料和化学制品制造业	Manufacture of Raw Chemical Materials and Chemical Products	1572.15	1.25	1.94	238.93
医药制造业	Manufacture of Medicines	126.43	0.86	1.26	19.65
化学纤维制造业	Manufacture of Chemical Fibres	27.82	0.01	0.02	3.60
橡胶和塑料制品业	Manufacture of Rubber and Plastics	25.50	0.38	0.92	24.16
非金属矿物制品业	Manufacture of Non-metal Mineral Products	1218.40	1.08	8.42	151.93
黑色金属冶炼和压延加工业	Smelting an Processing of Ferrous Metals	578.66	0.38	2.35	200.61
有色金属冶炼和压延加工业	Smelting an Processing of Non-ferrous Metals	71.03	0.08	0.91	62.60
金属制品业	Manufacture of Metal Products	31.76	0.66	1.66	28.45
通用设备制造业	Manufacture of General Purpose Machinery	14.19	0.55	1.52	18.01
专用设备制造业	Manufacture of Special Purpose Machinery	6.07	0.52	0.65	9.33
汽车制造业	Manufacture of Automobile	149.92	1.98	3.22	70.36
铁路、船舶、航空航天和其他运输设备制造业	Manufacture of Realway, Ship, Aircraft and Other Transport Equipment	0.87	0.25	0.79	6.74
电气机械和器材制造业	Manufacture of Electrical Machinery and Equipment	6.07	0.53	0.49	26.10
计算机、通信和其他电子设备制造业	Manufacture of Computers, Communication Equipment and Other Electronic Equipment	0.20	0.18	0.10	12.40
仪器仪表制造业	Manufacture of Measuring Instruments	0.26	0.09	0.06	1.41
其他制造业	Manufacture of Other Products	1.89	0.03	0.02	2.43
废弃资源综合利用业	Recycling and Disposal of Waste	1.76	0.03	0.27	0.59
金属制品、机械和设备修理业	Repairing of Metal Products and Mechanical Equipment	1.50	0.07	0.06	0.23
电力、燃气及水生产和供应业	**Electric Power, Gas and Water Production and Supply**	**3880.21**	**0.25**	**1.08**	**158.63**
电力、热力生产和供应业	Production and Supply of Electric Power and Heat Power	3880.20	0.10	0.98	150.36
燃气生产和供应业	Production and Supply of Gas	0.00	0.04	0.05	0.85
水的生产和供应业	Production and Supply of Water	0.01	0.12	0.06	7.42

6-4　全社会综合能源平衡表(等价值)
BALANCE SHEET OF DOMESTIC ENERGY (EQIVALENCE PRICE)

单位:万吨标准煤　　(10000 tons standardized coal)

项　　目	Item	2007	2008	2009	2010	2011	2012	2013
一、可供量	Quantity Available	12143	12845	13708	15138	16579	17675	18649
一次能源生产量	Primary Energy Production	4116	5336	5019	5331	4720	5583	5025
回收能	Recuperated Energy	54	424	489	336.6	448	443	443
外省(区、市)调入量	Engery moblized from other Province	10399	9863	10965	12329	13823	14057	16169
进　口　量	Import Volume							
我轮、机在外国加油量	Volume of Fuel Charged Abroad							
本省(区、市)调出量(－)	Engery moblized to other Province	2348	2711	2912	2975	1862	2049	2516
出　口　量(－)	Output Volume							
外轮、机在我国加油量(－)	Volume of Fuel Charged at Home			33				
年初年末库存差额	Storage Balance Difference between the Beginning and the End of the Year	-77	-67	181	117	-101	84	-29
年初库存量	Storage Volume at the Beginning of the Year	401	485	814	633	566	674	592
年末库存量(－)	Storage Volume by the End of the Year	478	551	633	517	667	591	621
二、消费量	Consumption	12143	12845	13708	15138	16579	17675	18649
消费量分组一	Consumption Group 1.	12142	12834	13662	15138	16579	17675	18649
1.农.林.牧.渔业	Agriculture, Forestry, Animal Husbandary, Fishing	422	438	460	436	437	464	493
2.工　　业	Industry	8574	8827	9304	10248	11331	12208	12602
3.建　筑　业	Construction	190	189	230	334	358	356	392
4.交通运输.仓储和邮政业	Transport communication, Storage, Post Service	1112	1291	1259	1330	1546	1549	1735
5.批发、零售业和住宿、餐饮业	Wholesale,Retail Sale, Hotel and Catering Industry	369	459	647	809	928	924	1014
6.其他	Others	288	291	345	433	515	595	683
7.生活消费	Living Consumption	1187	1338	1418	1466	1465	1578	1729
消费量分组二	Consumption Group 2.	12143	12845	13708	15138	16579	17675	18649
1. 终端消费	Terminal Consumption	11976	12799	13525	14628	16443	17489	18426
#工业	Industry	8411	8792	9166	9833	11195	12023	12380
2. 加工转换损失	Loss in Processing	160	38	88	129	-166	-153	-112
火力发电损失	Loss in Thermal Power Generation	1	3			0		
供热损失	Loss in Heating			1	228	239	248	266
洗选煤损失	Loss in Coal Seperation					0	0	1
炼焦损失	Loss in Coke Making	107	1	7	4	40	32	51
炼油损失	Loss in Oil Refining	23	4	71	27	0	7	10
制气损失	Loss in Gas Drying	29	30	6	27	2	2	2
煤制品加工损失	Loss in Coal Products Processing			3				1
3. 损　失　量	Loss in Processing	7	8	95	302	303	339	335
三、平衡差额	Balance							

6-5 全社会煤炭平衡表

BALANCE SHEET OF DOMESTIC COAL CONSUMPTION

单位:万吨 (10 000 tons)

项目	Item	2007	2008	2009	2010	2011	2012	2013
一、可供量	Quantity Available	10792	10196	11605	13470	15805	15799	16780
生产量	Production Capacity	1084	1205	1087	1292	953	887	856
外省(区、市)调入量	Engery moblized from other Province	9891	9189	10299	12096	15042	14810	15943
进口量	Import Volume							
本省(区、市)调出量(-)	Engery moblized to other Province							
出口量(-)	Output Volume							
年初年末库存差额	Storage Balance Difference between the Beginning and the End of the Year	-184	-198	219	82	-189	102	-18
年初库存量	Storage Volume at the Beginning of the Year	272	456	854	636	618	807	704
年末库存量(-)	Storage Volume by the End of the Year	456	654	635	554	807	704	723
二、消费量	Consumption	10792	10196	11605	13470	15805	15799	16780
消费量分组一	Consumption Group 1.	10792	10196	11605	13470	15805	15799	16780
1.农.林.牧.渔业	Agriculture, Forestry, Animal Husbandary, Fishing	89	89	121	157	213	221	232
2.工　业	Industry	9685	8983	10134	11616	13521	13764	14580
3.建 筑 业	Construction	91	98	98	133	162	128	131
4.交通运输.仓储和邮政业	Transport communication, Storage, Post Service	139	175	194	335	538	399	400
5.批发、零售业和住宿、餐饮业	Wholesale,Retail Sale, Hotel and Catering Industry	184	201	410	431	617	532	584
6.其　他	Others	61	68	77	167	244	273	315
7.生活消费	Living Consumption	543	583	546	632	512	483	538
消费量分组二	Consumption Group 2.	10792	10196	11605	13470	15805	15799	16780
1. 终端消费	Terminal Consumption	5847	5797	7196	8239	9849	10578	10841
#工业	Industry	4741	4584	5726	6385	7564	8543	8641
2. 用于加工转换	Coal Used for Processing	4944	4399	4405	5230	5957	5222	5939
火力发电	Thermal Power Generation	3480	2852	2888	3475	4077	3455	4092
供　热	Heating	310	396	334	397	443	442	475
洗煤损耗	Loss in Washing Coal		1	1		1	3	10
炼　焦	Coke Making	1118	1111	1146	1323	1421	1309	1349
制　气	Air Drying	37	38	32		15	12	12.49
型煤加工损耗	Loss in Standardlized Coal Processing			4	35		0.07	0.08
3. 损 失 量	Loss			4	1			
三、平衡差额	Balance							

6–6 全社会石油平衡表

BALANCE SHEET OF DOMESTIC PETROLEUM

单位:万吨 (10 000 tons)

项 目	Item	2007	2008	2009	2010	2011	2012	2013
一、可供量	Quantity Available	1689	1808	1668	1760	1852	1988	2198
生产量	Production Capacity	86	84	81	87	88	79	80
外省(区、市)调入量	Engery moblized from other Province	1560	1670	1590	1657	1783	1914	2138
进 口 量	Import Volume							
我轮、机在外国加油量	Volume of Fuel Charged Abroad							
本省(区、市)调出量(－)	Engery moblized to other Province				21	46	19	13
出 口 量(–)	Output Volume							
外轮、机在我国加油量(–)	Volume of Fuel Charged at Home							
年初年末库存差额	Storage Balance Difference between the Beginning and the End of the Year	44	54	20	38	27	14	-6
年初库存量	Storage Volume at the Beginning of the Year	129	90	119	109	74	43	29
年末库存量(–)	Storage Volume by the End of the Year	86	37	100	72	47	30	35
二、消费量	Consumption	1689	1808	1668	1760	1852	1988	2198
消费量分组一	Consumption Group 1.	1689	1802	1647	1760	1852	1988	2198
1.农.林.牧.渔业	Agriculture, Forestry, Animal Husbandary, Fishing	151	168	119	138	145	152	158
2.工 业	Industry	554	538	508	388	387	399	420
3.建 筑 业	Construction	62	59	85	135	138	149	162
4.交通运输.仓储和邮政业	Transport communication, Storage, Post Service	660	753	578	676	717	771	889
5.批发、零售业和住宿、餐饮业	Wholesale,Retail Sale, Hotel and Catering Industry	68	70	94	156	169	186	206
6.其他	Others	59	60	50	77	84	99	109
7.生活消费	Living Consumption	136	154	214	189	212	231	254
消费量分组二	Consumption Group 2.	1689	1808	1668	1760	1852	1988	2198
1. 终端消费	Terminal Consumption	1633	1783	1660	1702	1849	1985	2248
#工业	Industry	500	520	531	339	385	397	470
2. 加工转换损失	Coal Used for Processing	51	19	16	49	2	2	-50
火力发电	Thermal Power Generation	5	6	3	3	2	2	2
供 热	Heating	23	10	9	14	9	7	5
炼油损耗	Loss in Oil Refining	24	3	5	32	-9	-7	-56
制 气	Gas Making							
3. 损 失 量	Loss	5	6	8	9			
三、平衡差额	Balance							

6-7 全社会电力平衡表

BALANCE SHEET OF DOMESTIC ELECTRICITY

单位:亿千瓦时 (100 million kw/h)

项　目	Item	2007	2008	2009	2010	2011	2012	2013
一、可供量	Quantity Available	1561.00	1769.90	1797.77	2017.00	1572.59	1642.74	1775.43
生产量	Production Capacity	1561.00	1769.90	1797.77	2017.02	2101.67	2245.02	2235.16
火力发电	Thermal Power Generation	651.00	543.96	615.87	758.92	917.47	863.23	1053.92
水力发电、核发电、其它发电	Hydroelectricity Generation, Nuclearpower Generation, and others	910.00	1225.94	1181.90	1258.10	1184.20	1381.79	1181.24
外省(区、市)调入量	Engery moblized from other Province	115.00	76.25	228.53	262.53	250.89	310.95	293.68
进 口 量	Import Volume							
本省(区、市)调出量(-)	Engery moblized to other Province	667.00	769.91	843.26	861.72	779.97	913.23	753.41
出 口 量(-)	Output Volume							
二、消费量	Consumption	1009.00	1076.24	1183.04	1417.83	1572.59	1642.74	1775.43
消费量分组一	Consumption Group 1.	1009.00	1076.24	1183.04	1417.83	1572.59	1642.74	1775.43
1.农.林.牧.渔业	Agriculture, Forestry, Animal Husbandary, Fishing	38.00	35.84	36.84	37.23	24.05	26.85	30.24
2.工　业	Industry	728.00	772.83	829.48	1032.57	1162.83	1169.91	1242.68
3.建 筑 业	Construction	9.00	8.29	10.37	14.66	15.55	17.21	21.60
4.交通运输.仓储和邮政业	Transport communication, Storage, Post Service	12.00	10.86	12.71	20.41	25.47	29.43	34.81
5.批发、零售业和住宿、餐饮业	Wholesale,Retail Sale, Hotel and Catering Industry	37.00	44.30	51.70	56.77	63.31	71.96	79.39
6.其他	Others	44.00	43.55	62.91	61.67	70.34	81.91	95.26
7.生活消费	Living Consumption	141.00	160.57	179.03	194.52	211.04	245.47	271.45
消费量分组二	Consumption Group 2.	1009.00	1076.24	1183.04	1417.83	1572.59	1642.74	1775.43
1. 终端消费	Terminal Consumption	1009.00	1076.24	1153.06	1332.82	1481.48	1539.99	1672.42
#工业	Industry	728.00	772.83	799.50	947.56	1071.72	1067.16	1139.67
2. 输配电损失量	Distribution Loss			29.98	85.01	91.11	102.75	103.01
三、平衡差额	Balance							

6-8 分市州单位GDP能耗(2013)
UNIT GDP ENERGY CONSUMPTION OF SUB-CITY(2013)

地　区	Regions	2005年单位GDP能耗 2005 year Unit GDP energy consumption		2010年单位GDP能耗 2010year Unit GDP energy consumption		2013年单位GDP能耗 2013year Unit GDP energy consumption	
		指标值(吨标准煤/万元) Index value	"十一五"时期计划降低(±%) "Eleventh Five-Year" plan to reduce the period	指标值(吨标准煤/万元) Index value	比2005年降低(±%) Lower than in 2005	指标值(吨标准煤/万元) Index value	比2012年降低(±%) Lower than in 2012
全　省	**Total**	**1.51**	**-20**	**1.18**	**-21.67**	**0.84**	**-4.13**
武汉市	Wuhan	1.36	-20	1.06	-21.85	0.76	-3.51
黄石市	Huangshi	2.34	-20	1.83	-21.71	1.42	-6.06
十堰市	Shiyan	1.99	-20	1.59	-20.13	1.06	-5.99
宜昌市	Yichang	2.37	-20	1.87	-20.87	1.26	-5.50
襄阳市	Xiangyang	1.94	-20	1.52	-21.40	1.01	-3.77
鄂州市	Ezhou	2.57	-20	1.95	-22.83	1.25	-3.96
荆门市	Jingmen	1.91	-20	1.50	-21.15	1.03	-5.34
孝感市	Xiaogan	1.95	-20	1.51	-22.55	1.12	-5.69
荆州市	Jingzhou	1.31	-20	1.01	-21.93	0.75	-3.92
黄冈市	Huanggang	1.61	-20	1.26	-22.02	0.90	-4.03
咸宁市	Xianning	1.80	-20	1.40	-22.10	1.01	-3.72
随州市	Suizhou	1.02	-20	0.82	-20.04	0.74	-3.19
恩施州	Enshi Prefecture	1.31	-20	1.05	-20.20	0.96	-3.33
仙桃市	Xiantao	1.32	-20	1.06	-20.03	0.84	-2.75
潜江市	Qianjiang	1.98	-20	1.56	-20.91	1.10	-3.65
天门市	Tianmen	1.19	-20	0.94	-20.99	0.75	-2.77
神农架	Shennongjia	1.68	-20	1.34	-19.35	0.88	-2.48

注:2005年、2010年单位GDP能耗按2005年不变价计算,2013年单位GDP能耗按2010年不变价计算。单位GDP能耗降低率按照保留4位小数计算。
Note:The GDP energy consumptiom per unit of 2005、2010 is calculated by comparable price of 2005,The GDP energy consumptiom per unit of 2013 is calculated by comparable price of 2010。

主要统计指标解释

能源生产总量 指一定时期内，一次能源生产量的总和。该指标是观察能源生产水平、规模、构成和发展速度的总量指标。一次能源生产量包括原煤、原油、天然气、水电、核能及其他动力能(如风能、地热能等)发电量，不包括低热值燃料生产量、生物质能、太阳能等的利用和由一次能源加工转换而成的二次能源产量。

能源消费总量 指一定区域内（国家或地区）国民经济各行业和居民家庭在一定时期消费的各种能源的总和。能源消费总量分为三部分，即终端能源消费量、能源加工转换损失量和能源损失量。

(1)终端能源消费量：指一定时期内地区各行业和居民生活消费的各种能源在扣除了用于加工转换二次能源消费量和损失量以后的数量。

(2)能源加工转换损失量：指一定时期内地区投入加工转换的各种能源数量之和与产出各种能源产品之和的差额。该指标是观察能源在加工转换过程中损失量变化的指标。

(3)能源损失量：指一定时期内，能源在输送、分配、储存过程中发生的损失和由客观原因造成的各种损失量，不包括各种气体能源放空、放散量。

单位国内生产总值能耗 指一定时期内，一个国家或地区每生产一个单位的国内生产总值所消耗的能源。计算公式为：

$$\text{单位国内生产总值能耗}=\frac{\text{能源消费总量}}{\text{国内生产总值}}$$

Explanatory Notes on Main Statistical Indicators

Total Energy Production refers to the total production of primary energy by all energy producing enterprises in a given period of time. It is a comprehensive indicator to show the capacity, scale, composition and development of energy production. The production of primary energy includes that of coal, crude oil, natural gas, hydro-power and electricity generated by nuclear energy and other means such as wind power and geothermal power. However, it excludes the production of fuels of low calorific value, bio-energy, solar energy and the secondary energy converted from the primary energy.

Total Domestic Energy Consumption refers to the total consumption of energy of various kinds by material production sectors, non material production sectors and households in a given period of time. It is a comprehensive indicator to show the scale, composition and development of energy consumption. The total energy consumption includes that of coal, crude oil and their products, natural gas and electricity, However, it excludes the consumption of fuel of low calorific value, bio-energy and solar energy. Total domestic energy consumption can be divided into three parts: final energy consumption, loss during the process of energy conversion, and energy loss.

(1)Final Energy Consumption: It refers to the total energy consumption by material production sectors, non material production sectors and households in a given period of time, but excludes the consumption in conversion of the primary energy into the secondary energy and the loss in the process of energy conversion.

(2)Loss During the Process of Energy Conversion: It refers to the total input of various kinds of energy for conversion, minus the total output of various kinds of energy in a given period of time. It is an indicator to show the loss that occurs during the process of energy conversion.

(3)Energy Loss: It refers to the total of the loss of energy during the course of energy transport, distribution and storage and the loss caused by any objective reason in a given period of time. The loss of various kinds of gas due to gas discharges and stocktaking is excluded.

Energy Consumption per Unit of GDP refers to the energy consumption per unit of gross domestic production in a country or the gross region production in a region in the same reference period. The formula is:

Energy Consumption per Unit of GDP = Total Energy Consumption / Gross Domestic Production

7 财政、金融、保险

Government Finance, Banking and Insurance

资料整理：闵胜男

财政、金融、保险
GOVERNMENT FINANCE, BANKING AND INSURANCE
2013

地方公共财政收入	Local Public Financial Revenue(100 million yuan)	2191 (亿元)
地方公共财政支出	Local Public Financial Expenditure(100 million yuan)	4372 (亿元)
金融机构(含外资)人民币存款年末余额	Balance of RMB Deposits of Financial Organizations (including Foreign Funded Enterprises) By the End of the year(100 million yuan)	32636 (亿元)
#个人存款	#People's Savings Deposit	15905 (亿元)
金融机构(含外资)人民币贷款年末余额	Balance of RMB Loans of Financial Organizations (including Foreign Funded Enterprises) By the End of the year(100 million yuan)	20797 (亿元)

地方公共财政收入与地方公共财政支出(亿元)

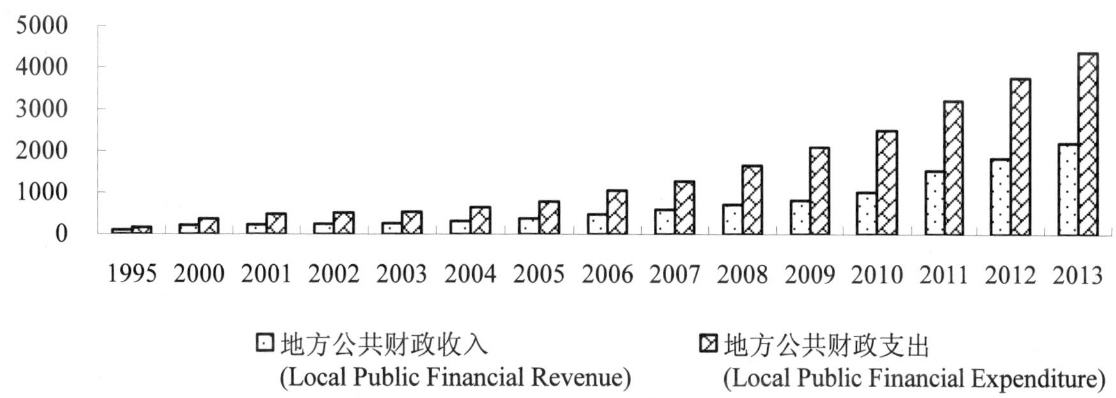

地方公共财政收入与地方公共财政支出(亿元)

Local Budgetary Revenue and Expenditure(100 million yuan)

年份(Year)	1995	2000	2002	2003	2004	2005	2006	2007	2008	2009	2010	2011	2012	2013
地方公共财政收入 (Local Public Financial Revenue)	100	214	243	260	311	376	476	590	711	815	1011	1527	1823	2191
地方公共财政支出 (Local Public Financial Expenditure)	162	369	511	540	646	779	1047	1274	1650	2091	2501	3215	3760	4372

7-1 历年地方财政收支额及指数

AMOVNT AND INDICES OF FINANCIAL REVENUE AND EXPENDITURE OVER THE YEARS

单位:亿元 (100 million yuan)

年份 Year	财政总收入 Total fiscal revenue	地方公共财政收入 Local Public Financial Revenue	地方公共财政支出 Local Public Financial Expenditure	指数(上年=100) Index (previous year=100)	
				收入 Revenue	支出 Expenditure
1952	3.81	3.81	1.96	100.0	100.0
1957	6.27	6.27	3.55	109.8	96.7
1965	11.26	11.26	6.85	97.4	105.2
1970	15.20	15.20	15.73	170.6	158.1
1975	24.05	24.05	17.52	139.5	103.9
1978	31.38	31.38	29.98	149.0	148.6
1980	34.01	34.01	26.53	107.6	94.5
1985	50.26	50.26	43.60	119.3	137.5
1990	77.85	77.85	84.82	100.8	106.1
1992	94.14	94.14	98.97	99.0	99.4
1993	115.07	115.07	114.58	122.2	115.8
1994	149.64	77.46	137.20		119.7
1995	180.57	99.69	162.43	128.7	118.4
1996	216.68	124.51	197.44	124.9	121.6
1997	246.35	139.89	223.70	112.4	113.3
1998	284.44	168.95	280.12	120.8	125.2
1999	314.91	194.44	336.46	115.1	120.1
2000	343.98	214.35	368.77	110.2	109.6
2001	374.15	231.94	484.40	108.2	131.4
2002	435.50	243.44	511.39	105.0	105.6
2003	483.90	259.76	540.44	106.7	105.7
2004	589.65	310.45	646.29	119.5	119.6
2005	727.61	375.52	778.72	121.0	120.5
2006	901.17	476.08	1047.00	126.8	134.5
2007	1115.47	590.36	1274.27	124.0	121.7
2008	1338.75	710.85	1650.28	120.4	129.5
2009	1541.55	814.87	2090.92	114.6	126.7
2010	1918.94	1011.23	2501.40	124.1	119.7
2011	2639.81	1526.91	3214.74	151.0	128.5
2012	3115.63	1823.05	3759.79	119.4	117.0
2013	3566.89	2191.22	4371.65	120.2	116.3

7-2 财政收支

FINANCIAL REVENUE AND EXPENDITURE

单位：亿元 (100 million yuan)

指标	Item	2010	2011	2012	2013
地方公共财政收入	**Local Public Financial Revenue**	**1011.23**	**1526.91**	**1823.05**	**2191.22**
#税收收入	Revenue	777.96	1067.11	1324.44	1604.85
#增值税25%	#25% Taxes on Value Added	125.57	148.36	162.39	225.68
营业税	Run Taxes	249.49	366.77	472.36	526.43
企业所得税	Enterprise Income Taxes	106.95	155.51	196.87	215.23
个人所得税	Individual Income Taxes	34.41	48.85	48.55	57.74
城市维护建设税	Taxes on City Maintenance and Construction	50.49	77.83	92.50	109.04
房产税	Real Estate Taxews	18.83	22.37	29.28	34.70
耕地占用税	Taxes on Use of Cultivated Land	56.25	50.63	69.29	80.39
地方公共财政支出	**Local Public Financial Expenditure**	**2501.40**	**3214.74**	**3759.79**	**4371.65**
1.一般公共服务	General Public Service	314.93	394.95	466.51	546.49
2.外交	Foreign Affairs				
3.国防	National Defence	2.00	2.51	2.99	4.12
4.公共安全	Public Security	166.87	188.40	204.53	227.04
5.教育	Education	366.57	488.16	732.37	690.63
6.科学技术	Science and Technology	30.09	44.19	54.39	77.21
7.文化体育与传媒	Culture, Sports and Media	36.67	47.09	62.47	72.44
8.社会保障和就业	Social Security and Employment	368.42	449.29	501.13	605.70
9.医疗卫生	Medical Care	179.13	247.30	267.99	322.08
10.节能环保	Environmental Protecction	96.31	101.11	95.63	109.72
11.城乡社区事务	Community Service in Urban and Rural Community	119.63	161.33	201.73	320.36
12.农林水事务	Water Affairs of Agriculture and Forestry	305.44	376.23	419.02	465.34
13.交通运输	Transportation	124.03	255.18	212.68	308.82
14.其他支出	Others	391.31	459.00	538.35	621.70

7-3 财政收入占地区生产总值的比重

FINANCIAL REVENUE AS PERCENTAGE TO GROSS DOMESTIC PRODUCT

年 份 Year	地方公共财政收入(亿元) Local Public Financial Revenue (100 million yuan)	地区生产总值(亿元) Gross Domestic Product (100 million yuan)	地方公共财政收入占地区生产总值的比重(%) Percentage of Local Financial Revenue to GDP (%)
1979	28.07	188.46	14.89
1980	26.53	199.38	13.31
1981	23.60	219.75	10.74
1982	25.47	241.55	10.54
1983	28.32	262.58	10.79
1984	31.72	328.22	9.66
1985	43.50	396.26	10.98
1986	58.04	442.04	13.13
1987	60.98	517.77	11.78
1988	68.66	626.52	10.96
1989	79.07	717.08	11.03
1990	84.82	824.38	10.29
1991	95.09	913.38	10.41
1992	94.14	1088.39	8.65
1993	115.07	1325.83	8.68
1994	77.46	1700.92	4.55
1995	99.69	2109.38	4.73
1996	124.51	2499.77	4.98
1997	139.89	2856.47	4.90
1998	168.95	3114.02	5.43
1999	194.44	3229.29	6.02
2000	214.35	3545.39	6.05
2001	231.94	3880.53	5.98
2002	243.44	4212.82	5.78
2003	259.76	4757.45	5.46
2004	310.45	5633.24	5.51
2005	375.52	6590.19	5.70
2006	476.08	7617.47	6.25
2007	590.36	9333.40	6.33
2008	710.85	11328.92	6.27
2009	814.87	12961.10	6.29
2010	1011.23	15967.61	6.33
2011	1526.91	19632.26	7.78
2012	1823.05	22250.45	8.19
2013	2191.22	24668.49	8.88

7-4 市州财政收入

FINANCIAL REVENUE OF CITIES AND PREFECTURE

单位：亿元 (100 million yuan)

市、州	Municipalities and Prefecrure	2003	2004	2005	2006	2007	2008	2009	2010	2011	2012	2013
全　　省	**Whole Province**	**259.76**	**310.45**	**375.52**	**476.08**	**590.36**	**710.85**	**814.87**	**1011.23**	**1526.91**	**1823.05**	**2191.22**
省　　级	Provinial Level	57.33	72.71	94.59	131.60	161.83	174.37	184.06	206.78	188.67	130.07	126.27
武汉市	Wuhan Municipality	80.44	104.02	138.82	178.60	221.68	277.32	316.07	390.19	673.26	828.58	978.52
黄石市	Huangshi Municipality	8.09	9.72	11.96	15.33	19.71	24.09	26.03	34.10	53.84	65.64	78.36
十堰市	Shiyan Municipality	8.47	10.17	11.37	13.20	15.59	19.89	25.76	43.77	66.71	76.93	73.53
荆州市	Jingzhou Municipality	13.28	13.45	12.05	12.86	15.24	18.71	22.36	27.60	44.33	56.76	71.95
宜昌市	Yichang Municipality	16.74	19.13	22.53	27.37	35.57	44.27	54.94	70.24	113.98	153.25	206.31
襄阳市	Xiangyang Municipality	16.90	17.85	18.40	20.62	24.02	30.06	37.02	51.01	97.41	139.85	191.53
鄂州市	Ezhou Municipality	3.58	3.97	4.93	6.46	8.51	10.70	13.02	15.66	26.31	33.02	38.43
荆门市	Jingmen Municipality	8.58	9.29	9.34	10.17	12.06	14.92	18.14	23.25	39.39	50.69	59.84
孝感市	Xiaogan Municipality	9.53	10.13	10.78	12.73	16.63	21.46	26.97	34.20	51.58	69.50	89.05
黄冈市	Huanggang Municipality	12.37	13.11	13.14	15.35	19.93	26.21	32.17	38.98	51.61	62.92	79.98
咸宁市	Xianning Municipality	5.68	6.40	7.43	8.71	11.10	14.33	18.14	23.34	35.56	45.82	58.71
恩施自治州	Enshi Prefecture	6.02	7.85	8.35	10.03	13.05	15.40	18.28	22.16	31.89	40.43	50.05
随州市	Suizhou Municipality	4.41	4.48	4.25	4.76	5.47	6.68	7.60	9.53	17.07	22.99	29.67
仙桃市	Xiantao Municipality	3.15	3.18	2.81	2.80	3.31	4.21	5.05	7.35	13.13	17.14	21.00
天门市	Tianmen Municipality	2.12	1.82	1.37	1.67	2.18	2.80	3.53	4.71	7.90	11.00	15.02
潜江市	Qianjiang Municipality	2.87	2.94	3.02	3.29	3.85	4.71	4.86	7.25	12.50	16.02	20.00
神农架林区	Shennongjia Forest Zone	0.18	0.25	0.42	0.50	0.60	0.73	0.87	1.10	1.77	2.44	3.00

7-5 市州财政支出

FINANCIAL EXPENDITURE OF CITIES AND PREFECTURES

单位：亿元 (100 million yuan)

市、州	Municipalities and Prefecrure	2003	2004	2005	2006	2007	2008	2009	2010	2011	2012	2013
全　　省	**Whole Province**	**540.44**	**646.29**	**778.73**	**1047**	**1274.27**	**1650.28**	**2090.92**	**2501.40**	**3214.74**	**3759.79**	**4371.65**
省　　级	Provinial Level	148.51	183.98	205.75	284.3	312.94	388.9	258.00	273.40	378.50	449.69	484.45
武汉市	Wuhan Municipality	117.78	142.62	176.88	257.81	307.23	377.88	503.64	583.55	765.04	885.55	1122.88
黄石市	Huangshi Municipality	15.26	18.34	23.47	31.43	40.90	53.06	80.85	102.56	128.69	140.43	150.79
十堰市	Shiyan Municipality	21.23	26.9	33.42	42.83	54.24	73.97	118.50	146.98	185.09	207.75	231.42
荆州市	Jingzhou Municipality	29.44	34.14	39.51	52.57	65.80	90.41	130.35	163.15	197.18	226.83	255.92
宜昌市	Yichang Municipality	34.3	38.92	47.63	62.76	79.78	105.86	156.50	196.51	241.13	297.45	364.44
襄阳市	Xiangyang Municipality	32.44	36.38	49.19	56.78	71.52	96.64	148.16	184.92	248.14	313.97	364.87
鄂州市	Ezhou Municipality	7.02	7.98	10.38	13.55	17.85	23.97	35.67	43.01	56.66	62.69	70.87
荆门市	Jingmen Municipality	16.26	19.47	24.58	29.33	38.65	49.18	81.66	95.46	125.34	142.20	158.79
孝感市	Xiaogan Municipality	23.68	26.23	32.5	41.89	54.60	74.64	109.79	133.58	172.61	201.79	227.90
黄冈市	Huanggang Municipality	31.77	37.1	44.4	57.13	76.23	104.47	155.09	188.13	225.54	278.92	305.16
咸宁市	Xianning Municipality	14.26	17.33	21.41	27.72	37.87	56.5	84.97	100.02	127.07	143.03	158.14
恩施自治州	Enshi Prefecture	22.03	26.19	32.12	41.92	54.89	71.04	102.25	129.79	160.14	179.69	216.69
随州市	Suizhou Municipality	10.33	11.45	14.11	18.08	23.10	31.73	46.11	57.23	72.32	85.55	100.04
仙桃市	Xiantao Municipality	6.4	7.44	8.29	9.81	13.30	17.03	26.25	32.91	42.34	47.71	50.08
天门市	Tianmen Municipality	4.09	5.18	6.22	8.11	10.79	15.14	23.44	28.27	38.51	41.84	46.53
潜江市	Qianjiang Municipality	4.37	5.34	6.99	8.62	11.43	15.36	23.03	28.60	37.68	42.01	46.80
神农架林区	Shennongjia Forest Zone	1.24	1.32	1.86	2.37	3.13	4.26	6.66	13.33	12.76	12.69	15.88

7-6 金融机构(含外资)人民币存款年末余额
BALANCE OF RMB DEPOSITS IN FINANCIAL ORGANIZATIONS (INCLUDING FOREIGN FUNDED ENTERPRISES) BY THE END

单位：亿元 (100 million yuan)

指 标	Item	2012	2013
各项存款	**Deposits**	**28006.36**	**32636.15**
1.单位存款	Corporate Deposits	12497.45	14569.65
其中：活期存款	Demand Deposits	6635.65	7286.91
定期存款	Time Deposits	2422.58	2997.64
通知存款	Notice Deposits	289.89	315.46
保证金存款	Margin Deposits	1503.69	1858.25
2.个人存款	Personal Deposits	13547.34	15905.45
储蓄存款	Saving Deposits	13419.72	15507.03
保证金存款	Margin Deposits	9.03	34.72
结构性存款	Structured Deposits	118.59	363.70
3.财政性存款	Public Financial Deposits	1483.72	1696.23
4.临时性存款	Temporary Deposits	42.04	42.55
5.委托存款	Entrusted Deposits	62.95	71.23
6.其他存款	Others	372.86	351.04

7-7 金融机构(含外资)人民币贷款年末余额
BALANCE OF RMB LOANS OF FINANCIAL ORGANIZTIONS (INCLUDING FOREIGN FUNDED ENTERPISES) BY THE END

单位：亿元 (100 million yuan)

指 标	Item	2012	2013
各项贷款	**Loans**	**18004.54**	**20796.86**
(一)境内贷款	**Domestil Loans**	**18001.09**	**20794.32**
1.短期贷款	Short-term Loans	6087.76	7479.38
个人贷款及透支	Individual Loans	1055.47	1424.89
单位普通贷款及透支	Commercial Loans	4291.60	5122.86
普通并购贷款	Construction Loans		
银团贷款	Agricnltural Loan	85.63	73.57
贸易融资	Loans to Township Enterprises	655.06	858.06
境外筹资转贷款	On-lending of Overseas Borrowing		
2.中长期贷款	Medium-term and Long-term Loans	11420.42	12820.21
个人贷款	Individual Loans	3122.05	3789.81
单位普通贷款	Commercial Loans	7185.25	7737.74
普通并购贷款	Construction Loans	28.07	35.13
银团贷款	Agricnltural Loan	962.84	1133.30
贸易融资	Loans to Township Enterprises	120.59	122.15
境外筹资转贷款	On-lending of Overseas Borrowing	1.62	2.08
3.融资租赁	Loans for Accomodation and Rent	170.44	190.51
4.票据融资	Bill Financing	314.55	291.65
5.各项垫款	Money Advanced Payment for Others	7.92	12.57
(二)境外贷款	**Foreign Loans**	**3.45**	**2.54**

7-8 保险业务主要指标

MAJOR INDICATORS OF INSURANCE BUSINESS

项　　目	Item	2010	2011	2012	2013
一、保险密度 (元/人)	Density of Insurance (yuan/person)	794.69	871.52	922.84	1012.94
二、保险深度 (%)	Depth of Insurance (%)	2.88	2.56	2.40	2.38
三、保费收入 (亿元)	Premium (100 million yuan)	454.88	501.82	533.31	587.40
(一)财产保险 (亿元)	Property Insurnce (100 million yuan)	98.20	114.71	135.26	169.35
1.财产险	Property Insurnce	6.74	7.04	10.13	11.04
2.机动车辆保险	Machine Driving Cars Insurnce	76.41	87.28	103.31	128.98
3.责任险	Responsibility Insurance	3.22	4.32	5.46	6.63
4.信用保证险	Credit Guarantee Insurance	1.29	3.26	4.60	8.40
5.其它	Others	10.54	12.81	11.76	14.29
(二)人身保险 (亿元)	Life Insurance (100 million yuan)	356.68	387.11	398.05	418.07
1.人身意外伤害保险	Accident Insurance	8.93	11.24	13.06	15.79
团体保险	Group Insurance	4.63	5.81	6.74	8.06
个人保险	Individual Insurance	4.30	5.43	6.32	7.73
2.健康险	Healthy Insurance	18.27	22.59	27.70	39.47
团体保险	Group Insurance	4.19	5.45	6.82	14.69
个人保险	Individual Insurance	14.08	17.14	20.88	24.78
3.寿险	Personal Insurance	329.47	353.28	357.29	362.81
团体保险	Group Insurance	1.77	1.65	3.99	1.80
个人保险	Individual Insurance	327.70	351.63	353.30	361.01
四、各项赔款和给付 (亿元)	Claim and Payment	85.05	101.09	128.55	187.61
(一)财产保险	Property Insurnce (100 million yuan)	45.13	52.92	68.34	86.32
1.财产险	Property Insurnce	1.77	3.08	3.53	4.01
2.机动车辆保险	Machine Driving Cars Insurnce	35.28	42.86	56.10	71.60
3.责任险	Responsibility Insurance	1.34	2.07	2.42	3.00
4.信用保证险	Credit Guarantee Insurance	0.17	0.60	0.46	0.50
5.其它	Others	6.57	4.31	5.83	7.21
(二)人身保险 (亿元)	Life Insurance (100 million yuan)	39.92	48.17	60.21	101.28
1.人身意外伤害保险	Accident Insurance	2.19	2.68	3.42	3.93
团体保险	Group Insurance	0.81	1.02	1.43	1.61
个人保险	Individual Insurance	1.38	1.66	1.99	2.32
2.健康险	Healthy Insurance	7.42	9.57	10.29	14.43
团体保险	Group Insurance	3.29	3.56	4.47	7.49
个人保险	Individual Insurance	4.13	6.01	5.82	6.94
3.寿险	Personal Insurance	30.31	35.93	46.50	82.92
团体保险	Group Insurance	5.70	6.56	7.57	7.69
个人保险	Individual Insurance	24.61	29.37	38.93	75.23

注：本表采用数据均为保险业新口径数据。

Note:Data from this table are based on the new standard.

主要统计指标解释

财政总收入 指地方一般预算收入与上划中央税收收入之和。

公共财政收入 是指各级政府为履行职能，按照国家法律、法规规定收取的纳入一般预算管理的各项税收及非税收入总和。主要包括：

（1）各项税收：包括国内增值税、国内消费税、进口货物增值税和消费税、出口货物退增值税和消费税、营业税、企业所得税、个人所得税、资源税、城市维护建设税、房产税、印花税、城镇土地使用税、土地增值税、车船税、船舶吨税、车辆购置税、关税、耕地占用税、契税、烟叶税等。

（2）非税收入：包括专项收入、行政事业性收费、罚没收入和其他收入。

公共财政支出 国家财政将筹集起来的资金进行分配使用，以满足经济建设和各项事业的需要。主要包括：

（1）一般公共服务：指政府提供基本公共管理与服务的支出，包括人大事务、政协事务、政府办公厅（室）及相关机构事务、发展与改革事务、统计信息事务、财政事务、税收事务、审计事务、海关事务、人力资源事务、纪检监察事务、人口与计划生育事务、商贸事务、知识产权事务、工商行政管理事务、国土资源事务、海洋管理事务、测绘事务、地震事务、气象事务、民族事务、宗教事务、港澳台侨事务、档案事务、共产党事务、民主党派事务及工商联事务、群众团体事务、彩票事务等。

（2）外交：指政府外交事务支出，包括外交行政管理、驻外机构、对外援助、国际组织、对外合作与交流、边界勘界联检等方面的支出。

（3）国防：指政府用于国防方面的支出，包括用于现役部队、预备役部队、民兵、国防科研事业、专项工程、国防动员等方面的支出。

（4）公共安全：指政府维护社会公共安全方面的支出，包括武装警察、公安、国家安全、检察、法院、司法行政、监狱、劳教、国家保密、缉私警察等。

（5）教育：指政府教育事务支出，包括教育行政管理、学前教育、小学教育、初中教育、普通高中教育、普通高等教育、初等职业教育、中专教育、技校教育、职业高中教育、高等职业教育、广播电视教育、留学生教育、特殊教育、干部继续教育、教育机关服务等。

（6）科学技术：指用于科学技术方面的支出，包括科学技术管理事务、基础研究、应用研究、技术研究与开发、科技条件与服务、社会科学、科学技术普及、科技交流与合作等。

（7）文化教育与传媒：指政府在文化、文物、体育、广播影视、新闻出版等方面的支出。

（8）社会保障和就业：指政府在社会保障与就业方面的支出，包括社会保障和就业管理事务、民政管理事务、财政对社会保险基金的补助、补充全国社会保障基金、行政事业单位离退休、企业改革补助、就业补助、抚恤、退役安置、社会福利、残疾人事业、城市居民最低生活保障、其他城镇社会救济、农村社会救济、自然灾害生活救助、红十字事务等。

（9）医疗卫生：指政府医疗卫生方面的支出，包括医疗卫生管理事务支出、医疗服务支出、医疗保障支出、疾病预防控制支出、卫生监督支出、妇幼保健支出、农村卫生支出等。

（10）节能环保：指政府环境保护支出，包括环境保护管理事务支出、环境监测与监察支出、污染治理支出、自然生态保护支出、天然林保护工程支出、退耕还林支出、风沙荒漠治理支出、退牧还草支出、已垦草原退耕还草、能源节约利用、污染减排、可再生能源和资源综合利用等支出。

（11）城乡社区事务：指政府城乡社区事务支出，包括城乡社区管理事务支出、城乡社区规划与管理支出、城乡社区公共设施支出、城乡社区住宅支出、城乡社区环境卫生支出、建设市场管理与监督支出等。

（12）农林水事务：指政府农林水事务支出，包括农业支出、林业支出、水利支出、扶贫支出、农业综合开发支出等。

（13）交通运输：指政府交通运输和邮政业方面的支出，包括公路运输支出、水路运输支出、铁路运输支出、民用航空运输支出、邮政业支出等。

信贷资金 指金融机构以信用方式积聚和分配的货币资金。金融机构信贷资金的来源有各项存款、金融债券发行、应付及暂收款、对国际金融机构负债、流通中货币、各项准备、所有者权益和其他项目等；信贷资金的运用有各项贷款、有价证券及投资、应收及预付款、委托投资、金银占款、外汇占款、库存现金、财政借款及在国际金融机构中的资产等。

存款 指企业、机关、团体或居民根据资金必须收回的原则，把货币资金存入银行或其他信贷机构保管并取得一定利息的一种信用活动形式。根据存款对象或性质的不同可划分为企业存款、财政存款、机关团体存款、基本建设存款、储蓄存款、农村存款、委托存款、其他存款等科目。它是银行信贷资金的主要来源。

贷款 指银行或其他信贷机构根据资金必须归还的原则，按一定利率，为企业、个人等提供资金的一种信用活动形式。我国银行贷款分为短期贷款、中期流动资金贷款、中长期贷款、信托贷款、融资租赁、委托贷款、票据融资、各项垫款等。

保险公司 在中国境内的、经过保险监督管理部门批准设立，并依法登记注册的各类商业保险公司。

保险金额 指保险人承担赔偿或者给付保险金责任的最高限额。

保费 指投保人为取得保险人在约定范围内所承担赔偿责任而支付给保险人的费用。

赔款 指保险人根据保险合同的规定，向被保险人支付的赔偿保险责任损失的金额。

给付 包括死伤医疗给付和满期给付。死伤医疗给付是指保险人根据人寿保险及长期健康保险合同的规定，因被保险人在保险期内发生保险责任范围内的保险事故支付给被保险人(或受益人)的金额。满期给付是指被保险人生存期满，保险人按人寿保险合同规定支付给被保险人的满期保险金额。

Explanatory Notes on Main Statistical Indicators

Total income refers to the local fiscal revenue and the general budget tax revenue and central planning.

Public Financial revenue is to perform its functions in accordance with national laws and regulations collected into the general budget of the revenue management and non-tax revenues combined.

Public Financial Expenditure refers to the distribution and use of the funds the government finances has risen, so as to meet the needs of economic construction and various causes. It includes the following main items:

(1) Expenditure for general public services: It refers to the spending on the basic public management and services which provided by governments, including the expense on affairs of People's Congress, affairs of People's Political Consultative Conference, affairs of government general office and relative institutions, affairs of development and reform, affairs of statistics, affairs of finance, affairs of taxation, affairs of audit, affairs of customs, affairs of human resources and social security, affairs of discipline inspection and supervision, affairs of population and family planning, affairs of commerce and trade, affairs of intellectual property, affairs of administration for industry and commerce, affairs of land and resources, affairs of oceanic administration, affairs of surveying and mapping, affairs of earthquake, ethnic affairs, religious affairs, affairs of Hong Kong, Macao, Taiwan, and Overseas Chinese, affairs of archives administration, affairs of Chinese Communist Party, affairs of democratic parties and federation of industry and commerce, affairs of mass organization, and affairs of lottery, etc.

(2) Expenditure for foreign affairs: It refers to the spending of government on foreign affairs, including the expense on administration of foreign affairs, missions overseas, external assistance, international organizations, foreign cooperation and

communication, surveying and joint inspection on borderline, etc.

(3) Expenditure for national defence: It refers to the spending of government on national defence, including the expense on active force, reserve force, militia, scientific research on national defence, special projects, mobilization of national defence, etc.

(4) Expenditure for public security: It refers to the spending of government on maintaining social and public security, including the expense on armed police force, public security, state security, prosecution, courts, justice, prison, labour education and rehabilitation, protection of state secrecy, anti-smuggling police, etc.

(5) Expenditure for education: It refers to the spending of government on education, including the expense on the administration of education, pre-primary education, primary education, secondary education, high school education, regular higher education, primary vocational education, secondary vocational education, technical school education, vocational high school education and higher vocational education, radio and television education, student abroad education, special education, on the job training of cadres, education authorities services, etc.

(6) Expenditure for science and technology: It refers to the spending of government on science and technology (S&T), including the expense on the administration of S&T, basic research, applied research, research and development, conditions and services of S&T, popularization of social science, science and technology, exchanges and cooperation of S&T, etc.

(7) Expenditure for culture, sport and media: It refers to the spending of government on culture, cultural heritage, sports, radio, film, television, press and publication, etc.

(8) Expenditure for social safety net and employment effort: It refers to the spending of government on social safety net and employment, including the expense on administration of social safety net and employment, civil affairs, budgetary subsidy on the social insurance funds, subsidy on National Social Security Fund, retirees of administrative units and institutions, subsidy on enterprise reform, subsidy on employment effort, pension, placement of ex-serviceman, social welfare, the handicapped undertakings, the system of cost of living allowances for urban residents, other urban social relief, rural social relief, living relief of natural disasters, affairs of Red Cross Society, etc.

(9) Expenditure for medical and health care: It refers to the spending of government on medical and health care, including the expense on administration of medical and health care, medical services, health care, disease prevention and control, health inspection and supervision, women and children's health, rural health care, etc.

(10) Expenditure for environment protection: It refers to the spending of government on environment protection, including the expense on administration of environment protection, environment monitoring and supervision, pollution control, natural ecology protection, project of virgin forests protection, reforesting farmland, controlling the sources of dust storms, returning pastureland to grassland, returning pastureland to grassland, returning cultivated land to grassland, energy conservation, emissions reduction, comprehensive utilization of renewable energy and resources, etc.

(11) Expenditure for urban and rural community affairs: It refers to the spending of government on urban and rural community affairs, including the expense on administration of urban and rural community, planning and management of urban and rural community, public facilities of urban and rural community, housing of urban and rural community, sanitation of urban and rural community, management and supervision on the construction market, etc.

(12) Expenditure for agriculture, forestry and water conservancy: It refers to the spending of government on agriculture, forestry

and water conservancy, including the expense on agriculture, forestry, water conservancy, poverty alleviation, comprehensive agricultural development, etc.

(13) Expenditure for transportation: It refers to the spending of government on transportation and postal services, including the expense on road transportation, waterway transportation, railway transportation, civil aviation transportation, and postal services.

Credit Funds refer to the funds issued as loans by banking institutions. The sources of credit funds of the banking institutions included deposits, issue of financial bonds, account-payable and temporary gathering, liabilities to international financial institutions, currency in circulation, various reserves, owners' rights and interests and other items. The credit funds can be used in forms of loans, securities and investment, account receivable and advance payment, entrusted investment, gold, foreign exchange, cash on hand, government debt and assets in the international financial institutions.

Deposit is a form of credit by which enterprises, institutions, organizations or households can put money into banks and other credit institutions for safekeeping and interest earning under the principle of free withdrawal. According to different depositors, deposits are divided into enterprise deposits, treasury deposits, deposits of government agencies and organizations, capital construction deposits, savings deposits, rural saving deposits, entrusted deposits and other deposits. Deposits are major sources of the credit funds of banks.

Loan is a form of credit by which banks and other credit institutions provide funds at certain interest rate to enterprises and individuals in the light of the principle of unconditional repayment. Loans from Chinese banks include circulating capital loans, fixed assets loans, loans to urban and rural individuals engaged in industrial and commercial business and agricultural loans.

Insurance Companies refer to commercial insurance companies of various forms registered by law and established in China with the approval of insurance regulatory agencies.

Amount Insured refers to the maximum that the insurant will get for the claim of the case insured.

Premium is the fee paid by the insurant to the insurer to obtain the obligation of compensation from the insurance within the agreed terms.

Settled Claim is the compensation paid by the insurer to the insurant in accordance with the insurance contract.

Payment includes payment for death, injury or medical treatment and mature payment. Payment for death, injury or medical treatment refers to the money paid to the insurant (or the beneficiary) in accordance with the life or health insurance contract when the insurant encounters accidents within the insured period covered in the contract. Mature payment refers to the mature payment to the insurant in accordance with the life insurance contract at the end of the insured period.

8 价格

Price

资料整理：文 峰 余 南 刘凯军

8-1　物　价　总　指　数（2013）
GENERAL PRICE INDICES(2013)

基　期	Base Period	商品零售价格总指数 General Rtail Price Index	居民消费价格总指数 General Consumption Price Index
以1950年价格为100	The Price of 1950 Equals 100	649.6	995.0
以1952年价格为100	The Price of 1952 Equals 100	576.0	875.3
以1957年价格为100	The Price of 1957 Equals 100	521.5	775.9
以1965年价格为100	The Price of 1965 Equals 100	467.3	682.7
以1970年价格为100	The Price of 1970 Equals 100	471.0	685.2
以1975年价格为100	The Price of 1975 Equals 100	471.6	678.5
以1978年价格为100	The Price of 1978 Equals 100	467.9	676.0
以1980年价格为100	The Price of 1980 Equals 100	441.1	617.2
以1985年价格为100	The Price of 1985 Equals 100	384.6	518.9
以1990年价格为100	The Price of 1990 Equals 100	238.6	327.2
以1995年价格为100	The Price of 1995 Equals 100	127.8	153.9
以2000年价格为100	The Price of 2000 Equals 100	130.1	143.3
以2005年价格为100	The Price of 2005 Equals 100	125.5	129.9
以2010年价格为100	The Price of 2010 Equals 100	110.2	111.9
以上年价格为100	The Price of Last Year Equals 100	101.8	102.8

8-2　各市、县物价指数(2013)
GENERAL PRICE INDICES(2013)

(上年=100) (preceding year = 100)

地　区	Region	居民消费价格指数 Consumer Price Index	商品零售价格指数 Retail Price Index	农业生产资料价格指数 Agricultural Production Material Price Index
湖北省	**Hubei Province**	**102.8**	**101.8**	**103.1**
武汉市	Wuhan Municipality	102.4	100.9	
黄石市	Huangshi Municipality	102.5	101.1	
十堰市	Shiyan Municipality	103.4	102.8	
竹山县	zhushan county	104.1	103.6	106.4
宜昌市	Yichang Municipality	103.3	101.7	
宜都市	Yidu Municipality	103.3	102.4	99.5
襄阳市	Xiangyang Municipality	102.9	102.2	
老河口市	Laohekou Municipality	103.7	102.7	100.7
鄂州市	Ezhou Municipality	102.7	101.9	
荆门市	Jingmen Municipality	103.2	102.8	
孝感市	Xiaogan Municipality	103.1	102.7	
大悟县	Dawu county	102.1	101.6	101.0
荆州市	Jingzhou Municipality	103.1	102.0	
洪湖市	Honghu Municipality	103.3	102.8	99.3
黄冈市		102.8	102.3	
浠水县	Xishui Municipality	103.8	102.5	103.1
麻城市	Macheng Municipality	103.3	102.3	104.4
咸宁市	Xianning Municipality	102.8	102.2	100.8
崇阳县	Chongyang County	103.1	102.4	100.0
恩施市	Enshi Municipality	102.3	101.1	99.7
随州市	Suizhou Municipality	102.5	101.5	
天门市	Tianmen Municipality	102.3	101.0	103.9

8-3 全省居民消费、商品零售价格分类指数(2013)

RETAIL PRICE INDICES BY CATEGORY OF COMMODITIES(2013)

(上年=100) (preceding year=100)

类别	Item	全省 Provincial Indices	城市 Urban Indices	农村 Rural Indices
居民消费价格总指数	**General Consumer Price Index**	**102.8**	**102.7**	**103.0**
*服务项目价格指数	Service Price Index	102.9	102.8	103.3
一、食品	Foods	104.9	104.5	105.7
二、烟酒及用品	Tobacco,Liquor and Articles	100.5	100.4	100.7
三、衣着	Clothing	102.2	102.5	101.5
四、家庭设备用品及维修服务	Household Facilities and Articles	101.9	102.1	101.5
五、医疗保健和个人用品	Medicine and Medical Articles	102.1	102.0	102.3
六、交通和通讯	Transportation and Communication	99.4	99.1	100.0
七、娱乐教育文化用品及服务	Receation, Education and Culture Articles and Services	101.5	101.3	101.8
八、居住	Housing Condition	103.1	103.4	102.5
商品零售价格总指数	**General Price Index**	**101.8**	**101.6**	**102.1**
一、食品	Foods	105.2	104.8	105.7
二、饮料、烟酒	Beverage, Tobacco and Liquor	101.2	100.8	101.7
三、服装、鞋帽	Garments, Shoes and Hats	101.7	102.2	101.1
四、纺织品	Texiles	102.3	103.3	101.1
五、家用电器及音像器材	Household Electric Appliance and Stereo	97.9	96.7	99.4
六、文化办公用品	Stationery and Business Articles	99.1	98.2	100.5
七、日用品	Daily Use Articles	101.0	101.1	100.9
八、体育娱乐用品	Sports and Receation Articles	100.5	100.6	100.4
九、交通、通信用品	Transportation and Communication Articles	93.5	92.9	94.2
十、家具	Furniture	100.8	101.7	99.5
十一、化妆品	Cosmetics	102.0	102.2	101.8
十二、金银珠宝	Gold, Silver and Pearls Jewelery	92.3	91.6	93.0
十三、中西药品及医疗保健用品	Chinese Traditional Medicine, Western Medicines and Health Care Appliances	102.7	102.8	102.6
十四、书报杂志及电子出版物	Books, Newspaper, Magzines and Electronic Publications	101.7	100.5	103.5
十五、燃料类	Fuels	100.5	100.6	100.4
十六、建筑材料及五金电料	Building and Decoration Materials	101.3	101.9	100.6
农业生产资料价格指数	**General Price Index of Means of Agricultural Production**	**103.1**		**103.1**

8-4 工业生产者出厂价格指数

EX-FACTORY PRICE INDICES OF INDUSTRIAL PRODUCTS

分 类	Group Name	上年=100 preceding year=100	1990年=100 1990=100	
		2013	2012	2013
总指数	General Indices	99.20	283.23	280.96
一、按轻重工业分	Grouped by Light Industry and Heavy Industry			
1.轻工业	Light Industry	101.60	222.02	225.57
以农产品为原料	Using Farm Products as Raw Material	101.80	253.17	257.73
以非农产品为原料	Using Non-Farm Products as Raw Material	101.00	147.20	148.67
2.重工业	Heavy Industry	98.30	339.33	333.56
采 掘	Mining and Quarrying	96.50	769.75	742.81
原 料	Raw Material	97.60	510.13	497.89
加 工	Processing	98.80	197.66	195.29
二、按两大部类分	Grouped by Two Sectors			
1.生产资料	Means of Production	98.10	331.38	325.08
采 掘	Mining and Quarrying	96.50	769.13	742.21
原 料	Raw Material	97.50	420.52	410.01
加 工	Processing	98.60	208.51	205.59
2.生活资料	Consumer Goods	101.70	200.58	203.99
食 品	Foods	102.00	269.91	275.31
衣 着	Clothing	105.30	214.28	225.64
一般日用品	Daily Use Articles	99.00	196.71	194.74
耐用消费品	Durable Consumer Goods	102.00	61.30	62.53

8–5 原材料、燃料、动力购进价格指数

RAW MATERIAL, FUEL, POWER PURCHASE PRICE INDICES

分类	Group Name	上年=100 preceding year=100	1990年=100 1990=100	
		2013	2012	2013
总指数	General Index	98.20	432.01	424.23
燃料、动力类	Fuel Powers	97.50	716.94	699.02
黑色金属材料类	Ferrous Metal	94.50	336.77	318.25
有色金属材料类	Non-ferrous Metal	95.50	349.02	333.31
化工原材料类	Chemical Materials	95.60	231.52	221.33
木材及纸浆类	Timber and Pulp	100.00	184.23	184.23
建筑材料及非金属矿类	Construction Materials and Non-Metal Mining Industry	99.40	326.80	324.84
其它工业原材料及半成品类	Other Industrial Raw Materials and Semi-Finished Products	100.80	191.76	193.29
农副产品类	Farm and Sideline Products	105.40	399.19	420.75
纺织原料类	Textile Raw Materials	101.50	210.12	213.27

8–6 固定资产投资价格指数

PRICE INDICES OF INVESTMENT IN FIXED ASSETS

分类	Name of Group	上年=100 preceding year=100	1990年=100 1990=100
		2013	2013
总指数	Total Indices	100.5	290.5
建筑安装工程	Construction and Installation	100.5	328.4
设备、工器具	Equipment and Devices	99.0	178.8
其他费用	Others	102.6	359.4

主要统计指标解释

居民消费价格指数　是反映一定时期内城乡居民所购买的生活消费品价格和服务项目价格变动趋势和程度的相对数，是对城市居民消费价格指数和农村居民消费价格指数进行综合汇总计算的结果。该指数可以观察和分析消费品的零售价格和服务价格变动对城乡居民实际生活费支出的影响程度。

城市居民消费价格指数　是反映一定时期内城市居民家庭所购买的生活消费品价格和服务项目价格变动趋势和程度的相对数。该指数可以观察和分析消费品的零售价格和服务项目价格变动对城镇职工货币工资的影响，作为研究职工生活和确定工资政策的依据。

农村居民消费价格指数　是反映一定时期内农村居民家庭所购买的生活消费品价格和服务项目价格变动趋势和程度的相对数。该指数可以观察农村消费品的零售价格和服务项目价格变动对农村居民生活消费支出的影响，直接反映农民生活水平的实际变化情况，为分析和研究农村居民生活问题提供依据。

商品零售价格指数　是反映一定时期内城乡商品零售价格变动趋势和程度的相对数。商品零售价格的变动直接影响到城乡居民的生活支出和国家的财政收入，影响居民购买力和市场供需的平衡，影响到消费与积累的比例关系。因此，该指数可以从一个侧面对上述经济活动进行观察和分析。

农业生产资料价格指数　指反映一定时期内农业生产资料价格变动趋势和程度的相对数。农业生产资料价格指数分为小农具、饲料、产品畜、役畜、半机械化农具、机械化农具、化学肥料、农药及农药械、农机用油、其他农业生产资料十大类。其编制目的是了解农业生产中物质资料投入价格的变动状况，服务于国民经济核算。1994 年以前，农业生产资料价格指数仅仅是商品零售价格指数的一个类别，此后，从商品零售价格指数中分离出来，单独编制。

农产品生产价格指数　是反映一定时期内，农产品生产者出售农产品价格水平变动趋势及幅度的相对数。该指数可以客观反映全国农产品生产价格水平和结构变动情况，满足农业与国民经济核算需要。其中某代表品生产价格指数是通过对全部有出售该产品行为的调查单位的个体指数进行几何平均求得的，类价格指数是通过对其所属的类（或代表品）的价格指数进行加权平均求得的。季度累计价格指数的计算方法与分季指数的计算方法相同。

工业生产者出厂价格指数　是反映一定时期内全部工业产品出厂价格总水平的变动趋势和程度的相对数，包括工业企业售给本企业以外所有单位的各种产品和直接售给居民用于生活消费的产品。该指数可以观察出厂价格变动对工业总产值及增加值的影响。

工业生产者购进价格指数　是反映工业企业作为生产投入，而从物资交易市场和能源、原材料生产企业购买原材料、燃料和动力产品时，所支付的价格水平变动趋势和程度的统计指标，是扣除工业企业物质消耗成本中的价格变动影响的重要依据。

目前，我国编制的原材料、燃料和动力购进价格指数所调查的产品包括燃料动力、黑色金属、有色金属、化工、建材等九大类的近 1800 种产品。

固定资产投资价格指数　是反映一定时期内固定资产投资品及项目的价格变动趋势和程度的相对数。固定资产投资额是由建筑安装工程投资完成额、设备工器具购置投资完成额和其他费用投资完成额三部分组成的。编制固定资产投资价格指数应首先分别编制上述三部分投资的价格指数，然后采用加权算术平均法求出固定资产投资价格总指数。

该指数可以准确地反映固定资产投资中涉及的各类投资品和取费项目价格变动趋势和变动幅度，消除按现价计算的固定资产投资指标中的价格变动因素，真实地反映固定资产投资的规模、速度、结构和效益，为国家科学地制定、检查固定资产投资计划并提高宏观调控水平，为完善国民经济核算体系提供科学的、可靠的依据。

房地产价格指数　是反映一定时期内房地产价格变动趋势和程度的相对数，包括房屋销售价格指数、房屋租赁价格指数、土地交易价格指数和物业管理价格指数。这四套指数的计算方法相似，均采用由下到上逐级汇总的方法。

Explanatory Notes on Main Statistical Indicators

Urban Consumer Price Indices reflect the trend and degree of changes in prices of consumer goods and services purchased by urban households during a given period. It can be used to observe and analyze the impact of price changes in consumer goods and services on wages (in monetary terms) of urban staff and workers, and provide basis for policy-making concerning the living cost and wages of staff and workers.

Rural Consumer Price Indices reflect the trend and degree of changes in prices of consumer goods and services purchased by rural households during a given period. It can be used to observe the impact of change in retail prices of consumer goods and service prices in rural areas on living expenditure of rural households, and to show the changes in the living standard of peasants. It provides basis for analysis and research on condition of life in rural areas.

Retail Price Indices reflect the trend and degree of change in retail prices of commodities during a given period. The change in retail prices of commodities directly affect the living expenditure of urban and rural residents, government revenue, purchasing power of residents and the equilibrium of market supply and demand, and the ratio of consumption to accumulation. Therefore, the retail price indices are useful to analyze the changes of the above economic activities.

Price Indices of Means of Agricultural Production reflect the trend and degree of changes in prices of means of agricultural production during a given period. Price indices of means of agricultural production are composed of 10 categories including small farm tools, feeds, domestic animals for meat, draught domestic animals, semi-mechanized farm machinery, mechanized farm machinery, chemical fertilizers, pesticides and spraying machinery, fuels for farm machinery and other means of agricultural production. Compilation of these indices helps to understand the changes in prices of input into agricultural production and facilitate the compilation of national account statistics. Before 1994, price indices of means of agricultural production was a sub-category in the in the retail price indices of commodities, and it has been compiled separately since 1994.

Indices of Producers' Prices for Farm Products reflect the trend and degree of changes in producers' prices received by farmers when they sell farm products during a given period. These indices depict the change in the level and structure of producers' prices of farm products of the country and meet the needs of agriculture statistics and national account statistics. The producers' price index of a given product is calculated through geometrical mean of individual indices of all surveyed units who sell such product, and the indices of a product category is obtained through weighted mean of price indices of all products in the category. Method for calculating accumulative quarterly indices is the same as for calculating the distinctive quarterly indices.

Ex-factory Price Indices of Industrial Products reflect the trend and degree of changes in general ex-factory prices of all industrial products during a given period, including sales of industrial products by an industrial enterprise to all units outside the enterprise, as well as sales of consumer goods to residents. It can be used to analyze the impact of ex-factory prices on gross output value and value-added of the industrial sector.

Indices of Purchasing Prices of Raw Materials, Fuels and Power reflect changes in the level and degree of prices paid by industrial enterprises when they purchase production input such as raw materials, fuels and power from the market or from other energy or raw materials producing enterprises. These indices provide important basis for measuring the material consumption of industrial enterprises after removing influence of price changes.

At present, close to 1,800 products in 9 categories, including fuels and power, ferrous metals, non-ferrous metals, chemicals, building materials, are covered in China for the survey to produce indices of purchasing prices of raw materials, fuels and power.

Price Indices of Investment in Fixed Assets reflect the trend and degree of changes in prices of investment goods and projects in fixed assets during a given period. The investment in fixed assets consists of three components, namely the investment in construction and installation, the investment in purchases of equipment and instrument, and the investment in other items. Price indices of investment in fixed assets are calculated as the weighted arithmetic mean of the price indices of the three components of investment in fixed assets.

Removing the factor of price change in the aggregates of investment at current prices, this indicator shows the changes in the prices of commodities and fees involved in the investment of fixed assets, and can be used to observe the actual size, growth, structure, and efficiency of investment in fixed assets and provides reliable and scientific data for government planning, management, decision-making, and further improving the current national accounting system.

Price Indices for Real Estate reflect the trend and degree of changes in prices of real estate during a given period, including price indices for selling houses and buildings, price indices for leasing houses and buildings and price indices for land transaction. The methods for the compilation of the three sets of indices are similar in that they all use bottom-up approach under which data are reported from lower level to higher level.

9 居民生活

People's Livelihood

资料整理：徐　菁　王　楠
王　道　闵胜男

9-1 居民生活水平情况
PEOPLE'S LIVING STANDARD

项　　目	Item	单位	unit	2000	2005	2010	2011	2012	2013
一、城乡就业	Employment								
每一农村劳动力负担人数	Average Person Supported by a Rural Laborer	人	person	1.49	1.34	1.27	1.27	1.28	1.31
每一城镇就业者负担人数	Average Person Supported by a Urban Laborer	人	person	1.73	1.96	2.01	1.97	1.95	1.81
城镇登记失业率	The Rate of Registered Unemployment	%	percentage	3.50	4.33	4.18	4.10	3.83	3.49
二、城乡居民收入	Revenue								
农村居民人均纯收入	Net Income of Rural Residents Per Capita	元	yuan	2267.00	3099.00	5832.00	6898.00	7852.00	8866.95
农村居民人均纯收入指数(1990=100)	Indices of Net Income of Rural Residents Per Capita (1990=100)	%	percentage	338.20	461.80	869.24	1028.31	1170.22	1321.48
城镇居民人均可支配收入	Annual Disposable Income of Urban Residents	元	yuan	5525.00	8786.00	16058.00	18374.00	20839.59	22906.42
城镇居民人均可支配收入指数(1990=100)	Indices of Net Annual Disposable Income of Urban Residents (1990=100)	%	percentage	387.10	615.80	1125.45	1287.41	1459.92	1604.71
国有职工平均工资	Average Wages of Staff and Workers in State-Owned Units	元	yuan	7989	14774	35981	40345	43438	46126
三、城乡居民人平消费水平	Consumption Level								
农村居民	Rural Residents	元	yuan	1302	2503	4758	5653	6705	7755
城镇居民	Urban Residents	元	yuan	6250	8051	13576	15935	17296	19156
四、储　蓄	Savings								
城乡居民人平储蓄存款余额	Balance of Saving Deposits of Rural and Urban Residents Per Capita	元	yuan	3209	7929	17216	19879	23589	27475
五、平均每人居住面积	Floor Area of Housing Per Capita								
城　市(大、中)	Municipalities (Large and Medium-sized)	平方米	sq.m	13.90	29.90	33.20	35.50	35.79	38.82
农　村	Rural Areas	平方米	sq.m	30.11	36.05	40.99	44.24	44.98	41.84
六、交　通	Transportations								
城镇每百户拥有汽车		辆	set			5.53	9.69	12.48	13.28
七、文　化	Culture								
每百人每天有报纸	Newspaper Owned Per 100 Persons Every Day	份	unit	6.17	8.89	8.70	9.53	9.77	9.36
每人每年有图书、杂志	Books and Magazines Owned Per Capita Anuually	册	unit	8.54	8.99	9.90	9.74	10.40	9.87
八、教　育	Education								
学龄儿童入学率	Emrollment Ratio of School-Age Children	%	percentsge	99.53	99.65	99.96	99.96	99.97	99.98
每万人口有大学生数	Number of University Students Per 10000 Persons	人	person	57.49	167.91	226.58	232.77	239.85	245.12
九、卫　生	Health Care								
每千人有医院病床数	Number of Hospital-Beds Owned By Per 1000 Person	张	unit	2.18	2.31	3.26	3.89	4.10	4.60
每千人有医生	Number of Doctors Owned By Per 1000 Persons	人	person	1.74	1.49	1.62	1.67	1.77	1.90

注：平均每人居住面积中，城市(大、中)从2002年起为建筑面积，以前年份为居住面积。
Notes: Of Average Housing Areas, it refers to Construction Area of Municipalities (large and medium-sized)areas.since 2002, before2002, it refers to living areas.

9–2 居民消费水平
PEOPLE'S CONSUMPTION LEVEL

年 份 year	居民消费 (亿元) People's Censurption (100 million yuan)	农村居民 rural residernts	城镇居民 wrban residernts	居民消费水平 (元) level of consumption	农村居民 rural residernts	城镇居民 wrban residernts
1981	106.26	72.84	33.42	225	184	440
1982	126.75	90.67	36.08	266	227	462
1983	141.49	101.17	40.32	293	251	502
1984	172.19	120.41	51.78	352	300	592
1985	203.23	129.78	73.45	411	328	738
1986	247.13	158.31	88.82	493	402	825
1987	271.22	172.47	98.75	533	434	891
1988	328.82	204.21	124.61	638	509	1092
1989	398.09	255.09	143.00	762	630	1218
1990	434.62	273.27	161.35	813	659	1341
1991	475.85	286.08	189.77	869	674	1541
1992	546.61	301.60	245.01	986	706	1926
1993	694.49	357.10	337.35	1236	831	2554
1994	845.14	413.40	431.75	1486	964	3086
1995	1095.97	504.10	591.85	1908	1183	3989
1996	1346.76	594.80	751.99	2323	1396	4892
1997	1438.12	614.90	823.26	2459	1441	5208
1998	1518.92	610.20	908.68	2579	1427	5632
1999	1507.12	558.40	948.69	2545	1302	5802
2000	1594.08	559.10	1034.96	2680	1302	6250
2001	1767.38	585.40	1181.96	2962	1365	7042
2002	1951.54	606.80	1344.70	3263	1418	7899
2003	2188.05	637.70	1550.36	3853	1926	6547
2004	2452.62	700.80	1751.85	4309	2134	7277
2005	2785.42	815.32	1970.10	4883	2503	8051
2006	3124.37	906.15	2218.22	5480	2813	8944
2007	3709.69	1051.82	2657.87	6513	3300	10593
2008	4225.38	1217.95	3007.43	7406	3864	11780
2009	4456.31	1277.72	3178.59	7791	4137	12080
2010	5136.78	1419.65	3717.13	8977	4758	13576
2011	6241.95	1597.69	4644.26	10873	5653	15935
2012	7085.46	1830.83	5254.63	12283	6705	17296
2013	8053.82	2064.74	5989.08	13912	7755	19156

9–3 居民消费水平指数

INDICES OF PEOPLE'S CONSUMPTION LEVEL

(1978年=100)

年 份 year	居民消费 (%) People's Censurption (%)	农村居民 rural residernts	城镇居民 wrban residernts	居民消费水平 (%) level of consumption(%)	农村居民 rural residernts	城镇居民 wrban residernts
1981	134.3	140.4	123.6	130.1	137.9	107.0
1982	156.2	169.2	132.3	149.0	164.2	111.5
1983	172.2	186.6	145.4	162.1	179.7	119.0
1984	196.6	205.4	181.4	183.3	198.7	136.6
1985	218.4	212.2	233.3	201.1	208.2	154.2
1986	253.2	247.7	267.4	229.7	244.3	163.5
1987	263.0	255.1	282.4	235.4	249.4	167.4
1988	268.8	257.1	295.6	237.8	248.6	170.4
1989	278.8	273.6	292.7	243.0	262.6	163.9
1990	290.5	281.2	312.9	247.6	263.3	170.8
1991	275.4	257.6	314.1	229.3	235.7	167.6
1992	281.7	254.0	339.6	231.8	230.5	175.3
1993	338.3	276.9	460.8	274.7	250.1	229.1
1994	380.3	292.4	553.4	304.9	264.6	259.6
1995	421.7	303.5	653.0	334.8	276.3	288.9
1996	474.9	340.2	737.9	373.6	310.0	315.2
1997	499.1	342.9	802.9	389.3	311.8	333.1
1998	549.5	354.6	927.3	425.5	321.8	377.1
1999	571.5	356.0	989.4	440.0	322.1	397.1
2000	599.5	361.0	1062.6	459.8	326.0	420.9
2001	661.3	377.2	1206.1	505.8	341.3	471.0
2002	738.6	391.9	1394.3	564.0	355.3	537.0
2003	807.3	393.9	1578.3	614.7	359.2	595.0
2004	868.7	405.3	1726.7	659.6	372.5	640.2
2005	963.4	458.4	1899.3	729.5	425.0	692.7
2006	1074.2	502.9	2132.9	826.5	480.7	777.9
2007	1191.3	557.2	2365.4	917.4	538.4	853.4
2008	1279.5	599.5	2540.4	984.4	585.8	900.3
2009	1352.4	631.3	2690.3	1038.5	625.0	935.4
2010	1507.9	676.1	3045.4	1156.9	693.1	1017.7
2011	1722.0	710.6	3584.4	1316.6	768.6	1125.6
2012	1897.6	785.9	3946.4	1444.3	880.0	1188.6
2013	2106.3	863.7	4396.3	1597.4	991.8	1286.1

注：2003年以前数据根据2004年第一次经济普查资料修订。
Notes:Data before 2003 is Gmended accordity to ecorymic survey 2004

9–4 城镇居民家庭基本情况

年份 Year	调查户数 (户) Number of Households Surveyed (household)	平均每户家庭人口 (人) Average Number of people Per Household (person)	平均每户就业人口 (人) Number of Employees Per Household (person)	每一就业者担负人数 (人) Average Persons Supported by a Labor (person)
1963	240	5.30	1.63	3.25
1964	299	5.36	1.61	3.33
1965	370	5.22	1.60	3.26
1980	571	4.20	2.32	1.81
1981	979	4.21	2.28	1.85
1982	981	4.16	2.32	1.79
1983	980	4.04	2.31	1.75
1984	980	3.97	2.30	1.73
1985	1658	3.84	2.15	1.79
1986	1910	3.76	2.13	1.77
1987	1900	3.73	2.12	1.76
1988	1950	3.61	2.07	1.74
1989	1990	3.52	2.05	1.72
1990	1990	3.47	2.04	1.70
1991	1990	3.45	2.04	1.69
1992	1940	3.36	2.02	1.66
1993	1890	3.29	1.98	1.66
1994	1330	3.23	1.95	1.66
1995	1330	3.22	1.92	1.68
1996	1390	3.24	1.95	1.66
1997	1790	3.23	1.89	1.71
1998	1640	3.19	1.90	1.68
1999	1540	3.15	1.86	1.69
2000	1540	3.14	1.81	1.73
2001	1540	3.10	1.77	1.75
2002	1600	3.07	1.64	1.87
2003	1600	3.06	1.68	1.82
2004	1700	3.03	1.65	1.83
2005	1800	2.98	1.52	1.96
2006	1800	2.96	1.55	1.91
2007	1850	2.95	1.59	1.86
2008	1900	2.96	1.50	1.97
2009	1900	2.94	1.48	1.99
2010	1900	2.93	1.46	2.01
2011	1900	2.90	1.47	1.97
2012	1900	2.89	1.48	1.95
2013	1718	2.77	1.53	1.81

注：由于2002年方法制度重新修订，部分指标有所变化：原“平均每人居住面积”现改为“平均每人建筑总面积”；原“平均每人实际收入”现改为“平均每人总收入”；原“平均每人实际支出”现改为“平均每人总支出”。

BASIC CONDITIONS OF URBAN HOUSEHOLDS

平均每户就业面 (%) Percentage of Employed Persons	平均每人 Per Capita 总收入 (元) Actual Income (yuan)	平均每人 Per Capita #可支配收入 (元) Disposable Income (yuan)	平均每人 Per Capita 总支出 (元) Actual Expenditures (yuan)	消费性支出 Living Expenditures	#食品 Food	平均每人建筑面积 (平方米) Average Living Floor Space Per
30.75	238.1	238.1	237.2	218.4	133.9	
30.04	232.9	232.9	228.3	211.7	122.7	
30.65	224.3	224.3	218.8	204.4	118.0	3.3
55.24	413.7	413.7	394.2	369.3	210.6	5.1
54.16	456.4	456.4	454.8	422.7	241.2	5.4
55.77	481.4	481.4	460.2	430.7	248.0	5.8
57.18	520.0	511.2	497.6	465.0	273.1	6.5
57.93	599.7	590.6	552.8	516.4	291.1	6.8
55.99	713.3	704.2	693.1	644.2	324.5	7.9
56.65	861.5	851.3	815.5	751.5	387.5	8.2
56.84	960.6	951.8	919.1	836.1	443.2	8.4
57.34	1136.4	1128.1	1153.1	1058.8	538.9	8.9
58.24	1271.6	1262.6	1250.0	1130.7	607.0	9.1
58.79	1437.1	1427.2	1349.4	1220.3	652.4	9.8
59.13	1603.7	1592.9	1538.2	1380.2	717.4	9.6
60.12	1886.4	1874.2	1799.9	1577.7	799.0	9.9
60.18	2453.5	2438.7	2358.1	2097.6	941.5	10.5
60.37	3360.0	3346.0	3588.6	2733.1	1307.1	11.1
59.63	4031.9	4016.7	3977.3	3433.8	1680.6	11.9
60.19	4367.0	4350.2	4290.6	3713.5	1731.4	11.8
58.51	4693.8	4673.2	4549.7	3855.6	1773.6	12.8
59.56	4849.4	4826.4	4903.1	4074.4	1787.7	12.7
59.04	5234.5	5212.8	5333.8	4340.6	1783.4	13.2
57.64	5542.6	5524.5	5643.6	4644.5	1779.4	13.9
57.10	5888.7	5856.0	5774.8	4804.8	1799.4	15.2
53.42	7142.2	6789.0	7159.7	5608.9	2087.8	26.2
54.90	7745.8	7322.0	7551.1	5963.3	2279.6	26.3
54.46	8522.1	8022.8	8076.1	6398.5	2516.2	27.3
51.01	9395.1	8786.0	8582.8	6737.0	2625.4	29.9
52.36	10533.3	9803.0	9839.7	7397.0	2868.4	31.0
53.90	12421.8	11485.0	11476.7	8701.0	3456.0	32.3
50.68	14174.3	13153.0	12471.0	9478.0	3996.0	32.0
50.34	15698.0	14367.0	13868.0	10294.0	4160.5	32.8
49.83	17572.8	16058.4	15612.3	11451.0	4429.3	33.2
50.69	20193.3	18373.9	18123.4	13163.8	5363.7	35.5
51.21	22903.9	20839.6	20107.1	14496.0	5837.9	35.8
55.23	25180.5	22906.4	20419.5	15749.5	6259.2	38.8

Note: The " Per Capita Living Floor Space (sq.m) " in the above table was changed into " Per Cappita Living Floor Space (sq.m) "; "Per Cappita Actual Income (yuan)" into "Per Capita Total Income (yuan)"; "Per Capita Actual Expenditures (yuan)" into "Per Capita Total Expenditures (yuan)", owing to the changes of items in the reversion of 2006 mearurement system.

9-5 城镇居民家庭收支情况(2013)

单位：元

项　　目	Item	总　计 Total
调查户数(户)	Households Surveyed	1718.00
比　　重(%)	Ratio	100.00
平均每户家庭人口(人)	Average Number of Residents Per Household	2.77
平均每户离退休人口(人)	Average Number of Retirees Per Household	0.35
平均每一就业者负担人数(人)	Average Persons supported by a Urban Labor	1.81
平均每户就业面(%)	Average Employment Rate Per Household	55.23
平均每人总收入	Per Capita Total Income	24516.05
#可支配收入	Disposable Income	22906.42
平均每人借贷收入	Income of Loans Per Capita	2599.86
#提取储蓄存款	Savings Withdrawn	2060.68
平均每人借贷支出	Expenditures of Loans Per Capita	4979.64
#存入储蓄款	Money Saved	4237.54
平均每人总支出	Total Expenditure Per Capita	20419.53
#消费性支出	Consumption Expenditure	15749.50
一、食　　品	Food	6259.22
粮油类	Oils Class	856.99
肉禽蛋水产品类	Meat, eggs and aquatic products	1595.49
蔬　菜　类	Vegetables	772.19
调　味　品	Flavorings	83.53
糖烟酒饮料	Sugar drink alcohol and tobacco	756.56
干鲜瓜果类	Dried and Fresh Melons and Fruits	367.88
糕点、奶及奶制品	Pastries, milk and milk products	346.80
其他食品	Others	173.20
饮食服务	Food Service	1306.59
二、衣　　着	Clothing	1881.85
服　　装	Garments	1338.13
衣着材料	Clothing Materials	12.66
鞋类	Shoes	394.48
其它衣着用品	Others	83.02
衣着加工服务费	Clothing Procecing and Service Fees	3.99
三、居　　住	Residence	1456.30
住　　房	Housing	501.34
水、电、燃料及其他	Water, Electricities, Fuel Materials and Others	826.23
居住服务	Residence Services	95.00
四、家庭设备、用品及服务	Facilities, Articals and Services	1059.22
耐用消费品	Durable Consumer Goods	434.84
室内装饰品	Interrior Decorations	20.23
床上用品	Bed Articals	86.15
家庭日用杂品	Daily Use Articals	435.51
家具材料	Furniture Materials	4.85
家庭服务	Households Service	57.59
五、医疗保健	Medicine and Medical Service	1033.46
医疗器具	Medical Equipments	7.82
保健器具	Health Products	6.75
药品费	Medicines	318.98
滋补保健品	Health Care Products	69.68
医疗费	Medical Service Fees	897.36
其　　他	Others	
六、交通和通信	Transportation and Communication	1745.05
交　　通	Transportation	1087.10
通　　信	Communication	657.75
七、娱乐、教育、文化服务	Recreation, Education and Cultural Services	1922.83
文化娱乐用品	Cultural Recreation Articals	228.44
文化娱乐服务	Cultural Recreation Services	594.46
教　　育	Education	1074.93
八、其他商品和服务	Miscellaneous Commodities and Services	391.57
其他商品	Miscellaneous Commodities	260.54
服务	Services	131.03

PER CAPITA INCOME AND EXPENDITURE OF URBAN HOUSEHOLDS(2013)

(yuan)

低收入户 Low Income Households	中低收入户 Lower Middle Income Households	中等收入户 Middle Income Households	中高收入户 Upper Middle Income Households	高收入户 High Income Households
345.00	345.42	345.33	341.50	340.33
20.08	20.11	20.10	19.88	19.81
3.32	3.19	2.76	2.51	2.28
0.22	0.33	0.47	0.38	0.34
2.07	1.86	1.82	1.72	1.53
48.23	53.86	54.84	58.07	65.38
11260.31	17923.42	23441.86	29318.97	48805.58
10348.82	16767.71	21715.93	27555.00	45866.35
1502.34	3014.60	1564.65	2392.41	5043.47
1086.60	1917.35	1400.55	1961.06	4554.26
1282.59	2698.96	4521.35	6175.48	12732.91
1055.59	2350.76	3769.15	5638.37	10487.14
11194.92	17154.52	18740.87	23581.46	36758.01
8745.15	12971.73	14438.88	18677.79	28051.31
3626.65	4830.67	5781.85	7157.69	9326.15
527.00	604.32	675.67	704.00	784.37
1020.19	1281.73	1542.62	1850.79	2057.84
534.52	636.79	759.27	836.62	963.65
53.07	68.44	80.08	96.23	107.84
348.68	599.95	653.44	865.96	1285.75
185.07	254.89	362.16	443.09	578.05
188.86	246.37	284.87	410.04	592.51
132.78	129.88	147.85	198.51	231.68
501.31	867.18	1130.54	1545.62	2547.70
753.20	1353.32	1637.72	2138.64	3559.24
519.46	979.22	1172.81	1495.13	2547.47
4.30	6.85	11.72	14.12	27.67
166.73	296.97	348.89	451.01	704.89
23.39	39.27	66.36	111.44	188.70
2.21	2.05	4.13	5.91	5.57
844.95	1182.48	1442.20	1771.17	2641.50
203.53	348.36	476.81	656.63	1089.84
595.20	755.16	845.37	962.18	1227.67
27.06	53.35	94.49	119.46	241.33
567.07	760.50	1003.51	1280.35	2010.57
233.94	300.86	415.07	529.46	832.01
5.35	11.18	19.58	26.69	48.03
41.32	52.34	75.15	103.61	192.29
244.16	349.03	417.96	512.06	768.34
0.22	1.39	9.88	1.56	13.86
22.04	33.21	45.69	78.40	134.58
713.45	616.97	962.34	1092.27	1698.87
0.76	2.61	1.39	6.98	30.91
2.52	1.22	9.67	8.28	12.82
241.39	203.64	360.41	297.26	442.16
9.01	26.31	39.47	94.62	199.75
660.89	651.51	734.50	967.45	1352.83
842.38	2089.36	1449.92	2592.19	4057.24
429.66	1438.08	580.92	1700.56	2764.40
412.72	651.28	869.00	890.31	1292.84
1191.02	1864.78	1714.99	2118.94	3487.98
99.27	187.17	203.17	295.73	476.20
123.04	409.87	446.12	684.60	1733.60
960.11	1238.85	1042.12	1106.96	1235.72
206.43	273.65	446.34	526.53	1269.75
122.35	192.22	291.12	337.04	873.22
84.08	81.44	155.23	189.49	396.53

9-6 城镇居民家庭平均每百户年末耐用品拥有量(2013)

品　　名		Item		总平均 Total Average	低收入户 Low Income Households
摩托车	(辆)	Motorcycles	unit	22.22	32.08
助力车	(辆)	Auxiliary Drving Bikes	unit	18.61	17.92
家用汽车	(辆)	Cars for Household Use	unit	13.28	5.82
洗衣机	(台)	Washing Machins	unit	90.15	82.87
电冰箱	(台)	Refrigerators	unit	94.71	89.78
彩色电视机	(台)	Color TV Sets	unit	117.13	106.74
家用电脑	(台)	Computers	unit	73.48	50.75
组合音响	(套)	Hi-Fi Stereo Systems	unit	11.10	8.70
摄像机	(台)	TV Cameras	unit	6.85	2.32
照相机	(架)	Cameras	unit	33.21	13.24
其他中高档乐器	(件)	Medium and High-Grade Musical Instruments	unit	3.22	
微波炉	(台)	Microwave Stove	unit	52.99	32.05
空调器	(台)	Air Conditioners	unit	122.03	84.18
淋浴热水器	(台)	Showers	unit	85.63	76.57
消毒碗柜	(台)	Disinfection cabinet	unit	9.60	2.46
洗碗机	(台)	Dishwasher	unit	1.93	0.29
健身器材	(件)	Health Care Instruments	unit	2.34	0.87
固定电话	(部)	Fixed telephone	set	39.22	33.23
移动电话	(部)	Mobile Phones	set	207.61	236.79

NUMBER OF DURABLE CONSUMER GOODS OWNED PER 100 URBAN HOUSEHOLDS AT THE YEAR-END BY INCOME LEVEL(2013)

中低收入户 Lower Middle Income Households	中等收入户 Middle Income Households	中高收入户 Upper Middle Income Households	高收入户 High Income Households
26.25	19.09	15.57	16.65
19.35	21.96	21.45	13.37
9.43	9.75	10.71	26.59
88.61	93.77	90.75	93.76
95.46	96.11	96.02	96.25
115.56	118.70	113.88	124.53
68.64	69.81	75.18	91.99
8.85	10.74	11.42	15.01
4.05	5.79	7.49	11.24
22.75	32.07	35.58	53.18
1.16	4.30	3.37	6.76
43.45	57.43	64.13	70.98
102.24	122.06	132.53	161.83
82.07	85.47	89.34	95.30
7.48	6.61	7.76	16.50
1.16	1.16	1.61	3.65
0.29	2.32	2.51	3.38
42.23	40.84	45.83	52.14
226.93	230.87	219.47	221.73

9-7 城镇居民家庭房屋居住分布情况
URABN HOUSEHOLDS HOUSING CONDITIONS

分 组	Group	各组户数占总户数比重(%) Percentage of Household in Each Group of the Total Households				
		2009	2010	2011	2012	2013
总 计	Total	1900	1900	1900	1900	1718
一、房屋产权	Building Property Right					
租赁公房	Leased Pubilc Houses	7.3	7.2	6.0	5.5	3.6
租赁私房	Leased Private Houses	3.1	2.9	1.9	1.9	7.5
原有私房	Original Private Houses	15.5	15.5	15.2	14.1	24.4
房改私房	Private Houses	51.1	50.9	44.5	44.1	28.3
商品房	Commercial Houses	21.4	21.6	30.1	32.4	32.8
借用房						1.4
其他	Others	1.7	1.9	2.4	1.0	1.9
二、住宅样式	Housing Pattens					
单栋住宅	Sole-Unit Houses	7.7	8.0	10.9	10.5	23.1
四居室	Four-Room Houses	4.0	4.1	4.6	4.9	3.8
三居室	Three-Room Houses	25.3	25.3	28.1	28.7	25.3
二居室	Two-Room Houses	42.4	42.4	42.9	43.6	35.2
一居室	One-Room Houses	5.1	4.7	3.9	4.2	5.8
普通楼房	Ordinary Houses	12.0	11.9	7.7	6.4	2.1
平房及其他	Bungalow and Others	3.6	3.6	1.9	1.7	4.6
三、用水情况	Waters					
独用自来水	Private Tap Water	99.5	99.5	99.8	99.8	97.8
公用自来水	Public Tap Water	0.2	0.2	0.2	0.2	
井、河水	Water from Rivers and Wells	0.3	0.3			1.5
其他	Others					0.7
四、卫生设备	Sanitary Faciities					
无卫生设备	Have not	2.0	2.1	0.9	0.7	3.5
有浴室厕所	Toilets with bth-room	82.0	82.0	90.5	91.9	87.2
有厕所无浴室	Toilets without bth-room	13.1	13.1	7.3	6.4	6.6
公用卫生设备	Public Health Facilities	2.9	2.9	1.3	1.0	2.6
五、取暖设备	Warming Facilities					
无取暖设备	Have not	36.9	36.0	24.7	22.5	29.5
空调设备	Air Conditioner	56.3	56.7	65.9	66.7	
暖 气	Heater	5.3	5.8	4.0	5.2	
其 他	Others	1.5	1.5	5.4	5.6	70.4
六、燃料使用情况	Fuel Material Usage Conditions					
煤	Coal	10.1	10.2	5.9	5.1	2.3
罐装液化石油气	LPG cylinders	56.2	55.7	43.4	43.0	47.5
管道液化石油气	LPG Pipeline	1.9	1.8	2.0	1.6	2.6
管道煤气	Piped Coal Gas	7.2	6.4	5.2	4.0	6.9
管道天然气	Gas pipeline	24.1	25.7	42.7	45.5	31.1
其 他	Others	0.3	0.3	0.9	0.8	9.2
七、通信设备使用情况	Telecommunication Facilities Usage Conditions					
1.每百户固定电话	Per 100 fixed telephone	72.4	71.9	61.2	59.3	39.2
2.每百户移动电话	Mobile Phones Per 100 Households	164.0	166.0	193.8	204.4	207.6

9-8 农民家庭基本情况
BASIC CONDITIONS OF RURAL HOUSEHOLDS

年 份	调查户数 Number of Households Surveyed	常住人口(人) Permanent Residents (person)	平均每户常住人口(人) Average Permanent Residents Per Households (person)	平均每户整半劳动力(人) Average Full-Time and Part-Time Labors Per Household (person)	平均每个劳动力负担人口(人) Average Person Supported by Each Labor (person)
1981	954	5497	5.76	2.67	2.16
1982	948	5364	5.66	2.73	2.08
1983	1470	8267	5.62	2.99	1.88
1984	1510	8317	5.51	3.02	1.83
1985	3300	16473	5.07	2.98	1.71
1986	3300	16432	4.98	2.96	1.68
1987	3300	16195	4.91	2.94	1.67
1988	3300	15966	4.84	2.93	1.65
1989	3300	15567	4.72	2.86	1.65
1990	3300	15411	4.67	2.84	1.65
1991	3300	15094	4.57	2.66	1.72
1992	3300	14900	4.52	2.63	1.71
1993	3300	14651	4.44	2.65	1.67
1994	3300	14466	4.38	2.72	1.61
1995	3300	14447	4.38	2.77	1.58
1996	3300	14053	4.26	2.75	1.55
1997	3200	13453	4.20	2.64	1.60
1998	3200	13239	4.14	2.62	1.58
1999	3200	13082	4.09	2.63	1.55
2000	3300	13557	4.11	2.76	1.49
2001	3300	13490	4.09	2.75	1.49
2002	3300	13420	4.07	2.78	1.46
2003	3300	13385	4.06	2.86	1.42
2004	3300	13356	4.05	2.92	1.39
2005	3300	13228	4.01	2.99	1.34
2006	3300	13259	4.02	3.03	1.34
2007	3300	13186	4.00	3.06	1.30
2008	3300	13163	3.99	3.08	1.29
2009	3300	13151	3.99	3.12	1.28
2010	3300	13123	3.98	3.14	1.27
2011	3300	13120	3.98	3.12	1.27
2012	3300	13140	3.98	3.12	1.28
2013	2096	7921	3.78	2.88	1.31

9-8 续表 1 continued

年 份 year	平均每户经营耕地面积(亩) Space of Cultivation land Per Household (mu)	平均每户年末拥有生产性固定资产原值(元) Value of Production Fixed Assets Per Household (yuan)	平均每户年内新建购房屋面积(平方米) Floor Space of Rooms Newly Built Per Household (sq.m)	平均每人年末使用房屋面积(平方米) Lving Space Per Capita (sq.m)
1981	0.52		6.51	15.31
1982	0.57	159.20	5.36	16.45
1983	8.95	389.97	5.65	18.04
1984	8.66	530.20	6.70	19.03
1985	7.60	557.86	8.24	21.18
1986	7.48	610.47	8.45	22.63
1987	7.31	672.87	7.79	23.50
1988	7.04	759.61	4.90	24.15
1989	6.95	819.53	5.50	25.10
1990	6.79	861.91	6.20	25.73
1991	6.58	1068.45	4.56	27.33
1992	6.47	1146.94	4.07	27.94
1993	6.36	1281.66	3.75	25.80
1994	6.69	1542.58	3.91	25.22
1995	6.73	1775.57	4.66	25.92
1996	6.82	2291.60	4.25	26.58
1997	6.56	2688.67	4.98	27.99
1998	6.08	2604.21	4.74	28.38
1999	6.08	2543.61	4.19	29.87
2000	5.93	2482.02	3.48	30.11
2001	5.94	2773.52	2.98	31.19
2002	6.01	2953.37	4.65	31.55
2003	6.03	2989.82	4.01	32.44
2004	6.15	3046.47	2.82	33.68
2005	6.15	4121.20	3.88	36.05
2006	6.12	4297.19	4.22	36.77
2007	6.41	4996.00	3.36	37.96
2008	6.36	5434.99	5.90	39.04
2009	6.51	6368.83	4.40	40.11
2010	6.73	7078.46	5.05	40.99
2011	6.44	9636.11	7.88	44.24
2012	6.80	10813.13	5.46	44.98
2013	7.08	13839.73	6.06	41.84

9–8 续表 2 continued

年 份	平均每户年末使用房屋价值(元) Value of Per Households Living Space (yuan)	平均每人总收入(元) Total Income Per Capita (yuan)	平均每人纯收入(元) Net Income Per Capita (yuan)	平均每人生活消费支出(元) Living Expenditures Per Capita (yuan)
1981	1249.13	232.64	217.44	183.78
1982	1261.51	311.51	286.07	226.96
1983	1688.93	405.14	299.24	252.47
1984	1786.54	525.86	392.29	305.03
1985	2068.78	569.74	421.24	334.63
1986	2319.44	605.67	445.13	373.53
1987	2514.22	638.64	460.66	408.69
1988	2751.40	710.47	497.84	450.62
1989	3095.15	820.70	571.84	540.13
1990	3545.50	957.01	670.80	607.58
1991	4661.58	936.57	626.92	615.40
1992	4885.77	1015.62	677.82	611.84
1993	5004.02	1135.77	783.18	722.09
1994	5887.81	1690.49	1170.06	1012.95
1995	6729.46	2184.20	1511.22	1245.10
1996	10050.26	2642.45	1863.62	1630.41
1997	11432.61	2913.16	2102.20	1660.13
1998	12966.45	2917.66	2172.24	1699.43
1999	13654.80	2871.62	2217.08	1572.90
2000	13717.28	3008.13	2268.50	1555.61
2001	16007.50	3124.10	2352.16	1649.18
2002	16581.94	3239.81	2444.06	1745.63
2003	19010.48	3378.80	2566.76	1801.63
2004	20254.50	3826.27	2890.01	2088.98
2005	24815.99	4221.81	3099.20	2430.19
2006	27772.00	4580.79	3419.35	2732.46
2007	31696.83	5365.78	3997.48	3090.00
2008	36250.27	6266.27	4656.38	3652.57
2009	41493.01	6663.13	5035.26	3725.40
2010	47606.56	7699.27	5832.27	4090.78
2011	61870.37	9387.20	6897.92	5010.74
2012	77338.15	10525.66	7851.71	5726.73
2013	101314.51	11896.06	8866.95	6279.52

9–9 农民家庭年人均纯收入及构成
ANNUAL NET INCOME OF RURAL HOUSEHOLDS PER CAPITA AND COMPOSITION

单位：元 (yuan)

指 标	Item	2003	2004	2005	2006	2007	2008	2009	2010	2011	2012	2013
全年总收入	Total Revenue	3378.80	3826.27	4221.81	4580.79	5365.78	6266.27	6663.13	7699.27	9387.20	10525.66	11896.06
全年纯收入	Annual Net Income	2566.76	2890.01	3099.20	3419.35	3997.48	4656.38	5035.26	5832.27	6897.92	7851.71	8866.95
工资性收入	Money Wage	706.79	755.23	941.64	1199.16	1454.50	1742.33	1900.54	2186.11	2703.05	3189.84	3648.20
家庭经营纯收入	House Business Revenue	1785.27	2051.62	2049.04	2095.15	2379.82	2690.83	2828.53	3234.94	3731.34	4123.49	4616.55
转移性收入	Transfer Income	58.95	66.96	91.71	99.13	125.46	182.40	247.81	304.30	379.08	472.51	518.07
财产性收入	Property Income	15.76	16.19	16.81	25.91	37.70	40.82	58.37	106.92	84.45	65.87	84.13
比重(纯收入=100)	Ratio (net income = 100)											
工资性收入	Money Wage	27.54	26.13	30.38	35.07	36.39	37.42	37.74	37.48	39.19	40.63	41.14
家庭经营纯收入	House Business Revenue	69.55	70.99	66.12	61.27	59.53	57.79	56.17	55.47	54.09	52.52	52.06
转移性收入	Transfer Income	2.30	2.32	2.96	2.90	3.14	3.92	4.92	5.22	5.50	6.02	5.84
财产性收入	Property Income	0.61	0.56	0.54	0.76	0.94	0.88	1.16	1.83	1.22	0.84	0.95

9–10 农民家庭年人均纯收入分组
RURAL HOUSEHOLDS GROUPED BY ANNUAL NET INCOME PER CAPITA

单位：户 (household)

指 标	Item	2002	2003	2004	2005	2006	2007	2008	2009	2010	2011	2012	2013
调查户总计	Total Households Surveyed	3300	3300	3300	3300	3300	3300	3300	3300	3300	3300	3300	2096
600元以下	Below 600 yuan	46	44	65	48	45	34	39	49	24	58	46	11
600–800元	600-800 yuan	68	64	79	69	61	34	27	22	6	10	3	2
800–1000元	800-1000 yuan	95	102	80	89	77	65	73	29	19	9	12	1
1000–1500元	1000-1500 yuan	468	410	280	269	182	138	115	138	85	57	30	14
1500–2000元	1500-2000 yuan	696	645	431	413	345	237	160	173	123	99	64	20
2000–3000元	2000-3000 yuan	1032	1007	1034	840	787	659	519	478	365	295	197	83
3000–4000元	3000-4000 yuan	495	513	611	702	684	660	559	492	419	313	289	127
4000–5000元	4000-5000 yuan	206	255	339	413	479	510	510	460	469	373	286	170
5000元以上	5000 yuan and Over	194	260	381	457	640	969	1298	1459	1790	2086	2373	1668

9-11 农民家庭年人均经营总收入

ANNUAL TOTAL INCME OF RURAL HOUSEHOLDS PER CAPITA

单位：元 (yuan)

指 标	Item	2003	2004	2005	2006	2007	2008	2009	2010	2011	2012	2013
家庭经营总收入	Total Income of Family Business	2527.03	2918.92	3167.19	3252.61	3743.44	4287.96	4435.68	5077.04	6134.62	6718.36	7022.00
农业收入	Farming	1562.57	1877.48	1933.74	2070.89	2316.71	2546.31	2638.00	3115.06	3682.89	4056.77	4049.41
林业收入	Forestry	31.56	34.10	47.83	54.10	60.37	61.54	59.33	65.63	79.26	88.49	140.80
牧业收入	Animal Husbandry	517.49	590.41	678.00	580.75	741.27	946.28	863.14	869.13	1013.07	1044.46	1077.50
渔业收入	Fishery	131.05	144.78	162.28	187.16	212.64	271.92	311.80	329.55	389.88	423.50	403.93
工业收入	Industry	60.78	47.22	53.92	49.43	46.53	53.95	58.65	69.15	135.22	144.59	60.66
建筑业收入	Construction	29.95	30.53	57.68	64.86	83.83	99.12	133.29	154.25	167.18	177.49	307.83
交通运输邮电业收入	Transportation, Post Services	57.61	57.41	80.59	91.21	106.20	116.66	127.96	155.76	277.54	322.49	328.76
批零贸易餐饮业收入	Wholesales, Retail Sales and Catering	75.63	84.13	99.04	104.48	118.82	133.06	164.99	220.55	273.17	317.95	401.46
社会服务和文教卫生业收入	Social Services and Cultural, Educational,and Public Health Services	28.19	23.63	32.79	34.93	44.40	44.70	63.47	78.53	91.43	113.54	177.96
其他家庭经营收入	Other Family Revenue	32.20	29.23	21.32	13.75	12.22	13.23	14.14	18.79	23.55	26.87	10.54

9-12 农民家庭年人均生产支出

ANNUAL PRODUCTION EXPENDITURES OF RURAL HOUSEHOLDS PER CAPITA

单位：元 (yuan)

指 标	Item	2004	2005	2006	2007	2008	2009	2010	2011	2012	2013
一、家庭经营费用支出	Expenditures of Family Business	765.03	1038.04	1071.50	1262.04	1493.00	1489.40	1713.15	2199.08	2402.73	2408.72
农业生产支出	Agricultural Expenditures	394.51	490.41	572.13	663.21	759.00	746.68	866.74	1029.67	1076.28	1049.49
林业生产支出	Forestry Expenditures	2.77	6.88	7.00	8.56	6.14	6.69	7.74	16.65	16.33	19.52
牧业生产支出	Animal Husbandary Expenditures	256.44	362.15	307.57	369.78	493.71	463.78	470.43	593.09	693.65	753.88
渔业生产支出	Fishery Expenditures	51.91	67.00	71.57	77.58	86.30	104.37	125.68	216.01	230.50	174.04
工业生产支出	Industrial Expenditures	16.86	19.53	16.80	19.20	14.56	16.37	18.89	54.66	84.17	28.31
建筑业支出	Construction Expenditures	2.81	22.14	27.51	32.56	37.45	45.15	54.95	61.78	54.28	120.30
交通运输邮电业支出	Expenditures of Transportation and Post Services	11.28	26.09	28.63	36.01	35.09	38.14	60.29	107.32	120.00	81.99
批零贸易餐饮业支出	Expenditures of Wholesales, Retail Sales and Catering	23.57	33.11	28.75	42.36	46.38	51.96	88.76	90.88	100.13	82.03
社会服务和文教卫生业支出	Expenditures of Social Services and Cultural, Educational, and Public Health Services	3.43	5.88	7.41	9.50	10.76	13.73	14.89	19.82	20.52	69.33
其他家庭经营支出	Other Family Expenditures	1.46	4.85	4.17	3.28	3.60	2.53	4.78	9.22	6.85	2.19
二、购置生产性固定资产及雇工支出	Expenditures of Purchasing Fixed Assets and employee	56.75	78.99	70.31	75.47	99.92	148.69	142.67	231.28	240.00	315.23
三、税费支出	Expenditures of Taxation	52.08	11.57	14.62	18.22	13.30	11.21	10.28	9.28	11.09	0

9–13 农民家庭年人均生活消费支出

LIVING EXPENDITURES OF RURAL HOUSEHOLDS PER CAPITA

单位：元 (yuan)

指 标	Item	2004	2005	2006	2007	2008	2009	2010	2011	2012	2013
全年总支出	Total Annual Expenditures	3180.49	3675.73	3999.48	4565.40	5402.06	5537.59	6131.23	7971.52	8923.73	9477.33
生活消费支出	Living Expenditures	2088.98	2430.19	2732.10	3090.00	3652.57	3725.40	4090.78	5010.74	5726.73	6279.52
一、食品消费	Food Consumption	1076.35	1192.26	1278.80	1479.04	1711.34	1668.35	1763.05	1954.62	2154.01	2308.45
主 食	Grain	291.96	266.31	279.99	305.79	323.50	320.19	329.34	334.56	350.86	334.10
副 食	Non-Staple Food	441.65	519.21	521.06	625.66	771.94	695.66	744.85	859.31	969.20	1037.53
其他食品	Others	206.65	260.45	291.72	329.14	369.51	392.37	413.46	480.38	542.32	514.98
在外饮食	Travelling Catering Service	126.78	136.37	176.71	209.62	237.24	249.14	264.06	273.91	282.94	393.63
二、衣着消费	Clothing Consumption	93.52	125.01	146.69	168.64	187.07	195.45	217.61	272.12	316.41	347.67
三、居住消费	Residence Consumption	274.10	310.27	377.20	434.91	651.50	702.62	816.42	1086.86	1206.16	1415.73
住 房	Housing	183.62	207.47	256.80	292.43	508.63	572.69	655.39	918.61	973.60	1013.20
电 费	Electricity Fees	24.78	30.44	38.17	46.43	58.77	70.08	80.50	85.04	112.57	138.37
燃 料	Fuel	53.06	57.53	66.00	70.34	63.96	39.16	50.14	55.28	91.16	197.33
四、家庭设备用品及服务	Familty facilities and Services	75.11	110.04	135.53	166.25	234.92	229.32	262.26	359.57	397.86	425.00
耐用消费品	Durable Consumer Goods	26.22	47.97	65.90	90.40	117.85	133.42	158.37	230.49	238.55	249.85
日用杂品	Daily Necessities	38.02	47.85	63.54	69.58	110.17	88.20	94.33	116.88	142.41	164.10
五、医疗保健消费	Medicine and Medical Services Fees	110.73	135.37	172.40	178.77	210.36	236.31	295.24	438.20	591.87	624.40
医疗保健用品	Health Care Supplies	41.96	56.01	64.76	60.17	64.34	71.18	71.61	102.19	117.28	127.71
医疗保健服务费	Health Care Service Fees	68.77	79.36	107.60	118.60	146.02	165.13	223.63	336.01	474.59	496.69
六、交通通讯消费	Transportation and Telecommunication Fees	162.65	223.16	246.07	281.12	290.44	307.22	331.35	414.36	496.10	605.95
交通工具	Transportation	47.44	60.98	74.82	92.97	97.88	108.82	124.59	186.09	235.85	324.51
通讯工具	Telecommunication	21.66	26.65	22.13	29.48	26.17	23.71	34.86	33.04	39.84	45.85
交通、邮电服务消费	Transport, postal services, consumer	92.20	132.88	149.12	158.66	166.38	174.70	171.90	195.23	220.41	235.48
七、文教娱乐用品及服务	Cultural, Educational and Receational Articles and Services	245.68	271.86	292.30	284.13	267.13	281.68	288.12	341.87	394.63	407.42
文教娱乐用品	Cultural, Educational and Receational Articles	46.61	52.90	55.12	53.97	53.40	61.71	62.30	94.96	107.87	104.20
学杂费	School Fees	176.31	189.93	201.25	185.74	156.51	146.81	102.61	139.02	136.21	159.18
技术培训费	Technical Training	5.12	3.09	2.94	5.30	5.23	5.44	7.19	10.43	12.85	28.88
文体休闲娱乐费	Sports recreation fee	3.39	4.49	5.92	7.52	11.03	9.92	13.81	17.44	23.05	35.58
八、其他商品和服务	Other Commdities and Services	50.85	62.23	83.24	97.13	99.80	104.29	116.73	143.14	169.68	144.90

9–14　农民家庭年人均现金收支
ANNUAL CASH REVENUE AND EXPENDITURE OF RURAL HOUSEHOLDS PER CAPITA

单位：元　　　　(yuan)

指　标	Item	2004	2005	2006	2007	2008	2009	2010	2011	2012	2013
期内现金收入合计	Total Cash Income at Year-End	2971.04	3454.30	3793.20	4498.98	5256.32	5718.37	6664.44	8232.92	9337.04	10819.88
一、工资性现金收入	Cash Income By Wages	754.47	941.18	1199.10	1454.46	1742.25	1898.93	2185.60	2696.32	3186.99	3858.97
二、家庭经营现金收入	Cash Income By Family Business	2070.50	2402.70	2470.20	2888.24	3289.11	3509.20	4063.37	5011.97	5546.68	5959.60
#农业	Farm Products	1197.84	1340.29	1443.51	1655.22	1782.47	1924.84	2306.34	2807.96	3096.78	3179.27
林业	Forestry Products	29.64	40.17	48.27	56.01	55.94	55.54	60.38	80.14	88.34	142.91
牧业	Animal husbandary Products	436.44	522.64	436.72	557.71	722.03	658.16	675.22	773.47	837.81	891.19
渔业	Fishery Products	136.17	155.67	182.48	206.85	266.99	307.25	323.77	380.89	418.62	395.83
工业	Industry Products	45.73	52.98	48.95	46.53	53.95	58.65	69.15	135.22	144.59	60.66
建筑业	Building Industry	30.49	57.68	64.86	83.83	98.93	133.29	154.25	167.18	177.49	307.83
交通运输邮电业	Transportation and Post Service	57.41	80.59	91.21	106.20	116.66	127.96	155.76	277.54	322.49	328.76
批零贸易餐饮业	Retail Sales and Catering	84.13	99.04	104.48	118.82	133.06	164.99	220.55	273.17	317.95	401.46
社会服务和文教卫生业	Social services and cultural and educational sector	23.63	32.79	34.93	44.40	44.70	63.47	78.53	91.43	113.54	177.96
其他家庭经营收入	Cash Income of Other Family Business	29.02	20.85	14.79	12.67	14.38	14.14	19.42	23.55	26.87	10.54
三、转移性现金收入	Transfer Cash Income	133.17	94.78	102.07	126.97	194.68	264.72	328.92	460.73	544.46	902.05
四、财产性现金收入	Property Cash Income	12.90	15.55	21.75	29.31	30.29	45.52	86.55	63.91	58.91	99.26
期内现金支出合计	Total Cash Expenditures at Year-End	2482.55	2974.75	3267.10	3740.56	4496.87	4723.52	5294.37	7194.75	8149.22	8563.81
一、家庭经营费用现金支出	Cash Expenditures By Family Business	683.75	953.96	972.70	1159.13	1383.60	1368.00	1562.32	2051.67	2285.75	2243.66
购买化肥	Fertilizers Purchases	191.90	215.34	234.63	255.96	340.71	313.95	320.80	377.07	374.44	396.06
购买农药	Purchases of Farm Chemical	43.55	51.93	74.54	81.13	94.78	87.72	94.03	125.52	129.82	112.80
购买农用薄膜	Purchase of Agricultural Film	4.21	4.82	5.27	5.18	5.42	3.40	5.07	6.80	6.31	4.80
二、购买生产性固定资产及雇工现金支出	Cash Expenditures of Purchasing Production Fixed Assets and Employee	56.75	78.99	70.31	75.47	99.92	148.38	142.17	231.28	240.00	315.23
三、税费现金支出	Cash Expenditures of Taxations	51.85	11.55	14.60	18.22	13.29	11.20	10.28	9.28	10.85	0
四、生活消费现金支出	Cash Expenditures of Living Consumption	1479.46	1813.40	2099.60	2368.68	2857.78	3033.37	3406.12	4382.95	5070.68	5531.07
五、转移性现金支出	Transfer Cash Expenditures	205.43	105.67	103.54	113.88	133.30	153.91	162.25	511.12	530.85	471.72
六、财产性现金支出	Property Cash Expenditures	5.31	10.88	6.23	5.17	8.97	8.33	10.74	8.45	11.10	2.13

9-15 农民家庭年人均出售主要农副产品情况
ANNUAL SELLING OF FARM AND SIDELINE PRODUCTS OF RURL HOUSEHOLDS PER CAPITA

单位：千克

品　名	Item	2003	2004	2005	2006	2007	2008	2009	2010	2011	2012	2013
粮 食	Grain	299.85	303.46	383.48	391.24	386.98	390.60	422.65	447.78	451.98	489.22	591.56
#小 麦	#Wheat	31.74	40.06	54.25	77.67	94.39	76.73	62.01	75.44	86.70	91.93	79.55
稻 谷	Paddy	236.27	234.53	302.70	288.86	268.94	292.78	320.27	331.71	302.69	329.15	432.85
棉 花	Cotton	33.83	55.99	55.95	69.22	81.48	70.09	76.43	55.03	88.30	93.94	72.29
油 料	Oil Producer	58.96	79.72	77.73	62.04	61.27	65.14	77.04	72.15	60.91	58.57	73.99
糖 料	Sugar	5.22	3.99	5.47	6.28	9.16	4.31	4.48	6.43	0.16	0.17	2.16
烟 草	Tobacco	1.65	1.30	2.34	2.07	1.55	2.11	2.92	2.77	2.97	3.82	7.89
蔬 菜	Vegetable	145.02	148.96	135.09	133.11	138.89	136.45	133.11	139.41	137.62	143.53	99.54
瓜 类	Melon	30.49	26.75	14.21	26.56	16.20	14.80	19.07	19.69	17.40	17.60	40.74
水 果	Fruits	54.72	66.57	69.54	76.41	82.72	90.38	99.70	78.09	66.13	109.87	62.86
茶 叶	Tea	0.70	0.80	1.24	1.25	1.56	1.56	1.29	1.95	4.17	8.08	5.02
猪 肉	Pork	31.38	26.67	29.70	30.80	26.03	26.38	28.70	30.92	22.91	25.68	28.51
家 禽	Poultry	1.48	1.63	4.47	5.19	4.44	7.16	7.29	8.38	2.28	2.80	1.65
蛋 类	Eggs	7.23	8.10	11.98	10.69	8.99	8.25	10.94	11.19	10.33	13.01	16.54
水产品	Aquatic Produc	28.84	25.59	28.59	33.06	35.66	37.26	42.12	38.70	43.09	43.25	39.61

9-16 农民家庭主要生活用品购买量
ANNUAL PURCHASES OF ARTICLES FOR BAILY USE OF RURAL HOUSEHOLDS PER CAPITA

品 名		Item		2004	2005	2006	2007	2008	2009	2010	2011	2012	2013
粮 食	(千克/人)	Grain	(Kg/person)	27.53	26.55	26.28	25.72	26.56	27.45	29.46	42.35	44.45	38.34
植物油	(千克/人)	Edible Vegetable	(Kg/person)	2.79	2.89	2.85	3.21	3.55	3.35	3.61	5.20	5.70	5.11
动物油	(千克/人)	Edible Animal O	(Kg/person)	0.64	0.73	0.63	0.50	0.47	0.38	0.33	0.43	0.39	0.27
蔬菜	(千克/人)	Vegetables	(Kg/person)	13.97	16.33	16.33	16.44	17.85	16.21	17.73	19.40	18.27	16.51
猪肉	(千克/人)	Pork	(Kg/person)	5.72	6.93	7.46	6.27	6.22	7.04	7.43	8.38	8.71	8.76
牛羊肉	(千克/人)	Beef and Mutton	(Kg/person)	0.28	0.37	0.42	0.49	0.41	0.41	0.51	0.56	0.47	0.54
家禽	(千克/人)	Poultry	(Kg/person)	0.67	0.79	0.79	1.08	1.21	1.16	1.17	1.26	1.24	0.97
鲜蛋	(千克/人)	Fresh Eggs	(Kg/person)	0.57	0.93	0.97	0.97	1.33	1.55	1.30	1.85	2.20	
鲜活鱼类	(千克/人)	Fresh Fish	(Kg/person)	5.72	6.64	7.07	7.69	7.29	6.97	6.99	7.11	7.06	
卷烟	(盒/人)	Tobacco	(pack/person)	25.72	30.53	30.98	29.06	28.88	27.51	27.50	31.12	31.42	26.93
酒	(千克/人)	Wine	(Kg/person)	8.15	10.13	11.90	12.30	11.70	11.35	10.72	11.37	11.06	10.06
水 果	(千克/人)	Fruits	(Kg/person)	5.40	6.84	6.34	6.87	6.80	6.72	6.22	6.87	8.27	
服 装	(件/人)	Clothing	(piece/person)	1.51	1.81	1.82	1.82	1.99	2.94	1.95	2.46	2.52	
鞋 类	(双/人)	Footwear	(Two/person)	1.32	1.42	1.45	1.35	1.43	1.28	1.36	1.39	1.80	
水 泥	(千克/人)	Cement	(Kg/person)	70.88	70.67	108.80	85.93	134.97	137.25	150.72	236.88	149.81	
钢 材	(千克/人)	Steel	(Kg/person)	3.76	4.52	6.66	5.84	10.45	10.11	10.21	13.85	9.72	
生活用煤	(千克/人)	Coal	(Kg/person)	58.08	52.97	52.65	49.44	32.82	20.22	19.70	14.77	13.18	
电视机	(台/百户)	TV Sets	(set/100 househol	7.00	6.88	6.79	5.79	4.95	3.97	3.70	6.67	6.48	5.76
洗衣机	(台/百户)	Washing Machin	(set/100 househol	0.82	1.85	1.79	1.92	2.73	2.67	3.21	6.09	5.09	4.44
电风扇	(台/百户)	Electric Fans	(set/100 househol	8.03	8.21	9.73	8.85	9.73	11.45	10.52	10.79	13.67	
电冰箱	(台/百户)	Refrigerators	(set/100 househol	0.48	1.66	2.67	4.18	5.64	7.06	7.00	8.30	7.12	6.16
自行车	(辆/百户)	Bycicle	(set/100 househol	6.45	5.29	4.50	3.91	4.83	5.29	2.42	3.73	3.09	2.39
摩托车	(辆/百户)	Motocycle	(set/100 househol	4.06	4.39	5.00	5.28	4.73	4.26	3.88	6.09	5.30	3.91
热水器	(台/百户)	Shower	(set/100 househol	0.30	1.24	1.67	2.06	3.11	3.79	4.36	6.18	5.70	3.58
电话机	(部/百户)	Telephone Sets	(set/100 househol	4.76	5.09	6.15	4.52	4.33	4.37	3.36	3.41	2.76	1.86
手 机	(部/百户)	Mobile Phones	(set/100 househol	7.36	9.64	8.30	12.97	13.82	14.42	18.92	25.39	28.00	33.40

9–17 农民家庭年人均主要食品消费量
RURAL HOUSEHOLD ANNUAL CONSUMPTION ON MAJOR FOOD PER CAPITA

单位：千克 (Kg)

品　名		2004	2005	2006	2007	2008	2009	2010	2011	2012	2013
一、粮 食	Grain	222.05	215.68	213.71	208.29	193.60	192.22	178.37	162.86	151.06	125.59
#小 麦	Wheat	22.52	22.58	23.11	21.80	22.02	19.87	17.60	17.41	15.55	10.17
稻 谷	Paddy	182.78	171.47	170.17	168.61	155.37	155.18	146.13	135.87	126.67	104.27
豆类	Bean	3.27	3.64	3.65	3.82	3.30	3.27	3.22	2.53	1.97	3.85
二、蔬菜及菜制品	Fresh Vegetables and	147.73	152.47	143.75	143.57	132.58	137.04	137.51	131.68	119.33	88.16
鲜 菜	Fresh Vegetables	140.34	147.06	138.12	140.57	130.05	134.69	136.22	130.67	118.25	86.56
三、油脂类	Oil and Fats	3.52	3.70	3.56	3.77	4.11	3.85	5.49	8.17	10.39	11.05
植物油	Edible Vegetable Oil	2.87	2.98	2.89	3.23	3.58	3.39	5.13	7.71	9.93	10.61
动物油	Edible Animal Oil	0.64	0.73	0.67	0.53	0.53	0.47	0.36	0.46	0.47	0.43
四、肉禽及其制品	Meat and Processed Products	20.81	24.79	25.27	22.70	22.21	22.99	22.79	22.90	22.80	22.91
猪 肉	Pork	17.49	20.63	20.91	17.83	17.51	18.14	17.98	17.40	17.63	18.11
牛羊肉	Beef and Mutton	0.37	0.44	0.53	0.52	0.50	0.48	0.57	0.65	0.53	0.63
家 禽	Poultry	2.48	3.02	2.91	3.30	3.23	3.22	2.91	3.23	2.94	2.87
五、蛋类及蛋制品	Eggs and Processed Products	3.99	4.14	4.15	4.17	4.69	4.93	4.47	5.03	5.02	4.68
六、奶及奶制品	Milk and Dariy Products	0.11	0.23	0.33	0.50	0.81	1.11	1.22	1.55	1.67	2.11
七、水产品	Aquatic Products	7.21	8.11	8.51	9.38	8.71	8.34	8.33	8.38	8.54	7.93
鱼 类	Ffish	6.97	7.81	8.18	9.03	8.40	7.97	7.93	8.03	8.09	7.58
八、瓜 类	Melons	4.99	4.79	8.08	6.28	4.67	5.87	5.56	7.06	5.80	6.34
九、酒 类	Liquor and Drinks	8.20	10.17	11.93	12.35	11.76	11.41	10.77	11.40	11.12	10.08
#白 酒	Wine Spirit	3.68	3.91	4.06	3.87	3.85	3.94	3.70	3.69	3.52	3.65
啤 酒	Beer	4.46	6.21	7.83	8.42	7.84	7.40	7.01	7.67	7.53	6.41
十、水果类	Fruit	9.85	10.62	10.87	11.51	10.37	9.97	9.31	8.44	10.17	6.24
十一、坚果及果仁制	Nuts and Grain Products	0.55	0.76	0.80	0.87	0.97	1.00	0.83	0.88	0.86	0.76

9-18 农民家庭每百户主要耐用消费品拥有量
POSSESSTION OF URABLE CONSUMER GOODS PER 100 RURAL HOUSEHOLDS

品名		Item		2004	2005	2006	2007	2008	2009	2010	2011	2012	2013
彩电	(台)	Color TV Set	(unit)	67.97	83.18	92.12	98.82	102.24	105.42	109.18	114.36	116.24	114.35
照相机	(架)	Camera	(unit)	2.18	1.88	1.76	1.82	2.06	2.58	2.64	3.55	3.64	5.24
洗衣机	(台)	Washing Machine	(unit)	21.58	26.39	30.12	34.68	37.12	41.70	47.97	57.09	62.42	53.79
电冰箱	(台)	Refrigerator	(unit)	11.06	14.82	19.18	26.18	30.52	41.36	51.48	73.73	80.18	75.82
摩托车	(辆)	Motocycle	(unit)	31.42	39.15	45.00	51.45	55.52	59.76	64.12	72.33	74.76	68.84
摄像机	(台)	Videorecorder	(unit)	0.30	0.55	0.76	1.06	0.91	0.52	0.70	1.42	1.52	0.62
抽油烟机	(台)	Ventilator	(unit)	2.00	3.12	3.72	5.03	6.10	7.70	10.03	13.70	15.82	10.94
空调机	(台)	Air Conditioner	(unit)	1.48	3.79	5.39	7.61	9.91	12.45	18.36	28.58	33.15	33.05
热水器	(台)	Shower	(unit)	3.85	6.21	8.79	12.21	16.03	22.73	32.00	48.24	55.91	52.16
电话机	(部)	Telephone Set	(set)	38.64	51.64	57.20	58.36	59.33	55.61	55.70	41.94	40.06	31.44
移动电话	(部)	Moblile Phone	(set)	37.12	71.18	90.10	104.67	117.88	134.21	152.27	204.82	215.06	211.52
家用计算机	(台)	PC	(unit)	1.18	1.09	2.33	2.00	3.00	5.15	7.39	15.58	19.73	22.14

9-19 市、州农民年人均纯收入
ANAUAL NET INCOME OF RURAL HOUCEHOLD PER CAPITA IN CITIES AND PREFERCTURES

单位：元 (yuan)

地区	Item	2004	2005	2006	2007	2008	2009	2010	2011	2012	2013
全省	Province	2890	3099	3419	3997	4656	5035	5832	6898	7852	8867
武汉市	Wuhan Municipality	3955	4341	4748	5371	6349	7161	8295	9814	11190	12713
黄石市	Huangshi Municipality	2626	2810	3182	3742	4374	4811	5524	6487	7477	8492
十堰市	Shiyan Municipality	1916	1990	2191	2490	2841	3110	3499	4044	4566	5226
宜昌市	Yichang Municipality	2938	3108	3433	4022	4686	5186	5980	7055	8046	9121
襄阳市	Xiangyang Municipality	3060	3191	3519	4114	4880	5440	6365	7549	8684	9785
鄂州市	Ezhou Municipality	3234	3495	3799	4393	5096	5718	6645	7909	9072	10210
荆门市	Jingmen Municipality	3629	3738	4059	4652	5332	5956	6951	8248	9387	10615
孝感市	Xiaogan Municipality	2874	3028	3336	3915	4636	5131	5943	7029	7988	9023
荆州市	Jingzhou Municipality	3002	3108	3502	4140	4889	5464	6453	7664	8710	9909
黄冈市	Huanggang Municipality	2485	2644	2861	3295	3744	4130	4634	5438	6142	6966
咸宁市	Xianning Municipality	2698	2911	3213	3737	4411	4873	5606	6588	7505	8480
随州市	Suizhou Municipality	3017	3223	3581	4177	4967	5457	6279	7427	8419	9490
恩施自治州	Enshi Municipality	1593	1643	1848	2143	2519	2810	3255	3939	4571	5235
仙桃市	Xiantao Municipality	3615	3818	4190	4695	5248	5856	6807	8006	9076	10365
天门市	Tianmen Municipality	3087	3273	3658	4207	4761	5326	6207	7407	8507	9608
潜江市	Qianjiang Municipality	3180	3398	3813	4378	4929	5531	6486	7684	8785	10017
神农架林区	Shennongjia Forest Zones	1906	2164	2394	2850	3330	3707	4083	4640	5110	5677

主要统计指标解释

城镇家庭人口 指居住在一起，经济上合在一起共同生活的家庭成员。凡计算为家庭人口的成员其全部收支都包括在本家庭中。

城镇就业面 指就业人口占家庭人口的百分比。

城镇就业者负担人数 指家庭人口与就业人口之比。

城镇家庭总收入 指家庭成员得到的工薪收入、经营净收入、财产性收入、转移性收入之和，不包括出售财物收入和借贷收入。

城镇家庭可支配收入 指家庭成员得到可用于最终消费支出和其它非义务性支出以及储蓄的总和，即居民家庭可以用来自由支配的收入。它是家庭总收入扣除交纳的所得税、个人交纳的社会保障支出以及记账补贴后的收入。计算公式为：

可支配收入=家庭总收入-交纳所得税-个人交纳的社会保障支出-记帐补贴

城镇家庭总支出 指除借贷支出以外的全部家庭支出。包括消费性支出、购房建房支出、转移性支出、财产性支出、社会保障支出。

城镇家庭消费性支出 指家庭用于日常生活的支出，包括食品、衣着、家庭设备用品及服务、医疗保健、交通和通信、娱乐教育文化服务、居住、杂项商品和服务等八大类支出。

城镇家庭服务性消费支出 指家庭用于支付社会提供的各种非商品性服务费用。

城镇家庭收入分组方法 是将所有调查户依户人均可支配收入由低到高排队，按 10%，10%，20%，20%，20%，10%，10%的比例依次分成：最低收入户、低收入户、中等偏下收入户、中等收入户、中等偏上收入户、高收入户、最高收入户等七组。总体中最低 5%的户为困难户。

恩格尔系数 指食物支出金额在消费性总支出金额中所占的比例。计算公式为：

$$\text{恩格尔系数}=\frac{\text{食品支出金额}}{\text{消费性总支出金额}}\times 100\%$$

农村住户 指农村常住户。农村常住户指长期(一年以上)居住在乡镇(不包括城关镇)行政管理区域内的住户，以及长期居住在城关镇所辖行政村范围内的农村住户。户口不在本地而在本地居住一年及以上的住户也包括在本地农村常住户范围内；有本地户口，但举家外出谋生一年以上的住户，无论是否保留承包耕地都不包括在本地农村住户范围内。

常住人口 指全年经常在家或在家居住 6 个月以上，而且经济和生活与本户连成一体的人口。外出从业人员在外居住时间虽然在 6 个月以上，但收入主要带回家中，经济与本户连为一体，仍视为家庭常住人口；在家居住，生活和本户连成一体的国家职工、退休人员也为家庭常住人口。但是现役军人、中专及以上(走读生除外)的在校学生、以及常年在外(不包括探亲、看病等)且已有稳定的职业与居住场所的外出从业人员，不算家庭常住人口。家庭常住人口主要作为计算农村住户平均每人收入、消费和积累水平及分析家庭人口状况的依据。

整、半劳动力 整劳动力指男子 18 周岁到 50 周岁，女子 18 周岁到 45 周岁；半劳动力指男子 16 周岁到 17 周岁，51 周岁到 60 周岁；女子 16 周岁到 17 周岁，46 周岁到 55 周岁，同时具有劳动能力的人。虽然在劳动年龄之内，但已丧失劳动能力的人，不应算为劳动力；超过劳动年龄，但能经常参加劳动，计入半劳动力数内。常住人口中的职工，若这些职工为劳动力，就包括在本户的整半劳动力中。

总收入 指调查期内农村住户和住户成员从各种来源渠道得到的收入总和。按收入的性质划分为工资性收入、家庭经营收入、财产性收入和转移性收入。

工资性收入 指农村住户成员受雇于单位或个人，靠出卖劳动而获得的收入。

家庭经营收入 指农村住户以家庭为生产经营单位进行生产筹划和管理而获得的收入。农村住户家庭经营活动按行业划分为农业、林业、牧业、渔业、工业、建筑业、交通运输业邮电业、批发和零售贸易餐饮业、社会服务业、文教卫生业和其他家庭经营。

财产性收入 指金融资产或有形非生产性资产的所有者向其他机构单位提供资金或将有形非生产性资产供其支配，作为回报而从中获得的收入。

转移性收入 指农村住户和住户成员无须付出任何对应物而获得的货物、服务、资金或资产所有权等，不包括无偿提供的用于固定资本形成的资金。一般情况下，是指农村住户在二次分配中的所有收入。

现金收入 指农村住户和住户成员在调查期内得到以现金形态表现的收入。按来源分成工资性收入、家庭经营现金收入、财产性收入、转移性收入。

纯收入 指农村住户当年从各个来源得到的总收入相应地扣除所发生的费用后的收入总和。计算方法：

纯收入=总收入−家庭经营费用支出−税费支出−生产性固定资产折旧−赠送农村外部亲友支出−记帐补贴

纯收入主要用于再生产投入和当年生活消费支出，也可用于储蓄和各种非义务性支出。“农民人均纯收入”按人口平均的纯收入水平，反映的是一个地区或一个农户农村居民的平均收入水平。

总支出 指农村住户用于生产、生活和再分配的全部支出。家庭经营费用支出、购置生产性固定资产支出、生产性固定资产折旧、税费支出、生活消费支出、财产性支出和转移性支出。

Explanatory Notes on Main Statistical Indicators

Population of Urban Households refer to members of the household living and sharing economically together. All income and expenditure of the population of the household are included in the income and expenditure of the household.

Proportion of Urban Employment refer to the proportion of employed population to the population of urban households.

Number of Dependents per Urban Employee refers to the ratio between number of persons in urban households and the number of dependents.

Total Income of Urban Households refers to the sum of wage and salary, net business income, income from properties, and income from transfers of members of the households, excluding income from selling of properties and income from borrowings.

Disposable Income of Urban Households refers to the actual income at the disposal of members of the households which can be used for final consumption, other non-compulsory expenditure and savings. This equals to total income minus income tax, personal contribution to social security and sample household subsidy for keeping diaries. Following formula is used:

Disposable income = total household income - income tax - personal contribution to social security - sample household subsidy for keeping diaries

Total Expenditure of Urban Households refer to all expenditure of the households except expenditure on leading. It includes expenditure on consumption, on purchasing or building houses, on transfers, on properties and on social security.

Consumption Expenditure of Urban Households refers to total expenditure of the sample households for consumption in daily life, including expenditure on eight categories such as food, clothing, household appliances and services, health care and medical services, transport and communications, recreation, education and cultural services, housing, miscellaneous goods and services.

Expenditure of Urban Households on Consumption of Services refers to expenditure of households on services of various kinds provided by the society.

Urban Households by Income Group All households in the sample are grouped, by per capita disposable income of the household, into groups of lowest income, low income, lower middle income, middle income, upper middle income, high income and highest income, each group consisting of 10%, 10%, 20%, 20%, 20%, 10% and 10% of all households respectively. The lowest 5% of households are also referred to as poor households.

Engel Coefficient refers to the percentage of expenditure on food in the total consumption expenditure, using the following formula:

Engel Coefficient = (expenditure on food / total consumption expenditure) x 100%

Rural Households refer to resident households in rural areas. Resident households in rural areas are the households residing for more than one year in the areas under the jurisdiction of administration of township governments (excluding county towns), and in the areas under the jurisdiction of administration of villages in county towns. Migrated households residing in the current addresses for over one year with their household registration in other places are included in the resident households of their current addresses. For households with their household registration in one place but all members of the households moving away for living in another place for over one year, they will not be included in the rural households of the area where they are registered, irrespective of whether they still keep their contracted land.

Resident Population refers to population staying at home permanently or for over 6 months during a year and sharing life economically with the household. Members of the household staying away from the household for over 6 months but keeping a close economic relation with the household by sending the majority of income to the household are regarded as resident population of the household. Government staff and workers or retirees living as close members of the household are also considered as resident population. However, servicemen, students of secondary technical schools or schools of higher education and persons with stable jobs and residence outside the household (excluding those visiting relatives or seeking medical service) are not included as resident population of the household. Resident population is used in calculating income, consumption, accumulation on per capita basis of rural households and in analyzing composition of rural households.

Full/Semi Labour Force Full labour force refers to persons capable of work, aged 18-50 for males and 18-45 for females. Semi labour force refers to persons capable of work, aged 16-17 and 51-60 for males and 16-17 and 46-55 for females. Persons at their working ages but not capable of work are not to be included as labour force. Persons not at working ages but participating regularly in work are included in semi labour force. For staff and workers as resident population of the household, they are included as full or semi labour force of the household if they are in the labour force.

Total Income refers to the sum of income earned from various sources by the rural households and their members during the reference period, and is classified as income from wages and salaries, income from household operations, income from properties and income from transfers.

Income from Wages and Salaries refers to income from labour earned by the members of rural households employed by other units or individuals.

Income from Household Operations refers to income by the rural households as units of production and operations. Operations by rural households are classified by economic activities as agriculture, forestry, animal husbandry, fishery, manufacturing, construction, transportation, post and telecommunications, wholesale, retail and catering, social service, culture, education, health, and other household operations.

Income from Properties refers to the income received as returns by owners of financial assets or tangible non-productive assets by providing capitals or tangible non-productive assets to other institutional units.

Income from Transfers refers to the receipt by rural households and their members of goods, services, capitals or rights of assets without giving or repaying accordingly, excluding capitals provided to them for the formation of fixed assets. In general, it refers to all income received by rural households through redistribution.

Cash Income refers to income received by rural households and their members in the form of cash during the reference period. It is classified, by source of income, into income from wages and salaries, cash income from household operations, income from properties and income from transfers.

Net Income refers to the total income of rural households from all sources minus all corresponding expenses. The formula for calculation is as follows:

Net income = total income - taxes and fees paid - household operation expenses - taxes and fees depreciation of fixed assets for production - subsidy for participating in household survey - gifts to non-rural relatives

Net income is mainly used as input for reproduction and as consumption expenditure of the year, and also used for savings and non-compulsory expenses of various forms. "Per capita net income of farmers" is the level of net income averaged by population which reflects the average income level of rural households in a given area.

Total Expenditure refers to total expenses of rural households on production, consumption and redistribution, including expenditure on household operations, on purchase of productive fixed assets, depreciation of productive fixed assets, taxes and fees, expenses on household consumption, expenses on properties and expenses on transfers.

10 城市概况

City Overview

资料整理：程文懿

10–1 主要城市土地面积、人口情况(2013)

LAND AREA AND PULATION OF MAJOR MUNICIPALITIES (2013)

城市	Municipalities	土地面积(平方公里) Land Area (sq.km)	常住人口(万人) Resident Population (10 000 persons)	当年出生人口(人) Births (persons)	当年死亡人口(人) Deaths (persons)	人口密度(人/平方公里) Population Desity (person/sq.km)
武 汉	Wuhan Municipality	8494	1022.00	92701	40941	1203.20
黄 石	Huangshi Municipality	4586	244.50	40408	9075	533.14
十 堰	Shiyan Municipality	23680	336.70	49495	22994	142.19
宜 昌	Yichang Municipality	21084	409.83	35174	25626	194.38
襄 阳	Xiangyang Municipality	19724	559.12	72722	68751	283.47
鄂 州	Ezhou Municipality	1596	105.70	11284	5794	662.28
荆 门	Jingmen Municipality	12404	288.72	26803	13938	232.76
孝 感	Xiaogan Municipality	8910	485.30	55790	29290	544.67
荆 州	Jingzhou Municipality	14067	573.94	49135	28252	408.00
黄 冈	Huanggang Municipality	17457	625.19	101788	27202	358.13
咸 宁	Xianning Municipality	10049	248.50	39525	9203	247.29
随 州	Suizhou Municipality	9636	218.01	31161	9120	226.25

10–2 主要城市就业情况(2013)

EMPLOYMENT OF MAJOR MUNICIPALITIES (2013)

单位：万人 (10 000 persons)

城市	Municipalities	年末单位从业人数 Employment (year-end)	从业人员按三次产业分 Employment Grouped by Type of Industry			#城镇私营和个体人数 #Employment in Private Enterprises and Self-employed Individuals of Urban Areas
			第一产业 Primary Industry	第二产业 Secondary Industry	第三产业 Tertiary Industry	
武 汉	Wuhan Municipality	198.54	0.38	102.28	95.88	212.25
黄 石	Huangshi Municipality	33.37	0.15	21.37	11.85	36.25
十 堰	Shiyan Municipality	60.90	0.66	31.71	28.53	59.60
宜 昌	Yichang Municipality	85.04	0.36	48.08	36.60	159.22
襄 阳	Xiangyang Municipality	84.91	0.78	48.85	35.28	63.18
鄂 州	Ezhou Municipality	20.35	0.01	13.24	7.10	10.59
荆 门	Jingmen Municipality	38.11	0.90	21.77	15.44	36.82
孝 感	Xiaogan Municipality	79.69	0.71	47.75	31.23	63.91
荆 州	Jingzhou Municipality	41.58	1.23	19.33	21.02	71.63
黄 冈	Huanggang Municipality	44.46	2.10	20.28	22.08	16.32
咸 宁	Xianning Municipality	23.55	0.07	9.87	13.61	20.07
随 州	Suizhou Municipality	15.03	0.07	7.12	7.84	54.37

10–3 主要城市地区生产总值及指数(2013)
GROSS DOMESTIC PRODUCTS OF MAJOR MUNICIPALITIES (2013)

城市	Municipalities	地区生产总值（当年价格）(亿元) Gross Domestic Product (100 million yuan)	第一产业 Primary Industry	第二产业 Secondary Industry	第三产业 Tertiary Industry	人均地区生产总值(元) Per Capita GDP(yuan)	地区生产总值指数(上年=100) GDP Index (preceding year=100)
武汉	Wuhan Municipality	9051.27	335.40	4396.17	4319.70	88999.71	110.0
黄石	Huangshi Municipality	1142.03	95.21	699.20	347.62	46749.90	109.8
十堰	Shiyan Municipality	1080.59	143.03	547.01	390.55	32142.24	110.4
宜昌	Yichang Municipality	2818.07	335.95	1693.77	788.35	68845.92	111.5
襄阳	Xiangyang Municipality	2814.02	386.45	1611.41	816.16	50509.22	111.4
鄂州	Ezhou Municipality	630.94	78.51	375.08	177.35	59790.57	110.5
荆门	Jingmen Municipality	1202.61	190.30	651.93	360.38	41667.59	110.5
孝感	Xiaogan Municipality	1238.93	243.13	602.31	393.49	25581.61	110.8
荆州	Jingzhou Municipality	1334.93	319.09	596.20	419.64	23299.65	110.4
黄冈	Huanggang Municipality	1332.55	356.79	521.28	454.48	21348.47	110.5
咸宁	Xianning Municipality	872.11	162.90	423.09	286.12	35165.73	110.6
随州	Suizhou Municipality	661.94	124.79	320.26	216.89	30376.76	110.6

10–4 主要城市固定资产投资(2013)
INVESTMENT IN FIXED ASSETS OF MAJOR MUNICIPALITIES (2013)

单位：亿元 (100 million yuan)

城市	Municipalities	固定资产投资 Investment in Fixed Assets	房地产开发投资 Investment in Real Estate	#住宅 #Residential Buildings	新增固定资产 Newly Increased Fixed Assets	商品房屋销售建筑面积(万平方米) Construction Floor Space of Commercial House Sold (10 000 sq.km)	#住宅 #Residential Buildings
武汉	Wuhan Municipality	5974.53	1905.60	1250.78	2021.16	1995.36	1750.43
黄石	Huangshi Municipality	947.69	84.68	64.78	605.17	187.14	168.17
十堰	Shiyan Municipality	853.52	101.11	69.62	530.64	177.85	169.71
宜昌	Yichang Municipality	2023.92	203.18	149.70	1398.38	460.13	406.54
襄阳	Xiangyang Municipality	1998.57	251.94	205.48	926.58	603.08	509.90
鄂州	Ezhou Municipality	567.19	16.28	12.89	365.57	56.78	53.18
荆门	Jingmen Municipality	978.50	87.79	63.31	723.85	195.47	178.46
孝感	Xiaogan Municipality	1215.35	111.13	88.39	940.78	242.78	233.73
荆州	Jingzhou Municipality	1287.40	76.79	56.41	776.79	174.39	166.92
黄冈	Huanggang Municipality	1365.57	132.73	104.16	951.08	421.31	393.62
咸宁	Xianning Municipality	953.00	112.06	78.98	675.59	271.31	245.31
随州	Suizhou Municipality	628.59	29.23	23.91	493.04	91.61	88.11

10-5 主要城市工业基本情况(2013)

BASIC STATISTICS ON INDUSTRY OF MAJOR MUNICIPALITIES (2013)

单位：亿元 (100 million yuan)

城市	Municipalities	工业企业单位数(个) Number of Industrial Enterprises (unit)	主营业务收入 Major Business Income	利润总额 Total Profits
武 汉	Wuhan Municipality	2340	10927.62	465.88
黄 石	Huangshi Municipality	687	2498.47	89.50
十 堰	Shiyan Municipality	696	1612.10	192.47
宜 昌	Yichang Municipality	1233	4269.99	414.78
襄 阳	Xiangyang Municipality	1529	4141.04	517.31
鄂 州	Ezhou Municipality	487	1179.50	42.44
荆 门	Jingmen Municipality	922	2545.50	131.56
孝 感	Xiaogan Municipality	1142	2160.33	120.97
荆 州	Jingzhou Municipality	861	1769.07	118.19
黄 冈	Huanggang Municipality	1134	1330.04	54.10
咸 宁	Xianning Municipality	830	1431.64	135.89
随 州	Suizhou Municipality	632	1024.92	78.94

10-6 主要城市工业总产值(2013)

GROSS OUTPUT VALUE OF INDUSTRY OF MAJOR MUNICIPALITIES (2013)

单位：亿元 (100 million yuan)

城市	Municipalities	工业总产值(当年价) Total Value of Industry	内资企业 Inner Funded Enterprises	外商港澳台投资企业 Foreign, Hongkong, Macao and Taiwan Funded Enterprises	#国有企业 #State-owned Enterprise
武 汉	Wuhan Municipality	11188.31	7943.52	3244.79	2881.22
黄 石	Huangshi Municipality	2095.64	1637.92	457.72	2.63
十 堰	Shiyan Municipality	1709.63	1128.29	581.34	31.42
宜 昌	Yichang Municipality	4396.28	4044.93	351.35	239.48
襄 阳	Xiangyang Municipality	5417.68	4728.60	689.08	111.53
鄂 州	Ezhou Municipality	1234.67	1152.02	82.65	120.77
荆 门	Jingmen Municipality	2605.44	2434.37	171.07	2.63
孝 感	Xiaogan Municipality	2198.59	1997.30	201.29	18.58
荆 州	Jingzhou Municipality	1896.66	1755.67	140.99	48.92
黄 冈	Huanggang Municipality	1495.37	1365.47	129.89	13.35
咸 宁	Xianning Municipality	1514.53	1367.00	147.53	2.46
随 州	Suizhou Municipality	1055.55	983.86	71.68	14.17

10-7 主要城市财政收支(2013)
GOVERNMENT REVENUE AND EXPENDITURES OF MAJOR MUNICIPALITIES (2013)

单位：亿元 (100 million yuan)

城市	Municipalities	公共财政收入 The public finance income	#各项税收 #Taxes	公共财政支出 The public finance expenditures	#文教科卫事业费 #Expenditures for Culture, Education, Science & Technology and Health Care	#社会保障和就业支出 #Subsides Expenditures for Social Security	#城乡社区事务支出 #Expenditures for City Maintenance
武 汉	Wuhan Municipality	1730.65	793.49	1122.88	259.43	149.25	190.54
黄 石	Huangshi Municipality	78.36	55.09	150.16	37.44	25.63	9.46
十 堰	Shiyan Municipality	73.53	56.13	231.42	55.01	33.53	10.09
宜 昌	Yichang Municipality	206.31	152.25	360.85	87.12	37.20	24.46
襄 阳	Xiangyang Municipality	191.53	141.38	364.87	91.07	53.41	24.21
鄂 州	Ezhou Municipality	38.43	27.90	70.85	17.44	8.51	5.97
荆 门	Jingmen Municipality	59.84	42.06	158.79	37.59	22.94	7.53
孝 感	Xiaogan Municipality	89.05	58.23	227.90	64.86	35.41	7.73
荆 州	Jingzhou Municipality	71.95	53.39	255.92	69.66	41.58	7.19
黄 冈	Huanggang Municipality	79.98	53.02	300.82	99.15	47.73	6.67
咸 宁	Xianning Municipality	58.71	41.13	156.69	43.72	18.86	5.22
随 州	Suizhou Municipality	29.67	21.79	100.04	29.05	16.48	3.83

10-8 主要城市金融机构存贷款余额(2013)
DEPOSITS AND LOANS BALANCE OF BANKING INSTITUTIONS OF MAJOR MUNICIPALITIES (2013)

单位：亿元 (100 million yuan)

城市	Municipalities	年末金融机构人民币各项存款余额 Deposit Balance	#居民储蓄存款 #Savings Deposits from Residents	年末金融机构人民币各项贷款余额 Loans Balance
武 汉	Wuhan Municipality	14915.69	5117.43	12803.87
黄 石	Huangshi Municipality	1138.90	597.18	737.35
十 堰	Shiyan Municipality	1436.58	786.93	731.51
宜 昌	Yichang Municipality	2370.61	1200.10	1724.39
襄 阳	Xiangyang Municipality	2181.96	1320.05	1244.79
鄂 州	Ezhou Municipality	397.82	236.75	270.99
荆 门	Jingmen Municipality	1121.25	732.74	560.42
孝 感	Xiaogan Municipality	1404.12	943.17	659.10
荆 州	Jingzhou Municipality	1738.91	1180.67	802.18
黄 冈	Huanggang Municipality	1719.43	1197.89	654.21
咸 宁	Xianning Municipality	776.62	448.83	442.58
随 州	Suizhou Municipality	724.41	499.16	323.91

10—9 主要城市贸易、外经(2013)

DOMESTIC TRADE AND FOREIGN ECONOMY OF MAJOR MUNICIPALITIES (2013)

城市	Municipalities	社会消费品零售总额(亿元) Total Retail Sales of consumer Goods (100 million yuan)	进出口总额(亿美元) Total Import and Export (USD 100 million)	进口 Imports	出口 Exports	当年实际使用外资金额(亿美元) ActualForeign Direct Investment (USD 100 million)
武 汉	Wuhan Municipality	3916.60	217.52	98.09	119.43	40.40
黄 石	Huangshi Municipality	468.86	28.53	16.48	12.05	4.90
十 堰	Shiyan Municipality	491.51	4.83	0.60	4.23	1.56
宜 昌	Yichang Municipality	881.93	23.50	3.33	20.17	2.70
襄 阳	Xiangyang Municipality	966.31	16.19	1.85	14.34	5.37
鄂 州	Ezhou Municipality	208.68	4.92	3.16	1.76	1.62
荆 门	Jingmen Municipality	414.68	7.77	1.59	6.18	2.63
孝 感	Xiaogan Municipality	608.68	10.25	2.45	7.80	2.75
荆 州	Jingzhou Municipality	781.36	13.66	2.39	11.27	1.08
黄 冈	Huanggang Municipality	635.02	5.37	0.85	4.51	0.67
咸 宁	Xianning Municipality	330.58	3.36	0.68	2.68	2.47
随 州	Suizhou Municipality	333.86	12.67	1.40	11.27	0.88

10—10 主要城市邮电、电力(2013)

POST SERVICF AND POWER IN MAJOR MUNICIPALITIES（2013）

城市	Municipalities	邮电业务收入(全市)(亿元) Revenue from Posts and Telecommunication Services(100 million yuan)	固定电话用户(万户) Telephones (10 000 Subscribers)	移动电话用户(万户) Mobile Telephones (10 000 Subscribers)	国际互联网用户(万户) Internet Service (10 000 Subscribers)	全年用电量(亿千瓦小时) Power Consumption (100 million kWh)	#城乡居民生活用电 #Urban and Rural Residents Power Consumption
武 汉	Wuhan Municipality	164.41	294.00	1662.00	369.00	437.23	83.01
黄 石	Huangshi Municipality	19.50	42.60	223.33	39.78	111.90	12.36
十 堰	Shiyan Municipality	18.40	48.50	267.51	68.48	94.81	12.88
宜 昌	Yichang Municipality	30.51	65.17	397.28	64.00	208.53	18.66
襄 阳	Xiangyang Municipality	34.62	78.00	413.80	62.00	123.94	21.63
鄂 州	Ezhou Municipality	16.36	21.68	95.00	16.16	58.93	5.22
荆 门	Jingmen Municipality	17.97	38.15	199.23	38.24	80.55	11.03
孝 感	Xiaogan Municipality	25.21	57.85	326.50	49.93	103.89	18.85
荆 州	Jingzhou Municipality	35.60	73.32	393.30	75.51	96.11	23.48
黄 冈	Huanggang Municipalit	29.28	87.43	369.27	56.17	92.28	21.01
咸 宁	Xianning Municipality	14.34	41.87	226.18	34.41	55.56	11.73
随 州	Suizhou Municipality	13.27	36.31	255.26	31.29	29.43	7.73

10-11 主要城市环境保护（2013）
ENVIRONMENTAL PROTECTION OF MAJOR MUNICIPALITIES(2013)

城 市	Municipalities	工业废水排放量(万吨) Industrial Waste Water Discharged (10,000 tons)	工业二氧化硫排放量(万吨) Industrial Sulphur Dioxide Emission (100 million tons)	工业固体废物综合利用率(%) Ratio of Industrial Solid Wastes Vtilized (%)	污水集中处理率(%) Ratio of Central Sewage Treatment (%)	生活垃圾无害化处理率(%) Ratio of Consumption Treated
武 汉	Wuhan Municipality	14700	9.76	95.0	92.5	100.0
黄 石	Huangshi Municipality	5037	8.24	94.3	90.4	100.0
十 堰	Shiyan Municipality	2144	1.81	39.6	90.7	97.0
宜 昌	Yichang Municipality	18419	5.51	47.9	91.0	91.6
襄 阳	Xiangyang Municipality	8619	4.40	98.1	90.3	98.9
鄂 州	Ezhou Municipality	2278	3.58	90.2	88.7	100.0
荆 门	Jingmen Municipality	3825	3.46	92.2	84.9	100.0
孝 感	Xiaogan Municipality	5111	4.30	69.3	91.0	100.0
荆 州	Jingzhou Municipality	10387	4.40	34.6	67.5	46.4
黄 冈	Huanggang Municipality	3045	1.74	92.3	56.9	58.8
咸 宁	Xianning Municipality	2018	2.40	56.2	91.0	100.0
随 州	Suizhou Municipality	1771	0.79	99.9	90.0	90.0

10-12 主要城市居民收支情况(2013)
INCOME AND EXPENDITURE OF MAJOR URBAN HOUSEHOLDS (2013)

单位：元 (yuan)

城 市	Municipalities	城镇居民人均可支配收入 Per Capita Disposable Income of Urban Residents	城镇居民人均消费性支出 Per Capita Living Expenditure of Urban Residents	人均住房建筑面积(平方米) Per Capita Utility Floor Space of Residential Buildings (sq.m)
武 汉	Wuhan Municipality	29821	20157	34.75
黄 石	Huangshi Municipality	21330	14964	31.11
十 堰	Shiyan Municipality	17694	16417	29.49
宜 昌	Yichang Municipality	20934	14743	40.00
襄 阳	Xiangyang Municipality	19329	14828	42.00
鄂 州	Ezhou Municipality	20878	12334	45.24
荆 门	Jingmen Municipality	19820	13993	40.06
孝 感	Xiaogan Municipality	19819	14438	39.90
荆 州	Jingzhou Municipality	18706	14062	40.00
黄 冈	Huanggang Municipality	18432	17438	30.50
咸 宁	Xianning Municipality	18581	15471	42.51
随 州	Suizhou Municipality	19806	14018	43.00

10-13 主要城市居民消费支出、价格(2013)
LIVING EXPENDITURES AND PRICE OF MAJOR URBAN HOUSEHOLDS (2013)

单位：元 (yuan)

城市	Municipalities	城镇居民人均消费性支出 Per Capita Living Expenditures for Consumption of Urban Residents				市辖区居民消费价格指数(上年=100) Consumer Price Index (preceding year=100)
		#医疗保健 #Medicine and Medicine and Medical Service	#交通和通讯 #Transport and Telecom-munication	#娱乐、教育、文化服务 #Recreation,Education and Cultural Services	#居住 #Residence	
武汉	Wuhan Municipality	1437	2546	2601	1649	102.4
黄石	Huangshi Municipality	615	2383	1897	1447	102.5
十堰	Shiyan Municipality	1292	1814	2182	1121	103.4
宜昌	Yichang Municipality	837	1635	1645	1294	103.3
襄阳	Xiangyang Municipality	1676	1018	1654	1448	103.0
鄂州	Ezhou Municipality	522	800	1379	1103	102.7
荆门	Jingmen Municipality	1271	1423	2068	1079	103.2
孝感	Xiaogan Municipality	834	1334	1445	1292	103.1
荆州	Jingzhou Municipality	921	1482	1527	1605	103.1
黄冈	Huanggang Municipality	1238	2198	2250	1430	103.0
咸宁	Xianning Municipality	1499	2133	1791	1272	102.8
随州	Suizhou Municipality	946	1437	1502	1131	102.5

10-14 主要城市文教、科技、卫生（2013）
CULTURE, EDUCATION, SCIENCE AND TECHNOLOGY AND PUBLIC HEALTH OF MAJOR MUNICIPALITIES (2013)

城市	Municipalities	高等学校在校学生数(万人) Number of Students Enrolled in Institutions of Higher Education (10 000 persons)	从事科技活动人员数(人) Number of Scientific and technical Personel (person)	公共图书馆图书总藏量(万册) Total Volume of Collection of Public Libraries (10 000 volumes)	医院、卫生院数(个) Number of Health Care Institutions (unit)	医院、卫生院数床位数(万张) Number of Beds In Health Care Intitutions (10 000 units)	执业(助理)医师(万人) Practioner Doctors (Assitant) (10 000 persons)
武汉	Wuhan Municipality	96.64		1223.70	242	5.84	2.78
黄石	Huangshi Municipality	3.67	13453	126.90	73	1.32	0.47
十堰	Shiyan Municipality	4.89	12317	94.78	171	2.26	0.84
宜昌	Yichang Municipality	5.98	24190	227.29	163	2.28	0.94
襄阳	Xiangyang Municipality	6.46	25398	157.00	208	2.75	1.02
鄂州	Ezhou Municipality	1.31	2754	38.90	473	0.44	0.17
荆门	Jingmen Municipality	2.12	6214	107.57	98	1.45	0.63
孝感	Xiaogan Municipality	3.77	55349	86.50	155	1.45	0.74
荆州	Jingzhou Municipality	11.35	8625	114.80	166	2.34	0.97
黄冈	Huanggang Municipality	4.83	7945	167.00	286	2.62	2.81
咸宁	Xianning Municipality	3.90	18000	84.79	92	1.03	0.60
随州	Suizhou Municipality	0.68	6010	226.25	103	0.82	0.35

主要统计指标解释

供水综合生产能力 指按供水设施取水、净化、送水、出厂输水干管等环节设计能力计算的综合生产能力。包括在原设计能力的基础上，经挖、革、改增加的生产能力。计算时，以四个环节中最薄弱的环节为主确定能力。

年末供水管道长度 指从送水泵至用户水表之间所有管道的长度。不包括新安装尚未使用的管道。

全年供水总量 指报告期供水企业(单位)供出的全部水量。包括有效供水量和漏损水量。

生活用水量 包括公共服务用水和居民家庭用水。公共服务用水指为城市社会公共生活服务的用水。包括行政事业单位、部队营区和公共设施服务、社会服务业、批发零售贸易业、旅馆饮食业以及其他公共服务业等单位的用水。居民家庭用水指城市范围内所有居民家庭的日常生活用水。包括城市居民、农民家庭、公共供水站用水。

用水普及率 指城市用水人口数与城市人口总数的比率。计算公式：

$$\text{用水普及率}=\frac{\text{城市用水人口数}}{\text{城市人口总数}}\times 100\%$$

供气管道长度 指报告期末从气源厂压缩机的出口或门站出口至各类用户引入管之间的全部已经通气投入使用的管道长度。不包括煤气生产厂、输配站、液化气储存站、灌瓶站、储配站、气化站、混气站、供应站等厂(站)内的管道。

全年供气总量 指全年燃气企业(单位)向用户供应的燃气数量。包括销售量和损失量。

用气普及率 指报告期末使用燃气的城市人口数与城市人口总数的比率。计算公式为：

$$\text{用气普及率}=\frac{\text{城市用气人口数}}{\text{城市人口总数}}\times 100\%$$

城市供热能力 指供热企业(单位)向城市热用户输送热能的设计能力。

城市供热总量 指在报告期供热企业(单位)向城市热用户输送全部蒸汽和热水的总热量。

城市供热管道长度 指从各类热源到热用户建筑物接入口之间的全部蒸汽和热水的管道长度。不包括各类热源厂内部的管道长度。

年末道路长度 指年末道路长度和与道路相通的广场、桥梁、隧道的长度，按车行道中心线计算。在统计时只统计路面宽度在3.5米(含3.5米)以上的各种铺装道路，包括开放型工业区和住宅区道路在内。

城市桥梁 指为跨越天然或人工障碍物而修建的构筑物。包括跨河桥、立交桥、人行天桥以及人行地下通道等。包括永久性桥和半永久性桥。

城市排水管道长度 指所有排水总管、干管、支管、检查井及连接井进出口等长度之和。

城市污水日处理能力 指污水处理厂(或处理装置)每昼夜处理污水量的设计能力。

年末运营车数 指年末公交企业(单位)用于运营业务的全部车辆数。以企业(单位)固定资产台帐中已投入运营的车辆数为准。

城市园林绿地面积 指报告期末用作园林和绿化的各种绿地面积。包括公共绿地、居住区绿地、单位附属绿地、防护绿地、生产绿地、道路绿地和风景林地面积。不包括：

1.屋顶绿化、垂直绿化、阳台绿化和室内绿化。

2.以物质生产为主的林地、耕地、牧草地、果园和竹园等。

3.城市总体规划中不列入绿地的水域。

公共绿地　指向公众开放的市级、区级、居住区级各类公园、街旁游园，包括其范围内的水域。其中居住区级公园应不小于 1 万平方米，街旁游园的宽度不小于 8 米，面积不小于 400 平方米。

Explanatory Notes on Main Statistical Indicators

Production Capacity of Water Supply refers to the designed comprehensive production capacity of water facilities, covering the 4 links of water collection, purification, conveyance, and outflow through trunk pipelines. Increase capacity through transformation and innovation projects are included as well. The capacity is determined mainly on the weakest of the above-mentioned 4 links.

Length of Water Supply Pipelines at the Year-end refers to the total length of all the pipelines between the water pumps and the user 抯 water meters, excluding pipelines newly installed but not used yet.

Annual Volume of Water Supply refers to the total volume of water supplied by water-works (units) during the reference period, including both the effective water supply and loss during the water supply.

Consumption of Water for Residential Use refers to the water consumption of households for daily life and the water consumption of public service facilities. The latter refers to water consumption for urban public services, including the consumption of government agencies and public institutions, military barracks, public facilities, wholesale and retail outlets, restaurants, hotels, and other units providing public services. Household water consumption refers to consumption of water for daily life of all households in the boundary of cities, including households of urban residents and farmers, and public water supply stations.

Percentage of Urban Population with Access to Tap Water refers to the ratio of the urban population with access to tap water to the total urban population. The formula is:

Percentage of population with access to tap water= (Urban population with access to tap water) / (Urban population)×100%

Length of Gas Pipelines refers to the total length of pipelines in use between the outlet of the compressor of gas-work or outlet of gas stations and the leading pipe of users, excluding pipelines within gasworks, delivery stations, LPG storage stations, refilling stations, gas-mixing stations and supply stations.

Volume of Gas Supply refers to the total volume of gas provided to users by gas-producing enterprises (units) in a year, including the volume sold and the volume lost.

Percentage of Urban Population with Access to Gas refers to the ratio of the urban population with access to gas to the total urban population at the end of the reference period. The formula is:

Percentage of population with access to gas = (Urban population with access to gas / Urban population) x 100%

Heating Capacity in Urban Area refers to the designed capacity of heating enterprises (units) in supplying heating energy to urban users during the reference period.

Quantity of Heat Supplied in Urban Area refers to the total quantity of heat from steam and hot water supplied to urban users by heating enterprises (units) during the reference period.

Length of Heating Pipelines refers to the total length of steam or hot water pipelines for sources of heat to the leading pipelines of the buildings of the users, excluding internal pipelines in heat generating enterprises.

Length of Paved Roads at the Year-end refers to the length of roads with paved surface including squares bridges and tunnels connected with roads by the end of the year. Length of the roads is measured by the central lines for vehicles for paved roads with a width of 3.5 meters and over, including roads in open-ended factory compounds and residential quarters.

Urban Bridges refer to bridges built to cross over natural or man-made barriers, including bridges over rivers, overpasses for traffic and for pedestrian, underpasses for pedestrian, etc. Both permanent and semi-permanent bridges are included.

Length of Urban Sewage Pipes refers to the total length of general drainage, trunks. branch and inspection wells, connection wells, inlets and outlets, etc.

Daily Disposal Capacity of Urban Sewage refers to the designed 24 hour capacity of sewage disposal by the sewage treatment works or facilities.

Number of Vehicles under Operation at the Year-end refers to the total number of vehicles under operation by public transport enterprises (units) at the end of the year, based on the records of operational vehicles by the enterprises (units).

Area of Urban Gardens and Green Areas refers to the total area occupied for green projects at the end of the reference period, including public green land, green land in residential quarters, green land attached to institutions, protection green land, production green land, roadside green land and forest in scenic spots. It does not include the following:

(1) Greenery and plants on roofs, balconies, indoors and vertical green areas;

(2) Forest, cultivated land, grassland, orchards and bamboo grooves that are for production purpose; and

(3) Water areas that are not included in urban master plan as green land.

Public Green Area refers to green areas open to the public such as municipal, community and neighborhood parks and roadside parks, including waters within parks. Neighborhood parks should occupy an area larger than 10,000 square meters, and the width of roadside parks should occupy an area larger than 400 square meters, with a width of more that 8 meters.

11 资源和环境

Resources and Environment

资料整理：苏　畅

11-1 “三废”排放和处理综合利用情况

"THREE WASTES" DISCHARGE AND TREATMENT UTILIZATION SITUATION

分类	Item	2010	2011	2012	2013
一、废水排放总量 (万吨)	Total Volume of Waste Water Discharged (10 000 ton)	270755	293064	290200	294054
工业废水排放总量 (万吨)	Total Volume of Industrial Waste Water Discharged	94593	104434	91609	84993
二、废气排放总量 (亿标立方米)	Total Volume of Waste Gas Discharged (100 million cu.m)	13865	22840	19512	19986
三、废气中污染物排放量 (万吨)	Pollutants Discharged in Waste Gas (10 000 ton)				
二氧化硫 (万吨)	Sulfur Dioxide (10 000 ton)	63.25	66.56	62.24	59.94
#工业二氧化硫 (万吨)	#Industrial Sulfur Dioxide (10 000 ton)	51.60	59.50	54.86	52.40
烟粉尘 (万吨)	Soot and Dust (10 000 ton)	19.31	30.74	34.97	35.95
四 、工业固体废物产生量 (万吨)	Volume of Industrial Solid Wastes Producced (10 000 ton)	6812.99	7595.79	7610.94	8180.61
已处置的 (万吨)	Teated (10 000 ton)	1097	1424	1561	1646
已综合利用的 (万吨)	Utilized In a Comprehensive Way (10 000 ton)	5521	6007	5737	6196
已贮存的 (万吨)	Stored (10 000 ton)	238	268	377	412
工业固体废物排放量 (万吨)	Volume of Industrial Solid Wastes Emission (10 000 ton)	4.17	16.64	1.06	0.80
五、锅炉总数 (台)	Total Number of Boiler (unit)	1982	2339	2451	2413
锅炉蒸吨数 (蒸吨)	Steam Tons of Boiler (steam ton)	64984	60862	72444	75469
六、工业炉窑 (座)	Number of Industrial Kiln Stove (unit)	2187	2494	2475	2298

11-2 工业污染治理情况

项　目		Item	Unit	1990	1995	2000
一、汇总工业企业单位数	(个)	Total Number of Industrial Enterprises	(unit)	991	613	583
二、污染治理项目本年投资来源合计	(万元)	Total Resource of Investment in Pollutant Treatment Projects	(10 000 yuan)	18051.00	27433.00	85237.90
国家预算内资金	(万元)	State Budgetary Funds	(10 000 yuan)	5568.00	3540.00	962.00
环境保护补助资金	(万元)	Environmental Protection Subsidy Funds	(10 000 yuan)	2531.00	5430.00	1282.40
环保贷款	(万元)	Environmental Protection Loans	(1 0000 yuan)	2149.00	3143.00	7579.40
其　他	(万元)	Others	(10 000 yuan)	1372.00	7966.00	61880.50
三、污染治理项目本年完成投资合计	(万元)	Total Investment in Pollutant Treatment Projects	(10 000 yuan)			85237.90
治理废水	(万元)	Waste Water	(10 000 yuan)	5637.00	12042.00	45653.40
治理废气	(万元)	Waste Gas	(10 000 yuan)	9891.00	9164.00	26667.70
治理固体废物	(万元)	Solid Waste	(10 000 yuan)	1371.00	5293.00	6072.30
治理噪声	(万元)	Noise Abatement	(10 000 yuan)	534.00	583.00	644.00
其　他	(万元)	Others	(10 000 yuan)	618.00	351.00	6200.50
四、本年施工项目数	(个)	Projects Carried Out in This Year	(unit)	1545	939	851
治理废水	(个)	Waste Water	(unit)	450	305	384
治理废气	(个)	Waste Gas	(unit)	758	367	361
治理固体废物	(个)	Solid Waste	(unit)	119	121	27
治理噪声	(个)	Noise Abatement	(unit)	139	109	31
其　他	(个)	Others	(unit)	79	37	48
五、本年竣工项目	(个)	Projects Completed in This Year	(unit)	1312	832	692
治理废水	(个)	Waste Water	(unit)	353	256	316
治理废气	(个)	Waste Gas	(unit)	662	339	286
治理固体废物	(个)	Solid Waste	(unit)	99	96	22
治理噪声	(个)	Noise Abatement	(unit)	126	106	26
其　他	(个)	Others	(unit)	72	35	42

STATISTICS ON TREATMENT OF INDUSTRIAL POLLUTION

2004	2005	2006	2007	2008	2009	2010	2011	2012	2013
254	336	354	342	307	225	159	232	171	147
98256.90	148096.50	148872.80	169404.70	161453.30	281332.30	277416.40	153811.62	154495.83	251744.96
3584.80	7590.80	9039.50	4433.50	4243.80	5602.00	3891.60	7216.00	4127.50	3667.00
4535.20	7384.50	2941.60	5543.00	3713.00	4092.00	1894.00	1290.00	675.70	210.00
90136.90		9574.00		3487.20			2950.00		
	133121.20	127317.70	159428.20	153496.50	271638.30	271630.80	145305.62	149692.63	247867.96
98256.90	148096.50	148872.80	169404.70	161453.30	281332.30	277416.40	153811.62	154495.83	251744.96
35561.00	48067.70	59631.70	78246.10	82634.80	54001.60	35627.30	84572.87	35867.60	15872.61
30140.40	40007.50	65821.70	74455.10	60834.40	213918.30	197292.80	47919.55	80510.24	216672.90
1889.80	11408.10	10240.60	2004.30	3959.90	5969.70	9579.60	10504.76	3565.00	1720.00
198.90	440.10	13178.80	1411.20	1041.10	674.80	866.60	1080.90	1114.20	52.00
29661.30	48173.10	649.80	13288.00	12983.10	6767.90	34050.10	9733.54	33438.79	17427.45
380	473	447	504	406	318	226	364	136	113
152	191	199	224	178	126	98	158	43	28
158	176	188	188	139	132	74	122	56	59
21	15	29	21	23	11	13	17	7	3
13	20	17	21	15	11	12	18	8	1
33	71	44	50	51	38	29	49	22	22
329	428	403	442	345	273	195	331	117	148
128	174	165	197	152	108	84	143	42	42
137	160	167	168	115	111	64	112	49	83
21	11	22	18	19	10	10	16	7	3
11	18	15	20	14	9	10	18	6	
32	65	34	39	45	35	27	42	13	20

11−3 排污费征收、使用和污染赔(罚)款情况

STATISTICS ON COLLECTION, REPARATIONS AND FINES ON POLLUTION DSICHARGES

项 目	Item	1990	1995	2000	2007	2008	2009	2010	2011	2012	2013
交纳排污费单位（个）	Number of Enterprises Charged (unit)	4072	9409	32581	25700	19607	15584	12017	10581	10895	7269
本年征收排污费数(万元)	Amount of Pollutant Fees (10 000 yuan)	7823	13870	20092	3981	40600	38176	40300	44975	50587	60161

11−4 工业企业废水处理设施情况

STATISTICS ON INDUSTRIAL WASTE WATER TREATMENT FACILITES

项 目	Item	2000	2005	2008	2009	2010	2011	2012	2013
汇总企业单位数 （个）	Total Number of Enterprises (unit)	2172	2313	2541	2552	2643	3911	3699	3590
治理设施数量 （套）	Number of Treatment Facilities	2120	2163	2050	2068	2093	5296	2110	2084
处理能力 （万吨/日）	Treatment Capacity(10 000 ton/day)		912.45	930.27	950.88	1037.41	1321.63	1023.14	1029.36
运行费用 （万元）	Operation Fees (10 000 yuan)	46651	77931	138821	134207	137920	344256	176058	168277

11-5 全省当年建成投产的建设项目“三同时”执行情况

STATISTICS ON IMPLEMENTATION OF "THREE MEANWHILE" OF CONSTRUCTION PROJECTS IN HUBEI PROVINCE

项　目	Item	1990	1995	2000	2005	2007	2008	2009	2010	2011	2012	2013
一、建设项目　(个)	Numberof Construction Projects (unit)	306	245	359	1437	4206	1498	2150	2107	3078	4912	3267
二、建设项目投资总额(亿元)	Total investmentin Construction Projects (100 million yuan)	12.72	33.60	69.61	1603.13	2140.50	315.73	2085.81	624.86	1099.26	3913.09	1180.10
#环保工程投资(亿元)	#Investment in Environmental Protection Projects (100 million yuan)	0.32	1.5	2.37	11.22	139.80	25.65	51.89	29.16	53.06	117.40	73.00
三、“三同时”执行情况(个)	Implementation of "Three Meanwhile" (unit)											
实际执行项目数　(个)	Number of Projects Actually Being Implemented (unit)	221	227	356	1336	1706	1491	2148	2107	3078	2076	3267
执行项目中合格的 (个)	Qualified (unit)	217	211	356	1191	1705	1481	2135	2087	2977	2032	3138

主要统计指标解释

工业废水排放量 指经过企业厂区所有排放口排到企业外部的工业废水量。包括生产废水、外排的直接冷却水、超标排放的矿井地下水和与工业废水混排的厂区生活污水，不包括外排的间接冷却水(清污不分流的间接冷却水应计算在内)。

工业废水排放达标量 指报告期内废水中各项污染物指标都达到国家或地方排放标准的外排工业废水量，包括未经处理外排达标的，经废水处理设施处理后达标排放的，以及经污水处理厂处理后达标排放的。

工业废水排放达标率 指工业废水排放达标量占工业废水排放量的百分率，计算公式为：

$$\text{工业废水排放达标率}=\frac{\text{工业废水排放达标量}}{\text{工业废水排放量}}\times 100\%$$

工业废气排放量 指报告期内企业厂区内燃料燃烧和生产工艺过程中产生的各种排入大气的含有污染物的气体的总量，以标准状态(273K，101325Pa)计算。测算公式为：

工业废气排放量 ＝ 燃料燃烧过程中废气排放量 ＋ 生产工艺过程中废气排放量

工业烟尘排放量 指企业厂区内燃料燃烧过程中产生的烟气中夹带的颗粒物排放量。

工业粉尘排放量 指企业在生产工艺过程中排放的能在空气中悬浮一定时间的固体颗粒物排放量。如钢铁企业的耐火材料粉尘、焦化企业的筛焦系统粉尘、烧结机的粉尘、石灰窑的粉尘、建材企业的水泥粉尘等。不包括电厂排入大气的烟尘。

工业固体废物产生量 指报告期内企业在生产过程中产生的固体状、半固体状和高浓度液体状废弃物的总量，包括危险废物、冶炼废渣、粉煤灰、炉渣、煤矸石、尾矿、放射性废物和其他废物等；不包括矿山开采的剥离废石和掘进废石(煤矸石和呈酸性或碱性的废石除外)。酸性或碱性废石指采掘的废石其流经水、雨淋水的pH值小于4或pH值大于10.5者。

工业固体废物综合利用量 指报告期内企业通过回收、加工、循环、交换等方式，从固体废物中提取或者使其转化为可以利用的资源、能源和其他原材料的固体废物量(包括当年利用往年的工业固体废物贮存量)，如用作农业肥料、生产建筑材料、筑路等。综合利用量由原产生固体废物的单位统计。

工业固体废物综合利用率 指工业固体废物综合利用量占工业固体废物产生量(包括综合利用往年贮存量)的百分率。计算公式为：

$$\text{工业固体废物综合利用率}=\frac{\text{工业固体废物综合利用量}}{\text{工业固体废物产生量}+\text{综合利用往年贮存量}}\times 100\%$$

生活垃圾无害化处理率 指报告期生活垃圾无害化处理量与生活垃圾产生量比率。在统计上，由于生活垃圾产生量不易取得，可用清运量代替。计算公式为：

$$\text{生活垃圾无害化处理率}=\frac{\text{生活垃圾无害化处理量}}{\text{生活垃圾产生量}}\times 100\%$$

Explanatory Notes on Main Statistical Indicators

Waste Water Discharged by Industry refers to the volume of waste water discharged by industrial enterprises through all their outlets, including waste water from production process, directly cooled water, groundwater from mining wells which does not meet discharge standards and sewage from households mixed with waste water produced by industrial activities, but excluding indirectly cooled water discharged (It should be included if the discharge is not separated with waste water).

Industrial Waste Water Meeting Discharge Standards refers to volume of industrial waste water discharge which, with or without treatment, reaches national or local standards with regard to all pollutants.

Ratio of Industrial Waste Water Meeting Discharge Standards refers to percentage of industrial waste water meeting discharge standards over total industrial waste water discharge. It is calculated as:

Ratio of industrial waste water meeting discharge standards = industrial waste water meeting discharge standards / total industrial waste water discharge

Industrial Waste Air Emission refers to discharge into atmosphere of waste air containing pollutants generated from fuel burning and production process in enterprises within a given period of time. It is calculated at standard status (273K, 101325Pa) as:

Industrial waste air emission = emission through fuel burning + emission through production process

Industrial Soot Emission refers to volume of soot in smoke emitted in process of fuel burning in premises of enterprises.

Industrial Dust Emission refers to volume of dust emitted by production process of enterprises and suspended in the air for a given period of time, including dust from refractory material of iron and steel works, dust from coke-screening systems and sintering machines of coke plants, dust from lime kilns and dust from cement production in building material enterprises, but excluding soot and dust emitted from power plants.

Industrial Solid Wastes Produced refers to total volume of solid, semi-solid and high concentration liquid residues produced by industrial enterprises from production process in a given period of time, including hazardous wastes, slag, coal ash, gangue, tailings, radioactive residues and other wastes, but excluding stones stripped or dug out in mining (gangue and acid or alkaline stones not included). A stone is acid or alkaline depending on the pH value of the water below 4 or above 10.5 when the stone is in, or soaked by, the water.

Industrial Solid Wastes Utilized refers to volume of solid wastes from which useful materials can be extracted or which can be converted into usable resources, energy or other materials by means of reclamation, processing, recycling and exchange (including utilizing in the year the stocks of industrial solid wastes of the previous year). Examples of such utilizations include fertilizers, building materials and road materials. The information shall be collected by the producing units of the wastes.

Ratio of Industrial Solid Wastes Utilized refers to the percentage of industrial solid wastes utilized over industrial solid wastes produced (including stocks of the previous years). It is calculated as:

Ratio of industrial solid wastes utilized = volume of industrial solid wastes utilized / (industrial solid wastes produced + stock of previous years) ×100%

Ratio of Consumption Wastes Treated refers to consumption wastes treated over that produced. In practical statistics, as it is difficult to estimate, the volume of consumption wastes produced is replaced with that transported. It is calculated as:

Ratio of consumption wastes treated = consumption wastes treated / consumption wastes produced×100%

12 农 业

Agriculture

资料整理：朱　江

12-1　农村基层组织和农业基本情况

BASIC CONDITIONS OF RURAL GRASSROOTS UNITS AND AGRICULTURE

指　标	Item	1990	1995	2000	2005	2010	2011	2012	2013
农村组织情况　　　(个	**Rural Units　　　(unit)**								
乡个数	Township	1121	1040	476	217	201	194	188	175
镇个数	Town Governments	844	861	853	737	742	742	746	757
村委会个数	Village Committees	3275	32802	32400	26678	26018	26025	25991	25452
村民小组个数	Villager Group	260847	260641	259250	212587	209598	206848	210432	210108
乡村户数、人口	**Rural Households,Population**								
乡村户数　(万户)	Rural Households　(10 000 units)	1005.32	1004.21	983.94	1015.72	1062.14	1071.75	1084.79	1088.01
乡村人口　(万人)	Rural Population　(10 000 persons)	4110.59	4041.67	3947.26	3991.47	4031.73	4057.10	4089.38	4092.19
乡村从业人员　(万人)	**Rural Employment (10 000 persons)**	1791.30	1810.44	1781.70	1931.15	2154.44	2665.02	2259.91	2280.14
按性别分	Grouped by Sex								
男	Male	944.72	955.74	937.67	1026.48	1154.45	1422.55	1208.63	1217.97
女	Female	846.58	854.70	844.03	904.67	999.99	1242.47	1051.28	1062.17
按行业分	Grouped by Sector								
农林牧渔业	Farming, Forestry, Animal husbandary and Fishery	1453.96	1329.18	1159.13	1101.29	900.14	885.63	863.49	869.79
国营农林牧渔场从业人员	Employees in State-run Agriculture, forestry,animal husbandry, fishery Farm	64.24	59.05	54.94	55.73	54.31	58.25	50.89	47.38
农业从业人员	Agriculture Employees	38.71	35.59	34.08	35.27	31.56	34.35	30.04	27.93
非农业从业人员	Non-agriculture Employees	25.53	23.46	20.86	20.46	22.37	23.90	20.85	19.45
年末实有耕地面积（千公顷	**Cultivated Areas (Year-End) (1 000 hectares)**	3476.77	3358.01	3282.96	3161.17	3323.92	3361.86	3390.00	3409.91
农业机械总动力(万千瓦)	Total Agricultural Machinery Power (10 000 kW)	1099.62	1174.34	1414.00	2057.37	2796.99	3571.23	3842.00	4081.05
化肥施用量　(万吨)	Consumption of Chemical Fertilizers (10 000 tons)	148.61	228.41	247.08	285.83	350.77	354.89	357.66	351.93
农村用电量（亿千瓦小时）	Electricity Consumed in Rural Areas (100 million kWh)	27.21	47.36	60.86	70.09	109.78	112.26	121.23	130.14
农作物总播种面积(千公顷)	Total Sown Area　(1 000 hectares)	7361.14	7413.71	7584.07	7391.30	7997.57	8009.57	8105.69	8106.19
#粮食	Grain Crops	5200.01	4776.65	4156.20	4068.15	4068.37	4122.07	4180.05	4258.40
主要农产品产量(万吨)	**Volume of Major Agricultural Products　(10 000 tons)**								
粮食	Grain Crops	2475.03	2463.84	2218.49	2177.38	2315.80	2388.53	2442.00	2501.30
棉花	Cotton Crops	51.73	58.60	30.43	37.50	47.18	52.58	53.15	45.97
油料	Oil-Bearing Crops	95.75	189.44	269.98	293.90	311.80	304.72	319.70	333.17
肉类产量	Output of Meat	146.83	279.40	271.19	342.63	379.42	381.87	412.30	430.08
水产品产量	Output of Aquatic Products	70.98	150.91	234.34	318.21	353.09	356.22	388.90	410.37

注：主要生产品产量2006、2007年数据按农业普查数据进行衔接、调整。

Note:Statistics of output of major farm products of 2006,2007 is adusted according to Second Agriculture Survey.

12–2 耕地面积

AREAS UNDER CULTIVATION

单位：千公顷 (1 000 hectares)

年 份 Year	年末实有耕地面积 Cultivated Areas (Year-End)	水 田 Paddy Fields	旱 地 Dry Fields	年内减少 Dereased in Cultivated Areas in This Year	#国家基建占地 Capital Construction	人均占有耕地(公顷) Per Capita Cultivated Area (sq.m) 按乡村人口计算 By Rural Population	按农林牧渔业劳动力计算 By Farming, Forestry, Animal husbandry and Fishery Laborers
1949	2742.58	1765.11	1977.47			0.12	0.29
1952	4015.90	1876.62	2139.28			0.16	0.39
1957	4172.31	1945.05	2227.26			0.16	0.37
1962	4271.33	1847.19	2424.56			0.15	0.39
1965	4239.93	1966.38	2273.55			0.14	0.37
1970	3964.01	1982.20	1981.81			0.11	0.31
1975	3823.00	1996.10	1826.77	54.10		0.10	0.28
1977	3779.89	1983.44	1796.45	34.37			
1978	3768.07	1959.63	1808.43	30.77	7.75	0.10	0.28
1979	3754.51	1940.27	1814.24	29.13	5.50	0.10	0.27
1980	3738.51	1929.50	1809.01	35.82	4.69	0.10	0.27
1981	3730.20	1924.66	1805.73	23.64	3.23	0.09	0.26
1982	3718.20	1916.53	1801.67	22.53	2.68	0.09	0.26
1983	3698.74	1907.51	1791.23	28.83	4.93	0.09	0.25
1984	3643.68	1892.89	1750.79	65.23	8.18	0.09	0.25
1985	3584.61	1864.15	1720.46	71.70	8.56	0.09	0.27
1986	3545.00	1847.63	1697.37	49.30	7.30	0.09	0.27
1987	3517.99	1845.17	1672.82	36.16	7.13	0.09	0.26
1988	3498.47	1838.37	1660.10	25.98	4.55	0.09	0.25
1989	3486.57	1858.25	1628.33	17.47	1.83	0.09	0.25
1990	3476.77	1871.77	1605.00	15.60	2.73	0.08	0.24
1991	3458.46	1869.19	1589.27	24.11	4.03	0.08	0.24
1992	3421.57	1845.31	1576.26	41.67	4.95	0.08	0.24
1993	3392.74	1815.75	1576.99	32.84	6.11	0.08	0.24
1994	3375.60	1805.42	1570.18	21.21	3.77	0.08	0.24
1995	3358.01	1780.40	1577.61	21.36	4.23	0.08	0.25
1996	3349.25	1800.00	1549.25	13.80	2.85	0.08	0.26
1997	3342.45	1796.07	1546.38	12.24	2.43	0.08	0.26
1998	3327.16	1788.95	1538.21	19.95	3.83	0.08	0.27
1999	3310.40	1786.34	1524.06	23.08	5.13	0.08	0.27
2000	3282.96	1757.63	1525.33	34.15	5.18	0.08	0.28
2001	3242.85	1742.69	1500.16	46.26	7.76	0.08	0.27
2002	3094.03	1708.58	1385.45	110.10	12.04	0.08	0.27
2003	3033.45	1665.49	1367.96	181.18	7.51	0.08	0.27
2004	3091.75	1789.10	1302.65	39.81	5.36	0.08	0.28
2005	3131.17	1856.17	1305.00	40.70	4.93	0.08	0.28
2006	3201.66	1881.74	1319.92	20.65	5.49	0.08	0.29
2007	3226.62	1890.04	1336.58	21.08	5.67	0.08	0.31
2008	3289.33	1914.07	1375.26	10.68	4.29	0.08	0.33
2009	3308.35	1928.67	1379.68	15.06	5.61	0.08	0.34
2010	3323.92	1932.05	1391.87	14.90	9.44	0.08	0.37
2011	3361.86	1954.61	1407.25	14.09	5.15	0.08	0.38
2012	3390.06	1963.13	1426.93	14.82	6.93	0.08	0.39
2013	3409.91	1976.12	1433.79	16.33	6.75	0.08	0.39

注：1996年及以后为农业普查接轨数(下同)。

Notes:Since 1996,the relative targers were in line with the data of agricultural gereral survey (the same as the following tables).

12-3 农林牧渔业总产值

GROSS OUTPUT VALUE OF FARMING, FORESTRY, ANIMAL HUSBANDRY AND FISHERY

单位：亿元 当年价格 (At current price, 100 million yuan)

年 份 Year	农林牧渔业总产值 Gross Output Value of FFAF	农业 Farming	林业 Foresty	畜牧业 Animal Husbandry	渔业 Fishery	农林牧渔服务业 Service Industry for Farming, Forestry, Animal husbandry and Fishery
1949	10.72	7.22	0.69	0.97	0.10	
1952	16.59	12.08	0.79	1.48	0.18	
1957	28.59	20.55	1.46	3.81	0.46	
1962	33.66	26.52	1.71	3.61	0.46	
1965	47.48	37.44	1.98	6.02	0.51	
1970	51.27	40.62	2.07	6.41	0.92	
1975	74.68					
1977	78.68					
1978	84.46					
1979	109.85					
1980	94.95	64.70	7.28	17.29	1.46	
1981	111.68	82.78	6.47	14.88	1.61	
1982	128.35	95.32	7.24	17.97	2.12	
1983	134.09	97.53	7.29	20.05	2.96	
1984	169.20	123.09	7.54	26.51	4.79	
1985	192.32	129.61	8.15	39.08	8.18	
1986	219.10	146.79	8.75	43.86	10.77	
1987	249.68	160.13	9.97	54.86	14.19	
1988	297.51	175.12	10.98	80.80	18.83	
1989	335.04	198.56	11.75	91.47	20.66	
1990	402.23	252.92	14.15	98.04	23.88	
1991	405.04	247.01	16.81	102.19	25.06	
1992	435.42	265.53	17.36	110.37	27.59	
1993	501.17	301.99	22.39	134.02	42.77	
1994	786.84	481.82	26.47	219.53	59.01	
1995	988.53	612.12	28.33	268.09	79.98	
1996	1140.76	670.27	33.62	337.02	99.86	
1997	1243.68	711.91	37.33	381.40	113.04	
1998	1222.58	688.06	41.29	371.37	121.86	
1999	1126.10	645.98	40.86	311.43	127.83	
2000	1125.64	615.74	40.24	338.77	130.89	
2001	1172.82	658.26	27.11	352.63	134.82	
2002	1203.30	671.20	28.33	354.84	148.93	
2003	1342.09	733.36	34.78	383.71	170.43	
2004	1695.44	921.59	31.78	514.52	205.68	21.87
2005	1775.58	932.15	37.30	545.40	236.49	24.24
2006	1842.20	995.46	40.50	487.09	221.42	97.73
2007	2296.84	1152.09	41.86	686.19	310.83	105.87
2008	2940.47	1395.76	49.69	1008.65	372.98	113.39
2009	2985.19	1511.49	57.67	881.78	413.14	121.11
2010	3501.99	1921.67	65.37	925.04	458.58	131.33
2011	4252.90	2299.30	86.10	1205.80	508.80	152.90
2012	4732.10	2488.10	100.10	1334.00	626.20	183.70
2013	5161.00	2678.10	122.00	1395.40	748.40	216.70

12-4 农、林、牧、渔业总产值指数
INDICES OF GROSS OUTPUT VALUE OF FARMING, FORESTRY, ANIMAL HUSBANDRY AND FISHERY

单位：% 上年=100 (preceding year=100)

年 份 Year	合 计 Total	农 业 Farming	林 业 Forestry	畜牧业 Animal Husbandry	渔 业 Fishery	农林牧渔服务业 Service Industry for Farming, Forestry, Animal husbandry and Fishery
1978	104.00	103.10	104.90	107.60	94.20	
1980	88.80	83.70	102.80	108.10	111.30	
1985	106.30	101.70	103.00	127.80	133.30	
1986	103.40	100.60	98.50	107.30	129.80	
1987	102.70	101.20	104.50	101.00	120.10	
1988	97.20	93.90	90.60	105.40	105.60	
1989	105.00	104.50	101.60	105.20	108.30	
1990	107.10	108.40	106.00	104.90	106.70	
1991	100.70	97.66	118.80	104.23	104.94	
1992	107.50	107.50	103.27	108.00	110.10	
1993	115.10	113.73	128.97	121.43	155.02	
1994	157.00	159.55	118.27	163.80	137.93	
1995	125.63	127.04	106.99	122.12	135.54	
1996	115.40	109.50	118.67	125.71	124.87	
1997	109.02	106.21	111.04	113.17	113.20	
1998	98.30	96.65	110.61	97.37	107.80	
1999	92.11	93.88	98.95	83.86	104.90	
2000	99.96	95.32	98.48	108.78	102.39	
2001	104.19	106.91	67.37	104.09	103.00	
2002	102.60	101.97	104.50	100.63	110.47	
2003	111.53	109.26	122.77	108.14	114.44	
2004	126.33	125.67	91.37	134.09	120.68	
2005	104.73	101.15	117.37	106.00	114.98	110.84
2006	105.37	109.29	108.58	96.04	109.87	116.05
2007	124.68	115.73	103.36	140.88	140.38	108.33
2008	128.02	121.15	118.17	146.99	119.99	107.10
2009	101.52	108.29	116.10	87.42	110.77	106.81
2010	109.95	121.28	113.35	94.12	106.86	100.16
2011	121.40	119.70	137.70	130.40	110.90	116.40
2012	111.30	108.20	116.30	110.60	123.10	120.10
2013	109.06	107.64	121.88	104.60	119.51	117.96

注:2009年畜牧业数据变动原因为与农普数衔接。

Note: 2009 data changes due to livestock and agricultural census data convergence.

12-5 农、林、牧、渔业总产值指数
INDICES OF GROSS OUTPUT VALUE OF FARMING, FORESTRY, ANIMAL HUSBANDRY AND FISHERY

单位：% 1978年=100 (year 1978 =100)

年份 Year	合计 Total	农业 Farming	林业 Forestry	牧业 Animal Husbandry	渔业 Fishery
1979	109.6	109.2	101.8	118.8	109.2
1980	97.3	91.4	104.7	127.9	121.5
1981	108.2	102.4	95.4	138.2	134.1
1982	122.6	116.5	104.1	135.6	156.8
1983	122.7	115.9	105.3	160.5	181.2
1984	148.4	140.0	110.6	164.7	254.0
1985	157.7	142.4	114.0	206.2	338.6
1986	163.1	143.3	112.3	263.5	439.5
1987	167.5	145.0	117.3	282.7	527.8
1988	162.9	136.1	106.3	285.5	557.3
1989	171.0	142.3	108.0	301.0	603.6
1990	183.1	154.2	114.5	315.7	644.0
1991	181.7	147.7	125.9	334.0	631.8
1992	194.4	158.7	120.1	360.7	689.3
1993	207.4	168.0	129.5	410.9	936.1
1994	227.8	175.0	152.0	461.7	1203.0
1995	259.9	195.3	156.0	535.1	1530.2
1996	277.6	198.0	168.5	611.1	1732.0
1997	304.0	213.4	179.3	671.6	2007.4
1998	307.3	209.1	204.6	682.3	2164.0
1999	309.5	220.2	196.7	627.9	2270.0
2000	318.1	226.3	194.2	650.4	2324.5
2001	327.6	238.7	141.6	669.6	2382.4
2002	334.2	233.1	145.9	700.2	2677.3
2003	351.8	237.2	167.2	730.8	2824.4
2004	374.7	257.9	153.9	760.8	2979.6
2005	392.4	260.9	180.6	806.4	3425.9
2006	171.8	137.9	58.7	502.2	2214.2
2007	214.3	159.6	60.7	707.4	3108.3
2008	274.3	193.3	72.0	1039.8	3729.8
2009	278.5	209.3	83.6	909.1	4131.4
2010	326.7	266.2	94.7	953.6	4585.8
2011	396.7	318.5	124.8	1243.1	5088.0
2012	441.4	344.6	145.1	1375.3	6262.0
2013	481.4	370.9	176.8	1438.6	7484.0

12-6 农、林、牧、渔业增加值(2013)
VALUE ADDED OF FARMING, FORESTRY, ANIMAL HUSBANDRY AND FISHERY(2013)

单位：亿元 (100 million yuan)

项目	Item	合计 Total	农业 Farming	林业 Forestry	牧业 Animal Husbandry	渔业 Fishery	农林牧渔服务业 Service Industry for Farming, Forestry,Animal husbandry and Fishery
一、总产值(现价)	Gross Output Value(current price)	5160.56	2678.08	122.01	1395.39	748.40	216.69
二、中间消耗	Intermedium-Consumption	2062.41	967.78	63.91	596.10	285.82	148.80
三、增加值	Value-Added	3098.16	1710.30	58.10	799.29	462.58	67.89

12-7 农作物播种面积

单位：千公顷

年份 Year	总播种面积 Total Sown Areas	粮食作物 Grain Crops	小麦 Wheat	稻谷 Rice	薯类 Tubers	玉米 Corn	大豆 Soybean	经济作物 Economic Crops
1978	7931.05	5544.78	1122.28	2894.63	427.23	403.14	173.43	971.53
1980	7477.06	5352.04	1292.29	2708.22	387.46	406.91	138.94	977.58
1985	7331.71	5108.25	1331.42	2538.57	354.01	374.17	134.64	1280.89
1990	7361.14	5200.01	1352.10	2636.47	391.90	386.11	164.65	1343.23
1991	7423.92	5194.50	1347.53	2622.79	402.38	395.19	150.61	1414.37
1992	7183.83	4955.35	1287.91	2537.49	392.59	376.18	140.23	1405.87
1993	7125.47	4812.05	1271.23	2377.82	384.33	365.96	181.69	1381.64
1994	7181.43	4797.95	1225.60	2373.26	203.39	373.02	201.52	1456.00
1995	7431.71	4776.65	1179.93	2408.66	397.65	393.77	188.01	1683.56
1996	7579.01	4880.28	1230.14	2448.58	419.53	405.07	174.71	1676.71
1997	7739.21	4944.66	1276.52	2467.51	415.74	400.30	182.51	1689.03
1998	7695.98	4737.15	1212.08	2244.74	431.02	442.84	201.32	1703.80
1999	7788.66	4673.11	1074.43	2284.98	448.72	460.82	207.01	1739.07
2000	7584.07	4156.20	845.10	1995.29	467.61	424.10	224.75	1984.76
2001	7488.99	4015.73	735.85	1953.77	237.75	401.11	218.01	1972.36
2002	7281.61	3816.08	679.02	1888.75	430.61	384.04	217.82	1981.04
2003	7153.24	3572.74	603.43	1808.75	208.56	349.81	196.47	2083.26
2004	7225.13	3817.89	605.08	2084.02	403.79	357.49	186.05	2079.51
2005	7391.30	4068.05	730.61	2162.39	397.75	428.79	179.79	1974.56
2006	7100.59	3902.27	1016.93	1975.07	218.67	431.93	118.40	1825.40
2007	7130.01	3981.43	1096.25	1978.82	219.19	436.34	114.75	1787.79
2008	7272.33	3906.69	1000.57	1978.94	216.09	470.37	206.79	1973.85
2009	7527.50	4012.53	993.36	2045.08	237.93	507.28	195.76	2018.78
2010	7997.57	4068.37	1000.11	2038.17	274.29	531.38	104.76	2116.92
2011	8009.57	4122.07	1013.61	2036.17	303.64	549.66	152.97	2127.49
2012	8105.69	4180.05	1065.50	2017.88	299.65	593.34	95.31	2204.36
2013	8106.19	4258.40	1094.80	2101.15	303.27	573.47	86.67	2159.12

注:2006、2007年度农业普查衔接数据。

TOTAL SOWN AREAS OF FARM CROPS

(1 000 hectares)

棉花 Cotton	油菜籽 Rape-Seed	花生 Peanuts	芝麻 Sesame	黄红麻 Jute and Ambary	甘蔗 Sugar-cane	甜菜 Beet-Roots	烤烟 Flue-Cured Tobacco	其他作物 Others
593.19	165.27	34.14	102.71	8.39	2.31	0.13	24.75	1414.73
591.67	175.75	40.76	113.51	12.17	1.49	0.12	9.69	1147.44
464.97	361.42	65.94	173.31	94.17	7.85	0.08	37.67	942.56
455.92	744.31	63.75	126.85	27.33	8.07	0.01	46.35	817.90
461.55	610.10	61.59	128.17	20.42	8.47	0.02	56.83	815.05
507.19	534.41	64.73	126.32	18.15	10.64	0.02	72.76	822.61
486.06	522.14	79.70	127.24	22.41	15.00	0.03	64.32	931.78
497.58	615.87	86.97	114.77	11.70	15.73		38.69	927.48
502.03	838.82	91.91	110.04	10.83	15.97	0.03	41.16	953.50
474.38	855.26	90.82	107.72	8.59	16.59		51.92	1022.02
480.56	829.80	95.20	107.35	10.10	18.00		70.99	1105.52
431.58	887.01	121.48	113.62	7.94	19.97		48.47	1255.03
310.70	1003.64	143.87	127.14	4.30	23.34		48.32	1376.48
318.07	1158.94	193.42	143.82	3.14	22.17		48.10	1443.11
346.65	1118.06	210.06	129.93	2.65	18.88		40.43	1500.90
286.37	1155.25	206.04	138.88	5.13	19.18		42.90	1484.49
355.02	1174.63	201.11	124.00	2.97	17.24		39.45	1497.24
408.30	1186.10	173.03	111.20	1.36	10.01		39.94	1327.73
360.95	1178.65	171.71	102.52	0.98	9.95		43.68	1348.69
496.40	1001.20	140.10	97.24	0.69	3.70		32.13	1372.92
514.22	927.10	137.80	94.67	0.59	3.60		32.70	1360.79
542.96	1089.61	142.26	92.18	0.50	6.62		46.78	1391.79
460.08	1165.88	183.73	99.64	0.35	10.35		55.87	1496.19
480.05	1159.88	189.26	92.46	0.11	8.05		40.76	1812.28
488.66	1141.38	192.17	89.16	0.10	7.80		47.65	1760.01
472.87	1167.33	239.80	88.19	0.09	7.75	0.03	52.06	1721.28
415.59	1226.30	200.35	84.37	0.08	7.50	0.02	49.64	1688.67

Note:Statistics of 2006 and 2007 are linkage data of Second Agricluture Survey.

12-8　主要农作物播种面积和产量(2013)
TOTAL SOWN AREAS AND OUTPUT OF FARM CROPS(2013)

指　标	Item	播种面积(千公顷) Sown Areas (1 000 hectares)	总产量(吨) Total Output(ton)
农作物总播种面积	**Total Sown Areas of Farm Crops**	**8106.19**	
粮食作物总计	**Total Grain**	**4258.40**	**25013000**
夏粮	Summer Grain	1392.93	5010000
小麦	Wheat	1094.80	4168000
大麦	Barley	22.99	87000
蚕豌豆	Broad and Dea Bean	58.48	104300
秋粮	Autumn Grain	2865.47	20003000
稻谷	Rice	2101.15	16766358
#中稻	#Semilate Rice	1265.65	11536037
双季晚稻	Late Double- crop Rice	449.89	3002821
#籼稻	#Long-grained Nonglutinous Rice		
薯类	Tubers	303.27	956827
玉米	Corn	573.47	2707505
高粱	Sorghum	1.33	6212
粟谷	Millet Grain		
其他秋粮	Others	0.60	1788
大豆	Soybeans	86.67	195760
杂豆	Miscellaneous Beans	15.13	17000
#绿豆	#Green Beans	11.88	15400
经济作物	**Economic Crops**	2159.12	
棉花	Cotton	415.59	459694
油料	Oil-Bearing Crops	1516.90	3331726
#花生	#Peanuts	200.35	681120
油菜籽	Rapeseed	1226.30	2504700
芝麻	Sesame	84.37	136034
麻类	Hemp Crops	11.19	26144
#黄麻	#Jute	0.08	147
苎麻	Ramie	11.10	25997
糖类	Sugar Crops	7.52	287211
#甘蔗	#Sugarcane	7.50	287162
烟叶	Tobacco Crops	64.35	126986
药材	Crude Drugs	143.57	
花卉种植面积	**Flower Gardening**	**44.06**	
其他农作物	**Others**	**1688.67**	
#蔬菜(含菜用瓜)	#Vegetable	1145.02	35783101
瓜果类	Melon and Fruits	101.42	3510422
绿肥	Organic Fertilizer	108.30	

12-9　主要农产品产量

OUTPUT OF MAJOR FARM CROPS

单位：万吨 (10 000 ton)

年 份 Year	粮 食 Grain	夏 粮 Summer Grain	秋 粮 Autumn Grain	棉 花 Cotton	油 料 Oil Bearing Crops	#花 生 Peanuts	#油菜籽 Rapeseed
1949	578.13	101.85	476.28	5.74	13.37	3.17	4.12
1952	747.54	148.81	598.73	12.17	22.34	4.56	7.09
1957	986.08	180.87	805.21	21.02	25.26	11.23	4.86
1962	960.41	246.34	714.07	14.22	18.30	3.81	4.29
1965	1241.34	255.01	986.33	38.29	22.32	5.15	6.76
1970	1268.67	187.06	1081.62	29.64	14.93	4.82	3.94
1975	1561.51	230.10	1331.41	40.61	21.44	5.12	10.65
1978	1725.60	315.04	1410.56	36.67	23.71	4.90	10.72
1980	1536.43	341.32	1195.11	31.63	20.58	5.85	11.59
1985	2216.13	429.58	1786.56	49.22	72.98	13.52	41.14
1990	2475.03	474.96	2000.07	51.73	95.75	12.79	70.90
1991	2244.10	476.20	1767.90	49.11	106.29	11.44	83.75
1992	2426.60	450.90	2022.83	60.99	99.74	15.72	70.86
1993	2325.70	471.87	1853.85	42.50	111.74	20.68	78.35
1994	2422.10	472.70	1949.40	45.00	137.77	24.81	98.07
1995	2463.84	447.20	2016.64	58.60	189.44	27.28	146.24
1996	2484.40	465.24	2019.16	43.01	181.82	30.77	134.88
1997	2634.40	542.60	2091.80	58.09	195.47	31.24	147.53
1998	2475.79	501.69	1974.10	32.50	216.69	42.87	154.76
1999	2451.88	392.71	2059.17	28.15	228.27	48.15	159.97
2000	2218.49	322.39	1896.10	30.43	269.98	53.46	192.40
2001	2138.49	319.14	1819.35	37.35	279.45	63.99	194.79
2002	2047.00	232.27	1841.73	32.26	245.29	72.25	151.40
2003	1921.02	255.65	1665.37	32.50	272.72	68.37	187.10
2004	2100.12	271.24	1828.96	39.54	314.38	63.19	235.12
2005	2177.38	302.49	1874.89	37.50	293.90	60.19	219.15
2006	2099.10	369.08	1730.02	55.20	254.45	48.40	191.83
2007	2185.44	406.44	1779.00	55.73	254.75	48.60	193.30
2008	2227.23	386.24	1840.99	51.30	283.56	49.41	214.89
2009	2309.10	398.45	1910.65	48.05	314.05	62.62	236.51
2010	2315.80	420.60	1895.18	47.18	311.80	64.45	232.57
2011	2388.53	425.83	1962.70	52.58	304.72	68.74	220.39
2012	2441.81	447.44	1994.37	53.15	319.66	74.34	230.03
2013	2501.30	501.00	2000.30	45.97	333.17	68.11	250.47

注：2006、2007年为农业普查衔接数据。

Note:Statistics 2006 and 2007 are linkage data of Second Agriculture Survey.

12-10 人均占有主要农产品产量

PER CAPITA OUTPUT OF MAJOR FARM PRODUCTS

单位：千克/人 (kg/person)

年 份 Year	粮 食 Grain	棉 花 Cotton	油 料 Oil Bearing Crops	猪、牛、羊肉 Output of Pork, Beef and Mutton	水产品 Output of Aquatic Products
1952	275	4.5	8.2		2.9
1957	327	7.0	8.4		4.0
1962	302	4.4	5.8		2.3
1965	359	11.1	6.4		3.3
1970	319	7.5	3.8		2.8
1975	357	9.3	4.9		2.6
1978	379	8.1	5.2		2.4
1980	330	6.8	4.4	11.9	2.9
1985	452	10.0	14.9	20.7	7.6
1990	467	9.8	18.1	27.7	13.4
1991	415	8.9	19.6	29.0	12.9
1992	443	11.1	18.2	31.9	14.9
1993	416	7.6	20.0	35.3	18.1
1994	431	8.0	24.5	41.8	23.0
1995	429	10.2	33.0	48.6	26.3
1996	428	7.4	31.4	40.4	30.1
1997	450	9.9	33.4	44.4	34.6
1998	419	5.5	36.7	44.2	37.0
1999	413	5.0	38.4	44.8	38.6
2000	372	5.1	45.3	45.5	39.3
2001	358	6.3	46.8	48.3	40.5
2002	342	5.4	41.0	49.4	45.4
2003	316	6.5	45.5	51.4	47.8
2004	349	6.6	52.3	54.1	50.2
2005	361	6.2	48.7	56.8	52.8
2006	365	7.4	46.2	42.0	46.7
2007	360	9.2	42.0	42.5	49.1
2008	390	9.0	49.7	49.8	54.9
2009	404	8.4	54.9	53.5	59.1
2010	405	8.2	54.5	54.6	61.7
2011	416	9.2	53.1	55.2	62.1
2012	423	9.2	55.4	59.7	67.4
2013	431	7.9	57.5	61.9	70.8

注：按全省常住人口计算的人均占有量。

Notes:The data is caculated by resident population.

12-11 蚕、茶、果生产情况

STATISTICS ON SILKWORM COCOONS, TEA AND FRUITS

指 标	Item	1990	1995	2000	2005	2010	2011	2012	2013
蚕茧产量 (万吨)	Silkworm Cocoons (10 000 tons)	0.79	2.24	1.22	1.07	0.71	0.84	0.82	0.77
茶叶产量 (万吨)	Tea (10 000 tons)	2.84	3.90	6.37	8.50	16.57	18.42	20.70	22.20
红毛茶	Red Tea	1.52	0.12		0.65	1.54	1.94	2.17	2.38
绿毛茶	Green Tea	0.55	3.05	5.15	6.72	13.71	14.85	16.50	17.04
其他茶	Others				0.18	0.33	0.37	0.46	0.44
园林水果产量 (万吨)	Garden fruit production (10 000 tons)	26.89	114.70	215.68	260.79	437.13	521.78	541.72	569.42
#苹果	#Apples	1.20	3.21	3.02	1.24	0.97	0.99	1.06	1.02
柑桔	Citrus	13.08	58.14	94.62	146.26	301.04	330.97	385.31	400.39
梨	Pears	5.98	26.02		46.80	48.05	46.29	53.64	56.31
葡萄	Grapes				4.97	13.12	15.19	20.49	23.68
桃子	Peaches	2.50	14.59	30.87	46.88	60.75	69.02	67.42	72.49
猕猴桃	Kiwi fruit				0.85	1.06	1.33	1.95	2.10
红枣	Dates				2.02	2.91	3.13	3.21	3.39
柿子	Persimmons				4.77	5.05	5.74	5.83	6.61
桑园面积 (千公顷)	Area of Mulberry Plantations (1 000 hectares)	14.83							
茶园面积 (千公顷)	Area of Tea Plantations (1 000 hectares)	76.38	113.39	121.02	138.43	214.61	242.98	260.13	291.77
#当年采摘面积	#Pick Area		7.42		101.62	155.92	174.70	189.36	205.39
果园 (千公顷)	Area of Orchards (1 000 hectares)	118.04	199.80	233.93	265.05	376.77	398.84	400.75	403.55
#苹果园	#Apples	6.58	13.66	8.98	3.30	0.17	1.94	2.01	1.63
柑桔园	Citrus	85.64	98.39	99.13	143.15	229.19	244.48	243.59	239.66
梨园	Pears	13.96	35.42	33.49	35.90	36.60	48.83	37.35	39.35
葡萄园	Grapes				4.77	5.57	8.45	10.21	10.01

12-12 林业生产情况
STATISTICS ON FORESTRY

单位：公顷 (hectare)

指标名称	Item	2013	增长（%）
造林面积	Build Forestry Areas	246858	24.3
用材林	Material Forests	83439	23.4
经济林	Economic Forests	58163	27.7
防护林	Windbreak Forests	103083	22.2
薪炭林	Firewood Forests	112	-48.4
特种用途林	Forests for Soecial Puppse	2061	139.7
更新造林	Updateing Areas	2952	-32.5
四旁（零星）植树	Planting	12014	-3.3
育苗面积	Raise Seedlings Areas	39353	1.1
本年新增	The Nw Seedlings	8181	8.6
主要林产品产量（吨）	Output of Forestry Products (ton)		
生漆	Lacquer	6897	-9.3
油桐籽	Tung-Oil Seeds	25290	33.0
乌桕籽	Tea-oil Seeds	18344	-8.2
油茶籽	Tallow Seeds	87483	2.8
五倍子	Gallnut	3710	34.1
棕片	palm pieces	3656	11.7
松脂	Turpentine	39867	11.1
竹笋干	Bamboo Shoots	8428	16.4
核桃	Walnut	93987	2.9
板栗	Chestnut	410983	2.8
花椒	Pepper	3324	2.2
八角	Star anise	18	-5.3
香菇	Mushroom	95996	-0.8
黑木耳	Jew's-ear	23784	19.3
木材采伐量（万立方米）	Output of Timber Cut(10 000 cu.m)	388.98	50.4
竹材采伐量（万根）	Output of Bamboo Cut (10 000 cu.m)	3297.30	9.6

12—13 畜牧业生产情况

STATISTICS ON LIVESTOCK

指 标	Item	1990	1995	2000	2005	2010	2011	2012	2013
牲畜年末存栏头数（万头）	(10 000 heads)								
大牲畜	Large Animals	356.64	413.86	431.50	384.32	327.54	321.80	334.90	345.29
牛	Cattles and Buffalloes	351.50	409.45	428.38	382.14	326.00	320.50	333.60	344.07
#良种及改良乳牛	Fine Improved Variety Cows	2.23	2.20		4.69	4.97	9.05	6.30	6.34
马	Horses	2.56	2.52	1.83	1.58	0.92	0.76	0.75	0.61
驴	Donkeys	2.28	1.60	0.98	0.44	0.46	0.39	0.36	0.41
骡	Mules	0.30	0.29	0.30	0.16	0.16	0.14	0.11	0.18
猪	Hogs	2063.55	2449.11	2132.79	2289.05	2476.10	2533.10	2543.20	2566.07
羊	Sheep (10 000 heads)	163.15	263.23	224.80	337.66	401.70	422.00	435.10	462.91
山羊	Goats	106.72	260.04	223.55	336.97	401.23	421.50	434.50	462.75
绵羊	Sheep	56.43	3.19	1.25	0.69	0.47	0.50	0.60	0.15
畜产品产量	**Livestock Products**								
猪牛羊出栏头数（万头）	Hogs, Sheep and Goats (10 000heads)	1805.44	3246.34	3023.96	3841.82	4459.80	4499.70	4823.50	5011.74
当年肉猪出栏头数	Hogs	1714.30	2981.48	2714.44	3345.18	3827.40	3871.40	4180.80	4356.43
当年出售和自宰的肉用牛	Ox by Sold and Killed	12.44	67.40	104.26	115.49	123.10	126.40	131.70	140.28
当年出售和自宰的肉用羊(万只	Sheep by Slod and Killed (10 000heads)	78.70	197.46	205.26	381.15	509.30	501.90	511.00	515.03
肉类产量 （万吨）	Output of Meat (10 000 tons)	146.83	279.40	271.19	342.63	379.42	381.87	412.30	430.08
猪肉	Pork	134.97	239.60	215.84	271.23	287.00	290.50	317.30	330.60
牛肉	Beef	1.34	8.33	13.80	16.91	17.70	18.20	18.90	20.17
羊肉	Mutton	1.07	2.78	3.04	6.00	8.10	8.00	8.20	8.22
禽肉	Poultry	9.45	28.69	38.51	48.49	65.80	64.30	67.00	70.11
其他禽产品产量 （吨）	Others (tons)								
牛奶产量	Milk Cow	51933	38214	56400	122223	140000	142000	153000	154048
绵羊毛产量	Sheep's Wool	83.00	14.16	34.57	4.00			3.30	3.56
山羊毛产量	Goats' Wool	15.00	11.01	52.17	16.00	13.73	8.40	74.90	73.82
蜂蜜	Cashmere	7904	1077	9187	7890	10182	17695	20071	23289
禽蛋 （万吨）	Poultry Eggs (10 000 tons)	51.87	87.92	102.56	121.25	132.60	137.00	139.40	145.05

12-14 水产品产量
OUTPUT OF AQUATIC PRODUCTS

指 标	Item	1990	1995	2000	2005	2010	2011	2012	2013
水产品产量 （万吨）	**Output of Aquatic Products (10 000 tons)**	**70.98**	**150.91**	**234.34**	**318.03**	**353.00**	**356.22**	**388.94**	**410.37**
鱼类产量	Fish	67.96	141.44	219.88	277.82	308.42	308.67	331.46	349.18
虾蟹产量	Shrimp, Prawn and Crab	1.56	3.52	7.51	7.71	35.93	40.03	46.25	51.00
贝类产量	Shell Fish	1.05	3.39	5.38	1.13	4.32	4.12	5.91	5.47
其它类产量	Others	0.42	2.56	1.58		3.66	3.40	5.32	4.72
养殖产量	Artificially Cultivated	60.79	131.69	194.84	274.45	321.56	335.62	350.23	371.06
捕捞产量	Captured	10.19	19.22	39.50	43.58	31.44	20.60	38.71	39.32
莲籽产量	Lotus Seed	0.26	0.93	3.02	2.97				
养殖按水面分类产量(万吨)	Grouped by waters (10 000 tons)	60.79	131.69	193.92	274.45	321.56	335.62	350.23	371.06
湖 泊	Lakes	9.78	15.24	20.84	28.44	33.03	31.38	33.17	32.96
水 库	Reservoir	3.88	6.51	8.15	12.52	19.96	19.24	19.58	19.56
塘 堰	Pools	19.72	31.26	33.05	38.87	26.61	29.07	31.03	32.60
精 养 池	Fine Cultivated Pools	25.92	73.10	122.96	177.54	224.86	239.98	264.23	283.98
河 沟	Rivers	1.28	2.25	2.90	6.03	2.03	1.74	1.84	1.78
其 它	Others	0.21	3.33	6.02	8.03	1.33	1.19	1.26	1.32
鱼苗产量 (亿尾)	Young Fry (100 million tons)	262.36	373.84	444.01	521.39	750.00	697.00	773.00	901.00
鱼种产量 (万吨)	Advanced Fry (10 000 tons)	14.15	25.58	38.79	54.04	82.03	86.00	94.30	100.26
投放鱼种量 (万吨)	Volume of Advanced Fry (10 000 tons)	13.24	25.55	40.16	57.08	80.74	84.00	92.31	97.54
水产养殖面积 （千公顷）	**Aquatic Raised Areas (1 000 hectares)**								
湖 泊	Lakes	249.71	229.64	196.46	175.34	196.17	209.36	212.73	207.66
水 库	Reservoir	152.15	144.92	166.07	102.18	110.77	127.52	140.35	150.53
塘 堰	Pools	153.15	141.09	134.79	119.20	87.44	422.09	440.88	447.90
精 养 池	Fine Cultivated Pools	55.65	125.88	156.33	220.37	252.96	263.00	275.13	275.15
河 沟	Rivers	16.63	18.67	20.86	21.89	5.71	22.91	23.56	22.91
其 它	Others		19.00	32.92	34.56	3.67	23.58	25.40	28.91

注：2008年为国家核定数据。
Note:Data for 2008 approved a number of countries.

12–15　农业现代化情况
STATISTICS ON AGRICULTURAL MODERNIZATION

单位：千公顷

指　标	Item	1990	1995	2000	2005	2010	2011	2012	2013
农业机械化情况	**Statistics on Agricultural Machinery**								
机耕面积	Areas Ploughed by Tractors	1097.23	1247.00	1969.55	2015.93	4517.14	4732.21	5118.70	5459.02
机播面积	Seeded Areas by Tractors	47.83	83.38	255.69	233.66	815.61	1107.84	1419.31	1821.53
机械植保面积	Plant Protection Area by Tractors	1064.75	1783.65	2426.95	2848.66	4074.38	4260.10	4430.36	4611.68
机械收获面积	Harvest Area by Tractors	97.56	130.95	643.65	1407.62	2780.52	3135.31	3461.33	3746.95
农村电气化情况	**Electrification of Rural Area**								
农村用电量　（亿千瓦小时）	Electricity Consumed in Rural Area (100 million kWh)	27.21	47.36	60.86	70.09	109.78	112.26	121.23	130.14
农用物资使用情况	**Used Agricultural Product Material**								
化肥施用量(折纯量)　（万吨）	Consumption of Chemical Fertilizers (10 000 tons)	148.61	228.41	247.08	285.83	350.77	354.89	357.66	351.93
每亩耕地施用化肥(折纯量)(千克	Per Mu Consumption of Chemical Fertilizers (kg)	28.50	45.35	50.17	60.28	70.35	70.38	70.34	68.81
农用塑料薄膜使用量　（万吨）	Used Plastic Film　(10 000 tons)				5.46	6.38	6.50	6.98	6.63
农用柴油使用量　（万吨）	Used Diesel Oil　(10 000 tons)			107.81	41.31	58.29	61.84	66.48	65.73
农药使用量　（万吨）	Used Agricultural Chemical Insecticid (10 000 tons)	4.63	11.24	11.54	11.02	14.00	13.95	13.59	12.72
农田水利情况	**Irrigation and Water Conservancy**								
有效灌溉面积	Effective Irrigation Area	2324.35	2172.08	2072.53	2064.59	2187.17	2227.63	2880.00	2791.40
#机电排灌面积	#Electrical Well		1257.70		1236.11	1320.53	1314.67	1713.60	1652.51
占有效灌溉面积的比重（%	Rate in Effective Irrigation Area (%)		57.9		59.9	60.4	59.0	59.5	59.2

12-16 主要农业机械和农产品加工机械拥有量

年 份 Year	农业机械总动力 (万千瓦) Total Power of Agricultural Machinery(1000 kW)	农用大中型拖拉机 (万台) Large and Medium Agricultural Tractors(10 000 units)	农用小型及手扶拖拉机(万台) Mini and Walking Agricultural Tractors (10 000 units)	农用排灌动力机械 (万千瓦) Machinery for Machinery for Agricultural Drainage and Irrigation (1000 kW)	农用水泵 (万台) Agricultual Water Pump(10 000 units)
1978	616.07	2.80	7.75		21.22
1980	772.53	3.60	10.90		23.70
1985	910.94	5.72	14.62	55.22	21.06
1990	1099.62	8.60	17.70	99.28	24.30
1991	1120.92	8.60	18.30	362.88	24.10
1992	1120.90	8.45	17.92	368.46	23.98
1993	1108.99	7.89	16.99	360.75	23.95
1994	1136.13	7.38	15.72	368.55	24.37
1995	1174.34	7.12	15.47	384.48	26.56
1996	1222.20	7.03	16.47	401.49	27.62
1997	1276.04	7.11	18.50	408.09	28.76
1998	1325.90	7.13	20.60	410.77	29.59
1999	1363.70	7.03	22.67	419.83	32.57
2000	1414.00	6.82	23.63	434.49	35.47
2001	1469.24	6.58	24.88	450.40	40.46
2002	1557.40	6.64	26.68	461.86	43.89
2003	1661.70	6.59	28.23	469.45	45.63
2004	1768.60	6.83	32.09	484.71	50.82
2005	2057.37	7.66	48.39	518.49	55.92
2006	2263.15	8.50	55.69	531.33	71.42
2007	2551.08	9.30	74.12	541.33	82.70
2008	2796.99	10.42	85.23	559.24	87.73
2009	3057.24	11.85	90.84	594.17	87.70
2010	3371.00	12.71	99.10	663.92	85.40
2011	3571.23	13.08	106.48	673.50	89.48
2012	3842.16	13.84	111.56	668.19	103.30
2013	4081.05	14.94	114.12	714.05	105.63

NUMBER OF AGRICULTURAL MACHINERY AND MACHINERY FOR PROCESSING FARM PRODUCTS OWNED AT YEAR-END

喷灌机械 (万套) Machinery for Sprinkling (10 000 units)	联合收割机 (台) Combine Hearvesters (unit)	机动脱粒机 (万台) Motorized Huller (10 000 units)	机动喷雾(粉)器 (万部) Motorized Duster (10 000 units)	饲料粉碎机 (万台) Fodder Grinder (10 000 units)	大中型拖拉机配套农具 (万部) Large and Medium Tractors Towing Farm Machinery (10 000 units)	小型拖拉机配套农具 (万部) Mini Tractors Towing Farm Machinery (10 000 units)
0.30	425	15.00	0.78	7.78	4.66	4.92
1.08	602	17.40	1.00	8.20	4.99	7.20
0.73	479	15.22	0.60	5.90	2.39	4.95
0.31	2335	12.60	3.70	5.60	2.70	10.14
0.34	455	12.50	4.60	5.55	3.00	11.87
0.60	390	12.35	4.70	5.32	3.86	12.30
0.48	345	11.97	4.77	5.12	3.05	11.64
0.47	346	11.39	5.29	5.50	2.91	12.38
0.72	312	11.25	6.44	5.32	2.85	15.48
0.72	553	12.33	6.74	8.70	3.05	23.02
7.75	1521	11.11	7.36	8.79	3.63	29.46
0.80	2338	11.56	8.27	9.65	4.33	37.75
0.71	2559	11.56	8.00	10.48	4.80	42.84
0.85	2704	12.25	8.70	10.73	4.81	37.48
1.01	3363	12.79	9.07	12.60	5.22	41.12
1.08	5722	12.81	9.72	9.59	5.97	46.44
1.17	6708	12.62	10.26	12.33	6.21	49.03
1.20	10585	12.88	11.86	15.01	7.45	59.31
1.55	16085	14.33	15.98	23.88	9.36	96.69
1.75	22407	12.54	25.44	26.37	11.18	111.02
1.81	29803	13.14	30.58	27.04	12.96	149.08
2.23	34983	12.99	35.41	29.94	15.49	169.69
2.21	41904	15.37	38.40	33.46	20.37	178.55
2.52	50509	18.09	43.56	35.50	21.49	204.66
2.88	58398	23.33	48.73	36.23	24.01	211.97
4.77	66860	24.28	55.07	32.30	25.74	214.51
10.73	73808	26.43	60.41	32.87	28.00	215.42

12-17 市、州乡村从业人员

RURAL EMPLOYMENT IN CITIES AND PREFECTURES

单位：万人

市、州	Municipalities and Prefecrures	2012	农林牧渔业从业人员 Employment in Farming, Forestry, Animal Husbandry and Fishery	2013	农林牧渔业从业人员 Employment in Farming, Forestry, Animal Husbandry and Fishery
全 省	**Province**	**2259.91**	**863.49**	**2280.14**	**869.49**
武汉市	Wuhan Municipality	141.32	49.94	145.32	47.05
黄石市	Huangshi Municipality	86.16	20.18	87.79	19.97
十堰市	Shiyan Municipality	134.81	52.08	136.76	47.20
荆州市	Jingzhou Municipality	230.97	104.23	235.37	101.16
宜昌市	Yichang Municipality	163.27	62.30	162.96	69.47
襄阳市	Xiangyang Municipality	231.82	83.84	220.47	83.47
鄂州市	Ezhou Municipality	40.00	18.90	40.30	19.03
荆门市	Jingmen Municipality	106.82	39.02	107.57	37.96
孝感市	Xiaogan Municipality	236.68	85.55	246.23	84.59
黄冈市	Huanggang Municipality	319.45	112.28	322.26	130.93
咸宁市	Xianning Municipality	106.32	42.61	108.60	40.21
随州市	Suizhou Municipality	105.96	40.47	106.28	39.79
恩施自治州	Enshi Prefecture	191.34	93.94	192.77	92.12
仙桃市	Xiantao Municipality	65.51	24.00	65.73	23.18
天门市	Tianmen Municipality	60.79	19.10	60.32	18.12
潜江市	Qianjiang Municipality	35.99	13.64	38.70	13.92
神农架林区	Shennongjia Forest Zone	2.70	1.41	2.71	1.32

12−18　市、州耕地面积

CULTIVATED AREA OF CITIES AND PREFECTURES

市、州	Municipalities and Prefecrures	1990 年末耕地面积(千公顷) Cultivated Area at Year-end(1 000 hectares)	1990 人平耕地(亩) Cultivated Area Per Capita(Mu)	2000 年末耕地面积(千公顷) Cultivated Area at Year-end(1 000 hectares)	2000 人平耕地(亩) Cultivated Area Per Capita(Mu)	2010 年末耕地面积(千公顷) Cultivated Area at Year-end(1000 hectares)	2010 人平耕地(亩) Cultivated Area Per Capita(Mu)	2012 年末耕地面积(千公顷) Cultivated Area at Year-end(1000 hectares)	2012 人平耕地(亩) Cultivated Area Per Capita(Mu)	2013 年末耕地面积(千公顷) Cultivated Area at Year-end(1000 hectares)	2013 人平耕地(亩) Cultivated Area Per Capita(Mu)
全省	**Province**	**3476.78**	**0.96**	**3282.96**	**0.83**	**3323.92**	**0.87**	**3390.06**	**0.88**	**3409.91**	**0.88**
武汉市	Wuhan Municipality	240.11	0.54	217.84	0.40	204.79	0.31	202.12	0.30	197.64	0.29
黄石市	Huangshi Municipality	84.08	0.60	79.32	0.48	89.80	0.55	89.57	0.55	89.39	0.55
十堰市	Shiyan Municipality	207.27	0.95	181.54	0.79	169.91	0.76	174.03	0.78	177.05	0.79
荆州市	Jingzhou Municipality	480.48	1.31	432.58	1.03	464.80	1.22	467.77	1.23	468.71	1.22
宜昌市	Yichang Municipality	275.72	1.07	257.71	0.94	230.14	0.85	258.69	0.95	266.44	0.98
襄阳市	Xiangyang Municipality	429.00	1.26	412.96	1.09	436.91	1.19	449.59	1.22	452.20	1.21
鄂州市	Ezhou Municipality	44.33	0.73	40.28	0.59	41.05	0.59	40.55	0.58	40.41	0.57
荆门市	Jingmen Municipality	240.96	1.34	256.53	1.29	255.69	1.33	265.02	1.38	266.69	1.39
孝感市	Xiaogan Municipality	296.41	0.83	247.10	0.74	261.27	0.81	262.31	0.81	266.84	0.82
黄冈市	Huanggang Municipality	335.85	0.77	312.36	0.65	337.52	0.82	343.48	0.83	343.63	0.82
咸宁市	Xianning Municipality	150.46	0.93	145.94	0.81	155.85	0.95	156.59	0.95	158.65	0.96
随州市	Suizhou Municipality	99.63	1.52	136.58	0.85	144.94	1.00	142.89	0.99	143.35	0.99
恩施自治州	Enshi Prefecture	291.61	1.22	280.59	1.11	255.89	1.17	260.49	1.18	260.29	1.18
仙桃市	Xiantao Municipality	108.29	1.17	98.68	1.01	90.59	1.16	90.54	1.15	90.54	1.15
天门市	Tianmen Municipality	110.63	1.08	107.62	1.00	108.36	1.15	109.80	1.22	109.66	1.28
潜江市	Qianjiang Municipality	73.39	1.27	66.99	1.01	70.22	1.11	72.08	1.14	72.10	1.14
神农架林区	Shennongjia Forest Zone	8.57	1.66	8.35	1.54	6.19	1.22	4.54	0.89	6.32	1.24

12-19 市、州农、林、牧、渔业总产值及指数

GROSS OUTPUT VALUE AND ITS INDICES OF FARMING, FORESTRY, ANIMAL HUSBANDRY AND FISHERY OF CITIES AND PREFECTURES

市、州	Municipalities and Prefecrures	绝对数(亿元) Absolute Number (100 milion yuan)					指数(%) Indices (%)				
		1995	2000	2010	2012	2013	1995	2000	2010	2012	2013
全 省	**Province**	**988.53**	**1125.64**	**3501.99**	**4732.12**	**5161.00**	**114.1**	**102.8**	**110.0**	**111.3**	**109.1**
武汉市	Wuhan Municipality	94.34	126.94	281.09	410.67	530.27	112.0	105.3	111.6	124.6	129.1
黄石市	Huangshi Municipality	23.75	27.63	83.91	122.85	133.76	109.0	104.2	115.3	120.3	108.9
十堰市	Shiyan Municipality	43.43	44.65	133.19	212.57	250.15	106.7	111.1	119.0	126.6	117.7
荆州市	Jingzhou Municipality	178.07	147.69	423.79	534.97	578.34	112.3	91.0	110.1	110.5	108.1
宜昌市	Yichang Municipality	80.26	97.19	294.05	502.96	555.63	116.4	102.6	117.4	125.6	110.5
襄阳市	Xiangyang Municipality	155.08	158.15	409.04	624.55	678.91	113.0	93.5	111.8	124.1	108.7
鄂州市	Ezhou Municipality	18.42	13.92	92.82	126.68	138.50	123.2	106.7	115.8	116.5	109.3
荆门市	Jingmen Municipality	103.56	100.13	253.14	316.65	337.93	115.3	103.0	109.2	108.5	106.7
孝感市	Xiaogan Municipality	124.45	111.63	306.61	417.57	452.40	115.0	90.7	117.7	117.3	108.3
黄冈市	Huanggang Municipality	119.17	127.48	374.79	505.72	532.22	108.9	102.4	115.0	109.0	105.2
咸宁市	Xianning Municipality	47.61	52.87	168.52	237.64	264.70	110.8	104.5	120.2	121.1	111.4
随州市	Suizhou Municipality	30.07	58.06	150.29	195.33	216.72	112.6	141.5	113.9	110.6	111.0
恩施自治州	Enshi Prefecture	48.32	76.78	174.25	209.20	227.22	111.0	102.3	114.3	108.3	108.6
仙桃市	Xiaotao Municipality	37.47	39.01	94.41	127.85	136.29	125.9	102.2	113.2	112.8	106.6
天门市	Tianmen Municipality	41.58	33.15	80.94	101.23	108.58	122.0	100.4	111.6	108.7	107.3
潜江市	Qianjiang Municipality	28.61	30.58	85.55	101.34	109.28	127.6	101.9	122.2	108.2	107.8
神农架林区	Shennongjia Forest Zone	0.84	0.99	2.59	3.16	3.56	103.2	87.1	112.6	111.0	112.4

注：本表产值按当年价格计算，指数按不变价格计算；全省合计数为调整数，故市、州相加不等于合计数。

Notes:The data of in this table is caculated at current prices of output valul,and the data of indices is calulaled at constort prices therefore,the total of provice is an adiusted number,and that of municipalities and prefecture if added are not egual to the total number.

12–20 市、州农、林、牧、渔业产值(现价)(2013)

GROSS OUTPUT VALUE OF FARMING, FORESTRY, ANIMAL HUSBANDRY AND FISHERY OF CITIES AND PREFECTURES (AT CURRENT PRICES)(2013)

单位：亿元 (100 million yuan)

市、州	Municipalities and Prefecrures	合计 Total	农业 Farming	林业 Forestry	牧业 nimal Husband	渔业 Fishery	农林牧渔服务业 Service Industry for Farming, Forestry, Animal Husbandry and Fishery
全省	**Province**	**5161.00**	**2678.10**	**122.00**	**1395.40**	**748.40**	**216.70**
武汉市	Wuhan Municipality	530.27	305.10	6.59	118.67	83.66	16.25
黄石市	Huangshi Municipality	133.76	52.56	1.55	42.08	36.19	1.38
十堰市	Shiyan Municipality	250.15	145.28	10.27	80.25	13.12	1.23
荆州市	Jingzhou Municipality	578.34	253.10	6.48	138.58	173.20	6.98
宜昌市	Yichang Municipality	555.63	296.30	6.36	200.44	39.00	13.52
襄阳市	Xiangyang Municipality	678.91	315.59	7.41	300.69	28.09	27.14
鄂州市	Ezhou Municipality	138.50	39.80	2.00	34.22	62.09	0.39
荆门市	Jingmen Municipality	337.93	149.99	5.34	112.35	62.31	7.94
孝感市	Xiaogan Municipality	452.40	194.59	10.24	166.85	72.37	8.35
黄冈市	Huanggang Municipality	532.22	268.05	7.84	184.59	60.74	11.00
咸宁市	Xianning Municipality	264.70	134.95	11.80	68.61	47.51	1.83
随州市	Suizhou Municipality	216.72	116.68	4.96	80.19	10.24	4.65
恩施自治州	Enshi Prefecture	227.22	128.92	8.93	86.45	1.18	1.74
仙桃市	Xiaotao Municipality	136.29	50.69	1.15	32.30	49.70	2.45
天门市	Tianmen Municipality	108.58	52.49	0.29	27.92	25.75	2.14
潜江市	Qianjiang Municipality	109.28	51.33	2.95	32.82	20.02	2.16
神农架林区	Shennongjia Forest Zone	3.56	2.12	0.30	1.08	0.02	0.04

注：全省数字第二次农业普查后国家统计局重新核定数，故今年市州汇总不等于全省。

Note:Note: The number of the second province after the National Bureau of Statistics agricultural census the number of re-approved, it summarizes the state does not mean the province this year.

12–21 市、州农、林、牧、渔业中间消耗(2013)

INTERMEDIATE-CONSUMPTION OF OF FARMING, FORESTRY, ANIMAL HUSBANDRY AND FISHERY OF CITIES AND PREFECTURES(2013)

单位：亿元 (100 million yuan)

市、州	Municipalities and Prefecrures	合计 Total	农业 Farming	林业 Forestry	牧业 Animal Husbandry	渔业 Fishery	农林牧渔服务业 Service Industry for Farming, Forestry, Animal Husbandry and Fishery
全省	**Province**	**2062.41**	**967.78**	**63.91**	**596.10**	**285.82**	**148.80**
武汉市	Wuhan Municipality	194.86	105.29	2.48	49.24	32.49	5.37
黄石市	Huangshi Municipality	38.55	13.70	0.34	14.80	9.20	0.50
十堰市	Shiyan Municipality	107.11	61.09	5.23	35.11	5.14	0.55
荆州市	Jingzhou Municipality	259.26	104.29	1.77	68.65	81.19	3.35
宜昌市	Yichang Municipality	219.68	114.29	2.66	81.12	15.56	6.05
襄阳市	Xiangyang Municipality	292.47	129.62	2.48	134.82	13.50	12.05
鄂州市	Ezhou Municipality	59.99	20.29	1.47	12.86	25.13	0.24
荆门市	Jingmen Municipality	147.63	67.80	2.27	45.84	28.71	3.01
孝感市	Xiaogan Municipality	209.26	82.45	4.32	83.12	35.26	4.11
黄冈市	Huanggang Municipality	175.43	76.76	3.51	69.56	22.28	3.33
咸宁市	Xianning Municipality	101.81	51.62	4.55	25.78	19.30	0.56
随州市	Suizhou Municipality	91.93	54.04	1.98	31.79	2.99	1.14
恩施自治州	Enshi Prefecture	93.93	53.66	3.96	35.33	0.33	0.65
仙桃市	Xiaotao Municipality	56.04	18.76	0.90	14.93	20.51	0.95
天门市	Tianmen Municipality	34.28	18.63	0.15	10.79	4.07	0.64
潜江市	Qianjiang Municipality	44.29	14.70	0.52	21.37	6.64	1.07
神农架林区	Shennongjia Forest Zone	1.78	1.10	0.11	0.53	0.02	0.02

注：全省中间消耗为省级核算数，故市、州相加不等于合计数。

Note:The statistics of Intermedium Consumption is checked by Provincial Statistical Burea,thus the total of municipalities and prefecture do not equal to the total of the whole province.

12-22　市、州农、林、牧、渔业增加值(2013)
VALUE ADDED OF FARMING, FORESTRY, ANIMAL HUSBANDRY AND FISHERY OF CITIES AND PREFECTURES(2013)

单位：亿元　　(100 million yuan)

市、州	Municipalities and Prefecrures	合计 Total	农业 Farming	林业 Forestry	牧业 Animal Husbandry	渔业 Fishery	农林牧渔服务业 Service Industry for Farming, Forestry, Animal Husbandry and Fishery
全省	**Province**	**3098.16**	**1710.30**	**58.10**	**799.29**	**462.58**	**67.89**
武汉市	Wuhan Municipality	335.40	199.81	4.11	69.43	51.17	10.88
黄石市	Huangshi Municipality	95.21	38.85	1.21	27.28	26.99	0.88
十堰市	Shiyan Municipality	143.03	84.19	5.05	45.14	7.98	0.68
荆州市	Jingzhou Municipality	319.09	148.81	4.71	69.92	92.01	3.63
宜昌市	Yichang Municipality	335.95	182.01	3.70	119.31	23.45	7.47
襄阳市	Xiangyang Municipality	386.45	185.97	4.92	165.87	14.59	15.09
鄂州市	Ezhou Municipality	78.51	19.50	0.53	21.36	36.96	0.15
荆门市	Jingmen Municipality	190.30	82.19	3.07	66.51	33.60	4.94
孝感市	Xiaogan Municipality	243.13	112.14	5.92	83.72	37.11	4.24
黄冈市	Huanggang Municipality	356.79	191.29	4.34	115.03	38.47	7.66
咸宁市	Xianning Municipality	162.90	83.33	7.25	42.83	28.21	1.27
随州市	Suizhou Municipality	124.79	62.64	2.98	48.40	7.25	3.51
恩施自治州	Enshi Prefecture	133.28	75.26	4.97	51.12	0.84	1.09
仙桃市	Xiaotao Municipality	80.25	31.93	0.26	17.38	29.19	1.50
天门市	Tianmen Municipality	74.30	33.86	0.14	17.12	21.68	1.50
潜江市	Qianjiang Municipality	65.00	36.63	2.44	11.45	13.38	1.09
神农架林区	Shennongjia Forest Zone	1.77	1.01	0.19	0.55	0.01	0.02

注：全省数为省级核算数，故分市州汇总不等于全省。

Note:The statistics of the whole province is checked by Provincial Statistical Burea, thus the total of municipalities and prefecture do not equal to the total of the whole province.

12–23 市、州主要农作物产量(2013)

单位：万吨

市、州	Municipalities and Prefecrures	粮食 Grain	稻谷 Rice	小麦 Wheat	玉米 Corn	薯类 Tubers	大豆 Soybean	棉花 Cotton
全省	**Province**	**2501.30**	**1676.64**	**416.80**	**270.75**	**95.68**	**19.58**	**45.97**
武汉市	Wuhan Municipality	126.87	102.05	7.05	9.42	4.25	2.32	3.32
黄石市	Huangshi Municipality	64.42	48.80	3.87	4.74	5.11	0.81	0.76
十堰市	Shiyan Municipality	116.06	27.28	24.26	37.61	19.72	4.59	0.02
荆州市	Jingzhou Municipality	386.06	327.65	42.43	5.58	4.12	2.74	13.88
宜昌市	Yichang Municipality	164.53	70.83	15.50	49.07	24.81	2.14	3.26
襄阳市	Xiangyang Municipality	502.81	188.11	210.23	80.83	18.62	1.77	4.18
鄂州市	Ezhou Municipality	35.51	29.38	1.25	0.60	3.04	0.42	0.70
荆门市	Jingmen Municipality	267.60	189.97	49.97	16.02	6.48	3.97	4.77
孝感市	Xiaogan Municipality	223.64	177.09	34.09	2.04	6.58	1.76	4.14
黄冈市	Huanggang Municipality	318.98	265.02	19.43	4.79	24.80	2.32	8.62
咸宁市	Xianning Municipality	104.67	83.56	2.62	8.46	7.34	1.17	0.55
随州市	Suizhou Municipality	158.18	98.61	42.46	5.89	8.46	0.70	1.94
恩施自治州	Enshi Prefecture	162.86	38.92	1.78	66.09	49.89	4.03	0.00
仙桃市	Xiaotao Municipality	80.99	62.73	8.52	5.63	1.12	1.75	2.93
天门市	Tianmen Municipality	71.50	49.15	15.39	1.72	2.49	2.59	4.93
潜江市	Qianjiang Municipality	52.00	36.95	10.63	2.38	1.05	0.77	3.97
神农架林区	Shennongjia Forest Zone	2.20	0.05	0.11	0.95	0.91	0.08	

OUTPUT OF MAJOR FARM CROPS OF CITIES AND PREFECTURES(2013)

(10 000tons)

油料 Oil Bearing Crops	花生 Peanuts	油菜籽 Rapeseed	芝麻 Sesame	麻类 Hemp Crops	苎麻 Ramie	糖类 Sugar Crops	甘蔗 Crane	烟叶 Tobacoo Crops	烤烟 Tobacco
333.17	**68.11**	**250.47**	**13.60**	**2.61**	**2.60**	**28.72**	**28.72**	**12.70**	**9.46**
18.66	4.23	12.34	2.08	0.27	0.27	4.75	4.75		
9.38	0.93	7.20	1.25	0.78	0.78	0.16	0.16		
13.20	4.49	6.88	1.65			1.43	1.43	2.04	1.72
62.75	0.65	61.02	1.08	0.01		4.31	4.31		
23.92	3.39	19.92	0.51			0.14	0.14	1.49	0.71
24.97	12.90	10.90	1.02	0.03	0.03	0.66	0.66	1.43	1.43
6.09	0.36	5.19	0.54	0.03	0.03	0.83	0.83		
38.80	8.43	29.37	1.00			2.64	2.64	0.00	
24.21	7.42	15.77	0.87	0.00	0.00	2.34	2.34		
55.39	15.64	38.44	1.31	0.53	0.53	3.29	3.29		
10.19	1.60	7.98	0.61	0.97	0.97	5.41	5.41		
7.37	3.80	2.74	0.83			0.49	0.49		
10.17	1.95	7.27	0.05	0.00	0.00	0.02	0.02	7.67	5.54
13.05	0.21	12.38	0.46			1.57	1.57		
11.46	1.58	9.68	0.20			0.41	0.41		
11.42	0.52	10.75	0.14			0.26	0.26		
0.05	0.01	0.04	0.00					0.06	0.06

12–24 市、州大牲畜、羊、猪年末存栏、出栏、肉产量(2013)

市、州	Municipalities and Prefecrures	大牲畜存栏 (万头) Large Animals in Stock(10 000 heads)	牛 Cattles and Bufflaoes	羊存栏 (万只) Sheep in Stock (10 000 heads)	山羊 Goats	年末生猪存栏 (万头) Hogs in Stock at Year-end(10 000 heads)
全省	**Province**	**345.29**	**344.07**	**462.91**	**462.75**	**2566.07**
武汉市	Wuhan Municipality	21.31	21.28	4.87	4.86	216.19
黄石市	Huangshi Municipality	7.99	7.99	7.09	7.09	101.43
十堰市	Shiyan Municipality	40.57	40.32	109.99	109.99	216.89
荆州市	Jingzhou Municipality	8.77	8.69	13.79	13.79	376.52
宜昌市	Yichang Municipality	17.91	17.91	113.68	113.68	501.77
襄阳市	Xiangyang Municipality	100.22	100.21	141.79	140.17	525.45
鄂州市	Ezhou Municipality	3.87	3.87	2.12	2.12	85.00
荆门市	Jingmen Municipality	22.37	22.25	43.25	43.25	313.19
孝感市	Xiaogan Municipality	44.88	44.58	29.74	29.74	297.54
黄冈市	Huanggang Municipality	103.74	103.73	91.44	91.41	478.64
咸宁市	Xianning Municipality	14.14	14.01	16.55	16.55	203.70
随州市	Suizhou Municipality	25.76	25.76	46.66	46.66	171.77
恩施自治州	Enshi Prefecture	42.85	42.68	88.37	88.35	470.84
仙桃市	Xiaotao Municipality	1.04	1.04	0.17	0.17	69.96
天门市	Tianmen Municipality	6.80	6.66	1.54	1.54	79.15
潜江市	Qianjiang Municipality	2.94	2.94	1.72	1.71	61.63
神农架林区	Shennongjia Forest Zone	0.72	0.71	2.70	2.70	3.83

STATISTICS ON LIVE ANIMALS, SHEEP, HOGS IN STOCK AND OUT OF STOCK AT YEAR-END AND OUTPUT OF MEAT OF CITIES AND PREFECTURES(2013)

年内出栏肉猪 (万头) Hogs out of Stock at Year-end(10 000 heads)	年内出栏羊 (万只) Sheep out of Stock at Year-end(10 000 heads)	出笼禽 (万只) Poultry out of Stock at Year-end(10 000 heads)	肉类总产量 (万吨) Total Output of Meat (10 000 tons)	猪肉产量 Output of Pork	羊 肉 Mutton	禽蛋产量 (万吨) Output of Eggs (10 000 tons)
5011.74	**515.03**	**52210.11**	**430.08**	**330.60**	**8.22**	**145.05**
308.20	4.77	5744.17	33.54	23.30	0.11	21.48
121.49	5.22	3038.01	14.53	9.11	0.10	4.14
198.73	100.19	3295.20	23.13	14.90	1.55	4.96
499.15	16.72	7708.29	50.97	38.19	0.22	18.62
623.40	147.53	3764.51	61.04	50.96	3.08	6.30
626.06	161.62	9013.59	82.38	48.52	3.55	26.24
120.00	2.35	1559.43	12.20	9.23	0.05	5.36
415.22	56.19	4994.55	42.28	30.46	1.39	15.13
388.73	24.27	13645.42	53.78	29.56	0.55	37.11
507.02	73.04	6054.09	58.48	37.71	1.57	58.22
264.74	17.44	4269.63	25.84	19.86	0.44	2.97
243.11	56.01	8094.79	31.95	18.00	1.05	7.58
501.59	79.69	1174.89	47.29	41.45	1.59	2.89
118.05	0.74	915.90	9.90	8.85	0.01	4.54
103.98	1.22	1257.40	9.59	7.80	0.02	5.17
111.05	2.49	1800.19	11.20	8.33	0.04	3.90
5.06	1.59	33.80	0.46	0.37	0.03	0.03

12-25 市、州主要土特产品产量(2013)

OUTPUT OF LOCAL SPECIALITY OF CITIES AND PREFECTURES(2013)

市、州	Municipalities and Prefecrures	茶叶 (万吨) Tea (10 000 tons)	绿毛茶 Green Tea	蚕茧 (吨) Silkworm Coccons (ton)	桑蚕茧 Mulbeery Silkworm Coccons	园林水果 (万吨) Fruits (10 000 tons)	桃子 Peaches	柑桔 Citrus	苹果 Apples	黑木耳 (吨) Jew's Ear (ton)
全省	**Province**	**22.20**	**17.04**	**7723.21**	**7618.21**	**569.42**	**72.49**	**400.39**	**1.02**	**23784**
武汉市	Wuhan Municipality	0.24	0.23			8.48	2.50	3.06		
黄石市	Huangshi Municipality	0.04	0.04	36.00	36.00	4.20	0.21	3.62	0.00	26.00
十堰市	Shiyan Municipality	1.31	1.14	812.00	812.00	36.63	0.89	33.18	0.07	2609.00
荆州市	Jingzhou Municipality	0.01	0.00	6.00	6.00	44.88	0.79	28.08	0.01	34.00
宜昌市	Yichang Municipality	5.60	4.49	1040.00	1040.00	283.20	3.21	275.89	0.05	632.00
襄阳市	Xiangyang Municipality	1.50	1.18	811.00	811.00	59.37	38.48	5.34	0.19	4382.00
鄂州市	Ezhou Municipality	0.01	0.01			3.79	0.36	2.80		
荆门市	Jingmen Municipality	0.02	0.02			44.62	2.72	17.16	0.03	1854.00
孝感市	Xiaogan Municipality	0.89	0.83	0.20	0.20	18.75	9.72	2.18	0.08	556.00
黄冈市	Huanggang Municipality	3.20	3.14	4827.00	4827.00	12.08	3.01	5.25	0.09	898.20
咸宁市	Xianning Municipality	2.67	1.07			6.54	0.71	3.75		164.00
随州市	Suizhou Municipality	0.25	0.24	105.00		13.95	8.53	0.74	0.17	12559.50
恩施自治州	Enshi Prefecture	6.44	4.65	86.01	86.01	25.15	0.52	17.77	0.33	9.00
仙桃市	Xiaotao Municipality					2.61	0.42	1.03		
天门市	Tianmen Municipality					1.66	0.11	0.37		
潜江市	Qianjiang Municipality					3.48	0.29	0.17		11.00
神农架林区	Shennongjia Forest Zone	0.01	0.01			0.04	0.01		0.00	49.00

注：根据国家报表制度变化，取消白木耳统计

12-26 市、州人平粮、棉、油、肉、水产品生产水平(2013)
PER CAPITA PRODUCTION LEVEL OF GRAIN,COTTON,OIL,MEAT AND AQUATIC PRODUCTS OF CITIES AND PREFECTURES(2013)

单位:千克 (kg)

市、州	Municipalities and Prefecrures	粮食 Grain	棉花 Cotton	油料 Oil Bearing Crops	肉类 Meat	水产品 Aquatic Products	禽蛋 Eggs
按常住人口平均	**Average of Total Population**						
全省	**Province**	**431.33**	**7.93**	**57.45**	**74.16**	**70.77**	**25.01**
武汉市	Wuhan Municipality	124.14	3.25	18.26	32.82	47.96	21.01
黄石市	Huangshi Municipality	263.49	3.10	38.36	59.43	82.78	16.92
十堰市	Shiyan Municipality	344.71	0.06	39.20	68.71	19.63	14.72
荆州市	Jingzhou Municipality	672.65	24.18	109.33	88.81	213.27	32.43
宜昌市	Yichang Municipality	401.46	7.96	58.36	148.94	45.98	15.36
襄阳市	Xiangyang Municipality	899.28	7.47	44.67	147.34	33.82	46.93
鄂州市	Ezhou Municipality	335.99	6.58	57.59	115.44	403.98	50.70
荆门市	Jingmen Municipality	926.86	16.52	134.38	146.45	170.30	52.40
孝感市	Xiaogan Municipality	460.83	8.52	49.88	110.81	85.61	76.47
黄冈市	Huanggang Municipality	510.22	13.78	88.60	93.54	76.50	93.12
咸宁市	Xianning Municipality	421.20	2.21	41.02	103.97	91.28	11.94
随州市	Suizhou Municipality	725.55	8.90	33.79	146.57	39.27	34.79
恩施自治州	Enshi Prefecture	491.73	0.01	30.71	142.78	2.15	8.73
仙桃市	Xiaotao Municipality	683.53	24.69	110.11	83.57	274.74	38.33
天门市	Tianmen Municipality	554.71	38.22	88.91	74.39	98.35	40.10
潜江市	Qianjiang Municipality	546.01	41.72	119.88	117.57	119.28	40.99
神农架林区	Shennongjia Forest Zone	287.21		5.87	60.69	2.95	3.63
按乡村人口平均	**Average of Country Population**						
全省	**Province**	**611.24**	**11.23**	**81.42**	**105.10**	**100.28**	**35.45**
武汉市	Wuhan Municipality	479.41	12.53	70.52	126.73	185.22	81.16
黄石市	Huangshi Municipality	401.27	4.73	58.42	90.51	126.06	25.77
十堰市	Shiyan Municipality	472.83	0.08	53.76	94.24	26.93	20.20
荆州市	Jingzhou Municipality	895.86	32.20	145.61	118.28	284.03	43.20
宜昌市	Yichang Municipality	607.41	12.04	88.30	225.34	69.57	23.25
襄阳市	Xiangyang Municipality	1342.39	11.15	66.68	219.93	50.49	70.05
鄂州市	Ezhou Municipality	461.16	9.02	79.04	158.45	554.48	69.59
荆门市	Jingmen Municipality	1401.57	24.98	203.20	221.46	257.53	79.23
孝感市	Xiaogan Municipality	535.71	9.91	57.99	128.82	99.52	88.89
黄冈市	Huanggang Municipality	548.27	14.81	95.21	100.52	82.20	100.07
咸宁市	Xianning Municipality	481.74	2.53	46.92	118.91	104.40	13.65
随州市	Suizhou Municipality	801.83	9.83	37.35	161.98	43.40	38.44
恩施自治州	Enshi Prefecture	472.22	0.01	29.49	137.11	2.07	8.38
仙桃市	Xiaotao Municipality	703.97	25.43	113.40	86.07	282.95	39.48
天门市	Tianmen Municipality	560.09	38.59	89.78	75.12	99.30	40.49
潜江市	Qianjiang Municipality	731.70	55.91	160.65	157.56	159.85	54.93
神农架林区	Shennongjia Forest Zone	464.14		9.49	98.08	4.77	5.86

12−27 市、州农业机械、用电、化肥、水利情况(2013)
AGRICULTURAL MACHINERY, ELECTRICITY CONSUMPTION, CHEMICAL FERTILIZERS AND IRRAGATION IN CITIES AND PREFECTURES(2013)

市、州	Municipalities and Prefecrures	农业机械总动力 (万千瓦特) Total Power of Agricultural Machinery (10 000kW)	当年实际机耕面积 (千公顷) Actual Sown Areas (1 000 hectares)	农村用电量 (万千瓦小时) Rural Electricity Consumption (1 000kW/h)	化肥施用量 (折纯量)(万吨) Consumption of Chemical Fertilizers (pure) (10 000tons)	有效灌溉面积 (千公顷) Effective Irrigation Area (1 000 hectares)
全省	**Province**	**4081.05**	**5459.02**	**1301417.00**	**351.93**	**2291.17**
武汉市	Wuhan Municipality			120729.00	14.87	162.10
黄石市	Huangshi Municipality			112684.00	5.41	52.18
十堰市	Shiyan Municipality			53103.00	14.25	36.58
荆州市	Jingzhou Municipality			148723.00	36.00	416.46
宜昌市	Yichang Municipality			97258.00	38.20	111.32
襄阳市	Xiangyang Municipality			93496.26	59.30	271.07
鄂州市	Ezhou Municipality			45042.00	9.76	27.75
荆门市	Jingmen Municipality			95612.30	35.03	208.13
孝感市	Xiaogan Municipality			117278.00	20.80	232.77
黄冈市	Huanggang Municipality			199119.80	39.83	236.87
咸宁市	Xianning Municipality			43367.38	11.94	92.31
随州市	Suizhou Municipality			44877.00	16.24	124.04
恩施自治州	Enshi Prefecture			45530.92	28.39	68.24
仙桃市	Xiaotao Municipality			45915.00	6.50	81.83
天门市	Tianmen Municipality			26648.92	7.56	109.66
潜江市	Qianjiang Municipality			10856.41	7.48	59.61
神农架林区	Shennongjia Forest Zone			1176.00	0.36	0.25

主要统计指标解释

农林牧渔业总产值　指以货币表现的农、林、牧、渔业全部产品和对农林牧渔业生产活动进行的各种支持性服务活动的价值总量，它反映一定时期内农林牧渔业生产总规模和总成果。1957 年以前的农林牧渔业总产值中包括了厩肥和农民自给性手工业(如农民自制衣服、鞋、袜，自己从事粮食初步加工等)。1958 年及以后，林业中增加了村及村以下竹木采伐产值；牧业中取消了厩肥产值；副业中取消了农民自给性手工业产值，增加了村及村以下办的工业产值；渔业中增加了海洋捕捞水产品产值。1980 年及以后，在副业中增加了农民家庭兼营工业商品部分的产值。从 1984 年起村及村以下工业产值划归工业。从 1993 年起取消副业，将野生动物的捕猎划入牧业，野生植物采集和农民家庭兼营商品性工业划归农业。从 2003 年起，执行新的国民经济行业分类标准，农林牧渔业总产值中包括了农林牧渔服务业产值。林业中增加了森林采运业产值。农业中取消了家庭兼营商品性工业产值，将野生林产品的采集划归林业。第一次农业普查以后，由于畜牧业产品年报数据与普查数据之间存在一定的差距，国家统计局农调总队对畜牧业年报数据与普查数据进行衔接，对畜牧业产值进行相应调整。

农林牧渔业总产值的计算方法通常是按农、林、牧、渔业产品及其副产品的产量分别乘以各自单位产品价格求得；少数生产周期较长，当年没有产品或产品产量不易统计的，则采用间接方法匡算其产值；然后将四业产品产值相加即为农林牧渔业总产值。

粮食产量　指全社会的产量。包括国有经济经营的、集体统一经营的和农民家庭经营的粮食产量，还包括工矿企业办的农场和其他生产单位的产量。粮食除包括稻谷、小麦、玉米、高粱、谷子及其他杂粮外，还包括薯类和豆类。其产量计算方法，豆类按去豆荚后的干豆计算；薯类(包括甘薯和马铃薯，不包括芋头和木薯)1963 年以前按每 4 公斤鲜薯折 1 公斤粮食计算，从 1964 年开始改为按 5 公斤鲜薯折 1 公斤粮食计算。城市郊区作为蔬菜的薯类(如马铃薯等)按鲜品计算，并且不作粮食统计。其他粮食一律按脱粒后的原粮计算。1989 年以前全国粮食产量数据主要靠全面报表取得，1989 年开始使用抽样调查数据。

棉花产量　指全社会的产量。包括春播棉和夏播棉。产量按皮棉计算。不包括木棉。

油料产量　指全部油料作物的生产量。包括花生、油菜籽、芝麻、向日葵籽、胡麻籽（亚麻籽）和其他油料。不包括大豆、木本油料和野生油料。花生以带壳干花生计算。

水产品产量　指人工养殖的水产品和天然生长的水产品的捕捞量。包括海水的鱼类、虾蟹类、贝类和藻类以及内陆水域的鱼类、虾蟹类和贝类，不包括淡水生植物。水产品产量是通过各级水产和统计部门逐级上报取得数据。1995 年及以前，贝类中牡蛎按鲜肉计算；蚶、蛤、蛙按 5 斤鲜品折 1 斤计算。1996 年以后则统一按鲜品计算。

猪、牛、羊肉产量　指当年出栏并已屠宰、除去头蹄下水后带骨肉(即胴体重)的重量。包括全社会范围内的产量。1996 年前为各级逐级上报数据。1996 年第一次农业普查以后，由于畜牧业产品年报数据与普查数据之间存在一定的差距，国家统计局农调总队对畜牧业年报数据与普查数据进行衔接。1999 年以后，国家统计局开展了猪、牛、羊、禽等主要畜禽品种的抽样调查，并用抽样数据作为国家定案数据使用。未开展抽样调查的品种，仍使用各级统计部门逐级上报数据。

期初(末)畜禽存栏头(只)数　指报告期初(末)农村各种合作经济组织和国营农场、农民个人、机关、团体、学校、工矿企业、部队等单位以及城镇居民饲养的大牲畜、猪、羊、家禽等畜禽的存栏数。数据上报方式及数据调整情况同猪、牛、羊肉产量。

常用耕地　是指耕地总资源中专门种植农作物并经常进行耕种、能够正常收获的土地。包括当年实际耕种的熟地；弃耕、休闲不满三年，随时可以复耕的地；开荒利用三年以上的土地。在统计口径上包括南方小于 1 米、北方小于 2 米宽的沟、渠、路和田埂。不包括临时种植农作物的坡度在 25 度以上的陡坡地；在河套、湖畔、库区临时开发的成片或零星土地；也不包括已列为国家和省（区、市）退耕计划但临时耕种的土地。常用耕地是国家需要重点保护的耕地，是反映我国农业综合生产能力的一个重要指标。

农作物播种面积 指实际播种或移植有农作物的面积。凡是实际种植有农作物的面积，不论种植在耕地上还是种植在非耕地上，均包括在农作物播种面积中。在播种季节基本结束后，因遭灾而重新改种和补种的农作物面积，也包括在内。它是反映我国耕地面积利用情况的一个重要指标。目前，农作物播种面积主要包括粮食、棉花、油料、糖料、麻类、烟叶、蔬菜和瓜类、药材和其他农作物九大类。

有效灌溉面积 指具有一定的水源，地块比较平整，灌溉工程或设备已经配套，在一般年景下，当年能够进行正常灌溉的耕地面积。在一般情况下，有效灌溉面积应等于灌溉工程或设备已经配备，能够进行正常灌溉的水田和水浇地面积之和。它是反映我国耕地抗旱能力的一个重要指标。

农用化肥施用量 指本年内实际用于农业生产的化肥数量，包括氮肥、磷肥、钾肥和复合肥。化肥施用量要求按折纯量计算数量。折纯量是指把氮肥、磷肥、钾肥分别按含氮、含五氧化二磷、含氧化钾的百分之百成份进行折算后的数量。复合肥按其所含主要成分折算。公式为：

折纯量=实物量×某种化肥有效成份含量的百分比

农业机械总动力 指主要用于农、林、牧、渔业的各种动力机械的动力总和。包括耕作机械、排灌机械、收获机械、农用运输机械、植物保护机械、牧业机械、林业机械、渔业机械和其他农业机械〔内燃机按引擎马力折成瓦(特)计算、电动机按功率折成瓦(特)计算〕。不包括专门用于乡、镇、村、组办工业、基本建设、非农业运输、科学试验和教学等非农业生产方面用的动力机械与作业机械。这个指标的统计数据主要来源于农机部门。

乡村从业人员 指乡村人口中劳动年龄在 16 周岁以上实际参加生产经营活动并取得实物或货币收入的人员，包括劳动年龄内经常参加劳动的人员，也包括超过劳动年龄但经常参加劳动的人员，但不包括户口在家的在外学生、现役军人和丧失劳动能力的人，也不包括待业人员和家务劳动者。从业人员按从事主业时间最长（时间相同按收入）分为农林牧渔业从业人员、工业从业人员、建筑业从业人员、交通运输业、仓储及邮电通信业从业人员、批零贸易业、餐饮业从业人员、其他非农行业从业人员。

Explanatory Notes on Main Statistical Indicators

Gross Output Value of Farming, Forestry, Animal Husbandry and Fishery refers to the total value of products of farming, forestry, animal husbandry and fishery, and total value of services rendered to support farming, forestry, animal husbandry and fishery activities. It reflects the total scale and results of agricultural production during a given period. Prior to 1957, Chinas gross agricultural output value included barnyard manure and handicraft products for self-consumption (clothes, shoes, stockings, and initial grain processing undertaken by peasants). Since 1958, cutting and felling of bamboo and trees by villages and other cooperative organizations under villages have been included in forestry; value of barnyard manure has been excluded from animal husbandry; self consumed handicrafts has been excluded from sideline occupations, while the output value of industries run by villages and cooperative organizations under village had been included in sideline occupations and the output value of fish catches by motor fishing boats has been added to fishery. Since 1980, the value of handicraft products made for sale by individuals in households had been added to sideline occupations. Since 1984, industries run by villages and under villages have been included in the sector of industry. Since 1993, the subdivision of sideline occupations has been canceled, and the hunting of wild animals has been classified into animal husbandry, and the gathering of wild plants and commodity industry run by rural household have been included in farming. A new industrial classification of economic activities was introduced in 2003. Under the new classification, value of services to farming, forestry, animal husbandry and fishery is included in the gross output value of agriculture, value of wood felling and transport is included in forestry, value of industrial output by rural households is not included in agriculture, and the collection of wild forest products is taken from agriculture and included in the forestry. The first agriculture census of China revealed some discrepancy between the production of animal products from the annual reports and that from the census. Efforts were made by the Rural Socio-economic Survey Organization of NBS to adjust the output value of animal husbandry to make the figures from the annual reports consistent with the census data.

Gross output value of agriculture is obtained by first multiplying the output of each product or by product by its price, resulting in the output value of each single item. For a small number of products, annual output of which is not available or difficult to get due to the long production (growing) process involved, the output value is estimated through an indirect approach. The sum of output value of all products of farming, forestry, animal husbandry and fishery is then equal to the gross output value of agriculture.

Grain Output refers to the total output in the whole country including grains produced by state farms, collective units, rural households, as well as by farms affiliated to industrial and mining enterprises and other production units. Grain includes rice, wheat, corn, sorghum, millet and other miscellaneous grains as well as tubers and bean. Output of beans refers to dry beans without pods. The output of tubers (sweet potatoes and potatoes, not including taros and cassava) was converted into that of grain at the ratio 4:1, i.e. 4 kilograms of fresh tubers was equivalent to 1 kilogram of grain up to 1963. Since 1964 the ratio for conversion has been 5:1. Tubers supplied as vegetables (such as potatoes) in cities and suburbs are calculated as fresh vegetables and their output is not included in the output of grain. Output of all other grains refers to husked grain. Data on grain production before 1989 were obtained through Comprehensive Statistical Reporting System. Since 1989, data from sample surveys are used.

Cotton Output refers to the cotton production in the whole country including cotton sown in spring and in autumn. Output is measured as the weight of ginned cotton. Ceiba is not included.

Output of Oil-bearing Crops refers to the total production of oil-bearing crops of various kinds, including peanuts, (dry, in shell) rapeseeds, sesame, sunflower seeds, flax seeds, and other oil-bearing crops. Soybeans, oil-bearing woody plants, and wild oil-bearing crops are not included.

Output of Aquatic Products refers to catches of both artificially cultured and naturally grown aquatic products, including fish, shrimps, crabs and shellfish in sea and inland water as well as seaweed. Freshwater plants are not included. Data on output of aquatic products are reported by aquatic product and statistical agencies level by level. Before 1995, among the shellfish, the oyster was counted as fresh meat; 5 kilograms of ark shell, clams and frogs are equivalent to 1 kilogram of fresh aquatic products; they are all counted as fresh aquatic products since 1996.

Output of Pork, Beef, and Mutton refers to the meat of slaughtered hogs, cattle, sheep and goats with head, feet, and offal taken away. Data refers to the production of the whole country. The first agriculture census of China in 1996 revealed some discrepancy between the production of animal products from the annual reports and that from the census. Efforts were made by the Rural Socio-economic Survey Organization of NBS to adjust the output value of animal husbandry to make the figures from the annual reports consistent with the census data. Since 1999, NBS conducted sample survey for the major animal husbandry products, such as hogs, cattle, sheep and goats and fowls, and the data from sample surveys are used as national finalized data. Those products, which are not covered by the sample survey, are still reported by statistical agencies level by level.

Number of Livestock or Poultry in Stock at Beginning (or End) refers to the total number of large animals, pigs, sheep, fowls, etc. raised by rural cooperative organizations, state farms, rural individuals, government agencies, schools, industrial and mining enterprises, army, and urban residents at the beginning (or end) of the reference period. Data reporting system and data adjustment are the same as that in the output of pork, beef and mutton.

Regularly Cultivated Land refers to farmland among the total land resources, which is exclusively used for farming and is under regular cultivation with harvest in normal years. Included are currently cultivated land, land that has been abandoned or put in idle for less than 3 years and could be re-used for cultivation at any time, and new-claimed land that has been put into cultivation for more than 3 years. According to statistical coverage, it includes the gouges, dykes, roads and ridges of field with 1 meter wide in Southern areas and 2 meters wide in Northern areas. Excluded under this category are steep slope land over 25 degrees under temporary cultivation, land (large or small plots) that is claimed along river bends, lake sides or banks of reservoirs, as well as land that has been designated under the "Green for Grain" programme of the state and provincial governments but is still temporarily under cultivation. The regularly cultivated land is the key protection land of the nation, an important indicator reflecting the comprehensive productivity of agriculture of China.

Sown Area of Crops refers to area of land sown or transplanted with crops regardless of being in cultivated area or non-cultivated area. Area of land re-sown due to natural disasters is also included. This is an important indicator that can reflect the utilization condition of the cultivated land in China. At present, the sown area of crops mainly include the following 9 categories of crops: grain, cotton, oil-bearing crops, sugar crops, fiber crops, Tobacco, Vegetables and melons, medicinal materials and other farm crops.

Irrigated Area refers to areas that are effectively irrigated, i.e. level land, which has water source and complete sets of irrigation facilities to lift and move adequate water for irrigation purpose under normal conditions. Under normal conditions, irrigated area is the sum of watered fields and irrigated fields where irrigation systems or equipment have been installed for regular irrigation purpose. This important indicator reflects drought resistance capacity of the cultivated land in China.

Consumption of Chemical Fertilizers in Agriculture refers to the quantity of chemical fertilizers applied in agriculture in the year, including nitrogenous fertilizer, phosphate fertilizer, potash fertilizer, and compound fertilizer. The consumption of chemical fertilizers is required in calculation to convert the gross weight into weight containing 100% effective component (e.g. 100% nitrogen content in nitrogenous fertilizer, 100% phosphorous pent oxide contents in phosphate fertilizer, 100% potassium oxide contents in potash fertilizer). Compound fertilizer is converted with its major component. The formula is :

Volume of effective component= physical quantity x effective component of certain chemical fertilizer (%)

Total Power of Farm Machinery refers to total mechanical power of machinery used in farming, forestry, animal husbandry, and fishery, including ploughing, irrigation and drainage, harvesting, transport, plant protection, stock breeding, forestry and fishery. The power of internal combustion engines is required to convert horsepower into watts and the power of electric motors is required to be converted into watts. Machinery employed for non-agricultural purposes, such as the machines used in township run and village-run industry, construction, non-agricultural transport, scientific experiments and teaching, is excluded. Data are mainly from agricultural machinery agencies.

Rural Employed Persons refer to rural labor forces aged over 16 years old who are engaged in real production and management activities and receive payment in kind or wages, including those covered within the age frame and regularly participating in production activities, and those who are out of the range of age frame and also participating in production activities regularly. Excluding students studying in other places with their permanent residence registered in local areas, servicemen and persons incapable of working; also excluding those who are waiting for jobs and those engaged in household work. Persons employed are classified as persons engaged in agriculture, forestry, animal husbandry or fishery activities; persons engaged in industrial activities; persons engaged in construction activities; persons engaged in transport, storage and telecommunications activities; persons engaged in whole sales and retail sales trade and catering activities; and persons engaged in other non-agriculture activities, depending upon the longest period of employment in major activities (or using income indicator when period of employment is the same).

13 工　业

Industry

资料整理：何良伟　陶　禹

工　业

INDUSTRY

2013

规模以上工业企业	**Industrial Enterprises Above Designated Size**	
工业总产值(现价)	Total Output Value (at current price)	39208.98 （亿元）
#轻工业	Light Industry	13405.24 （亿元）
重工业	Heavy Industry	25803.74 （亿元）
#大型企业	Large Scale Enterprises	15449.76 （亿元）
中型企业	Medium Scale Enterprises	8807.05 （亿元）
资产总计	Total Assets	30633.98 （亿元）
负债合计	Total Liability	17570.58 （亿元）
主营业务收入	Income from Major Business	38183.39 （亿元）
利税总额	Total Revenue	4451.87 （亿元）
从业人员年平均人数	Annually Average number of Employment	346.29 （万人）

规模以上工业总产值构成（%）
Composition of Industry above desginated size

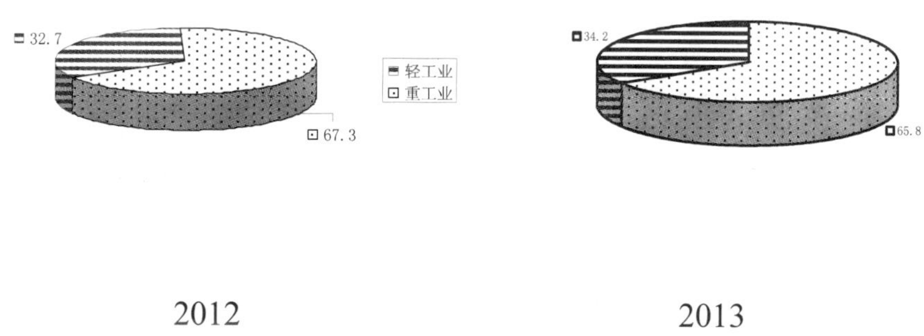

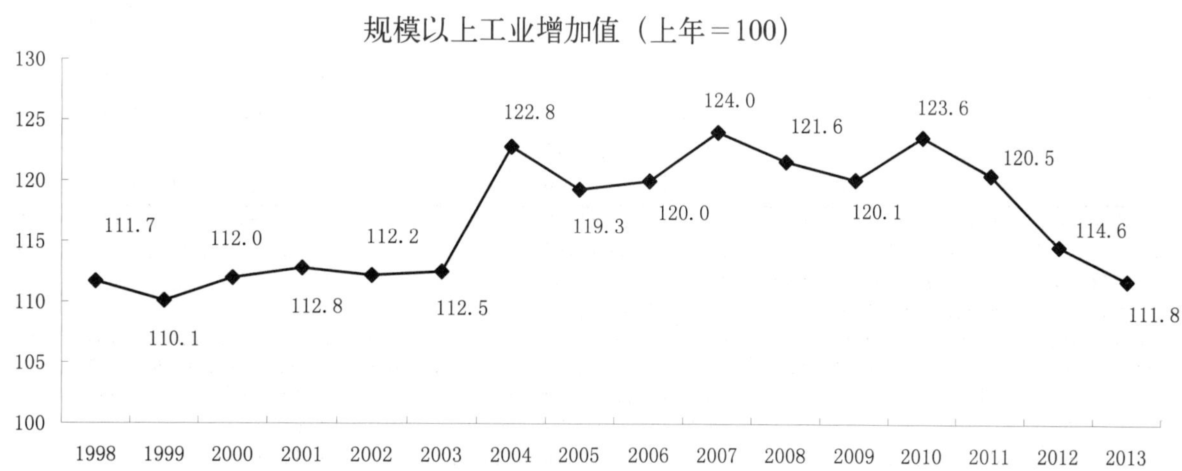

13-1 工业发展基本情况

THE BASIC SITUATION OF INDUSTRIAL DEVELOPMENT

年份 Year	工业企业单位数(个) Number of Industrial Enterprises (unit)	轻工业 Light industry	重工业 Heavy industry	工业总产值(当年价)(亿元) Total Output Value(currentprice) (100 million yuan)	轻工业 Light industry	重工业 Heavy industry
1979	16073	10100	5973	220.82	93.45	107.37
1980	16609	10582	6027	228.02	110.14	117.88
1981	17032	11192	5840	249.72	131.13	118.59
1982	18066	11960	6106	272.08	137.66	134.42
1983	18926	12325	6637	319.21	157.33	161.88
1984	22713	14664	8049	371.93	182.57	189.36
1985	25011	15309	9702	467.22	216.47	250.75
1986	27697	16890	10807	538.28	256.06	282.22
1987	26294	15528	10766	659.19	315.49	343.70
1988	26016	15279	10737	834.84	405.13	429.71
1989	25999	15035	10964	976.93	463.35	513.58
1990	25913	14885	11028	1008.20	476.76	531.44
1991	25204	14317	10887	1136.02	531.26	604.76
1992	23985	13428	10557	1373.66	605.11	768.55
1993	22600	11958	10642	1992.31	770.20	1222.11
1994	23275	12096	11179	3024.72	1360.78	1663.94
1995	27815	14827	12988	3697.91	1870.12	1827.79
1996	25986	13618	12368	4836.33	2470.90	2365.43
1997	24498	12723	11775	5977.00	3158.47	2818.53
1998	7399	3581	3818	6731.31	3534.67	3196.64
1999	6874	3308	3566	2831.70	1109.92	1721.78
2000	6282	3026	3256	3064.43	1177.24	1887.18
2001	6197	2981	3216	3239.51	1194.90	2044.61
2002	6183	2947	3236	3589.26	1184.78	2404.48
2003	6271	2789	3482	3631.29	1192.46	2438.82
2004	6232	2632	3600	4960.25	1180.07	3780.17
2005	6813	2953	3860	6066.96	1503.00	4563.95
2006	7546	3272	4274	7454.07	1898.34	5555.73
2007	8996	3808	5188	9601.52	2492.88	7108.64
2008	12067	4806	7261	13454.94	3344.80	10110.14
2009	14027	5515	8512	15567.02	4234.52	11332.50
2010	16106	6326	9780	21623.12	5935.78	15687.33
2011	10633	4347	6286	28072.73	8370.27	19702.45
2012	12441	5012	7429	33450.66	10941.70	22508.95
2013	14650	5855	8795	39208.98	13405.24	25803.74

注：1.本表规模以上工业1997年及以前统计范围为乡及乡以上工业。1998—2006年为全部国有工业及年销售收入500万元以上非国有工业企业;2007年—2010年为主营业务收入500万元以上工业企业。2011年起为主营业务收入2000万元及以上的工业法人企业。(下表同)

2."国有及国有控股经济"一栏，1998年以前统计范围为国有工业。

3.2011年行业小类码按照《国民经济行业分类》(GB/T4754—2011)填写。(下表同)

Note:1.The scopes of industrial statistics are all township and above town industrial enterprises before 1998.The scopes are all state-owned industrial enterprises and non-state-owned industrial enterprise with revenue from principal business over 5 million yuan from 1998 to 2006.For 2007 to 2010,the scopes are all industrial enterprices with revenue from principal business over 5 million yuan.From 2011,the scopes are all industrial enterprises with revenue from principal business over 20 millon yuan.The same applies to the talbe following.

2."State-owned and state-controlled economy"a column,prior to 1998 statistics the range of state-owned industries.

3.Accordring to GB/T4754-2011,the small classes code of industries are filled in the table from 2011.The same applies to the talbe following.

13-1 续表　continued

单位:亿元　(100 million yuan)

年份 Year	主营业务收入 (亿元) Main business income (100 million yuan)	利润总额 (亿元) Total profit (100 million yuan)	利税总额 (亿元) Total profits and taxes (100 million yuan)	职工人数 (万人) Number of employees (1000 persons)
1979	163.52	20.70	34.19	161.98
1980	197.52	25.45	41.54	173.29
1981	210.15	25.71	43.53	185.80
1982	239.64	27.50	47.82	197.62
1983	268.98	31.77	53.46	202.80
1984	308.66	37.33	62.38	292.49
1985	381.43	43.64	80.82	306.83
1986	438.95	40.22	82.14	333.63
1987	526.95	48.54	96.16	343.43
1988	654.72	58.85	117.28	356.43
1989	706.99	50.99	112.12	360.88
1990	705.97	26.73	88.40	358.65
1991	800.01	31.79	103.46	367.41
1992	1041.66	43.19	127.15	357.74
1993	1500.71	67.00	167.92	357.97
1994	1690.94	74.06	190.29	381.45
1995	2066.38	52.26	181.57	379.84
1996	2305.57	43.93	181.41	369.80
1997	2681.36	57.71	221.53	362.50
1998	2433.92	44.71	195.96	274.43
1999	2602.26	68.82	232.24	250.07
2000	2870.36	106.47	29.36	230.36
2001	3043.82	134.49	335.36	212.48
2002	3378.31	175.60	404.23	205.82
2003	3993.99	194.40	444.96	198.60
2004	4832.43	270.98	559.28	176.70
2005	5962.54	371.84	727.48	188.30
2006	7314.81	454.00	897.19	190.85
2007	9390.43	647.85	1229.16	200.35
2008	13081.90	909.03	1761.47	235.90
2009	15331.62	1092.47	1987.88	272.39
2010	21151.56	1668.55	2950.08	294.97
2011	27072.02	1864.46	3093.57	279.59
2012	32325.95	2046.28	3528.80	311.13
2013	38183.39	2475.07	4451.87	346.29

13-2 规模以上工业企业单位数和产销总值 (2013)

单位:亿元

项 目	Item	企业单位数(个) Number of Enterprises (unit)
总 计	**Total**	**14650**
一、按登记注册类型分组:	**Grouped by Type of Registration**	
内资企业	Inner Funded Enterprises	13798
国有企业	State Owned Enterprises	155
中央企业	Central Enterprises	51
地方企业	Local Enterprises	104
集体企业	Collective-owned Enterprise	128
股份合作企业	Share Holding Cooperative Enterprises	26
联营企业	Joint Owned Enterprise	7
国有联营企业	State Joint Ownership	
集体联营企业	Collective Joint Ownership	2
国有与集体联营企业	Joint State- Collective Ownership	1
其他联营企业	Other Joint Owned Enterprise	4
有限责任公司	Responsibility Co. Ltd	5081
国有独资公司	State Solely Funded Co.	113
其他有限责任公司	Others	4968
股份有限公司	Share Holding Co.Ltd.	609
私营企业	Private - owned enterprises	7686
私营独资企业	Solely Private - owned enterprises	321
私营合伙企业	Private Joint Venture	67
私营有限责任公司	Private Responsibility Co. Ltd	6853
私营股份有限公司	Private Share Holding Co.Ltd.	445
其他企业	Others	106
港、澳、台商投资企业	Hongkong, Macao and Taiwan Funded Enterprises	374
合资经营企业(港或澳、台资)	Joint Venture with Hongkong, Macao and Taiwan	173
合作经营企业(港或澳、台资)	Cooperate with Hongkong, Macao and Taiwan Funded	6
港澳台商独资经营企业	Enterprises Solely Funded by Hongkong, Macao and Taiwan Businessmen	179
港澳台商投资股份有限公司	Share Holding Co.Ltd. With Hongkong, Macao and Taiwan Investment	15
外商投资企业	Foreign Funded Enterprises	478
中外合资经营企业	Sino - Foreign Joint Funded Enterprises	264
中外合作经营企业	Sino - Foreign Cooperative Funded Enterprises	11
外资企业	Foreign Solely Funded Enterprises	191
外商投资股份有限公司	Foreign Funded Share Holding Co.Ltd.	11
二、在总计中:亏损企业	**Of the Total: enterprises running under deficit**	**1046**
在总计中:国有控股企业	Of the Total: State-Owned Share Holding Enterprises	724
在总计中:农村工业	Of the Total: Rural Industry	119
在总计中:轻工业	Of the Total: Light Industry	5855
重工业	Heavy Industry	8795
在总计中:大型企业	Of the Total: Large Scale Enterprises	344
中型企业	Medium Scale Enterprises	1935
小型企业	Small Enterprises	12371

THE NUMBER OF UNITS OF INDUSTRIAL ENTERPRISES ABOVE DESIGNATED SIZE AND GROSS SALES(2013)

工业总产值（当年价格） Total Output Value (current price)	工业销售产值（当年价格） Output Value of Industrial Products Sales(current price)	出口交货值 Delivery Value for Export
39208.98	**38107.78**	**1544.19**
32790.62	31897.03	1004.15
3633.54	3615.63	247.42
3475.52	3459.78	230.85
158.02	155.85	16.57
148.98	145.06	
21.89	20.69	
17.20	16.66	
4.14	3.91	
0.76	0.76	
12.31	11.99	
12229.04	11833.01	299.39
1797.61	1731.48	51.39
10431.42	10101.53	248.00
4118.04	4048.95	148.01
12467.09	12064.72	306.69
396.95	385.25	6.09
87.49	85.06	1.20
10965.14	10624.47	265.27
1017.51	969.94	34.13
154.84	152.30	2.64
2006.04	1928.01	378.46
1260.05	1220.77	275.17
10.06	9.99	
678.27	642.72	91.67
44.44	42.55	11.62
4412.32	4282.74	161.57
3350.85	3228.83	76.79
41.99	41.60	1.01
797.32	786.96	83.19
221.96	225.16	0.58
2803.39	**2715.24**	**90.70**
11293.00	11094.35	434.03
189.47	185.42	1.54
13405.24	12956.33	616.21
25803.74	25151.45	927.98
15449.76	15160.48	921.48
8807.05	8484.15	357.53
14952.17	14463.15	265.18

13-2 续表 continued

单位:亿元

项 目	Item	企业单位数（个） Number of Enterprises(unit)
按行业分	Grouped by sector	
采矿业	**Mining and Qarrying**	
煤炭开采和洗选业	Coal Mining and Processing	147
石油和天然气开采业	Petroleum and Natural Gas Extraction	1
黑色金属矿采选业	Ferrous Metals Mining and Processing	145
有色金属矿采选业	Non-ferrous Metals Mining and Processing	54
非金属矿采选业	Non-metal Minerals Mining and Processing	420
开采辅助活动	Mining Auxiliary Activities	5
其他采矿业	Other Minerals Mining and Processing	2
制造业	**Manufacturing**	
农副食品加工业	Food Processing	1596
食品制造业	Food Production	370
酒、饮料和精制茶制造业	Wine,Beverage and Refined Tea Production	376
烟草制品业	Tobacco Processing	7
纺织业	Textile Industry	1016
纺织服装、服饰业	Textile,Garments, and Fashion Industry	527
皮革、毛皮、羽毛及其制品和制鞋业	Leather, Furs,Down and Related Products	110
木材加工和木、竹、藤、棕、草制品业	Timber Processing, Wood, Bamboo, Cane, Palm and Sraw Products	242
家具制造业	Furniture Manufacturing	101
造纸和纸制品业	Papermaking and Paper Products	246
印刷和记录媒介复制业	Printing and Record Processing	188
文教、工美、体育和娱乐用品制造业	Stationery, Education and Sports Goods	94
石油加工、炼焦和核燃料加工业	Petroleum Processing, Coking Products and Nuclear Fuel Processing	48
化学原料和化学制品制造业	Raw Chemical Material and Chemical Products	1028
医药制造业	Medical and pharmaceutical Products	359
化学纤维制造业	Chemical Fibers	20
橡胶和塑料制品业	Rubber and plastic products	582
非金属矿物制品业	Nonmetal Material Products	1685
黑色金属冶炼和压延加工业	Smelting and Pressing of Ferrous Metals	346
有色金属冶炼和压延加工业	Smelting and Pressing of Nonferrous Metals	173
金属制品业	Metal Products	674
通用设备制造业	Ordinary Machinery Manufacturing	667
专用设备制造业	Special Purpose Equipment Manufacturing	556
汽车制造业	Motor manufacturing	1306
铁路、船舶、航空航天和其他运输设备制造业	Railway,Watercraft,Aviation and other Transporlation Equipment manufacturing	154
电气机械和器材制造业	Electric Machinery and Equipment	604
计算机、通信和其他电子设备制造业	Telecommunication Computer,Equipment and Other Electronic Equipment Manufacturing	277
仪器仪表制造业	Instruments and Meters, Manufacturing	113
其他制造业	Other Manufacturing	70
废弃资源综合利用业	Waste Comprehensive Vtilization of Resources Industry	40
金属制品、机械和设备修理业	Metal products,Machinery and Equipment Repairing	21
电力、燃气及水的生产和供应业	**Electric Power, Gas and Water Production and Supply**	
电力、热力生产和供应业	Electric Power, Steam and Hot Water Production and Supply	157
燃气生产和供应业	Gas Production and Supply	55
水的生产和供应业	Tap Water Production and Supply	68

(100 million Yuan)

工业总产值 (当年价格) Total Output Value(current price)	工业销售产值 (当年价格) Output Value of Industrial Products Sales(current price)	出口交货值 Delivery Value for Export
113.73	112.91	
82.89	82.85	0.54
436.91	427.17	
85.66	83.02	
527.30	513.84	0.65
62.70	62.65	0.10
1.38	1.38	
4018.14	3884.31	125.74
865.58	837.44	63.99
1321.02	1269.88	3.27
519.20	503.55	1.34
1948.70	1881.02	125.75
832.44	809.71	89.61
129.78	125.51	39.32
360.96	345.40	1.60
117.48	114.33	1.02
469.12	453.00	4.02
263.72	252.33	2.23
146.27	140.33	11.87
870.38	846.40	
3362.24	3270.48	123.56
862.28	820.79	65.35
77.43	75.79	2.84
949.15	922.23	8.12
2584.87	2505.27	25.68
3079.07	3047.10	67.88
1000.78	973.35	30.74
1244.25	1196.94	28.40
1185.99	1136.39	35.14
913.92	875.23	17.70
5008.32	4915.01	64.36
587.12	568.93	186.71
1653.16	1587.76	75.29
1460.27	1426.28	334.26
123.09	116.33	2.13
132.95	128.52	4.63
97.75	94.47	
36.53	33.57	0.36
1530.97	1521.36	
98.68	99.95	
46.82	44.98	

13-3 规模以上工业企业主要经济指标（2013）

单位：亿元

项 目	Item	企业单位数(个) Number of Enterprises (unit)
总 计	**Total**	**14650**
一、按登记注册类型分组：	**Grouped by Type of Registration**	
内资企业	Inner Funded Enterprises	13798
国有企业	State Owned Enterprises	155
中央企业	Central Enterprises	51
地方企业	Local Enterprises	104
集体企业	Collective-owned Enterprise	128
股份合作企业	Share Holding Cooperative Enterprises	26
联营企业	Joint Owned Enterprise	7
国有联营企业	State Joint Ownership	
集体联营企业	Collective Joint Ownership	2
国有与集体联营企业	Joint State- Collective Ownership	1
其他联营企业	Other Joint Owned Enterprise	4
有限责任公司	Responsibility Co. Ltd	5081
国有独资公司	State Solely Funded Co.	113
其他有限责任公司	Others	4968
股份有限公司	Share Holding Co.Ltd.	609
私营企业	Private - owned enterprises	7686
私营独资企业	Solely Private - owned enterprises	321
私营合伙企业	Private Joint Venture	67
私营有限责任公司	Private Responsibility Co. Ltd	6853
私营股份有限公司	Private Share Holding Co.Ltd.	445
其他企业	Others	106
港、澳、台商投资企业	Hongkong, Macao and Taiwan Funded Enterprises	374
合资经营企业(港或澳、台资)	Joint Venture with Hongkong, Macao and Taiwan	173
合作经营企业(港或澳、台资)	Cooperate with Hongkong, Macao and Taiwan Funded	6
港澳台商独资经营企业	Enterprises Solely Funded by Hongkong, Macao and Taiwan Businessmen	179
港澳台商投资股份有限公司	Share Holding Co.Ltd. With Hongkong, Macao and Taiwan Investment	15
外商投资企业	Foreign Funded Enterprises	478
中外合资经营企业	Sino - Foreign Joint Funded Enterprises	264
中外合作经营企业	Sino - Foreign Cooperative Funded Enterprises	11
外资企业	Foreign Solely Funded Enterprises	191
外商投资股份有限公司	Foreign Funded Share Holding Co.Ltd.	11
二、在总计中：亏损企业	**Of the Total: enterprises running under deficit**	**1046**
在总计中：国有控股企业	Of the Total: State-Owned Share Holding Enterprises	724
在总计中：农村工业	Of the Total: Rural Industry	119
在总计中：轻工业	Of the Total: Light Industry	5855
重工业	Heavy Industry	8795
在总计中：大型企业	Of the Total: Large Scale Enterprises	344
中型企业	Medium Scale Enterprises	1935
小型企业	Small Enterprises	12371

MAJOR ECONOMIC INDICATORS OF INDUSTRIAL ENTERPRISES ABOVE DESIGNATED SCALE (2013)

(100 million Yuan)

资产总计 Total Assets	流动资产合计 Circulating Funds	应收帐款净额 Net Value of Account Received	固定资产合计 Total Fixed Assets
30633.98	**13838.57**	**3091.73**	**12044.51**
25864.47	11358.06	2503.66	10446.27
6004.38	1539.86	254.64	3401.98
5832.53	1456.40	239.97	3331.04
171.85	83.46	14.68	70.94
51.61	28.53	9.47	18.43
10.47	6.69	2.61	3.00
3.38	1.37	0.51	0.93
0.57	0.25	0.04	0.24
0.84	0.66	0.43	0.18
1.97	0.46	0.04	0.51
9468.78	4708.26	1126.64	3539.82
1968.91	985.35	208.61	686.52
7499.86	3722.91	918.03	2853.30
4967.11	2407.35	494.33	1343.95
5305.56	2640.30	610.37	2113.83
101.83	45.61	11.02	44.91
23.85	12.36	3.46	9.11
4770.88	2391.83	555.79	1888.71
409.00	190.50	40.09	171.10
53.18	25.69	5.07	24.32
1252.81	567.64	149.68	542.18
769.20	348.93	72.22	331.69
11.18	5.12	0.42	5.10
418.69	186.55	68.92	188.68
49.70	24.37	7.67	15.97
3516.70	1912.86	438.40	1056.07
2539.21	1443.55	295.92	658.60
33.42	7.29	2.04	24.86
658.79	385.66	125.86	214.95
284.59	75.89	14.22	157.59
3279.04	**1485.46**	**355.01**	**1290.38**
14835.46	5677.06	1062.13	6438.75
82.64	43.79	11.16	28.04
7081.48	3839.92	707.85	2365.82
23552.50	9998.64	2383.88	9678.69
16681.44	6897.94	1274.65	6854.24
6188.42	3133.88	754.63	2113.77
7764.11	3806.75	1062.45	3076.49

13-3 续表 1 continued

单位:亿元

项 目	Item	企业单位数(个) Number of Enterprises(unit)
按行业分	Grouped by sector	**14650**
采矿业	**Mining and Qarrying**	
煤炭开采和洗选业	Coal Mining and Processing	147
石油和天然气开采业	Petroleum and Natural Gas Extraction	1
黑色金属矿采选业	Ferrous Metals Mining and Processing	145
有色金属矿采选业	Non-ferrous Metals Mining and Processing	54
非金属矿采选业	Non-metal Minerals Mining and Processing	420
开采辅助活动	Mining Auxiliary Activities	5
其他采矿业	Other Minerals Mining and Processing	2
制造业	**Manufacturing**	
农副食品加工业	Food Processing	1596
食品制造业	Food Production	370
酒、饮料和精制茶制造业	Wine,Beverage and Refined Tea Production	376
烟草制品业	Tobacco Processing	7
纺织业	Textile Industry	1016
纺织服装、服饰业	Textile,Garments, and Fashion Industry	527
皮革、毛皮、羽毛及其制品和制鞋业	Leather, Furs,Down and Related Products	110
木材加工和木、竹、藤、棕、草制品业	Timber Processing, Wood, Bamboo, Cane, Palm and Sraw Products	242
家具制造业	Furniture Manufacturing	101
造纸和纸制品业	Papermaking and Paper Products	246
印刷和记录媒介复制业	Printing and Record Processing	188
文教、工美、体育和娱乐用品制造业	Stationery, Education and Sports Goods	94
石油加工、炼焦和核燃料加工业	Petroleum Processing, Coking Products and Nuclear Fuel Processing	48
化学原料和化学制品制造业	Raw Chemical Material and Chemical Products	1028
医药制造业	Medical and pharmaceutical Products	359
化学纤维制造业	Chemical Fibers	20
橡胶和塑料制品业	Rubber and Plastic Products	582
非金属矿物制品业	Nonmetal Material Products	1685
黑色金属冶炼和压延加工业	Smelting and Pressing of Ferrous Metals	346
有色金属冶炼和压延加工业	Smelting and Pressing of Nonferrous Metals	173
金属制品业	Metal Products	674
通用设备制造业	Ordinary Machinery Manufacturing	667
专用设备制造业	Special Purpose Equipment Manufacturing	556
汽车制造业	Motor manufacturing	1306
铁路、船舶、航空航天和其他运输设备制造业	Railway,Watercraft,Aviation and other Transporlation Equipment manufacturing	154
电气机械和器材制造业	Electric Machinery and Equipment	604
计算机、通信和其他电子设备制造业	Telecommunication Computer,Equipment and Other Electronic Equipment Manufacturing	277
仪器仪表制造业	Instruments and Meters, Manufacturing	113
其他制造业	Other Manufacturing	70
废弃资源综合利用业	Waste Comprehensive Vtilization of Resources Industry	40
金属制品、机械和设备修理业	Metal products,Machinery and Equipment Repairing	21
电力、燃气及水的生产和供应业	**Electric Power, Gas and Water Production and Supply**	
电力、热力生产和供应业	Electric Power, Steam and Hot Water Production and Supply	157
燃气生产和供应业	Gas Production and Supply	55
水的生产和供应业	Tap Water Production and Supply	68

(100 million Yuan)

资产总计 Total Assets	流动资产合计 Circulating Funds	应收帐款净额 Net Value of Account Received	固定资产合计 Total Fixed Assets
30633.98	**13838.57**	**3091.73**	**12044.51**
68.90	26.08	3.35	35.73
205.34	31.62	3.42	173.71
127.96	57.53	14.74	56.73
49.68	25.19	3.88	18.21
275.92	129.71	32.34	83.83
75.98	21.15	12.39	40.77
0.96	0.57	0.53	0.24
1416.22	691.56	108.26	553.46
432.46	205.19	43.01	168.82
1001.73	650.32	73.34	237.13
417.90	329.11	31.20	32.55
823.32	388.91	66.55	367.20
396.74	234.39	38.73	126.10
63.49	28.82	5.75	26.44
205.06	98.35	12.11	82.91
79.77	31.02	5.88	43.21
276.92	132.38	42.32	105.77
156.61	85.78	26.09	48.85
74.73	45.42	5.60	19.72
220.55	86.26	16.77	121.50
2531.73	1001.54	166.64	1027.26
710.41	341.80	74.82	227.70
47.14	20.76	3.73	17.77
478.47	252.03	69.82	173.02
1619.44	654.28	164.12	741.84
3414.68	1133.54	150.24	1515.57
549.36	317.66	39.14	147.57
841.71	460.45	119.49	286.92
1225.91	642.11	191.44	313.85
873.49	546.97	165.80	267.71
4577.55	2541.51	567.33	886.50
676.58	418.91	127.66	176.93
1085.47	664.55	245.65	316.74
1306.16	931.73	328.86	270.70
126.30	71.71	25.51	45.52
114.11	71.46	11.26	30.50
51.28	36.73	6.51	11.72
21.32	14.01	4.99	5.83
3631.05	272.38	64.78	3086.90
147.31	50.74	6.26	66.22
234.29	94.33	11.40	84.86

13-3 续表 2 continued

单位:亿元

项 目	Item	固定资产原价 Original Price of Fixed Assets
总　　计	**Total**	**22158.39**
一、按登记注册类型分组:	**Grouped by Type of Registration**	
内资企业	Inner Funded Enterprises	19213.75
国有企业	State Owned Enterprises	5262.76
中央企业	Central Enterprises	5119.34
地方企业	Local Enterprises	143.41
集体企业	Collective-owned Enterprise	33.49
股份合作企业	Share Holding Cooperative Enterprises	4.97
联营企业	Joint Owned Enterprise	1.33
国有联营企业	State Joint Ownership	
集体联营企业	Collective Joint Ownership	0.39
国有与集体联营企业	Joint State- Collective Ownership	0.38
其他联营企业	Other Joint Owned Enterprise	0.57
有限责任公司	Responsibility Co. Ltd	5831.08
国有独资公司	State Solely Funded Co.	1071.75
其他有限责任公司	Others	4759.33
股份有限公司	Share Holding Co.Ltd.	2206.09
私营企业	Private - owned enterprises	5841.67
私营独资企业	Solely Private - owned enterprises	152.40
私营合伙企业	Private Joint Venture	12.63
私营有限责任公司	Private Responsibility Co. Ltd	5280.91
私营股份有限公司	Private Share Holding Co.Ltd.	395.73
其他企业	Others	32.36
港、澳、台商投资企业	Hongkong, Macao and Taiwan Funded Enterprises	1028.68
合资经营企业(港或澳、台资)	Joint Venture with Hongkong, Macao and Taiwan	628.89
合作经营企业(港或澳、台资)	Cooperate with Hongkong, Macao and Taiwan Funded	6.03
港澳台商独资经营企业	Enterprises Solely Funded by Hongkong, Macao and Taiwan Businessmen	368.52
港澳台商投资股份有限公司	Share Holding Co.Ltd. With Hongkong, Macao and Taiwan Investment	24.35
外商投资企业	Foreign Funded Enterprises	1915.96
中外合资经营企业	Sino - Foreign Joint Funded Enterprises	1287.67
中外合作经营企业	Sino - Foreign Cooperative Funded Enterprises	39.86
外资企业	Foreign Solely Funded Enterprises	359.83
外商投资股份有限公司	Foreign Funded Share Holding Co.Ltd.	228.54
二、在总计中:亏损企业	**Of the Total: enterprises running under deficit**	**1992.44**
在总计中:国有控股企业	Of the Total: State-Owned Share Holding Enterprises	10023.07
在总计中:农村工业	Of the Total: Rural Industry	111.41
在总计中:轻工业	Of the Total: Light Industry	5800.34
重工业	Heavy Industry	16358.05
在总计中:大型企业	Of the Total: Large Scale Enterprises	11421.93
中型企业	Medium Scale Enterprises	4385.31
小型企业	Small Enterprises	6351.15

(100 million Yuan)

资产总计 Total Assets		负债合计	流动负债合计	应付账款
累计折旧 Accumulated Depreciation	在建工程 Construction in process	Total Liability	Total Circulating Liability	Account Payable
10836.13	**1386.69**	**17570.58**	**13340.58**	**3338.22**
9525.41	1188.37	14677.29	10970.19	2535.13
2012.32	358.38	3635.99	2660.38	538.44
1922.62	349.87	3523.33	2581.24	521.28
89.71	8.51	112.65	79.14	17.16
18.00	1.26	27.06	22.36	8.52
2.30	0.08	6.21	4.35	1.20
0.48	0.03	1.23	1.09	0.38
0.14		0.23	0.23	0.09
0.24	0.03	0.60	0.60	0.26
0.10		0.40	0.27	0.03
2568.14	439.43	5876.24	4378.38	1086.76
421.17	112.83	1258.71	981.22	270.68
2146.97	326.60	4617.53	3397.16	816.08
983.66	216.92	2603.72	1978.82	392.51
3930.56	171.08	2504.80	1906.80	502.26
110.88	2.67	36.67	27.35	7.00
4.35	0.10	8.86	5.42	1.46
3571.04	155.71	2264.53	1724.39	463.02
244.29	12.60	194.73	149.64	30.78
9.97	1.19	22.06	18.01	5.05
524.53	60.30	687.04	454.53	146.33
325.08	50.16	454.19	269.34	83.69
3.45		3.43	3.17	0.98
186.73	7.83	206.78	161.94	52.49
9.11	2.08	19.13	16.57	5.76
786.18	138.02	2206.25	1915.87	656.76
544.01	102.29	1611.95	1461.10	513.61
18.15	2.50	21.18	11.40	3.09
153.01	17.65	379.66	320.69	107.13
71.01	15.44	192.81	122.03	32.72
817.97	232.63	**2459.23**	**1852.01**	**486.42**
3831.54	770.17	8998.11	6783.97	1662.58
88.87	2.68	41.68	32.04	8.08
3653.78	260.86	3628.37	2912.32	641.86
7182.35	1125.83	13942.21	10428.26	2696.36
4970.92	848.42	10089.44	7660.49	1881.01
2282.65	235.28	3560.32	2737.87	730.35
3582.56	302.99	3920.81	2942.23	726.86

13-3 续表 3 continued

单位:亿元

项 目	Item	固定资产原价 Original Price of Fixed Assets
按行业分	Grouped by sector	
采矿业	**Mining and Qarrying**	
煤炭开采和洗选业	Coal Mining and Processing	41.81
石油和天然气开采业	Petroleum and Natural Gas Extraction	295.58
黑色金属矿采选业	Ferrous Metals Mining and Processing	83.51
有色金属矿采选业	Non-ferrous Metals Mining and Processing	27.42
非金属矿采选业	Non-metal Minerals Mining and Processing	192.63
开采辅助活动	Mining Auxiliary Activities	62.47
其他采矿业	Other Minerals Mining and Processing	0.32
制造业	**Manufacturing**	
农副食品加工业	Food Processing	2038.98
食品制造业	Food Production	422.37
酒、饮料和精制茶制造业	Wine,Beverage and Refined Tea Production	326.88
烟草制品业	Tobacco Processing	81.79
纺织业	Textile Industry	844.69
纺织服装、服饰业	Textile,Garments, and Fashion Industry	262.59
皮革、毛皮、羽毛及其制品和制鞋业	Leather, Furs,Down and Related Products	42.56
木材加工和木、竹、藤、棕、草制品业	Timber Processing, Wood, Bamboo, Cane, Palm and Sraw Products	150.69
家具制造业	Furniture Manufacturing	107.73
造纸和纸制品业	Papermaking and Paper Products	329.39
印刷和记录媒介复制业	Printing and Record Processing	102.80
文教、工美、体育和娱乐用品制造业	Stationery, Education and Sports Goods	54.66
石油加工、炼焦和核燃料加工业	Petroleum Processing, Coking Products and Nuclear Fuel Processing	197.73
化学原料和化学制品制造业	Raw Chemical Material and Chemical Products	2256.86
医药制造业	Medical and pharmaceutical Products	344.85
化学纤维制造业	Chemical Fibers	36.26
橡胶和塑料制品业	Rubber and Plastic Products	551.70
非金属矿物制品业	Nonmetal Material Products	1187.55
黑色金属冶炼和压延加工业	Smelting and Pressing of Ferrous Metals	2651.67
有色金属冶炼和压延加工业	Smelting and Pressing of Nonferrous Metals	229.20
金属制品业	Metal Products	573.99
通用设备制造业	Ordinary Machinery Manufacturing	592.80
专用设备制造业	Special Purpose Equipment Manufacturing	527.15
汽车制造业	Motor manufacturing	1469.15
铁路、船舶、航空航天和其他运输设备制造业	Railway,Watercraft,Aviation and other Transporlation Equipment manufacturing	216.23
电气机械和器材制造业	Electric Machinery and Equipment	635.48
计算机、通信和其他电子设备制造业	Telecommunication Computer,Equipment and Other Electronic Equipment Manufacturing	494.75
仪器仪表制造业	Instruments and Meters, Manufacturing	66.57
其他制造业	Other Manufacturing	41.33
废弃资源综合利用业	Waste Comprehensive Vtilization of Resources Industry	13.77
金属制品、机械和设备修理业	Metal products,Machinery and Equipment Repairing	19.41
电力、燃气及水的生产和供应业	**Electric Power, Gas and Water Production and Supply**	
电力、热力生产和供应业	Electric Power, Steam and Hot Water Production and Supply	4376.75
燃气生产和供应业	Gas Production and Supply	82.17
水的生产和供应业	Tap Water Production and Supply	124.16

(100 million Yuan)

资产总计 Total Assets		负债合计 Total Liability	流动负债合计 Total Circulating Liability	应付账款 Account Payable
累计折旧 Accumulated Depreciation	在建工程 Construction in process			
10.86	5.06	33.63	26.95	5.25
151.71	7.67	100.50	85.97	12.63
30.63	5.15	71.52	59.92	20.77
13.99	2.97	24.64	22.25	2.80
116.89	10.24	148.50	110.85	16.02
21.05	8.70	58.41	57.68	13.55
0.07		0.54	0.01	
1531.46	45.40	666.91	498.35	87.85
264.47	14.94	186.76	124.14	31.49
124.86	44.74	631.32	570.59	82.45
49.63	8.37	203.20	202.58	63.69
501.46	22.71	400.15	311.67	53.88
145.05	8.68	184.66	154.54	30.59
20.58	3.37	34.85	26.87	6.49
69.76	4.48	81.42	51.96	10.70
73.27	3.28	31.65	25.48	6.77
231.39	13.60	147.62	114.93	27.71
55.78	4.47	79.28	60.01	16.72
36.64	2.04	42.43	36.43	4.65
84.70	10.86	131.64	117.49	15.29
1134.34	131.26	1594.01	1103.07	219.37
134.98	40.05	346.43	252.36	49.93
19.21	0.50	25.87	20.46	3.83
399.64	20.12	227.62	184.04	44.87
490.69	70.07	838.83	614.90	151.65
1167.95	261.71	2266.56	1740.93	316.66
92.27	34.38	373.77	291.16	47.59
303.23	48.80	470.76	375.21	104.33
303.34	28.53	729.17	598.17	99.16
289.35	18.41	538.77	406.50	144.33
699.16	158.70	2394.08	2094.79	799.73
69.33	48.00	472.88	402.69	126.02
354.05	51.81	630.95	525.63	197.45
239.26	39.72	792.09	571.17	260.61
23.93	2.26	78.23	71.63	14.13
20.66	3.34	73.40	41.76	11.76
3.87	1.79	37.71	20.09	3.74
13.76	0.40	11.36	10.67	5.18
1469.64	164.67	2191.19	1199.26	210.56
17.02	14.45	97.24	74.55	9.95
56.21	21.02	120.01	82.89	8.08

13-3　续表 4　continued

单位:亿元

项　目	Item	非流动负债合计	所有者权益合计 Total Rights of Owners
总　　计	**Total**	**3180.21**	**12904.96**
一、按登记注册类型分组:	**Grouped by Type of Registration**		
内资企业	Inner Funded Enterprises	2767.04	11047.75
国有企业	State Owned Enterprises	942.27	2366.47
中央企业	Central Enterprises	913.99	2307.58
地方企业	Local Enterprises	28.28	58.89
集体企业	Collective-owned Enterprise	3.30	24.19
股份合作企业	Share Holding Cooperative Enterprises	0.41	4.20
联营企业	Joint Owned Enterprise	0.14	2.16
国有联营企业	State Joint Ownership		
集体联营企业	Collective Joint Ownership		0.35
国有与集体联营企业	Joint State- Collective Ownership		0.24
其他联营企业	Other Joint Owned Enterprise	0.14	1.57
有限责任公司	Responsibility Co. Ltd	1053.47	3533.51
国有独资公司	State Solely Funded Co.	217.90	710.25
其他有限责任公司	Others	835.57	2823.27
股份有限公司	Share Holding Co.Ltd.	484.37	2348.84
私营企业	Private - owned enterprises	280.16	2737.83
私营独资企业	Solely Private - owned enterprises	2.92	64.60
私营合伙企业	Private Joint Venture	0.81	14.08
私营有限责任公司	Private Responsibility Co. Ltd	251.59	2449.43
私营股份有限公司	Private Share Holding Co.Ltd.	24.84	209.73
其他企业	Others	2.91	30.55
港、澳、台商投资企业	Hongkong, Macao and Taiwan Funded Enterprises	159.94	551.66
合资经营企业(港或澳、台资)	Joint Venture with Hongkong, Macao and Taiwan	115.83	312.15
合作经营企业(港或澳、台资)	Cooperate with Hongkong, Macao and Taiwan Funded	0.26	7.74
港澳台商独资经营企业	Enterprises Solely Funded by Hongkong, Macao and Taiwan Businessmen	41.30	200.69
港澳台商投资股份有限公司	Share Holding Co.Ltd. With Hongkong, Macao and Taiwan Investment	2.56	30.55
外商投资企业	Foreign Funded Enterprises	253.23	1305.55
中外合资经营企业	Sino - Foreign Joint Funded Enterprises	131.29	923.59
中外合作经营企业	Sino - Foreign Cooperative Funded Enterprises	6.87	12.23
外资企业	Foreign Solely Funded Enterprises	44.25	278.04
外商投资股份有限公司	Foreign Funded Share Holding Co.Ltd.	70.82	91.63
二、在总计中:亏损企业	**Of the Total: enterprises running under deficit**	**369.88**	**819.43**
在总计中:国有控股企业	Of the Total: State-Owned Share Holding Enterprises	1977.20	5808.13
在总计中:农村工业	Of the Total: Rural Industry	5.94	40.09
在总计中:轻工业	Of the Total: Light Industry	441.26	3392.46
重工业	Heavy Industry	2738.96	9512.50
在总计中:大型企业	Of the Total: Large Scale Enterprises	2077.62	6556.45
中型企业	Medium Scale Enterprises	521.55	2581.39
小型企业	Small Enterprises	581.05	3767.12

(100 million Yuan)

实收资本 Assets Recevied	国家资本 National Assets	所有者权益合计 Total Rights of Owners 集体资本 Collective Assets	法人资本 Corperative Assets	个人资本 Individual Assets	港澳台资本 Assets from Hongkong, Maco and Taiwan Funded Enterprises
5668.78	**1572.25**	**102.60**	**1871.43**	**1385.08**	**163.32**
4626.94	1399.42	91.85	1639.13	1358.58	2.81
561.64	494.18	1.69	17.75	45.90	0.02
536.75	478.66	0.42	15.18	42.65	0.02
24.89	15.52	1.27	2.57	3.25	
11.06	1.13	6.56	2.11	1.26	
3.31		0.55	1.57	1.19	
1.32		0.08	1.12	0.11	
0.12			0.07	0.05	
0.14		0.08	0.05		
1.06			1.01	0.06	
1784.76	587.60	54.71	703.53	416.76	1.81
353.72	285.63	0.73	65.73	1.53	
1431.03	301.96	53.99	637.80	415.23	1.81
791.08	309.28	11.86	200.57	265.88	0.26
1462.31	7.19	16.36	708.89	619.69	0.71
29.84	0.01	0.15	6.72	22.79	
6.34		0.79	2.13	3.43	
1343.16	6.57	14.69	659.40	553.01	0.71
82.97	0.61	0.73	40.64	40.46	
11.46	0.04	0.03	3.58	7.80	0.01
316.19	14.22	4.22	71.59	11.71	131.92
183.03	10.97	3.55	53.51	6.10	54.61
5.91			3.75	0.55	0.13
117.66	3.03		9.32	3.92	74.81
8.81	0.21	0.67	5.01	0.35	2.37
725.66	158.61	6.53	160.72	14.79	28.58
502.40	156.20	6.27	133.73	11.28	10.79
12.32		0.20	6.45	0.16	0.22
195.38	0.56	0.07	14.20	3.35	17.51
15.50	1.84		6.35		0.06
888.24	**383.04**	**11.73**	**214.29**	**169.94**	**20.83**
2180.25	1514.77	15.04	405.59	101.99	2.67
16.74	0.01	2.26	6.15	7.94	0.12
1487.94	87.22	25.40	603.07	542.66	61.85
4180.83	1485.03	77.20	1268.37	842.42	101.46
2159.52	1274.47	12.94	370.88	281.11	57.60
1305.32	164.69	41.02	564.32	280.76	60.75
2203.93	133.08	48.64	936.23	823.22	44.97

13-3 续表 5 continued

单位:亿元

项 目	Item	非流动负债合计	所有者权益合计 Total Rights of Owners
按行业分	Grouped by sector		
采矿业	**Mining and Qarrying**		
煤炭开采和洗选业	Coal Mining and Processing	4.54	34.88
石油和天然气开采业	Petroleum and Natural Gas Extraction	14.53	104.84
黑色金属矿采选业	Ferrous Metals Mining and Processing	6.40	55.37
有色金属矿采选业	Non-ferrous Metals Mining and Processing	1.51	24.84
非金属矿采选业	Non-metal Minerals Mining and Processing	25.08	122.03
开采辅助活动	Mining Auxiliary Activities	0.73	17.58
其他采矿业	Other Minerals Mining and Processing		0.41
制造业	**Manufacturing**		
农副食品加工业	Food Processing	83.55	721.28
食品制造业	Food Production	23.61	239.01
酒、饮料和精制茶制造业	Wine,Beverage and Refined Tea Production	45.13	363.00
烟草制品业	Tobacco Processing	0.62	214.70
纺织业	Textile Industry	57.57	417.00
纺织服装、服饰业	Textile,Garments, and Fashion Industry	19.46	211.32
皮革、毛皮、羽毛及其制品和制鞋业	Leather, Furs,Down and Related Products	6.82	27.82
木材加工和木、竹、藤、棕、草制品业	Timber Processing, Wood, Bamboo, Cane, Palm and Sraw Products	17.76	122.82
家具制造业	Furniture Manufacturing	2.87	47.58
造纸和纸制品业	Papermaking and Paper Products	17.78	129.71
印刷和记录媒介复制业	Printing and Record Processing	11.44	75.27
文教、工美、体育和娱乐用品制造业	Stationery, Education and Sports Goods	4.02	31.41
石油加工、炼焦和核燃料加工业	Petroleum Processing, Coking Products and Nuclear Fuel Processing	13.33	88.85
化学原料和化学制品制造业	Raw Chemical Material and Chemical Products	301.27	927.34
医药制造业	Medical and pharmaceutical Products	82.49	360.79
化学纤维制造业	Chemical Fibers	3.79	21.27
橡胶和塑料制品业	Rubber and plastic products	22.54	247.33
非金属矿物制品业	Nonmetal Material Products	174.74	765.35
黑色金属冶炼和压延加工业	Smelting and Pressing of Ferrous Metals	455.54	1145.89
有色金属冶炼和压延加工业	Smelting and Pressing of Nonferrous Metals	74.50	172.51
金属制品业	Metal Products	76.24	366.89
通用设备制造业	Ordinary Machinery Manufacturing	109.12	491.51
专用设备制造业	Special Purpose Equipment Manufacturing	28.06	329.08
汽车制造业	Motor manufacturing	208.09	2167.40
铁路、船舶、航空航天和其他运输设备制造业	Railway,Watercraft,Aviation and other Transporlation Equipment manufacturing	59.64	201.29
电气机械和器材制造业	Electric Machinery and Equipment	81.03	447.01
计算机、通信和其他电子设备制造业	Telecommunication Computer,Equipment and Other Electronic Equipment Manufacturing	123.80	509.44
仪器仪表制造业	Instruments and Meters, Manufacturing	4.83	47.97
其他制造业	Other Manufacturing	6.31	39.26
废弃资源综合利用业	Waste Comprehensive Vtilization of Resources Industry	1.48	13.57
金属制品、机械和设备修理业	Metal products,Machinery and Equipment Repairing	0.27	9.95
电力、燃气及水的生产和供应业	**Electric Power, Gas and Water Production and Supply**		
电力、热力生产和供应业	Electric Power, Steam and Hot Water Production and Supply	957.46	1428.07
燃气生产和供应业	Gas Production and Supply	21.07	49.11
水的生产和供应业	Tap Water Production and Supply	31.21	114.20

(100 million Yuan)

实收资本 Assets Recevied	国家资本 National Assets	所有者权益合计 Total Rights of Owners			
		集体资本 Collective Assets	法人资本 Corperative Assets	个人资本 Individual Assets	港澳台资本 Assets from Hongkong, Maco and Taiwan Funded Enterprises
77.00	1.19	1.48	6.61	7.16	0.39
115.34	115.34				
33.69	14.15	2.01	9.73	7.80	
8.78	4.21	0.06	2.25	2.16	
59.46	0.81	3.05	24.36	31.11	
29.65	24.63		5.01	0.01	
0.25	0.04	0.06		0.15	
281.12	9.68	7.20	103.48	137.70	3.87
111.78	10.68	0.50	52.89	30.51	4.41
167.06	3.56	3.00	42.97	85.33	15.35
23.29	0.13		23.15		
185.05	5.59	2.29	82.27	82.88	10.67
125.00	0.73	0.77	78.56	37.36	5.75
20.98		0.20	5.21	8.10	0.74
60.85	0.72	0.15	39.71	20.03	0.10
11.80	0.25	0.01	4.86	5.85	0.04
107.05	1.49	1.80	29.44	23.43	0.78
33.01	3.91	1.07	13.62	12.40	0.92
13.94	0.93	0.10	6.21	4.54	1.65
129.33	113.32	0.04	2.88	3.15	
439.04	37.00	16.36	181.42	102.18	6.33
147.14	12.48	5.83	70.96	41.35	13.71
17.51			7.75	2.43	
114.44	3.20	5.03	45.38	54.58	2.31
362.91	14.35	11.65	162.61	135.88	4.85
397.70	197.21	3.46	71.25	86.86	2.32
89.53	56.26	1.11	13.00	16.89	0.09
190.30	43.17	4.00	61.08	71.85	7.59
170.89	38.54	4.06	59.28	57.17	2.88
198.42	44.98	1.25	113.65	32.73	0.33
717.70	296.60	12.19	162.50	109.85	3.80
129.50	59.23	0.24	56.43	12.79	
238.94	17.31	5.75	101.10	69.39	12.35
186.47	37.99	2.18	86.94	26.21	25.74
20.66	2.97	0.37	9.11	6.42	0.66
10.43	4.12		3.00	3.31	
9.68	0.47	0.51	6.10	1.81	0.78
6.25	0.51	1.02	3.94	0.78	
558.98	362.83	3.52	100.22	49.75	31.35
25.07	6.47	0.13	9.59	1.52	3.57
42.79	25.19	0.17	12.92	1.65	

13-3 续表 6 continued

单位:亿元

项　目	Item	所有者权益合计 Total owner 外商资本 Total Rights of the Owners Foreign Assets
总　　计	**Total**	**406.82**
一、按登记注册类型分组:	**Grouped by Type of Registration**	
内资企业	Inner Funded Enterprises	22.38
国有企业	State Owned Enterprises	2.32
中央企业	Central Enterprises	0.02
地方企业	Local Enterprises	2.30
集体企业	Collective-owned Enterprise	
股份合作企业	Share Holding Cooperative Enterprises	
联营企业	Joint Owned Enterprise	
国有联营企业	State Joint Ownership	
集体联营企业	Collective Joint Ownership	
国有与集体联营企业	Joint State- Collective Ownership	
其他联营企业	Other Joint Owned Enterprise	
有限责任公司	Responsibility Co. Ltd	14.06
国有独资公司	State Solely Funded Co.	
其他有限责任公司	Others	14.06
股份有限公司	Share Holding Co.Ltd.	1.79
私营企业	Private - owned enterprises	4.21
私营独资企业	Solely Private - owned enterprises	
私营合伙企业	Private Joint Venture	
私营有限责任公司	Private Responsibility Co. Ltd	4.08
私营股份有限公司	Private Share Holding Co.Ltd.	0.13
其他企业	Others	
港、澳、台商投资企业	Hongkong, Macao and Taiwan Funded Enterprises	78.60
合资经营企业(港或澳、台资)	Joint Venture with Hongkong, Macao and Taiwan	53.80
合作经营企业(港或澳、台资)	Cooperate with Hongkong, Macao and Taiwan Funded	1.47
港澳台商独资经营企业	Enterprises Solely Funded by Hongkong, Macao and Taiwan Businessmen	23.13
港澳台商投资股份有限公司	Share Holding Co.Ltd. With Hongkong, Macao and Taiwan Investment	0.20
外商投资企业	Foreign Funded Enterprises	305.84
中外合资经营企业	Sino - Foreign Joint Funded Enterprises	135.94
中外合作经营企业	Sino - Foreign Cooperative Funded Enterprises	5.28
外资企业	Foreign Solely Funded Enterprises	157.30
外商投资股份有限公司	Foreign Funded Share Holding Co.Ltd.	7.26
二、在总计中:亏损企业	**Of the Total: enterprises running under deficit**	**88.85**
在总计中:国有控股企业	Of the Total: State-Owned Share Holding Enterprises	92.60
在总计中:农村工业	Of the Total: Rural Industry	
在总计中:轻工业	Of the Total: Light Industry	119.38
重工业	Heavy Industry	287.44
在总计中:大型企业	Of the Total: Large Scale Enterprises	162.42
中型企业	Medium Scale Enterprises	136.41
小型企业	Small Enterprises	107.99

(100 million Yuan)

营业收入 Proceeds Of Business	主营业务收入 Revenue of Major Business	营业成本 Operating Costs	主营业务成本 Cost of Major Business	营业税金及附加 Tax of Major Business	主营业务税金及附加 Tax of Major Business	其他业务收入 Revenue of Other Business	其他业务利润 Profit from Other Business	销售费用 Selling Expenses
39033.75	**38183.39**	**33195.67**	**32183.61**	**795.44**	**775.09**	**850.37**	**72.41**	**1169.77**
32878.93	32307.27	28193.31	27434.44	655.16	635.69	571.66	44.09	891.23
4117.91	4020.32	3848.61	3583.93	17.87	11.53	97.59	5.50	42.01
3960.17	3867.67	3712.14	3451.96	16.96	10.63	92.50	4.48	38.29
157.73	152.65	136.47	131.97	0.91	0.91	5.08	1.02	3.72
137.85	137.46	122.60	122.33	3.04	3.03	0.39	0.02	3.07
20.09	20.05	16.31	16.26	0.25	0.25	0.04		0.89
15.91	15.91	14.62	14.62	0.05	0.05			0.11
3.54	3.54	3.06	3.06					
0.76	0.76	0.67	0.67	0.01	0.01			0.02
11.62	11.62	10.88	10.88	0.04	0.04			0.09
12618.01	12280.66	10659.89	10310.78	414.45	406.58	337.35	24.00	333.51
2074.65	1836.07	1522.07	1274.65	337.65	331.99	238.57	6.62	38.11
10543.36	10444.58	9137.82	9036.14	76.80	74.59	98.78	17.38	295.40
3874.63	3794.24	3185.48	3106.98	98.30	97.13	80.40	10.51	183.08
11947.49	11892.61	10219.76	10154.66	119.77	115.69	54.88	4.04	326.29
388.55	388.23	327.43	324.76	5.41	5.35	0.33	0.12	10.71
84.97	84.88	72.66	72.58	1.08	1.06	0.09		1.89
10543.24	10493.71	9032.53	8977.48	104.36	101.07	49.53	3.87	283.31
930.72	925.79	787.14	779.83	8.92	8.21	4.93	0.05	30.38
147.03	146.02	126.05	124.90	1.43	1.42	1.01	0.02	2.27
1883.01	1775.52	1633.21	1524.47	7.87	7.59	107.49	2.87	68.47
1201.87	1121.93	1060.92	983.39	3.64	3.41	79.94	2.57	33.26
9.96	9.94	8.82	8.80	0.06	0.06	0.02		0.49
616.91	589.99	518.40	487.69	3.82	3.79	26.92	0.28	32.87
41.01	40.48	33.42	33.06	0.35	0.33	0.52	0.01	1.69
4271.82	4100.60	3369.15	3224.70	132.40	131.81	171.22	25.46	210.08
3261.40	3107.19	2574.88	2442.94	124.47	124.02	154.21	24.32	152.13
41.48	41.14	33.98	33.79	0.23	0.23	0.34	0.14	0.78
767.20	751.93	607.26	597.91	5.37	5.22	15.27	4.70	43.99
201.22	199.82	152.56	149.59	2.34	2.34	1.40	-3.70	13.16
2767.36	**2678.02**	**2520.41**	**2435.44**	**126.32**	**125.99**	**89.34**	**2.57**	**78.83**
12394.47	11834.52	10513.02	9808.50	553.66	540.39	559.95	48.91	310.48
180.20	180.00	157.91	157.49	1.76	1.76	0.21	0.01	3.50
12981.83	12711.62	10678.83	10394.78	397.46	389.10	270.21	12.72	523.87
26051.93	25471.77	22516.84	21788.83	397.98	385.99	580.15	59.70	645.90
16172.25	15566.19	13774.51	13019.64	586.19	572.72	606.06	48.10	498.38
8581.83	8401.40	7249.93	7061.74	68.65	66.33	180.43	15.23	271.09
14279.68	14215.80	12171.23	12102.23	140.60	136.04	63.88	9.08	400.30

13-3 续表 7 continued

单位:亿元

项 目	Item	所有者权益合计 Total owner 外商资本 Total Rights of the Owners Foreign Assets
按行业分	Grouped by sector	
采矿业	**Mining and Qarrying**	
煤炭开采和洗选业	Coal Mining and Processing	
石油和天然气开采业	Petroleum and Natural Gas Extraction	
黑色金属矿采选业	Ferrous Metals Mining and Processing	
有色金属矿采选业	Non-ferrous Metals Mining and Processing	0.10
非金属矿采选业	Non-metal Minerals Mining and Processing	0.02
开采辅助活动	Mining Auxiliary Activities	
其他采矿业	Other Minerals Mining and Processing	
制造业	**Manufacturing**	
农副食品加工业	Food Processing	18.69
食品制造业	Food Production	12.78
酒、饮料和精制茶制造业	Wine,Beverage and Refined Tea Production	16.68
烟草制品业	Tobacco Processing	
纺织业	Textile Industry	1.22
纺织服装、服饰业	Textile,Garments, and Fashion Industry	1.32
皮革、毛皮、羽毛及其制品和制鞋业	Leather, Furs,Down and Related Products	3.29
木材加工和木、竹、藤、棕、草制品业	Timber Processing, Wood, Bamboo, Cane, Palm and Sraw Products	0.14
家具制造业	Furniture Manufacturing	0.34
造纸和纸制品业	Papermaking and Paper Products	9.93
印刷和记录媒介复制业	Printing and Record Processing	0.17
文教、工美、体育和娱乐用品制造业	Stationery, Education and Sports Goods	0.49
石油加工、炼焦和核燃料加工业	Petroleum Processing, Coking Products and Nuclear Fuel Processing	9.91
化学原料和化学制品制造业	Raw Chemical Material and Chemical Products	51.53
医药制造业	Medical and pharmaceutical Products	2.64
化学纤维制造业	Chemical Fibers	7.34
橡胶和塑料制品业	Rubber and plastic products	2.07
非金属矿物制品业	Nonmetal Material Products	32.47
黑色金属冶炼和压延加工业	Smelting and Pressing of Ferrous Metals	36.60
有色金属冶炼和压延加工业	Smelting and Pressing of Nonferrous Metals	2.08
金属制品业	Metal Products	2.58
通用设备制造业	Ordinary Machinery Manufacturing	7.35
专用设备制造业	Special Purpose Equipment Manufacturing	5.17
汽车制造业	Motor manufacturing	126.88
铁路、船舶、航空航天和其他运输设备制造业	Railway,Watercraft,Aviation and other Transporlation Equipment manufacturing	0.78
电气机械和器材制造业	Electric Machinery and Equipment	31.21
计算机、通信和其他电子设备制造业	Telecommunication Computer,Equipment and Other Electronic Equipment Manufacturing	5.44
仪器仪表制造业	Instruments and Meters, Manufacturing	0.98
其他制造业	Other Manufacturing	0.01
废弃资源综合利用业	Waste Comprehensive Vtilization of Resources Industry	
金属制品、机械和设备修理业	Metal products,Machinery and Equipment Repairing	
电力、燃气及水的生产和供应业	**Electric Power, Gas and Water Production and Supply**	
电力、热力生产和供应业	Electric Power, Steam and Hot Water Production and Supply	11.04
燃气生产和供应业	Gas Production and Supply	2.72
水的生产和供应业	Tap Water Production and Supply	2.85

(100 million Yuan)

营业收入 Proceeds Of Business	主营业务收入 Revenue of Major Business	营业成本 Operating Costs	主营业务成本 Cost of Major Business	营业税金及附加 Tax of Major Business	主营业务税金及附加 Tax of Major Business	其他业务收入 Revenue of Other Business	其他业务利润 Profit from Other Business	销售费用 Selling Expenses
113.70	113.04	88.62	88.27	3.10	3.09	0.66	0.01	2.84
107.69	82.98	76.30	51.40	15.47	15.36	24.71	-0.19	1.31
423.86	423.53	380.17	376.21	3.67	3.66	0.32	0.07	9.63
82.53	81.14	63.29	63.11	1.33	1.33	1.39	0.03	0.85
494.50	493.05	382.43	380.82	13.27	12.75	1.45	0.31	15.59
80.34	79.27	75.70	74.86	1.80	1.79	1.08	0.25	0.04
1.24	1.24	0.84	0.84					0.02
3898.23	3882.59	3441.50	3425.67	23.95	22.64	15.64	0.91	92.06
825.18	821.84	670.76	667.17	6.99	6.78	3.34	0.18	47.23
1240.03	1229.67	919.30	906.21	30.11	29.72	10.36	4.87	122.37
667.39	489.63	286.80	108.21	285.14	279.26	177.76	-0.84	16.08
1897.55	1885.96	1639.56	1625.95	15.94	15.78	11.59	0.34	45.84
793.81	789.53	682.82	678.68	7.20	6.99	4.28	0.28	25.50
120.42	120.41	104.29	104.06	1.13	1.07	0.01		2.33
341.89	341.23	287.35	285.51	4.72	4.63	0.66	0.03	8.67
112.68	112.50	94.44	94.19	1.14	1.14	0.18	0.02	4.06
450.41	447.22	392.50	388.44	3.53	3.40	3.19	0.23	15.78
239.42	238.29	201.29	199.38	1.70	1.63	1.13	0.48	7.47
141.64	141.49	118.29	118.02	1.25	1.22	0.15	0.05	4.78
866.53	836.98	750.04	720.62	97.81	97.78	29.54	0.13	2.79
3383.35	3347.22	2908.46	2883.92	23.99	22.78	36.14	8.51	104.19
820.50	816.59	628.43	625.01	5.72	5.69	3.91	0.20	63.15
75.50	75.39	68.32	68.23	0.38	0.38	0.11	0.03	1.18
910.79	906.08	768.20	763.84	7.42	7.13	4.71	0.41	25.40
2430.74	2422.95	2001.88	1989.91	29.10	28.47	7.79	1.81	84.54
3625.08	3454.16	3542.62	3193.43	12.67	6.31	170.93	5.53	40.59
1485.42	1473.16	1427.23	1416.17	2.46	2.44	12.27	1.36	7.97
1220.30	1164.39	1053.57	995.77	10.54	10.33	55.90	0.81	34.83
1105.98	1101.27	897.10	889.04	12.80	12.60	4.71	-1.18	34.07
845.77	841.72	715.22	707.16	6.30	6.23	4.06	0.49	25.21
4771.00	4602.63	3900.93	3757.50	128.61	127.25	168.37	32.09	189.88
546.73	535.97	477.02	465.60	3.74	3.70	10.76	1.27	7.69
1510.26	1474.80	1293.84	1258.90	8.72	8.66	35.46	4.28	48.00
1315.91	1303.76	1138.84	1127.48	6.68	6.46	12.15	4.42	53.23
114.40	113.65	88.31	87.08	0.86	0.86	0.75	0.13	4.99
129.45	128.82	108.59	108.02	1.62	1.60	0.63	0.03	3.09
97.21	96.69	90.49	90.02	0.41	0.41	0.53		0.84
33.71	33.68	28.20	28.18	0.37	0.37	0.03	0.01	0.83
1550.01	1521.78	1268.81	1245.21	12.36	12.02	28.23	3.08	7.57
111.18	109.26	87.75	86.23	0.88	0.83	1.91	0.76	4.08
51.39	47.83	45.57	39.30	0.55	0.52	3.57	1.20	3.21

13-3 续表 8 continued

单位:亿元

项 目	Item	管理费用 Management Expense
总 计	**Total**	**1625.62**
一、按登记注册类型分组:	**Grouped by Type of Registration**	
内资企业	Inner Funded Enterprises	1358.92
国有企业	State Owned Enterprises	165.44
中央企业	Central Enterprises	156.16
地方企业	Local Enterprises	9.28
集体企业	Collective-owned Enterprise	7.58
股份合作企业	Share Holding Cooperative Enterprises	0.92
联营企业	Joint Owned Enterprise	0.32
国有联营企业	State Joint Ownership	
集体联营企业	Collective Joint Ownership	0.08
国有与集体联营企业	Joint State- Collective Ownership	0.10
其他联营企业	Other Joint Owned Enterprise	0.14
有限责任公司	Responsibility Co. Ltd	503.49
国有独资公司	State Solely Funded Co.	86.65
其他有限责任公司	Others	416.84
股份有限公司	Share Holding Co.Ltd.	235.33
私营企业	Private - owned enterprises	441.89
私营独资企业	Solely Private - owned enterprises	10.91
私营合伙企业	Private Joint Venture	2.65
私营有限责任公司	Private Responsibility Co. Ltd	394.15
私营股份有限公司	Private Share Holding Co.Ltd.	34.19
其他企业	Others	3.94
港、澳、台商投资企业	Hongkong, Macao and Taiwan Funded Enterprises	77.16
合资经营企业(港或澳、台资)	Joint Venture with Hongkong, Macao and Taiwan	48.83
合作经营企业(港或澳、台资)	Cooperate with Hongkong, Macao and Taiwan Funded	0.39
港澳台商独资经营企业	Enterprises Solely Funded by Hongkong, Macao and Taiwan Businessmen	25.05
港澳台商投资股份有限公司	Share Holding Co.Ltd. With Hongkong,	2.80
外商投资企业	Foreign Funded Enterprises	189.54
中外合资经营企业	Sino - Foreign Joint Funded Enterprises	136.15
中外合作经营企业	Sino - Foreign Cooperative Funded Enterprises	0.69
外资企业	Foreign Solely Funded Enterprises	42.08
外商投资股份有限公司	Foreign Funded Share Holding Co.Ltd.	10.60
二、在总计中:亏损企业	**Of the Total: enterprises running under deficit**	**148.61**
在总计中:国有控股企业	Of the Total: State-Owned Share Holding Enterprises	559.10
在总计中:农村工业	Of the Total: Rural Industry	5.47
在总计中:轻工业	Of the Total: Light Industry	547.46
重工业	Heavy Industry	1078.16
在总计中:大型企业	Of the Total: Large Scale Enterprises	667.00
中型企业	Medium Scale Enterprises	385.41
小型企业	Small Enterprises	573.21

(100 million Yuan)

税金 Tax	财务费用 Financial Expense	利息收入 Interest Income	利息支出 Interest Expense
90.11	**476.04**	40.93	**457.65**
77.13	444.94	35.66	412.74
8.93	92.30	7.33	107.26
8.48	90.49	7.24	105.65
0.45	1.81	0.08	1.60
0.50	0.77	0.03	0.64
0.01	0.21		0.11
0.01	0.02		0.01
	0.01		
24.62	160.35	15.60	152.96
2.81	26.87	2.93	29.53
21.81	133.48	12.67	123.43
14.04	49.16	9.02	52.13
28.80	141.12	3.66	98.89
1.09	4.02	0.03	2.82
0.08	0.73	0.02	0.53
25.15	125.96	3.21	87.24
2.48	10.41	0.40	8.30
0.22	1.01	0.02	0.75
4.20	17.73	1.22	15.94
2.79	11.97	0.76	11.61
0.03	0.06		0.04
1.20	4.88	0.45	3.68
0.14	0.79	0.02	0.57
8.78	13.37	4.05	28.97
5.75	1.00	2.77	15.01
0.03	0.81	0.03	0.79
2.32	4.50	1.00	6.04
0.68	7.06	0.26	7.12
5.49	**47.84**	2.64	**44.88**
22.67	174.50	23.97	210.12
0.23	1.75	-0.03	1.47
39.04	138.84	10.80	115.89
51.07	337.20	30.13	341.76
36.32	202.90	28.33	238.88
22.05	108.21	9.21	97.04
31.74	164.93	3.39	121.72

13-3 续表 9 continued

单位:亿元

项 目	Item	管理费用 Management Expense
按行业分	Grouped by sector	
采矿业	**Mining and Qarrying**	
煤炭开采和洗选业	Coal Mining and Processing	6.89
石油和天然气开采业	Petroleum and Natural Gas Extraction	21.63
黑色金属矿采选业	Ferrous Metals Mining and Processing	17.48
有色金属矿采选业	Non-ferrous Metals Mining and Processing	4.33
非金属矿采选业	Non-metal Minerals Mining and Processing	22.16
开采辅助活动	Mining Auxiliary Activities	7.08
其他采矿业	Other Minerals Mining and Processing	0.22
制造业	**Manufacturing**	
农副食品加工业	Food Processing	113.67
食品制造业	Food Production	40.87
酒、饮料和精制茶制造业	Wine,Beverage and Refined Tea Production	63.11
烟草制品业	Tobacco Processing	24.45
纺织业	Textile Industry	79.28
纺织服装、服饰业	Textile,Garments, and Fashion Industry	32.90
皮革、毛皮、羽毛及其制品和制鞋业	Leather, Furs,Down and Related Products	6.31
木材加工和木、竹、藤、棕、草制品业	Timber Processing, Wood, Bamboo, Cane, Palm and Sraw Products	9.83
家具制造业	Furniture Manufacturing	5.53
造纸和纸制品业	Papermaking and Paper Products	15.76
印刷和记录媒介复制业	Printing and Record Processing	17.94
文教、工美、体育和娱乐用品制造业	Stationery, Education and Sports Goods	6.01
石油加工、炼焦和核燃料加工业	Petroleum Processing, Coking Products and Nuclear Fuel Processing	11.89
化学原料和化学制品制造业	Raw Chemical Material and Chemical Products	115.09
医药制造业	Medical and pharmaceutical Products	49.31
化学纤维制造业	Chemical Fibers	5.03
橡胶和塑料制品业	Rubber and plastic products	35.33
非金属矿物制品业	Nonmetal Material Products	99.33
黑色金属冶炼和压延加工业	Smelting and Pressing of Ferrous Metals	142.75
有色金属冶炼和压延加工业	Smelting and Pressing of Nonferrous Metals	23.75
金属制品业	Metal Products	52.70
通用设备制造业	Ordinary Machinery Manufacturing	55.35
专用设备制造业	Special Purpose Equipment Manufacturing	44.17
汽车制造业	Motor manufacturing	255.09
铁路、船舶、航空航天和其他运输设备制造业	Railway,Watercraft,Aviation and other Transporlation Equipment manufacturing	31.81
电气机械和器材制造业	Electric Machinery and Equipment	69.41
计算机、通信和其他电子设备制造业	Telecommunication Computer,Equipment and Other Electronic Equipment Manufacturing	74.19
仪器仪表制造业	Instruments and Meters, Manufacturing	9.94
其他制造业	Other Manufacturing	7.63
废弃资源综合利用业	Waste Comprehensive Vtilization of Resources Industry	7.91
金属制品、机械和设备修理业	Metal products,Machinery and Equipment Repairing	2.59
电力、燃气及水的生产和供应业	**Electric Power, Gas and Water Production and Supply**	
电力、热力生产和供应业	Electric Power, Steam and Hot Water Production and Supply	26.66
燃气生产和供应业	Gas Production and Supply	4.38
水的生产和供应业	Tap Water Production and Supply	5.87

(100 million Yuan)

税金 Tax	财务费用 Financial Expense	利息收入 Interest Income	利息支出 Interest Expense
0.54	0.65	0.12	0.61
0.11	1.48	0.05	1.53
0.67	3.56	0.04	3.00
0.20	0.38	0.07	0.35
0.62	8.79	0.14	6.01
0.72	1.21	0.02	1.07
0.12			
7.99	36.81	0.82	29.40
3.23	9.87	2.51	9.50
9.14	10.93	3.92	13.36
0.49	3.15	0.26	3.51
4.45	29.77	0.40	18.63
2.97	7.81	0.64	6.19
0.60	1.64	0.09	1.54
0.94	4.04	0.05	2.82
0.21	1.08	0.01	0.94
1.07	5.61	0.39	4.71
1.30	2.22	0.12	1.81
0.30	1.84	0.03	1.64
0.33	2.77	0.27	2.86
6.77	49.86	1.89	45.27
2.85	11.75	0.87	10.99
0.04	0.98	0.11	1.00
2.04	11.00	0.42	8.40
6.52	35.34	1.25	29.07
7.43	53.80	5.35	66.16
1.14	10.52	3.32	8.79
2.12	14.06	0.54	12.03
2.11	15.67	1.75	14.43
2.35	13.32	0.67	11.09
11.56	8.60	8.80	22.63
1.16	3.59	0.68	4.04
3.57	10.80	1.09	9.61
1.38	8.10	1.73	8.81
0.34	1.37	0.07	1.02
0.24	1.66	0.09	1.23
0.06	1.13	0.02	1.00
0.06	0.32	0.01	0.36
1.67	86.97	2.06	88.64
0.28	1.51	0.26	1.60
0.45	2.05	0.01	2.01

13-3 续表 10 continued

单位:亿元

项 目	Item	营业利润 Operating Profit
总 计	**Total**	**2466.15**
一、按登记注册类型分组:	**Grouped by Type of Registration**	
内资企业	Inner Funded Enterprises	2013.25
国有企业	State Owned Enterprises	157.12
中央企业	Central Enterprises	151.82
地方企业	Local Enterprises	5.30
集体企业	Collective-owned Enterprise	10.59
股份合作企业	Share Holding Cooperative Enterprises	1.00
联营企业	Joint Owned Enterprise	0.45
国有联营企业	State Joint Ownership	
集体联营企业	Collective Joint Ownership	0.20
国有与集体联营企业	Joint State- Collective Ownership	-0.05
其他联营企业	Other Joint Owned Enterprise	0.30
有限责任公司	Responsibility Co. Ltd	692.44
国有独资公司	State Solely Funded Co.	104.46
其他有限责任公司	Others	587.98
股份有限公司	Share Holding Co.Ltd.	297.58
私营企业	Private - owned enterprises	844.78
私营独资企业	Solely Private - owned enterprises	29.73
私营合伙企业	Private Joint Venture	5.45
私营有限责任公司	Private Responsibility Co. Ltd	713.84
私营股份有限公司	Private Share Holding Co.Ltd.	95.76
其他企业	Others	9.28
港、澳、台商投资企业	Hongkong, Macao and Taiwan Funded Enterprises	108.38
合资经营企业(港或澳、台资)	Joint Venture with Hongkong, Macao and Taiwan	58.20
合作经营企业(港或澳、台资)	Cooperate with Hongkong, Macao and Taiwan Funded	0.16
港澳台商独资经营企业	Enterprises Solely Funded by Hongkong, Macao and Taiwan Businessmen	46.35
港澳台商投资股份有限公司	Share Holding Co.Ltd. With Hongkong, Macao and Taiwan Investment	3.13
外商投资企业	Foreign Funded Enterprises	344.52
中外合资经营企业	Sino - Foreign Joint Funded Enterprises	266.27
中外合作经营企业	Sino - Foreign Cooperative Funded Enterprises	4.98
外资企业	Foreign Solely Funded Enterprises	56.46
外商投资股份有限公司	Foreign Funded Share Holding Co.Ltd.	16.80
二、在总计中:亏损企业	**Of the Total: enterprises running under deficit**	**-141.75**
在总计中:国有控股企业	Of the Total: State-Owned Share Holding Enterprises	680.97
在总计中:农村工业	Of the Total: Rural Industry	12.24
在总计中:轻工业	Of the Total: Light Industry	919.10
重工业	Heavy Industry	1547.05
在总计中:大型企业	Of the Total: Large Scale Enterprises	903.42
中型企业	Medium Scale Enterprises	584.17
小型企业	Small Enterprises	978.56

(100 million Yuan)

补贴收入 Income from subsidy	营业外收入 Non-operating Income	营业外支出 Non-operating Expense	利润总额 Total Profit	应交所得税 Income Tax	亏损企业 亏损总额 Total Loss of Enterprises Running under Deficit
72.44	**166.13**	**97.21**	**2475.07**	**288.59**	**136.46**
64.79	146.93	90.68	2046.23	215.80	112.87
29.56	51.91	5.54	204.68	33.37	11.21
29.28	49.88	5.27	197.57	31.43	10.16
0.27	2.03	0.27	7.11	1.94	1.05
0.05	0.18	0.11	10.71	1.15	0.29
	0.03	0.05	0.98	0.02	0.02
0.05	0.05		0.50	0.01	
			0.20	0.01	
0.05	0.05				
			0.30		
20.74	52.45	34.88	689.17	80.25	54.55
5.46	18.08	7.61	96.91	17.10	11.72
15.28	34.37	27.28	592.26	63.15	42.83
9.51	24.32	9.48	311.39	33.23	33.16
4.87	17.82	39.93	820.05	66.61	12.92
	0.34	0.67	29.44	2.96	0.01
		0.21	5.40	0.38	
4.53	15.91	23.81	703.07	58.45	12.06
0.33	1.57	15.24	82.14	4.81	0.85
0.02	0.17	0.69	8.75	1.15	0.73
2.60	6.04	0.85	114.09	14.02	4.58
2.46	4.91	0.43	63.22	8.63	2.52
	0.02	0.01	0.17	-0.01	0.07
0.13	1.00	0.41	46.92	4.87	1.30
0.01	0.12	0.02	3.23	0.53	0.70
5.05	13.16	5.68	314.74	58.77	19.01
2.58	6.27	3.88	232.09	44.56	7.12
0.02	0.09	0.03	5.05	1.46	0.09
0.48	4.56	1.49	58.85	12.42	10.85
1.98	2.23	0.28	18.75	0.32	0.95
3.87	**17.20**	**10.89**	**-136.46**	**1.11**	**136.46**
48.42	99.95	21.56	706.10	106.54	68.21
0.03	0.39	2.30	10.24	1.02	0.22
13.11	33.72	35.44	895.23	101.44	24.90
59.33	132.42	61.77	1579.83	187.15	111.57
47.81	97.68	31.42	915.43	132.92	65.21
14.61	39.75	20.61	600.04	66.61	38.09
10.02	28.71	45.18	959.59	89.07	33.17

13-3 续表 11 continued

单位:亿元

项 目	Item	营业利润 Operating Profit
按行业分	Grouped by sector	
采矿业	**Mining and Qarrying**	
煤炭开采和洗选业	Coal Mining and Processing	12.24
石油和天然气开采业	Petroleum and Natural Gas Extraction	-8.38
黑色金属矿采选业	Ferrous Metals Mining and Processing	18.62
有色金属矿采选业	Non-ferrous Metals Mining and Processing	12.63
非金属矿采选业	Non-metal Minerals Mining and Processing	50.23
开采辅助活动	Mining Auxiliary Activities	-5.61
其他采矿业	Other Minerals Mining and Processing	0.02
制造业	**Manufacturing**	
农副食品加工业	Food Processing	265.57
食品制造业	Food Production	57.39
酒、饮料和精制茶制造业	Wine,Beverage and Refined Tea Production	118.42
烟草制品业	Tobacco Processing	57.25
纺织业	Textile Industry	110.68
纺织服装、服饰业	Textile,Garments, and Fashion Industry	50.03
皮革、毛皮、羽毛及其制品和制鞋业	Leather, Furs,Down and Related Products	5.14
木材加工和木、竹、藤、棕、草制品业	Timber Processing, Wood, Bamboo, Cane, Palm and Sraw Products	26.07
家具制造业	Furniture Manufacturing	6.43
造纸和纸制品业	Papermaking and Paper Products	25.30
印刷和记录媒介复制业	Printing and Record Processing	15.76
文教、工美、体育和娱乐用品制造业	Stationery, Education and Sports Goods	8.84
石油加工、炼焦和核燃料加工业	Petroleum Processing, Coking Products and Nuclear Fuel Processing	0.23
化学原料和化学制品制造业	Raw Chemical Material and Chemical Products	221.01
医药制造业	Medical and pharmaceutical Products	71.38
化学纤维制造业	Chemical Fibers	4.66
橡胶和塑料制品业	Rubber and plastic products	67.78
非金属矿物制品业	Nonmetal Material Products	195.00
黑色金属冶炼和压延加工业	Smelting and Pressing of Ferrous Metals	26.45
有色金属冶炼和压延加工业	Smelting and Pressing of Nonferrous Metals	19.43
金属制品业	Metal Products	67.72
通用设备制造业	Ordinary Machinery Manufacturing	71.92
专用设备制造业	Special Purpose Equipment Manufacturing	43.92
汽车制造业	Motor manufacturing	481.73
铁路、船舶、航空航天和其他运输设备制造业	Railway,Watercraft,Aviation and other Transporlation Equipment manufacturing	25.16
电气机械和器材制造业	Electric Machinery and Equipment	89.90
计算机、通信和其他电子设备制造业	Telecommunication Computer,Equipment and Other Electronic Equipment Manufacturing	32.23
仪器仪表制造业	Instruments and Meters, Manufacturing	9.33
其他制造业	Other Manufacturing	6.82
废弃资源综合利用业	Waste Comprehensive Vtilization of Resources Industry	2.48
金属制品、机械和设备修理业	Metal products,Machinery and Equipment Repairing	1.23
电力、燃气及水的生产和供应业	**Electric Power, Gas and Water Production and Supply**	
电力、热力生产和供应业	Electric Power, Steam and Hot Water Production and Supply	168.12
燃气生产和供应业	Gas Production and Supply	13.97
水的生产和供应业	Tap Water Production and Supply	19.05

(100 million Yuan)

补贴收入 Income from subsidy	营业外收入 Non-operating Income	营业外支出 Non-operating Expense	利润总额 Total Profit	应交所得税 Income Tax	亏损企业亏损总额 Total Loss of Enterprises Running
0.04	0.03	0.79	11.47	1.70	1.04
	0.19	0.39	-8.58	0.27	8.58
0.01	0.25	0.80	17.93	1.93	0.73
0.08	0.13	0.12	12.64	2.49	0.10
0.02	0.77	0.69	50.66	3.21	0.41
0.33	0.59	0.35	-5.37	0.13	5.40
			0.02		
2.77	7.63	10.11	261.40	17.64	1.67
0.57	1.38	3.11	55.61	4.72	3.11
0.99	4.35	3.39	119.09	20.02	1.25
0.04	0.25	1.48	56.03	12.56	
0.75	2.56	1.47	111.90	10.95	3.80
0.16	1.55	1.66	49.92	4.96	0.83
0.04	0.27	0.08	5.32	0.28	0.12
0.17	1.28	0.31	27.16	2.18	0.10
	0.03	0.08	6.41	0.93	0.06
0.52	1.35	4.52	21.74	2.83	2.43
0.20	0.66	0.25	15.80	2.06	0.86
0.18	0.27	0.12	8.99	0.88	0.81
0.04	0.53	0.55	0.22	0.78	3.33
3.50	13.81	20.74	213.44	18.24	13.22
3.57	6.16	3.57	73.56	8.96	1.39
0.05	0.11	0.16	4.60	0.09	1.43
0.72	1.28	3.09	66.22	7.18	0.82
4.89	9.84	7.41	197.93	19.34	5.10
0.82	22.96	2.22	46.71	5.98	7.51
0.77	1.46	0.79	20.14	2.13	5.71
1.48	2.81	4.19	65.03	7.20	4.10
2.14	6.52	1.26	77.47	7.24	5.89
1.02	2.07	0.74	45.07	5.29	5.33
9.84	20.00	7.70	457.29	55.17	19.18
2.33	2.69	2.39	26.25	5.02	4.40
2.38	5.63	4.88	88.81	11.55	2.85
9.06	17.08	1.19	48.09	5.91	13.98
0.43	1.92	0.12	11.12	0.86	0.11
0.08	0.24	0.08	7.17	0.34	0.03
0.71	0.75	0.02	3.22	0.56	0.65
0.22	0.22	0.52	0.93	0.05	0.26
21.15	24.58	5.00	187.71	33.33	8.37
0.01	0.63	0.61	13.95	3.33	0.12
0.37	1.27	0.28	1.99	0.32	1.35

13-3 续表 12 continued

单位:亿元 (100 million Yuan)

项 目	Item	利税总额 Total Profit	本年应付职工薪酬 Wages Welfarism payable This Year
总 计	**Total**	**4451.87**	**1862.54**
一、按登记注册类型分组:	**Grouped by Type of Registration**		
内资企业	Inner Funded Enterprises	3668.07	1562.76
国有企业	State Owned Enterprises	340.05	304.22
中央企业	Central Enterprises	328.58	291.42
地方企业	Local Enterprises	11.47	12.80
集体企业	Collective-owned Enterprise	20.61	9.05
股份合作企业	Share Holding Cooperative Enterprises	1.91	0.70
联营企业	Joint Owned Enterprise	0.65	0.37
国有联营企业	State Joint Ownership		
集体联营企业	Collective Joint Ownership	0.23	0.07
国有与集体联营企业	Joint State- Collective Ownership	0.06	0.12
其他联营企业	Other Joint Owned Enterprise	0.36	0.18
有限责任公司	Responsibility Co. Ltd	1478.06	568.80
国有独资公司	State Solely Funded Co.	528.43	90.59
其他有限责任公司	Others	949.63	478.21
股份有限公司	Share Holding Co.Ltd.	530.13	230.52
私营企业	Private - owned enterprises	1281.28	442.70
私营独资企业	Solely Private - owned enterprises	45.28	12.34
私营合伙企业	Private Joint Venture	8.21	2.90
私营有限责任公司	Private Responsibility Co. Ltd	1103.86	392.64
私营股份有限公司	Private Share Holding Co.Ltd.	123.94	34.83
其他企业	Others	15.39	6.39
港、澳、台商投资企业	Hongkong, Macao and Taiwan Funded Enterprises	174.20	85.68
合资经营企业(港或澳、台资)	Joint Venture with Hongkong, Macao and Taiwan	94.25	48.71
合作经营企业(港或澳、台资)	Cooperate with Hongkong, Macao and Taiwan Funded	0.52	0.57
港澳台商独资经营企业	Enterprises Solely Funded by Hongkong, Macao and Taiwan Businessmen	73.25	33.12
港澳台商投资股份有限公司	Share Holding Co.Ltd. With Hongkong, Macao and Taiwan Investment	5.12	3.24
外商投资企业	Foreign Funded Enterprises	609.60	214.10
中外合资经营企业	Sino - Foreign Joint Funded Enterprises	483.84	155.24
中外合作经营企业	Sino - Foreign Cooperative Funded Enterprises	7.38	1.70
外资企业	Foreign Solely Funded Enterprises	86.93	44.61
外商投资股份有限公司	Foreign Funded Share Holding Co.Ltd.	31.42	12.54
二、在总计中:亏损企业	**Of the Total: enterprises running under deficit**	**45.77**	**173.77**
在总计中:国有控股企业	Of the Total: State-Owned Share Holding Enterprises	1677.20	735.41
在总计中:农村工业	Of the Total: Rural Industry	16.52	6.88
在总计中:轻工业	Of the Total: Light Industry	1701.82	578.64
重工业	Heavy Industry	2750.06	1283.90
在总计中:大型企业	Of the Total: Large Scale Enterprises	2004.08	888.44
中型企业	Medium Scale Enterprises	944.49	474.50
小型企业	Small Enterprises	1503.31	499.60

13-3 续表 13 continued

单位:亿元

项　目	Item	利税总额 Total Profit	本年应付职工薪酬 Wages Welfarism Payable this year
按行业分	Grouped by sector		
采矿业	**Mining and Qarrying**		
煤炭开采和洗选业	Coal Mining and Processing	21.42	15.87
石油和天然气开采业	Petroleum and Natural Gas Extraction	10.24	18.29
黑色金属矿采选业	Ferrous Metals Mining and Processing	31.62	13.13
有色金属矿采选业	Non-ferrous Metals Mining and Processing	18.26	4.75
非金属矿采选业	Non-metal Minerals Mining and Processing	85.75	19.72
开采辅助活动	Mining Auxiliary Activities	0.64	16.30
其他采矿业	Other Minerals Mining and Processing	0.03	0.11
制造业	**Manufacturing**		
农副食品加工业	Food Processing	365.82	99.62
食品制造业	Food Production	93.72	39.90
酒、饮料和精制茶制造业	Wine,Beverage and Refined Tea Production	193.65	57.04
烟草制品业	Tobacco Processing	401.76	11.07
纺织业	Textile Industry	180.11	105.38
纺织服装、服饰业	Textile,Garments, and Fashion Industry	78.59	58.47
皮革、毛皮、羽毛及其制品和制鞋业	Leather, Furs,Down and Related Products	9.67	11.62
木材加工和木、竹、藤、棕、草制品业	Timber Processing, Wood, Bamboo, Cane, Palm and Sraw Products	43.53	15.30
家具制造业	Furniture Manufacturing	12.33	7.52
造纸和纸制品业	Papermaking and Paper Products	38.03	18.06
印刷和记录媒介复制业	Printing and Record Processing	25.50	13.80
文教、工美、体育和娱乐用品制造业	Stationery, Education and Sports Goods	14.47	7.89
石油加工、炼焦和核燃料加工业	Petroleum Processing, Coking Products and Nuclear Fuel Processing	115.35	10.61
化学原料和化学制品制造业	Raw Chemical Material and Chemical Products	325.27	104.78
医药制造业	Medical and pharmaceutical Products	114.62	47.91
化学纤维制造业	Chemical Fibers	6.66	3.90
橡胶和塑料制品业	Rubber and plastic products	102.23	42.23
非金属矿物制品业	Nonmetal Material Products	321.26	111.95
黑色金属冶炼和压延加工业	Smelting and Pressing of Ferrous Metals	125.48	175.03
有色金属冶炼和压延加工业	Smelting and Pressing of Nonferrous Metals	36.52	24.85
金属制品业	Metal Products	105.93	57.26
通用设备制造业	Ordinary Machinery Manufacturing	120.59	57.19
专用设备制造业	Special Purpose Equipment Manufacturing	72.81	52.44
汽车制造业	Motor manufacturing	754.65	265.80
铁路、船舶、航空航天和其他运输设备制造业	Railway,Watercraft,Aviation and other Transporlation Equipment manufacturing	42.33	44.14
电气机械和器材制造业	Electric Machinery and Equipment	134.51	76.37
计算机、通信和其他电子设备制造业	Telecommunication Computer,Equipment and Other Electronic Equipment Manufacturing	85.36	85.30
仪器仪表制造业	Instruments and Meters, Manufacturing	16.51	11.94
其他制造业	Other Manufacturing	11.25	9.20
废弃资源综合利用业	Waste Comprehensive Vtilization of Resources Industry	6.91	2.82
金属制品、机械和设备修理业	Metal products,Machinery and Equipment Repairing	2.33	3.59
电力、燃气及水的生产和供应业	**Electric Power, Gas and Water Production and Supply**		
电力、热力生产和供应业	Electric Power, Steam and Hot Water Production and Supply	304.32	126.33
燃气生产和供应业	Gas Production and Supply	17.28	5.69
水的生产和供应业	Tap Water Production and Supply	4.59	9.37

13-3 续表 14 continued

单位:亿元 (100 million Yuan)

项 目	Item	应交税金及附加 Tax and Extra Charges	本年应交增值税 Value Added Payable of the Current Year	全部从业人员年平均人数(万人) Average Number of Empolyment of the Current Year (10000 persons)
总 计	**Total**	**2355.51**	**1181.37**	**346.29**
一、按登记注册类型分组:	**Grouped by Type of Registration**			
内资企业	Inner Funded Enterprises	1914.77	966.68	298.60
国有企业	State Owned Enterprises	177.67	117.49	29.07
中央企业	Central Enterprises	170.91	114.05	26.15
地方企业	Local Enterprises	6.75	3.45	2.92
集体企业	Collective-owned Enterprise	11.54	6.85	2.45
股份合作企业	Share Holding Cooperative Enterprises	0.96	0.67	0.22
联营企业	Joint Owned Enterprise	0.17	0.10	0.13
国有联营企业	State Joint Ownership	0.00		
集体联营企业	Collective Joint Ownership	0.04	0.03	0.02
国有与集体联营企业	Joint State- Collective Ownership	0.06	0.05	0.04
其他联营企业	Other Joint Owned Enterprise	0.07	0.02	0.07
有限责任公司	Responsibility Co. Ltd	893.77	374.44	114.81
国有独资公司	State Solely Funded Co.	451.43	93.87	12.55
其他有限责任公司	Others	442.33	280.57	102.26
股份有限公司	Share Holding Co.Ltd.	266.00	120.44	37.93
私营企业	Private - owned enterprises	556.65	341.47	112.60
私营独资企业	Solely Private - owned enterprises	19.89	10.43	3.54
私营合伙企业	Private Joint Venture	3.27	1.72	0.75
私营有限责任公司	Private Responsibility Co. Ltd	484.40	296.43	99.69
私营股份有限公司	Private Share Holding Co.Ltd.	49.09	32.88	8.62
其他企业	Others	8.02	5.21	1.39
港、澳、台商投资企业	Hongkong, Macao and Taiwan Funded Enterprises	78.33	52.24	18.95
合资经营企业(港或澳、台资)	Joint Venture with Hongkong, Macao and Taiwan	42.45	27.38	10.19
合作经营企业(港或澳、台资)	Cooperate with Hongkong, Macao and Taiwan Funded	0.37	0.29	0.12
港澳台商独资经营企业	Enterprises Solely Funded by Hongkong, Macao and Taiwan Businessmen	32.40	22.51	8.00
港澳台商投资股份有限公司	Share Holding Co.Ltd. With Hongkong, Macao and Taiwan Investment	2.55	1.53	0.63
外商投资企业	Foreign Funded Enterprises	362.41	162.46	28.74
中外合资经营企业	Sino - Foreign Joint Funded Enterprises	302.06	127.29	18.43
中外合作经营企业	Sino - Foreign Cooperative Funded Enterprises	3.82	2.11	0.23
外资企业	Foreign Solely Funded Enterprises	42.83	22.72	8.33
外商投资股份有限公司	Foreign Funded Share Holding Co.Ltd.	13.68	10.33	1.74
二、在总计中:亏损企业	**Of the Total: enterprises running under deficit**	**188.83**	**55.91**	**32.60**
在总计中:国有控股企业	Of the Total: State-Owned Share Holding Enterprises	1100.30	417.43	83.59
在总计中:农村工业	Of the Total: Rural Industry	7.52	4.52	1.74
在总计中:轻工业	Of the Total: Light Industry	947.06	409.13	137.07
重工业	Heavy Industry	1408.45	772.25	209.22
在总计中:大型企业	Of the Total: Large Scale Enterprises	1257.88	502.46	118.80
中型企业	Medium Scale Enterprises	433.10	275.80	102.31
小型企业	Small Enterprises	664.53	403.12	125.19

13-3 续表 15 continued

单位:亿元 (100 million Yuan)

项　目	Item	应交税金及附加 Tax and Extra Charges	本年应交增值税 Value Added Payable of the Current Year	全部从业人员年平均人数(万人) Average Number of Empolyment of the Current Year (10000 persons)
按行业分	Grouped by sector			
采矿业	**Mining and Qarrying**			
煤炭开采和洗选业	Coal Mining and Processing	12.19	6.85	3.29
石油和天然气开采业	Petroleum and Natural Gas Extraction	19.20	3.35	1.89
黑色金属矿采选业	Ferrous Metals Mining and Processing	16.29	10.02	2.89
有色金属矿采选业	Non-ferrous Metals Mining and Processing	8.30	4.29	1.03
非金属矿采选业	Non-metal Minerals Mining and Processing	38.92	21.82	4.96
开采辅助活动	Mining Auxiliary Activities	6.86	4.21	1.98
其他采矿业	Other Minerals Mining and Processing	0.13	0.01	0.03
制造业	**Manufacturing**			
农副食品加工业	Food Processing	130.04	80.46	23.45
食品制造业	Food Production	46.06	31.13	9.50
酒、饮料和精制茶制造业	Wine,Beverage and Refined Tea Production	103.72	44.45	10.85
烟草制品业	Tobacco Processing	358.78	60.59	0.81
纺织业	Textile Industry	83.61	52.27	29.03
纺织服装、服饰业	Textile,Garments, and Fashion Industry	36.60	21.46	16.66
皮革、毛皮、羽毛及其制品和制鞋业	Leather, Furs,Down and Related Products	5.22	3.22	3.42
木材加工和木、竹、藤、棕、草制品业	Timber Processing, Wood, Bamboo, Cane, Palm and Sraw Products	19.49	11.64	3.84
家具制造业	Furniture Manufacturing	7.07	4.79	1.58
造纸和纸制品业	Papermaking and Paper Products	20.17	12.75	4.67
印刷和记录媒介复制业	Printing and Record Processing	13.07	8.01	3.04
文教、工美、体育和娱乐用品制造业	Stationery, Education and Sports Goods	6.66	4.23	1.97
石油加工、炼焦和核燃料加工业	Petroleum Processing, Coking Products and Nuclear Fuel Processing	116.24	17.32	1.18
化学原料和化学制品制造业	Raw Chemical Material and Chemical Products	136.84	87.84	21.72
医药制造业	Medical and pharmaceutical Products	52.86	35.34	10.47
化学纤维制造业	Chemical Fibers	2.18	1.67	0.85
橡胶和塑料制品业	Rubber and plastic products	45.22	28.58	9.96
非金属矿物制品业	Nonmetal Material Products	149.19	94.23	24.72
黑色金属冶炼和压延加工业	Smelting and Pressing of Ferrous Metals	92.18	66.10	18.84
有色金属冶炼和压延加工业	Smelting and Pressing of Nonferrous Metals	19.65	13.92	5.11
金属制品业	Metal Products	50.22	30.36	11.48
通用设备制造业	Ordinary Machinery Manufacturing	52.47	30.33	11.59
专用设备制造业	Special Purpose Equipment Manufacturing	35.38	21.44	10.04
汽车制造业	Motor manufacturing	364.09	168.75	39.39
铁路、船舶、航空航天和其他运输设备制造业	Railway,Watercraft,Aviation and other Transporlation Equipment manufacturing	22.26	12.33	6.94
电气机械和器材制造业	Electric Machinery and Equipment	60.82	36.98	14.98
计算机、通信和其他电子设备制造业	Telecommunication Computer,Equipment and Other Electronic Equipment Manufacturing	44.56	30.59	13.76
仪器仪表制造业	Instruments and Meters, Manufacturing	6.59	4.53	2.34
其他制造业	Other Manufacturing	4.66	2.46	2.18
废弃资源综合利用业	Waste Comprehensive Vtilization of Resources Industry	4.31	3.28	0.69
金属制品、机械和设备修理业	Metal products,Machinery and Equipment Repairing	1.50	1.02	0.92
电力、燃气及水的生产和供应业	**Electric Power, Gas and Water Production and Supply**			
电力、热力生产和供应业	Electric Power, Steam and Hot Water Production and Supply	151.60	104.25	11.35
燃气生产和供应业	Gas Production and Supply	6.94	2.45	0.85
水的生产和供应业	Tap Water Production and Supply	3.36	2.05	2.03

13-4 国有控股工业企业单位数和主要经济指标（2013）

单位:亿元

项 目	Item	企业单位数(个) Number of Enterprises(unit)	工业总产值(当年价格) Total Output Value(current price)
总　　计	**Total**	**724**	**11293.00**
在总计中:	Of the Total		
亏损企业	Enterprises running under Deficit	140	1279.37
在总计中:	Of the Total:		
中央企业	Central Enterprises	50	3470.58
地方企业	Local Enterprises	104	158.02
在总计中:	Of the Total:		
轻工业	Light Industry	206	1281.39
重工业	Heavy Industry	518	10011.61
在总计中:	Of the Total:		
大型企业	Large Scale Enterprises	118	9636.10
中型企业	Medium Scale Enterprises	225	1082.19
小型企业	Small Enterprises	381	574.71
按行业分	Grouped by sector		
采矿业	**Mining and Qarrying**		
煤炭开采和洗选业	Coal Mining and Processing	7	6.92
石油和天然气开采业	Petroleum and Natural Gas Extraction	1	82.89
黑色金属矿采选业	Ferrous Metals Mining and Processing	3	63.67
有色金属矿采选业	Non-ferrous Metals Mining and Processing	4	13.55
非金属矿采选业	Non-metal Minerals Mining and Processing	9	7.76
开采辅助活动	Mining Auxiliary Activities	4	61.67
其他采矿业	Other Minerals Mining and Processing		
制造业	**Manufacturing**		
农副食品加工业	Food Processing	49	171.67
食品制造业	Food Production	10	34.62
酒、饮料和精制茶制造业	Wine,Beverage and Refined Tea Production	10	49.56
烟草制品业	Tobacco Processing	6	518.14
纺织业	Textile Industry	18	61.59
纺织服装、服饰业	Textile,Garments, and Fashion Industry	9	23.08
皮革、毛皮、羽毛及其制品和制鞋业	Leather, Furs,Down and Related Products		
木材加工和木、竹、藤、棕、草制品业	Timber Processing, Wood, Bamboo, Cane, Palm and Sraw Products	4	9.90
家具制造业	Furniture Manufacturing	1	0.66
造纸和纸制品业	Papermaking and Paper Products	2	8.70
印刷和记录媒介复制业	Printing and Record Processing	15	52.53
文教、工美、体育和娱乐用品制造业	Stationery, Education and Sports Goods	2	0.65
石油加工、炼焦和核燃料加工业	Petroleum Processing, Coking Products and Nuclear Fuel Processing	6	704.94
化学原料和化学制品制造业	Raw Chemical Material and Chemical Products	46	848.42
医药制造业	Medical and pharmaceutical Products	15	53.23
化学纤维制造业	Chemical Fibers	1	0.92
橡胶和塑料制品业	Rubber and plastic products	10	64.05
非金属矿物制品业	Nonmetal Material Products	60	167.25
黑色金属冶炼和压延加工业	Smelting and Pressing of Ferrous Metals	15	2006.48
有色金属冶炼和压延加工业	Smelting and Pressing of Nonferrous Metals	7	362.39
金属制品业	Metal Products	26	145.65
通用设备制造业	Ordinary Machinery Manufacturing	36	231.04
专用设备制造业	Special Purpose Equipment Manufacturing	32	122.98
汽车制造业	Motor manufacturing	77	2722.51
铁路、船舶、航空航天和其他运输设备制造业	Railway,Watercraft,Aviation and other Transporlation Equipment manufacturing	25	378.42
电气机械和器材制造业	Electric Machinery and Equipment	28	315.22
计算机、通信和其他电子设备制造业	Telecommunication Computer,Equipment and Other Electronic Equipment Manufacturing	29	484.03
仪器仪表制造业	Instruments and Meters, Manufacturing	14	18.56
其他制造业	Other Manufacturing	9	41.30
废弃资源综合利用业	Waste Comprehensive Vtilization of Resources Industry	2	2.33
金属制品、机械和设备修理业	Metal products,Machinery and Equipment Repairing	2	1.39
电力、燃气及水的生产和供应业	**Electric Power, Gas and Water Production and Supply**		
电力、热力生产和供应业	Electric Power, Steam and Hot Water Production and Supp	81	1380.88
燃气生产和供应业	Gas Production and Supply	10	40.82
水的生产和供应业	Tap Water Production and Supply	39	32.63

THE NUMBER OF STATE-OWNED SHARE HOLDING INDUSTRIAL ENTERPRISES AND THEIR TOTAL OUTPUT OF PRODUCTION AND SALES (2013)

(100 million yuan)

工业销售产值(当年价格) Output Value of Industrial Products Sales (current price)	出口交货值 Delivery Value for Export	资产总计 Total Assets	流动资产合计 Circulating Funds	固定资产合计 Total Fined Assets	固定资产原价 Original Value of Fixed Assets	主营业务收入 Revenue of Major Business	全部从业人员年平均人数(万人) Average Number of Empolyment of the Curreat Year(10 000 Bersons)
11094.35	**434.03**	**14835.46**	**5677.06**	**6438.75**	**10023.07**	**11834.52**	**83.59**
1263.57	28.87	1288.80	501.91	648.42	1034.24	1279.52	12.43
3454.83	230.85	5826.13	1451.43	3331.04	5119.34	3862.03	26.03
155.85	16.57	171.85	83.46	70.94	143.41	152.65	2.92
1240.71	27.76	1261.75	791.32	283.69	509.21	1203.61	11.41
9853.64	406.27	13573.71	4885.73	6155.07	9513.86	10630.91	72.17
9498.10	408.29	12385.54	4683.30	5421.51	8357.17	10160.23	64.71
1047.31	15.59	1617.84	723.70	512.18	1003.78	1111.57	13.82
548.94	10.15	832.08	270.06	505.06	662.12	562.72	5.06
6.85		13.30	8.53	4.45	5.25	7.36	0.71
82.85	0.54	205.34	31.62	173.71	295.58	82.98	1.89
65.05		27.00	6.61	15.27	30.69	65.09	0.38
13.38		17.41	5.23	7.71	10.26	13.27	0.25
8.03		15.66	10.99	1.23	2.24	12.20	0.12
61.64	0.10	75.84	21.06	40.71	62.40	78.26	1.97
168.11	4.26	70.38	38.78	24.41	62.54	166.45	0.74
35.04	0.20	70.31	37.39	18.90	42.30	45.56	0.58
47.37		29.87	16.04	9.92	18.62	37.72	0.66
502.49	1.34	415.65	327.81	32.03	80.86	488.57	0.79
54.17	2.98	46.78	26.76	17.14	55.51	76.02	1.12
21.73	5.68	48.30	38.26	6.29	6.98	23.59	1.15
9.58		4.20	3.32	0.44	0.64	8.98	0.10
0.67		0.64	0.50	0.17	0.12	0.67	0.02
9.33		29.04	13.18	3.95	7.68	8.60	0.11
46.05	1.81	39.87	22.96	9.32	18.55	38.28	0.53
0.64		1.08	0.70	0.11	0.14	0.80	0.02
695.58		150.43	57.08	88.18	156.26	712.83	0.78
							5.09
815.70	57.28	1200.34	370.37	515.42	877.80	917.16	5.09
51.89	3.36	76.63	37.98	22.11	30.85	59.47	0.88
0.92		6.74	3.44	0.87	3.01	1.06	0.07
62.72	0.23	57.64	41.65	12.40	25.60	63.34	0.56
159.70	1.90	195.49	66.12	90.84	146.30	149.81	1.65
2003.52	40.46	2654.38	814.19	1233.74	2135.61	2431.47	12.00
357.40	24.71	351.80	204.51	78.82	119.28	877.87	1.84
122.02	3.14	224.84	154.21	38.66	64.73	140.53	1.71
225.75	5.30	311.88	165.05	118.19	150.12	212.01	2.58
111.44	4.89	214.91	146.21	52.19	89.05	92.35	2.40
2689.18	17.12	3042.30	1589.39	465.04	778.22	2445.80	16.04
368.19	186.27	567.15	359.87	137.37	163.27	344.60	4.67
302.52	13.84	269.34	184.66	60.13	80.02	267.66	2.53
487.91	57.99	683.12	496.41	138.01	240.78	444.54	5.38
18.01	0.34	47.81	19.20	28.27	30.45	18.08	0.48
39.57	0.30	62.63	43.44	17.40	17.28	39.20	1.07
2.32		1.78	1.42	0.35	0.40	2.36	0.03
1.39		0.77	0.40	0.30	0.53	1.39	0.11
1373.80		3326.69	203.11	2867.96	4067.03	1376.87	10.57
40.56		69.31	20.20	35.03	44.71	48.98	0.35
31.29		208.85	88.38	71.71	101.39	32.76	1.68

13-5 集体工业企业单位数和主要经济指标（2013）

单位:亿元

项 目	Item	企业单位数(个) Number of Enterprises (unit)	工业总产值(当年价格) Total Output Value (current price)
总 计	**Total**	**353**	**898.40**
在总计中:	Of the Total:		
亏损企业	Enterprises running under Deficit	40	110.44
在总计中:	Of the Total:		
农村工业	Rural Industry	29	71.92
在总计中:	Of the Total:		
轻工业	Light Industry	78	301.70
重工业	Heavy Industry	275	596.70
在总计中:	Of the Total:		
大型企业	Large Scale Enterprises	16	364.65
中型企业	Medium Scale Enterprises	79	252.79
小型企业	Small Enterprises	258	280.96
按行业分	Grouped by sector		
采矿业	**Mining and Qarrying**		
煤炭开采和洗选业	Coal Mining and Processing	11	19.44
石油和天然气开采业	Petroleum and Natural Gas Extraction		
黑色金属矿采选业	Ferrous Metals Mining and Processing	12	94.69
有色金属矿采选业	Non-ferrous Metals Mining and Processing	1	0.57
非金属矿采选业	Non-metal Minerals Mining and Processing	35	70.35
开采辅助活动	Mining Auxiliary Activities		
其他采矿业	Other Minerals Mining and Processing	1	0.62
制造业	**Manufacturing**		
农副食品加工业	Food Processing	9	33.80
食品制造业	Food Production	4	6.60
酒、饮料和精制茶制造业	Wine,Beverage and Refined Tea Production	8	23.37
烟草制品业	Tobacco Processing		
纺织业	Textile Industry	11	27.89
纺织服装、服饰业	Textile,Garments, and Fashion Industry	9	12.14
皮革、毛皮、羽毛及其制品和制鞋业	Leather, Furs,Down and Related Products		
木材加工和木、竹、藤、棕、草制品业	Timber Processing, Wood, Bamboo, Cane, Palm and Saw Products	1	8.96
家具制造业	Furniture Manufacturing	1	0.31
造纸和纸制品业	Papermaking and Paper Products	6	69.55
印刷和记录媒介复制业	Printing and Record Processing	5	4.91
文教、工美、体育和娱乐用品制造业	Stationery, Education and Sports Goods	1	3.39
石油加工、炼焦和核燃料加工业	Petroleum Processing, Coking Products and Nuclear Fuel Processing		
化学原料和化学制品制造业	Raw Chemical Material and Chemical Products	22	30.44
医药制造业	Medical and pharmaceutical Products	10	41.67
化学纤维制造业	Chemical Fibers		
橡胶和塑料制品业	Rubber and plastic products	14	13.30
非金属矿物制品业	Nonmetal Material Products	33	65.91
黑色金属冶炼和压延加工业	Smelting and Pressing of Ferrous Metals	16	13.76
有色金属冶炼和压延加工业	Smelting and Pressing of Nonferrous Metals	9	6.15
金属制品业	Metal Products	16	11.93
通用设备制造业	Ordinary Machinery Manufacturing	23	25.81
专用设备制造业	Special Purpose Equipment Manufacturing	7	45.35
汽车制造业	Motor manufacturing	31	137.78
铁路、船舶、航空航天和其他运输设备制造业	Railway,Watercraft,Aviation and other Equipment manufacturing	4	5.85
电气机械和器材制造业	Electric Machinery and Equipment	18	100.98
计算机、通信和其他电子设备制造业	Telecommunication Computer,Equipment and Oth Electronic Equipment Manufacturing	2	2.16
仪器仪表制造业	Instruments and Meters, Manufacturing	4	1.80
其他制造业	Other Manufacturing		
废弃资源综合利用业	Waste Comprehensive Vtilization of Resources Ind	10	8.22
金属制品、机械和设备修理业	Metal products,Machinery and Equipment Repairi	7	4.55
电力、燃气及水的生产和供应业	**Electric Power, Gas and Water Production and Supply**		
电力、热力生产和供应业	Electric Power, Steam and Hot Water Production a	4	2.32
燃气生产和供应业	Gas Production and Supply	1	1.04
水的生产和供应业	Tap Water Production and Supply	7	2.82

THE NUMBER OF COLLECTIVE-OWNED INDUSTRIAL ENTERPRISES(2013)

(100 million yuan)

工业销售产值(当年价格) Output Value of Industrial Products Sales (current price)	出口交货值 Delivery Value for Export	资产总计 Total Assets	流动资产合计 Circulating Funds	固定资产合计 Total Fined Assets	固定资产原价 Original Value of Fixed Assets	主营业务收入 Revenue of Major Business	全部从业人员年平均人数(万人) Average Number of Empolyment of the Curreat Year (10 000 Bersons)
891.59	**30.53**	**578.30**	**349.35**	**166.59**	**406.87**	**864.44**	**11.78**
109.30	9.57	99.13	64.75	23.54	36.70	101.56	1.90
71.26	0.51	31.40	14.41	10.72	55.20	71.65	0.69
291.49	12.07	182.48	94.54	68.11	223.25	273.85	3.50
600.10	18.46	395.82	254.81	98.49	183.61	590.59	8.28
374.74	17.89	268.44	172.50	73.40	172.14	349.83	3.97
246.63	9.10	151.40	88.14	47.12	155.14	257.62	4.77
270.23	3.54	158.46	88.72	46.07	79.59	256.99	3.03
19.28		4.47	1.74	2.36	3.29	18.96	0.38
91.89		13.29	8.04	4.56	8.82	91.54	0.74
0.57		0.08	0.06	0.01	0.03	0.55	0.01
68.04		46.06	21.25	12.57	14.39	65.13	0.77
0.62		0.69	0.52	0.17	0.23	0.48	0.01
32.56	0.46	23.88	10.97	12.43	15.51	23.58	0.24
6.46		1.76	0.79	0.69	1.05	6.43	0.06
24.77	0.51	6.42	3.20	2.26	2.90	24.51	0.15
27.38	0.48	21.68	10.50	9.63	20.76	24.62	0.85
12.14		2.71	1.85	0.63	19.75	11.73	0.18
8.91		3.04	1.12	1.91	3.45	8.91	0.19
0.30	0.29	0.67	0.17	0.43	0.43	0.29	0.03
63.53	0.19	12.36	5.07	7.25	120.54	60.33	0.26
4.83		5.27	2.36	1.68	3.52	5.97	0.11
3.39		1.34	0.19	1.15	1.16	3.39	0.06
28.05	3.97	16.25	9.51	5.86	8.58	29.06	0.42
39.26	9.20	47.10	22.77	17.26	23.08	51.95	0.88
12.84		9.63	5.43	2.71	3.60	12.74	0.33
64.56	3.38	21.72	11.25	10.26	11.47	64.90	0.67
12.80		8.93	4.58	2.57	11.52	13.52	0.47
6.21		4.31	2.88	1.05	1.32	6.62	0.17
11.81	0.21	8.05	5.62	1.23	2.38	11.04	0.44
25.08		18.66	10.69	4.00	5.89	23.14	0.42
43.90	0.14	54.83	40.47	12.06	53.59	43.53	0.34
154.93	10.75	139.71	101.89	24.58	39.02	147.90	1.61
5.57		2.82	1.80	0.70	0.90	4.39	0.14
99.35	0.93	73.52	48.02	15.81	16.87	83.96	0.78
2.28		3.56	2.77	0.35	0.71	2.19	0.04
1.80		1.56	1.38	0.14	0.29	1.31	0.06
8.11		8.14	5.86	1.93	3.08	11.13	0.40
4.33		5.48	4.72	0.36	0.64	4.85	0.50
2.25		7.42	1.46	6.07	5.51	2.05	0.05
1.04		1.31	0.15	0.69	1.04	1.04	0.01
2.74		1.59	0.25	1.22	1.54	2.70	0.03

13-6 外商投资和港澳台商投资工业企业单位数和主要经济指标（2013）

单位:亿元

项 目	Item	企业单位数(个) Number of Enterprises (unit)
总计		**593**
在总计中：	Of the Total:	
亏损企业	Enterprises running under Deficit	98
在总计中：	Of the Total:	
港、澳、台商投资企业	Hongkong, Macao and Taiwan Funded Enterprises	264
合资经营企业(港或澳、台资)	Joint Venture with Hongkong, Macao and Taiwan	78
合作经营企业(港或澳、台资)	Cooperate with Hongkong, Macao and Taiwan Funded	4
港澳台商独资经营企业	Enterprises Solely Funded by Hongkong, Macao and Taiwan Businessmen	166
港澳台商投资股份有限公司	Share Holding Co.Ltd.With Hongkong,Macao and Taiwan Businessmen	15
其他港澳台投资	Othes	1
外商投资企业	Foreign Funded Enterprises	315
中外合资经营企业	Sino - Foreign Joint Funded Enterprises	116
中外合作经营企业	Sino - Foreign Cooperative Funded Enterprises	4
外资企业	Foreign Solely Funded Enterprises	184
外商投资股份有限公司	Foreign Funded Share Holding Co.Ltd.	11
其他外商投资	Othes	
在总计中：	Of the Total:	
国有控股企业	State-Owned Share Holding Enterprises	
在总计中：	Of the Total:	
农村工业	Rural Industry	1
在总计中：	Of the Total:	
轻工业	Light Industry	268
重工业	Heavy Industry	325
在总计中：	Of the Total:	
大型企业	Large Scale Enterprises	47
中型企业	Medium Scale Enterprises	172
小型企业	Small Enterprises	374
按行业分	Grouped by sector	
采矿业	**Mining and Oarrying**	
煤炭开采和洗选业	Coal Mining and Processing	1
石油和天然气开采业	Petroleum and Natural Gas Extraction	
黑色金属矿采选业	Ferrous Metals Mining and Processing	
有色金属矿采选业	Non-ferrous Metals Mining and Processing	1
非金属矿采选业	Non-metal Minerals Mining and Processing	2
开采辅助活动	Mining Auxiliary Activities	
其他采矿业	Other Minerals Mining and Processing	
制造业	**Manufacturing**	
农副食品加工业	Food Processing	32
食品制造业	Food Production	22
酒、饮料和精制茶制造业	Wine,Beverage and Refined Tea Production	26
烟草制品业	Tobacco Processing	
纺织业	Textile Industry	40
纺织服装、服饰业	Textile,Garments, and Fashion Industry	31
皮革、毛皮、羽毛及其制品和制鞋业	Leather, Furs,Down and Related Products	11
木材加工和木、竹、藤、棕、草制品业	Timber Processing, Wood, Bamboo, Cane, Palm and Sraw Products	4
家具制造业	Furniture Manufacturing	5
造纸和纸制品业	Papermaking and Paper Products	15
印刷和记录媒介复制业	Printing and Record Processing	7
文教、工美、体育和娱乐用品制造业	Stationery, Education and Sports Goods	10
石油加工、炼焦和核燃料加工业	Petroleum Processing, Coking Products and Nuclear Fuel Processing	3
化学原料和化学制品制造业	Raw Chemical Material and Chemical Products	29
医药制造业	Medical and pharmaceutical Products	25
化学纤维制造业	Chemical Fibers	2
橡胶和塑料制品业	Rubber and plastic products	21
非金属矿物制品业	Nonmetal Material Products	30
黑色金属冶炼和压延加工业	Smelting and Pressing of Ferrous Metals	5
有色金属冶炼和压延加工业	Smelting and Pressing of Nonferrous Metals	2
金属制品业	Metal Products	18
通用设备制造业	Ordinary Machinery Manufacturing	24
专用设备制造业	Special Purpose Equipment Manufacturing	10
汽车制造业	Motor manufacturing	112
铁路、船舶、航空航天和其他运输设备制	Railway,Watercraft,Aviation and other Transporlation Equipment manufacturing	2
电气机械和器材制造业	Electric Machinery and Equipment	40
计算机、通信和其他电子设备制造业	Telecommunication Computer,Equipment and Other Electronic Equipment Manufacturing	32
仪器仪表制造业	Instruments and Meters, Manufacturing	6
其他制造业	Other Manufacturing	1
废弃资源综合利用业	Waste Comprehensive Vtilization of Resources Industry	1
金属制品、机械和设备修理业	Metal products,Machinery and Equipment Repairing	
电力、燃气及水的生产和供应业	**Electric Power, Gas and Water Production and Supply**	
电力、热力生产和供应业	Electric Power, Steam and Hot Water Production and Supply	4
燃气生产和供应业	Gas Production and Supply	17
水的生产和供应业	Tap Water Production and Supply	2

THE NUMBER OF FOREIGN FUNDED AND HONGKONG MACO AND TAIWAN FUNDED INDUSTRIAL ENTERPRISES AND THEIR TOTAL OUTPUT OF PRODUCTION AND SALES (2013)

(100 million yuan)

工业总产值(当年价格) Total Output Value (current price)	工业销售产值(当年价格) Output Value of Industrial Products Sales (current price)	出口交货值 Delivery Value for Export	资产总计 Total Assets	流动资产合计 Circulating Funds	固定资产合计 Total Fined Assets	固定资产原价 Original Value of Fixed Assets	主营业务收入 Revenue of Major Business	全部从业人员年平均人数(万人) Average Number of Empolyment of the Curreat Year (10 000 Bersons)
3190.91	**3068.40**	**430.23**	**2369.06**	**1156.25**	**977.02**	**1661.36**	**2876.36**	**29.46**
204.90	201.66	32.75	287.74	116.74	124.94	205.51	188.96	3.77
1487.97	1425.03	320.40	922.47	422.53	410.00	767.30	1267.11	14.08
800.92	773.50	227.21	470.57	218.93	209.95	380.12	670.33	6.28
4.16	4.07		1.75	0.78	0.55	1.18	4.00	0.04
625.22	592.94	81.57	396.41	175.78	182.80	360.75	539.12	7.12
44.44	42.55	11.62	49.70	24.37	15.97	24.35	40.48	0.63
13.23	11.98		4.04	2.67	0.74	0.90	13.18	0.01
1678.88	1619.61	108.79	1419.16	722.41	554.78	877.37	1585.95	15.12
653.71	601.25	28.59	480.81	266.12	181.49	287.49	626.86	5.25
22.54	22.23		5.87	2.22	2.53	5.48	21.85	0.12
780.67	770.97	79.62	647.89	378.17	213.18	355.86	737.42	8.01
221.96	225.16	0.58	284.59	75.89	157.59	228.54	199.82	1.74
4.57	4.93	0.02	3.34	3.18	0.17	4.69	4.43	0.02
1163.29	1092.70	94.00	710.65	379.28	259.54	471.56	1066.55	13.49
2027.62	1975.70	336.23	1658.40	776.96	717.48	1189.81	1809.82	15.97
1415.20	1363.98	316.81	951.08	424.96	436.76	682.75	1241.92	13.44
1141.87	1090.01	73.91	896.64	470.66	332.89	624.49	1046.53	11.44
633.84	614.41	39.51	521.33	260.63	207.36	354.13	587.92	4.58
0.61	0.61		0.69	0.37	0.32	0.33	0.61	0.05
1.52	1.52		0.33	0.18	0.15	0.16	1.52	0.01
0.69	0.70		0.70	0.59	0.11	0.02	0.69	
201.84	180.34	2.75	89.41	53.79	26.81	47.15	214.19	0.87
145.33	138.69	5.23	63.90	24.41	26.63	58.40	120.05	1.26
277.74	250.35		207.35	115.64	71.29	117.13	241.90	1.93
98.33	92.39	18.80	69.33	27.59	36.35	60.94	91.70	1.79
57.14	55.01	15.55	24.36	15.80	6.23	11.99	52.46	1.37
21.53	20.70	10.98	15.09	4.43	10.23	8.20	16.45	1.66
5.34	5.20		2.12	0.97	1.15	1.53	4.81	0.13
5.16	5.14	0.21	2.73	1.53	0.90	1.23	4.98	0.09
41.96	40.08	1.43	35.16	17.77	14.16	18.32	45.64	0.53
18.43	17.79		16.63	11.21	4.30	11.13	17.69	0.19
14.55	13.09	2.76	16.81	9.52	4.94	15.62	14.16	0.37
54.60	52.31		24.89	6.13	15.98	19.95	25.40	0.07
82.78	86.22	9.57	76.57	32.37	22.63	69.65	79.55	0.74
90.75	86.12	7.92	69.29	35.09	25.29	35.76	82.22	1.71
13.26	12.33	1.25	10.72	3.52	6.79	10.07	12.08	0.08
40.85	40.30	0.07	46.04	27.21	9.74	13.48	39.31	0.46
242.49	246.60	0.41	358.20	101.00	198.96	282.10	232.57	2.09
178.60	178.05	23.15	138.33	47.09	83.53	177.25	178.84	0.88
26.06	25.86		12.16	4.53	6.51	7.14	21.45	0.15
69.90	62.70	9.03	57.54	22.15	32.21	53.34	61.45	0.44
46.93	46.07	3.80	57.97	34.57	16.44	21.27	46.45	0.57
36.11	35.73	10.44	32.88	25.73	6.66	10.12	35.18	0.70
541.83	524.08	18.07	418.85	278.98	107.33	205.23	507.95	4.68
3.36	3.47	0.04	4.33	4.01	0.32	0.93	3.70	0.03
240.63	233.94	37.03	158.38	82.23	67.61	113.06	210.48	2.07
513.61	494.47	250.82	188.84	126.28	54.24	132.17	392.72	3.73
8.75	7.92	0.93	4.33	2.40	1.70	2.31	8.71	0.35
0.23	0.23		0.60	0.60			0.23	0.01
12.04	10.68		4.76	4.01	0.04	0.05	10.68	
68.52	68.52		114.60	18.20	95.19	129.22	68.31	0.09
28.35	30.12		36.35	14.45	17.62	20.32	31.14	0.27
1.06	1.06		8.81	1.90	4.65	5.77	1.07	0.08

13-7 私营工业企业单位数和主要经济指标（2013）

单位:亿元

项 目	Item	企业单位数(个) Number of Enterprises (unit)	工业总产值(当年价格) Total Output Value (current price)
总计		**12171**	**21704.87**
在总计中：	Of the Total:		
亏损企业	Enterprises running under Deficit	679	889.83
在总计中：	Of the Total:		
轻工业	Light Industry	4990	9957.64
重工业	Heavy Industry	7181	11747.24
在总计中：	Of the Total:		
大型企业	Large Scale Enterprises	140	3263.75
中型企业	Medium Scale Enterprises	1324	5719.26
小型企业	Small Enterprises	10707	12721.86
按行业分	Grouped by Sector		
采矿业	**Mining and Qarrying**		
煤炭开采和洗选业	Coal Mining and Processing	115	78.03
石油和天然气开采业	Petroleum and Natural Gas Extraction		
黑色金属矿采选业	Ferrous Metals Mining and Processing	126	269.14
有色金属矿采选业	Non-ferrous Metals Mining and Processing	47	69.75
非金属矿采选业	Non-metal Minerals Mining and Processing	362	427.22
开采辅助活动	Mining Auxiliary Activities	1	1.03
其他采矿业	Other Minerals Mining and Processing	1	0.76
制造业	**Manufacturing**		
农副食品加工业	Food Processing	1439	3420.28
食品制造业	Food Production	313	642.92
酒、饮料和精制茶制造业	Wine,Beverage and Refined Tea Production	323	954.96
烟草制品业	Tobacco Processing		
纺织业	Textile Industry	896	1650.68
纺织服装、服饰业	Textile,Garments, and Fashion Industry	452	706.55
皮革、毛皮、羽毛及其制品和制鞋业	Leather, Furs,Down and Related Products	97	105.10
木材加工和木、竹、藤、棕、草制品业	Timber Processing, Wood, Bamboo, Cane, Palm and Sraw Products	221	315.12
家具制造业	Furniture Manufacturing	90	108.30
造纸和纸制品业	Papermaking and Paper Products	209	330.09
印刷和记录媒介复制业	Printing and Record Processing	148	180.23
文教、工美、体育和娱乐用品制造业	Stationery, Education and Sports Goods	78	123.98
石油加工、炼焦和核燃料加工业	Petroleum Processing, Coking Products and Nuclear Fuel Processing	35	109.46
化学原料和化学制品制造业	Raw Chemical Material and Chemical Products	868	2152.09
医药制造业	Medical and pharmaceutical Products	270	532.28
化学纤维制造业	Chemical Fibers	14	55.15
橡胶和塑料制品业	Rubber and plastic products	502	768.47
非金属矿物制品业	Nonmetal Material Products	1499	1995.42
黑色金属冶炼和压延加工业	Smelting and Pressing of Ferrous Metals	291	806.27
有色金属冶炼和压延加工业	Smelting and Pressing of Nonferrous Metals	146	579.13
金属制品业	Metal Products	571	933.58
通用设备制造业	Ordinary Machinery Manufacturing	540	679.80
专用设备制造业	Special Purpose Equipment Manufacturing	472	655.22
汽车制造业	Motor manufacturing	1008	1335.06
铁路、船舶、航空航天和其他运输设备制造业	Railway,Watercraft,Aviation and other Transporlation Equipment manufacturing	117	194.15
电气机械和器材制造业	Electric Machinery and Equipment	475	892.23
计算机、通信和其他电子设备制造业	Telecommunication Computer,Equipment and Oth Electronic Equipment Manufacturing	185	285.08
仪器仪表制造业	Instruments and Meters, Manufacturing	78	80.56
其他制造业	Other Manufacturing	54	82.34
废弃资源综合利用业	Waste Comprehensive Vtilization of Resources Inc	25	71.33
金属制品、机械和设备修理业	Metal products,Machinery and Equipment Repairi	12	30.60
电力、燃气及水的生产和供应业	**Electric Power, Gas and Water Production and Supply**		
电力、热力生产和供应业	Electric Power, Steam and Hot Water Production a	56	50.69
燃气生产和供应业	Gas Production and Supply	18	22.44
水的生产和供应业	Tap Water Production and Supply	17	9.41

THE NUMBER OF PRIVATE-OWNED INDUSTRIAL ENTERPRISES AND THEIR MAJOR ECONOMIC INDICATORS (2013)

(100 million yuan)

工业销售产值(当年价格) Output Value of Industrial Products Sales(current price)	出口交货值 Delivery Value for Export	资产总计 Total Assets	流动资产合计 Circulating Funds	固定资产合计 Total Fined Assets	固定资产原价 Original Value of Fixed Assets	主营业务收入 Revenue of Major Business	全部从业人员年平均人数(万人) Average Number of Empolyment of the Curreat Year (10 000 Bersons)
20996.59	**529.12**	**10903.12**	**5609.29**	**3938.21**	**9030.31**	**20538.60**	**200.83**
832.98	16.09	1269.98	563.47	425.46	593.80	767.67	12.14
9650.43	421.82	4381.32	2326.81	1548.14	4123.87	9479.05	99.81
11346.15	107.30	6521.80	3282.48	2390.07	4906.43	11059.55	101.03
3162.99	125.94	2166.96	1131.51	730.81	1829.09	3023.65	30.31
5519.87	207.49	3002.05	1582.27	1044.50	2241.38	5412.56	64.86
12313.72	195.69	5734.11	2895.50	2162.90	4959.83	12102.39	105.66
77.23		47.74	14.98	26.38	30.12	77.39	1.99
260.83		82.17	38.65	35.70	42.64	257.87	1.65
67.33		31.73	19.65	10.30	16.94	65.55	0.74
416.71	0.65	200.70	90.21	66.43	149.57	397.07	3.82
1.01		0.14	0.09	0.05	0.07	1.01	0.01
0.76		0.27	0.05	0.08	0.09	0.76	0.02
3318.96	99.67	1088.91	550.91	413.24	1687.96	3295.86	20.08
622.12	52.88	275.90	131.43	114.68	280.70	615.48	7.31
934.50	2.76	735.72	499.22	151.12	185.78	912.12	7.95
1599.56	96.36	632.65	296.71	285.32	655.42	1581.14	23.53
687.99	63.99	306.70	170.18	107.43	215.93	671.61	13.29
101.66	25.55	46.66	23.52	15.80	33.92	100.81	1.72
300.76	1.60	162.24	65.50	74.25	138.97	297.68	3.28
105.34	0.52	73.65	27.94	41.02	105.18	103.73	1.36
321.28	2.41	181.82	86.94	73.53	172.56	314.03	3.47
176.16	0.42	88.40	45.16	32.20	67.01	169.07	2.02
119.56	9.09	54.23	34.51	12.82	36.69	119.48	1.47
97.14		44.71	22.75	17.11	21.24	97.48	0.32
2096.38	35.38	1113.90	532.76	437.09	1202.43	2078.63	13.98
505.59	32.10	375.92	185.63	112.46	179.08	485.56	5.53
54.66	0.05	16.10	7.42	6.46	13.11	54.44	0.39
745.73	2.46	328.55	159.86	132.14	484.76	735.35	7.94
1926.88	19.98	946.97	439.35	397.40	684.89	1870.28	19.10
785.12	4.08	573.02	245.39	180.54	297.25	764.11	5.12
559.52	2.13	169.40	97.42	58.50	97.57	541.92	2.78
918.90	12.79	520.83	262.69	204.61	440.68	869.67	8.32
645.55	5.34	385.38	207.80	129.52	320.59	638.03	6.68
632.82	1.84	486.86	271.64	182.81	333.26	613.70	6.01
1277.17	10.77	763.05	432.05	235.74	351.59	1236.89	13.34
186.80	0.40	96.88	50.26	37.61	49.67	178.36	1.97
850.40	15.60	492.49	289.75	149.49	396.80	802.19	8.04
267.58	25.11	275.79	173.95	60.52	100.40	262.17	4.00
76.01	0.50	61.09	41.94	12.52	29.86	72.93	1.29
79.71	4.33	40.63	20.24	11.72	22.29	79.66	0.89
69.59		35.13	24.09	9.28	10.17	68.76	0.25
27.85	0.36	15.07	8.89	5.17	18.23	27.44	0.31
49.96		111.71	24.47	80.27	129.25	47.72	0.51
22.41		28.97	12.15	10.25	12.93	22.27	0.19
9.01		11.05	3.15	6.66	14.72	10.41	0.19

13-8 大中型工业企业单位数和产销总值（2013）

单位:亿元

项　目	Item	企业单位数(个) Number of Enterprises (unit)
总　　计	**Total**	**2279**
一、按登记注册类型分组:	**Grouped by Type of Registration**	
内资企业	Inner Funded Enterprises	1956
国有企业	State Owned Enterprises	70
中央企业	Central Enterprises	37
地方企业	Local Enterprises	33
集体企业	Collective-owned Enterprise	21
股份合作企业	Share Holding Cooperative Enterprises	1
联营企业	Joint Owned Enterprise	2
国有联营企业	State Joint Ownership	
集体联营企业	Collective Joint Ownership	
国有与集体联营企业	Joint State- Collective Ownership	1
其他联营企业	Other Joint Owned Enterprise	1
有限责任公司	Responsibility Co. Ltd	828
国有独资公司	State Solely Funded Co.	62
其他有限责任公司	Others	766
股份有限公司	Share Holding Co.Ltd.	223
私营企业	Private - owned enterprises	805
私营独资企业	Solely Private - owned enterprises	13
私营合作企业	Private Joint Venture	4
私营有限责任公司	Private Responsibility Co. Ltd	721
私营股份有限公司	Private Share Holding Co.Ltd.	67
其他企业	Others	6
港、澳、台商投资企业	Hongkong, Macao and Taiwan Funded Enterprises	148
合资经营企业(港或澳、台资)	Joint Venture with Hongkong, Macao and Taiwan	73
合作经营企业(港或澳、台资)	Cooperate with Hongkong, Macao and Taiwan Funded	1
港澳台商独资经营企业	Enterprises Solely Funded by Hongkong, Macao and Taiwan Businessmen	68
港澳台商投资股份有限公司	Share Holding Co.Ltd. With Hongkong, Macao and Taiwan Investment	6
其他港澳台投资	Others	
外商投资企业	Foreign Funded Enterprises	175
中外合资经营企业	Sino - Foreign Joint Funded Enterprises	96
中外合作经营企业	Sino - Foreign Cooperative Funded Enterprises	3
外资企业	Foreign Solely Funded Enterprises	70
外商投资股份有限公司	Foreign Funded Share Holding Co.Ltd.	6
其他外商投资	Others	
二、在总计中:亏损企业	**Of the Total: enterprises running under deficit**	236
在总计中:国有控股企业	Of the Total: State-Owned Share Holding Enterprises	343
在总计中:农村工业	Of the Total: Rural Industry	15
在总计中:轻工业	Of the Total: Light Industry	1118
重工业	Heavy Industry	1161
在总计中:大型企业	Of the Total: Large Scale Enterprises	344
中型企业	Medium Scale Enterprises	1935
按行业分	Grouped by Sector	
采矿业	**Mining and Qarrying**	

NUMBER OF LARGE AND MEDIUM SCALE INDUSTRIAL ENTERPRISES AND THEIR TOTAL VALUE OF PRODUCTION AND SALES (2013)

(100 million yuan)

工业总产值(当年价格) Total Output Value (current price)	工业销售产值(当年价格) Output Value of Industrial Products Sales (current price)	出口交货值 Delivery Value for Export
24256.81	**23644.63**	**1279.01**
18731.03	18303.02	804.66
3540.54	3524.62	247.38
3457.79	3442.34	230.85
82.74	82.28	16.53
44.45	43.24	
0.65	0.65	
9.71	9.62	
0.76	0.76	
8.95	8.86	
7219.53	6988.72	251.34
1730.30	1667.36	47.06
5489.23	5321.36	204.29
3491.53	3449.41	138.96
4390.39	4252.63	166.54
42.99	40.56	6.09
19.11	19.03	
3859.77	3746.35	138.81
468.52	446.69	21.64
34.23	34.13	0.44
1623.14	1553.28	355.63
1040.34	1006.32	268.17
4.19	4.25	
547.50	513.29	77.01
31.11	29.41	10.44
3902.65	3788.33	118.72
3060.89	2948.09	53.22
22.84	22.59	
605.21	600.71	64.92
213.70	216.94	0.58
2222.74	2160.50	70.65
10718.29	10545.42	423.88
92.28	90.10	1.00
7434.58	7180.84	431.51
16822.23	16463.79	847.50
15449.76	15160.48	921.48
8807.05	8484.15	357.53

13－8 续表 continued

单位:亿元

项 目	Item	企业单位数(个) Number of Enterprises(unit)
煤炭开采和洗选业	Coal Mining and Processing	23
石油和天然气开采业	Petroleum and Natural Gas Extraction	1
黑色金属矿采选业	Ferrous Metals Mining and Processing	16
有色金属矿采选业	Non-ferrous Metals Mining and Processing	9
非金属矿采选业	Non-metal Minerals Mining and Processing	21
开采辅助活动	Mining Auxiliary Activities	3
其他采矿业	Other Minerals Mining and Processing	
制造业	**Manufacturing**	
农副食品加工业	Food Processing	158
食品制造业	Food Production	80
酒、饮料和精制茶制造业	Wine,Beverage and Refined Tea Production	54
烟草制品业	Tobacco Processing	1
纺织业	Textile Industry	310
纺织服装、服饰业	Textile,Garments, and Fashion Industry	161
皮革、毛皮、羽毛及其制品和制鞋业	Leather, Furs,Down and Related Products	14
木材加工和木、竹、藤、棕、草制品业	Timber Processing, Wood, Bamboo, Cane, Palm and Sraw Products	25
家具制造业	Furniture Manufacturing	10
造纸和纸制品业	Papermaking and Paper Products	41
印刷和记录媒介复制业	Printing and Record Processing	27
文教、工美、体育和娱乐用品制造业	Stationery, Education and Sports Goods	18
石油加工、炼焦和核燃料加工业	Petroleum Processing, Coking Products and Nuclear Fuel Processing	6
化学原料和化学制品制造业	Raw Chemical Material and Chemical Products	145
医药制造业	Medical and pharmaceutical Products	70
化学纤维制造业	Chemical Fibers	9
橡胶和塑料制品业	Rubber and plastic products	78
非金属矿物制品业	Nonmetal Material Products	183
黑色金属冶炼和压延加工业	Smelting and Pressing of Ferrous Metals	53
有色金属冶炼和压延加工业	Smelting and Pressing of Nonferrous Metals	40
金属制品业	Metal Products	73
通用设备制造业	Ordinary Machinery Manufacturing	76
专用设备制造业	Special Purpose Equipment Manufacturing	55
汽车制造业	Motor manufacturing	212
铁路、船舶、航空航天和其他运输设备制造业	Railway,Watercraft,Aviation and other Transporlation Equipment manufacturing	36
电气机械和器材制造业	Electric Machinery and Equipment	93
计算机、通信和其他电子设备制造业	Telecommunication Computer,Equipment and Other Electronic Equipment Manufacturing	71
仪器仪表制造业	Instruments and Meters, Manufacturing	19
其他制造业	Other Manufacturing	18
废弃资源综合利用业	Waste Comprehensive Vtilization of Resources Industry	5
金属制品、机械和设备修理业	Metal products,Machinery and Equipment Repairing	8
电力、燃气及水的生产和供应业	**Electric Power, Gas and Water Production and Supply**	
电力、热力生产和供应业	Electric Power, Steam and Hot Water Production and Supply	33
燃气生产和供应业	Gas Production and Supply	6
水的生产和供应业	Tap Water Production and Supply	18

(100 million yuan)

工业总产值(当年价格) Total Output Value	工业销售产值(当年价格) Output Value of Industrial Products Sales(current price)	出口交货值 Delivery Value for Export
31.19	30.93	
82.89	82.85	0.54
190.18	188.96	
32.41	32.04	
94.91	92.01	
61.67	61.64	0.10
1665.11	1600.51	63.42
496.82	478.18	53.95
968.45	930.14	0.60
501.68	486.16	1.34
1155.83	1117.88	104.46
491.47	479.01	78.30
40.59	39.90	14.69
115.11	109.88	
38.75	38.01	0.29
259.32	250.30	0.44
97.66	91.30	1.83
66.07	63.64	4.41
808.82	790.85	
2057.96	1998.32	97.01
486.33	463.44	57.58
49.09	47.58	1.78
421.99	411.37	6.20
956.14	934.77	14.56
2679.89	2661.20	65.20
733.89	714.82	26.18
520.48	485.77	18.97
587.85	565.32	31.98
374.27	352.63	15.41
3833.76	3791.22	51.02
438.09	426.67	183.67
1068.73	1019.66	67.23
1275.05	1249.57	314.94
51.43	47.55	1.75
84.52	81.59	0.80
5.33	5.07	
21.12	18.75	0.36
1345.63	1338.01	
43.89	45.41	
22.42	21.72	

13-8 续表 continued

单位:亿元

项 目	Item	资产总计 Total Assets
总 计	**Total**	**22869.87**
一、按登记注册类型分组:	Grouped by Type of Registration	
内资企业	Inner Funded Enterprises	18828.48
国有企业	State Owned Enterprises	5934.36
中央企业	Central Enterprises	5813.75
地方企业	Local Enterprises	120.61
集体企业	Collective-owned Enterprise	20.53
股份合作企业	Share Holding Cooperative Enterprises	0.71
联营企业	Joint Owned Enterprise	1.28
国有联营企业	State Joint Ownership	
集体联营企业	Collective Joint Ownership	
国有与集体联营企业	Joint State- Collective Ownership	0.84
其他联营企业	Other Joint Owned Enterprise	0.44
有限责任公司	Responsibility Co. Ltd	6406.31
国有独资公司	State Solely Funded Co.	1863.05
其他有限责任公司	Others	4543.27
股份有限公司	Share Holding Co.Ltd.	4493.62
私营企业	Private - owned enterprises	1955.58
私营独资企业	Solely Private - owned enterprises	13.18
私营合作企业	Private Joint Venture	2.23
私营有限责任公司	Private Responsibility Co. Ltd	1729.46
私营股份有限公司	Private Share Holding Co.Ltd.	210.71
其他企业	Others	16.08
港、澳、台商投资企业	Hongkong, Macao and Taiwan Funded Enterprises	967.02
合资经营企业(港或澳、台资)	Joint Venture with Hongkong, Macao and Taiwan	593.49
合作经营企业(港或澳、台资)	Cooperate with Hongkong, Macao and Taiwan Funded	8.60
港澳台商独资经营企业	Enterprises Solely Funded by Hongkong, Macao and Taiwan Businessmen	322.01
港澳台商投资股份有限公司	Share Holding Co.Ltd. With Hongkong, Macao and Taiwan Investment	42.92
其他港澳台投资	Others	
外商投资企业	Foreign Funded Enterprises	3074.37
中外合资经营企业	Sino - Foreign Joint Funded Enterprises	2291.31
中外合作经营企业	Sino - Foreign Cooperative Funded Enterprises	4.91
外资企业	Foreign Solely Funded Enterprises	495.12
外商投资股份有限公司	Foreign Funded Share Holding Co.Ltd.	283.03
其他外商投资	Others	
二、在总计中:亏损企业	**Of the Total: enterprises running under deficit**	2437.58
在总计中:国有控股企业	Of the Total: State-Owned Share Holding Enterprises	14003.38
在总计中:农村工业	Of the Total: Rural Industry	35.29
在总计中:轻工业	Of the Total: Light Industry	4609.77
重工业	Heavy Industry	18260.09
在总计中:大型企业	Of the Total: Large Scale Enterprises	16681.44
中型企业	Medium Scale Enterprises	6188.42
按行业分	Grouped by Sector	
采矿业	**Mining and Qarrying**	

(100 million yuan)

流动资产合计 Circulating Funds	固定资产合计 Total Fined Assets	固定资产原价 Original Value of Fixed Assets	主营业务收入 Revenue of Major Business	全部从业人员年平均人数（万人） Average Number of Empolyment of the Curreat Year (10 000 Bersons)
10031.82	**8968.02**	**15807.24**	**23967.59**	**221.10**
7900.79	7671.21	13349.82	18935.67	180.05
1501.40	3380.15	5195.70	3927.21	27.93
1444.60	3324.41	5108.93	3848.03	25.94
56.81	55.74	86.77	79.17	1.99
11.11	7.20	17.82	45.65	1.27
0.28	0.44	1.26	0.65	0.03
1.03	0.24	0.45	9.27	0.09
0.66	0.18	0.38	0.76	0.04
0.37	0.06	0.07	8.51	0.05
3226.35	2304.61	3815.78	7554.01	71.80
950.55	623.26	991.59	1772.47	11.78
2275.81	1681.35	2824.19	5781.55	60.02
2165.81	1174.45	1920.67	3186.84	33.26
984.57	799.13	2392.09	4182.21	45.36
6.35	4.43	5.51	42.60	0.71
1.33	0.86	1.10	19.00	0.15
880.48	703.95	2213.78	3715.19	39.88
96.40	89.88	171.70	405.42	4.63
10.24	5.00	6.04	29.83	0.30
449.13	406.97	845.11	1416.37	16.23
289.42	234.52	503.00	920.64	8.89
3.75	4.35	4.35	4.25	0.06
134.32	154.93	317.24	463.51	6.75
21.65	13.17	20.53	27.97	0.53
1681.90	889.83	1612.31	3615.54	24.82
1308.04	567.24	1131.49	2831.44	16.27
2.18	2.70	5.97	22.21	0.14
296.66	162.94	247.82	569.97	6.71
75.02	156.95	227.03	191.92	1.71
1073.13	976.74	1553.01	2139.14	23.87
5407.00	5933.69	9360.95	11271.80	78.53
18.28	11.59	77.95	84.96	0.83
2636.73	1387.18	3390.03	7039.27	85.65
7395.08	7580.83	12417.21	16928.32	135.45
6897.94	6854.24	11421.93	15566.19	118.80
3133.88	2113.77	4385.31	8401.40	102.31

13-8 续表 continued

单位:亿元

项 目	Item	资产总计 Total Assets
煤炭开采和洗选业	Coal Mining and Processing	25.03
石油和天然气开采业	Petroleum and Natural Gas Extraction	205.34
黑色金属矿采选业	Ferrous Metals Mining and Processing	59.44
有色金属矿采选业	Non-ferrous Metals Mining and Processing	23.79
非金属矿采选业	Non-metal Minerals Mining and Processing	52.60
开采辅助活动	Mining Auxiliary Activities	75.84
其他采矿业	Other Minerals Mining and Processing	
制造业	**Manufacturing**	
农副食品加工业	Food Processing	630.27
食品制造业	Food Production	261.77
酒、饮料和精制茶制造业	Wine,Beverage and Refined Tea Production	814.77
烟草制品业	Tobacco Processing	397.08
纺织业	Textile Industry	535.87
纺织服装、服饰业	Textile,Garments, and Fashion Industry	294.13
皮革、毛皮、羽毛及其制品和制鞋业	Leather, Furs,Down and Related Products	25.15
木材加工和木、竹、藤、棕、草制品业	Timber Processing, Wood, Bamboo, Cane, Palm and Sraw Products	66.04
家具制造业	Furniture Manufacturing	39.45
造纸和纸制品业	Papermaking and Paper Products	158.32
印刷和记录媒介复制业	Printing and Record Processing	69.26
文教、工美、体育和娱乐用品制造业	Stationery, Education and Sports Goods	31.44
石油加工、炼焦和核燃料加工业	Petroleum Processing, Coking Products and Nuclear Fuel Processing	198.79
化学原料和化学制品制造业	Raw Chemical Material and Chemical Products	1894.46
医药制造业	Medical and pharmaceutical Products	509.47
化学纤维制造业	Chemical Fibers	36.76
橡胶和塑料制品业	Rubber and plastic products	229.49
非金属矿物制品业	Nonmetal Material Products	887.60
黑色金属冶炼和压延加工业	Smelting and Pressing of Ferrous Metals	3235.23
有色金属冶炼和压延加工业	Smelting and Pressing of Nonferrous Metals	455.33
金属制品业	Metal Products	519.64
通用设备制造业	Ordinary Machinery Manufacturing	875.31
专用设备制造业	Special Purpose Equipment Manufacturing	497.03
汽车制造业	Motor manufacturing	3876.94
铁路、船舶、航空航天和其他运输设备制造业	Railway,Watercraft,Aviation and other Transporlation Equipment manufacturing	601.53
电气机械和器材制造业	Electric Machinery and Equipment	689.50
计算机、通信和其他电子设备制造业	Telecommunication Computer,Equipment and Other Electronic Equipment Manufacturing	1141.36
仪器仪表制造业	Instruments and Meters, Manufacturing	73.26
其他制造业	Other Manufacturing	93.68
废弃资源综合利用业	Waste Comprehensive Vtilization of Resources Industry	7.42
金属制品、机械和设备修理业	Metal products,Machinery and Equipment Repairing	15.17
电力、燃气及水的生产和供应业	**Electric Power, Gas and Water Production and Supply**	
电力、热力生产和供应业	Electric Power, Steam and Hot Water Production and Supply	3016.41
燃气生产和供应业	Gas Production and Supply	62.39
水的生产和供应业	Tap Water Production and Supply	187.49

(100 million yuan)

流动资产合计 Circulating Funds	固定资产合计 Total Fined Assets	固定资产原价 Original Value of Fixed Assets	主营业务收入 Revenue of Major Business	全部从业人员年平均人数（万人） Average Number of Empolyment of the Curreat Year (10 000 Bersons)
14.33	9.56	12.70	31.11	1.66
31.62	173.71	295.58	82.98	1.89
23.83	27.95	48.29	184.95	1.42
10.24	9.00	13.25	32.67	0.51
24.97	11.63	38.88	74.69	1.23
21.06	40.71	62.40	78.26	1.89
294.67	257.15	1148.73	1636.15	10.45
118.15	102.32	265.31	464.35	6.00
572.15	152.85	201.71	909.84	7.74
314.33	27.43	71.94	473.15	0.69
257.90	238.10	563.22	1124.74	19.78
191.12	75.59	140.80	467.72	11.32
8.59	13.26	11.49	34.54	2.31
29.67	32.66	72.73	109.26	1.56
13.45	25.35	50.25	37.25	0.63
76.05	60.74	197.86	250.26	2.39
41.24	17.22	33.25	89.28	1.31
20.78	6.38	27.12	61.99	1.02
72.06	115.62	190.21	766.12	0.92
694.49	796.36	1522.19	2092.47	13.78
244.77	158.68	227.81	467.49	7.30
16.46	12.62	29.65	47.22	0.74
129.37	80.38	317.17	403.85	5.08
292.72	441.25	635.23	882.93	10.77
1035.23	1444.29	2499.70	3062.59	16.04
259.81	120.03	175.60	1220.03	3.92
294.22	163.86	255.15	485.82	5.69
456.76	200.44	316.36	535.40	5.86
298.22	170.21	322.42	324.20	5.09
2127.04	685.22	1172.37	3518.92	28.54
371.96	157.05	187.09	393.57	5.63
438.25	193.59	333.99	923.94	10.01
824.49	234.46	444.47	1125.88	11.41
35.72	34.15	37.94	47.01	1.49
60.22	22.53	27.39	82.31	1.63
4.86	2.49	3.31	8.67	0.36
10.34	4.07	6.98	18.48	0.77
203.48	2554.69	3722.20	1341.36	10.30
18.84	34.05	44.09	53.11	0.50
78.36	60.31	80.44	23.05	1.48

13-9 规模以上工业企业生产能力表（2013）
OUTPUT OF MAJOR PRODUCTS OF INDUSTRY ABOVE DESIGNATED SIZE (2013)

产品名称		Item		年初生产能力 Capacity at the Beginning of the Year	年末生产能力 Capacity at the End of the Year
原煤	吨	Coal	ton	18107481	17433140
天然原油	吨	Crude Petroleum Oil	ton	787950	787950
卷烟	万支	Cigarettes	10000 pieces	18670230	19880730
棉纺锭/纺纱量	锭/吨	Knitting Spindle/Capacity	spindle/ton	10050163	10295777
气流纺锭/纺纱量	头/吨	Air Spindle/Capacity	spindle/ton	443280	439196
棉布织机/布	台/万米	Cotton Loom/Cloth	piece/10000 meters	258618	299745
原油加工能力/原油加工量	吨/吨	Crude Oil Processing Capacity	ton/ton	13830000	13792949
焦炭	吨	Coke	ton	10546000	10546000
烧碱（折100%）	吨	Caustic Soda (100%)	ton	970850	1072872
碳化钙（电石，折 300升/千克）	吨	Calcium Carbide (300 L/kg)	ton	983000	874017
农用氮、磷、钾化学肥料总计（折纯）	吨	Chemical Fertilizers	ton	14174010	15633600
初级形态塑料	吨	Primary Plastic	ton	1042849	1173056
化学纤维	吨	Chemical Fiber	ton	232509	234721
硅酸盐水泥熟料	吨	Portland Cement Clinker	ton	67199129	68046203
水泥	吨	Cement	ton	130784402	135428505
平板玻璃	重量箱	Plain Glass	weight case	99989808	111566075
生铁	吨	Pig Ion	ton	27088390	28518271
粗钢	吨	Crude Steel	ton	39932151	40170000
钢材	吨	Rolled Steel	ton	49377151	49406471
铁合金	吨	Ferroalloy	ton	615200	615500
原铝（电解铝）	吨	Electrolyzed Aluminum	ton	283350	297050
金属切削机床	台	Metal-cutting Machine Tools	piece	19768	19616
汽车	辆	Automobile	unit	1999240	2214550
其中：基本型乘用车（轿车）	辆	Cars	unit	835040	1036000
家用电冰箱	台	Home Refrigerators	piece	4800000	4800000
房间空气调节器	台	Air Conditioners	piece	12700000	13900000
移动通信手持机（手机）	台	Mobile Phones	piece	6600000	34000000
彩色电视机	台	Color Television Sets	piece	180000	215000
发电设备容量总计/发电量	万千瓦/万千瓦小时	Generating Capacity	10000 kwh	5547.30	5578.50
其中：火电设备容量/发电量		Thermal Power	10000 kwh	1908.30	2022.30
水电设备容量/发电量		Hydropower	10000 kwh	3556.10	3455.50
核电设备容量/发电量		Nuclear Power	10000 kwh		
风电设备容量/发电量		Wind Power	10000 kwh	14.50	22.10

13-10 规模以上工业主要产品产量(2013)
SCALE INDUSTRIAL OUTPUT OF MAIN ProduCTS (2013)

名 称	计量单位	name		产品产量
原煤	吨	Original Coal	ton	8558750
1.无烟煤	吨	1.Anthracite	ton	5900670
2.烟煤	吨	2.Bituminous Coal	ton	2658080
其中:一般烟煤	吨	General Bituminous Coal	ton	2658080
洗煤	吨	Washed Coal	ton	302138
其中：洗精煤	吨	Cleaned Coal	ton	302138
天然原油	吨	Natural Oil	ton	800775
天然气	万立方米	Natural Gas	10000 cu.m	30898
铁矿石原矿	吨	Iron Ore	ton	28050990
铜金属含量	吨	Copper	ton	66161
锌金属含量	吨	Zinc	ton	9119
锑金属含量	吨	Antimony	ton	532
钨精矿折合量(折三氧化钨6 5 %)	吨	Tungsten Concentrate Equivalent Amount (65% of Tungsten Trioxide)	ton	421
钼精矿折合量(折纯钼4 5 %)	吨	Molybdenum Concentrate Equivalent Amoun (45% of Pure Mo)	ton	1369
硫铁矿石(折含硫35%)	吨	Pyrite Stone (35% of Sulfur)	ton	222996
磷矿石(折含五氧化二磷30%)	吨	Phosphate Rock (30% of Phosphorus Pentoxide)	ton	41321138
原盐	吨	Crude Salt	ton	4649528
小麦粉	吨	Wheat Flour	ton	3892595
大米	吨	Rice	ton	22417728
饲料	吨	Feed	ton	12255560
其中:配合饲料	吨	Compoud Feed	ton	6745977
混合饲料	吨	Mixed feed	ton	2756900
精制食用植物油	吨	Refined Edible Vegetable oil	ton	6023583
成品糖	吨	Sugar	ton	
鲜、冷藏肉	吨	Fresh and Chilled Meat	ton	1559475
冷冻水产品	吨	Frozen Seafood	ton	211571
糖果	吨	Candy	ton	196842
速冻米面食品	吨	Frozen Rice\Flour Food	ton	45545
方便面	吨	Instant Noodles	ton	200849
乳制品	吨	Dairy Products	ton	778348
其中:液体乳	吨	Liquid Dairies	ton	754013
乳粉	吨	Milk Powder	ton	1435
罐头	吨	Can	ton	1279996
酱油	吨	Soy Sauce	ton	93720
冷冻饮品	吨	Frozen Drinks	ton	215904
食品添加剂	吨	Food Additives	ton	260367
发酵酒精(折96度,商品量)	千升	Fermentation of Alcohol (of 96 degrees, the amount of goods)	kl	33008

13-10 续表-1 continued

名　称	计量单位	name		产品产量
饮料酒	千升	Alcoholic Beverage	kl	3447892
其中:白酒(折65度,商品量)	千升	Liquor (of 65 degrees, the amount of goods)	kl	721512
啤酒	千升	Beer	kl	2546916
葡萄酒	千升	Wine	kl	1533
软饮料	吨	Soft Drinks	ton	8625356
其中:碳酸饮料类(汽水)	吨	Carbonated Beverages (soft drinks)	ton	719461
包装饮用水类	吨	Packaging of Drinking Water	ton	2629651
果汁和蔬菜汁饮料类	吨	Fruit Juice and Vegetable Juice	ton	915557
精制茶	吨	Refined Tea	ton	340361
卷烟	万支	Cigarette	10000 pieces	13979928
纱	吨	Yarn	ton	3019997
1、棉纱	吨	Cotton Yarn	ton	1945133
2、棉混纺纱	吨	Cotton Blended Yarn	ton	429048
3、化学纤维纱	吨	Chemical Fiber Yarn	ton	645816
布	万米	Fabric	10000 meters	792521
其中：色织布(含牛仔布)	万米	Dyed Fabric (including jean)	10000 meters	1738
其中：1.棉布	万米	1.Cotton	10000 meters	656357
2.棉混纺布	万米	2.Cotton Blended Cloth	10000 meters	111122
3.化学纤维布	万米	3.Chemical-Fiber Cloth	10000 meters	25042
印染布	万米	Dyed Cloth	10000 meters	36045
亚麻布(含亚麻≥55%)	万米	Linen Fabric (containing linen≥ 55%)	10000 meters	229
苎麻布(含苎麻≥55%)	万米	Ramie fabric (containing linen ≥ 55%)	10000 meters	866
蚕丝	吨	Silk	ton	1007
蚕丝被	万条	Silk Quilt	10000 pieces	330
无纺布(无纺织物)	吨	Non-woven Fabric	ton	140201
服装	万件	Clothing	10000 pieces	103379
1.梭织服装	万件	Tated Garments	10000 pieces	78047
其中:羽绒服	万件	Down Jacket	10000 pieces	222
西服套装	万件	Western-style	10000 pieces	2760
衬衫	万件	Shirt	10000 pieces	1286
2.针织服装	万件	Knitted Garments	10000 pieces	25331
轻革	平方米	Light Leather	sq.m	2643987
天然毛皮服装	件	Leather Clothes	piece	154985
皮革鞋靴	万双	Leather Footwear	10000 pairs	781
人造板	立方米	Artificial Board	cu.m	10044561
其中:胶合板	立方米	Plywood	cu.m	3300870
纤维板	立方米	FibreBoard	cu.m	2980629
刨花板	立方米	Shaving Board	cu.m	428195
人造板表面装饰板	立方米	Artificial Board for Surface Decoration	cu.m	46423874

13-10 续表-2 continued

名 称	计量单位	name		产品产量
复合木地板	立方米	Composite Wood Flooring	cu.m	33582115
家具	件	Furniture	piece	4124625
其中:木质家具	件	Wood Furniture	piece	1616620
金属家具	件	Metal Furniture	piece	290294
软体家具	件	Upholstered Furniture	piece	352509
纸浆(原生浆及废纸浆)	吨	Pulp (original pulp and waste paper pulp)	ton	96760
机制纸及纸板(外购原纸加工除外)	吨	Machine Made Paper and PaperBoard (excludingprocessing outsourcing base paper)	ton	2108091
其中:未涂布印刷书写用纸	吨	Uncoating Writing Paper	ton	738027
其中:新闻纸	吨	Newsprint	ton	15847
卫生用纸原纸	吨	Toilet Paper	ton	128126
箱纸板	吨	Case Board	ton	161769
纸制品	吨	Paper Products	ton	2681613
其中：瓦楞纸箱	吨	Corrugated Case	ton	1324694
单色印刷品	令	Monochrome Print	ream	4114218
多色印刷品	对开色令	Multi-color Print	lio color ream	13308448
原油加工量	吨	Crude Oil Processing Capacity	ton	11678102
汽油	吨	Gasoline	ton	2813397
煤油	吨	Kerosene	ton	637839
柴油	吨	Diesel Fuel	ton	4642809
润滑油	吨	Lubricating Oil	ton	157209
燃料油	吨	Fuel Oil	ton	117441
石脑油	吨	Naphtha	ton	632110
溶剂油	吨	Megilp	ton	2159
液化石油气	吨	LPG	ton	543564
石油焦	吨	Petroleum Coke	ton	964997
石油沥青	吨	Petroleum Pitch	ton	99457
焦炭	吨	Coke	ton	9434213
其中:机焦	吨	Organic	ton	7985766
硫酸(折100%)	吨	Sulfuric Acid (100% discount)	ton	6801072
盐酸(氯化氢,含量31%)	吨	Hydrochloric Acid (hydrogen chloride, 31%)	ton	634730
浓硝酸(折100%)	吨	Concentrated Nitric Acid (100% discount)	ton	43163
烧碱(折100%)	吨	Caustic Soda (100% discount)	ton	992257
其中：离子膜法烧碱(折100%)	吨	Ionic Membrane Method(100% discount)	ton	805635
纯碱(碳酸钠)	吨	Soda Ash (sodium carbonate)	ton	1322247
精甲醇	吨	Refined Methanol	ton	309262
合成氨(无水氨)	吨	Anhydrous Amonia	ton	4878452
农用氮、磷、钾化学肥料总计(折纯)	吨	Agricultural Nitrogen, Phosphorus and Potass	ton	11866858
1、氮肥(折含N100%)	吨	1.N (of N 100%)	ton	5915905
其中：尿素(折含N100%)	吨	Urea (of N 100%)	ton	1876377

13-10 续表-3 continued

名　称	计量单位	name		产品产量
2、磷肥(折五氧化二磷100 %)	吨	2.P (of 100% phosphorus pentoxide)	ton	5722991
3、钾肥(折氧化钾100%)	吨	3.K (of 100% potassium hydroxide)	ton	227962
磷酸一铵(实物量)	吨	MAP (physical quantity)	ton	6936104
磷酸二铵(实物量)	吨	DAP (physical quantity)	ton	4379478
化学农药原药(折有效成分100%)	吨	Chemical Pesticide Active Compound	ton	272477
其中:杀虫剂原药	吨	Pesticide Active Compound	ton	77895
除草剂原药	吨	Herbicide Active Compound	ton	147542
涂料	吨	Paint	ton	304731
初级形态的塑料	吨	Primary Form Plastic	ton	991168
聚丙烯树脂	吨	Polypropylene Resin	ton	278911
聚氯乙烯树脂	吨	PVC Resin	ton	491535
聚苯乙烯树脂	吨	Polystyrene Resin	ton	23183
ABS树脂	吨	ABS Resin	ton	17175
合成橡胶	吨	Synthetic Rubber	ton	39812
合成纤维聚合物	吨	Synthetic Fiber Polymer	ton	19237
化学试剂	吨	Chemical Reagent	ton	171297
单晶硅	千克	Single Crystal Silion	kg	
多晶硅	千克	Polycrystalline Silion	kg	385348
合成洗涤剂	吨	Synthetic Detergent	ton	253631
其中:合成洗衣粉	吨	Synthetic Washing Powder	ton	5041
化学药品原药	吨	Original Drug Chemicals	ton	258987
中成药	吨	Chinese Patent Medicine	ton	402072
化学纤维用浆粕	吨	Chemical Fiber Pulp	ton	74495
化学纤维	吨	Chemical Fiber	ton	216737
其中：人造纤维(纤维素纤维)	吨	Artificid Fiber	ton	106981
其中:粘胶短纤维	吨	Fibranne	ton	89355
粘胶纤维长丝	吨	Viscose Filament	ton	14949
合成纤维	吨	Synthetic Fiber	ton	109756
其中:锦纶纤维	吨	Polyamide Fiber	ton	
涤纶纤维	吨	Polyester Fiber	ton	29008
丙纶纤维	吨	Polypropylene Fiber	ton	63776
橡胶轮胎外胎	条	Rubber Cover Tyre	piece	8092431
其中：子午线轮胎外胎	条	Radial Tire	piece	7773257
塑料制品	吨	Plastic Products	ton	3328074
其中:塑料薄膜	吨	Plastic Film	ton	208191
其中：农用薄膜	吨	Agricultural Film	ton	27593
泡沫塑料	吨	Foam	ton	58707
塑料人造革、合成革	吨	Plastic Leather and Synthetic Leather	ton	44345
日用塑料制品	吨	Household Plastic Products	ton	326205
硅酸盐水泥熟料	吨	Cement Clinker	ton	57339446
其中:窑外分解窑水泥熟料	吨	Cement Kiln Clinker	ton	36915849

13-10 续表-4 continued

名　称	计量单位	name		产品产量
水泥	吨	Cement	ton	110565197
其中:强度等级42.5水泥(含R型)	吨	Strength Grade 42.5 Cement (including R-ty	ton	14969485
强度等级52.5水泥(含R型)	吨	Strength Grade 52.5 Cement (including R-ty	ton	161962
商品混凝土	立方米	Concrete	cu.m	41048206
水泥混凝土排水管	千米	Concrete Drainage Pipe	km	8287
水泥混凝土压力管	千米	Concrete Pressure Pipe	km	5159
水泥混凝土电杆	根	Cement Concrete Pole	piece	522902
预应力混凝土桩	米	Prestressed Concrete Pile	meter	12362951
石膏板	万平方米	Gypsum Board	10000 sq.m	42245
砖	万块	Brick	10000 pieces	5036494
瓦	万片	Tile	10000 pieces	57244
瓷质砖	平方米	Porcelain Tile	sq.m	286928508
陶质砖	平方米	Ceramic Tile	sq.m	99030534
天然大理石建筑板材	平方米	Natural Marble Building Boards	sq.m	23493756
天然花岗石建筑板材	平方米	Natural Granite Building Boards	sq.m	12267356
沥青和改性沥青防水卷材	平方米	Asphalt and Modified Bitumen Sheet	sq.m	21664354
平板玻璃	重量箱	Plate Glass	weight case	81327534
钢化玻璃	平方米	Tempered Glass	sq.m	9129825
夹层玻璃	平方米	Laminated Glass	sq.m	1443703
中空玻璃	平方米	Insulating Glass	sq.m	18662736
日用玻璃制品	吨	Daily Glass Products	ton	552491
玻璃包装容器	吨	Glass Containers	ton	1294731
玻璃纤维纱	吨	Glass Fiber Yarn	ton	14785
纤维增强塑料制品	吨	Fiber Reinforced Plastic Products	ton	8168
卫生陶瓷制品	件	Sanitary Ceramic Products	piece	16884270
耐火材料制品	吨	Refractory Products	ton	1218355
石墨及炭素制品	吨	Graphite and Carbon Products	ton	309276
生铁	吨	Pig Iron	ton	24162299
粗钢	吨	Crude Steel	ton	30009847
铸铁件	吨	Iron Casting	ton	2285344
铸钢件	吨	Steel Casting	ton	394236
钢材	吨	Steel	ton	33449213
1.铁道用钢材	吨	1. Railway Steel	ton	842361
重轨	吨	Heavy Rail	ton	810864
2.大型型钢	吨	2. Large-scale Steel	ton	9359
3.中小型型钢	吨	3. Small and Medium Scale Steel	ton	1399292
4.棒材	吨	4. Bar	ton	2092293
5.钢筋	吨	5. Steel Bar	ton	6073418
6.线材(盘条)	吨	6. Wire (coil)	ton	2133655
7.特厚板	吨	7. Special Plate	ton	179389

13—10 续表—5 continued

名　称	计量单位	name		产品产量
8.厚钢板	吨	8. Thick Steel Plate	ton	437034
9.中板	吨	9. Middle Plate	ton	1360629
10.热轧薄板	吨	10. Hot-rolled Sheet	ton	71268
11.冷轧薄板	吨	11. Cold-rolled Sheet	ton	1586839
12.中厚宽钢带	吨	12. Thick Wide Strip	ton	4995364
13.热轧薄宽钢带	吨	13. Hot-rolled Thin Wide Strip	ton	1302556
14.冷轧薄宽钢带	吨	14. Cold-rolled Wide Strip	ton	2377395
15.热轧窄钢带	吨	15. Hot-rolled Narrow Strip	ton	624710
16.冷轧窄钢带	吨	16. Cold-rolled Narrow Strip	ton	124382
17.镀层板(带)	吨	17. Coated Plate	ton	3188343
18.涂层板(带)	吨	18. Coated Plate	ton	254218
锰硅合金	吨	Silicon Manganese Alloy	ton	162306
十种有色金属	吨	10 Kinds of Nonferrous Metals	ton	1078235
精炼铜(电解铜)	吨	Refined Copper (electrolytic copper)	ton	502466
铅	吨	Lead	ton	337617
锌	吨	Zinc	ton	7082
氧化铝	吨	Alumina	ton	
原铝(电解铝)	吨	Electrolytic Aluminum	ton	231071
黄金	千克	Gold	kg	17656
白银(银锭)	千克	Silver (silver bullion)	kg	554290
铝合金	吨	Aluminum Alloy	ton	116071
铜材	吨	Copper	ton	246592
铝材	吨	Aluminum	ton	895391
金属切削工具	万件	Metal Cutting Tools	10000 pieces	34130
钢丝	吨	Wire	ton	203034
钢丝绳	吨	Wire Rope	ton	36290
钢绞线	吨	Strand	ton	166592
锻件	吨	Forge Piece	ton	463131
粉末冶金零件	吨	Powder Metallurgy	ton	63666
工业锅炉	蒸发量吨	Industrial Boiler	ton	3755
发动机	千瓦	Engine	kw	88644674
其中：汽车用发动机	千瓦	Automotive Engine	kw	85604732
电站用汽轮机	千瓦	Power Plant Steam Turbine	kw	1815000
电站水轮机	千瓦	Turbine	kw	25150
金属切削机床	台	Metal Cutting Machine	piece	2462
其中:数控金属切削机床	台	CNC Metal Cutting Machine	piece	886
金属成形机床	台	Metal Forming Machine	piece	2969
其中：数控金属成形机床(数控锻压设备	台	CNC Metal Forming Machine	piece	184

13-10 续表-6 continued

名 称	计量单位	name		产品产量
铸造机械	台	Foundry Machine	piece	51708
电焊机	台	Electric Welding Machine	piece	114
机床数控装置	套	Machine Digital Control Device	piece	10980
起重机	吨	Crane	piece	48971
电动车辆(电动叉车)	台	Electric Vehicles (electric forklift)	piece	25063
内燃叉车	台	Internal Combustion Forklift	piece	355
输送机械(输送机和提升机)	吨	Transportation Machinery (conveyors and ele	ton	134908
泵	台	Pump	piece	161120
其中:真空泵	台	Vacuum Pump	piece	3895
气体压缩机	台	Gas Compressor	piece	28148540
其中:制冷设备用压缩机	台	Refrigeration Equipment with Compressor	piece	28143841
阀门	吨	Valve	ton	43193
液压元件	件	Hydraulic Components	piece	741003
气动元件	件	Pneumatic components	piece	84197
滚动轴承	万套	Roller	10000 pieces	5686
齿轮	吨	Gear	ton	255296
风机	台	Fans	piece	24729
包装专用设备	台	Special Equipment Package	piece	6051
金属密封件	万件	Metal Sealing Element	10000 pieces	418
金属紧固件	吨	Metal Fastenings	ton	18191
弹簧	吨	Spring	ton	54446
减速机	台	Reducer	piece	226056
矿山专用设备	台	Mining Special Equipment	ton	92472
挖掘、铲土运输机械	台	Digging and Scraper Transport Machinery	piece	621
其中:挖掘机	台	Excavator	piece	621
水泥专用设备	吨	Cement Special Equipment	ton	18700
混凝土机械	台	Concrete Machinery	piece	964
金属冶炼设备	吨	Metal Smelting Equipment	ton	13173
金属轧制设备	吨	Metal Rolling Equipment	ton	6367
炼油、化工生产专用设备	吨	Oil Refining and Chemical Production Specia	ton	744099
塑料加工专用设备	台	Plastics Processing Special Equipment	piece	243
模具	套	Mold	piece	33993
农产品初加工机械	台	Equipment for Agricultural Products Pretreati	piece	789480
饲料生产专用设备	台	Equipment for Feed Production	piece	49
印刷专用设备	吨	Printing Special Equipment	ton	885
中型拖拉机	台	Medium-size Tractors	piece	543
小型拖拉机	台	Small Tractor	piece	93502
收获机械	台	Harvesting Machinery	piece	9535
其中:谷物收获机械	台	Cereal Harvesting Machinery	piece	910

13−10 续表−7 continued

名　称	计量单位	name		产品产量
收获后处理机械	台	Post-harvesting Processing Machinery	piece	35292
环境污染防治专用设备	台(套)	Equipment for Environmental Pollution Contı	piece	67059
其中:大气污染防治设备	台	Air Pollution Control Equipment	piece	13639
水质污染防治设备	台(套)	Water Pollution Control Equipment	piece	346
固体废弃物处理设备	台	Solid Waste Handling Equipment	piece	448
汽车	辆	Car	piece	1586961
其中：基本型乘用车(轿车)	辆	Passenger Vehicles	piece	665868
1升<排量≤1.6升	辆	(1) 1.0 Liter < Displacement ≤ 1.6 Liter	piece	426752
1.6升<排量≤2.0升	辆	(2) 1.6 Liter < Displacement ≤ 2.0 Liter	piece	213933
2.0升<排量≤2.5升	辆	(3) 2.0 Liter < Displacement ≤ 2.5 Liter	piece	25180
2.5升<排量≤3.0升	辆	(4) 2.5 Liter < Displacement ≤ 3.0 Liter	piece	3
多功能乘用车(MPV)	辆	MPV	piece	73651
运动型多用途乘用车(SUV)	辆	SUV	piece	245887
客车	辆	Bus	piece	222165
(1)大型客车(车长>10米)	辆	(1) Large Passenger Bus (car length>10 m)	piece	121
(2)中型客车(7米<车长≤10米)	辆	(2) Medium Passenger Bus(7 m<car length	piece	16472
(3)轻型客车(车长≤7米)	辆	(3) light buses (car length≤ 7 m)	piece	205572
载货汽车	辆	Lorry	piece	379238
改装汽车	辆	Modified Cars	piece	210037
低速载货汽车	辆	Low Speed Truck	piece	6515
铁路货车	辆	Railway Wagon	piece	9165
民用钢质船舶	载重吨	Civil Steel Ships	ton	2298404
电动自行车	辆	Electric Bicycle	piece	419072
发电机组(发电设备)	千瓦	Generating Units (power equipment)	kw	1457000
其中：水轮发电机组	千瓦	Generator Group	kw	4000
汽轮发电机	千瓦	Turbonator	kw	1453000
交流电动机	千瓦	AC Motors	kw	1753234
变压器	千伏安	Transformer	kva	16836946
其中：电力变压器(额定容量≥8000kVA，电压≥500kV)	千伏安	Power Transformer	kva	1370050
互感器	台	Mutual Inductor	kva	40054
高压开关板	面	High-voltage Switch Board	piece	136393
低压开关板	面	Low-voltage Switch Board	piece	197783
高压开关设备(11万伏以上)	台	High Voltage Switchgear (11 KV and above)	piece	67294
通信及电子网络用电缆	对千米	Communication and Electronic Networks Cal	km	289010
电力电缆	千米	Power Cable	km	724768
光缆	芯千米	Optical Cable	km	38194943
绝缘制品	吨	Insulation Products	ton	36005

13-10 续表-8 continued

名 称	计量单位	name		产品产量
锂离子电池	只(自然只)	Li-ion Battery	piece	119715291
铅酸蓄电池	千伏安时	Lead-acid Battery	kvah	21855751
碱性蓄电池	只(自然只)	Alkaline Battery	piece	7031600
原电池及原电池组(折R20标准只)	万只	Primary Cells and Primary Batteries (of R20 standard only)	10000 pieces	9542
太阳能电池	千瓦	Solar Battery	kw	722194
家用电冰箱	台	Household Refrigerator	piece	2260666
家用冷柜(家用冷冻箱)	台	Household Refrigerator (household freezers)	piece	1319928
房间空气调节器	台	Room Air Conditioners	piece	11893719
家用吸排油烟机	台	Home Ventilator	piece	8078
家用洗衣机	台	Household Washing Machines	piece	1376181
家用电热水器	台	Water Heater	piece	2214808
家用吸尘器	台	Household Vacuum Cleaner	piece	
家用燃气灶具	台	Kitchen Range	piece	2547511
太阳能热水器	平方米	Solar Water Heater	sq.m	36883
电光源	万只	Light Sources	10000 pieces	157616
其中：白炽灯泡	万只	Incandescent Bulb	10000 pieces	51583
荧光灯	万只	Fluorescent Lamp	10000 pieces	12477
灯具及照明装置	套(台、个)	Lamps and Lighting Fittings	pieces	16524301
电子计算机整机	台	Computers	pieces	979114
微型计算机设备	台	Micro-computer Equipment	pieces	979114
显示器	台	Monitor	pieces	13735601
程控交换机	线	SPC Exchange	line	561003
移动通信手持机(手机)	台	Mobile Handset (cell phone)	pieces	7147571
组合音响	台	Music Center	pieces	
半导体分立器件	万只	Semiconductor Discrete Devices	10000 pieces	1282784
集成电路	万块	IC	10000 pieces	53
集成电路圆片	万片	IC Wafer	10000 pieces	11
光电子器件	万只(片、套)	Optoelectronic Devices	10000 pieces	779928
其中：发光二极管(LED)	万只	Light-emitting Diode (LED)	10000 pieces	446693
电子元件	万只	Electronic Component	10000 pieces	655474
其中：射频元器件	万只	RF Components	10000 pieces	2881
印制电路板	平方米	Printed Board	sq.m	373610
工业自动调节仪表与控制系统	台(套)	Automatic Adjustment and Control System of Industrial Instrumentation	piece	16758
电工仪器仪表	台	Electric Instrument	piece	
分析仪器及装置	台(套)	Analytical Instrument	piece	924
汽车仪器仪表	台	Car Instrument	piece	3574208
光学仪器	台(个)	Optical Instrument	piece	5145557
船舶修理	载重吨	Ship Repair	ton	63
发电量	万千瓦小时	Power Generation	10000 kwh	21188168
其中：火力发电量	万千瓦小时	Thermal Capacity	10000 kwh	9565026
水力发电量	万千瓦小时	Hydroelectricity	10000 kwh	11535110
风力发电量	万千瓦小时	Wind Power Capacity	10000 kwh	88032
煤气生产量	万立方米	Coal Gas	10000 cu.m	
自来水生产量	万立方米	Water Production	10000 cu.m	154401

13-11 规模以上工业企业主要经济效益指标（2013）

项 目	Item	企业亏损面（%） Enterprises deficit (%)
总　　计	**Total**	**7.14**
一、按登记注册类型分组：	**Grouped by Type of Registration**	
内资企业	Inner Funded Enterprises	6.59
国有企业	State Owned Enterprises	23.23
中央企业	Central Enterprises	23.53
地方企业	Local Enterprises	23.08
集体企业	Collective-owned Enterprise	7.81
股份合作企业	Share Holding Cooperative Enterprises	3.85
联营企业	Joint Owned Enterprise	
国有联营企业	State Joint Ownership	
集体联营企业	Collective Joint Ownership	
国有与集体联营企业	Joint State- Collective Ownership	
其他联营企业	Other Joint Owned Enterprise	
有限责任公司	Responsibility Co. Ltd	9.21
国有独资公司	State Solely Funded Co.	16.81
其他有限责任公司	Others	9.04
股份有限公司	Share Holding Co.Ltd.	10.18
私营企业	Private - owned enterprises	4.24
私营独资企业	Solely Private - owned enterprises	0.93
私营合作企业	Private Joint Venture	1.49
私营有限责任公司	Private Responsibility Co. Ltd	4.38
私营股份有限公司	Private Share Holding Co.Ltd.	4.94
其他企业	Others	5.66
港、澳、台商投资企业	Hongkong, Macao and Taiwan Funded Enterprises	15.78
合资经营企业(港或澳、台资)	Joint Venture with Hongkong, Macao and Taiwan	19.65
合作经营企业(港或澳、台资)	Cooperate with Hongkong, Macao and Taiwan Funded	16.67
港澳台商独资经营企业	Enterprises Solely Funded by Hongkong, Macao and Taiwan Businessmen	11.73
港澳台商投资股份有限公司	Share Holding Co.Ltd. With Hongkong, Macao and Taiwan Investment	20.00
外商投资企业	Foreign Funded Enterprises	16.32
中外合资经营企业	Sino - Foreign Joint Funded Enterprises	15.15
中外合作经营企业	Sino - Foreign Cooperative Funded Enterprises	18.18
外资企业	Foreign Solely Funded Enterprises	18.32
外商投资股份有限公司	Foreign Funded Share Holding Co.Ltd.	9.09
二、在总计中：亏损企业	**Of the Total: enterprises running under deficit**	100.00
在总计中：国有控股企业	Of the Total: State-Owned Share Holding Enterprises	**19.34**
在总计中：农村工业	Of the Total: Rural Industry	5.88
在总计中：轻工业	Of the Total: Light Industry	5.69
重工业	Heavy Industry	8.11
在总计中：大型企业	Of the Total: Large Scale Enterprises	11.63
中型企业	Medium Scale Enterprises	10.13
小型企业	Small Enterprises	6.55

MAJOR ECONOMIC INDICATORS OF INDUSTRIAL ENTERPRISES ABOVE DESIGNATED SIZE (2013)

总资产贡献率（%） Contributing Ratie of Tatal Assets(%)	资产负债率（%） Assets Liability Ratio(%)	流动资产周转率（次/年） Current Asset Tuinover (Times/year)	成本费用利润率（%） Ratio of Riofits to Industrial Cost(%)	产品销售率（%） Propovtion of Produts Sold(%)
15.89	**57.36**	**2.82**	**6.79**	**97.19**
15.64	56.75	2.89	6.62	97.27
7.33	60.56	2.67	4.93	99.51
7.32	60.41	2.72	4.94	99.55
7.56	65.55	1.89	4.70	98.63
41.12	52.43	4.83	7.99	97.37
19.24	59.27	3.00	5.36	94.55
19.37	36.25	11.62	3.29	96.86
40.14	39.63	14.19	6.31	94.55
7.42	70.97	1.14	0.17	100.21
18.43	20.48	25.34	2.67	97.43
17.06	62.06	2.68	5.91	96.76
28.19	63.93	2.11	5.79	96.32
14.14	61.57	2.83	5.93	96.84
11.54	52.42	1.61	8.52	98.32
25.94	47.21	4.53	7.37	96.77
47.20	36.01	8.52	8.34	97.05
36.55	37.16	6.87	6.93	97.22
24.90	47.47	4.41	7.15	96.89
32.23	47.61	4.89	9.53	95.32
30.31	41.48	5.72	6.57	98.36
15.08	54.84	3.32	6.35	96.11
13.66	59.05	3.44	5.47	96.88
5.03	30.72	1.95	1.78	99.37
18.27	49.39	3.31	8.07	94.76
11.41	38.49	1.68	8.36	95.75
18.04	62.74	2.23	8.32	97.06
19.54	63.48	2.26	8.10	96.36
24.35	63.39	5.69	13.92	99.08
13.96	57.63	1.99	8.43	98.70
13.45	67.75	2.65	10.22	101.44
2.68	75.00	1.86	-4.88	96.86
12.56	60.65	2.18	6.11	98.24
21.79	50.44	4.12	6.07	97.86
25.52	51.24	3.38	7.53	96.65
13.00	59.20	2.61	6.43	97.47
13.28	60.48	2.34	6.05	98.13
16.68	57.53	2.74	7.49	96.33
20.89	50.50	3.75	7.21	96.73

13-11 续表 continued

项　目	Item	企业亏损面（%）Enterprises Deficit(%)
按行业分	Grouped by Sector	
采矿业	**Mining and Qarrying**	
煤炭开采和洗选业	Coal Mining and Processing	8.84
石油和天然气开采业	Petroleum and Natural Gas Extraction	100.00
黑色金属矿采选业	Ferrous Metals Mining and Processing	8.28
有色金属矿采选业	Non-ferrous Metals Mining and Processing	12.96
非金属矿采选业	Non-metal Minerals Mining and Processing	3.10
开采辅助活动	Mining Auxiliary Activities	60.00
其他采矿业	Other Minerals Mining and Processing	
制造业	**Manufacturing**	
农副食品加工业	Food Processing	2.63
食品制造业	Food Production	4.59
酒、饮料和精制茶制造业	Wine,Beverage and Refined Tea Production	6.65
烟草制品业	Tobacco Processing	
纺织业	Textile Industry	6.89
纺织服装、服饰业	Textile,Garments, and Fashion Industry	3.98
皮革、毛皮、羽毛及其制品和制鞋业	Leather, Furs,Down and Related Products	7.27
木材加工和木、竹、藤、棕、草制品业	Timber Processing, Wood, Bamboo, Cane, Palm and Sraw Products	2.07
家具制造业	Furniture Manufacturing	3.96
造纸和纸制品业	Papermaking and Paper Products	12.60
印刷和记录媒介复制业	Printing and Record Processing	8.51
文教、工美、体育和娱乐用品制造业	Stationery, Education and Sports Goods	5.32
石油加工、炼焦和核燃料加工业	Petroleum Processing, Coking Products and Nuclear Fuel Processing	18.75
化学原料和化学制品制造业	Raw Chemical Material and Chemical Products	7.20
医药制造业	Medical and pharmaceutical Products	6.69
化学纤维制造业	Chemical Fibers	15.00
橡胶和塑料制品业	Rubber and plastic products	6.01
非金属矿物制品业	Nonmetal Material Products	4.87
黑色金属冶炼和压延加工业	Smelting and Pressing of Ferrous Metals	8.96
有色金属冶炼和压延加工业	Smelting and Pressing of Nonferrous Metals	15.03
金属制品业	Metal Products	6.97
通用设备制造业	Ordinary Machinery Manufacturing	9.45
专用设备制造业	Special Purpose Equipment Manufacturing	7.91
汽车制造业	Motor manufacturing	10.18
铁路、船舶、航空航天和其他运输设备制造业	Railway,Watercraft,Aviation and other Transporlation Equipment manufacturing	4.55
电气机械和器材制造业	Electric Machinery and Equipment	9.77
计算机、通信和其他电子设备制造业	Telecommunication Computer,Equipment and Other Electronic Equipment Manufacturing Other Electronic Equipment Manufacturing	14.08
仪器仪表制造业	Instruments and Meters, Manufacturing	7.08
其他制造业	Other Manufacturing	5.71
废弃资源综合利用业	Waste Comprehensive Vtilization of Resources Industry	15.00
金属制品、机械和设备修理业	Metal products,Machinery and Equipment Repairing	19.05
电力、燃气及水的生产和供应业	**Electric Power, Gas and Water Production and Supply**	
电力、热力生产和供应业	Electric Power, Steam and Hot Water Production and Supply	24.20
燃气生产和供应业	Gas Production and Supply	3.64
水的生产和供应业	Tap Water Production and Supply	22.06

总资产贡献率（%） Contributing Ratie of Tatal Assets(%)	资产负债率（%） Assets Liability Ratio(%)	流动资产周转率（次/年） Current Asset Tuinover (Times/year)	成本费用利润率（%） Ratio of Riofits to Industrial Cost(%)	产品销售率（%） Propovtion of Produts Sold(%)
31.80	48.81	4.36	11.59	99.28
5.71	48.94	3.41	-8.52	99.95
27.02	55.89	7.37	4.36	97.77
37.32	49.60	3.28	18.37	96.92
33.20	53.82	3.81	11.81	97.45
2.22	76.87	3.80	-6.39	99.93
3.43	56.67	2.16	1.85	100.00
27.85	47.09	5.64	7.10	96.67
23.29	43.19	4.02	7.23	96.75
20.28	63.02	1.91	10.67	96.13
96.91	48.62	2.03	16.95	96.99
24.09	48.60	4.88	6.24	96.53
21.21	46.54	3.39	6.67	97.27
17.51	54.90	4.18	4.65	96.71
22.58	39.70	3.48	8.76	95.69
16.62	39.68	3.63	6.09	97.32
15.29	53.31	3.40	5.06	96.56
17.36	50.62	2.79	6.90	95.68
21.52	56.77	3.12	6.87	95.94
53.47	59.69	10.05	0.03	97.25
14.56	62.96	3.38	6.72	97.27
17.56	48.76	2.40	9.77	95.19
16.02	54.88	3.64	6.10	97.88
23.03	47.57	3.61	7.88	97.16
21.55	51.80	3.72	8.91	96.92
5.46	66.38	3.20	1.24	98.96
7.64	68.04	4.68	1.37	97.26
13.95	55.93	2.65	5.63	96.20
10.87	59.48	1.72	7.73	95.82
9.53	61.68	1.55	5.65	95.77
16.79	52.30	1.88	10.50	98.14
6.75	69.89	1.31	5.05	96.90
13.18	58.13	2.27	6.25	96.04
7.08	60.64	1.41	3.77	97.67
13.83	61.94	1.60	10.64	94.51
10.86	64.33	1.81	5.93	96.67
15.38	73.53	2.65	3.20	96.65
12.56	53.30	2.41	2.92	91.90
10.77	60.35	5.69	13.50	99.37
12.64	66.01	2.19	14.28	101.28
2.81	51.22	0.54	3.51	96.08

13–12 规模以上工业企业产销总值及主要经济指标(分地区) (2013)

单位:亿元

地区	Region	企业单位数(个) Number of Enterprises(unit)	亏损企业 Enterprises Running under Deficit
全省	**Province**	**14650**	**1046**
武汉	Wuhan Municipality	2353	327
黄石	Huangshi Municipality	688	72
十堰	Shiyan Municipality	856	71
宜昌	Yichang Municipality	1387	108
襄阳	Xiangyang Municipality	1714	99
鄂州	Ezhou Municipality	484	19
荆门	Jingmen Municipality	971	57
孝感	Xiaogan Municipality	1150	61
荆州	Jingzhou Municipality	1001	52
黄冈	Huanggang Municipality	1248	53
咸宁	Xianning Municipality	829	50
随州	Suizhou Municipality	631	30
恩施	Enshi Municipality	428	13
仙桃	Xiantao Municipality	364	10
潜江	Qianjiang Municipality	252	15
天门	Tianmen Municipality	281	4
林区	Shennongjia Forest Zone	13	5

13–12 续表 1 continued

单位:亿元

地区	Region	资产总计 Total Assets	流动资产合计 Circulating Funds	应收帐款净额 Net Account Received
全省	**Province**	**30633.98**	**13838.57**	**3091.73**
武汉	Wuhan Municipality	10925.87	5395.75	1371.21
黄石	Huangshi Municipality	1753.10	870.06	125.19
十堰	Shiyan Municipality	2573.63	1203.49	236.82
宜昌	Yichang Municipality	4836.04	1466.81	270.46
襄阳	Xiangyang Municipality	2467.39	1279.36	345.16
鄂州	Ezhou Municipality	519.55	189.52	42.11
荆门	Jingmen Municipality	1030.29	422.74	71.26
孝感	Xiaogan Municipality	1176.78	531.65	126.42
荆州	Jingzhou Municipality	1154.09	574.87	148.69
黄冈	Huanggang Municipality	881.71	411.34	101.90
咸宁	Xianning Municipality	769.38	335.16	67.10
随州	Suizhou Municipality	458.24	224.50	57.28
恩施	Enshi Municipality	419.07	108.94	22.31
仙桃	Xiantao Municipality	379.03	175.40	46.73
潜江	Qianjiang Municipality	777.03	404.39	33.35
天门	Tianmen Municipality	473.50	229.58	24.62
林区	Shennongjia Forest Zone	39.29	14.99	1.11

TOTAL VALUE OF PRODUCTION AND SALES AND MAJOR ECONOMIC INDICATORS OF INDUSTRIAL ENTERPRISES ABOVE DESIGNATED SIZE (BY REGIONS) (2013)

(100 million yuan)

工业总产值(当年价格) Total Output Value(current price)	工业销售产值(当年价格) Output Value of Industrial Products(current price)	出口交货值 Delivery Value for Export
39208.98	**38107.78**	**1544.19**
11423.98	11095.02	656.23
2101.17	2052.87	83.20
1709.63	1676.88	30.12
4560.37	4420.79	146.28
4532.08	4397.18	84.48
1221.53	1203.33	9.24
2605.44	2539.73	45.28
2159.88	2113.34	45.55
1900.57	1825.12	74.91
1533.37	1450.60	31.14
1504.07	1474.13	31.24
1057.72	1039.60	83.59
328.20	318.45	6.32
973.28	948.45	111.49
946.79	921.17	56.75
642.62	623.28	48.34
8.29	7.83	0.02

(100 million yuan)

固定资产合计 Total Value of Fixed Assets	固定资产原价 Original Price of Fixed Assets	资产总计 Total Assets	
		累计折旧 Accumulated	在建工程 Construction in Process
12044.51	**22158.39**	**10836.13**	**1386.69**
3687.44	6097.81	2556.83	599.94
663.90	866.15	265.96	100.27
449.79	647.76	265.88	62.14
2612.35	3562.31	1021.89	259.84
895.18	1146.71	346.21	103.71
277.13	398.07	133.10	14.59
475.45	1393.48	954.87	50.53
587.01	2938.41	2383.98	22.39
465.75	2367.18	1936.04	41.19
359.65	436.92	110.40	34.35
368.89	451.78	122.96	21.98
178.26	209.72	45.19	13.54
266.41	336.73	91.21	24.98
178.03	352.30	187.94	14.65
343.79	512.70	205.73	15.28
221.04	421.35	202.18	5.50
14.46	19.02	5.75	1.80

13-12 续表 2 continued

单位:亿元

地区	Region	负债合计 Total Liability	流动负债合计 Total Circulating Liability	应付账款 Account	非流动负债合计 Tatal Non-current Liability	所有者权益合计 Total Rights of Owners
全省	**Province**	**17570.58**	**13340.58**	**3338.22**	**3180.21**	**12904.96**
武汉	Wuhan Municipality	7024.06	5672.24	1676.16	1014.44	3887.77
黄石	Huangshi Municipality	1126.02	867.19	183.55	234.40	623.79
十堰	Shiyan Municipality	1173.46	965.10	302.03	171.26	1392.92
宜昌	Yichang Municipality	2915.01	1951.49	259.88	870.59	1907.78
襄阳	Xiangyang Municipality	1319.01	1016.85	279.24	209.97	1096.79
鄂州	Ezhou Municipality	313.29	248.65	59.98	54.31	205.10
荆门	Jingmen Municipality	515.68	402.57	67.97	84.78	508.29
孝感	Xiaogan Municipality	604.00	321.93	77.07	113.66	570.24
荆州	Jingzhou Municipality	600.58	462.20	119.38	65.96	548.45
黄冈	Huanggang Municipality	461.11	313.96	70.12	58.24	404.54
咸宁	Xianning Municipality	348.79	249.20	61.15	75.47	406.97
随州	Suizhou Municipality	213.95	176.07	42.35	19.75	236.02
恩施	Enshi Municipality	247.84	139.16	19.05	92.06	169.56
仙桃	Xiantao Municipality	164.95	136.53	41.75	16.61	210.62
潜江	Qianjiang Municipality	284.76	235.98	46.95	39.39	486.48
天门	Tianmen Municipality	226.12	158.20	30.35	50.65	242.28
林区	Shennongjia Forest Zone	31.94	23.27	1.25	8.67	7.35

13-12 续表 3 continued

单位:亿元

地区	Region	所有者权益合计 Total Rights of the Owners	主营业务收入 Revenue of Major Business	主营业务成本 Cost of Major Business
		外商资本 Foreign Assets		
全省	**Province**	**406.82**	**38183.39**	**32183.61**
武汉	Wuhan Municipality	187.66	11123.30	9228.91
黄石	Huangshi Municipality	68.07	2503.73	2273.94
十堰	Shiyan Municipality	14.91	1612.07	1370.85
宜昌	Yichang Municipality	23.59	4428.57	3563.90
襄阳	Xiangyang Municipality	21.93	4220.08	3644.34
鄂州	Ezhou Municipality		1179.83	1064.00
荆门	Jingmen Municipality	5.91	2545.50	2176.21
孝感	Xiaogan Municipality	13.72	2116.74	1773.84
荆州	Jingzhou Municipality	31.54	1772.44	1525.62
黄冈	Huanggang Municipality	11.56	1389.25	1202.96
咸宁	Xianning Municipality	2.37	1420.88	1176.46
随州	Suizhou Municipality	1.22	1046.18	863.34
恩施	Enshi Municipality	0.66	315.79	241.07
仙桃	Xiantao Municipality	20.72	953.52	754.86
潜江	Qianjiang Municipality	2.20	921.35	814.15
天门	Tianmen Municipality	0.77	626.31	503.25
林区	Shennongjia Forest Zone		7.84	5.92

(100 million Yuan)

		所有者权益合计 Total Rights of Owners			
实收资本 Assets Recevied	国家资本 National Assets	集体资本 Collective Assets	法人资本 Corperative Assets	个人资本 Individual Assets	港澳台资本 Assets from Hongkong,Maco and Taiwan
5668.78	**1572.25**	**102.60**	**1871.43**	**1385.08**	**163.32**
1565.59	587.13	23.72	479.56	171.54	61.51
251.45	67.95	8.04	63.40	39.22	3.92
423.00	273.61	8.21	55.83	68.05	0.94
727.85	198.18	15.64	161.61	251.20	16.85
410.60	84.09	8.02	160.12	126.06	4.00
161.03	64.48	0.62	70.94	24.42	0.09
243.57	56.56	2.83	77.83	97.12	3.28
375.95	28.93	2.55	110.87	170.85	7.66
269.84	14.94	12.85	72.00	136.52	0.75
217.03	5.75	8.90	92.34	84.06	14.40
158.73	3.26	3.14	61.51	56.34	31.98
120.26	1.52	1.42	42.95	71.43	1.72
110.65	41.89	2.46	33.56	31.73	0.16
96.31	2.09	0.68	43.19	14.72	15.05
445.64	140.24	3.16	288.30	11.23	0.51
86.66	1.09	0.36	55.52	28.43	0.50
4.61	0.54		1.89	2.17	

(100 million Yuan)

主营业务税金及附加 Tax of Major Business	其他业务收入 Revenue of Other Business	其他业务利润 Profit from Other Business	销售费用 Selling Expenses	管理费用 Management Expense	税金 Tax
775.09	**850.37**	**72.41**	**1169.77**	**1625.62**	**90.11**
468.28	420.53	27.34	374.02	489.18	18.99
14.54	123.41	8.99	53.21	69.32	4.09
13.30	85.98	7.21	63.57	112.50	4.79
39.94	42.24	8.21	165.83	176.68	11.23
45.81	51.58	6.93	91.04	212.44	7.12
7.31	38.15	3.94	22.96	55.04	1.24
64.02	9.61	1.17	63.18	79.04	5.68
27.94	18.50	0.68	66.01	80.35	3.00
11.01	12.83	3.00	57.41	71.39	15.47
10.17	6.96	0.45	33.22	59.90	2.54
22.44	4.00	1.09	39.24	37.10	1.90
6.79	3.15	0.55	33.43	34.58	1.63
6.54	2.37	0.37	12.14	14.49	2.15
5.23	3.66	2.33	57.88	57.87	6.96
27.36	26.86	0.11	10.97	40.23	1.51
3.90	0.51	0.04	25.51	35.00	1.72
0.51	0.02		0.13	0.54	0.10

13-12 续表 4 continued

单位:亿元

地区	Region	财务费用 Financial Expense	利息支出 Interest Expense	营业利润 Operating Profit	补贴收入 Income from Subsidy
全省	**Province**	**476.04**	**457.65**	**2466.15**	**72.44**
武汉	Wuhan Municipality	104.42	127.83	489.65	19.69
黄石	Huangshi Municipality	26.41	27.73	86.82	4.07
十堰	Shiyan Municipality	9.02	15.97	186.40	5.48
宜昌	Yichang Municipality	110.18	107.20	447.65	26.49
襄阳	Xiangyang Municipality	41.82	34.43	343.18	9.01
鄂州	Ezhou Municipality	9.31	9.84	41.85	0.22
荆门	Jingmen Municipality	25.33	22.05	132.62	0.81
孝感	Xiaogan Municipality	35.61	18.77	118.43	0.76
荆州	Jingzhou Municipality	19.99	14.06	118.25	2.72
黄冈	Huanggang Municipality	16.56	14.13	106.61	1.19
咸宁	Xianning Municipality	14.28	11.14	133.75	0.77
随州	Suizhou Municipality	16.41	12.01	107.13	0.41
恩施	Enshi Municipality	9.16	9.27	33.22	0.19
仙桃	Xiantao Municipality	10.78	10.27	69.39	0.06
潜江	Qianjiang Municipality	10.24	7.68	10.16	0.52
天门	Tianmen Municipality	15.63	14.80	41.17	0.03
林区	Shennongjia Forest Zone	0.90	0.47	-0.15	

13-12 续表 5 continued

单位:亿元

地区	Region	应交税金及附加 Tax alafor Business	本年应付工资薪酬 Wases Welfarism Payable This Year
全省	**Province**	**2355.51**	**1862.54**
武汉	Wuhan Municipality	935.64	647.19
黄石	Huangshi Municipality	83.89	87.18
十堰	Shiyan Municipality	79.51	143.08
宜昌	Yichang Municipality	311.34	221.25
襄阳	Xiangyang Municipality	214.55	154.59
鄂州	Ezhou Municipality	45.87	35.75
荆门	Jingmen Municipality	131.45	66.79
孝感	Xiaogan Municipality	87.75	84.63
荆州	Jingzhou Municipality	88.02	74.63
黄冈	Huanggang Municipality	64.01	67.82
咸宁	Xianning Municipality	93.20	56.38
随州	Suizhou Municipality	48.39	36.66
恩施	Enshi Municipality	29.96	17.84
仙桃	Xiantao Municipality	59.86	59.55
潜江	Qianjiang Municipality	47.03	59.59
天门	Tianmen Municipality	33.28	48.91
林区	Shennongjia Forest Zone	1.76	0.71

(100 million Yuan)

营业外收入 Non-operating Income	营业外支出 Non-operating Expense	利润总额 Total Profit	应交所得税 Income Tax	亏损企业亏损总额 Total Loss of Enterprises Running under Deficit	利税总额 Total Profit
166.13	**97.21**	**2475.07**	**288.59**	**136.46**	**4451.87**
64.55	17.05	480.54	89.57	58.49	1307.62
6.59	2.25	89.77	15.42	8.15	154.15
12.29	5.77	192.47	7.34	5.05	259.85
33.70	33.61	448.24	56.07	15.49	692.29
15.74	4.44	351.67	36.40	4.89	522.70
3.12	2.58	42.44	5.73	1.18	81.35
3.56	4.53	131.56	7.89	7.91	249.43
4.23	1.54	121.83	7.68	6.92	198.90
7.81	7.64	118.38	11.44	3.08	179.49
4.63	12.79	98.55	7.46	1.33	152.56
2.67	1.06	135.60	20.76	1.08	206.14
4.71	1.60	110.23	5.45	2.14	151.54
0.87	1.13	32.78	2.90	1.09	57.68
0.28	0.08	69.60	8.55	2.93	113.95
1.21	0.88	10.49	2.27	15.71	53.74
0.11	0.22	41.06	3.47	0.06	69.16
0.05	0.03	-0.13	0.19	0.96	1.33

(100 million Yuan)

本年应交增值税 Value Added Payable of the Current Year	全部从业人员年平均人数(万人) Average Number of Empolyment of the Current Year (10000 persons)
1181.37	**346.29**
345.92	85.00
49.74	19.49
53.55	20.58
203.50	36.10
122.60	35.80
31.45	8.02
52.99	16.21
48.77	24.14
50.05	17.91
43.29	18.49
46.86	13.98
34.43	10.25
18.29	4.74
39.12	12.93
15.77	11.58
24.10	10.93
0.95	0.14

13-13　分市州规模以上工业企业主要经济效益指标（2013）

单位：%

地　区	Item	企业亏损面 Loss Making Rate of Enterprises
全省	**Province**	**7.14**
武汉市	Wuhan Municipality	13.90
黄石市	Huangshi Municipality	10.47
十堰市	Shiyan Municipality	8.29
宜昌市	Yichang Municipality	7.79
襄阳市	Xiangyang Municipality	5.78
鄂州市	Ezhou Municipality	3.93
荆门市	Jingmen Municipality	5.87
孝感市	Xiaogan Municipality	5.30
荆州市	Jingzhou Municipality	5.19
黄冈市	Huanggang Municipality	4.25
咸宁市	Xianning Municipality	6.03
随州市	Suizhou Municipality	4.75
恩施市	Enshi Prefecture	3.04
仙桃市	Xiantao Municipality	2.75
潜江市	Qianjiang Municipality	5.95
天门市	Tianmen Municipality	1.42
神农架林区	Shennongjia Forest Zone	38.46

MAJOR INDICATORS OF ECONOMIC BENEFITS OF ABOVE DESIGNATED SIZE INDUSTRIAL ENTERPRISES BY REGION(2013)

总资产贡献率 Contributing Rate of Total Assets	资产负债率 Assets Liability Ratio	流动资产周转率（次/年） Current Asset Turnover(Times/Year)	成本费用利润率 Ratio of Profits to Industrial Cost	产品销售率 Proportion of Products Sold
15.89	**57.36**	**2.82**	**6.79**	**97.19**
13.04	64.29	2.14	4.46	97.12
9.97	64.23	3.02	3.53	97.70
10.34	45.60	1.41	11.68	98.08
16.42	60.28	3.05	11.06	96.94
22.45	53.46	3.34	8.70	97.02
17.44	60.30	6.43	3.56	98.51
26.32	50.05	6.04	5.59	97.48
18.46	51.33	4.02	6.17	97.85
16.72	52.04	3.11	7.02	96.03
18.84	52.30	3.39	7.45	94.60
28.13	45.33	4.25	10.65	98.01
35.65	46.69	4.67	11.59	98.29
15.93	59.14	2.92	11.72	97.03
32.75	43.52	5.46	7.87	97.45
7.87	36.65	2.34	1.16	97.29
17.73	47.75	2.73	7.08	96.99
4.40	81.28	0.52	-1.74	94.44

主要统计指标解释

工业　指从事自然资源的开采，对采掘品和农产品进行加工和再加工的物质生产部门。具体包括：(1)对自然资源的开采，如采矿、晒盐等(但不包括禽兽捕猎和水产捕捞)；(2)对农副产品的加工、再加工，如粮油加工、食品加工、缫丝、纺织、制革等；(3)对采掘品的加工、再加工，如炼铁、炼钢、化工生产、石油加工、机器制造、木材加工等，以及电力、自来水、煤气的生产和供应等；(4)对工业品的修理、翻新，如机器设备的修理、交通运输工具(如汽车)的修理等。

工业统计调查单位为独立核算法人工业企业。

独立核算法人工业企业指从事工业生产经营活动的单位。独立核算法人工业企业应同时具备以下条件：①依法成立，有自己的名称、组织机构和场所，能够承担民事责任；②独立拥有和使用资产，承担负债，有权与其他单位签订合同；③独立核算盈亏，并能够编制资产负债表。

本年鉴中涉及的企业登记注册类型：

国有及国有控股企业　指国有企业加上国有控股企业。国有企业(即原全民所有制工业或国营工业)指企业全部资产归国家所有，并按《中华人民共和国企业法人登记管理条例》规定登记注册的非公司制的经济组织。包括国有企业、国有独资公司和国有联营企业。1957 年以前的公私合营和私营工业，后均改造为国营工业，1992 年改为国有工业，这部分工业的资料不单独分列时，均包括在国有企业内。国有控股企业是对混合所有制经济的企业进行的“国有控股”分类。它是指这些企业的全部资产中国有资产(股份)相对其他所有者中的任何一个所有者占资(股)最多的企业。该分组反映了国有经济控股情况。

集体企业　指企业资产归集体所有，并按《中华人民共和国企业法人登记管理条例》规定登记注册的经济组织。是社会主义公有制经济的组成部分。包括城乡所有使用集体投资举办的企业，以及部分个人通过集资自愿放弃所有权并依法经工商行政管理机关认定为集体所有制的企业。

股份合作企业　指以合作制为基础，由企业职工共同出资入股，吸收一定比例的社会资产投资组建，实行自主经营，自负盈亏，共同劳动，民主管理，按劳分配与按股分红相结合的一种集体经济组织。

联营企业　指两个及两个以上相同或不同所有制性质的企业法人或事业单位法人，按自愿、平等、互利的原则，共同投资组成的经济组织。联营企业包括：

国有联营企业指国有企业与国有企业间的联营；

集体联营企业指集体企业与集体企业间的联营；

国有与集体联营企业指国有企业与集体企业间的联营。

有限责任公司　指根据《中华人民共和国公司登记管理条例》规定登记注册，由两个以上，五十个以下的股东共同出资，每个股东以其所认缴的出资额对公司承担有限责任，公司以其全部资产对其债务承担责任的经济组织。

有限责任公司包括国有独资公司以及其他有限责任公司。

股份有限公司　指根据《中华人民共和国企业法人登记管理条例》规定登记注册，其全部注册资本由等额股份构成并通过发行股票筹集资本，股东以其认购的股份对公司承担有限责任，公司以其全部资产对其债务承担责任的经济组织。

私营企业　指由自然人投资设立或由自然人控股，以雇佣劳动为基础的营利性经济组织。包括按照《公司法》、《合伙企业法》、《私营企业暂行条例》规定登记注册的私营有限责任公司、私营股份有限公司、私营合伙企业和私营独资企业。

港、澳、台商投资企业　指企业注册登记类型中的港、澳、台资合资、合作、独资经营企业和股份有限公司之和。

外商投资企业　指企业注册登记类型中的中外合资、合作经营企业、外资企业和外商投资股份有限公司之和。

“三资”企业系指港、澳、台商投资企业和外资企业的简称。

轻工业　指主要提供生活消费品和制作手工工具的工业。按其所使用的原料不同，可分为两大类：(1)以农产品为原料的轻工业，是指直接或间接以农产品为基本原料的轻工业。主要包括食品制造、饮料制造、烟草加工、纺织、缝纫、皮革和毛皮制作、造纸以及印刷等工业；(2)以非农产品为原料的轻工业，是指以工业品为原料的轻工业。主要包括文教体育用品、化学药品制造、合成纤维制造、日用化学制品、日用玻璃制品、日用金属制品、手工工具制造、医疗器械制造、文化和办公用机械制造等工业。

重工业　指为国民经济各部门提供物质技术基础的主要生产资料的工业。按其生产性质和产品用途，可以分为下列三类：(1)采掘(伐)工业，是指对自然资源的开采，包括石油开采、煤炭开采、金属矿开采、非金属矿开采等工业；(2)原材料工业，指向国民经济各部门提供基本材料、动力和燃料的工业。包括金属冶炼及加工、炼焦及焦炭、化学、化工原料、水泥、人造板以及电力、石油和煤炭加工等工业；(3)加工工业，是指对工业原材料进行再加工制造的工业。包括装备国民经济各部门的机械设备制造工业、金属结构、水泥制品等工业，以及为农业提供的生产资料如化肥、农药等工业。

根据上述划分原则，修理业中以重工业产品为修理作业对象的划为重工业，反之划为轻工业。

工业总产值

(1)定义：

工业总产值是以货币形式表现的，工业企业在一定时期内生产的工业最终产品或提供工业性劳务活动的总价值量。它反映一定时间内工业生产的总规模和总水平。

(2)计算原则：

工业生产的原则，即凡是企业在报告期生产的经检验合格的产品，不管是否在报告期销售，均包括在内。

最终产品的原则，即凡是计入工业总产值的产品，必须是本企业生产的经检验合格的，不需要再进行任何加工的最终产品。如果企业有中间产品(半成品)对外销售，则对外销售的中间产品应视为企业的最终产品。

工厂法原则，即工业总产值是以工业企业作为基本计算(核算)单位，即按企业的最终产品计算工业总产值。按这种方法计算的工业总产值，不允许同一产品价值在企业内部重复计算，不能把企业内部各个车间(分厂)生产的成果相加，但允许企业间的重复计算。

(3)内容及计算方法：

1995 年全国工业普查对工业总产值(原规定)的内容及计算原则和方法做了某些修订，修订后的工业总产值(新规定)包括三项内容：即本期生产成品价值、对外加工费收入、在制品半成品期末期初差额价值三部分。

本期生产成品价值：指企业本期生产，并在报告期内不再进行加工，经检验、包装入库的全部工业成品(半成品)价值合计，包括企业生产的自制设备及提供给本企业在建工程、其他非工业部门和福利部门等单位使用的成品价值。本期生产成品价值为按自备原材料生产的产品的数量乘以本期不含增值税(销项税额)的产品实际销售平均单价计算;会计核算中按成本价格转帐的自制设备和自产自用的成品，按成本价格计算生产成品价值。生产成品价值中不包括用定货者来料加工的成品(半成品)价值。

对外加工费收入：指企业在报告期内完成的对外承接的工业品加工(包括用定货者来料加工产品)的加工费收入和对外工业修理作业所取得的加工费收入。对外加工费收入按不含增值税(销项税额)的价格计算，可根据会计“产品销售收入”科目的有关资料取得。

对于本企业对内非工业部门提供的加工修理、设备安装的劳务收入，如果企业会计核算基础较好，能取得这部分资料，而且这部分价值所占比重较大，应包括在对外加工费收入中。

自制半成品在制品期末期初差额价值：指企业报告期在制品期末减期初的差额价值，本指标一般可以从会计核算资料中取得。如果会计产品成本核算中不计算半成品、在制品的成本，则总产值中也不包括这部分价值，反之则包括。

(4)工业总产值统计范围变化和计算方法修订情况：

1984 年以前工业总产值不包括村办工业，村办工业总产值划归农业。1984 年以后工业总产值包括村办工业。

1995 年工业普查对工业总产值计算方法做了修订，即从 1995 年始按新修订(新规定)方法计算工业总产值。新规定与原规定的区别如下：

全价与加工费的计算原则不同：新规定为凡自备原材料，不论其生产繁简程度如何，一律按全价计算工业总产值；凡来料加工，允许按加工费计算工业总产值。原规定则视生产加工的繁简程度不同，规定哪些行业按全价，哪些行业按加工费计算工业总产值。

自制半成品、在产品期末期初差额价值的计算原则不同：新规定要求，凡会计产品成本核算时计算了成本的差额价值，总产值中就应包括，否则可不包括；原规定则按生产周期六个月的界限区分，凡生产周期六个月以上的企业，总产值计算中应包括这部分差额价值，否则可不包括。

计算价格不同：新规定按不含增值税(销项税额)的价格计算；原规定则按含增值税(销项税额)的价格计算。

工业增加值　指工业企业在报告期内以货币表现的工业生产活动的最终成果。

工业增加值有两种计算方法：一是生产法，即工业总产出减去工业中间投入加上应交增值税；二是收入法，即从收入的角度出发，根据生产要素在生产过程中应得到的收入份额计算，具体构成项目有固定资产折旧、劳动者报酬、生产税净额、营业盈余，这种方法也称要素分配法。本年鉴中的工业增加值是以生产法计算的。

生产法工业增加值的计算方法为：

工业增加值=工业总产出−工业中间投入+应交增值税

(1)工业总产出：指工业企业在一定时期内工业生产活动的总成果。工业总产出包括：成品生产价值，对外加工费收入，自制半成品、在产品期末期初差额价值。1995 年后用新规定计算的工业总产值代替。

(2)工业中间投入：指工业企业在工业生产活动中消耗的外购物质产品和对外支付的服务费用。服务费用包括支付给物质生产部门(工业、农业、批发零售贸易业、建筑业、运输邮电业)的服务费用和支付给非物质生产部门(如保险、金融、文化教育、科学研究、医疗卫生、行政管理等)的服务费用。工业中间投入的确定须遵循以下原则：必须从外部购入的，并已计入工业总产出的产品和服务价值；必须是本期投入生产，并一次性消耗掉(包括本期摊销的低值易耗品等)的产品和服务价值。

工业中间投入包括直接材料费用、制造费用中的工业中间投入、管理费用中的工业中间投入、销售费用中的工业中间投入和利息支出五部分。

资产总计　指企业拥有或控制的能以货币计量的经济资源，包括各种财产、债权和其他权利。资产按流动性分为流动资产、长期投资、固定资产、无形资产、递延资产和其他资产。该指标根据企业会计“资产负债表”中“资产总计”项目的期末数增列。

流动资产　指企业可以在一年内或者超过一年的一个生产周期内变现或者耗用的资产，包括现金及各种存款、短期投资，应收及预付款项、存货等。

流动资产平均余额　指企业在报告期内全部流动资产的平均余额。

固定资产原价　指企业在建造、购置、安装、改建、扩建、技术改造某项固定资产时所支出的全部货币总额。它一般包括买价、包装费、运杂费和安装费等。

固定资产净值年平均余额　指固定资产净值在报告期内余额的平均数。计算公式为：

$$\text{固定资产净值年平均余额}=\frac{\text{1至12月各月月初、月末固定资产净值之和}}{24}$$

该指标根据“资产负债表”中“固定资产原价”、“累计折旧”指标的期初、期末数计算填列。

固定资产净值指固定资产原价减去历年已提折旧额后的净额。计算公式为：

固定资产净值=固定资产原价−累计折旧

负债合计　指企业所承担的能以货币计量，将以资产或劳务偿付的债务，偿还形式包括货币、资产或提供劳务。负债一般按偿还期长短分为流动负债和长期负债。根据会计“资产负债表”中“负债合计”的年末数填列。

所有者权益　指企业投资人对企业净资产的所有权。企业净资产等于企业全部资产减去全部负债后的余额，包括企业投资人对企业的最初投入的实际到位的资产及资本公积金、盈余公积金和未分配利润。所有者权益合计数小于零，表示企业资不抵债。

主营业务收入　指会计“利润表”中对应指标的本年累计数。未执行 2001 年《企业会计制度》的企业，用“产品销售收入”的本期累计数代替。

主营业务成本　指会计“利润表”中对应指标的本年累计数。未执行 2001 年《企业会计制度》的企业，用“产品销售成本”的本期累计数代替。

主营业务税金及附加　指会计“利润表”中对应指标的本年累计数。未执行 2001 年《企业会计制度》的企业，用“产品销售税金及附加”的本期累计数代替。

利润总额　指企业生产经营活动的最终成果，是企业在一定时期内实现的盈亏相抵后的利润总额(亏损以“−”号表示)，它等于营业利润加上补贴收入加上投资收益加上营业外净收入再加上以前年度损益调整。

本年应交增值税　指企业在报告期内应交纳的增值税额。它等于本年销项税额加上出口退税加上进项税额转出数减去本年进项税额。小规模纳税企业直接按全年计税销售额乘以征收率计算取得。

从业人员平均人数　是指报告期内每天拥有的从业人员人数。其计算公式为：

$$\text{季平均人数}=\frac{\text{季内各月平均人数之和}}{3}$$

$$\text{月平均人数}=\frac{\text{报告月内每天实有人数之和}}{\text{报告月日历日数}}$$

$$\text{年平均人数}=\frac{\text{年内各月平均人数之和}}{12}$$

总资产贡献率　反映企业全部资产的获利能力，是企业经营业绩和管理水平的集中体现，是评价和考核企业盈利能力的核心指标。计算公式为：

$$\text{总资产贡献率（\%）}=\frac{\text{利润总额+税金总额+利息支出}}{\text{平均资金总额}}\times 100\%$$

公式中：税金总额为产品销售税金及附加与应交增值税之和；平均资产总额为期初期末资产之和的算术平均值。

资产负债率　该指标既反映企业经营风险的大小，也反映企业利用债权人提供的资金从事经营活动的能力。计算公式为：

$$\text{资产负债率（\%）}=\frac{\text{负债总额}}{\text{资产总额}}\times 100\%$$

资产与负债均为报告期期末数。

流动资产周转次数　指一定时期内流动资产完成的周转次数，反映投入工业企业流动资金的周转速度。计算公式为：

$$\text{流动资产周转资转次数}=\frac{\text{产品销售收入}}{\text{全部流动资产平均余额}}$$

公式中：全部流动资产平均余额为期初和期末的流动资产之和的算术平均值。

成本费用利润率 反映企业投入的生产成本及费用的经济效益，同时也反映企业降低成本所取得的经济效益。计算公式为：

$$\text{成本费用利润率（\%）} = \frac{\text{利润总额}}{\text{成本费用总额}} \times 100\%$$

公式中：成本费用总额为产品销售成本、销售费用、管理费用、财务费用之和。

全员劳动生产率 该指标反映企业的生产效率和劳动投入的经济效益。计算公式为：

$$\text{全员劳动生产率（元/人）} = \frac{\text{工业增加值}}{\text{全部从业人员平均人数}}$$

产品销售率 该指标反映工业产品已实现销售的程度，是分析工业产销衔接情况，研究工业产品满足社会需求的指标。计算公式为：

$$\text{产品销售率（\%）} = \frac{\text{工业销售产值}}{\text{工业总产值（现价）}} \times 100\%$$

Explanatory Notes on Main Statistical Indicators

Industry refers to the material production sector which is engaged in extraction of natural resources and processing and reprocessing of minerals and agricultural products, including (1) extraction of natural resources, such as mining, salt production (but not including hunting and fishing); (2) processing and reprocessing of farm and sideline produces, such as rice husking, flour milling, wine making, oil pressing, silk reeling, spinning and weaving, and leather making; (3) manufacture of industrial products, such as steel making, iron smelting, chemicals manufacturing, petroleum processing, machine building, timber processing; water and gas production and electricity generation and supply; (4)repairing of industrial products such as the repairing of machinery and means of transport (including cars).

Units of industrial statistics survey corporate industrial enterprises with independent accounting system.

Corporate industrial enterprises with independent accounting system refer to enterprises engaging in industrial production activities, which meet the following requirements: (1)They are established legally, having their own names, organizations, location, able to take civil liability; (2)They possess and use their assets independently, assume liabilities, and are entitled to sign contracts with other units; (3)They are financially independent and compile their own balance sheets.

Enterprises covered in the industrial statistics in the Yearbook include following categories by their registration:

State-owned and State-holding Enterprises refer to state-owned enterprises plus state-holding enterprises. State-owned enterprises (originally known as state-run enterprises with ownership by the whole society) are non-corporate economic entities registered in accordance with the Regulation of the People's Republic of China on the Management of Registration of Legal Enterprises, where all assets are owned by the state. Included in this category are state-owned enterprises, state-funded corporations and state-owned joint-operation enterprises. Joint state-private industries and private industries, which existed before 1957, were transformed into state-run industries since 1957, and into state-owned industries after 1992. Statistics on those enterprises are included in the state-owned industries instead of grouping them separately. State-holding enterprises is a sub-classification of enterprises with mixed ownership, referring to enterprises where the percentage of state assets (or shares by the state) is larger than any other single share holder of the same enterprise. This sub-classification illustrates the control of the state over a particular industry.

Collective-owned Enterprises refer to economic entities registered in accordance with the Regulation of the People's Republic of China on the Management of Registration of Legal Enterprises, where assets are owned by collectively. Collective enterprises constitute an integral part of the socialist economy with public ownership. They include urban and rural enterprises invested by collectives, and some enterprises registered in industrial and commercial administration agency as collective units where funds are pulled together by individuals who voluntarily give up their right of ownership.

Share-holding Cooperative Enterprises refer to economic units set up on cooperative basis, with funding partly from members of the enterprise and partly from outside investment, where the operation and management is decided by the members who also participate in the production, and the distribution of income is based both on work (labour input) and on shares (capital input).

Joint-operation enterprises refer to economic units that are established by joint investment by two or more corporate enterprises or institutions of the same or different types of ownership on voluntary, equal and mutual-beneficial basis. They include:

a) state-owned joint-operation enterprises (joint operation between state-owned enterprises);

b) collective joint-operation enterprises (joint operation between collective enterprises; and

c) state-collective joint-operation enterprises (joint operation between state and collective enterprises).

Limited Liability Corporations refer to economic units registered in accordance with the Regulation of the People's Republic of China on the Management of Registration of Corporations, with capitals from 2 to 49 investors, each investor bears limited liability to the corporation depending on his/her holding of shares, and the corporation bears liability to its debt to the maximum of its total assets.

Share-holding Corporations Ltd. refer to economic units registered in accordance with the Regulation of the People's Republic of China on the Management of Registration of Corporate Enterprises, with total registered capitals divided into equal shares and raised through issuing stocks. Each investor bears limited liability to the corporation depending on the holding of shares, and the corporation bears liability to its debt to the maximum of its total assets.

Private Enterprises refer to economic units invested or controlled (by holding the majority of the shares) by natural persons who hire labours for profit-making activities. Included in this category are private limited liability corporations, private share-holding corporations Ltd., private partnership enterprises and private sole investment enterprises registered in accordance with the Corporation Law, Partnership Enterprise Law and Tentative Regulation on Private Enterprises.

Enterprises with Funds from Hong Kong, Macao and Taiwan refers to all industrial enterprises registered as the joint-venture, cooperative, sole (exclusive) investment industrial enterprises and limited liability corporations with funds from Hong Kong, Macao and Taiwan.

Foreign Funded Enterprises refers to all industrial enterprises registered as the joint-venture, cooperative, sole (exclusive) investment industrial enterprises and limited liability corporations with foreign funds.

Enterprise with Hong Kong, Macao, Taiwan and foreign fund refer to all the enterpries with funds from Hong Kong Macao and Taiwan and foreign funded enterprises.

Light Industry refers to the industry that produces consumer goods and hand tools. It consists of two categories, depending on the materials used:

(1) Industries using farm products as raw materials. These are branches of light industry which directly or indirectly use farm

products as basic raw materials, including the manufacture of food and beverages, tobacco processing, textile, clothing, fur and leather manufacturing, paper making, printing, etc.

(2) Industries using non farm products as raw materials. These are branches of light industry which use manufactured goods as raw materials, including the manufacture of cultural, educational articles and sports goods, chemicals, synthetic fiber, chemical products for daily use, glass products for daily use, metal products for daily use, hand tools, medical apparatus and instruments, and the manufacture of cultural and clerical machinery.

Heavy Industry refers to the industry which produces capital goods, and provides various sectors of the national economy with necessary material and technical basis. It consists of the following three branches according to the purpose of production or the use of products:

(1) Mining, quarrying and logging industry refers to the industry that extracts natural resources, including extraction of petroleum, coal, metal and non-metal ores.

(2) Raw materials industry refers to the industry that provides various sectors of the national economy with raw materials, fuels and power. It includes smelting and processing of metals, coking and coke chemistry, chemical materials and building materials such as cement, plywood, and power, petroleum refining and coal dressing.

(3) Manufacturing industry refers to the industry that processes raw materials. It includes machine-building industry which equips sectors of the national economy, industries of metal structure and cement products, industries producing means of agricultural production, such as chemical fertilizers and pesticides.

According to the above principle of classification, the repairing trades, which are engaged primarily in repairing products of heavy industry are classified into heavy industry while these engaged in repairing products of light industry are classified into light industry.

Gross Industrial Output Value

(1) Definition: Gross industrial output value is the total volume of final industrial products produced and industrial services provided during a given period. It reflects the total achievements and overall scale of industrial production during a given period.

(2) Principles for calculation:

Statistics on industrial production follow the principle that all products produced by the enterprises and accepted during the reference period are to be included no matter whether they are sold or not during the reference period.

Determination of final products follow the principle that all products that are included in the calculation of grow industrial output value are the final products of the enterprise which have been accepted through quality check and require no further processing. If an enterprise has intermediate (semi-finished) products to sell, these intermediate products are considered as the final products of the enterprise.

Gross industrial output value is calculated following the principle of factory approach, i.e. industrial enterprise is used as the basic accounting unit in calculating the gross industrial output value. By this approach, value of the same product is not to be double counted, and the output value of different workshops (branch factories) should not be added. However, this approach does not exclude the possibility of double counting between enterprises.

(3) Content and calculation method: The old definition of gross industrial output value was modified during the national industrial census in 1995. The revised (new) definition of gross industrial output value consists of 3 components: value of the finished products during the reference period, income from external processing, and value of change in semi-finished products at the end and at the beginning of the reference period.

Value of the finished products during the reference period: refers to the value of all finished (semi-finished) industrial products that are produced during the reference period without the need for further processing, checked for acceptance, packed and put into the warehouse of the enterprise, including the value of own-produced equipment and the value of products provided to the projects under construction of the enterprise, and to other non-industrial or welfare units. Value of finished products during the reference period is calculated by the quantity of products produced using own materials multiplied by the average unit prices at which products are sold (excluding value-added tax). Own-produced equipment and products produced for own use are value at cost prices as in the case of enterprise accounting. Value of finished products does not include the value of finished products (semi-finished products) that are produced using the materials from the clients who make the orders.

Income from external processing: refers to income from contracted external processing of industrial products (including processing of industrial products using materials from the clients), and the income from industrial repairing work provided to other units. Income from external processing is calculated using information from the item "products sales income" in the enterprise accounting at the prices excluding value-added tax.

For income from services such as processing, repairing and installation of equipment provided to non-industrial units within the enterprise, if the accounting work of the enterprise is good enough to separate it from other records, and the share of such services is significant, it should also be included in the income from external processing.

Value of change in semi-finished products at the end and at the beginning of the reference period: refers to the value of change in semi-finished products at the end and at the beginning of the reference period, which generally can be obtained from accounting records of enterprises. If the enterprise accounting excludes the cost of semi-finished products, then it should not be included in the gross industrial output value, and vice versa.

(4) Changes in the coverage and method of calculation of gross industrial output value

Prior to 1984, the value of rural industry run by villages was classified into agriculture instead of industry. Since 1984, it has been included in the gross industrial output value. Method of calculation for the gross industrial output value was modified in the industrial census in 1995. The difference in the new method as compared with the old one is outlined below:

Principle in using full value vs. processing fee: The new method stipulates that all products produced using own materials are to be calculated with full value in reporting the gross industrial output value irrespective of sophistication of production, and for external processing, it allows calculation using processing fee. In the old method, however, the use of full value or processing fee was determined by the degree of sophistication of production in different branches of industries.

Principle in determining the value of change in semi-finished products: The new method requires that value of the change in semi-finished products should be included in the gross industrial output value if it is included in the accounting record of the enterprise, otherwise it should not be included. By the old method, it is determined by the type of enterprises in terms of production cycle. If the production cycle is over 6 months, the value of change in semi-finished products is included in the gross industrial output value, otherwise it is excluded.

Difference in prices: The new method uses prices excluding value-added tax in the calculation of gross industrial output value, while the old method used prices including value-added tax.

Value-added of Industry refers to the final results of industrial production of industrial enterprises in money terms during the reference period.

Industrial value-added can be calculated by two approaches: the production approach, i.e. gross industrial output value minus intermediate input plus value-added tax, and the income approach, i.e. income for various factors used in the course of production, including depreciation of fixed assets, remuneration of labourers, net of production tax, and operating surplus. Value-added of industry in the Yearbook is calculated by production approach as following:

Value-added of industry = gross industrial output industrial intermediate input + value-added tax

(1) Gross industrial output: refers to the total achievements of industrial production during a given period. Gross industrial output includes value of finished products, income from external processing, and value of change in semi-finished products at the end and at the beginning of the reference period. Since 1995, it was substituted by the gross industrial output value by new method.

(2) Industrial intermediate input: refers to purchased goods and paid services consumed during the industrial production of enterprises. Fees paid for services include fees paid for the services provided by material production sectors (industry, agriculture,

wholesale and retail trade, construction, transport, post and telecommunications) and by non-material production sectors (insurance, banking, culture, education, scientific research, health and medical care, public administration, etc.). The determination of industrial intermediate input follows the principle that the goods and services must be purchased from outside and included in the gross industrial output, and that the goods and services are inputted into production and consumed (include low-value consumables) during the reference period.

Industrial intermediate input includes 5 components, namely direct consumption of materials, industrial intermediate input in manufacturing cost, industrial intermediate input in management cost, industrial intermediate input in marketing cost and expenditure on interest.

Total Assets refer to all economic resources, in monetary terms, that is owned or controlled by enterprises, including properties, creditors equity and other economic rights of all forms. Classified by the degree of equitability, total assets include circulating assets, long-term investment, fixed assets, intangible assets and deferred assets, and other assets. Data on this indicator can be obtained by the year-end figures of total assets in the Assets and Liability Table of accounting records of enterprises.

Working Capitals refer to capitals that an enterprise can cash or use during one year or one production cycle that may exceeds one year, including cash and savings deposits of various forms, short-term investment, money receivable and prepaid money, inventories, etc.

Annual Average Value of Working Capitals refers to the average value of all working capitals of the enterprise during the reference period.

Original Value of Fixed Assets refers to the total value, in monetary terms, that an enterprise spent on fixed assets, through construction, purchase, installation, transformation, expansion or technical upgrading. Generally, it covers cost of purchase, packing, transportation and installation, etc.

Annual Average of Net Value of Fixed Assets refer to average of the net value of fixed assets during the reference period, calculated with the following formula:

Annual Average of Net Value of Fixed Assets = sum of net value of fixed assets at the beginning and at the end of each month from January to December / 24.

Information on this indicator can be obtained from the beginning and ending figures of the original value of fixed assets and cumulative depreciation from the Assets and Liability Table of enterprises.

Net value of fixed assets refers to the original value of fixed assets minus depreciation over the years, i.e.:

Net value of fixed assets = original value of fixed assets cumulative depreciation

Total Liabilities refer to payable liabilities of enterprises that have to repay in terms of money, assets or labour services. In terms of payment, it can be divided into liquid liabilities and long-term liabilities. Data on this item is obtained from the ending figures on total liabilities from the Assets and Liability Table from the enterprises.

Owner's Equity refers to the ownership of net assets of enterprise by its investors. The net assets equal the total assets minus total liabilities of the enterprise, including the actual assets invested into the enterprise by investors, accumulation of capitals and operating surplus and non-distributed profits. The enterprise's assets is less than its liabilities if the sum of owner's equity is smaller than zero.

Revenue from Principal Business refers to the annual accumulation of corresponding item in the "profit table" of the accountant. For enterprises that do not follow the 2001 Enterprise Accounting Standards, the year-end accumulation of revenue from the sales of products is used as a substitute.

Cost of Principal Business refers to the annual accumulation of corresponding item in the "profit table" of the accountant. For enterprises that do not follow the 2001 Enterprise Accounting Standards, the year-end accumulation of cost for the sales of products is used as a substitute.

Tax and Extra Charges from Principal Business refer to the annual accumulation of corresponding item in the "profit table"

of the accountant. For enterprises that do not follow the 2001 Enterprise Accounting Standards, the year-end accumulation of tax and extra charges from the sales of products is used as a substitute.

Total Profits refer to the final achievements of production and operation of the enterprises, represented by the total profits after deducting losses (loss is expressed by the negative figure). It is the sum of profits from operation, income from subsidies, investment earnings, net income from activities other than operation, and adjustment of profits and losses of previous years.

Value-added Tax Payable refers to the amount of the value-added tax which should be paid by the enterprises during the reference period. It is the sum of tax on sales, export rebate, and transferred tax on purchases of the current year, minus the tax on purchases of the current year. Value-added tax payable of small-size enterprises is determined by the taxable sales of the year multiplied by the tax rate.

Average Annual Number of Employed Persons Employed persons refer to all those who are employed in enterprises and receive remunerations therefrom, including currently working employees, retirees who are re-employed, teachers of local-run schools, as well as foreigners, staff from Hong Kong, Macao and Taiwan, part-time employees and persons with second job who are employed by the enterprise, and employees of other units temporarily working in the enterprises, but excluding former employees who left the enterprise with their employment records still kept by the enterprises.

Average number of employed persons refers to the number of employees everyday during the reference period, calculated with the following formula:

Monthly average number = sum of actual employees everyday in reference month/number of calendar dates in reference month

Quarterly average number = sum of monthly average number in reference quarter/3

Annual average number = sum of monthly average number in reference year/12

Ratio of Profits, Taxes and Interests to Average Assets reflects the profit-making capability of all assets of the enterprise and is a key indicator manifesting the performance and management and evaluating the profit-making potential of the enterprise. It is calculated as follows:

Ratio of Profits, Taxes and Interests to Average Assets (%) = [(total profits + total taxes + interest payment) / average assets]×100%

In the above formula, total taxes is the sum of tax and extra charges on the sales of products and value-added tax payable; and average assets is the arithmetic mean of the sum of beginning assets and ending assets.

Ratio of Debts to Assets reflect both the operation risk and the capability of the enterprise in making use of the capital from the creditors. It is calculated as follows:

Ratio of Debts to Assets (%) = (total debts / total assets)×100%

Both assets and debts are figures at the end of the reference period.

Turnover of Working Capitals refers to the number of times of turnover of working capital in a given period of time, which reflects the speed of the turnover of working capital of industrial enterprises, and is calculated as follows:

Turnover of Working Capital=(sales revenue of products) / (average balance of total working capital)

In the above formula, average balance of total working capital refers to the arithmetic mean of the sum of working capital at the beginning and at the end of the reference period.

Ratio of Profits to Total Industrial Costs refers to the ratio of profits realized in a given period to the total costs in the same period, which reflects the economic efficiency of input cost and is calculated as follows:

Ratio of Profits to Total Industrial Cost (%)=(total profits/ total costs)×100%

Total costs in the above formula is the sum of cost of products sold, marketing cost, management cost and financial cost.

Overall Labour Productivity is an indicator reflecting the production efficiency of an enterprise and the economic efficiency of its labour input, calculated by the formula:

Overall Labour Productivity (yuan/person) = industrial value-added / average of all persons engaged

Sales Ratio of Products is an indicator reflecting the actual sale of industrial products, analyzing the production-selling and supply-demand relations. It is calculated as:

Sales Ratio of Products (%) = value of industrial sales / gross industrial output value (current prices) * 100%

14 建筑业

Construction

资料整理：樊喜珍

建　　筑　　业
Construction
2013

建筑施工企业个数	Number of Construction Enterprises	3376	(个)
建筑施工企业职工平均人数	Average Number of Staff and Workers in Construction Enter[	174.2	(万人)
建筑业总产值	Total Output Value of Construction Industry	8465.5	(亿元)
房屋建筑竣工面积	Floor Space of Building Completed	22773.7	(万平方米)
建筑业全员劳动生产率	Overall Labor Productivity of Construction Industry	48.6	(万元/人)
建筑业技术装备率	Technical Equipment Ratio of Construction Enterprises	19058.6	(元/人)

建筑业产值构成　(%)
Composition of Output Value(%)

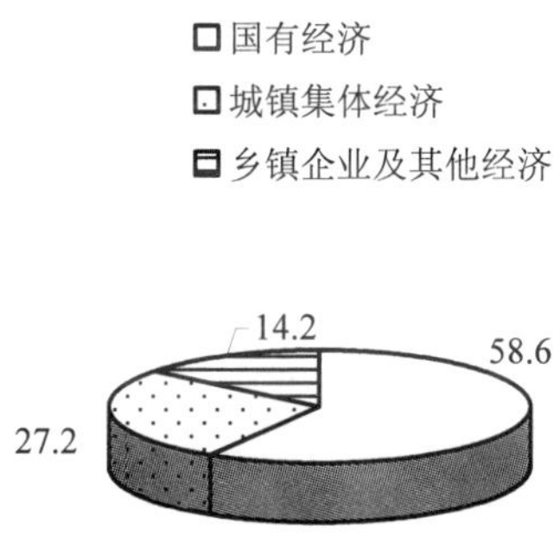

2000

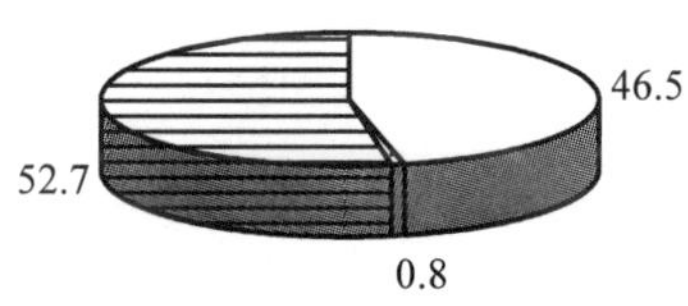

2013

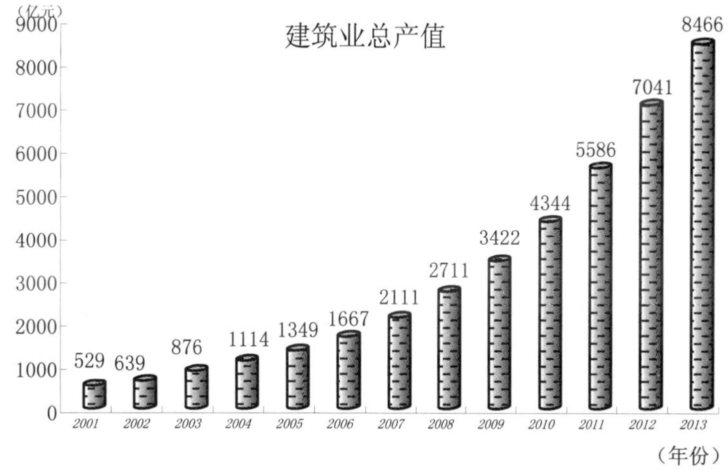

附：建筑业产值构成(%)

	2003	2006	2007	2008	2009	2010	2011	2012	2013
国有经济	61.1	32.7	50.5	49.2	47.4	52.6	52.5	48.7	46.5
城镇集体经济	9.5	4.3	3.2	2.1	2.3	1.4	1.5	1.9	0.8
乡镇企业及其他经济	29.4	63.0	46.3	51.3	50.3	45.9	45.9	49.4	52.7

14-1 建筑企业概况
BASIC STATISTICS ON CONSTRUCTION ENTERPRISES

项 目 Item	总 计 Total	国有经济 State-Owned	地 方 Local - Owned	中 央 Central- Owned	城镇集体经济 Urban Collective- Owned	其他经济 Others
企业单位个数(个) Number of Enterprises (unit)						
1990	570	174	132	42	396	
1991	575	179	137	42	396	
1992	603	184	142	42	419	
1993	898	241	208	40	642	15
1994	823	307	268	39	492	24
1995	912	323	277	46	539	50
1996	1696	403	250	53	1198	95
1997	1761	429	378	51	1207	125
1998	1838	433	379	54	1206	199
1999	2120	491	432	59	1297	332
2000	2070	488	440	48	1175	409
2001	1661	393	350	43	809	459
2002	1625	363	327	36	480	782
2003	1808	558	488	70	344	906
2004	2357	433	378	55	358	2566
2005	2114	524	448	76	268	1322
2006	2238	320	279	41	223	1695
2007	2516	449	383	66	191	1876
2008	2975	440	374	66	161	2374
2009	2878	396	331	65	152	2330
2010	2845	388	334	54	142	2315
2011	2640	376	330	46	130	2134
2012	2952	390	335	55	122	2440
2013	3376	399	334	66	98	2879
职工平均人数(万人) Average Staff and Workers (10000 persons)						
1990	41.88	29.35	13.97	15.38	12.53	
1991	43.08	30.34	14.52	15.82	12.74	
1992	46.13	30.92	14.89	16.03	15.21	
1993	55.75	36.41	19.65	16.76	19.15	0.19
1994	52.66	36.83	19.07	17.76	15.43	0.40
1995	57.28	38.05	18.86	19.19	16.62	2.61
1996	76.51	36.83	18.58	18.25	36.20	3.48
1997	76.09	36.36	18.60	17.76	35.96	3.77
1998	82.63	38.22	19.22	19.00	38.82	5.59
1999	85.72	39.57	22.57	17.00	36.69	9.46
2000	82.76	36.58	21.73	14.83	35.36	10.82
2001	83.11	36.16	19.99	16.44	29.30	17.65
2002	93.50	34.20	21.25	12.95	23.50	35.80
2003	108.82	50.20	30.72	19.48	16.98	41.64
2004	105.30	44.40	28.10	16.30	12.20	48.70
2005	110.09	41.70	22.85	18.85	11.60	56.79
2006	114.25	27.26	15.18	12.08	10.28	76.71
2007	136.14	39.73	19.52	20.21	9.44	86.97
2008	137.61	38.51	18.40	20.11	6.61	92.49
2009	146.02	41.68	18.76	22.92	7.22	97.12
2010	170.71	54.40	22.31	32.09	5.57	110.74
2011	141.88	42.61	15.06	27.55	4.78	94.49
2012	169.33	50.83	15.10	35.73	4.21	114.29
2013	174.18	40.50	14.83	25.67	3.04	130.64

14−1 续表 1 continued

项 目 Item	总 计 Total	国有经济 State-Owned	地 方 Local - Owned	中 央 Central- Owned	城镇集体经济 Urban Collective- Owned	其他经济 Others
建筑业总产值(亿元) Gross Output Value of Construction Enterprises (100 million yuan)						
1990	49.30	38.92	16.34	22.58	10.38	
1991	57.56	44.19	19.16	25.03	13.37	
1992	78.44	59.51	25.03	34.47	18.93	
1993	119.90	90.27	36.17	54.10	29.10	0.53
1994	169.28	140.29	56.95	83.34	27.75	1.24
1995	227.41	178.51	58.96	119.55	33.70	15.19
1996	284.43	187.00	60.83	126.17	79.14	18.29
1997	305.97	199.53	63.59	135.94	84.70	21.75
1998	343.65	223.80	73.98	149.82	93.15	26.70
1999	399.02	246.58	88.07	158.51	107.32	45.13
2000	454.35	266.03	106.76	159.27	123.46	64.86
2001	529.02	279.39	112.32	167.07	117.70	131.93
2002	639.11	301.93	143.90	158.03	98.90	238.29
2003	876.26	535.71	227.72	307.99	82.99	257.56
2004	1114.33	676.45	285.29	391.16	67.25	370.63
2005	1349.32	776.70	268.77	507.92	69.92	502.71
2006	1667.00	545.64	184.87	360.77	72.44	1048.92
2007	2110.80	1065.26	234.03	831.23	68.69	976.85
2008	2710.80	1333.87	241.63	1092.24	57.52	1319.41
2009	3421.89	1621.66	191.86	1429.80	77.86	1722.37
2010	4344.39	2287.08	414.78	1872.30	61.21	1996.10
2011	5586.45	2934.99	501.47	2433.52	85.04	2566.42
2012	7040.65	3428.40	627.89	2800.51	133.55	3478.70
2013	8465.50	3933.36	757.54	3175.82	66.75	4465.39
施工房屋面积(万平方米) Floor Space of Buildings Under Construction (10000 sq.m)						
1990	1684.90	1061.40	746.10	315.30	623.50	
1991	1839.90	1103.30	758.10	345.20	736.60	
1992	2128.40	1190.40	829.90	360.50	938.10	
1993	2579.10	1439.30	989.10	450.20	1131.20	8.60
1994	2843.50	1894.50	1319.10	575.40	922.30	26.70
1995	3284.30	2122.80	1185.20	937.60	867.60	293.90
1996	4548.80	2224.60	1203.30	1021.30	2008.40	315.80
1997	4604.20	2330.60	1226.90	1103.70	1885.30	388.30
1998	5310.00	2488.80	1288.80	1200.00	2247.50	573.70
1999	5797.00	2703.40	1578.40	1125.00	2329.40	764.20
2000	6256.50	2889.10	1564.50	1324.60	2448.20	919.20
2001	6662.59	2792.50	1480.20	1312.30	2053.00	1817.10
2002	7215.88	2836.00	1452.00	1384.00	1742.00	2637.90
2003	8933.44	3817.50	2102.60	1714.90	1574.80	3541.10
2004	11772.31	5089.10	2522.60	2566.50	1348.90	5334.30
2005	12091.16	4568.90	1993.30	2575.60	1264.80	6257.50
2006	14478.24	3811.18	1016.18	2795.00	1021.60	9545.40
2007	16679.70	5503.80	1666.40	3837.40	1036.10	10139.80
2008	18376.50	5703.90	1060.40	4643.50	752.00	11920.60
2009	20499.30	5672.40	522.50	5149.90	799.40	14027.50
2010	25046.70	6752.80	968.80	5784.00	633.70	17660.30
2011	31023.80	9209.70	1549.00	7660.70	782.30	21031.70
2012	39112.20	10747.20	1661.70	9085.50	905.90	27459.10
2013	48937.96	14424.51	1734.33	12690.18	599.26	33914.19

14-1 续表 2 continued

项　　目 Item	总　计 Total	国有经济 State-Owned	地　方 Local - Owned	中　央 Central- Owned	城镇集体经济 Urban Collective- Owned	其他经济 Others
竣工房屋面积(万平方米) Floor Space of Buildings Completed (10000 sq.m)						
1990	785.9	455.9	351.6	104.3	330.0	
1991	852.4	474.9	338.7	136.2	377.5	
1992	1002.8	508.4	378.5	129.9	494.4	
1993	1114.9	481.0	384.4	96.1	632.9	1.0
1994	1070.9	577.5	485.2	92.3	481.6	11.8
1995	1175.9	622.2	466.9	155.3	484.3	69.4
1996	1880.7	653.3	501.3	152.0	1123.5	103.9
1997	1982.3	765.3	522.1	243.2	1124.5	92.5
1998	2374.0	836.0	624.0	212.0	1298.6	239.4
1999	2873.0	1023.1	776.1	247.0	1484.3	365.6
2000	3150.1	1096.3	836.1	260.2	1572.0	481.8
2001	3673.4	1237.0	828.3	408.7	1334.1	1102.3
2002	4146.6	1261.8	889.3	372.5	1146.0	1738.8
2003	4840.8	1578.8	1143.4	435.4	993.7	2268.3
2004	6647.1	2561.3	1563.2	998.1	820.5	3265.3
2005	6896.9	2125.6	923.7	1201.9	791.5	3979.8
2006	7376.2	1137.1	450.4	686.7	678.8	5560.3
2007	8425.0	1620.9	858.6	762.3	608.8	5895.3
2008	9256.1	1386.0	537.9	848.1	476.1	7394.0
2009	10280.7	1587.1	255.9	1331.2	494.7	8198.9
2010	12813.4	2185.7	364.5	1821.2	452.8	10174.9
2011	16468.1	2593.0	600.0	1993.0	600.9	13274.2
2012	20395.2	1938.0	649.8	1288.3	705.2	17751.9
2013	22773.7	2278.0	571.7	1706.3	418.6	20077.1
房屋建筑面积竣工率(%) Rate of Floor Space of Buildings Completed (%)						
1990	46.6	43.0	47.1	33.1	52.9	
1991	46.3	43.0	44.7	39.5	51.2	
1992	47.1	42.7	45.6	36.0	52.7	
1993	43.2	33.9	38.9	21.3	56.0	11.6
1994	37.7	30.5	36.8	16.0	52.2	44.2
1995	35.8	41.2	39.4	16.6	55.8	23.6
1996	41.3	29.4	41.7	14.9	55.9	32.9
1997	43.1	32.7	42.6	22.0	59.6	23.8
1998	44.7	33.6	48.4	17.7	57.8	41.7
1999	49.6	37.8	49.2	22.0	63.7	47.8
2000	50.3	37.9	53.4	19.6	64.2	52.4
2001	55.1	44.3	56.0	31.1	65.0	60.7
2002	57.5	44.5	61.2	26.9	65.8	65.9
2003	54.2	41.3	51.1	25.4	63.1	64.1
2004	56.5	50.3	62.0	38.9	60.8	61.2
2005	57.0	46.5	46.3	46.7	60.8	63.6
2006	50.9	29.8	44.3	24.6	66.4	58.3
2007	50.5	29.5	51.5	19.9	58.8	58.1
2008	50.4	24.3	50.7	18.3	63.3	62.0
2009	50.2	28.0	49.0	25.8	61.9	58.4
2010	51.2	32.4	37.6	31.5	71.5	57.6
2011	53.1	28.2	38.7	26.0	76.8	63.1
2012	52.1	18.0	39.1	14.2	77.8	64.6
2013	46.5	15.8	33.0	13.4	69.9	59.2

注：本表资料包括施工总承包和专业承包企业，不含劳务分包企业(下同)。

Note: In this table, the data including general contract and specilized contract enterprises under construction, excluding labor divided contract (the same as the following tables)

14-2 按行业分建筑业主要经济指标（2013）
MAJOR ECONOMIC INDICATORS OF CONSTRUCTION ENTRPRISES BY SECTOR(2013)

指 标	Item	房屋和土木工程建筑业 Housing and Civil Engineering Construction	房屋工程 Housing Construction	土木工程 Civil Engineering	建筑安装业 Construction and Installation	建筑装饰业 Building Decorative Construction
施工企业个数(个)	Number of Construction Enterprises (unit)	2058	1435	623	455	485
建筑业总产值(亿元)	Gross Output Value of Construction Enterprises (100 million yuan)	7731.43	4800.62	2930.81	456.17	152.73
#建筑工程	Construction	7022.63	4261.17	2761.46	266.46	69.86
安装工程	Construction and Installation	532.57	434.79	97.78	155.18	54.77
固定资产折旧	Depreciation on Fixed Assets	80.07	33.17	46.90	4.64	1.37
本年应付工资总额	Wages Payable of This Year	760.51	544.96	215.55	53.95	15.69
本年应付福利费总额	Welfare Costs Payable of This Year					
工程结算税金及附加	Taxes abd Added Taxes of Settle Accounts	292.74	182.56	110.18	14.70	5.40
竣工产值(亿元)	Building Completed Output Value (100 million yuan)	3885.29	3201.21	684.08	300.04	114.34
房屋建筑施工面积(万平方米)	Floor Space Of Buildings under Construction (10000 sq.m)	47452.46	45070.45	2382.01	1382.88	27.70
#本年新开工	Beginning Projects inThis Year	25827.92	24554.56	1273.36	817.83	16.64
投标承包面积	Floor Space of Bidding System	34028.33	32120.51	1907.81	1033.32	8.95
房屋建筑竣工面积(万平方米)	Floor Space of Buildings Completed (10000 sq.m)	21870.46	21185.45	685.01	838.68	16.47
自有机械设备总台数(万台)	Number of Machinery and Equipment Owned (10000 units)	122.13	101.62	20.51	3.55	1.32
自有机械设备总功率(万千瓦)	Total Power of Machinery and Equipment Owned (10000 Kw)	1308.15	639.44	668.71	65.63	14.01
自有机械设备净值(亿元)	Net Value of Machinery and Equipment Owned (100 million yuan)	306.21	127.41	178.79	16.58	3.06
职工平均人数(万人)	Annual Average Number of Staff and Workers (10000 person)	156.71	122.41	34.30	11.03	3.78
全员劳动生产率(元/人)	Overall Labor Productivity (yuan/person)	493349.44	392178.58	854362.40	413718.29	404260.42
技术装备率(元/人)	Value of Machines Per Laborer (yuan/person)	19539.22	10408.87	52119.52	15034.70	8090.20
动力装备率(千瓦/人)	Motive Power Per Labor (kW/person)	8.35	5.22	19.49	5.95	3.71
利润总额(亿元)	Total Profits (100 million yuan)	344.22	219.88	124.34	27.21	8.82

14-3 按登记注册类型分建筑业主要经济指标（2013）

指 标		tem		合 计 Total	内资企业 Domestic Funded	#国 有 State - Owned
施工企业个数	（个）	Number of Construction Enterprises	(unit)	3212	3194	190
建筑业总产值	（亿元）	Gross Output Value of Construction Enterprises	(100 million yuan)	8465.50	8422.92	276.07
#建筑工程		Construction		7450.82	7409.08	207.12
安装工程		Construction and Installation		757.26	756.78	28.33
固定资产折旧		Depreciation on Fixed Assets		87.68	87.60	2.99
本年应付工资总额		Wages Payable of This Year		841.08	836.61	36.58
工程结算税金及附加		Taxes abd Added Taxes of Settle Accounts		316.88	315.53	9.43
竣工产值	（亿元）	Building Completed Output Value (100 million yuan)		4380.00	4362.42	174.57
房屋建筑施工面积	（万平方米）	Floor Space Of Buildings under Construction	(10000 sq.m)	48937.96	48697.71	413.37
#本年新开工		Beginning Projects inThis Year		26721.34	26556.71	244.86
#投标承包面积		Floor Space of Bidding System		35117.40	34881.73	281.71
房屋建筑竣工面积	（万平方米）	Floor Space of Buildings Completed	(10000 sq.m)	22773.72	22691.42	227.86
自有机械设备总台数	（万台）	Number of Machinery and Equipment Owned	(10000 units)	127.90	127.60	2.43
自有机械设备总功率	（万千瓦）	Total Power of Machinery and Equipment Owned	(10000 Kw)	1420.45	1418.09	64.81
自有机械设备净值	（亿元）	Net Value of Machinery and Equipment Owned	(100 million yuan)	331.97	331.32	13.92
职工平均人数	（万人）	Annual Average Number of Staff and Workers	(10000 person)	174.18	173.26	7.76
全员劳动生产率	（元/人）	Overall Labor Productivity	(yuan/person)	486008.21	486134.60	355802.45
技术装备率	（元/人）	Value of Machines Per Laborer	（yuan/person)	19058.64	19122.33	17933.92
动力装备率	（千瓦/人）	Motive Power Per Labor	(kW/person)	8.15	8.18	8.35
利润总额	（亿元）	Total Profits	(100 million yuan)	387.72	384.48	13.85

MAJOR ECONOMIC INDICATORS OF CONSTRUCTION ENTRPRISES BY REGISTRATION STATUS(2013)

#集 体 Collective - Collective - Owned	#股份合作 ShareHolding Cooperative Enterprises	#联 营 Joint - Owned Enterprises	#有限责任 Limited Liability Enterprises	#股份有限 Limited ShareHolding Enterprises	#私 营 Private - Owned Enterprises	#其 他 Others	港澳台商投资企业 Hongkong, Macao and Taiwan Funded Enterprises	外商投资企业 Foreign Funded Enterprises
91	6	3	1352	150	1401	1	14	4
65.68	7.87	2.05	5950.55	473.53	1647.16	0.01	7.00	35.58
57.64	6.97	1.39	5305.56	415.44	1414.95	0.01	6.17	35.57
7.53	0.90	0.03	518.27	31.87	169.85		0.48	
0.79	0.07	0.07	63.83	4.01	15.84	0.01	0.04	0.04
9.97	0.79	0.31	541.57	44.76	202.63	0.00	1.19	3.29
2.76	0.26	0.11	221.97	17.25	63.75	0.00	0.25	1.10
50.98	4.07	0.92	2667.57	275.41	1188.89	0.01	5.16	12.41
592.50	33.06	6.76	32444.35	3222.74	11984.92		4.58	235.67
419.66	6.63	5.39	16939.11	1948.90	6992.17		2.56	162.08
365.46	32.24	5.39	23322.73	2597.95	8276.26			235.67
411.87	18.50	6.76	13453.95	1564.45	7008.04		2.02	80.28
1.22	0.08	0.02	38.97	69.10	15.79	0.00	0.13	0.17
18.68	0.76	0.43	932.92	139.14	261.01	0.35	1.38	0.98
3.29	0.19	0.05	233.12	16.01	64.71	0.04	0.11	0.54
2.98	0.22	0.07	100.82	10.30	51.10	0.00	0.31	0.61
220277.03	351518.54	274366.80	590210.26	459873.61	322319.87	26538.46	224652.66	583796.36
11036.79	8262.62	6228.92	23122.16	15550.80	12662.44	155961.54	3661.00	8827.70
6.26	3.40	5.75	9.25	13.51	5.11	135.12	4.42	1.61
5.72	0.38	0.23	244.81	20.40	99.09	0.00	0.31	2.93

14-4 按登记注册类型分建筑业财务状况（2013）

单位：亿元

指 标	Item	合 计 Total	内资企业 Domestic Funded	#国 有 State - Owned
流动资产合计	Circulating Funds	4826.82	4806.26	188.58
#存货	Stock	1404.18	1403.22	38.34
固定资产合计	Total Fixed Assets	1008.55	1007.37	35.62
固定资产原价合计	Total Original Value of Fixed Assets	1059.05	1057.27	47.57
累计折旧	Total Depreciation Drawn Accumulated	420.21	419.53	20.01
#本年折旧	Depreciation Drawn This Year	87.68	87.60	2.99
在建工程	Projets Under Construction	79.82	79.75	4.59
资产总计	Total Assets	6457.93	6427.72	233.85
流动负债合计	Total Circulating Liability	3765.94	3755.11	147.01
负债合计	Total Long-Term Liability	4502.20	4488.28	164.89
所有者权益合计	Creditor's Equity	1955.63	1939.34	68.96
工程结算收入	Projets Settlement Revenue	8395.12	8356.29	281.42
工程结算成本	Cost of Projets Settlement Accounts	7274.16	7240.98	239.60
工程结算税金及附加	Tax and Extra Charges on Projets Settlement Accounts	316.88	315.53	9.43
营业利润	Profits of Projets Settlement Accounts	384.48	381.11	13.95
其他业务利润	Other Profits	11.05	11.04	3.84
管理费用	Management Expenses	288.82	288.06	13.80
#税金	Taxes	14.17	14.14	0.66
利润总额	Total Profits	387.72	384.48	13.85
应交所得税	Payable Income Taxes	77.81	76.62	2.35
应付利润	Payable Profits			
本年应付工资总额	Payable Total Wages This Year	841.08	836.61	36.58
亏损企业个数(个)	Number of Lossing-Making Enterprises	270	264	8

FINANCIAL INDICATORS OF CONSTRUCTION BY REGISTERATION STATUS (2013)

(100 million yuan)

#集 体 Collective - Owned	#股份合作 ShareHolding Cooperative Enterprises	#联 营 Joint - Owned Enterprises	#有限责任 Limited y Liabilit Enterprises	#股份有限 Limited ShareHolding Enterprises	#私营 Private - Owned Enterprises	#其他 Others	港澳台商投资企业 Hongkong, Macao and Taiwan Funded Enterprises	外商投资企业 Foreign Funded Enterprises
19.29	6.12	2.02	3535.57	310.00	744.00	0.05	12.35	8.21
3.65	1.01	1.15	1140.65	49.88	168.53	0.02	0.48	0.48
9.80	0.63	0.50	744.18	43.21	173.39	0.04	0.43	0.75
10.76	1.28	0.51	745.33	48.80	202.92	0.09	0.76	1.03
2.96	0.74	0.24	312.39	18.10	65.05	0.04	0.39	0.29
0.79	0.07	0.07	63.83	4.01	15.84	0.01	0.04	0.04
0.87	0.09		44.95	8.09	21.17		0.06	0.01
30.38	7.76	2.54	4758.98	406.44	987.67	0.11	20.14	10.07
12.08	3.80	1.87	2932.70	268.23	389.41	0.01	10.18	0.64
15.27	4.47	1.93	3520.29	283.68	497.74	0.01	10.19	3.73
15.11	3.29	0.61	1238.58	122.76	489.93	0.11	9.95	6.34
59.82	7.67	2.18	5983.54	453.36	1568.31	0.01	7.49	31.34
47.99	6.60	1.70	5232.14	394.53	1318.41	0.00	6.33	26.85
2.76	0.26	0.11	221.97	17.25	63.75	0.00	0.25	1.10
5.64	0.37	0.22	243.05	20.04	97.83	0.00	0.44	2.93
0.01			5.77	0.47	0.95		0.01	
2.35	0.31	0.11	203.10	14.67	53.71	0.00	0.37	0.39
0.30	0.01	0.01	7.13	1.14	4.89		0.00	0.02
5.72	0.38	0.23	244.81	20.40	99.09	0.00	0.31	2.93
1.04	0.08	0.03	47.11	3.89	22.11		0.12	1.07
9.97	0.79	0.31	541.57	44.76	202.63	0.00	1.19	3.29
5			108	3	139	1	5	1

14-5 按行业分建筑业财务状况（2013）

FINANCIAL INDICATORS OF CNSTRUCTION BY SECTOR (2013)

单位：亿元 (100 million yuan)

指 标	Item	房屋和土木工程建筑业 Housing and Civil Engineering Construction	房屋工程 Housing Construction	土木工程 Civil Engineering	建筑安装业 Construction and Installation	建筑装饰业 Building Decorative Construction
流动资产合计	Circulating Funds	4318.84	2037.63	2281.21	350.26	88.95
#存货	Stock	1294.53	557.67	736.86	76.21	21.51
固定资产合计	Total Fixed Assets	926.73	324.16	602.57	50.14	15.52
固定资产原价合计	Total Original Value of Fixed Assets	947.33	388.77	558.56	72.89	18.45
累计折旧	Total Depreciation Drawn Accumulated	373.72	126.80	246.91	32.70	5.95
#本年折旧	Depreciation Drawn This Year	80.07	33.17	46.90	4.64	1.37
在建工程	Projets Under Construction	66.55	36.28	30.27	8.84	2.46
资产总计	Total Assets	5825.00	2700.12	3124.87	432.30	109.42
流动负债合计	Total Circulating Liability	3416.94	1442.22	1974.72	250.91	50.06
负债合计	Total Long-Term Liability	4126.25	1656.91	2469.34	270.18	52.91
所有者权益合计	Creditor's Equity	1698.75	1043.21	655.54	162.12	56.41
工程结算收入	Projets Settlement Revenue	7643.71	4563.50	3080.21	493.14	149.72
工程结算成本	Cost of Projets Settlement Accounts	6647.73	3958.93	2688.80	418.98	120.72
工程结算税金及附加	Tax and Extra Charges on Projets Settlement Accounts	292.74	182.56	110.18	14.70	5.40
营业利润	Profits of Projets Settlement Accounts	341.94	219.75	122.19	27.34	7.91
其他业务利润	Other Profits	7.32	4.55	2.77	3.39	0.29
管理费用	Management Expenses	245.72	126.35	119.37	28.14	8.63
#税金	Taxes	12.44	9.76	2.69	1.14	0.29
利润总额	Total Profits	344.22	219.88	124.34	27.21	8.82
应交所得税	Payable Income Taxes	69.04	49.77	19.26	5.00	2.04
本年应付工资总额	Payable Total Wages This Year	760.51	544.96	215.55	53.95	15.69
亏损企业个数(个)	Number of Lossing-Making Enterprises	108	59	49	66	72

14-6 分市州建筑业企业生产情况(2013)
STATISTICS ON PRODUCTION OF CONSTRUCTION ENTERPRISES OF CITIES AND PREFECTURE(2013)

单位：亿元 (100 million yuan)

项目	Item	建筑业总产值 Total Output Value of Construction Industry	建筑工程产值 Output Value of Construction Projects	安装工程产值 Output Value of Installation Projects	其他产值 Output Value of Other Projects	竣工产值 Output Value of Projects Completed
湖北省	**Hubei Province**	**8465.50**	**7450.82**	**757.26**	**257.42**	**4380.00**
武汉市	Wuhan Municipality	4879.24	4252.93	463.86	162.45	2246.75
黄石市	Huangshi Municipality	243.67	223.25	15.77	4.64	181.84
十堰市	Shiyan Municipality	305.83	293.15	9.53	3.15	112.99
宜昌市	Yichang Municipality	701.04	631.99	51.73	17.32	220.86
襄阳市	Xiangyang Municipality	581.04	512.30	58.63	10.10	327.59
鄂州市	Ezhou Municipality	95.79	69.57	16.45	9.76	61.93
荆门市	Jingmen Municipality	93.65	84.44	5.90	3.31	70.82
孝感市	Xiaogan Municipality	314.29	291.49	15.69	7.11	228.89
荆州市	Jingzhou Municipality	197.11	179.82	10.33	6.96	155.09
黄冈市	Huanggang Municipality	649.30	558.40	76.36	14.53	486.71
咸宁市	Xianning Municipality	98.40	89.20	5.58	3.62	73.16
随州市	Suizhou Municipality	65.80	58.29	3.01	4.51	55.83
恩施自治州	Enshi Prefecture	86.77	79.71	4.90	2.16	60.98
仙桃市	Xiantao Municipality	22.90	22.13	0.52	0.26	18.63
潜江市	Qianjiang Municipality	88.44	70.97	14.96	2.51	49.34
天门市	Tianmen Municipality	36.75	28.65	3.23	4.87	23.85
神农架林区	Shennongjia Forest Zone	5.49	4.51	0.81	0.17	4.75

14-7 分市州建筑业企业财务状况（2013）

单位：亿元

项目	Item	资产合计 Total Assets	流动资产合计 Total Circulating Assets	固定资产合计 Total Fixed Assets
湖北省	Hubei Province	**6457.93**	**4826.82**	**1008.55**
武汉市	Wuhan Municipality	4419.52	3384.09	654.31
黄石市	Huangshi Municipality	209.15	174.22	27.57
十堰市	Shiyan Municipality	180.02	147.05	26.81
宜昌市	Yichang Municipality	495.43	295.23	78.56
襄阳市	Xiangyang Municipality	316.83	248.08	42.66
鄂州市	Ezhou Municipality	49.41	35.67	10.06
荆门市	Jingmen Municipality	70.49	50.88	14.79
孝感市	Xiaogan Municipality	113.91	81.66	26.35
荆州市	Jingzhou Municipality	111.78	73.74	29.68
黄冈市	Huanggang Municipality	190.98	139.82	42.58
咸宁市	Xianning Municipality	68.47	49.96	14.81
随州市	Suizhou Municipality	33.75	23.14	8.88
恩施自治州	Enshi Prefecture	53.53	37.37	11.66
仙桃市	Xiantao Municipality	18.94	14.88	3.15
潜江市	Qianjiang Municipality	71.28	57.46	10.60
天门市	Tianmen Municipality	48.98	10.64	3.97
神农架林区	Shennongjia Forest Zone	5.46	2.92	2.11

FINANCIAL INDICATORS OF CONSTRUCTION ENTERPRISES BY CITIES AND PREFECTURE (2013)

(100 million yuan)

流动负债合计 Total Circulating Liability	负债合计 Total Long-Term Liability	所有者权益合计 Creditor's Equity	工程结算收入 Projects Settlement Revenue	营业利润 Operating Profits	利润总额 Total profits
3765.94	**4502.20**	**1955.63**	**8395.12**	**384.48**	**387.72**
2765.08	3360.05	1059.37	4998.50	170.05	174.72
129.56	138.15	71.01	242.74	13.20	13.30
113.35	122.11	57.91	282.60	12.75	12.65
254.47	293.88	201.54	702.42	56.03	55.76
178.36	203.98	112.85	527.87	34.30	33.78
22.89	23.36	26.05	91.68	4.52	4.49
31.74	35.62	34.87	91.26	6.45	6.41
37.30	45.42	68.48	285.17	16.77	16.35
39.33	48.30	63.48	184.91	10.96	11.27
73.21	85.25	105.72	589.63	34.93	34.67
29.84	34.77	33.70	88.25	5.10	5.27
9.33	13.03	20.72	65.16	3.92	3.90
23.73	26.03	27.50	83.72	7.44	7.29
7.91	8.61	10.34	25.35	1.23	1.23
35.89	44.68	26.60	94.28	4.05	3.82
10.77	15.66	33.32	35.76	2.55	2.59
3.19	3.29	2.16	5.82	0.20	0.20

14-8 分市州建筑业企业工程完成情况(2013)
STATISTICS ON PROJECTS COMPLETION OF CONSTRUCTION ENTERPRISES BY CITIES AND PREFECTURES (2013)

单位：万平方米 (10 000 sq.m)

项　目	Item	房屋建筑施工面积 Floor Space of Housing Construction	本年新开工面积 Beginning projects in This Year	实行投标承包面积 Actual Floor Space by Contracts and Bids	房屋建筑竣工面积 Floor Space of Housing Projects Completed	#住　宅 Residential Buildings	#办公用房 Office Buildings
湖北省	**Hubei Province**	**48937.96**	**26721.34**	**35117.40**	**22773.72**	**15182.75**	**1447.18**
武汉市	Wuhan Municipality	26369.04	12151.09	18622.25	10103.98	6585.10	698.67
黄石市	Huangshi Municipality	1802.44	1100.35	1423.87	1019.45	699.46	50.89
十堰市	Shiyan Municipality	1249.87	702.50	741.28	508.43	346.57	40.57
宜昌市	Yichang Municipality	2100.62	1327.25	1613.91	1021.90	758.01	58.05
襄阳市	Xiangyang Municipality	3901.11	2194.21	3266.07	1664.91	1123.16	42.91
鄂州市	Ezhou Municipality	843.62	525.18	526.36	453.87	361.26	1.42
荆门市	Jingmen Municipality	771.85	509.87	744.65	388.88	270.41	19.06
孝感市	Xiaogan Municipality	3081.61	2360.19	1650.58	1804.50	1381.97	129.21
荆州市	Jingzhou Municipality	1471.55	895.51	995.47	776.19	508.55	35.38
黄冈市	Huanggang Municipality	4219.89	2853.17	3301.86	3140.59	1952.54	243.02
咸宁市	Xianning Municipality	643.59	511.17	388.84	504.19	388.60	18.25
随州市	Suizhou Municipality	689.02	445.49	524.72	452.50	259.79	49.06
恩施自治州	Enshi Prefecture	675.21	417.66	417.27	383.73	239.88	21.85
仙桃市	Xiantao Municipality	214.27	141.96	169.58	143.43	105.44	6.30
潜江市	Qianjiang Municipality	545.21	341.87	479.97	240.16	118.85	6.74
天门市	Tianmen Municipality	318.52	206.76	226.44	151.81	70.22	24.90
神农架林区	Shennongjia Forest Zone	40.54	37.11	24.25	15.19	12.93	0.89

主要统计指标解释

建筑业统计单位 指从事房屋、构筑物建造和设备安装活动的法人企业。建筑业法人企业应具有建筑业资质并能够独立核算，同时其应具备以下条件：①依法成立，有自己的名称、组织机构和场所，能够承担民事责任；②独立拥有和使用资产，承担负债，有权与其他单位签订合同；③独立核算盈亏，能够编制资产负债表。

建筑业总产值 是以货币形式表现的建筑业企业在一定时期内生产的建筑业产品和提供的服务的总和。建筑业总产值包括：

⑴建筑工程产值：指列入建筑工程预算内的各种工程价值。

⑵安装工程产值：指设备安装工程价值，不包括被安装设备本身的价值。

⑶其他产值：建筑业总产值中除建筑工程、安装工程以外的产值。包括房屋构筑物修理产值、非标准设备制造产值、总包企业向分包企业收取的管理费以及不能明确划分的施工活动所完成的产值。

a.房屋构筑物修理产值：指房屋和构筑物修理所完成的产值，但不包括被修理房屋、构筑物本身价值和生产设备的修理产值。

b.非标准设备制造产值：指加工制造没有定型的非标准生产设备的加工费和原材料价值(如化工厂、炼油厂用的各种罐、槽，矿井生产统一使用的各种漏斗、三角槽、阀门等)以及附属加工厂为本企业承建工程制作的非标准设备的价值。

建筑业增加值 指建筑业企业在报告期内以货币形式表现的建筑业生产经营活动的最终成果。

从 2004 年第一次全国经济普查开始，建筑业现价增加值按生产法和分配法(收入法)两种方法计算，以收入法的计算结果为准，即从收入的角度出发，根据生产要素在生产过程中应得的收入份额计算。具体计算方法：经济普查年度建筑业增加值按照《经济普查年度 GDP 核算方案》计算，非经济普查年度建筑业增加值按照《非经济普查年度 GDP 核算方案》计算。

房屋建筑施工面积 指在报告期内施过工的全部房屋建筑面积，包括本期新开工的房屋面积、上期施工跨入本期继续施工的房屋面积、上期停缓建在本期恢复施工的房屋面积、本期竣工的房屋面积及本期施工后又停缓建的房屋面积。

房屋建筑竣工面积 指在报告期内房屋建筑按照设计要求全部完工，达到了使用条件，经验收鉴定合格，正式移交使用单位的房屋建筑面积。

Explanatory Notes on Main Statistical Indicators

Statistical Unit in Construction refers to corporate enterprise engaged in the construction of buildings and structures and in the installation of equipment. A corporate construction enterprise should have qualification certificates with independent accounting system, and should meet the following 3 requirements: a) being set up in line with relevant legal basis, having its full name, organization and location, and capable of taking civil liabilities; b) independently possessing and using its assets and assuming its liabilities, and entitled to sign contracts with other institutions; and c) making independent accounts of its profits and losses, and capable of compiling its own balance sheet.

Gross Output Value of Construction refers to total of construction products and services, expressed in money terms, produced or rendered by construction and installation enterprises during a given period of time. It includes:

(1) Output value of construction projects, that is the value of projects covered by the project budgets;

(2) Output value of installation projects, that is the value of the installation of equipment, (excluding the value of the equipment

to be installed);

(3) Output value of others, that is the output value of construction industry excluding that of construction projects and installation projects. It includes: output value of repair of buildings and structures; output value of non-standard equipment manufacturing; overhead expenses received by contracted enterprises to the sub-contracted enterprises and the completed output value of construction activities that have no clear definition.

a. Output value of repair of buildings and structures, that is the value created through the repairs of buildings or structures, but does not include the value of buildings or structures being repaired and the value of the repair of production equipment;

b. Output value of manufactured non-standard equipment, that is the value of non-standard production equipment including raw materials and manufacturing cost made for the construction project (i.e., chemical plant; kettles or tanks used by refineries; various fillers, triangle tanks, valves used by mines), and the output value of equipment manufactured by subsidiary workshops.

Value-added of Construction refers to the final result of the activities of production and management of construction industry in monetary terms in the reference period.

Starting from the 2004 economic census, value-added of construction is calculated by both production approach and income approach, with the income approach as the final approach, where the calculation is based on the share of production factor in the production process. Specifically, value-added of construction for census years is calculated in accordance with the Programme of Compilation of GDP and National Accounts for the Year of Economic Census, and value-added of construction for other years is calculated in accordance with the Programme of Compilation of GDP and National Accounts for the Non Economic Census Years.

Floor Space of Buildings Under Construction refers to floor space of buildings under construction during the reference period, including newly started buildings, buildings started earlier and continued during the reference period, and buildings suspended earlier but restarted during the reference period, buildings completed during the reference period, and buildings under construction and then suspended during the reference period.

Floor Space of Buildings Completed refers to the floor space of buildings that are completed in the reference period in accordance with the requirements of the design, up to the standard for putting them into use, and have been checked and accepted by concerned departments as qualified ones.

15 交通运输、邮电

Transportation, Post and Telecommunications Services

资料整理：朱　焰

交通运输、邮电

Transportation,Post and Telecommunication Service

2013

全社会客运量	Passenger Capacity of The Whole Society	143100.28	(万人)
#公路	Public Road	129533.75	(万人)
全社会货运量	Volume of Freight Traffic	139740.26	(万吨)
#公路	Public Road	108824.21	(万吨)
邮电业务总量	Postal Service Portfolio	547.62	(亿元)
#函件	Letters	1.05	(亿件)
年末固定电话用户	Local Telephone Subscriber End of Year	984.00	(万户)
年末移动电话用户	Mobile Phone Subscriber End of Year	4416.80	(万户)

全 社 会 客 货 运 量

Passenger Capactity of The Whole Society

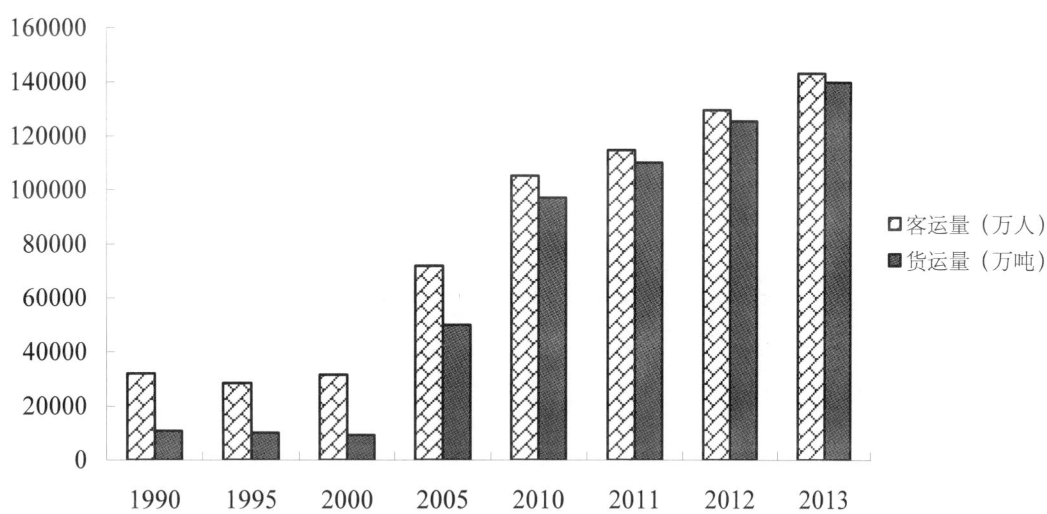

附：全社会客货运量

Passenger Capacity of The Whole Society

年份 Year	客运量（万人） Passenger Capacity (10 000 persons)	货运量（万吨） volume of freight traffic (10 000 tons)
1990	32146	10916
1995	28508	10174
2000	31593	9345
2005	71892	49924
2010	105132	96938
2011	114737	110168
2012	129511	126195
2013	143100	139740

15-1 交通运输业基本情况

指 标	Item	1990	1995
运输线路长度 (公里)	Length of Transportation Routes (km)		
铁路营业里程	Total Railway's Length in Operation	1634	1940
公路通车里程	Total Highway in Operation	47511	48728
#等级公路里程	Length of Expressway and Class I to IV Highway	24532	30910
#高速公路	Expressway		
一级公路	Class I Highway	196	641
二级公路	Class II Highway	1973	4967
内河航道里程	Navigable Inland Waterways	8960	8969
客运量总计 (万人)	Total Passenger Traffic (10 000 persons)	32145.93	28508.20
铁路	Railway	2107.00	2300.00
公路	Highway	27333.00	24315.00
水运	Waterway	2693.00	1745.00
民用航空	Civil Aviation	12.93	150.00
旅客周转量 (亿人公里)	Turnover Volume of Passenger Traffic (100 million persons-km)	225.85	285.29
货物运输量总计 (万吨)	Total Freight Traffic (10 000 tons)	10916.10	10173.62
铁路	Railway	3901.00	3986.00
公路	Highway	2941.00	2600.00
水运	Waterway	3784.00	3585.00
货物周转量 (亿吨公里)	Turnover Volume of FreightTraffic (100 million tons-km)	670.53	776.44
民用车辆拥有量 (万辆)	Civil Moto Vehicles		
#民用汽车拥有量	Civil Vehicles	20.32	34.89
#载客汽车	Passenger Vehicles	6.08	14.96
载货汽车	Trucks	13.04	18.61
#营运汽车	Moto Vehicles in Operation		
#私人汽车	Private Vehicles		
民用运输船舶拥有量 (艘)	Civil Transpot Vessels (units)		
机动船	Moto Vessels		
驳船	Barges		
港口货物吞吐量 (万吨)	Cargo Handled at Ports (10 000 tons)		

TRANSPORTATION

2000	2005	2009	2010	2011	2012	2013
2025	2758	3662	3032	3340	3463	3551
57850	91131	197196	206212	212746	218151	226912
48062	76075	168834	187812	196452	203145	212893
569	1649	3283	3674	4006	4006	4333
611	1092	1725	2210	2395	2515	2789
7911	15225	16261	16159	16852	17233	17576
8309	8988	8988	8988	8988	8988	8988
31593.00	71892.00	96219.00	105415.50	114736.92	129510.90	143100.28
3469.00	4615.00	6440.00	7281.30	8503.80	9177.40	12101.80
27184.00	66183.00	88703.00	96873.00	104971.00	118369.00	129533.75
679.00	601.00	371.00	375.80	347.60	443.50	528.00
261.00	494.00	705.00	885.40	914.52	933.50	936.73
398.32	803.90	1096.30	1262.26	1444.66	1576.97	1761.10
9345.19	49923.52	82714.00	97006.94	110167.83	126194.64	139740.26
3857.00	8491.00	9839.00	10145.60	10059.40	9177.40	9010.40
2228.00	33481.00	59563.00	71020.00	82741.00	97136.00	108824.21
3255.00	7944.00	13305.00	15832.00	17358.00	19070.00	21897.00
831.64	1682.48	2808.46	3370.37	4044.45	4351.80	4883.01
	393.90	760.97	761.11	822.68	879.01	967.23
47.55	103.04	187.02	224.60	264.82	305.07	363.68
24.69	53.40	119.81	151.51	186.72	277.76	282.29
21.72	30.96	46.07	53.29	59.72	62.69	68.62
	20.33	32.20	36.60	40.28	40.37	42.04
41.72	59.66	131.56	165.39	200.38	238.64	292.00
5905	5362	5460	5502	5505	4895	4938
4188	4158	4175	4634	4884	4531	4794
1717	1204	1285	868	621	364	144
4113.46	13992.51	16671.77	18782.67	21662.91	23518.12	26219.00

15-2 客 运 量

PASSENGER TRAFFIC

单位：万人 (10 000 persons)

年份 Year	总计 Total	铁路 Railway	公路 Highway	水运 Waterway	民用航空 Civil Aviation
1978	12009.20	2854.00	7429.00	1722.00	4.20
1980	16629.26	3217.00	11282.00	2123.00	7.26
1985	28178.22	3353.00	22378.00	2433.00	14.22
1990	32145.93	2107.00	27333.00	2693.00	12.93
1991	33982.62	2016.00	29279.00	2654.00	33.62
1992	34726.00	2077.00	29635.00	2894.00	120.00
1993	30152.00	2265.00	25116.00	2665.00	106.00
1994	29607.00	2358.00	24819.00	2210.00	120.00
1995	28508.20	2300.00	24315.00	1743.00	150.00
1996	29045.40	2248.00	25180.00	1449.00	168.00
1997	29503.08	2127.00	25684.00	1538.00	154.08
1998	28208.00	2218.00	24540.00	1306.00	144.00
1999	29360.14	2545.00	25596.00	1080.00	139.14
2000	63306.00	3469.00	58897.00	679.00	261.00
2001	62696.00	3632.00	58018.00	767.00	279.00
2002	63382.00	3813.00	58623.00	638.00	308.00
2003	62880.00	3602.00	58371.00	573.00	334.42
2004	68167.00	4072.00	63127.00	522.00	446.11
2005	71892.00	4615.00	66183.00	601.00	494.00
2006	75440.00	4850.00	69335.00	706.00	549.00
2007	84088.00	5125.00	77514.00	736.00	712.70
2008	89720.00	6027.00	82532.00	388.00	774.00
2009	96219.00	6440.00	88703.00	371.00	705.00
2010	105415.50	7281.30	96873.00	375.80	885.40
2011	114736.92	8503.80	104971.00	347.60	914.52
2012	129510.90	9764.90	118369.00	443.50	933.50
2013	143100.28	12101.80	129533.75	528.00	936.73

注:2003年以后为全社会口径

Note: It's the whole society caliber after 2003.

15-3 旅 客 周 转 量

TURNOVER VOLUME OF PASSENGER TRAFFIC

单位：亿人公里 (100 million person-kms)

年份 Year	总计 Total	铁路 Railway	公路 Highway	水运 Waterway	民用航空 Civil Aviation
1978	69.38	30.72	24.85	13.54	0.17
1980	95.88	41.79	36.20	17.52	0.37
1985	185.25	84.00	81.33	19.40	0.52
1990	225.85	82.83	112.83	29.28	0.91
1991	257.68	98.09	126.70	30.19	2.70
1992	286.35	104.89	135.61	34.72	11.13
1993	281.28	113.60	123.64	33.50	10.54
1994	283.98	121.91	121.40	28.71	11.96
1995	285.29	129.47	117.76	22.71	15.35
1996	285.04	121.17	124.97	21.09	17.81
1997	282.53	118.62	123.39	24.14	16.38
1998	278.66	126.68	118.51	18.79	14.68
1999	300.38	146.54	124.46	14.09	15.29
2000	563.78	232.00	297.46	8.84	25.48
2001	574.24	248.00	293.35	5.87	27.02
2002	633.6.9	283.00	317.02	3.60	30.07
2003	617.68	271.00	309.00	4.00	33.68
2004	703.95	322.80	334.00	3.20	43.95
2005	803.90	389.40	358.00	4.20	52.30
2006	847.42	408.10	374.80	5.10	59.42
2007	947.71	440.80	423.80	5.30	77.81
2008	1077.68	474.01	522.57	2.30	78.80
2009	1096.31	466.70	562.34	2.49	64.78
2010	1262.26	528.90	631.39	2.92	99.05
2011	1444.66	639.15	700.06	2.49	102.97
2012	1576.00	663.60	804.07	2.94	106.36
2013	1761.10	756.40	892.25	3.14	109.31

15-4 货 运 量
FREIGHT TRAFFIC

单位：万吨 (10 000 tons)

年份 Year	总计 Total	铁路 Railway	公路 Highway	水运 Waterway	#内河 Inland Waterway	#海运 Seashipping
1978	10199	3513	3556	3130		
1980	8420	3211	2199	3110		
1985	11059	2659	3852	3463		
1990	10916	3901	2941	3784		
1991	11217	3957	2999	3996		
1992	11565	4018	2828	4364		
1993	11184	4029	2734	4248		
1994	10663	3964	2666	3641		
1995	10174	3986	2600	3585		
1996	9928	3779	2537	3268		
1997	9389	3882	2280	3119		
1998	10154	3999	2009	4040		
1999	10517	3964	2141	4313		
2000	40949	6558	27863	6270	6202	68
2001	41476	7094	29851	4275	4198	77
2002	42064	7400	28777	5630	5390	240
2003	44661	7825	30348	6195	5830	365
2004	47073	7872	31584	7259	6823	436
2005	50317	8491	33481	7944	7466	478
2006	52885	8990	35361	8242	7679	536
2007	58523	9728	39568	9027	7765	1262
2008	75778	10202	52759	12681	8182	4499
2009	82714	9839	59563	13305	8108	5197
2010	97007	10145	71020	15832	9916	6082
2011	110168	10059	82741	17358	10817	6536
2012	125392	9177	97136	19070	11836	7275
2013	139740	9010	108824	21897	13575	8042

15-5 货物周转量

TURNOVER VOLUME OF FREIGHT TRAFFIC

单位：亿吨公里 (100 million ton-km)

年份 Year	总计 Total	铁路 Railway	公路 Highway	水运 Waterway	#内河 Inland Waterway	#沿海 Seashipping
1978	281.09	191.72	9.22	80.15		
1980	326.85	206.14	9.85	110.85		
1985	507.57	320.37	16.59	169.94		
1990	670.53	415.17	14.72	235.04		
1991	720.23	455.00	14.67	245.41		
1992	757.00	461.81	13.89	272.70		
1993	753.52	477.64	11.99	259.90		
1994	743.21	505.57	10.23	222.32		
1995	776.44	544.40	9.62	222.20		
1996	775.79	552.32	9.93	208.05		
1997	725.34	501.77	8.72	212.21		
1998	696.62	465.81	7.59	220.63		
1999	696.27	457.70	8.25	227.76		
2000	1156.57	618.37	227.16	305.29	295.07	10.22
2001	1097.60	634.90	218.97	237.31	226.15	11.16
2002	1212.82	680.00	211.49	313.60	271.30	42.29
2003	1313.13	703.80	224.00	377.00	315.38	61.61
2004	1485.76	781.83	235.60	461.08	395.75	65.33
2005	1689.86	987.60	251.00	443.20	391.05	105.00
2006	1730.93	1021.40	266.10	437.90	379.81	58.10
2007	1902.17	1138.20	302.09	458.00	361.93	95.83
2008	2699.97	1096.90	789.37	810.46	416.17	394.29
2009	2808.46	1032.40	930.10	845.18	402.82	442.36
2010	3370.37	1144.60	1079.13	1145.52	547.77	470.00
2011	4044.45	1226.80	1277.71	1538.83	625.26	609.61
2012	4693.61	1194.10	1565.45	1590.65	740.76	683.36
2013	4883.01	1195.70	1818.18	1868.08	946.02	756.69

15-6 全省民用车辆拥有量(2013)
NUMBER OF CIVIL MOTOR VEHICLES OWNED BY WHOLE PROVINCE(2013)

单位：辆 (unit)

指标	Item	总计 Total	营运 Working	非营运 Non-Working
合计	Total	9672257	733314	8933771
汽车	Civil Vehicles	3636753	597620	3033961
载客汽车	Passenger Vehicles	2822917	116143	2701602
#大型	Lage Scale	48994	34769	11179
中型	Medium Scale	40898	13879	25076
小型	Small Scale	2694183	66433	2627579
#轿车	Cars	1804109	60369	1743740
载货汽车	Trucks	686161	420383	265778
#重型	Heavy Scale	133109	122396	10713
中型	Medium Scale	84916	76205	8711
轻型	Light Scale	463797	220056	243741
#普通载货	Ordinary Trucks	320727	120706	200021
其他汽车	Other Vehicles	127675	61094	66581
#三轮汽车	Tricycle Motocars	24696	8722	15974
低速汽车	Low Speed Vehicles	68084	44348	23736
摩托车	Motorear	4805462	102510	4702952
#普通	Ordinary Motor	4735945	102457	4633488
轻便	Light Motor	69517	53	69464
拖拉机	Tractors	1195439		1195439
大中型	Large	77		77
小型方向盘式	Small Scale	1195295		1195295
挂车	Freight Trailers	34005	32873	1132
其他类型车	Other Motor Vehicles	598	239	359

注：本表“其他汽车”中，包括三轮和四轮农用运输车。
Note:Tricycles and four-wheel farming vehicles are inclued in "Other Vehicles".

15-7　私人车辆拥有量
NUMBER OF PRIVATE - OWNED VEHICLES

单位：辆　　　　(unit)

指　标	Item	2000	2005	2010	2011	2012	2013
民用汽车	Civil Vehicles	475500	596601	1653948	2003831	2386393	2919992
载客汽车	Passenger Vehicles	245500	297095	1153728	1473193	1861548	2366962
#大型	Lage Scale	29200	3312	2939	2840	1258	1011
轿车	Cars		177650	773727	982237	1234812	1556798
载货汽车	Ordinary Trucks	211400	135352	327509	373852	405060	452886
#重型	#Heavy Scale		8766	33281	40982	45874	51217
其它汽车	Others		164154	172711	156786	119785	100144
摩托车	Motors	1241000	2853113	4971619	5182441	4946723	4793599
载货挂车	Freight Trailers	4400	1714	6467	7866	8927	10255

15-8　水路运输工具拥有量(2013)
NUMBER OF WATER TRANSPORT TOOLS(2013)

指　标	Item	机动船 Power Boat	客船 Passenger Ship	货船 Cargo Ship	拖船 Tugboat
数量　(艘)	Quantity　(ship)	4562	852	3566	144
总载重量　(吨位)	Total Carrying Capacity　(tonage)	7454589		7454589	
净载重量　(吨位)	Net Load　(tonage)	7340799		7340799	
载客量　(客位)	Passenger Carrying Capacity　(person)	41611	41611		
标准箱	TEU	1127		1127	
功率　(千瓦)	Power　(kw)	1892374	108527	1725949	57898

15-9 分市、州公路旅客运输完成情况(2013)
STATISTICS ON HIGHWAY PASSFNGER TRANSPORTATION OF CITIES AND PREFECTURES(2013)

地区	Region	旅客运输量(万人) Passenger Traffic (10,000 person)	增长速度(%) Growth Rate (%)	旅客周转量(亿人公里) Turnover Volume of Passenger Traffic (100 million person-km)	增长速度(%) Growth Rate (%)
全　省	**Province**	**129533.75**	**9.4**	**892.25**	**11.0**
#武汉市	Wuhan Municipality	16521	-1.6	124.76	-2.1
黄石市	Huangshi Municipality	5031	11.4	40.48	15.3
十堰市	Shiyan Municipality	7933	13.1	70.51	14.5
宜昌市	Yichang Municipality	14969	14.1	79.36	16.1
襄阳市	Xiangyang Municipality	15938	14.1	89.86	16.1
鄂州市	Ezhou Municipality	2399	15.0	14.42	15.0
荆门市	Jingmen Municipality	8008	12.4	55.41	15.6
孝感市	Xiaogan Municipality	8971	9.0	65.14	14.7
荆州市	Jingzhou Municipality	10397	11.1	83.58	14.7
黄冈市	Huanggang Municipality	12959	5.4	93.70	5.7
咸宁市	Xianning Municipality	6704	10.8	44.16	17.1
随州市	Suizhou Municipality	5947	10.8	31.69	11.2
恩施自治州	Enshi Municipality	3011	11.2	33.03	10.2
仙桃市	Xiantao Municipality	3292	13.0	21.42	13.1
潜江市	Qianjiang Municipality	3290	2.6	17.63	3.3
天门市	Tianmen Municipality	3706	15.5	23.59	16.7
神农架林区	Shennongjia Forest Zone	459	11.1	3.51	15.4

15-10 分市、州公路货物运输完成情况(2013)
STATISTICS ON HIGHWAY FREIGHT TRANSPORTATION OF CITIES AND PREFECTURES(2013)

地区	Region	货物运输量(万吨) Freight Traffic (10 000 ton)	增长速度(%) Growth Rate (%)	货物周转量 Turnover Volume of Freight Traffic (100 million ton-km)	增长速度(%) Growth Rate (%)
全 省	**Province**	**108824.00**	**12.0**	**1818.18**	**16.1**
#武汉市	Wuhan Municipality	25023.00	2.8	468.35	14.0
黄石市	Huangshi Municipality	7407.00	15.1	114.51	17.5
十堰市	Shiyan Municipality	5883.00	14.7	110.26	13.7
宜昌市	Yichang Municipality	13693.00	15.6	193.68	17.9
襄阳市	Xiangyang Municipality	15033.00	15.6	221.92	17.9
鄂州市	Ezhou Municipality	1975.00	15.0	18.97	15.0
荆门市	Jingmen Municipality	12066.00	14.9	217.96	17.0
孝感市	Xiaogan Municipality	3315.00	14.5	55.30	17.1
荆州市	Jingzhou Municipality	5239.00	13.0	103.25	17.0
黄冈市	Huanggang Municipality	3597.00	16.1	51.25	16.8
咸宁市	Xianning Municipality	3530.00	16.3	60.43	17.7
随州市	Suizhou Municipality	3143.00	15.2	68.74	16.2
恩施自治州	Enshi Municipality	3401.00	15.0	52.14	17.5
仙桃市	Xiantao Municipality	1283.00	13.2	16.29	13.6
潜江市	Qianjiang Municipality	2249.00	15.3	41.03	15.4
天门市	Tianmen Municipality	1598.00	15.5	18.60	15.7
神农架林区	Shennongjia Forest Zone	400.00	13.9	5.52	14.0

15-11 邮电业务基本情况
BASIC CONDITIONS OF THE POST AND TELECOMMUNICATION SERVICES

指　　标		Item		2000	2005	2010	2012	2013
邮电业务总量	**(亿元)**	**Total Volume of Post and Telecommunication Services**	**(100 million yuan)**		**373.63**	**1028.09**	**491.46**	**547.62**
邮政业务总量		Postal Services		21.50	23.40	55.71	52.55	74.15
电信业务总量		Telecommunication Services			350.20	972.38	438.91	473.47
函件	(亿件)	Letters	(100 million pcs)	3.60	1.30	1.00	1.31	1.05
包件	(万件)	Parcels	(10 000 pcs)	473.00	320.00	210.10	174.70	170.20
快递业务量	(万件)	Special Express	(10 000 pcs)	428.00	685.30	5476.60	11629.80	21991.00
报刊期发数	(万份)	Newspaper and Magzines Circulation	(10 000 pcs)	1368.00	643.00	55102.50	67384.00	72770.50
固定电话用户	(万户)	Fixed telephone subscribers	(10 000 subscribers)	726.00	1236.00	1026.40	1003.60	984.00
年末城市电话	(万户)	Urban Telephone Subscribers at Year-end	(10 000 subscribers)	546.00	900.00	670.70	666.20	662.90
年末农村电话	(万户)	Rural Telephones	(10 000 subscribers)	180.00	336.00	355.70	337.40	321.10
年末移动电话用户	(万户)	Mobile Telephone Subscribers at Year-end	(10 000 subscribers)		1401.00	3454.70	4554.10	4416.80
互联网宽带接入用户	(万户)	Internet Users	(10 000 subscribers)		128.00	459.40	708.00	813.30
邮政局所、服务网点合计	(处)	Post and Telecommunication Offices		2047	1933	2022	1678	1672
邮路总长度(单程)	(公里)	Length of Postal Routes and Rural Delivery (One Way)	(km)			57483	57125	57223
邮路线路总条数	(条)	Routes				411	577	578
农村投递线路条数	(条)	Highway Routes				4198	3747	3747
农村投递线路长度(单程)	(公里)	Railway Routes(One Way)	(km)			194656.00	211898.00	211898.00
邮电通信工具拥有量		Telecommunication Facilities						
固定电话局用交换机容量	(万门)	City Swicthboard Capacity	(10 000 units)		1587.00	1690.80	1560.20	1482.60
移动电话交换机容量	(万户)	Mobile Telephone Swicthboard Capacity	(10 000 units)			5862.70	6805.70	7245.20
固定长途电话交换机容量	(万路端)	Capacity of Long Distance Telephone Switchborad	(circuit)		46.60	49.00	49.10	49.10
长途光缆线路长度	(万公里)	Length of Long Distance Optical Cable	(km)			2.70	2.77	2.81

注：邮电业务总量统计口径2011年发生变化，与以前各年份不可比。

Note:The statistic on total volume of post and telecommunication have been reconfigured from 2011.Datas of other year can not compare with the data of 2011.

15-12 邮电通信水平
LEVEL OF POST AND TELECOMMUNICATION SERVICES

指　　标	Item	2000	2005	2010	2011	2012	2013
每百人平均函件量 (件/百人)	Average Number of Letters Mailed Per 100 Persons (unit/100 person)	638.8	228.0	174.7	182.4	226.6	181.1
每百人平均订阅报刊量 (份/百人)	Average Number of Newspaper and Periodicals Subscribed Per 100 Persons (unit/100 person)	1798.8	977.9	962.7	971.2	1166.0	1254.9
每百人平均包件 (件/百人)	Average Number of Parcels Per 100 Persons (unit/100 person)	8.3	5.6	3.4	3.4	3.0	2.9
电话普及率 (部/百人)	Rate of Popularization of Telephone (unit/100 person)		43.9	78.3	86.9	96.2	93.1
移动电话普及率 (部/百人)	Rate of Popularization of Mobile Phones (unit/100 person)		23.3	60.4	68.7	78.8	76.2

主要统计指标解释

铁路营业里程 又称营业长度(包括正式营业和临时营业里程)，指办理客货运输业务的铁路正线总长度。凡是全线或部分建成双线及以上的线路，以第一线的实际长度计算；复线、站线、段管线、岔线和特殊用途线以及不计算运费的联络线都不计算营业里程。该指标可以反映铁路运输业基础设施的发展水平，也是计算客货周转量、运输密度和机车车辆运用效率等指标的基础资料。

公路里程 指在一定时期内实际达到《公路工程[WTBZ]技术标准 JTJ01-88》规定的等级公路，并经公路主管部门正式验收交付使用的公路里程数。包括大中城市的郊区公路以及通过小城镇街道部分的公路里程和桥梁、渡口的长度，不包括大中城市的街道、厂矿、林区生产用道和农业生产用道的里程。两条或多条公路共同经由同一路段，只计算一次，不得重复计算里程长度。该指标可以反映公路建设的发展规模，也是计算运输网密度等指标的基础资料。

内河航道里程 也称内河通航里程，指在一定时期内，能通航运输船舶及排筏的天然河流、湖泊水库、运河及通航渠道的长度。包括全年季节性通航累计三个月以上的航道，不包括仅供零散流放竹、木排的河道。该指标可以反映内河水运网的规模、水平和发展情况。

民用航空航线里程 指民航运输定期班机飞行的航线长度的总和。航线长度按机场之间的距离计算，通常有两种计算方法：一是将每条航线长度相加称为重复计算航线里程；一是将两线或两条以上航线经过同一区段里程，只计算一次航线长度称为不重复计算航线里程。一般常用的是后者，该指标可以确切反映民航运输网的规模，是表明民航事业为国民经济服务和方便人民生活程度的主要指标。

货(客)运量 指在一定时期内，各种运输工具实际运送的货物(旅客)数量。该指标是反映运输业为国民经济和人民生活服务的数量指标，也是制定和检查运输生产计划、研究运输发展规模和速度的重要指标。货运按吨计算，客运按人计算。货物不论运输距离长短、货物类别，均按实际重量统计。旅客不论行程远近或票价多少，均按一人一次客运量统计；半价票、小孩票也按一人统计。

货物(旅客)周转量 指在一定时期内，由各种运输工具运送的货物(旅客)数量与其相应运输距离的乘积之总和。该指标可以反映运输业生产的总成果，也是编制和检查运输生产计划，计算运输效率、劳动生产率以及核算运输单位成本的主要基础资料。计算货物周转量通常按发出站与到达站之间的最短距离，也就是计费距离计算。计算公式为：

货物（旅客）周转量=Σ（货物（旅客）运输量×运输距离）

民用汽车拥有量 指报告期末，在公安交通管理部门按照《机动车注册登记工作规范》，已注册登记领有民用车辆牌照的全部汽车数量。汽车拥有量统计的主要分类：根据汽车结构分为载客汽车、载货汽车及其他汽车；根据汽车所有者不同分为个人(私人)汽车、单位汽车；根据汽车的使用性质分为营运汽车、非营运汽车；根据汽车大小规格不同载客汽车分为大型、中型、小型和微型，载货汽车分为重型、中型、轻型和微型。

邮电业务总量 指以价值量形式表现的邮电通信企业为社会提供各类邮电通信服务的总数量。邮电业务量按专业分类包括函件、包件、汇票、报刊发行、邮政快件、特快专递、邮政储蓄、集邮、公众电报、用户电报、传真、长途电话、出租电路、无线寻呼、移动电话、分组交换数据通信、出租代维等。计算方法为各类产品乘以相应的平均单价(不变价)之和，再加上出租电路和设备、代用户维护电话交换机和线路等的服务收入。该指标综合反映了一定时期邮电业务发展的总成果，是研究邮电业务量构成和发展趋势的重要指标。计算公式为：

邮电业务总量=Σ（各类邮电业务量×不变单价）+出租代维及其他业务收入

=邮政业务总量+电信业务总量

移动电话用户 指通过移动电话交换机进入移动电话网、占用移动电话号码的各类电话用户。包括签约用户和智能网预付费用户。一个移动电话号码统计为一户。

互联网上网人数 指平均每周使用互联网至少 1 小时的中国公民人数。

本地电话用户 指接入本地电信运营商固定电话网上的电话用户。包括：住宅用户、单位用户、公用电话用户等。按电话用户位置又分为市内电话用户和农村电话用户。1997 年以前，“市内电话用户”是指接入县城及县以上城市的电话网上的电话用户；“农村电话用户”是指接入县邮电局农话台及县以下农村电话交换点,以县城为中心(除市话用户外)联通县、乡(镇)、行政村、村民小组的用户。从 1997 年起，电话用户数分组调整为以用户所在区域划分为“城市电话用户”和“乡村电话用户”，与过去的按市内电话和农村电话划分方法不同。而电话用户总数、电话机总部数统计范围不变。

城市电话用户 指直辖市、省辖市、地级市、县级市的市区、市郊区及县城(包括县人民政府所在地的县城关区或行政建制相当于县人民政府所在地的镇)范围内接入局用交换机的电话用户数，包括分布在农村地区的独立工矿区、林区、驻军等电话用户数。

农村电话用户 指按行政区划属于城市范围以外的乡(镇)、村的电话用户数。

住宅电话用户 指安装在居民住宅或农民家里并按照住宅电话用户登记注册和收费的电话用户。包括私人付费、单位付费和按规定免费安装的住宅电话用户。

长途电话交换机容量 指用于接入长途电话网的电话交换机设备的额定容量，包括国际电话交换机容量。

局用交换机容量 指安装在电信运营企业内用于接续本地固定电话的电话交换机容量，包括现用和备用的人工或自动交换机的全部容量。不包括用户交换机容量。

移动电话交换机容量 指移动电话交换机根据一定话务模型和交换机处理能力计算出来的最大同时服务用户的数量。

Explanatory Notes on Main Statistical Indicators

Length of Railways in Operation refers to the total length of the trunk line under passenger and freight transportation (including both full operation and temporary operation). The calculation is based on the actual length of the first line even if this line has a full or partial double track or more tracks, excluding double tracks, station sidings, tracks under the charge of stations, branch lines, special-purpose lines and the non-payable connecting lines. The length of railways in operation is an important indicator to show the development of the infrastructure for the railway transport, and also the essential data to calculate volume of passenger freight transport, traffic density and utilization efficiency of the locomotives and carriages.

Length of Electrified Railways refers to the length of the section of railways in operation in which the power supply lines and other equipment are installed for the running of electrified locomotives. The proportion of the length of electrified railways to the total length of railways in operation is an important indicator to show the modernization of railways.

Automatic-blocking and Semi-automatic-blocking Length of Railways refer to length of railways installed with equipment to perform automatic or manual blocking of trains. Blocking is a spacing technique by which a section of the railway only allows one train to pass at a time in the aim of ensuring the traffic safety. the proportion of automatic/semi-automatic blocking length to the total length of railways in operation is an important indicator to show the modernization of railways.

Length of Highways refers to the length of highways which are built in conformity with the grades specified by the highway engineering standard formulated by the Ministry of Communications, and have been formally checked and accepted by the departments of highways and put into use. The length of highways includes that of the suburb highways at large and medium-sized cities, highways passing through streets at small cities and towns, and also the length of bridges and ferries. It does not include the length of streets in big and medium-sized cities and highways built for the production purpose at factories, mines, forest areas and agricultural areas. If two or more highways go the same section of the way, the length of the section is only calculated for once and no duplication is allowed. The length of highways is an important indicator to show the development of the highway construction and to provide essential information to calculate the transport network density.

Length of Navigable Inland Waterways it is an indicator reflecting the size and development of inland water network, it refers to the length of the natural rivers, lakes, reservoirs, canals, and ditches open to navigation during a given period, which enables the transport by ships and rafts. It includes the channels open to navigation for over an accumulative 3 months in a year, yet this does not include the river courses, which are only used to float odd logs and bamboo rafts. This indicator can reflect the scale, level and development situation of the inland waterway network.

Length of Civil Aviation Routes refers to the length of all routes for regular civil aviation flights. There are usually two ways to calculate the distance between airports connected by the route length: One is to put the length of all air routes together, called duplicated calculation of the length of the routes; the other is not to allow the duplication in calculation when two or more routes passing the same section of aviation routes. The latter is usually used, as it can precisely show the size of the civil aviation network and indicate the extent of civil aviation serving the national economy and the people.

Length of Oil (Gas) Pipelines used as an indicator to show the development, scale and level of the pipeline transportation, it refers to the actual transport distance of oil (or gas) products, and is in general calculated in the length of single pipeline. If the length of the double pipelines and alternate pipeline are included, it is called the extension length of the oil (gas) pipelines, which indicates the actual length of the pipelines built, excluding double pipelines.

Freight (Passenger) Traffic refers to the volume of freight (passenger) transported with various means. Freight transport is calculated in tons and passenger traffic is calculated in the number of persons. Despite the type of freight and traveling distance, the freight transport is calculated in the actual weight of the goods: and despite the traveling distance and ticket price, the passenger traffic is calculated by the principle that one person can be counted only once in one travel. The passengers who travel with a half price ticket or a child ticket is also calculated as one person. The freight (passenger) traffic provides a quantitative measure to show how the transport industry serves the national economy and people, and is also an important indicator for planning the transport industry and for studying the development scale and speed of the transport industry.

Freight (Passenger) Traffic Density refers to the freight (passenger) traffic volume carried by a particular means of transportation during a given period through one kilometer of a specific section of transportation route. The formula is as follows:

Freight (Passenger) traffic density=[freight ton-kilometers (passenger-kilometers)] / (length of route in operation)

Freight (passenger) traffic density reflects the degree of business of freight (passenger) traffic on transportation routes, and therefore provides important information for balancing transport capability, planning construction and upgrading of transport routes and studying the distribution of transport network.

Freight Ton-kilometers (Passenger-kilometers) refer to the sum of the products of the volume of transported cargo (passengers) multiplying by the transport distance. It is an important indicator to reflect the achievement of transportation industry. Normally, the shortest distance between the departure station and the destination station (i.e., the payable distance) is the basis to calculate the freight ton-kilometers. This is an important indicator to show the total results of the transport industry, to prepare and examine the transport plan and to measure the efficiency, the labour productivity and the unit cost of transport.

The formula is as follows:

Freight ton-kilometers (passenger-kilometers) =Σ {freight (passenger) traffic × distance of transportation}

Possession of Civil Motor Vehicles refer to the total numbers of vehicles that are registered and received vehicles license tags according to the Work Standard for Motor Vehicles Registration formulated by transport management office under department of public security at the end of reference period. They are divided into following categories according to the structure of motor vehicles: passenger vehicles, trucks and others; and private vehicles and vehicles for units use according to ownerships; working vehicles and non-working vehicles according to kind of usage; large passenger vehicles, medium passenger vehicles, small passenger vehicles and mini passenger vehicle, heavy trucks, light-heavy trucks, light trucks and mini trucks according to sizes of vehicles.

Business Volume of Post and Telecommunications refers to the total amount of post and telecommunication services, expressed in value terms, provided by the post and telecommunications departments for the society. Post and telecommunication services can be classified as letters, parcels, remittance, issue of newspapers and magazines, fast mail service, express mail service, savings deposits, stamps for collection, public and individual telegraph service, facsimiles, long-distance telephone service, leasing of telephone lines, urban paging service, mobile telephone service, data transfer and transmission, etc. The accounting approach is to multiply the service products of all types with their average unit price (constant price) to get sum of business value, plus income from other services such as leasing of telephone lines and equipment, maintenance of telephone switchboards and lines on behalf of customers. This indicator reflects the overall results of post and telecommunications service during a given period, and is important to study the composition of business service and the development of post and telecommunications service.

The formula is as follows:

Business volume of post and telecommunications=Σ(Transaction of post and telecommunication service x constant price) + Income from leasing, maintenance and other services = business volume of postal service + business volume of telecommunications service

Subscribers of Wireless Paging Services Wireless paging service refers the service by which telephone users send audio, digital or character signals to persons carrying small-size pagers within the designated areas through wireless paging centers. The page carriers who have registered in paging centers are counted as paging subscribers.

Mobile Telephone Subscribers refer to the persons who own mobile telephone numbers and are connected with the mobile telephone communication network through the mobile telephone switchboards, including contracted subscribers and pre-paid subscribers for intelligent network. One mobile telephone is taken as a subscriber.

Internet Users refer to the number of Chinese citizens who use Internet at least for one hour each week.

Local Telephone Subscribers refer to subscribers that are connected to the local telecommunication service provider through fix line network, including household subscribers, institutional subscribers and public telephones. They are also classified as city subscribers and rural subscribers according to locations. Before 1997, city subscribers referred to those connected to city telephone networks in county towns and cities, while village subscribers referred to those connected to village telephone stations at and below counties. Since 1997, the classification of telephone subscribers was modified on the basis of physical location of the subscribers as urban telephone subscribers and rural telephone subscribers, which is different from the previous classification of categorizing local telephones and rural telephones, while the definition of total subscribers and total number of telephones remain unchanged.

Urban Telephone Subscribers refer to number of telephone subscribers, located at municipalities, cities under the jurisdiction of province, cities at prefecture level, downtown and suburb of city at county level town and county towns (including country towns where county government located, and towns of county level according to the administrative organizational system), that are connected to the public line telephone network, including rural mineral area, forest area, military area.

Rural Telephone Subscribers refer to telephone subscribers, located at counties (towns) and villages outside the range of cities according to administrative jurisdiction.

Household Telephone Subscribers refer to telephone sets installed in the dwelling units of urban or rural residents, and registered as residence subscribers for payment, including 3 types of payment for the service: private payment, public payment and free service.

Capacity of Long Distance Telephone Exchanges refers to the rated capacity of telephone exchanges to connect long distance telephone network, including capacity of international telephone exchanges.

Capacity of Office Telephone Exchanges refers to the capacity (measured in gate) of telephone exchanges installed in the offices of telecommunication service providers for communication between fixed telephones. It includes the capacity of both manual and automatic exchanges in use and for stand-by purpose, excluding the capacity of subscribers exchanges.

Capacity of Mobile Telephone Exchanges refers to the capacity of the maximum services provided to subscribers at one time basing on a certain model and transacting capacity of the mobile telephone exchanges.

16 国内贸易

Domestic Trade

资料整理：陈彬彬　朱　莉

国 内 贸 易

Domestic Trade

2013

社会消费品零售总额	Total Retail Sales of Consumption Goods	10885.9	（亿元）
商品零售额	Retail Sales	9813.0	（亿元）
餐饮收入额	Amount of Food and beverage revenue	1072.9	（亿元）

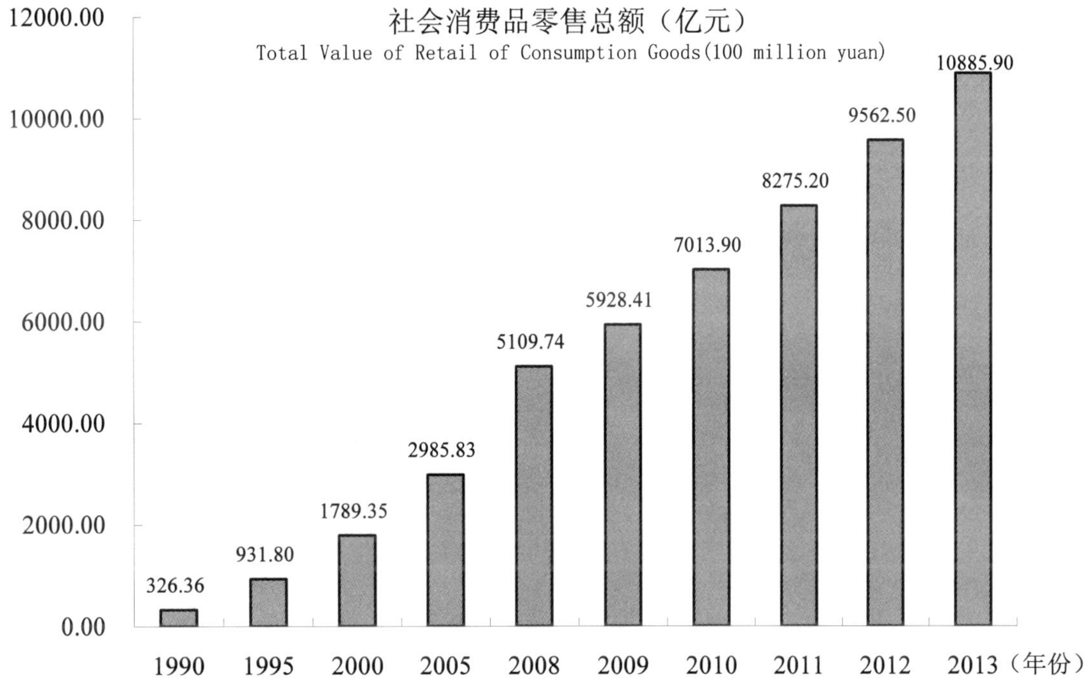

社会消费品零售总额（亿元）

Total Value of Retail Sales of Consumption Goods(100 million yuan)

年份 year	1990	1995	2000	2005	2008	2009	2010	2011	2012	2013
社会消费品零售总额 Total Value of Retail of Consumption Goods	326.36	931.80	1789.35	2985.83	5109.74	5928.41	7013.90	8275.20	9562.50	10885.90

16-1 按地区分社会消费品零售总额

TOTAL RETAIL SALES OF CONSUMER GOODS BY REGION

单位：亿元 (100 million yuan)

年份 Year	零售额 Total Retail Sales of Consumer Goods	市 City	县 County	县以下 Below County Level
1978	59.84	19.24	16.56	24.04
1980	81.91	28.98	17.01	35.92
1982	99.83			
1983	112.44			
1984	137.34			
1985	181.17	75.26	31.64	74.17
1986	200.20	81.83	35.54	82.83
1987	234.06	103.21	38.23	92.62
1988	295.80	142.49	42.08	111.23
1989	320.68	159.89	43.78	117.01
1990	326.36	166.44	45.62	114.30
1991	362.26	190.65	50.04	121.57
1992	411.52	221.59	55.04	134.89
1993	521.35	293.82	68.88	158.65
1994	723.75	411.63	101.74	210.38
1995	931.80	539.79	127.76	264.25
1996	1145.73	688.40	130.28	327.05
1997	1345.34	802.37	146.61	396.36
1998	1481.38	896.08	156.07	429.23
1999	1617.14	1019.58	150.95	446.61
2000	1789.35	1128.47	177.65	483.23
2001	1975.16	1267.09	194.21	513.86
2002	2129.38	1429.83	200.69	498.86
2003	2358.69	1603.34	222.86	587.66
2004	2619.47	1819.80	246.21	277.44
2005	2985.83	2081.31	279.43	625.09
2006	3461.09	2430.05	325.66	705.38
2007	4115.78	2889.08	393.38	833.33
2008	5109.74	3587.49	491.44	1030.80
2009	5928.41	4128.16	586.81	1213.45
2010	7013.90	(城镇)5937.80	(城区)5030.80	(乡村)1076.10
2011	8275.20	(城镇)7003.70	(城区)5954.80	(乡村)1271.50
2012	9562.50	(城镇)8112.60	(城区)6873.80	(乡村)1449.90
2013	10885.90	(城镇)9163.80	(城区)7682.40	(乡村)1722.10

注：1.1996年及以后社会消费品零售总额及各分组指标中不含售给城乡居民生活用住房的零售额。
2.2004、2008年为经普数据，2005-2007年为按国家统计局制定的修订方法修订数据，1993-2003年原则根据原各年环比发展速度和2004年经济普查数据调整。
3.2010年起采用国家新制定的城乡划分标准：城镇(其中:城区)、乡村

a) Since 1996, the residential house was exclued in the total retail sales of consumer goods and all the targets by groups.

b) The figures of 2004 and 2008 were from general economic Survey, that of the 2005-2007 were from statistics according to the reqirment of general economic survey; while the figures of 1993-2003 were from each year's indices (previous year =100) and readjusted according to the data of general economic survey.

c)Since 2010,a new towm and country division national standard is applied:town(including urban area),country.

16-2 分市、州社会消费品零售总额

TOTAL RETAIL SALES OF CONSUMER GOODS BY DISTRICT

单位：亿元 (100 million yuan)

地区	Region	2006	2007	2008	2009	2010	2011	2012	2013
全省	**Province**	**3461.09**	**4115.78**	**5109.74**	**5928.41**	**7013.90**	**8275.20**	**9562.50**	**10885.90**
武汉	Wuhan Municipality	1293.33	1518.30	1895.89	2164.09	2570.40	3031.79	3467.37	3916.60
黄石	Huangshi Municipality	148.27	174.97	221.60	256.09	301.63	355.05	413.50	468.86
十堰	Shiyan Municipality	144.72	170.19	217.17	254.25	308.88	364.18	424.80	491.51
宜昌	Yichang Municipality	262.20	311.34	399.41	470.41	552.72	656.00	766.19	881.93
襄阳	Xiangyang Municipality	277.97	328.87	425.01	500.56	613.34	721.51	839.51	966.31
鄂州	Ezhou Municipality	71.56	84.58	107.89	126.68	135.55	159.68	182.20	208.68
荆门	Jingmen Municipality	128.11	151.57	194.26	228.82	263.08	311.25	362.85	414.68
孝感	Xiaogan Municipality	183.52	218.19	278.18	326.90	388.77	459.70	535.50	608.68
荆州	Jingzhou Municipality	254.07	299.59	381.19	445.42	505.34	595.66	688.36	781.36
黄冈	Huanggang Municipality	184.47	223.66	292.33	340.07	408.71	482.10	559.37	635.02
咸宁	Xianning Municipality	88.01	105.86	140.72	165.88	209.63	247.89	289.54	330.58
随州	Suizhou Municipality	103.59	122.76	156.67	182.05	215.21	254.09	293.51	333.86
恩施	Enshi Prefecture	63.13	75.94	97.49	114.04	136.76	161.65	188.82	218.28
仙桃	Xiantao Municipality	70.32	82.52	108.87	127.87	146.79	172.64	200.81	229.00
潜江	Qianjiang Municipality	49.44	58.05	74.40	86.36	101.13	117.83	137.36	156.31
天门	Tianmen Municipality	76.69	90.57	115.42	135.21	151.57	179.04	206.91	237.50
林区	Shennongjia Forest Zone	2.25	2.57	3.25	3.72	4.38	5.14	5.92	6.75

注：1.本表各市、州数据包含了"其他"部分的全口径数据；
2.2008年以前的全省的数据根据经济普查的结果进行了调整。

Notes:a)"Others " was included in the total retail sales of consumer goods in the form.
b)Before 2008,Total was adjusted accoding to the economic census data.

16-3 批发和零售业连锁经营情况

BASIC CONDITIONS OF WHOLESALES, RETAIL SALES, CATERING CHAIN STORES INDUSTRIES

指标名称	Item	合计 Total		直营店 Direct Sales Store		加盟店 League Store	
		2012	2013	2012	2013	2012	2013
一、门店总数 (个)	Number of Stores (unit)	5182	5923	4847	5345	335	578
其中:批发业 (个)	Number of Stores (unit)	290	291	290	291		
零售业 (个)	Number of Stores (unit)	4892	5632	4557	5054	335	578
二、营业面积 (百平方米)	Floor Space of Business (100 sq.m)	59172	66657	58537	66240	636	417
其中:批发业 (百平方米)	Floor Space of Business (100 sq.m)	1328	1342	1328	1342		
零售业 (百平方米)	Floor Space of Business (100 sq.m)	57844	65315	57209	64898	636	417
三、从业人员 (人)	Person Engaged (person)	144640	148470	141007	145882	3633	2588
其中:批发业 (人)	Person Engaged (person)	7258	7225	7258	7225		
零售业 (人)	Person Engaged (person)	137382	141245	133749	138657	3633	2588
四、商品购进总额 (亿元)	Total Value of Commodities Purchaesd (100 000 000 yuan)	1359.98	1493.14	1356.23	1491.23	3.75	1.92
#统一配送商品购进额	#Total Purchasing Value	1034.69	1101.60	1031.12	1099.81	3.57	1.79
#自有配送中心配送商品购进额	#Commodities Purchased From Dispatching Center	789.89	844.87	786.82	843.54	3.07	1.33
#非自有配送中心配送商品购进额	#Commodities Purchased From Nondispatching Center	63.77	78.39	63.33	77.99	0.44	0.40
五、商品销售额 (亿元)	Sales Amount (100 000 000 yuan)	1552.62	1710.92	1547.58	1708.30	5.04	1459.58
#零售额	#Retail Sales	1270.83	1459.58	1265.79	1456.95	5.04	2.62

16-4 住宿和餐饮业连锁经营情况

BASIC CONDITIONS OF HOTELS AND CATERING SERVICES

指标名称	Item	合计 Total		直营店 Direct Sales Store		加盟店 League Store	
		2012	2013	2012	2013	2012	2013
一、门店总数 （个）	Number of Stores (unit)	544	590	541	588	3	2
二、营业面积 （百平方米）	Floor Space of Business (100 sq.m)	4542	4605	4528	4595	14	10
三、从业人员 （人）	Person Engaged (person)	33835	34360	33660	34230	175	130
四、客房数 （间）	Number of Hotel Rooms (unit)	7777	6898	7715	6836	62	62
五、床位数 （个）	Number of Beds (unit)	11011	9123	10913	9025	98	98
六、餐位数 （位）	Restaurant Seating Capacity (unit)	153429	153724	151551	152666	1878	1058
七、商品购进总额 （万元）	Total Value of Commodities Purchaesd (10 000 yuan)	267517	214112	267027	213753	490	359
#统一配送商品购进额	#Total Purchasing Value	247694	198098	247205	197739	489	359
#自有配送中心配送商品购进额	#Commodities Purchased From Dispatching Center	199677	133206	489	359	199188	132847
#非自有配送中心配送商品购进额	#Commodities Purchased From Nondispatching Center	13330	36818	13330	36818		
八、连锁门店销售额（万元）	Sales of the Chain Stores (10 000 yuan)	506739	517506	505570	516371	1170	1135
#餐费收入	Meals Revenue	483879	495990	483075	495198	804	792
#商品销售额	Merchandise Sales	1811	1771	1808	1767	4	3

16-5 限额以上批发零售业基本情况(2013)
BASIC CONDITIONS OF ENTERPRISES ABOVE DESIGNATED SIZE IN WHOLESALES AND RETAILSALES TRADE (2013)

(按登记注册类型分)

(Grouped by Registration Type)

登记注册类型	Type of Registration	法人企业数(个) Number of Corperations (unit)	年末从业人数(人) Person Engaged at Year-end (person)	零售营业面积(万平方米) Floor Space of Retail Business (10 000 sq.m)
总　计	**Total**	**8078**	**570471**	**2223.14**
一、批发业	**Wholesales**	**3019**	**203399**	**610.83**
按登记注册类型分组	Grouped by Registration Type			
内资	**Domestic Funded Enterprises**	**2986**	**191361**	**608.03**
国有	State-owned Enterprises	108	17632	36.92
集体	Collective-owned Enterprises	12	2066	1.69
股份合作	Cooperative Enterprises	6	296	4.17
联营企业	Joint Ownership Enterprises	1	18	
国有联营	State Joint Ownership Enterprises			
集体联营	Collective Joint Ownership Enterprises			
国有与集体联营	Joint State-collective Enterprises			
其他联营	Other Joint Ownership Enterprises	1	18	
有限责任公司	Limited Liability Corporations	1123	61182	178.94
国有独资公司	State Sole Funded Corporations	31	8736	10.92
其他有限责任公司	Other Limited Liability Corporations	1092	52446	168.02
股份有限公司	Share-holding Corporations Ltd.	78	50569	88.05
私营企业	Private Enterprises	1491	51851	256.85
私营独资	Private-funded Enterprises	70	1162	9.23
私营合伙	Private Partnership Enterprises	2	66	0.08
私营有限责任公司	Private Limited Liability Corporations	1390	49495	241.03
私营股份有限公司	Private Share-holding Corporations Ltd.	29	1128	6.51
其他	Other Enterprises	167	7747	41.41
港澳台商投资企业	**Enterprises with Funds from Hongkong, Macao and Taiwan**	**15**	**3761**	**2.30**
合资经营	Joint-venture Enterprises	4	381	0.06
合作经营	Cooperative Enterprises			
独资经营	Enterprises with Sole Investment	11	3380	2.23
独资股份有限公司	Sole Investment Co. Ltd. With Investment			
外商投资企业	**Foreign Funded Enterprises**	**18**	**8277**	**0.51**
中外合资经营	Sino-foreign Joint-venture Enterprises	8	777	0.27
外资企业	Enterprises with Sole Foreign Investment	8	6294	0.24
外商投资股份有限公司	Share-holding Co. Ltd. with Foreign Investment	1	13	
其他外资企业	Other Enterprises with Sole Foreign Investment	1	1193	

16-5 续表 continued

登记注册类型	Type of Registration	法人企业数(个) Number of Corperations (unit)	年末从业人数(人) Person Engaged at Year-end (person)	零售营业面积(万平方米) Floor Space of Retail Business (10 000 sq.m)
二、零售业	**Retail Trade**	**5059**	**367072**	**1612.30**
按登记注册类型分组	Grouped by Registration Type			
内资	**Domestic Funded Enterprises**	**5003**	**341601**	**1532.26**
国有	State-owned Enterprises	137	9653	19.31
集体	Collective-owned Enterprises	108	12429	51.88
股份合作	Cooperative Enterprises	8	299	2.61
联营企业	Joint Ownership Enterprises	4	209	0.42
国有联营	State Joint Ownership Enterprises			
集体联营	Collective Joint Ownership Enterprises	1	20	0.20
国有与集体联营	Joint State-collective Enterprises	2	175	0.16
其他联营	Other Joint Ownership Enterprises	1	14	0.06
有限责任公司	Limited Liability Corporations	1774	147446	606.12
国有独资公司	State Sole Funded Corporations	21	5217	25.71
其他有限责任公司	Other Limited Liability Corporations	1753	142229	580.40
股份有限公司	Share-holding Corporations Ltd.	123	60281	424.67
私营企业	Private Enterprises	2748	107387	416.54
私营独资	Private-funded Enterprises	516	9400	46.97
私营合伙	Private Partnership Enterprises	29	718	2.81
私营有限责任公司	Private Limited Liability Corporations	2138	94083	350.61
私营股份有限公司	Private Share-holding Corporations Ltd.	65	3186	16.14
其他	Other Enterprises	101	3897	10.71
港澳台商投资企业	**Enterprises with Funds from Hongkong, Macao and Taiwan**	**31**	**10689**	**29.85**
合资经营	Joint-venture Enterprises	8	1090	2.18
合作经营	Cooperative Enterprises			
独资经营	Enterprises with Sole Investment	23	9599	27.67
独资股份有限公司	Sole Investment Co. Ltd. With Investment			
外商投资企业	**Foreign Funded Enterprises**	**25**	**14782**	**50.19**
中外合资经营	Sino-foreign Joint-venture Enterprises	8	4750	8.10
外资企业	Enterprises with Sole Foreign Investment	15	9770	40.79
外商投资股份有限公司	Share-holding Co. Ltd. with Foreign Investment	1	260	1.30
其他外资企业	Other Enterprises with Sole Foreign Investment	1	2	

16-6 限额以上批发零售业基本情况(2013)
BASIC CONDITIONS OF ENTERPRISES ABOVE DESIGNATED SIZE IN WHOLESALES AND RETAILSALES TRADE (2013)

(按国民经济行业分)

(Grouped by Sector)

项　目	Item	法人企业数(个) Number of Corperations (unit)	年末从业人数(人) Person Engaged at Year-end (person)	零售营业面积(万平方米) Floor Space of Retail Business (10 000 sq.m)
总　计	**Total**	**8078**	**570471**	**2223.14**
一、批发业	**Wholesales**	**3019**	**203399**	**610.83**
农、林、牧产品批发业	Wholesales of Agriculture, Forestry and Animal Husbandry Products	296	16651	152.33
食品、饮料及烟草制品批发业	Wholesales of Foods, Beverage and Tobacco	544	54220	135.05
米、面制品及食用油批发业	Wholesales of Rice, Noodles and Edible Oil	80	3987	21.28
烟草制品批发业	Wholesales of Tobacco	42	12770	4.70
纺织、服装及日用品批发业	Wholesales of Textile Products, Garments and Daily Used Articles	182	10490	14.04
服装批发业	Wholesales of Garments	62	3142	8.28
家用电器批发业	Wholesales of Home Appliances	38	3267	1.70
文化、体育用品及器材批发业	Wholesales of Cultural and Sports Goods and Equipments	44	7418	6.03
医药及医疗器材批发业	Wholesales of Medicnes and Medical Appliances	257	29560	26.56
矿产品、建材及化工产品批发业	Wholesales of Mineral Products, Building Materials and Chemical Products	1109	65704	221.77
煤炭及制品批发业	Wholesales of Coal and Coal-made Products	168	4537	24.64
石油及制品批发业	Wholesales of Petroleum Products	94	37681	92.08
非金属矿及制品批发	Wholesales of Non-metal and Non-metal Mines	34	885	4.68
金属及金属矿批发业	Wholesales of Metal and Metal Mines	420	8116	18.54
建材批发业	Wholesales of Construction Materials	142	3731	21.88
化肥批发业	Wholesales of Chemical Fertilizers	101	7409	17.07
机械设备、五金交电及电子产品批发	Wholesales of Machinery Equipment, Hardware, Transport and Electronic Products	486	14561	31.07
汽车批发业	Wholesales of Cars	84	2987	7.44
计算机、软件及辅助设备批发业	Wholesales of Computers, Softwares and Assisted Equipments	26	1031	0.29
贸易经纪与代理	Trade Agent	11	1858	0.33
其他批发业	Other Wholesales	90	2937	23.66
二、零售业	**Retail Sales**	**5059**	**367072**	**1612.30**
综合零售业	Retail Sales of Department	870	161900	857.14
百货零售业	Department Stores	391	64944	492.16
超级市场零售业	Supermarkets	347	88064	330.79
食品、饮料及烟草制品专门零售业	Monopoly Retail of Foods, Beverage and Tobacco	649	28318	67.48
纺织、服装及日用品专门零售业	Monopoly Retail of Textile, Garments,and Daily Used Articles	367	26425	72.69
服装零售业	Retail Sales of Garments	214	19129	55.18
文化、体育用品及器材专门零售业	Monopoly Retail of Cultural, Sports Products and Equipments	226	8357	21.62
体育用品零售业	Retail Sales of Sports Products	8	319	1.78
图书报刊零售业	Retail Sales of Books, Newspapers and Periodicals	85	4119	9.45
医药及医疗器材专门零售业	Monopoly Retail of Medicine and Medical Appliances	294	21042	50.47
药品零售业	Retail Sales of Medicine	258	20308	49.22
汽车、摩托车、燃料及零配件专门	Monopoly Retail of Cars, and Motorcars Parts	1193	75939	264.54
汽车零售业	Retail Sales of Cars	856	62219	197.95
机动车燃料零售业	Retail Sales of Motor Vehicles Fuels	134	9382	41.36
家用电器及电子产品专门零售业	Monopoly Retail of Home Appliances and Electronic Products	796	24860	134.55
家用电器零售业	Retail Sales of Home Appliances	402	14974	105.33
计算机、软件及辅助设备零售业	Retail Sales of Computers, Softwares and Assisted Equipments	177	4023	7.71
		39	1391	2.7612
通讯设备零售业	Retail Sales of Communication Equipments	26	542	1.19
五金、家具及室内装修材料专门零售业	Monopoly Retail of Hardware, Furnitures and Decorative Materials	482	12821	109.71
无店铺及其他零售业	Retail Sales of Storeless and Others	182	7410	34.09
互联网零售	Retail Sales of Internet	10	1418	

16-7 限额以上住宿和餐饮业基本情况(2013)
BASIC CONDITIONS OF ENTERPRISES ABOVE DESIGNATED SIZE IN HOTELS AND CATERING SERVICES (2013)

(按登记注册类型分)

(Grouped by Registeration Type)

项 目	Item	法人企业数(个) Number of Corperations (unit)	年末从业人数(人) Person Engaged at Year-end (person)	餐饮营业面积(万平方米) Floor Space of Catering Business (10 000 sq.m)
总 计	**Total**	**2703**	**197088**	**520.17**
一、住宿业	**Hotel Trade**	**846**	**70619**	**159.98**
按登记注册类型分组	**Grouped by Registration Type**			
内资	**Domestic Funded Enterprises**	**824**	**65483**	**154.86**
国有	State-owned Enterprises	65	7694	16.60
集体	Collective-owned Enterprises	13	1478	2.07
股份合作	Cooperative Enterprises	6	314	1.86
联营企业	Joint Ownership Enterprises	1	70	0.05
国有联营	State Joint Ownership Enterprises			
集体联营	Collective Joint Ownership Enterprises	1	70	0.05
国有与集体联营	Joint State-collective Enterprises			
其他联营	Other Joint Ownership Enterprises			
有限责任公司	Limited Liability Corporations	295	28053	56.82
国有独资公司	State Sole Funded Corporations	12	1492	1.85
其他有限责任公司	Other Limited Liability Corporations	283	26561	54.98
股份有限公司	Share-holding Corporations Ltd.	21	2951	6.46
私营企业	Private Enterprises	399	24117	68.31
私营独资	Private-funded Enterprises	47	1429	4.83
私营合伙	Private Partnership Enterprises	12	501	3.11
私营有限责任公司	Private Limited Liability Corporations	318	20516	57.00
私营股份有限公司	Private Share-holding Corporations Ltd.	22	1671	3.37
其他	Other Enterprises	24	806	2.68
港澳台商投资企业	**Enterprises with Funds from Hongkong, Macao and Taiwan**	**17**	**4522**	**4.08**
合资经营	Joint-venture Enterprises	4	1356	0.90
合作经营	Cooperative Enterprises	2	816	0.32
独资经营	Enterprises with Sole Investment	8	1752	2.25
投资股份有限公司	Share-holding Co. Ltd. With Investment	3	598	0.62
外商投资企业	**Foreign Funded Enterprises**	**5**	**614**	**1.04**
中外合资经营	Sino-foreign Joint-venture Enterprises	1	238	0.20
中外合作经营	Sino-foreign Cooperative Enterprises			
外资企业	Enterprises with Sole Foreign Investment	3	301	0.54
外商投资股份有限公司	Share-holding Co. Ltd. with Foreign Investment	1	75	0.30
二、餐饮业	**Catering Trade**	**1857**	**126469**	**360.19**
按登记注册类型分组	**Grouped by Registration Type**			
内资	**Domestic Funded Enterprises**	**1821**	**100826**	**340.03**
国有	State-owned Enterprises	30	1704	5.88
集体	Collective-owned Enterprises	8	355	1.59
股份合作	Cooperative Enterprises	2	230	0.24
联营企业	Joint Ownership Enterprises	1	262	0.50
国有联营	State Joint Ownership Enterprises			
集体联营	Collective Joint Ownership Enterprises	1	262	0.50
国有与集体联营	Joint State-collective Enterprises			
其他联营	Other Joint Ownership Enterprises			
有限责任公司	Limited Liability Corporations	569	44762	129.42
国有独资公司	State Sole Funded Corporations	7	1540	1.02
其他有限责任公司	Other Limited Liability Corporations	562	43222	128.40
股份有限公司	Share-holding Corporations Ltd.	22	1859	4.46
私营企业	Private Enterprises	1125	49992	188.66
私营独资	Private-funded Enterprises	348	9008	43.32
私营合伙	Private Partnership Enterprises	14	572	2.32
私营有限责任公司	Private Limited Liability Corporations	737	38418	137.41
私营股份有限公司	Private Share-holding Corporations Ltd.	26	1994	5.61
其他	Other Enterprises	64	1662	9.28
港澳台商投资企业	**Enterprises with Funds from Hongkong, Macao and Taiwan**	**20**	**3053**	**4.94**
合资经营	Joint-venture Enterprises	6	426	1.39
合作经营	Cooperative Enterprises			
独资经营	Enterprises with Sole Investment	12	2558	3.34
投资股份有限公司	Share-holding Co. Ltd. With Investment	2	69	0.22
外商投资企业	**Foreign Funded Enterprises**	**16**	**22590**	**15.22**
中外合资经营	Sino-foreign Joint-venture Enterprises	2	727	1.60
外资企业	Enterprises with Sole Foreign Investment	12	21733	13.12
外商投资股份有限公司	Share-holding Co. Ltd. with Foreign Investment			
其他外商投资企业	Other Enterprises with Sole Foreign Investment	2	130	0.49

16-8 限额以上住宿和餐饮业基本情况(2013)
BASIC CONDITIONS OF ENTERPRISES ABOVE DESIGNATED SIZE IN HOTELS AND CATERING SERVICES (2013)

(按国民经济行业分)

(Grouped by Sector)

行业	Item	法人企业数(个) Number of Corperations (unit)	年末从业人数(人) Person Engaged at Year-end (person)	餐饮营业面积(万平方米) Floor Space of Catering Business (10 000 sq.m)
总计	**Total**	**2703**	**197088**	**520.17**
一、住宿业	**Hotel**	**846**	**70619**	**159.98**
按国民经济行业分组	Grouped by Sector			
旅游饭店	Tourist Hotel	448	51473	109.31
一般旅馆	Regular Hotel	379	17671	46.64
其他住宿服务	Other Accomodation Service	19	1475	4.03
二、餐饮业	**Catering**	**1857**	**126469**	**360.19**
按国民经济行业分组	Grouped by Sector			
正餐服务业	Dinner	1806	101119	342.03
快餐服务业	Fast Food	33	22663	14.47
饮料及冷饮服务业	Beverage and Cold Drink Services	10	1642	1.88
其他餐饮服务业	Others	8	1045	1.81

16-9 限额以上住宿和餐饮业经营情况(2013)
BUSINESS OF ENTERPRISES ABOVE DESIGNATED SIZE OF HOTELS AND CATERING SERVICES (2013)

(按国民经济行业分)
(Grouped by Sector)

行业	Item	营业额(亿元) Turnover (100 million yuan)	客房收入 Revnue from Guest Rooms	餐费收入 Revenue from Catering Bills	商品销售收入 Revenue from Commodity Sales	其他收入 Revenue from Others	年末住宿和餐饮企业拥有床位数(万个) Number of Beds owned by Hotels and Catering Enterprises at Year-end (10 000 units)	年末住宿和餐饮企业拥有餐位数(万位) Number of Seats owned by Hotels and Catering Enterprises at Year-end (10 000 units)
总计	**Total**	**349.42**	**81.37**	**245.04**	**12.91**	**10.10**	**24.56**	**101.56**
一、住宿业	**Hotel**	**123.63**	**61.81**	**49.51**	**4.80**	**7.52**	**17.47**	**26.02**
按国民经济行业分组	Grouped by Sector							
旅游饭店	Tourist Hotel	87.57	42.11	36.52	2.78	6.16	11.17	18.71
一般旅馆	Regular Hotel	32.90	18.39	12.41	0.91	1.19	5.93	6.68
其他住宿服务	Other Accomodation Service	3.17	1.31	0.58	1.11	0.17	0.37	0.63
二、餐饮业	**Catering**	**225.79**	**19.56**	**195.53**	**8.11**	**2.58**	**7.10**	**75.55**
按国民经济行业分组	Grouped by Sector							
正餐服务业	Dinner	185.73	19.38	155.81	7.99	2.55	7.04	69.70
快餐服务业	Fast Food	32.68	0.06	32.57	0.05	0.00	0.02	4.88
饮料及冷饮服务业	Beverage and Cold Drink Services	3.28	0.02	3.19	0.07	0.00	0.01	0.69
其他餐饮服务业	Others	4.10	0.10	3.96	0.01	0.02	0.03	0.28

16-10 限额以上住宿和餐饮业经营情况(2013)

(按登记注册类型分)

单位：亿元

项 目	Item	营业额 Turnover	客房收入 Revnue from Guest Rooms
总 计	**Total**	**349.42**	**81.37**
一、住宿业	**Hotels**	**123.63**	**61.81**
按登记注册类型分组	**Grouped by Registration Type**		
内资	**Domestic Funded Enterprises**	**113.55**	**56.62**
国有	State-Owned Enterprises	12.18	6.65
集体	Collective-owned Enterprises	3.04	1.05
股份合作	Cooperative Enterprises	0.35	0.11
联营企业	Joint Ownership Enterprises	0.08	0.02
国有联营	State Joint Ownership Enterprises		
集体联营	Collective Joint Ownership Enterprises	0.08	0.02
国有与集体联营	Joint State-collective Enterprises		
其他联营	Other Joint Ownership Enterprises		
有限责任公司	Limited Liability Corporations	44.61	23.94
国有独资公司	State Sole Funded Corporations	4.21	1.60
其他有限责任公司	Other Limited Liability Corporations	40.40	22.34
股份有限公司	Share-holding Corporations Ltd.	4.49	2.04
私营企业	Private Enterprises	46.51	21.83
私营独资	Private-funded Enterprises	4.32	2.49
私营合伙	Private Partnership Enterprises	1.07	0.30
私营有限责任公司	Private Limited Liability Corporations	35.32	17.81
私营股份有限公司	Private Share-holding Corporations Ltd.	5.80	1.23
其他	Other Enterprises	2.29	0.98
港澳台商投资企业	**Enterprises with Funds from Hongkong, Macao and Taiwan**	**9.37**	**4.84**
合资经营	Joint-venture Enterprises	3.42	1.57
合作经营	Cooperative Enterprises	1.42	0.80
独资经营	Enterprises with Sole Investment	3.13	1.59
投资股份有限公司	Share-holding Co. Ltd. With Investment	1.40	0.87
外商投资企业	**Foreign Funded Enterprises**	**0.71**	**0.35**
中外合资经营	Sino-Foreign Joint-venture Enterprises	0.29	0.16
外资企业	Enterprises with Sole Foreign Investment	0.33	0.17
外商投资股份有限公司	Share-holding Co. Ltd. with Foreign Investment	0.09	0.02
其他外商投资企业	Other Foreign Founded Enterprises		
二、餐饮业	**Catering Trade**	**225.79**	**19.56**
按登记注册类型分组	**Grouped by Registration Type**		
内资	**Domestic Funded Enterprises**	**187.53**	**19.18**
国有	State-Owned Enterprises	3.31	0.95
集体	Collective-owned Enterprises	1.04	0.12
股份合作	Cooperative Enterprises	0.32	0.08
联营企业	Joint Ownership Enterprises	4.68	
国有联营	State Joint Ownership Enterprises		
集体联营	Collective Joint Ownership Enterprises	4.68	
国有与集体联营	Joint State-collective Enterprises		
其他联营	Other Joint Ownership Enterprises		
有限责任公司	Limited Liability Corporations	72.05	7.86
国有独资公司	State Sole Funded Corporations	1.21	0.20
其他有限责任公司	Other Limited Liability Corporations	70.85	7.66
股份有限公司	Share-holding Corporations Ltd.	2.56	0.44
私营企业	Private Enterprises	99.08	9.38
私营独资	Private-funded Enterprises	23.64	1.92
私营合伙	Private Partnership Enterprises	0.92	0.12
私营有限责任公司	Private Limited Liability Corporations	71.15	6.95
私营股份有限公司	Private Share-holding Corporations Ltd.	3.37	0.39
其他	Other Enterprises	4.48	0.34
港澳台商投资企业	**Enterprises with Funds from Hongkong, Macao and Taiwan**	**6.37**	**0.19**
合资经营	Joint-venture Enterprises	0.75	0.12
合作经营	Cooperative Enterprises		
独资经营	Enterprises with Sole Investment	5.54	0.07
投资股份有限公司	Share-holding Co. Ltd. With Investment	0.08	0.00
外商投资企业	**Foreign Funded Enterprises**	**31.89**	**0.20**
中外合资经营	Sino-Foreign Joint-venture Enterprises	0.79	0.05
外资企业	Enterprises with Sole Foreign Investment	30.92	0.14
外商投资股份有限公司	Share-holding Co. Ltd. with Foreign Investment		
其他外商投资企业	Other Foreign Funded Enterprises	0.18	

BUSINESS OF ENTERPRISES ABOVE DESIGNATED SIZE OF HOTELS AND CATERING SERVICES (2013)

(Grouped by Registeration Type)

(100 million yuan)

餐费收入 Revenue from Catering Bills	商品销售收入 Revenue from Commodity Sales	其他收入 Revenue from Others	年末床位数 (万个) Number of Beds at Year-end (10 000 units)	年末餐位数 (万位) Number of Seats at Year-end (10 000 units)
245.04	**12.91**	**10.10**	**24.56**	**101.56**
49.51	**4.80**	**7.52**	**17.47**	**26.02**
45.69	**4.66**	**6.58**	**16.73**	**24.92**
4.38	0.51	0.63	1.52	2.69
1.70	0.05	0.24	0.20	0.54
0.18	0.02	0.04	0.09	0.21
0.05	0.01	0.00	0.01	0.00
0.05	0.01	0.00	0.01	0.00
16.04	1.23	3.41	6.98	9.63
1.77	0.26	0.57	0.41	0.49
14.27	0.97	2.84	6.57	9.14
1.85	0.21	0.39	0.56	1.03
20.22	2.60	1.86	7.14	10.31
1.73	0.08	0.01	0.51	0.60
0.73	0.04	0.01	0.14	0.33
13.91	2.14	1.46	6.04	8.54
3.85	0.34	0.38	0.47	0.84
1.28	0.02	0.01	0.25	0.50
3.55	**0.12**	**0.85**	**0.61**	**0.87**
1.47	0.06	0.32	0.19	0.22
0.56	0.00	0.06	0.07	0.18
1.01	0.06	0.46	0.24	0.34
0.51	0.00	0.02	0.11	0.13
0.27	**0.01**	**0.08**	**0.12**	**0.23**
0.10	0.00	0.03	0.03	0.08
0.14	0.01	0.01	0.07	0.13
0.02		0.05	0.02	0.02
195.53	**8.11**	**2.58**	**7.10**	**75.55**
158.05	**8.03**	**2.27**	**6.96**	**69.89**
2.11	0.06	0.18	0.30	1.00
0.91	0.01	0.00	0.07	0.28
0.24			0.02	0.09
2.92	1.76			0.40
2.92	1.76			0.40
61.42	1.77	1.00	2.84	28.88
0.98	0.01	0.00	0.08	0.60
60.43	1.76	1.00	2.76	28.28
1.67	0.27	0.18	0.18	0.70
84.96	3.90	0.85	3.42	36.63
20.60	0.97	0.14	0.66	8.98
0.76	0.03	0.01	0.05	0.62
60.93	2.64	0.63	2.57	25.93
2.67	0.25	0.06	0.15	1.10
3.83	0.26	0.06	0.14	1.93
5.84	**0.08**	**0.26**	**0.06**	**1.37**
0.39	0.00	0.23	0.04	0.15
5.37	0.07	0.03	0.02	1.19
0.08			0.01	0.03
31.65	**0.00**	**0.04**	**0.07**	**4.29**
0.73	0.00	0.01	0.02	0.31
30.74		0.04	0.05	3.91
0.18				0.08

16-11 限额以上批发和零售业商品购、销、存总额(2013)
TOTAL PURCHASES, SALES AND STOCK OF ENTERPRISES ABOVE DESIGNATED SIZE OF WHOLESALE AND RETAIL TRADES(2013)

(按登记注册类型分)

(Grouped by Registeration Type)

单位：亿元 (100 million yuan)

项目	Item	购进总额 Total Purchasing Value	销售总额 Total Sales Value	批发 Whole-sales	零售 Retail Sales	年末库存总额 Total Value of Inventory at Year-end
总计	**Total**	**14413.23**	**15446.84**	**10076.82**	**5370.02**	**1041.54**
一、批发业	**Wholesales**	**9878.13**	**10459.51**	**9686.44**	**773.07**	**614.33**
按登记注册类型分组	**Grouped by Registration Type**					
内资	**Domestic Funded Enterprises**	**9604.10**	**10116.63**	**9350.89**	**765.73**	**589.92**
国有	State-owned Enterprises	1205.01	1277.36	1249.72	27.64	150.49
集体	Collective-owned Enterprises	15.54	18.31	17.95	0.36	1.58
股份合作	Cooperative Enterprises	3.44	3.78	3.44	0.34	0.15
联营企业	Joint Ownership Enterprises	0.15	0.15	0.15		0.00
国有联营	State Joint Ownership Enterprises					
集体联营	Collective Joint Ownership Enterprises					
国有与集体联营	Joint State-collective Enterprises					
其他联营	Other Joint Ownership Enterprises	0.15	0.15	0.15		0.00
有限责任公司	Limited Liability Corporations	4728.49	4955.79	4723.83	231.96	199.82
国有独资公司	State Sole Funded Corporations	2174.95	2269.64	2240.85	28.79	41.94
其他有限责任公司	Other Limited Liability Corporations	2553.54	2686.15	2482.98	203.17	157.89
股份有限公司	Share-holding Corporations Ltd.	1938.92	2023.84	1717.83	306.01	107.90
私营企业	Private Enterprises	1609.31	1727.24	1548.38	178.86	118.13
私营独资	Private-funded Enterprises	22.39	23.80	18.91	4.89	1.11
私营合伙	Private Partnership Enterprises	0.47	1.19	1.13	0.06	0.02
私营有限责任公司	Private Limited Liability Corporations	1552.90	1665.40	1495.58	169.83	115.01
私营股份有限公司	Private Share-holding Corporations Ltd.	33.54	36.85	32.76	4.09	1.98
其他	Other Enterprises	103.25	110.15	89.59	20.56	11.85
港澳台商投资企业	**Enterprises with Funds from Hongkong, Macao and Taiwan**	**64.13**	**77.91**	**73.00**	**4.91**	**13.05**
合资经营	Joint-venture Enterprises	13.22	13.79	10.81	2.98	1.84
合作经营	Cooperative Enterprises					
独资经营	Enterprises with Sole Investment	50.90	64.12	62.19	1.93	11.21
投资股份有限公司	Share-holding Co. Ltd. With Investment					
外商投资企业	**Foreign Funded Enterprises**	**209.90**	**264.97**	**262.54**	**2.43**	**11.36**
中外合资经营	Sino-foreign Joint-venture Enterprises	68.81	78.95	77.12	1.84	6.05
外资企业	Enterprises with Sole Foreign Investment	138.11	180.81	180.22	0.59	5.24
外商投资股份有限公司	Share-holding Co. Ltd. with Foreign Investment	0.66	0.86	0.86		
其它外商投资企业	Other Foreign Funded Enterprises	2.32	4.34	4.34		0.06
二、零售业	**Retail Trade**	**4535.11**	**4987.33**	**390.38**	**4596.95**	**427.21**
按登记注册类型分组	**Grouped by Registration Type**					
内资	**Domestic Funded Enterprises**	**4232.44**	**4654.53**	**385.86**	**4268.67**	**395.77**
国有	State-owned Enterprises	206.25	226.28	13.69	212.60	8.39
集体	Collective-owned Enterprises	125.34	155.62	13.97	141.64	14.29
股份合作	Cooperative Enterprises	3.09	3.08	0.13	2.94	0.10
联营企业	Joint Ownership Enterprises	3.01	3.02		3.02	0.04
国有联营	State Joint Ownership Enterprises					
集体联营	Collective Joint Ownership Enterprises	0.40	0.42		0.42	0.01
国有与集体联营	Joint State-collective Enterprises	2.48	2.48		2.48	0.02
其他联营	Other Joint Ownership Enterprises	0.13	0.13		0.13	0.00
有限责任公司	Limited Liability Corporations	1754.81	1913.70	171.49	1742.21	165.24
国有独资公司	State Sole Funded Corporations	179.48	226.54	58.13	168.40	3.25
其他有限责任公司	Other Limited Liability Corporations	1575.33	1687.16	113.35	1573.81	161.99
股份有限公司	Share-holding Corporations Ltd.	926.60	1034.55	109.37	925.18	69.31
私营企业	Private Enterprises	1171.44	1273.34	76.31	1197.03	136.43
私营独资	Private-funded Enterprises	87.59	98.58	2.66	95.93	7.54
私营合伙	Private Partnership Enterprises	5.61	7.05	0.00	7.05	0.38
私营有限责任公司	Private Limited Liability Corporations	996.94	1082.21	65.77	1016.44	118.78
私营股份有限公司	Private Share-holding Corporations Ltd.	81.31	85.50	7.89	77.61	9.73
其他	Other Enterprises	41.89	44.94	0.90	44.05	1.96
港澳台商投资企业	**Enterprises with Funds from Hongkong, Macao and Taiwan**	**139.42**	**146.24**	**2.78**	**143.46**	**18.55**
合资经营	Joint-venture Enterprises	5.27	7.25		7.25	1.76
合作经营	Cooperative Enterprises					
独资经营	Enterprises with Sole Investment	134.16	138.99	2.78	136.21	16.79
投资股份有限公司	Share-holding Co. Ltd. With Investment					
外商投资企业	**Foreign Funded Enterprises**	**163.24**	**186.56**	**1.74**	**184.82**	**12.89**
中外合资经营	Sino-foreign Joint-venture Enterprises	19.65	25.00	1.57	23.43	1.31
外资企业	Enterprises with Sole Foreign Investment	127.03	144.05	0.17	143.87	11.36
外商投资股份有限公司	Share-holding Co. Ltd. with Foreign Investment	1.28	1.18		1.18	0.22
其它外商投资企业	Other Foreign Funded Enterprises	15.29	16.33		16.33	

16-12 限额以上批发和零售业商品购、销、存总额(2013)
TOTAL PURCHASES, SALES AND STOCK OF ENTERPRISES ABOVE DESIGNATED SIZE OF WHOLESALE AND RETAIL TRADES (2013)

(按国民经济行业分)

(Grouped by Sector)

单位：亿元 (100 million yuan)

行业	Item	购进总额 Total Purchasing Value	销售总额 Total Sales Value	批发 Whole-sales	零售 Retail Sales	年末库存总额 Total Value of Inventory at Year-end
总计	**Total**	**14413.23**	**15446.84**	**10076.82**	**5370.02**	**1041.54**
一、批发业	**Wholesales**	**9878.13**	**10459.51**	**9686.44**	**773.07**	**614.33**
农、林、牧产品批发业	Wholesales of Agriculture, Forestry and Animal Husbandry Products	368.88	351.24	317.88	33.36	100.99
食品、饮料及烟草制品批发业	Wholesales of Foods, Beverage and Tobacco	1331.89	1516.49	1310.04	206.46	122.62
米、面制品及食用油批发业	Wholesales of Rice, Noodles and Edible Oil	103.13	72.59	60.44	12.15	41.99
烟草制品批发业	Wholesales of Tobacco	482.51	616.74	607.07	9.67	42.64
纺织、服装及日用品批发业	Wholesales of Textile Products, Garments and Daily Used Articles	272.60	306.58	271.47	35.12	39.81
服装批发业	Wholesales of Garments	62.09	86.99	72.42	14.57	5.50
家用电器批发业	Wholesales of Home Appliances	3.26	3.96	3.96		0.27
文化、体育用品及器材批发业	Wholesales of Cultural and Sports Goods and Equipments	112.68	123.75	113.84	9.91	20.22
医药及医疗器材批发业	Wholesales of Medicnes and Medical Appliances	732.80	733.93	623.32	110.61	81.30
矿产品、建材及化工产品批发业	Wholesales of Mineral Products, Building Materials and Chemical Products	5645.44	5947.18	5617.70	329.49	178.17
煤炭及制品批发业	Wholesales of Coal and Coal-made Products	316.81	332.69	306.24	26.45	9.12
石油及制品批发业	Wholesales of Petroleum Products	3413.70	3617.49	3348.72	268.78	60.51
非金属及金属矿批发业	Wholesales of Non-metellic Mineral and Metal Industry	28.59	28.95	26.84	2.11	1.63
金属及金属矿批发业	Wholesales of Metal and Metal Mines	1452.52	1507.27	1497.03	10.23	70.31
建材批发业	Wholesales of Construction Materials	68.13	80.66	70.24	10.42	4.24
化肥批发业	Wholesales of Chemical Fertilizers	204.93	198.78	194.48	4.30	24.97
机械设备、五金交电及电子产品批发	Wholesales of Machinery Equipment, Hardware, Transport and Electronic Products	504.59	570.28	530.21	40.07	41.48
汽车批发业	Wholesales of Cars	133.08	143.15	131.17	11.98	16.58
计算机、软件及辅助设备批发业	Wholesales of Computers, Softwares and Assisted Equipments	107.93	109.18	98.68	10.50	2.43
贸易经纪与代理	Trade Agent	842.05	840.55	840.54	0.01	24.49
其他批发业	Other Wholesales	67.19	69.49	61.45	8.04	5.27
二、零售业	**Retail Sales**	**4535.11**	**4987.33**	**390.38**	**4596.95**	**427.21**
综合零售业	Retail Sales of Department	1518.80	1689.93	100.23	1589.69	154.35
百货零售业	Department Stores	817.84	893.87	55.19	838.68	75.25
超级市场零售业	Supermarkets	591.57	676.76	31.25	645.51	72.51
食品、饮料及烟草制品专门零售业	Monopoly Retail of Foods, Beverage and Tobacco	332.56	372.08	33.86	338.23	19.47
纺织、服装及日用品专门零售业	Monopoly Retail of Textile, Garments,and Daily Used Articles	141.13	168.63	6.26	162.36	23.27
服装零售业	Retail Sales of Garments	83.01	102.19	4.69	97.51	13.17
文化、体育用品及器材专门零售业	Monopoly Retail of Cultural, Sports Products and Equipments	84.58	89.49	3.69	85.80	11.92
体育用品零售业	Retail Sales of Sports Products	2.37	3.46	0.02	3.45	0.17
图书报刊零售业	Retail Sales of Books, Newspapers and Periodicals	32.40	32.24	2.10	30.15	6.21
医药及医疗器材专门零售业	Monopoly Retail of Medicine and Medical Appliances	290.44	305.53	70.69	234.83	21.95
药品零售业	Retail Sales of Medicine	282.70	296.72	70.36	226.36	21.45
汽车、摩托车、燃料及零配件专门零售	Monopoly Retail of Cars, and Motorcars Parts	1454.52	1535.43	104.49	1430.93	134.58
汽车零售业	Retail Sales of Cars	1011.65	1054.38	28.01	1026.38	124.68
机动车燃料零售业	Retail Sales of Motor Vehicles Fuels	389.94	417.71	73.95	343.76	5.59
家用电器及电子产品专门零售业	Monopoly Retail of Home Appliances and Electronic Products	385.28	414.56	30.73	383.83	46.60
家用电器零售业	Retail Sales of Home Appliances	224.47	234.99	16.29	218.69	20.03
计算机、软件及辅助设备零售业	Retail Sales of Computers, Softwares and Assisted Equipments	48.34	54.18	3.72	50.47	3.94
通讯设备零售业	Retail Sales of Communication Equipments	28.98	39.07	5.32	33.75	15.40
五金、家具及室内装修材料专门零售业	Monopoly Retail of Hardware, Furnitures and Decorative Materials	148.11	182.95	8.35	174.60	7.45
无店铺及其他零售业	Retail Sales of Storeless and Others	179.68	228.74	32.08	196.66	7.61
互联网零售	Retail Sales of Internet	70.09	71.03	0.12	70.91	4.66

16-13 限额以上批发和零售业企业资产及负债(2013)
ASSETS AND LIABILITIES OF ENTERPRISES ABOVE DESIGNATED SIZE OF WHOLESALE AND RETAIL TRADES (2013)

单位: 亿元 (100 million yuan)

项目	Item	流动资产合计 Total Circulating Funds	固定资产原价 Original Price of Fixed Assets	资产总计 Total Assets	负债合计 Total Liabilities	所有者权益合计 Total Creditor's Equity
总计	**Total**	**3800.50**	**1119.55**	**5340.22**	**3789.62**	**1551.16**
一、批发业	**Wholesales**	**2522.55**	**533.90**	**3273.60**	**2357.65**	**915.95**
1.按登记注册类型分组	**Grouped by Registration Type**					
内资	**Domestic Funded Enterprises**	**2406.71**	**524.79**	**3144.66**	**2236.01**	**908.66**
国有	State-owned Enterprises	449.82	72.65	547.61	369.00	178.62
集体	Collective-owned Enterprises	8.86	1.32	10.32	9.48	0.83
股份合作	Cooperative Enterprises	0.65	0.17	0.78	0.54	0.24
联营企业	Joint Ownership Enterprises	0.13	0.01	0.14	0.13	0.01
国有联营	State Joint Ownership Enterprises					
集体联营	Collective Joint Ownership Enterprises					
国有与集体联营	Joint State-collective Enterprises					
其他联营	Other Joint Ownership Enterprises	0.13	0.01	0.14	0.13	0.01
有限责任公司	Limited Liability Corporations	1062.25	152.22	1311.40	986.42	324.98
国有独资公司	State Sole Funded Corporations	125.06	45.01	203.31	154.62	48.69
其他有限责任公司	Other Limited Liability Corporations	937.19	107.21	1108.09	831.80	276.28
股份有限公司	Share-holding Corporations Ltd.	246.68	186.26	485.50	276.73	208.78
私营企业	Private Enterprises	622.86	99.71	758.13	577.81	180.32
私营独资	Private-funded Enterprises	2.97	3.95	7.61	2.33	5.27
私营合伙	Private Partnership Enterprises	0.08	0.07	0.11	0.05	0.06
私营有限责任公司	Private Limited Liability Corporations	613.02	92.39	739.85	569.16	170.70
私营股份有限公司	Private Share-holding Corporations Ltd.	6.79	3.30	10.56	6.26	4.29
其他	Other Enterprises	15.46	12.46	30.78	15.91	14.87
港澳台商投资企业	**Enterprises with Funds from Hongkong, Macao and Taiwan**	**33.40**	**6.84**	**43.70**	**30.09**	**13.61**
合资经营	Joint-venture Enterprises	6.88	0.25	7.06	4.75	2.31
合作经营	Cooperative Enterprises					
独资经营	Enterprises with Sole Investment	26.51	6.59	36.64	25.34	11.30
投资股份有限公司	Share-holding Co. Ltd. With Investment					
外商投资企业	**Foreign Funded Enterprises**	**82.44**	**2.27**	**85.24**	**91.55**	**-6.31**
中外合资经营	Sino-foreign Joint-venture Enterprises	24.67	1.54	26.25	19.25	7.00
外资企业	Enterprises with Sole Foreign Investment	56.11	0.65	57.25	70.45	-13.20
外商投资股份有限公司	Share-holding Co. Ltd. with Foreign Investment	0.28	0.01	0.28	0.12	0.16
其他外资企业	Other Enterprises with Sole Foreign Investment	1.38	0.08	1.45	1.73	-0.28
2.按国民经济行业分组	**Grouped by Sector**					
农、林、牧产品批发业	Wholesales of Agriculture, Forestry and Animal Husbandry Products	174.73	42.36	221.64	162.44	59.20
食品、饮料及烟草制品批发业	Wholesales of Foods, Beverage and Tobacco	465.11	138.02	616.22	337.60	278.63
米、面制品及食用油批发业	Wholesales of Rice, Noodles and Edible Oil	15.83	12.97	29.00	17.50	11.50
烟草制品批发业	Wholesales of Tobacco	157.47	59.05	208.27	69.85	138.42
纺织、服装及日用品批发业	Wholesales of Textile Products, Garments and Daily Used Articles	132.55	8.96	145.91	124.35	21.56
服装批发业	Wholesales of Garments	35.07	4.07	42.08	31.73	10.35
家用电器批发业	Wholesales of Home Appliances	76.95	1.64	79.97	75.01	4.96
文化、体育用品及器材批发业	Wholesales of Cultural and Sports Goods and Equipments	55.14	13.12	71.68	45.50	26.18
医药及医疗器材批发业	Wholesales of Medicnes and Medical Appliances	291.19	34.59	344.98	266.38	78.60
矿产品、建材及化工产品批发业	Wholesales of Mineral Products, Building Materials and Chemical Products	929.13	259.56	1321.25	974.83	346.42
煤炭及制品批发业	Wholesales of Coal and Coal-made Products	101.30	12.53	123.73	97.88	25.85
石油及制品批发业	Wholesales of Petroleum Products	137.23	203.13	405.50	221.08	184.41
非金属及金属矿批发业	Wholesales of Non-metellic Mineral and Metal Industry	13.02	1.43	14.54	11.59	2.95
金属及金属矿批发业	Wholesales of Metal and Metal Mines	565.61	22.55	636.38	538.18	98.21
建材批发业	Wholesales of Construction Materials	18.52	7.76	27.01	17.36	9.65
化肥批发业	Wholesales of Chemical Fertilizers	53.70	7.21	63.95	50.57	13.37
机械设备、五金交电及电子产品批发	Wholesales of Machinery Equipment, Hardware, Transport and Electronic Products	201.03	24.89	233.86	180.02	53.84
汽车批发业	Wholesales of Cars	52.95	5.52	58.83	48.07	10.75
计算机、软件及辅助设备批发业	Wholesales of Computers, Softwares and Assisted Equipments	15.39	0.20	16.62	10.78	5.84
贸易经纪与代理	Trade Agent	248.39	3.76	282.47	243.76	38.70
其他批发业	Other Wholesales	25.29	8.64	35.58	22.76	12.82

16-13 续表 continued

单位：亿元 (100 million yuan)

项　目	Item	流动资产合计 Total Circulating Funds	固定资产原价 Original Price of Fixed Assets	资产总计 Total Assets	负债合计 Total Liabilities	所有者权益合计 Total Creditor's Equity
二、零售业	**Retail Trade**	**1277.95**	**585.65**	**2066.62**	**1431.98**	**635.20**
1.按登记注册类型分组	**Grouped by Registration Type**					
内资	**Domestic Funded Enterprises**	**1153.10**	**548.38**	**1901.19**	**1304.53**	**597.22**
国有	State-owned Enterprises	45.10	16.55	67.63	49.45	18.18
集体	Collective-owned Enterprises	16.86	18.39	33.54	26.09	7.44
股份合作	Cooperative Enterprises	0.53	0.72	1.11	0.47	0.64
联营企业	Joint Ownership Enterprises	0.40	0.20	0.59	0.12	0.48
国有联营	State Joint Ownership Enterprises					
集体联营	Collective Joint Ownership Enterprises	0.07	0.08	0.15	0.06	0.09
国有与集体联营	Joint State-collective Enterprises	0.31	0.11	0.43	0.06	0.37
其他联营	Other Joint Ownership Enterprises	0.02	0.00	0.02	0.00	0.02
有限责任公司	Limited Liability Corporations	594.47	205.22	938.74	663.18	276.12
国有独资公司	State Sole Funded Corporations	7.80	25.91	49.19	29.42	19.77
其他有限责任公司	Other Limited Liability Corporations	586.68	179.32	889.55	633.76	256.35
股份有限公司	Share-holding Corporations Ltd.	170.05	153.80	356.20	246.35	109.84
私营企业	Private Enterprises	320.36	147.84	491.43	313.22	178.21
私营独资	Private-funded Enterprises	14.35	19.04	32.65	10.10	22.55
私营合伙	Private Partnership Enterprises	1.16	2.08	3.50	0.99	2.51
私营有限责任公司	Private Limited Liability Corporations	282.33	119.04	422.37	280.17	142.21
私营股份有限公司	Private Share-holding Corporations Ltd.	22.52	7.67	32.91	21.97	10.94
其他	Other Enterprises	5.34	5.67	11.94	5.64	6.30
港澳台商投资企业	**Enterprises with Funds from Hongkong, Macao and Taiwan**	**72.40**	**10.09**	**82.57**	**62.25**	**20.32**
合资经营	Joint-venture Enterprises	2.26	0.93	3.59	3.20	0.40
合作经营	Cooperative Enterprises					
独资经营	Enterprises with Sole Investment	70.14	9.17	78.97	59.05	19.92
投资股份有限公司	Share-holding Co. Ltd. With Investment					
外商投资企业	**Foreign Funded Enterprises**	**52.45**	**27.17**	**82.87**	**65.20**	**17.67**
中外合资经营	Sino-foreign Joint-venture Enterprises	6.35	3.18	12.90	9.91	2.99
外资企业	Enterprises with Sole Foreign Investment	35.98	23.17	59.00	45.24	13.76
外商投资股份有限公司	Share-holding Co. Ltd. with Foreign Investment	0.28	0.82	1.13	0.97	0.16
其他外资企业	Other Enterprises with Sole Foreign Investment	9.84	0.00	9.84	9.07	0.76
2.按国民经济行业分组	**Grouped by Sector**					
综合零售业	Retail Sales of Department	349.58	262.97	659.17	475.44	184.29
百货零售业	Department Stores	191.66	146.74	372.22	268.87	103.88
超级市场零售业	Supermarkets	146.73	107.22	267.91	194.17	73.77
食品、饮料及烟草制品专门零售业	Monopoly Retail of Foods, Beverage and Tobacco	64.09	35.74	106.92	45.73	61.19
纺织、服装及日用品专门零售业	Monopoly Retail of Textile, Garments,and Daily Used Articles	55.44	29.39	84.49	49.73	34.76
服装零售业	Retail Sales of Garments	37.41	21.70	58.82	36.04	22.79
文化、体育用品及器材专门零售业	Monopoly Retail of Cultural, Sports Products and Equipments	37.74	18.26	62.45	35.02	27.43
体育用品零售业	Retail Sales of Sports Products	0.57	0.18	1.33	1.36	-0.02
图书报刊零售业	Retail Sales of Books, Newspapers and Periodicals	17.48	9.10	28.07	12.89	15.18
医药及医疗器材专门零售业	Monopoly Retail of Medicine and Medical Appliances	142.40	17.83	173.59	132.91	40.68
药品零售业	Retail Sales of Medicine	138.96	17.60	169.91	130.11	39.80
汽车、摩托车、燃料及零配件专门零售业	Monopoly Retail of Cars, and Motorcars Parts	431.97	133.20	657.23	480.06	177.17
汽车零售业	Retail Sales of Cars	410.51	79.26	575.23	434.27	140.95
机动车燃料零售业	Retail Sales of Motor Vehicles Fuels	11.07	46.76	64.73	36.76	27.97
家用电器及电子产品专门零售业	Monopoly Retail of Home Appliances and Electronic Products	108.71	46.54	164.42	105.67	58.74
家用电器零售业	Retail Sales of Home Appliances	76.05	36.35	120.73	79.88	40.85
计算机、软件及辅助设备零售业	Retail Sales of Computers, Softwares and Assisted Equipments	14.65	2.24	17.37	10.83	6.54
通讯设备零售业	Retail Sales of Communication Equipments	3.67	1.58	5.12	3.53	1.59
五金、家具及室内装修材料专门零售业	Monopoly Retail of Hardware, Furnitures and Decorative Materials	54.70	20.96	88.24	59.18	29.06
无店铺及其他零售业	Retail Sales of Storeless and Others	33.31	20.76	70.12	48.23	21.89
互联网零售	Retail Sales of Internet	16.76	0.41	17.44	17.49	-0.05

16-14 限额以上批发和零售业企业主要财务指标(2013)
MAIN FINANCIAL INDICATORS OF ENTERPRISES ABOVE DESIGNATED SIZE OF WHOLESALE AND RETAIL TRADES (2013)

单位：亿元 (100 million yuan)

项目	Item	主营业务收入 Revenue of Major Business	主营业务成本 Cost of Major Business	其他业务利润 Profits of Other Business	利润总额 Total Profits
总计	**Total**	**13262.32**	**11864.04**	**46.92**	**475.09**
一、批发业	**Wholesales**	**9009.09**	**8246.35**	**11.40**	**277.77**
1.按登记注册类型分组	**Grouped by Registration Type**				
内资	**Domestic Funded Enterprises**	**8709.50**	**8006.25**	**10.69**	**276.39**
国有	State-owned Enterprises	1124.54	965.69	4.21	70.29
集体	Collective-owned Enterprises	16.50	15.26		0.32
股份合作	Cooperative Enterprises	3.26	2.72	-0.01	0.15
联营企业	Joint Ownership Enterprises	0.13	0.13		0.00
国有联营	State Joint Ownership Enterprises				
集体联营	Collective Joint Ownership Enterprises				
国有与集体联营	Joint State-collective Enterprises				
其他联营	Other Joint Ownership Enterprises	0.13	0.13		0.00
有限责任公司	Limited Liability Corporations	4330.18	4054.69	2.84	116.57
国有独资公司	State Sole Funded Corporations	1918.96	1871.63	0.05	24.28
其他有限责任公司	Other Limited Liability Corporations	2411.22	2183.06	2.79	92.28
股份有限公司	Share-holding Corporations Ltd.	1697.31	1590.09	0.84	25.90
私营企业	Private Enterprises	1431.13	1284.79	2.60	54.38
私营独资	Private-funded Enterprises	23.18	17.14	0.06	2.95
私营合伙	Private Partnership Enterprises	1.16	1.01		0.02
私营有限责任公司	Private Limited Liability Corporations	1372.23	1234.72	2.51	50.70
私营股份有限公司	Private Share-holding Corporations Ltd.	34.56	31.92	0.03	0.71
其他	Other Enterprises	106.45	92.90	0.20	8.79
港澳台商投资企业	**Enterprises with Funds from Hongkong, Macao and Taiwan**	**69.42**	**54.46**	**0.60**	**1.14**
合资经营	Joint-venture Enterprises	11.79	10.72	0.01	-0.01
合作经营	Cooperative Enterprises				
独资经营	Enterprises with Sole Investment	57.63	43.74	0.59	1.16
投资股份有限公司	Share-holding Co. Ltd. With Investment				
外商投资企业	**Foreign Funded Enterprises**	**230.17**	**185.64**	**0.11**	**0.24**
中外合资经营	Sino-foreign Joint-venture Enterprises	71.54	65.42	0.01	3.77
外资企业	Enterprises with Sole Foreign Investment	153.61	117.39	0.10	-3.63
外商投资股份有限公司	Share-holding Co. Ltd. with Foreign Investment	0.74	0.56		0.09
其他外资企业	Other Enterprises with Sole Foreign Investment	4.29	2.26		0.01
2.按国民经济行业分组	**Grouped by Sector**				
农、林、牧产品批发业	Wholesales of Agriculture, Forestry and Animal Husbandry Products	324.87	286.60	0.81	13.83
食品、饮料及烟草制品批发业	Wholesales of Foods, Beverage and Tobacco	1235.81	932.75	1.89	117.45
米、面制品及食用油批发业	Wholesales of Rice, Noodles and Edible Oil	67.59	56.41	0.23	2.54
烟草制品批发业	Wholesales of Tobacco	552.38	408.07	0.37	68.82
纺织、服装及日用品批发业	Wholesales of Textile Products, Garments and Daily Used Articles	274.39	239.70	1.42	8.37
服装批发业	Wholesales of Garments	80.78	65.63	0.08	0.54
家用电器批发业	Wholesales of Home Appliances	120.20	111.38	0.49	3.68
文化、体育用品及器材批发业	Wholesales of Cultural and Sports Goods and Equipments	111.17	97.45	0.03	3.24
医药及医疗器材批发业	Wholesales of Medicnes and Medical Appliances	636.33	579.36	0.47	16.16
矿产品、建材及化工产品批发业	Wholesales of Mineral Products, Building Materials and Chemical Products	5182.80	4939.55	2.50	97.79
煤炭及制品批发业	Wholesales of Coal and Coal-made Products	291.36	269.11	0.31	8.60
石油及制品批发业	Wholesales of Petroleum Products	3077.22	2958.49	1.06	41.46
非金属及金属矿批发业	Wholesales of Non-metellic Mineral and Metal Industry	25.79	21.42		1.70
金属及金属矿批发业	Wholesales of Metal and Metal Mines	1349.61	1300.94	0.55	21.29
建材批发业	Wholesales of Construction Materials	77.79	64.23	0.11	7.03
化肥批发业	Wholesales of Chemical Fertilizers	198.39	180.64	0.36	7.54
机械设备、五金交电及电子产品批发	Wholesales of Machinery Equipment, Hardware, Transport and Electronic Products	472.45	418.68	0.87	15.04
汽车批发业	Wholesales of Cars	126.91	110.74	0.01	4.75
计算机、软件及辅助设备批发业	Wholesales of Computers, Softwares and Assisted Equipments	73.40	68.77	0.04	1.74
贸易经纪与代理	Trade Agent	696.85	690.80	3.38	0.45
其他批发业	Other Wholesales	74.41	61.46	0.02	5.44

16-14 续表 continued

单位：亿元 (100 million yuan)

项　目	Item	主营业务收入 Revenue of Major Business	主营业务成本 Cost of Major Business	其他业务利润 Profits of Other Business	利润总额 Total Profits
二、零售业	**Retail Trade**	**4253.23**	**3617.69**	**35.52**	**197.32**
1.按登记注册类型分组	**Grouped by Registration Type**				
内资	**Domestic Funded Enterprises**	**3961.54**	**3365.93**	**21.96**	**179.08**
国有	State-owned Enterprises	208.69	183.44	0.23	12.15
集体	Collective-owned Enterprises	132.25	116.04	0.20	2.78
股份合作	Cooperative Enterprises	3.04	2.49	0.00	0.32
联营企业	Joint Ownership Enterprises	2.89	2.64		0.08
国有联营	State Joint Ownership Enterprises				
集体联营	Collective Joint Ownership Enterprises	0.42	0.40		
国有与集体联营	Joint State-collective Enterprises	2.35	2.12		0.07
其他联营	Other Joint Ownership Enterprises	0.13	0.12		0.00
有限责任公司	Limited Liability Corporations	1787.45	1538.38	10.37	73.01
国有独资公司	State Sole Funded Corporations	193.83	184.39	0.21	2.34
其他有限责任公司	Other Limited Liability Corporations	1593.62	1353.99	10.16	70.67
股份有限公司	Share-holding Corporations Ltd.	626.92	533.36	8.85	21.09
私营企业	Private Enterprises	1156.93	954.34	2.28	66.88
私营独资	Private-funded Enterprises	96.56	73.76	0.04	9.12
私营合伙	Private Partnership Enterprises	6.85	5.48	0.02	0.41
私营有限责任公司	Private Limited Liability Corporations	973.30	807.93	2.01	53.45
私营股份有限公司	Private Share-holding Corporations Ltd.	80.22	67.17	0.20	3.89
其他	Other Enterprises	43.35	35.25	0.03	2.78
港澳台商投资企业	**Enterprises with Funds from Hongkong, Macao and Taiwan**	**126.31**	**109.46**	**11.97**	**13.92**
合资经营	Joint-venture Enterprises	5.64	4.05	0.05	0.34
合作经营	Cooperative Enterprises				
独资经营	Enterprises with Sole Investment	120.67	105.41	11.92	13.58
投资股份有限公司	Share-holding Co. Ltd. With Investment				
外商投资企业	**Foreign Funded Enterprises**	**165.39**	**142.30**	**1.59**	**4.31**
中外合资经营	Sino-foreign Joint-venture Enterprises	21.46	16.89	0.03	0.35
外资企业	Enterprises with Sole Foreign Investment	128.78	111.45	1.56	3.55
外商投资股份有限公司	Share-holding Co. Ltd. with Foreign Investment	1.18	0.74		0.06
其他外资企业	Other Enterprises with Sole Foreign Investment	13.96	13.22		0.35
2.按国民经济行业分组	**Grouped by Sector**				
综合零售业	Retail Sales of Department	1198.72	986.53	28.48	59.34
百货零售业	Department Stores	593.47	494.09	24.14	34.28
超级市场零售业	Supermarkets	490.89	398.49	4.26	19.69
食品、饮料及烟草制品专门零售业	Monopoly Retail of Foods, Beverage and Tobacco	354.02	278.16	0.42	29.92
纺织、服装及日用品专门零售业	Monopoly Retail of Textile, Garments,and Daily Used Articles	149.31	112.68	0.37	9.95
服装零售业	Retail Sales of Garments	93.40	68.64	0.27	5.62
文化、体育用品及器材专门零售业	Monopoly Retail of Cultural, Sports Products and Equipments	81.08	63.46	0.28	5.63
体育用品零售业	Retail Sales of Sports Products	3.23	2.88	0.00	-0.21
图书报刊零售业	Retail Sales of Books, Newspapers and Periodicals	29.62	22.70	0.22	2.15
医药及医疗器材专门零售业	Monopoly Retail of Medicine and Medical Appliances	277.43	247.49	0.86	7.56
药品零售业	Retail Sales of Medicine	269.54	240.86	0.79	7.38
汽车、摩托车、燃料及零配件专门零售业	Monopoly Retail of Cars, and Motorcars Parts	1464.92	1312.75	1.99	44.10
汽车零售业	Retail Sales of Cars	1035.26	925.23	1.91	28.43
机动车燃料零售业	Retail Sales of Motor Vehicles Fuels	368.38	339.15	0.06	10.72
家用电器及电子产品专门零售业	Monopoly Retail of Home Appliances and Electronic Products	351.13	291.41	2.30	24.45
家用电器零售业	Retail Sales of Home Appliances	210.32	175.63	1.82	11.94
计算机、软件及辅助设备零售业	Retail Sales of Computers, Softwares and Assisted Equipments	48.04	41.02	0.12	3.33
通讯设备零售业	Retail Sales of Communication Equipments	11.77	10.35	0.03	0.29
五金、家具及室内装修材料专门零售业	Monopoly Retail of Hardware, Furnitures and Decorative Materials	166.10	132.77	0.19	11.70
无店铺及其他零售业	Retail Sales of Storeless and Others	210.52	192.43	0.64	4.67
互联网零售	Retail Sales of Internet	69.50	66.25		0.23

16-15 限额以上餐饮业企业资产及负债(2013)
ASSETS AND LIABILITIES OF ENTERPRISES ABOVE DESIGNATED SIZE OF CATERING SERVICES (2013)

单位：亿元 (100 million yuan)

项 目	Item	流动资产合计 Total Circulating Funds	固定资产原价 Original Price of Fixed Assets	资产总计 Total Assets	负债合计 Total Liabilities	所有者权益合计 Total Creditor's Equity
总 计	**Total**	**85.37**	**123.32**	**234.43**	**149.59**	**84.84**
1.按国民经济行业分组	**Grouped by Sector**					
正餐服务业	Dinner	80.31	114.93	214.80	135.21	79.59
快餐服务业	Fast Food	3.26	6.89	15.82	12.20	3.63
饮料及冷饮服务业	Beverage and Cold Drink Services	0.43	0.79	1.83	1.00	0.83
其他餐饮服务业	Others	1.37	0.70	1.97	1.18	0.79
2.按登记注册类型分组	**Grouped by Registration Type**					
内资	**Domestic Funded Enterprises**	**80.46**	**110.10**	**209.38**	**128.19**	**81.19**
国有	State-Owned Enterprises	1.13	4.03	4.74	2.47	2.27
集体	Collective-owned Enterprises	0.10	0.62	0.62	0.49	0.13
股份合作	Cooperative Enterprises	0.02	0.08	0.10	0.01	0.09
联营企业	Joint Ownership Enterprises	0.41	0.81	1.11	0.20	0.90
国有联营	State Joint Ownership Enterprises					
集体联营	Collective Joint Ownership Enterprises	0.41	0.81	1.11	0.20	0.90
国有与集体联营	Joint State-collective Enterprises					
其他联营	Other Joint Ownership Enterprises					
有限责任公司	Limited Liability Corporations	41.90	47.73	100.60	74.23	26.37
国有独资公司	State Sole Funded Corporations	2.65	3.36	7.32	4.34	2.98
其他有限责任公司	Other Limited Liability Corporations	39.25	44.37	93.28	69.89	23.39
股份有限公司	Share-holding Corporations Ltd.	1.16	3.41	4.33	2.90	1.43
私营企业	Private Enterprises	34.69	51.05	94.33	47.09	47.24
私营独资	Private-funded Enterprises	3.68	10.81	14.36	4.07	10.29
私营合伙	Private Partnership Enterprises	0.24	0.62	0.80	0.22	0.58
私营有限责任公司	Private Limited Liability Corporations	29.70	37.82	75.67	40.88	34.79
私营股份有限公司	Private Share-holding Corporations Ltd.	1.07	1.80	3.51	1.92	1.59
其他	Other Enterprises	1.04	2.38	3.57	0.81	2.76
港澳台商投资企业	**Enterprises with Funds from Hongkong, Macao and Taiwan**	**1.58**	**4.06**	**6.46**	**5.54**	**0.92**
合资经营	Joint-venture Enterprises	0.50	2.05	2.52	2.48	0.05
合作经营	Cooperative Enterprises					
独资经营	Enterprises with Sole Investment	1.04	1.94	3.86	3.01	0.85
投资股份有限公司	Share-holding Co. Ltd. With Investment	0.04	0.06	0.08	0.06	0.02
外商投资企业	**Foreign Funded Enterprises**	**3.33**	**9.16**	**18.59**	**15.85**	**2.73**
中外合资经营	Sino-Foreign Joint-venture Enterprises	0.60	0.52	1.67	1.68	-0.01
外资企业	Enterprises with Sole Foreign Investment	2.69	8.64	16.86	14.14	2.72
外商投资股份有限公司	Share-holding Co. Ltd. with Foreign Investment					
其他外商投资企业	Other Enterprises with Sole Foreign Investment	0.04	0.01	0.06	0.04	0.02

16-16 限额以上餐饮业企业主要财务指标(2013)
MAIN FINANCIAL INDICATORS OF ENTERPRISES ABOVE DESIGNATED SIZE OF CATERING SERVICES (2013)

单位：亿元 (100 million yuan)

项　目	Item	主营业务收入 Revenue of Major Business	主营业务成本 Cost of Major Business	其他业务利润 Profits of Other Business	利润总额 Total Profits
总　计	**Total**	**221.13**	**123.16**	**1.61**	**13.89**
1.按国民经济行业分组	**Grouped by Sector**				
正餐服务业	Dinner	181.20	104.04	1.60	11.57
快餐服务业	Fast Food	32.59	14.96	0.00	1.84
饮料及冷饮服务业	Beverage and Cold Drink Services	3.26	0.98		0.38
其他餐饮服务业	Others	4.07	3.18		0.09
2.按登记注册类型分组	**Grouped by Registration Type**				
内资	**Domestic Funded Enterprises**	**182.88**	**106.27**	**1.59**	**11.93**
国有	State-Owned Enterprises	3.26	2.00	0.05	0.35
集体	Collective-owned Enterprises	1.04	0.61	0.00	0.20
股份合作	Cooperative Enterprises	0.32	0.17		0.09
联营企业	Joint Ownership Enterprises	4.68	3.03		0.28
国有联营	State Joint Ownership Enterprises				
集体联营	Collective Joint Ownership Enterprises	4.68	3.03		0.28
国有与集体联营	Joint State-collective Enterprises				
其他联营	Other Joint Ownership Enterprises				
有限责任公司	Limited Liability Corporations	70.62	38.38	0.95	1.39
国有独资公司	State Sole Funded Corporations	1.23	0.87	0.01	0.04
其他有限责任公司	Other Limited Liability Corporations	69.39	37.51	0.94	1.35
股份有限公司	Share-holding Corporations Ltd.	2.57	1.44	0.00	0.35
私营企业	Private Enterprises	96.16	57.93	0.59	8.58
私营独资	Private-funded Enterprises	22.74	14.63	0.14	3.41
私营合伙	Private Partnership Enterprises	0.89	0.56	0.01	0.11
私营有限责任公司	Private Limited Liability Corporations	69.25	40.88	0.44	4.86
私营股份有限公司	Private Share-holding Corporations Ltd.	3.29	1.86	0.00	0.20
其他	Other Enterprises	4.22	2.72	0.00	0.70
港澳台商投资企业	**Enterprises with Funds from Hongkong, Macao and Taiwan**	**6.38**	**2.30**	**0.01**	**0.19**
合资经营	Joint-venture Enterprises	0.75	0.20		-0.07
合作经营	Cooperative Enterprises				
独资经营	Enterprises with Sole Investment	5.55	2.05		0.27
独资股份有限公司	Sole Investment Co. Ltd. With Investment	0.08	0.05	0.01	-0.01
外商投资企业	**Foreign Funded Enterprises**	**31.87**	**14.59**	**0.01**	**1.78**
中外合资经营	Sino-Foreign Joint-venture Enterprises	0.79	0.61	0.01	-0.03
外资企业	Enterprises with Sole Foreign Investment	30.89	13.87	0.00	1.79
外商投资股份有限公司	Share-holding Co. Ltd. with Foreign Investment				
其他外商投资企业	Other Enterprises with Sole Foreign Investment	0.18	0.11		0.01

主要统计指标解释

社会消费品零售总额 指批发和零售业、餐饮业、新闻出版业、邮政业和其他服务业等，售予城乡居民用于生活消费的商品和社会集团用于公共消费的商品之总量。社会消费品零售总额包括:

一、批发和零售业企业（单位):

1.售予城乡居民的各种生活消费品;

2.售予入境旅游的外国人、华侨、港澳台同胞的各类商品;

3.售予行政事业单位、社会团体、军队和武警等机构的商品，以及以零售方式售予各类企业的商品。具体包括: 用于非生产和社会交往的办公用品，如通讯设备、计算器具和设备、电讯网络设备、文印设备、音像视听器材和设备、纸张、本册、文具及装订文印材料、家具、日用电器、针纺织品、清洁卫生用品、文体用品、奖品、纪念品、礼品等; 供内部人员乘坐的交通工具和燃料; 用于办公设施修缮的各类配件、材料、工具等; 用于取暖和防暑降温的设备、燃料、材料及食品等; 专用于教学的用品和设备; 非营利医疗机构的中、西药品、中药材和医疗设备器材; 非专用的劳动保护用品; 不对外营业的内部食堂用的餐具、炊具、设备、清洁卫生工具和食品、燃料等; 军队、武警用于其人员生活的衣着品和个人用品; 其他各类非生产性设备和用品。

二、餐饮业出售的主食、菜肴、烟酒饮料和其他商品。

三、新闻出版业、邮政业售予城乡居民、企事业单位、军队和武警等机构的书报杂志、音像制品、邮品等。

四、其他服务业出售的食品、烟酒饮料、服装鞋帽、日常生活用品、医药保健用品、艺术品、工艺美术品、玩具、殡葬用品以及其他消费品。

批发零售业商品购、销、存总额 指各种登记注册类型的批发、零售业企业(单位)以本企业(单位)为总体的，从国内、国外市场购进的商品总量，销售和出口的商品总量、库存商品总量等情况。该指标可以反映商品流转过程中商品的购进、销售、库存之间的比例关系和存在的问题。

商品购进总额 指从本企业(单位)以外的单位和个人购进(包括从境外直接进口)作为转卖或加工后转卖的商品总额。它反映批发零售贸易业从国内、国外市场上购进商品的总量。商品购进总额包括: (1)从工农业生产者购进的商品; (2)从出版社、报社的出版发行部门购进的图书、杂志和报纸; (3)从各种登记注册类型的批发零售贸易企业(单位)购进的商品; (4)从其他单位购进的商品，如从机关、团体、企业等单位购进的剩余物资，从餐饮业、服务业购进的商品，从海关、市场管理部门购进的缉私和没收的商品，从居民手中收购的废旧商品等; (5)从国(境)外直接进口的商品。不包括企业(单位)为自身经营用和未通过买卖行为而收入的商品以及销售退回、商品升溢等。

商品销售总额 指对本企业(单位)以外的单位和个人出售(包括对境外直接出口)的商品总额。它反映批发零售贸易业在国内市场上销售商品以及出口商品的总量。商品销售总额包括: (1)售给城乡居民和社会集团消费用的商品; (2)售给工业、农业、建筑业、运输邮电业、批发零售贸易业、餐饮业、服务业等作为生产、经营使用的商品; (3)售给批发零售贸易业作为转卖或加工后转卖的商品; (4)对国(境)外直接出口的商品。不包括出售本企业(单位)自用的废旧包装用品、未通过买卖行为付出的商品、经本单位介绍，由买卖双方直接结算，本单位只收取手续费的业务、购货退出的商品以及商品损耗和损失等。

批发零售业库存 指报告期末各种登记注册类型的批发零售贸易企业(单位)已取得所有权的商品。它反映批发零售贸易企业(单位)的商品库存情况和对市场商品供应的保证程度。期末库存包括: (1)存放在批发零售贸易业经营单位(如门市部、批发站、经营处)仓库、货场、货柜和货架中的商品; (2)挑选、整理、包装中的商品; (3)已记入购进而尚未运到本单位的商品，即发货单或银行承兑凭证已到而货未到的部分; (4)寄放他处的商品，如因购货方拒绝承付而暂时存放在购货方的商品和已办完加工成品收回手续而未提回的商品; (5)委托其他单位代销(未作销售或调出)尚未售出的商品; (6)代其他单位购进尚未交付的商品。不包括所有权不属于本单位的商品、拨付除批发零售贸易业以外的其他行业所属独立核算加工厂等加工生产尚未收回成品的商品、代国家物资储备部门保管的商品等。

库存总额采用的计算价格是：农副产品采购单位按购进价计算；批发单位按进货价计算；零售单位按核算价格计算，即按什么价格核算就按什么价格计算。

住宿餐饮业营业额 指住宿和餐饮业法人企业、产业活动单位在经营活动中因提供服务或销售商品等取得的收入，包括客房收入、餐费收入、商品销售收入和其他收入。客房收入指住宿和餐饮业法人企业、产业活动单位在经营活动中因提供住宿服务取得的客房收入。餐费收入指住宿和餐饮业法人企业、产业活动单位因为顾客提供就餐服务取得的收入，包括经烹饪、调制加工后出售的各种食品，如主食、炒菜、凉拌菜等的收入。商品销售收入指住宿和餐饮业法人企业、产业活动单位伴随服务而出售商品所取得的收入。其他收入指营业收入中除客房收入、餐费收入、商品销售收入以外的其他收入，包括娱乐、健身和商务服务等。

亿元商品交易市场成交额 指年成交额达到亿元以上，经工商部门批准、专门从事商品批发、零售业务活动的市场。其市场所有摊位成交总额称为商品交易市场成交额。

连锁企业（或称连锁店、连锁公司） 指在核心企业或总店的领导下，由分散的、经营同类商品或服务的企业或活动单位，采取共同方针，实行集中采购和分散销售的有机结合，通过规范化经营，实现规模效益的经济联合组织形式。一般连锁店应由若干个分店组成。其经营特征：(1)经营同类商品；(2)使用统一商号；(3)统一采购配送，采购与销售相分离（部分商品可根据物流合理和保质保鲜原则，由供应商直接送货到门店，其余均由总部统一配送）。

连锁门店包括下列三种形式：

直营连锁：也叫正规连锁。连锁门店均由总部独资或控股开设，在总部的直接领导下统一经营。总部采取纵深似的管理方式，直接下令掌管所有的零售门店，零售门店也必须完全接受总部指挥。他是大型垄断商业资本通过吞并、兼并或独资、控股等途径，发展壮大自身实力和规模的一种形式。

特许连锁：各连锁门店（被特许人）通过合同形式，取得使用总部（特许人）商标、商号、经营技术和销售总部开发的商品的特许权，各加盟连锁门店为独立法人，在总部指导下统一经营。

自由连锁：也称自愿连锁。连锁公司的门店均为独立法人，各自的资产所有权关系不变，在公司总部的指导下共同经营。各成员店使用共同的店名，与总部订阅有关购、销、宣传等方面的合同，并按合同开展经营活动。在合同规定的范围之外，各成员店可以自由活动。根据自愿原则，各成员店可自由加入连锁体系，也可自由退出。

特许连锁加上自由连锁等于加盟连锁。

Explanatory Notes on Main Statistical Indicators

Total Retail Sales of Consumer Goods refer to the sum of retail sales of commodities sold by wholesale, retail, catering, publishing, post and telecommunications and other service industries to urban and rural households for private consumption and to social institutions for public consumption. Retail sales of consumer goods include:

1) Sales by wholesale and retail units:

a) of consumer goods sold to urban and rural households

b) of commodities sold to foreigners, overseas Chinese and Chinese compatriots from Hong Kong, Macao and Taiwan visiting in China

c) of commodities sold to government agencies, institutions, social organizations, military and armed police units, and commodities sold to enterprises in the form of retail sales. More specifically, they include: office facilities and articles for non-production purposes such as communications equipment, computing equipment and instruments, TV and network equipment, printing and copying equipment, audio-visual equipment and instruments, paper, notebooks, stationeries, furniture, electric appliances, knitwear, sanitation and cleaning articles, cultural and sport articles, articles for prizes, souvenirs, etc.; transport vehicles and fuels for employees; materials, spare parts and tools for the maintenance of office facilities; equipment, fuels, materials and food for winter heating or summer cooling purposes; articles and equipment for teaching purpose; Chinese and western medicines and medical equipment and facilities purchased by non profit-making medical institutes; non-specialized work safety articles; cooking utensils, tableware, equipment, cleaning articles, food and fuels purchased by internal cafeterias; clothes and personal articles purchased by military or armed police units for their officials and soldiers; and other equipment and articles for non-production purposes.

2) Sales of stable food, cooked dishes, beverages, tobaccos and other articles by catering units.

3) Sales of books, newspapers, magazines, audio-visual products and post products by publishing, post and telecommunications departments to urban and rural households and to enterprises, institutions, military and armed police units.

4) Sales of food, beverages, tobaccos, clothing, hats, footwear, articles for daily use, medicines, medical and health articles, work of art, handicrafts, toys, funeral articles and other articles by other service industries.

Purchase, Sales and Stock of Commodities by Wholesale and Retail Trades refer to the total volume of commodities purchased, total volume of sales and exports, and the stock of commodities by wholesale and retail enterprises (establishments) of different status of registration from domestic and overseas markets. This indictor reflects the relationship among purchase, sales and stock of commodities in the circulation of goods and reveals the existing problems.

Total Purchases of Commodities refer to the total value of purchases of commodities by the enterprises (establishments) from other establishments or individuals (including direct import from abroad) for the purpose of re-selling, either with or without further processing of the commodities purchased. This indicator is used to show the total value of purchases of commodities by wholesale and retail establishments from domestic and overseas markets. The total purchases include: (1) agricultural and industrial products purchased from producers; (2) books, magazines and newspapers purchased from distribution departments of the publishers; (3) commodities purchased from wholesale and retail establishments of different status of registration; (4) commodities purchased from other units, such as surplus materials purchased from government agencies, enterprises or institutions, commodities purchased from catering and service establishments, confiscated goods purchased from customs authorities or market management agencies, second-hand goods and wastes purchased from residents; and (5) commodities directly imported from abroad. Excluded are commodities purchased by enterprises (establishments) for use in their own business operation, commodities obtained without buying or selling procedures, rejected commodities, etc.

Total Sales of Commodities refer to value of commodities sold by the establishments to other establishments and individuals (including direct export). This indicator is used to show the total value of sales of commodities at domestic markets and export. The total sales include: (1) commodities sold to urban and rural residents and social groups for their consumption; (2) commodities sold to establishments in industry, agriculture, construction, transportation, post and telecommunications, wholesale and retail trades, catering trade and public utility for their production and operation; (3) commodities sold to wholesale and retail establishments for re selling, with or without further processing; and (4)commodities for direct export to other countries. Excluded are selling of waste packaging materials used by the establishments (units) themselves, commodities transferred without buying or selling procedures, commission income from brokerage in transactions whose settlement is directly handled by buyers and sellers, rejected commodities in the purchase, loss in commodities, etc.

Commodity Stock of Wholesale and Retail Enterprises refers to total commodities possessed by wholesale and retail enterprises (units) of various types of registration status at the end of the reference period, which reflects the commodity stock level of various wholesale and retail enterprises and the potential for market supply. It includes: (1) commodities located in storage, garages, counters, and shelves of operating units (such as sale stores, wholesale centers, and operating offices) of wholesale and retail enterprises; (2) commodities in the process of selecting, sorting, and packing; (3) commodities not arrived but recorded as purchase in the account, i.e. commodities not arrived but payment receipts for the commodities from the sellers or the banks arrived; (4) commodities deposited in other places rather than places mentioned above, for instance: commodities in the hold of purchasers temporarily due to the refusal of payment and commodities not taken back after going through the formalities; (5) commodities entrusted to other units to sell but not sold yet; (6) commodities purchased for other units but not delivered yet. Commodities not included as stock are those not owned by the enterprises (units), those allocated to financially independent factories rather than wholesale and retail enterprises for processing but not taken back yet, and finally those put in stock by wholesale and retail enterprises on behalf of the state material reserves units.

For the calculation of the value of commodities stock, the value is calculated at purchasing prices in agricultural goods purchasing units and wholesale units, and at the accounting prices in retail units.

Business Revenue of Hotels and Catering Services refer to revenue received from providing services or selling commodities by corporate enterprises and establishments engaged in hotel and catering services, including income from hotel rooms, from catering services, from selling of commodities and from other services. Income from hotel rooms refers to income of corporate enterprises and establishments by providing lodging services. Income from catering services refers to income of corporate enterprises and establishments by providing catering services, including selling of cooked or prepared foods such as stable food, cooked dishes or cold dishes. Income from selling of commodities refers to income of corporate enterprises and establishments by selling commodities that accompany the services they provide. Income from other activities refers to income received other than income from hotel rooms, catering services or selling of commodities, such as income from providing recreation, fitness or business services.

Volume of Transaction at Large Commodity Markets (with transaction value over 100 million yuan) refers to markets approved by the industrial and commercial administration departments, which specialize in wholesale and retail of commodities with an annual transaction of over 100 million yuan. The sum of sales of all sellers in the markets makes up the transaction value of the markets.

Chain Enterprises (also called chain stores or chain corporations) refer to a form of joint economic entities under which scattered enterprises or establishments engaged in providing homogeneous commodities or services, with the central leadership of core enterprise or headquarters and guided by common policies, conduct centralized purchase and distributed selling of commodities, in order to gain better efficiency through standardized operation. Consisting of a number of branch stores, the chain stores have in general following features: 1) homogeneous commodities, 2) unique name of stores, 3) centralized purchase and delivery which is separated from distributed selling operation (most commodities are delivered from the headquarters except some items which, from logistics, quality or freshness considerations, might be delivered by the suppliers directly).

Chain stores have 3 categories:

a) Chain stores under direct management: These are formal chain stores invested or controlled by the headquarters. They operate under the direct and unified management from the headquarters. Adopting a direct management approach, the headquarters give orders and control all retail stores, which follow completely the directives from the headquarters. Large monopolized commercial companies develop and expand their business through purchasing, merging, direct investment and controlling of shares.

b) Chain stores through special permit: Through contracts, chain stores (or their owners) obtain licenses from the headquarters to use designated trade marks, names, operation know-how, and to sell the commodity developed by the headquarters. Under this arrangement, each store in the chain is an independent legal entity and operates under the guidance from the headquarters.

c) Chain stores through voluntary arrangement: Under this arrangement, all stores operate together under the guidance of the headquarters, while maintaining their status of independent legal entities with full ownership of their assets. They use the same store name, sign contracts with the headquarters concerning purchase, sale, publicity, etc. and operate under the contract. They are free to engage in other activities which are not bounded in the contract. They could join or leave the chain on voluntary basis.

Chain stores through special permit and those through voluntary arrangement make up chain stores through license arrangement.

17 科技和教育

Science，Technology and Education

资料整理：徐晓颖　谢　涛

17-1 科技活动基本情况
BASIC STATISTICS ON PERSONEL ENGAGED IN SCIENTIFIC AND TECHNICAL ACTIVITIES

项　目	Item	2008	2009	2010	2011	2012	2013
科技活动人员 (人)	Personels Engaged in Scientific and Technical Activities (person)	210911	274963	282604	310240	339786	365502
R&D人员 (人)	R & D Personels	73042	131680	142683	166357	185703	205172
R&D经费内部支出 (万元)	Inner Expenditures of R & D Funds (10 000 yuan)	1490636	2134490	2637885	3230128	3845239	4462690
基础研究	Basic Research	54136	89327	102494	139256	203953	218994
应用研究	Practical Research	204439	335189	472497	471732	561485	679021
实验发展	Experiment Development	1141009	1709975	2062893	2619140	3079800	3564675

17-2 科技活动项目、成果与机构情况
BASIC STATISTICS ON SCIENTIFIC AND TECHNICAL PROJECTS, ACHIEVEMENT AND INSTITUTIONS

项　目	Item	2009	2010	2011	2012	2013
发表科技论文 (篇)	Scientific Research Papers Published (piece)	83533	84660	88826	89714	90209
出版科技专著数 (种)	Scientific and Techincal Books Published (kind)	2625	2679	2401	2672	2618
科技项目(课题)数 (个)	Number of Scientific Projects (unit)	42856		45457	48669	53088
科技项目经费支出 (万元)	Expenses for Scientific Projects (10 000 yuan)	2436985		2440630	3208902	3433884
科学研究与开发机构数 (个)	Number of Scientific Research Institutions and Development Organizations (unit)	1500	1557	1471	1744	1946
科研机构R&D人员数 (人)	R & D Staff (person)	50199	57274	72747	67997	74696
科研机构R&D内部支出(万元)	Inner Expenditures of R & D Funds (10 000 yuan)	1002444	1235013	1237563	1464692	1938710
科研机构年末仪器设备资产原价 (万元)	Original Price of Fixed Assets of Scientific Research Institutions and Organizations at Year-end (10 000 yuan)	1399607	1738151	2037951	2293613	2553205

17-3 政府部门所属科学研究与开发机构科技活动情况
BASIC STATISTICS ON STATE-OWNED RESAEARCH AND DEVELOPMENT INSTITUTIONS

项 目	Item	机构(个) Number of Institu-tions (unit)	科技活动人员(人) Persons Engaged (person)	大学本科及以上学历 Bachelor's Degrees and Above	#R&D人员 Research and Development Persons	收费收入(万元) Revenue (10 000 yuan)	#政府拨款 Government Appropriations
2010年总计	**Total of 2010**	**274**	**9217**	**5513**	**4937**	**223085**	**171558**
一、自然科学和技术领域	Natural Science and Technology	253	8299	4833	4937	207805	158368
县级政府部门属	Department of County	136	1120			4273	3112
市、州级政府部门属	Department of Cities and Prefecture	72	1737	846	384	21536	13075
省政府部门属	Department of Province	54	3718	2620	1156	98362	59496
国务院部门属	Department of State Council	12	2642	2047	3397	142559	104718
#中科院武汉分院属	#Chinese Academy of Science Wuhan Branch	7	1397	1195	2809	83068	70497
二、社会、人文科学领域	Sosiety and Humanity	10	406	333		7436	7181
2011年总计	**Total of 2011**	**274**	**9731**	**6307**	**4303**	**277585**	**229273**
一、自然科学和技术领域	Natural Science and Technology	253	8785	5568	4303	260274	214727
县级政府部门属	Department of County	137	1181	216		4505	2760
市、州级政府部门属	Department of Cities and Prefecture	71	1727	875	458	26759	13104
省政府部门属	Department of Province	54	3764	2750	1300	134026	87459
国务院部门属	Department of State Council	12	3059	2466	3494	169331	137807
#中科院武汉分院属	#Chinese Academy of Science Wuhan Branch	7	1631	1437	3078	94785	83664
二、社会、人文科学领域	Sosiety and Humanity	10	425	352		9057	8222
2012年总计	**Total of 2012**	**273**	**9929**	**6770**	**5423**	**317269**	**254809**
一、自然科学和技术领域	Natural Science and Technology	252	8938	5974	4933	296724	237331
县级政府部门属	Department of County	138	1177	232	103	4846	3447
市、州级政府部门属	Department of Cities and Prefecture	70	1704	940	477	30407	14551
省政府部门属	Department of Province	54	3841	2952	2027	150760	81231
国务院部门属	Department of State Council	11	3207	2646	3769	211957	174455
#中科院武汉分院属	#Chinese Academy of Science Wuhan Branch	7	1820	1590	3283	125113	113833
二、社会、人文科学领域	Sosiety and Humanity	10	437	374	267	11788	10671
2013年总计	**Total of 2013**	**268**	**9880**	**6997**	**6627**	**330002**	**262430**
一、自然科学和技术领域	Natural Science and Technology	249	8944	6240	6083	309814	244642
县级政府部门属	Department of County	135	1144	239	113	5135	3572
市、州级政府部门属	Department of Cities and Prefecture	68	1693	964	448	32952	17648
省政府部门属	Department of Province	53	3822	2958	2185	163291	98118
国务院部门属	Department of State Council	12	3221	2836	3881	210591	160783
#中科院武汉分院属	#Chinese Academy of Science Wuhan Branch	7	1876	1722	3487	112661	92969
二、社会、人文科学领域	Sosiety and Humanity	8	363	302	320	8003	7490

17-3 续表 continued

项　目	Item	经费支出（万元）Expenditures (10 000 yuan)	#科技经费支出 Expenditure on Science & Technology	#R&D经费内部支出 Inner Expenditure of R & D	研究课题数（个）Number of Projects	课题经费投入(万元) Investment on Subject Study (10 000 Yuan)	参加课题组(人年) Number of Persons Engaged in Subjects Study (person/year)
2010年总计	**Total of 2010**	**245449**	**199514**	**100506**	**3100**	**103270**	**5616**
一、自然科学和技术领域	Natural Science and Technology	23793	185405	100506	2985	102101	5289
县级政府部门属	Department of County	8530	4301		45	759	141
市、州级政府部门属	Department of Cities and Prefecture	19380	14833	2717	237	3142	591
省政府部门属	Department of Province	92437	61376	16315	807	16990	1873
国务院部门属	Department of State Council	133632	119003	81474	2011	82377	3012
#中科院武汉分院属	#Chinese Academy of Science Wuhan Branch	75685	66492	61821	1372	51418	2169
二、社会、人文科学领域	Sosiety and Humanity	13568	11916		88	844	144
2011年总计	**Total of 2011**	**321449**	**242197**	**108026**	**3179**	**104278**	**6024**
一、自然科学和技术领域	Natural Science and Technology	302879	227074	108026	3024	103074	5723
县级政府部门属	Department of County	12363	4532		39	568	109
市、州级政府部门属	Department of Cities and Prefecture	24342	18547	4167	240	3311	585
省政府部门属	Department of Province	128210	83563	21533	820	18640	2222
国务院部门属	Department of State Council	156534	135554	82325	2080	81757	3108
#中科院武汉分院属	#Chinese Academy of Science Wuhan Branch	85065	74178	68477	1425	51010	2277
二、社会、人文科学领域	Sosiety and Humanity	9722	7826		82	375	87
2012年总计	**Total of 2012**	**386332**	**283475**	**145490**	**3550**	**112506**	**6467**
一、自然科学和技术领域	Natural Science and Technology	364349	265746	138462	3385	110018	6067
县级政府部门属	Department of County	10957	5712	709	41	830	133
市、州级政府部门属	Department of Cities and Prefecture	27836	21223	5198	240	3871	604
省政府部门属	Department of Province	148703	82733	26417	3632	19049	2085
国务院部门属	Department of State Council	198834	173806	113165	2377	88755	3645
#中科院武汉分院属	#Chinese Academy of Science Wuhan Branch	117503	104469	99484	1544	57134	2485
二、社会、人文科学领域	Sosiety and Humanity	11522	9345	4841	84	403	100
2013年总计	**Total of 2013**	**414914**	**310410**	**158077**	**3738**	**126673**	**6523**
一、自然科学和技术领域	Natural Science and Technology	393283	292941	153014	3599	123807	6106
县级政府部门属	Department of County	15898	6576	850	49	1037	153
市、州级政府部门属	Department of Cities and Prefecture	31822	24529	5428	220	3907	542
省政府部门属	Department of Province	163291	78747	31809	936	22159	2151
国务院部门属	Department of State Council	217520	185486	119988	2533	99569	3678
#中科院武汉分院属	#Chinese Academy of Science Wuhan Branch	123903	111453	107873	1644	62085	2674
二、社会、人文科学领域	Sosiety and Humanity	8046	6545	2119	77	726	199

注：1.本表数据没有包括科技情报文献机构数据，但包括了县政府所属科技综合服务机构数。
　　2.科技部门的课题数包括生产性活动课题。

Notes:a)The data of intelligence literature is not included in this table.
　　b)The number of projects in science and technology department includes projects of production activities.

17-4 科学情报文献机构情况

STATISTICS ON SCIENTIFIC INTELLIGENCE LITERATURE ORGANIZATIONS

项 目	Item	1995	2000	2005	2009	2010	2011	2012	2013
机构 (个)	Institutions (unit)	12	14	12	11	11	11	11	11
职工总数 (人)	Total Number of Employees (person)	609	564	546	539	553	560	596	610
从事科技活动人员	Persons engaged in Scientific Activities	158	511	456	489	512	521	554	573
#大学本科及以上学历	#Bachelor's degrees and Above	329	337	306	336	347	387	422	455
经费收入总额 (万元)	Funds (10 000 yuan)	1529.2	2629.3	6676.8	7743.6	8706.0	8253.0	11650.0	15472.0
#政府拨款	#Government Appropriations	934.5	1679.2	5209.6	6637.3	6009.0	6323.0	8476.0	12131.0
经费支出总额 (万元)	Expendtitures (10 000 yuan)	1480.0	2339.9	6778.2	8292.3	7955.0	7296.0	10460.0	13584.0
#劳务费	#Service Charge	448.2	970.2	1178.8	2272.0	2668.0	3255.0	4038.0	4105.0

17-5 高等院校科技活动情况

BASIC STATISTICS ON SCIENTIFIC AND TECHNICAL ACTIVITIES OF INSTITUTIONS OF HIGHER EDUCATION

项 目	Item	2012			2013		
		合 计 Total	自然科学和技术领域 Natural Science and Technology	社会、人文科学领域 Sosiety and Humanity	合 计 Total	自然科学和技术领域 Natural Science and Technology	社会、人文科学领域 Sosiety and Humanity
科学研究与开发机构数 (个)	Institutions of Research and Development (unit)	482	319	163	517	339	178
科技活动人员数 (人)	Number of Personels in Scientific and Technical Activities (person)	70909	47792	23117	73886	48586	25300
研究与发展经费内部支出	Inner Expenditures of Research and Development	416891	359643	57248	448844	383763	65081
研究课题数 (个)	Number of Research Projects (unit)	36241	26210	15225	38828	22306	16522
项目(课题)经费投入 (万元)	Funds Invested in Research Projects (10 000 yuan)	369694	325694	44000	389182	338504	50677
项目(课题)参加人员折合全时当量	Number of Persons Engaged in Projects (10 000 persons)	12847	9444	3403	15420	11343	4077

17-6 大中型工业企业科技活动情况

STATISTICS ON SCIENTIFIC AND TECHNICAL ACTIVITIES OF LAREGE AND MEDIUM-SIZED INDUSTRIAL ENTERPRISES

单位：万元 (10 000 yuan)

项目	Item	2000	2005	2010	2011	2012	2013
大中型企业个数 （个）	Large and Medium Enterprises (unit)	848	803	1421	1881	2022	2274
有R&D活动的企业数 （个）	Number of Enterprises with Scientific Activities (unit)	484	303	559	491	478	584
从事科技活动人员数 （个）	Number of Persons Engaged in Scientific Activities (person)	69678	60811	120581	136661	155116	157520
#大学本科以上学历	#Bachelor's Degree and Above						49624
研究与发展人员数 （个）	Persons Engaged in Research and Development (person)	26614	32005	64329	81444	93825	99563
企业办科技开发机构数 （个）	Number of Scientific development Organizations Opened by Enterprises (unit)	306	253	457	352	454	478
R&D项目数 （个）	Number of R&D Projects (unit)	5482	4306	4602	5222	5668	6095
全部R&D项目经费支出（万元）	Expenses for Development Projects (10 000 yuan)	217040	462619	1193793	1331576	1978154	1892653
研究与发展经费支出	Expenditures for Research and Development	140828	307880	1429050	1835717	2287148	2521324
新产品开发费支出	Expenditures for Developing New Products	162302	354130	1760964	2113832	2488079	2606672
技术改造经费支出	Expenditures for Technical Innovation	323734	1253563	1326521	891890	921059	883841
技术引进经费支出	Expenditures for Technology Introduction	106801	83022	190418	81194	153336	121278
消化吸收经费支出	Expenditures for Technology Utilization	9092	16312	29408	29911	42406	39464
购买国内技术经费支出	Expenditures for Purchasing Domestic Technology	12919	7387	21561	26716	38037	72594

17-7 有科技活动的规模以上工业企业主要分组指标

指　标	Item	有R&D活动企业(个) Number of Enterprises with R & D Activities (unit)	
		2012	2013
总　计	**Total**	**1285**	**1714**
一、按登记注册类型分	**Grouped by Type of Registration**		
内资企业	Domestic-funded Enterprises	1151	1565
国有企业	State-owned Enterprises	64	27
集体企业	Collective-owned Enterprises	4	4
股份合作企业	Cooperative Enterprises	5	3
联营企业	Associated Enterprises	2	
有限责任公司	Limited Liability Companies	515	758
股份有限公司	Share Holding Co., Ltd	160	193
私营企业	Private Enterprises	367	575
其他企业	Others	34	5
港、澳、台商投资企业	Hongkong, Maco and Taiwan-invested Enterprises	54	59
合资经营企业(港或澳、台资)	Joint Ventures (Hongkong, Maco or Taiwan Invested Enterprises)	31	36
合作经营企业(港或澳、台资)	Cooperative Ventures(Hongkong, Maco or Taiwan Invested Enterprises)	1	1
港、澳、台商独资经营企业	Enterprises Solely Funded by hongkong, Maco and Taiwan Businessmen	19	18
港、澳、台商投资股份有限公司	Hongkong, Maco and Taiwan Funded Share Holding Co.Ltd.	3	4
其他港澳台投资企业	Other Hongkong, Maco and Taiwan Funded Share Holding Co., Ltd.		
外商投资企业	Foreign-invested Enterprises	80	90
中外合资经营企业	Sino-Foreign Joint Ventures	59	68
中外合作经营企业	Sino-Foreign Contractual Joint Ventures		
外资企业	Foreign Funded Enterprises	19	20
外商投资股份有限公司	Foreign Funded Share Holding Co., Ltd.	2	2
其他外商投资企业	Other Enterprises Invested by Foreign Businessmen		
二、按行业分	**Grouped by Sector**		
煤炭开采和洗选业	Coal Mining and Processing		
石油和天然气开采业	Petroleum and Natural Gas Extraction		1
黑色金属矿采选业	Ferrous Metals Mining and Processing		3
有色金属矿采选业	Non-ferrous Metals Mining and Processing	1	
非金属矿采选业	Non-metal Minerals Mining and Processing	7	7
开采辅助活动	Mining Auxiliary	1	1
其他采矿业	Other Mining	1	1
农副食品加工业	Primary Products and Food Processing Industry	77	120

MAJOR INDIENTORS OF INDUSTRIAL ABOVE DESIGNATED ENTERPRISES WITH SCIENTIFIC AND TECHNOLOGICAL ACTIVITIES

有科技机构的企业(个) Nuber of Persons Engaged in Scientific and Technical Activities (person)		R&D人员合计(人) R & D Personels (person)		R&D经费支出(万元) Funding for R & D Expenditure (10 000 yuan)		新产品开发经费支出(万元) Funding for New Product Development Expenditures (10 000 yuan)		新产品销售收入(万元) Revenue of New Product Sales (10 000 yuan)	
2012	2013	2012	2013	2012	2013	2012	2013	2012	2013
763	**903**	**112554**	**128952**	**2633099.2**	**3117986.6**	**2937086.1**	**3317174.7**	**36984124.9**	**46544784.4**
695	849	95916	111419	2270443.1	2620092.0	2385259.9	2706002.5	26097196.5	32592755.8
42	19	22826	15278	842185.3	675366.5	781544.9	576989.8	6759408.3	4014580.6
1	1	144	211	2160.8	2024.6	4574.0	1565.6	86254.0	17790.1
6		277	117	2380.9	1339.2	3707.7	961.0	115233.7	2325.0
1		303		7424.4		9900.0		251929.4	16680.0
285	355	37181	50587	657961.2	994218.0	752020.4	1028045.2	8739400.8	14123588.6
106	126	24410	28206	520727.9	579808.3	524982.9	648700.6	6083519.4	7043368.6
235	345	9663	16821	212798.4	364711.4	276749.6	445697.2	3695906.9	7361003.7
19	3	1112	199	24804.2	2624.0	31780.4	4043.1	365544.0	13419.2
33	24	5844	7032	154528.2	178303.4	164856.7	151333.8	2103332.1	1988952.5
23	19	4881	4606	116236.1	132328.5	121525.4	108631.3	1187558.3	1009759.3
	1	11	15	53.6	80.8	913.2	135.2	254.8	266.5
10	4	798	2298	35511.5	42832.0	37947.6	38235.2	892235.1	966938.1
		154	113	2727.0	3062.1	4470.5	4332.1	23283.9	11988.6
35	30	10794	10501	208127.9	319591.2	386969.5	459838.4	8783596.3	11963076.1
25	23	6922	7049	140285.6	257023.4	301262.6	397234.1	8121204.4	10919253.8
						603.0	512.5	3865.5	3012.5
8	5	1488	1524	28579.7	30470.1	28224.2	51644.1	482574.1	690338.9
2	2	2384	1928	39262.6	32097.7	56879.7	10447.7	175952.3	350470.9
	1		584		7650.2		993.3		1145.0
1			74		254.0		35.0	348.1	
	1	9		48.0		875.1	900.4		
2	5	69	78	5908.5	1345.1	416.0	1279.2	24089.4	10757.6
1		1003	242	7035.7	2091.4	4466.0	734.8	1045.0	
1	1	64	27	443.6	187.8	381.3	279.8		
63	79	1913	3167	65170.4	102229.3	70447.3	112952.0	1575375.4	2695208.7

17-7 续表 continued

指 标	Item	有R&D活动企业(个) Number of Enterprises with R & D Activities (unit)	
		2012	2013
食品制造业	Food Production	19	28
酒、饮料和精制茶制造业	Beverage Production	22	38
烟草制品业	Tabacco Processing	2	2
纺织业	Textile Industry	35	37
纺织服装、服饰业	Textile Wearing Apparel and Accessaries	5	8
皮革、毛皮、羽毛及其制品和制鞋业	Leather, Fur, Feather and Related Products	1	1
木材加工及木、竹、藤、棕、草制品业	Timber Processing and Wood, Bamboo, Rattan, Palm and Sraw Products	9	14
家具制造业	Furniture Manufacturing	1	2
造纸及纸制品业	Papermaking and Paper Products	6	15
印刷和记录媒介复制业	Printing and Record Processing	9	14
文教、工美、体育和娱乐用品制造业	Stationery, Education, Art, Sport and Entertainment Products	2	7
石油加工、炼焦及核燃料加工业	Petroleum Processing, Coking Products and Nuclear Fuel Processing	5	5
化学原料及化学制品制造业	Raw Chemical Material and Chemical Products	149	179
医药制造业	Medical and pharmaceutical Products	106	127
化学纤维制造业	Chemical Fibers	6	6
橡胶和塑料制品业	Rubber Products and Plastic Products	30	45
非金属矿物制品业	Nonmetal Material Products	72	82
黑色金属冶炼及压延加工业	Smelting and Processing of ferrous Metals	25	34
有色金属冶炼及压延加工业	Smelting and Processing of Nonferrous Metals	21	19
金属制品业	Metal Products	61	76
通用设备械制造业	Ordinaryly Machinery Manufacturing	107	137
专用设备制造业	Special Purpose Equipment Manufacturing	81	120
汽车制造业	Automobile Manufacturing	158	226
铁路、船舶、航空航天和其他运输设备制造业	Realway, Ship, Aircraft and Other Transport Equipment Manufacturing	24	32
电气机械及器材制造业	Electric Machinery and Equipment	112	168
通信设备、计算机及其他电子设备制造业	Telecommunication Equipment, Computer and Other Electronic Equipment Manufacturing	78	105
仪器仪表及文化办公用机械制造业	Instruments, Meters, Cultural and Official Machinery	33	35
其他制造业	Other Manufacturing	7	5
废弃资源和废旧材料回收加工业	Waste Resources and Junk Material Recycled		2
金属制品、机械和设备修理业	Repairing of Metal and Mechanical Equipment	2	4
电力、热力的生产和供应业	Electric Power, Steam and Hot Water Production and Supply	10	8
煤气生产和供应业	Gas Production and Supply		
水的生产和供应业	Tap Water Production and Supply		

有科技机构的企业(个) Number of Enterprises with R & D Units (unit)		R&D人员合计(人) R & D Personels (person)		R&D经费支出(万元) Funding for R & D Expenditure (10 000 yuan)		新产品开发经费支出(万元) Funding for New Product Development Expenditures (10 000 yuan)		新产品销售收入(万元) Revenue of New Product Sales (10 000 yuan)	
2012	2013	2012	2013	2012	2013	2012	2013	2012	2013
12	17	591	821	22211.9	29994.7	33757.4	54061.6	348209.0	428227.5
24	33	926	1094	11551.9	28497.3	38571.2	62875.0	619545.0	762724.2
1	1	527	549	22699.3	20140.7	19768.3	21085.8	101500.1	59524.1
24	23	1364	2675	27765.7	33639.8	53192.1	40176.4	489301.6	452173.5
5	9	570	856	12609.5	12408.2	19812.3	15908.1	151192.5	158316.0
1	1	6	13	19.5	238.0	661.9	274.9	1985.0	2004.8
4	8	332	428	5021.2	8980.1	6665.7	11319.8	89411.2	174048.8
2	1	66	92	802.8	1446.0	1292.1	1458.0	25256.5	36708.1
7	7	443	437	6612.7	12683.0	12459.6	15107.2	93388.1	121077.3
6	5	557	592	10584.1	12613.2	15177.6	9945.4	81851.8	93443.1
1	3	139	326	4143.4	3770.2	4915.7	5484.2	52043.7	52751.3
1	1	333	275	8941.1	8779.4	689.2	8527.2	90459.2	2308.0
86	107	9853	10522	258690.5	255467.8	170266.7	183102.3	3757160.0	4679114.8
73	72	9299	10713	125431.5	160514.0	122321.1	149695.4	1667391.4	1741568.3
5	1	130	390	3485.2	8969.7	3061.0	4203.2	66280.3	36279.4
26	30	2785	3249	28977.5	38615.6	39273.6	62836.9	874791.7	1187589.3
37	47	3672	5973	67210.2	95992.4	79056.5	79398.5	474443.8	1359356.5
16	17	8364	7954	544445.2	550585.9	550833.7	470171.7	4259333.9	4252496.7
14	16	1230	1422	74822.2	90545.3	27153.1	41846.3	1944367.7	2082481.6
40	39	5420	6410	98362.2	103934.7	114901.4	102090.4	854770.2	1149135.7
51	59	6648	7643	105857.7	137428.9	101787.7	148760.3	1489544.8	1687971.5
35	52	5881	6691	103213.6	124972.9	113388.3	157327.0	952695.9	1267283.8
94	113	13117	15928	285115.2	411601.3	499270.8	622541.2	10619542.1	13661279.6
16	18	9270	10246	135723.6	166098.3	144547.6	160028.9	1423378.7	1367077.8
48	64	8100	11057	157583.2	190447.6	192437.7	214400.9	2274195.9	3696835.0
47	48	14136	14905	381613.8	440823.8	432675.9	504570.4	2311884.9	2885790.5
11	14	1584	1575	21177.6	23402.0	26125.9	29286.8	142589.3	224998.3
3	3	1255	460	18202.0	11704.1	24944.7	15207.3	90151.8	93394.0
	2		24		617.1		540.7		48538.6
2	3	67	345	2789.2	7582.1	4663.5	5323.5	6308.2	12764.9
2	1	2831	1115	8829.5	11734.7	6828.1	2444.9	28512.7	58762.1
1	1							1780.0	1648.0

17-8 全省高新技术产业发展情况(2013)

STATISTICS ON NEW AND HIGH TECHNIC INDUSTRY DEVELOPMENT IN THE WHOLE PROVINCE(2013)

单位:亿元 (100 million yuan)

项目	Item	全省 the Whole Province	增幅(%) Increase(%)
高新技术产业增加值	Added Value of High-tech Industry	3604.96	16.1
高新服务业增加值	Added Value of High-tech Service	337.9	12.2
高新制造业产值	Output Value of High-tech Manufacturing	11853.15	14.4
高新制造业增加值	Added Value of High-tech Manufacturing	3267.06	16.5
1.电子信息	1.Electronic Information	504.16	22.8
2.先进制造	2.Advanced Manufacturing	1345.42	17.9
3.新材料	3.New Material	715.1	15.4
4.生物医药与医疗机械	4.Bio-medicine and Medical Instrument	260.79	19.1
高新制造业产品出口交货值	Export Value of High-tech Manufacturing	958.92	7.2
高新制造业产品销售收入	Revenue of High-tech Manufacturing	11483.77	14.8
高新制造业利税总额	Tax on High-tech Manufacturing	876.42	13.6

17-9 市州高新技术产业发展情况(2013)

STATISTICS ON THE DEVELOPMENT OF HIGH AND NEW TECHNOLOGY INDUSTRIE OF CITIES AND PREFECTURE (2013)

单位:亿元 (100 million yuan)

		增加值 Value Added	总产值(制造业) Total Output Value	产品出口交货值(制造业) Value of Export	产品销售收入(制造业) Sales Revenue of Products	利税总额(制造业) Total Value of Taxes
全省合计	**Total of the Province**	**3604.96**	**11853.15**	**958.92**	**11483.77**	**876.42**
武汉市	Wuhan Municipality	1700.19	5051.60	452.96	4958.95	394.97
黄石市	Huangshi Municipality	177.13	699.42	57.66	668.96	44.41
十堰市	Shiyan Municipality	126.49	423.10	5.78	412.63	35.38
宜昌市	Yichang Municipality	345.02	1223.09	207.51	1249.73	96.39
襄阳市	Xiangyang Municipality	494.16	1720.57	59.95	1565.77	107.07
鄂州市	Ezhou Municipality	90.20	317.46	13.44	295.43	25.41
荆门市	Jingmen Municipality	114.27	435.33	16.55	408.74	21.92
孝感市	Xiaogan Municipality	143.89	489.86	13.00	457.47	32.57
荆州市	Jingzhou Municipality	107.63	399.64	43.35	401.18	38.42
黄冈市	Huanggang Municipality	96.77	344.48	19.44	310.37	23.36
咸宁市	Xianning Municipality	46.61	161.77	9.08	137.60	11.24
随州市	Suizhou Municipality	64.09	225.08	21.85	221.48	16.09
恩施州	Enshi Prefecture	5.59	19.44	2.18	19.13	1.12
仙桃市	Xiantao Municipality	41.10	148.61	6.07	139.37	13.25
潜江市	Qianjiang Municipality	24.20	97.86	17.27	118.88	4.97
天门市	Tianmen Municipality	27.62	95.82	12.84	118.08	9.83
神农架林区	Shennongjia Forest Zone					

17-10 申报登记省、部级以上成果分类及经济效益
CLASSIFICATION AND ECONOMIC BENEFITS OF SCIENTIFIC ACHIEVEMENTS APPLIED AND REGISTERED ABOVE PROVINCIAL AND MINISTRIAL LEVEL

单位：项 (unit)

项 目	Item	2000	2005	2008	2009	2010	2011	2012	2013
成果总类	**Total Calsses of Achievement**	**571**	**717**	**800**	**740**	**750**	**1200**	**1567**	**1621**
一、按成果水平分类	Grouped by Level								
国际首创/领先	International Innovation/ Leading	19	28	73	56	52	94	101	81
国际先进	Internationl Advanced Technology	97	172	214	217	195	210	254	326
国内首创/领先	Domestic Innovation/ Leading	276	394	393	353	362	559	745	751
国内先进	Domestic Advanced Technology	84	72	64	60	69	133	176	177
其它	Others	18	3	6	7	39	154	14	31
二、按成果类型分类	Grouped by Type								
基础理论研究	Basic Theory Research	37	15	19	20	15	21	24	22
应用开发研究	Applicable Development	494	669	750	693	717	1150	1507	1570
其它	Others	40	33	31	27	18	29	36	29
三、按成果产业属性分类	Grouped by Sector Property								
工业类成果	Industrial Achievements	145	225	179	178	226	355	532	514
农业类成果	Agricultural Achievements	79	129	142	113	124	209	197	251
医学类成果	Medical Achievements	199	291	263	214	231	385	414	441
其他类成果	Others	148	74	216	235	169	251	424	415
四、按成果完成单位分类	Grouped by Units								
高等院校完成	Institutions of Higher Education	149	169	174	144	137	168	160	246
研究单位完成	Scientific Research Institutions	92	92	74	70	64	110	86	74
厂矿企业完成	Industrial and Mineral Enterprises	137	176	259	272	303	513	1136	911
其他单位完成	Others	193	280	293	267	246	409	185	390
五、经济效益 （亿元）	Economic Benefits (100 million yuan)								
本年度新增产值	Newly Added Output Value	78.33	199.50					1212.78	331.33
本年度节约资金	Capital Saved in This Year	6.33	28.28	36.54		36.85	169.65	401.37	56.38

17-11 科学技术协会组织与活动

ORGANIZATIONS AND ACTIVITIES OF SCIENTIFIC AND TECHNOLOGICAL ASSOCIATION

项目		Item		2012	2013
一、机构与人员		**Organizations and Personels**			
1.省级学会	(个)	Provincal Institute	(unit)	133	133
会员	(人)	Members	(person)	151194	155183
高级(资深)会员	(人)	Senoir Members	(person)	32349	22736
外国会员	(人)	Foreign Members	(person)	10	38
2.市、州学会数	(个)	City and Prefecture Institute	(unit)	542	546
3.省级科协	(个)	Provincal Scientific Assosiations	(unit)	1	1
市、州科协	(个)	City and Prefecture Scientific Assosiations	(unit)	13	13
县(区)科协	(个)	County (District) Scientific Assosiations	(unit)	104	104
二、学术活动		**Academic Activities**			
省级学会及县以上科协		**Provincial Institutes and Scientific Assosiations above County level**			
国内学术会议	(次)	Domestic Academic Conference	(time)	985	642
参加人数	(人次)	Number of Person Participated	(person-time)	93912	60327
论文数	(篇)	Number of Scholary Paper	(piece)	18171	13739
境内国际学术会议	(次)	Domestic International Academic Conference	(time)	65	36
参加人数	(人次)	Number of Person Participated	(person-time)	8751	3006
论文数	(篇)	Number of Scholary Paper	(piece)	3840	1499
三、科普活动		**Science and Technology Popularization Activities**			
省级学会及县以上科协		**Provincial Institutes and Scientific Assosiations above County level**			
举办科普宣讲活动	(次)	Events of Science Popularization Lectures	(time)	8099	7608
宣讲活动受众人数	(人次)	People Participated	(person-time)	6235127	7040613
举办实用技术培训	(次)	Technical Training	(time)	9711	7536
实用技术培训人数	(人次)	People Participated	(person-time)	1870323	1701324
播放科技广播、影视节目	(分钟)	Scientific Radio and Video Programs	(mimute)	187850	644039
参加活动科技人员	(人次)	People Participated	(person-time)	296664	83466
四、青少年科技教育		**Education in Science and Technology for the Adolescents**			
省级学会及县以上科协		**Provincial Institutes and Scientific Assosiations above County level**			
举办青少年科技竞赛	(项)	Adolescent Technology Competition	(unit)	633	487
参加人数	(人次)	Number of Person Participated	(person-time)	2906456	2157230
获奖人数	(人次)	Number of Person Rewarded	(person-time)	53695	81605
举办青少年科学营	(次)	Adolescent Technology Campus		166	129
参加人数	(人次)	Number of Person Participated	(person-time)	12260	10435
举办青少年科技教育培训	(次)	Adolescent Technology Education Training		809	807
培训人数	(人次)	Number of Person Participated	(person-time)	526150	524014
五、科普基础设施建设		**Infrastructure Construction of Science Popularization**			
县以上科协		**Scientific Assosiations above County Level**			
科技场馆	(个)	Science and Technology Museum	(unit)	60	61
建筑面积	(平方米)	Construction Area	(square metre)	163738	178317
展厅面积	(平方米)	Exhibition Area	(square metre)	59606	70039
全年参观人数	(人次)	Year-round Visitor	(person-time)	1456639	1912890
科普活动站	(个)	Science Popularization Station	(unit)	8743	9879
科普画廊建筑面积	(平方米)	Science Popularization Gallery Construction Area	(square metre)	65255	107212
省级科普教育基地	(个)	Provincial Education Base of Science Popularization	(unit)	45	80
农村科普示范基地	(个)	Rural Demonstration Base of Science Popularization	(unit)	1083	1204
六、为科技工作者服务		**Serve for Scientists**			
省级学会及县以上科协		**Provincial Institutes and Scientific Assosiations above County level**			
反映科技工作者建议	(条)	Reported Suggestions of Scientists		1910	2171
其中：获上级领导批示的建议	(条)	Answered by Leaders		417	415
答复人大政协代表(委员)提案	(件)	Replied Proposal of NPC and CPPCC Representatives(Con	(piece)	130	113
走访看望(慰问)科技工作者	(人次)	Visit Scientific Workers	(person-time)	2200	2556
科学道德与学风建设宣讲活动	(场次)	Preach Ethics of Science		1	1
宣讲活动受众人数	(人次)	Number of Audience	(person-time)	1100	1500
参加宣讲活动专家数	(人次)	Number of Specialists	(person-time)	2	1
技术创新方法培训班	(场次)	Technology Innovation Training Class			13
继续教育培训班	(场次)	Continuing Education Class		94	70
培训结业人数	(人次)	Number of People Completed Courses	(person-time)	5609	5858
宣传科技工作者人数	(人)	Propagating Scientific and Technology Workers	(person)	566	466
表彰奖励科技工作者	(人次)	Rewarded Scientific and Technology Workers	(person-time)	5103	3870

17-12 专利受理量、批准量及分布状况
NUMBER OF PATENT APPLICATIONS EXAMINATION, APPROVAL AND DISTRITUTION

单位：项 (unit)

项 目	Item	受理量 Number of Patent Applications Examined				批准量 Number of Patent Applications Approved			
		2000	2005	2010	2013	2000	2005	2010	2013
合 计	**Total**	**3486**	**11534**	**31311**	**50816**	**2198**	**3860**	**17362**	**28760**
发 明	Creations and Inventions	771	2038	7410	18189	156	733	2025	4052
实用新型	Utility Models	2102	4835	12792	26163	1573	2238	10431	19655
外观设计	Designs	613	4661	11109	6464	469	889	4906	5053
在合计中	**Of This Total**								
个 人	Individual	2411	7400	10844	16437	1502	2189	4990	7996
大专院校	Universities and Colleges	205	1365	3265	6320	92	574	1972	3008
科研单位	Insitutions of Scientific Research	128	182	1112	1611	82	101	532	742
工矿企业	Industrial and Mineral Enterprises	721	2305	15856	23813	509	901	9744	16739
机关团体	Government Agencies and Organizations	21	283	234	2635	13	98	124	275

17-13 按市州分三种专利申请与授权状况(2013)
THREE KINDS OF PATENT APPICATION AND AUTHORIZATION BY MUNICIPALITIES AND PREFECTURES(2013)

市、州	Municipalities and Prefecture	申请 当年累计 Patent Application Total of 2013	发明 Invention	实用新型 New type of practicial Utility	外观设计 Design	授权 当年累计 Authorization Total of 2013	发明 Invention	实用新型 New type of practicial Utility	外观设计 Design
全省合计	**Total of the Province**	**50816**	**18189**	**26163**	**6464**	**28760**	**4052**	**19655**	**5053**
武 汉	Wuhan	25619	9726	14006	1887	15856	3168	10984	1704
黄 石	Huangshi	2306	975	763	568	1142	61	707	374
十 堰	Shiyan	1613	450	1011	152	1079	49	870	160
荆 州	Jingzhou	1499	319	848	332	1004	81	688	235
宜 昌	Yichang	4971	1683	2246	1042	2907	203	1820	884
襄 阳	Xiangfan	5347	2033	2971	343	2064	100	1560	404
鄂 州	Ezhou	632	358	213	61	221	21	179	21
荆 门	Jingmen	1380	447	692	241	828	37	595	196
孝 感	Xiaogan	1654	460	804	390	990	124	620	246
黄 冈	Huanggang	1668	493	877	298	831	64	518	249
咸 宁	Xianning	845	261	319	265	362	29	218	115
随 州	Suizhou	832	220	488	124	472	20	317	135
恩施州	Enshi	497	174	201	122	252	37	133	82
仙 桃	Xiantao	622	227	294	101	281	37	185	59
潜 江	Qianjiang	534	174	233	127	221	9	120	92
天 门	Tianmen	765	174	182	409	216	7	127	82
神农架林区	Shennongjia Forest District	32	15	15	2	34	5	14	15

17-14 各类技术合同签定及执行情况

SIGNING AND IMPEMENTATION OF VARIOUS TECHNICAL CONTRACTS

项　目	Item	合同数(项) Number of Contracts (unit)	合同金额(万元) Value of Contracts (10 000 yuan)
2007	**2007**	**8298**	**525216**
技术开发合同	Technology Development Contracts	3317	284859
技术转让合同	Technology Transfer Contracts	234	44577
技术咨询合同	Technology Consultation Contracts	1305	37977
技术服务合同	Technology Service Contracts	3442	157803
2008	**2008**	**7147**	**628971**
技术开发合同	Technology Development Contracts	3703	379092
技术转让合同	Technology Transfer Contracts	235	45101
技术咨询合同	Technology Consultation Contracts	1237	42571
技术服务合同	Technology Service Contracts	1972	162207
2009	**2009**	**5694**	**779700**
技术开发合同	Technology Development Contracts	2391	337341
技术转让合同	Technology Transfer Contracts	216	239272
技术咨询合同	Technology Consultation Contracts	1144	42747
技术服务合同	Technology Service Contracts	1943	160339
2010	**2010**	**6641**	**909167**
技术开发合同	Technology Development Contracts	2390	502290
技术转让合同	Technology Transfer Contracts	199	126505
技术咨询合同	Technology Consultation Contracts	1321	71932
技术服务合同	Technology Service Contracts	2731	208439
2011	**2011**	**7799**	**1214103**
技术开发合同	Technology Development Contracts	4101	661014
技术转让合同	Technology Transfer Contracts	327	99063
技术咨询合同	Technology Consultation Contracts	1358	88232
技术服务合同	Technology Service Contracts	2013	365793
2012	**2012**	**12908**	**2345655**
技术开发合同	Technology Development Contracts	7698	1000226
技术转让合同	Technology Transfer Contracts	447	482601
技术咨询合同	Technology Consultation Contracts	1391	87457
技术服务合同	Technology Service Contracts	3372	775371
2013	**2013**	**14909**	**4187410**
技术开发合同	Technology Development Contracts	9473	1614052
技术转让合同	Technology Transfer Contracts	574	342631
技术咨询合同	Technology Consultation Contracts	1082	238981
技术服务合同	Technology Service Contracts	3780	1991746

17-15 全省技术买卖情况(2013)

PURCHASE AND SELLING OF TECHNOLOGY IN THE WHOLE PROVINCE (2013)

卖方类别 Type of the Seller / 买方类别 Type of the Buyer		合 计 Total		机关法人 Organ Corporations		事业法人 Institutions Corporations		社团法人 Associations Corporations	
		合同数(项) Number of Contracts	成交额(万元) Contracted Value (10 000 yuan)	合同数(项) Number of Contracts	成交额(万元) Contracted Value (10 000 yuan)	合同数(项) Number of Contracts	成交额(万元) Contracted Value (10 000 yuan)	合同数(项) Number of Contracts	成交额(万元) Contracted Value (10 000 yuan)
总计	**Total**	**14909**	**4187410**	**55**	**54366**	**8205**	**1010922**	**8**	**521**
机关法人	Departments	1801	924402	49	51077	869	530474		
事业法人	Institutions	2585	279522			2074	162780	1	78
社团法人	Social Groups	30	1600			21	1204		
企业法人	Corporations	10355	2925744	6	3289	5211	312166	7	443
自然人	Natural Person	53	8036			13	1044		
其他组织	Other Organizations	85	48107			17	3255		

17-15 续表 continued

卖方类别 Type of the Seller / 买方类别 Type of the Buyer		企业法人 Corporations		自然人 Natural Person		其他组织 Other Organizations	
		合同数(项) Number of Contracts	成交额(万元) Contracted Value (10 000 yuan)	合同数(项) Number of Contracts	成交额(万元) Contracted Value (10 000 yuan)	合同数(项) Number of Contracts	成交额(万元) Contracted Value (10 000 yuan)
总计	**Total**	**6600**	**3107506**	**7**	**2415**	**34**	**11680**
机关法人	Departments	880	336367			3	6484
事业法人	Institutions	505	116207			5	458
社团法人	Social Groups	9	396				
企业法人	Corporations	5102	2603127	6	2259	23	4460
自然人	Natural Person	39	6835	1	156		
其他组织	Other Organizations	65	44575			3	278

17-16 地震观测及地方地震工作情况

STATISTICS ON EARTHQUAKE OBSERVATION AND LOCAL EFFORTS ON EARTHQUAKE WORKS

项　　目	Item	2000	2005	2010	2013
职工总数 (人)	Total Number of Staff and Workers (person)	589	528	464	474
专业技术人员 (人)	Professtional Technical Personel (person)	386	295	314	335
高级技术人员 (人)	Senior Technical Personel (person)	107	91	83	77
市州级地震局 (个)	Number of Earthquake Agency (unit)	12	17	17	17
重点县地震办公室 (个)	Number of Earthquake Offices in Key Counties (unit)	52	35	35	32
地方地震工作人员 (人)	Local Seismologist (person)	255	267	271	374
地震观测台(网)人员 (人)	Number of Staff in Earthquake Observation Station (person)	74	70	71	67
#观测技术人员 (人)	#Technical Personel (person)	64	60	50	46
地震台站 (个)	Earthquake Observation Station (unit)	11	9	10	48
基准台	Norm Station	4	1	1	5
基本台	Basic Station		4	4	
省级台	Provincial Station		4	5	43
GPS测量 (千米/点)	GPS Measurement (km/point)		75000/85	110000/206	120000/230
流动重力测量 (千米/点)	Flow Gravity Measurement (km/point)		40000/300	459500/782	75000/465

17-17 气象部门基本情况

BASIC CONDITIONS OF METEOROLOGICAL DEPARTMENT

项目	tem	2000	2005	2009	2010	2011	2012	2013
一、气象观测人员总数（人）	Total Number of Staff in Meteorological Depaartment (person)	333	375	455	378	398	388	415
地面观测	Groud Observation	285	320	350	330	350	340	367
高空观测	Upper Air Observation	24	18	20	18	18	16	14
雷达观测	Radar Observation	24	20	25	30	30	32	34
特种观测	Special Observation			60				
二、气象台站总数（个）	Total Number of Meteorological Obervatory (unit)	85	87	87	87	87	87	89
气象台	Meteorological Obervatory	13	14	14	14	14	14	14
气象站	Weather Station	70	71	71	71	71	71	73
独立农试站	Independent Agricultural Station	2	2	2	2	2	2	2
三、卫星云图接收站点数（个）	Number of Stations Receiving Satellite Image (unit)	11	25	15	15	15	10	17
极轨卫星	Polar Orbiting Meteorological Satellite	2	23	5	5	5	3	4
同步卫星	Geostationary Satellite	9	7	10	10	10	7	13
接收卫星云图图片数	Number of Satellite Image Pictures Received							
使用云图单位数	Number of Pictures Used	144						
四、拥有计算机数（台）	Number of Computers (unit)	1019	1695	2408	2752	2982	3153	3160
大型机					1	1	1	3
中小型机	Small and Medium-size	8	1	1	1	1	159	159
微型机	Microcomputer	950	1694	2407	2751	2981	2993	2998
袖珍机	Pocket-computer	61						
五、拥有雷达数（部）	Number of Radar Owned (unit)	11	12	14	15	14	14	17
701测风	701 Wind Sensing	4	4					
3厘米	3 cm	2	2	1	1	1	1	1
5厘米	5 cm	2	1	1	1	1		1
10厘米	10 cm	3	5	9	10	9	10	7
1波段	1 Wave Band			3	3	3	3	8

17-18 质量技术监督检查情况

STATISTICS ON SUPERVISION AND EXAMINATION OF QUALITY TECHNOLOGY

年 份 Year	机构(个) Institutions (unit)	职工人数(人) Number of Staff and Workers (person)	#专业技术人员 #Professional Technic Personel	经费收入(万元) Revenue (10 000 yuan)	经费支出(万元) Expenditures (10 000 yuan)	固定资产(万元) Fixed Assets (10 000 yuan)	#仪器设备 #Equipment and Devices	计量器具检定台(万套件) Number of Measuring Equipment Tested (10 000 units)	#衡 具 #Measuring Instrument	#强制检定 #Compulsory Test
1980	88	1211	327	308	306	1667	512	60		
1985	107	1668	356	640	515	3234	1402	146	36	
1990	105	3299	1409	3063	2610	7994	3760	136	68	118
1995	167	6275	2121	10095	10374	21213	6327	150	64	140
1996	102	2265	1252	3237	3177	6985	3261	136	61	108
1997	101	2337	1337	3491	3418	6751	3680	150	62	110
1998	106	2479	1439	4 079	4034	6314	3810	126	50	100
1999	105	2531	1446	4 515	4532	6732	3713	120	43	103
2000	104	2790	1478	4 568	4853	8829	5286	150	43	105
2001	91	1632	911	3005	2899	6537	3881	132	33	65
2002	360	9583	4059	36371	34024	39461	9806	165	40	138
2003	403	9137	3960	44450	41317	47323	12114	154	45	118
2004	376	9034	4703	50520	48383	53579	14549	128	23	114
2005	398	9046	3953	59089	56152	62607	19986	120	22	98
2006	398	9050	4094	67864	64078	72440	23840	119	22	110
2007	393	9065	4072	79698	75988	81822	26984	119	19	102
2008	392	9055	3732	93140	89653	94547	27832	109	16	96
2009	395	9077	3718	111477	110965	111627	35047	128	18	107
2010	388	9133	3815	116319	109915	129113	38963	125	17	119
2011	387	8828	3693	134901	135563	150114	44143	142	15	135
2012	385	8997	3645	153332	146310	159772	45440	175	16	155
2013	383	8981	3655	197287	180390	183786	57740	199	15	188

17-19 标准事业基本情况

BASIC STATISTICS ON STANDARD ENTERPRISES

项目	Item	1995	2000	2005	2010	2011	2012	2013
质量监督机构 (个)	Quality Supervision Institution (unit)	85	86	99	99	99	99	99
固定人员 (人)	Fixed Personel (person)	1 019	1 007					
制定标准 (项)	Standard Established (unit)	15	29	36	81	96	101	69
修定标准 (项)	Standard Revised (unit)				4	18	8	4
废止标准 (项)	Standard Abolished (unit)							
当年采用国际标准(项)	International Standard Adopted (unit)		4	129	193	130	101	106
受检产品质量监督(种)	Number of Products under Quality Supervision (kind)	92	99					
质量监督检测 (批次)	Quality Supervision Test (batch)	29105	20093	26548	40288	34734	35117	40317
标准文件馆藏 (万件)	Standard Document Collection (10 000 units)	21	25	22	30	46	57	121

17-20 档案事业基本情况

BASIC STATISTICS ON ARCHIVES

项目	Item	2000	2005	2010	2011	2012	2013
1.机构数 (个)	Number of Institutions (unit)	553	988	12574	12580	12580	12580
#档案馆	#Archives	148	150	170	175	175	175
2.专职人员数 (人)	Number of Full-time Personel (person)	3597	4166	10500	10509	11012	10895
#副研究馆员以上	#Associate Research Fellow of Archives and Above	136	257	262	262	297	308
馆员	Member of Archives	911	964	1173	1225	1028	1053
助理馆员	Assistant Member of Archives	707	573	1092	1215	879	891
管理员	Administors	268	263	1226	1140	1444	1449
3.馆藏档案卷宗 (个)	Volumes Stored In Archives (unit)	13005	14206	14444	14580	14628	15403
案卷 (万个)	Files (10 000 units)	837.00	1178.00	1367.06	1432.33	1527.00	1659.54
案卷总长度 (万米)	Total Length of Files (10 000 m)	12.67	33.54	54.00	57.00	45.00	56.31
零散文件长度 (米)	Total Length of Scattered Files (m)	1 234	200	3185	5076	1162	1221
馆藏资料册数 (万册)	Number of Material Stored (10 000 Volumes)	201.00	255.00	268.00	240.26	258.41	291.08
举办展览 (个)	Display Organized (unit)			172	149	566	604
接待参观 (万人次)	Visitors (10 000 person-times)			35.03	24.18	33.50	41.15
4.本年度利用档案人次(万人次)	Use of Material This Year (10 000 times)	11.47	17.70	37.55	36.33	28.78	30.08
利用档案卷次 (万卷次)	Number of Archives Used (10 000 volume-times)	39.95	74.05	100.40	95.30	68.63	72.00
利用资料册数 (万册数)	Number of Data Used (10 000 volume-times)	5.94	5.58	5.40	5.56	2.66	6.07
5.本年编研档案资料	Materials Edited This Year						
公开出版种数 (种)	Number of Materials Open Published (kind)	507	140	84	77	85	76
公开出版字数 (万字)	Number of Words Open Published (10 000 wordds)	1259.00	993.00	1970.00	2187.00	2142.70	1929.56
内部参考种数 (种)	Number of Materials for Inner Reference (kind)	218	197	164	214	172	197
内部参考字数 (万字)	Number of Words for Inner Reference (10 000 words)	909	1762	1704	1598	1860	2063
库房面积 (万平方米)	Floor Space of Storehouse (10 000 sq.m)	22.14	11.90	11.63	11.52	12.14	12.46

17-21 各级各类学校数
NUMBER OF SCHOOLS OF VARIOUS LEVELS

单位：所 (unit)

学校分类	Type of Shool	2000	2005	2007	2008	2009	2010	2011	2012	2013
普通高等学校	Regular Institutions of Higher Education	54	85	86	87	120	120	122	122	123
#地方院校	#Local Schools	45	77	78	79	112	112	114	114	115
中等职业学校	Secondary Vocation Schools	203	437	478	462	402	413	341	332	310
#中师	#Secondary Teacher School	23			10	7	7	3	3	3
普通中学	Regular Middle School	3 261	3231	3108	3011	2897	2787	2707	2622	2576
#初中	#Junior High Schools	2 678	2578	2440	2356	2275	2184	2122	2047	2013
城市	Urban	757	465	435	431	383	362	507	507	509
县镇	Township	189	487	539	564	622	671	929	953	945
农村	Rural	1 732	1635	1466	1361	1270	1151	686	587	559
高中	Senior High School	583	653	668	655	622	603	585	575	563
城市	Urban	371	306	292	295	267	243	313	318	318
县镇	Township	111	235	289	271	268	278	222	220	212
农村	Rural	101	112	87	89	87	82	50	37	33
小学	Primary School	23 372	12631	10210	9302	8544	7749	7415	6614	5746
城市	Urban	3 319	949	831	845	722	685	1015	1007	997
县镇	Township	1 155	627	693	715	847	937	1636	1629	1536
农村	Rural	18 898	11055	8686	7742	6975	6127	4764	3978	3213
特殊教育学校	Special Education School	74	77	76	76	76	76	76	77	80
幼儿园	Kindergarten	3 748	2336	2572	2880	2995	4395	4670	5321	6011
技工学校	School of Technology	204	208	208	208		206			

17-22 各级各类学校在校学生数

ENROLLMENT IN SCHOOLS OF VARIOUS LEVELS

单位：人 (person)

学校分类	Type of Shool	2000	2005	2008	2009	2010	2011	2012	2013
普通高等学校	Regular Institutions of Higher Education	346568	1012665	1184915	1249061	1296920	1340298	1386086	1421434
#地方院校	#Local Schools	205615	824960	991819	1053341	1098570	1129010	1183416	1217155
中等职业学校	Secondary Vocation Schools	278602	606014	1037294	1041759	903834	720915	500540	411194
普通中学	Regular Middle School	3509318	4466879	3934445	3650102	3418299	3208399	2652208	2471869
#初中	#Junior High Schools	2810909	3172392	2612455	2363351	2180937	2040702	1577701	1483710
城市	Urban	772160	494739	515470	452518	413930	561141	543902	529708
县镇	Township	232916	750903	821270	811217	848967	994830	743679	689455
农村	Rural	1805833	1926750	1275715	1099616	918040	484731	290120	264547
高中	Senior High School	698409	1294487	1321990	1286751	1237362	1167697	1074507	988159
城市	Urban	424406	541404	536578	512139	427334	596728	580248	555182
县镇	Township	171592	553411	625120	608803	633319	465734	435656	386923
农村	Rural	102411	199672	160292	165809	176709	105235	58603	46054
小学	Primary School	6677422	4291881	3607744	3592629	3655512	3773446	3267498	3282579
城市	Urban	1585037	787812	748768	717749	713491	1005861	1027061	1050497
县镇	Township	457132	593090	705023	812990	974019	1273914	1160375	1187536
农村	Rural	4635253	2910979	2153953	2061890	1968002	1493671	1080062	1044546
特殊教育学校	Special Education School	9739	9444	13374	13959	15349	12893	10557	10576
幼儿园	Kindergarten	726712	594481	742531	831399	1118360	1324714	1355395	1473371
技工学校	School of Technology	55812	136000	245246		229000			

17–23 各级各类学校招生数
NEW ENROLLMENT IN SCHOOLS OF VARIOUS LEVELS

单位：人 (person)

学校分类	Type of Shool	2000	2005	2008	2009	2010	2011	2012	2013
普通高等学校	Regular Institutions of Higher Education	139666	315560	375512	395929	387612	413600	406957	403860
#地方院校	#Local Schools	94524	269042	326845	346525	337621	358933	356113	352544
中等职业学校	Secondary Vocation Schools	62418	273789	390641	367161	283610	212318	143530	130995
普通中学	Regular Middle School	1352592	1469777	1214750	1120047	1053418	981191	838372	804312
#初中	#Junior High Schools	1075527	1011186	775634	696261	657947	619213	510866	487841
城市	Urban	281648	162324	159646	139712	132571	179751	181591	177436
县镇	Township	89106	241579	244207	240542	251823	295975	237380	225227
农村	Rural	704773	607283	371781	316007	273553	143487	91895	85178
高中	Senior High School	277065	458591	439116	423786	395471	361978	327506	316471
城市	Urban	168541	187976	175774	169309	138260	184335	178360	179553
县镇	Township	68314	197496	209698	199571	199177	144925	131519	123402
农村	Rural	40210	73119	53644	54906	58034	32718	17627	13516
小学	Primary School	904559	567411	626247	642190	680166	692317	634766	607979
城市	Urban	239984	113284	123171	117466	126070	179176	186695	188925
县镇	Township	75192	81622	117355	144972	176073	228466	220893	211576
农村	Rural	589383	372505	385721	379752	378023	284675	227178	207478
特殊教育学校	Special Education School	1655	1038	2183	2167	2047	1622	1483	1788
幼儿园	Kindergarten	523542	396082	497716	537579	761044	807017	785848	825253
技工学校	School of Technology	23052	73000	110338		57000			

17-24 各级各类学校毕业生数

NUMBER OF GRADUATES FROM SCHOOLS OF VARIOUS LEVELS

单位：人 (person)

学校分类	Type of Shool	2000	2005	2008	2009	2010	2011	2012	2013
普通高等学校	Regular Institutions of Higher Education	51932	187920	351854	328202	331303	362991	353014	361572
#地方院校	#Local Schools	26461	144529	306770	282718	285599	312189	305545	313748
中等职业学校	Secondary Vocation Schools	125593	129436	264826	307813	335776	307701	272883	200196
#中师	#Secondary Teacher School	14908							
普通中学	Regular Middle School	883828	1438503	1410673	1373676	1288944	1200425	988034	924920
#初中	#Junior High Schools	718015	1055083	960997	923759	854395	771362	575799	533709
城市	Urban	198402	169257	170316	161959	149922	203090	183511	176905
县镇	Township	61909	239870	297268	319137	326945	381043	277376	257033
农村	Rural	457704	645956	493413	442663	377528	187229	114912	99771
高中	Senior High School	165813	383420	449676	449917	434549	429063	412235	391211
城市	Urban	98353	161281	184590	181546	147307	219472	216107	216067
县镇	Township	41382	164517	212750	208682	228146	169153	173191	157143
农村	Rural	26078	57622	52336	59689	59096	40438	22937	18001
小学	Primary School	1160203	1020710	715128	646753	611620	583417	513818	489395
城市	Urban	281706	149766	136872	126806	120208	162925	162653	162408
县镇	Township	84207	134340	128750	143354	160359	201483	177913	180709
农村	Rural	794290	736604	449506	376593	331053	219009	173252	146278
特殊教育学校	Special Education School	1310	1498	1530	1675	2261	1535	1292	1227
幼儿园	Kindergarten								572085

17-25 各级各类学校教职工数

NUMBER OF FACULTIES AT SCHOOLS OF VARIOUS LEVELS

单位：人 (person)

学校分类	Type of Shool	2000	2005	2008	2009	2010	2011	2012	2013
普通高等学校	Regular Institutions of Higher Education	72265	107459	120816	123693	123491	127363	127921	128185
#地方院校	#Local Schools	35120	73079	86217	89339	89205	92721	94170	94777
中等职业学校	Secondary Vocation Schools	28816	36658	44847	42244	40985	36980	33442	30845
#中师	#Secondary Teacher School	3384							
普通中学	Regular Middle School	237500	273146	271629	267265	263055	270838	259884	254716
教育部门和集体办	Run by Ministry of Education and the Collective	216338	253955	251185	247068	243222	249476	238671	232762
其他部门办	Run by Other Departments	15483	6585	1528	1488	646	1024	971	734
社会力量办	Run by Non-Governmental Sectors	2316	12606	18916	18709	19187			
私立	Private Owned	3363						20242	21189
城市	Urban	97054	75581	78734	74103	68468	101691	104952	105801
县镇	Township	28889	78027	95035	99653	107371	119012	115008	110983
农村	Rural	111557	119538	97860	93509	87216	50135	39924	37932
小学	Primary Schools	299994	232888	216119	213347	211247	197395	193609	198262
城市	Urban	84877	47727	47349	43738	42100	51939	54139	55015
县镇	Township	23515	33532	38615	44738	51059	64920	67003	69933
农村	Rural	191602	151629	130155	124871	118088	80536	72467	73314
特殊教育学校	Special Education School	1676	1679	1694	1708	1744	1811	1826	1921
幼儿园	Kindergarten	40484	33094	41920	46867	66202	79659	92024	110376
技工学校	School of Technology	13070	9934	12884					

17-26 各级各类学校专任教师数
NUMBER OF FULL-TIME TEACHERS AT SCHOOLS OF VARIOUS LEVELS

单位：人 (person)

学校分类	Type of Shool	2000	2005	2008	2009	2010	2011	2012	2013
普通高等学校	Regular Institutions of Higher Education	30363	59009	70617	73159	74685	78952	80665	81784
#地方院校	#Local Schools	15995	43240	53797	56013	57264	60910	62913	64032
中等职业学校	Secondary Vocation Schools	15549	24036	30689	29148	28476	26208	23796	22555
普通中学	Regular Middle School	198486	233517	233878	231452	227962	225628	212305	205306
#初中	#Junior High Schools	154543	169084	163666	160662	156836	154295	141409	135580
城市	Urban	49752	31803	34487	31574	30409	43589	44766	44122
县镇	Township	13138	39851	50178	54203	59014	75088	69143	65457
农村	Rural	91653	97430	79001	74885	67413	35618	27500	26001
高中	Senior High School	43943	64433	70212	70790	71126	71333	70896	69726
城市	Urban	27663	28330	30242	29754	26883	38552	39579	40383
县镇	Township	10336	27235	32372	32913	35091	26573	27221	26097
农村	Rural	5944	8868	7598	8123	9152	6208	4096	3246
小学	Primary School	274979	215693	201356	198188	196078	194851	191699	196556
城市	Urban	75377	42127	42413	39274	37873	52716	55297	56547
县镇	Township	21459	30351	35653	41273	47480	63542	65828	68204
农村	Rural	178143	143215	123290	117641	110725	78593	70574	71805
特殊教育学校	Special Education School	1231	1317	1427	1444	1477	1527	1560	1647
幼儿园	Kindergarten	29889	20018	24795	27440	38494	43141	49153	57736
技工学校	School of Technology	6182	7064	10561					

17-27 各级各类学校专任教师学历分类

STATISTICS ON ACADEMIC DEGREE OF FULL-TIME TEACHERS AT SCHOOLS OF VARIOUS LEVELS

单位：人 (person)

学历分类	Type of School	2009	2010	2011	2012	2013
一、中等职业学校	Secondary Vocational School	29148	28476	26208	23796	22555
高等学校本科毕业及以上	Graduated from Universities and Above	22922	22972	21322	19604	19172
高等学校专科毕业	Graduated from Colleges	5803	5170	4550	3861	3148
高中阶段及以下	Degree Below Senior High School	423	334	336	331	235
二、普通中学	Regular Secondary Schools	231452	227962	225628	212305	205306
高等学校本科毕业及以上	Graduated from Universities and Above	146936	150502	154668	156745	156715
高等学校专科毕业	Graduated from Colleges	78549	72490	66739	52938	47284
中专、高中毕业的	Graduated from Secondary and High Schools	5819	4877	4132	2521	1257
三、小学	Primary School	198188	196078	194851	191699	196556
中师、高中毕业及以上的	Graduated from Teacher Schools and Degrees Above	196647	194809	194079	191282	196300
四、幼儿园(不包括园长)	Kindergarten (President is Excluded)	27440	38494	43141	49153	57736
中师、高中毕业及以上的	Graduate from Teacher Schools and Degrees Above	26658	36869	41455	47040	55669

17-28 高等学校分类别情况

单位：所、人

学校分类	Type of School	2000				2005			
		学校数 Number of Colleges and Universities	在校生数 Students Enrollment in Schools	招生数 New Enroll-ment	毕业生数 Graduates	学校数 Number of Colleges and Universities	在校生数 Students Enrollment in Schools	招生数 New Enroll-ment	毕业生数 Graduates
总　计	**Total**	**54**	**346568**	**139666**	**51932**	**85**	**989754**	**306775**	**184706**
综合大学	Comprehensive Universities	6	79303	28489	13871	10	196454	48591	48617
理工院校	Colleges and Universities of Science	11	124501	47724	18603	49	545277	181363	92857
农业院校	Colleges and Universities of Agriculture	2	13111	4311	1775	1	15715	3999	2763
林业院校	Colleges and Universities of Forestry	4	10770	4095	1068	1	1678	1062	121
医药院校	Colleges and Universities of Medicine	7	39694	17186	5950	3	26534	7686	5238
师范院校	Colleges and Universities of Teacher-Training	4	26218	9923	4466	5	52581	15687	12960
财经院校	Colleges and Universities of Finance	1	2482	974	448	6	93524	30319	12771
政法院校	Colleges and Universities of Politics and Law	1	2787	915	515	3	12389	3416	2369
体育院校	Colleges and Universities of Physical Education	2	2255	749	318	1	8837	2735	1154
艺术院校	Colleges and Universities of Art	2	12719	4298	2584	4	8834	4378	814
民族院校	Colleges and Universities of Minority Groups	14	32728	21002	2334	2	27931	7539	5042

CLASSIFICATION OF HIGHER EDUCATION INSTITUTIONS

(unit, person)

2010				2012				2013			
学校数 Number of Colleges and Universities	在校生数 Students Enrollment in Schools	招生数 New Enroll-ment	毕业生数 Graduates	学校数 Number of Colleges and Universities	在校生数 Students Enrollment in Schools	招生数 New Enroll-ment	毕业生数 Graduates	学校数 Number of Colleges and Universities	在校生数 Students Enrollment in Schools	招生数 New Enroll-ment	毕业生数 Graduates
120	**1290243**	**386984**	**327208**	**122**	**1383741**	**406271**	**351348**	**123**	**1419094**	**403226**	**361004**
8	166008	44736	39434	8	178505	48337	39621	8	181239	45191	41403
74	773095	238873	202148	76	827552	249084	220237	76	851991	252535	224369
1	18239	4600	3892	1	18408	4682	4332	1	18625	4774	4335
1	5721	2051	1461	1	7156	2691	1893	1	8740	3629	2045
4	38173	10979	10031	4	39980	11125	8387	4	41375	11161	9682
7	78905	24018	18007	7	87097	25541	21792	8	89303	25122	22605
12	123204	37315	30366	11	129462	37515	33162	11	130324	35572	33885
4	11698	2877	4157	4	11210	3725	3640	4	12284	4105	2995
2	14826	4298	2855	3	16378	4423	3593	3	16692	4180	3787
5	26179	8000	6898	5	28534	8198	6766	5	27532	6522	7208
2	34195	9237	7959	2	39459	10950	7925	2	40989	10435	8690

17-29 大学、中专专任教师职称情况
STATISTICS ON RANKS AND TITLES OF FULL-TIME TEACHERS AT SCHOOLS OF VARIOUS LEVELS

单位：人 (person)

职称	Ranks and Titles	2000	2005	2008	2009	2010	2011	2012	2013
普通高等学校专任教师数	**Number of Full-Time Teachers of Regular Higher Education Institutions**	**30363**	**59009**	**70617**	**73159**	**74685**	**78952**	**80665**	**81784**
正高级	Senoir	3253	6434	7707	8297	8674	9378	9998	10217
副高级	Associate Senoir	9448	17843	20623	21608	22047	23013	24373	24959
中　级	Junior	9847	19169	23380	24978	26077	29013	30244	31147
初　级	Primary	5741	10311	14402	13817	13656	13475	11883	11242
无职称	No Title	2074	5252	4505	4459	4231	4073	4167	4219
中等职业学校专任教师数	**Number of Full-Time Teachers of Specialized Schools**	**15549**	**24036**	**30689**	**29148**	**28476**	**26208**	**23796**	**22555**
副高级	Associate Senoir	3523	5152	6752	6541	6441	5958	5644	5495
中　级	Junior	7229	11467	14460	13366	12935	11960	10760	10187
初　级	Primary	4399	5889	7564	7403	7229	6856	6082	5762
无职称	No Title	398	1528	1913	1838	1871	1434	1310	1111

17-30 各级各类学校校舍建筑面积情况
STATISTICS ON FLOOR SPACE OF SCHOOL HOUSES UNDER CONSTRUCTION IN SCHOOLS OF VARIOUS LEVELS

单位：万平方米 (10 000 sq.m)

项　目	Item	2000	2005	2008	2009	2010	2011	2012	2013
中等职业学校	**Secondary Vocational School**	**736.78**	**833.01**	**999.97**	**899.28**	**952.02**	**852.4**	**862.85**	**857.84**
中等技术学校	Secondary School of Technology	647.55							
中等师范学校	Secondary Normal School	89.23							
普通中学	**Regular Middle School**	**3140.54**	**3745.41**	**4004.21**	**3991.6**	**4000.87**	**4012.05**	**4102.65**	**4183.53**
城市	Urban	1251.43	1121.26	1240.22	1175.05	1070.06	1484.08	1569.82	1642.53
县镇	Township	381.35	1083.29	1381.34	1484.82	1633.3	1781.12	1863.59	1902.28
农村	Rural	1507.76	1540.86	1382.65	1331.73	1297.51	746.85	669.24	638.72
职业中学	**Vocational Middle School**	**235.91**	**20.51**	**11.38**	**6.71**				
城市	Urban	149.14	3.34		0.1				
县镇	Township	44.53	3.21	3.36	0.08				
农村	Rural	42.24	13.96	8.01	6.52				
小学	**Primary School**	**3603.03**	**2926.92**	**2690.59**	**2648.74**	**2641.13**	**2496.01**	**2611.49**	**2749.99**
城市	Urban	781.80	414.55	432.74	400.48	390.94	505.47	575.87	620.2
县镇	Township	251.07	319.56	379.31	469.32	521.74	727.75	846.45	933.77
农村	Rural	2570.17	2192.81	1878.53	1778.94	1728.45	1262.79	1189.17	1196.02

17-31 初中毕业生升入高中和小学毕业生升入初中的升学率
STATISTICS ON PROPORTION OF MIDDLE-SCHOOL STUDENTS ENTERING HIGH SCHOOL AND PROPORTION OF PRIMARY-SCHOOL STUDENTS ENTERING MIDDLE SCHOOL

年份 Year	初中毕业生升入高中升学率 Proportion of Middle-School Students Entering High-School			小学毕业生升学率 Proportion of Primary-School Students Entering Middle-School		
	初中毕业生数(万人) Number of Middle-School Graduates (10 000 persons)	高中招生数(万人) Number of High-School Graduates (10 000 persons)	升学率(%) Proportion of Students Entering Schools of Higher Level(%)	小学毕业生数(万人) Number of Primary School Graduates (10 000 persons)	初中招生数(万人) Number of Middle-School Graduates (10 000 persons)	升学率(%) Proportion of Students Entering Schools of Higher Level(%)
1965	7.60	3.75	49.4	29.60	24.95	84.3
1975	49.25	31.26	63.5	116.05	110.11	94.9
1978	98.80	43.33	43.9	132.37	119.46	90.3
1980	52.23	25.04	47.7	107.64	88.93	82.6
1985	49.92	19.13	38.3	104.89	69.21	66.0
1990	51.71	16.78	32.5	89.96	66.63	74.1
1995	57.85	19.88	34.4	90.76	80.53	88.7
1996	59.33	19.86	33.5	90.19	83.59	92.7
1997	64.70	21.29	32.9	95.35	89.30	93.7
1998	69.23	24.53	35.4	103.75	96.10	92.6
1999	69.60	27.20	39.1	111.24	101.40	91.2
2000	71.80	31.43	43.8	116.02	109.06	94.0
2001	76.34	35.31	46.3	121.00	113.49	93.8
2002	82.93	42.45	51.2	122.17	120.07	98.3
2003	91.61	39.61	43.2	118.70	117.83	99.3
2004	99.32	42.97	43.3	109.93	109.69	99.8
2005	105.51	45.86	43.5	102.07	101.85	99.8
2006	106.18	45.55	42.9	94.66	97.07	102.6
2007	99.77	43.98	44.1	83.29	87.27	104.8
2008	96.10	43.91	45.7	71.51	77.75	108.7
2009	92.38	42.38	45.9	64.68	69.63	107.7
2010	85.44	39.55	46.3	61.16	65.79	107.6
2011	77.14	36.20	46.9	58.34	61.92	106.1
2012	57.58	32.75	56.9	51.38	51.09	99.4
2013	53.37	31.65	59.3	48.94	48.78	99.7

17-32 小学学龄儿童入学率
STATISTICS ON PROPORTION OF CHILDREN AT SCHOOLING AGE ENTERING PRIMARY SCHOOLS

年份 Year	学龄儿童数(万人) Number of Children at Schooling Age (10 000 person)	已入学学龄儿童数(万人) Number of Children Entering School (10 000 persons)	入学率(%) Proportion of Students Entering Schools of Higher Level (%)
1975	629.50	611.00	97.1
1978	616.86	597.73	96.9
1980	594.80	576.86	97.0
1985	496.69	489.38	98.5
1990	485.00	480.32	99.0
1991	556.39	549.35	98.7
1992	571.44	563.44	98.6
1993	574.54	566.84	98.7
1994	599.47	593.88	99.1
1995	637.12	632.34	99.2
1996	661.72	658.38	99.5
1997	681.52	678.95	99.6
1998	685.87	682.53	99.5
1999	669.16	665.88	99.5
2000	641.60	638.57	99.5
2001	585.99	583.29	99.5
2002	538.02	535.98	99.6
2003	490.29	488.68	99.7
2004	440.03	438.66	99.7
2005	397.52	396.11	99.7
2006	363.99	362.14	99.5
2007	345.49	344.77	99.8
2008	340.59	340.08	99.9
2009	343.63	342.74	99.7
2010	350.95	350.82	99.96
2011	362.77	362.74	99.96
2012	317.15	317.06	99.97
2013	320.48	320.41	99.98

17-33 各级各类学校服务的人口及每万人口中在校学生数
STATISTICS ON THE NUMBER OF POPULATION SERVED BY SCHOOLS OF VARIOUS LEVELS AND THE NUMBER OF STUDENTS AT SCHOOL PER 10000 PERSONS

项 目	Item	2000	2005	2008	2009	2010	2011	2012	2013
每一学校服务的人口数（万人）	**Number of Population Served by Each School (10 000 persons)**								
普通高等学校	Regular Institutions of Higher Education	111.63	70.95	65.64	47.67	47.70	47.20	47.37	47.15
成人高等学校	Adults Higher Education	188.37	354.76	380.73	408.57	408.86	411.29	412.79	414.21
普通中等专业学校	Specialized Secondary School	29.69	13.80	12.36	14.23	13.86	16.89	17.41	18.71
普通中学	Regualr Middle School	1.85	1.87	1.90	1.97	2.05	2.13	2.20	2.25
小学	Primary School	0.26	0.48	0.61	0.67	0.74	0.78	0.87	1.01
幼儿园	Kindergarten	1.61	2.58	1.98	1.91	1.30	1.23	1.09	0.96
每万人口中的学生数（人）	**Number of Students at School per 10 000 Persons (person)**								
普通高等学校	Regular Institutions of Higher Education	57.49	167.91	207.48	218.37	226.58	232.77	239.85	245.12
成人高等学校	Adults Higher Education	35.94	37.05	49.89	48.27	45.79	46.19	47.59	48.77
普通中等专业学校	Specialized Secondary School	46.22	100.48	181.63	182.13	157.90	125.20	86.61	70.91
普通中学	Regualr Middle School	582.19	740.65	688.92	638.13	597.19	557.21	458.94	426.26
小学	Primary School	1107.77	711.64	631.72	628.08	638.63	655.34	565.41	566.06
幼儿园	Kindergarten	120.56	98.57	130.02	145.35	195.38	230.06	234.54	254.07

17-34 各级各类学校每个专任教师负担的学生数
STATISTICS ON STUDENT-TEACHER RATIO BY LEVELS OF SCHOOL

单位：人 (person)

项 目	Item	2000	2005	2006	2007	2008	2009	2010	2011	2012	2013
普通高等学校	Regular Institutions of Higher Education	11.41	15.86	15.30	15.35	15.29	15.70	17.37	16.98	17.18	17.35
中等职业学校	Secondary Vocation School	17.92	25.21	29.77	31.89	33.80	35.74	31.74	27.51	21.03	18.23
普通中学	Regular High School	17.68	19.13	18.49	17.66	16.82	15.77	15.00	14.22	12.49	12.04
#初中	#Junior Middle Schools	18.19	18.76	17.97	17.06	15.96	14.71	13.91	13.23	11.16	10.94
高中	Senior High School	15.89	20.09	19.79	19.11	18.829	18.18	17.40	16.37	15.16	14.17
职业中学	Vocational Secondary School	13.47	20.28	18.07	15.52	13.81					
#高中	#Senior School	12.41									
小学	Primary School	24.28	19.90	18.69	18.07	17.92	12.09	18.64	20.46	17.04	16.70
幼儿园	Kindergarten	24.31	29.70	29.90	29.45	29.947	18.13	29.05	30.71	27.58	25.52

17-35 各级学校女学生和女教师数
NUMBER OF FEMALE STUDENTS AND FEMALE TEACHERS AT SCHOOL OF VARIOUS LEVELS

单位：万人 (10 000 persons)

项　　目	Item	2000	2005	2008	2009	2010	2011	2012	2013
一、女学生数	Number of Female Students	506.17	473.27	445.01	436.92	426.07	416.40	360.95	350.98
普通高等学校	Regular Institutions of Higher Education	11.93	44.11	55.00	58.90	62.25	65.13	67.70	69.12
中等专业学校	Specialized Secondary School	14.33	29.14	49.13	49.73	44.22	34.96	24.58	19.84
普通中学	Regualr High School	155.66	203.98	178.81	166.26	154.98	145.44	119.94	112.14
小学	Primary School	317.45	194.85	161.74	161.82	164.62	170.87	148.73	149.88
二、女学生占学生总数 %	Percentage of Female Students in School	46.2	45.5	45.5	45.8	46.2	46.1	46.2	46.3
普通高等学校	Regular Institutions of Higher Education	34.4	43.6	46.4	47.2	48.0	48.6	48.8	48.6
中等专业学校	Specialized Secondary School	51.4	48.1	47.4	47.7	48.9	48.5	49.1	48.3
普通中学	Regualr High School	44.4	45.7	45.4	45.6	45.3	45.3	45.2	45.4
小学	Primary School	47.5	45.4	44.8	45.0	45.0	45.3	45.5	45.7
三、女教师数	Number of Female Teachers	20.33	21.58	22.29	22.35	22.43	22.61	22.4	22.8
普通高等学校	Regular Institutions of Higher Education	1.02	2.34	2.94	3.07	3.16	3.42	3.51	3.59
中等专业学校	Specialized Secondary School	0.60	0.94	1.23	1.19	1.17	1.07	0.99	0.94
普通中学	Regualr High School	6.26	7.94	8.31	8.37	8.4	8.43	8.22	8.15
小学	Primary School	12.07	10.32	9.79	9.71	9.7	9.69	9.68	10.13
四、女教师占教师总数 %	Percentage of Female Teachers in School	38.3	40.4	41.5	41.9	42.5	43.0	44.0	45.1
普通高等学校	Regular Institutions of Higher Education	33.6	39.7	41.6	42.0	42.3	43.3	43.5	43.9
中等专业学校	Specialized Secondary School	38.5	39.1	40.1	40.7	41.0	40.8	41.5	41.5
普通中学	Regualr High School	31.5	34.0	35.5	36.1	36.9	37.4	38.7	39.7
小学	Primary School	43.9	47.9	48.6	49.0	49.5	49.7	50.5	51.5

17-36 各级各类成人学校在校学生数
NUMBER OF ADULT STUDENTS ENROLLED AT SCHOOLS OF VARIOUS LEVELS

单位：万人 (10 000 persons)

各类学校	Items	2000	2005	2008	2009	2010	2011	2012	2013
成人高等学校	Adult Higher Education	21.66	22.34	28.49	27.61	26.21	26.60	27.5	28.28
广播电视大学	Radio and TV Universities	2.78	2.52	1.29	0.76	0.54	0.61	0.45	0.43
职工大学	Schools of Higher Education for Staff	1.36	0.22	0.33	0.30	0.04	0.01	0.01	0.004
管理干部学院	Colleges for Management and Caders	0.90	0.60	0.71	0.48	0.35	0.20	0.06	0.04
教育学院	Pedagogical College	0.94	0.89	0.36	0.42	0.37	0.26	0.24	0.24
普通高等学校办函授部、夜大学	Correspondence and Evening College Run by Regualr High Education	15.16	18.11	25.81	25.64	24.91	25.52	26.74	27.57
成人中等学校	Secondary Schools for Adults	139.75	35.90	85.83	64.40	81.77	49.27	43.85	45.06
中学	Middle School	0.61	2.42	4.71	3.00	3.69	2.64	4.57	4.24
技术培训学校	Technical Training Schools	131.86	33.48	81.12	55.28	78.08	46.63	39.28	40.82
成人初等学校	Primary Schools for Adults	12.50	2.20	1.10	0.81	0.73	0.86	0.15	0.05
#扫盲班	#Class for Illiteracy	6.43	0.82	0.15	0.34	0.39	0.03	0.01	0.03

注：成人高等学校学生数是本、专科学生数。

Note:The number of students in Adults Higher Education refers to the number of students in vocational schools.

17-37 研究生基本情况

BASIC CONDTIONS ABOUT POST-GRADUATES

单位：人 (person)

项 目	Item	2010	2011	2012	2013
高等学校在校研究生数	Number of Post-graduates at School in Institutions of Higher Education	100841	104879	108528	112707
攻读博士学位研究生	Post-graduate Studying for Doctor's Degree	19232	19905	20927	22367
攻读硕士学位研究生	Post-graduate Studying for Master's Degree	81609	84974	87601	90340
招收研究生数	New Students Enrollment	35341	36358	37371	39027
攻读博士学位研究生	Post-graduate Studying for Doctor's Degree	4551	4706	4766	5070
攻读硕士学位研究生	Post-graduate Studying for Master's Degree	30790	31652	32605	33957
毕业研究生数	Number of Graduates	22228	30510	32201	34585
攻读博士学位研究生	Post-graduate Studying for Doctor's Degree	3516	3763	3692	3948
攻读硕士学位研究生	Post-graduate Studying for Master's Degree	18712	26747	28509	30637
科研单位在学研究生数	Number of Post-graduates Studying in Research Institutions	2299	2288	2328	2362
攻读博士学位研究生	Post-graduate Studying for Doctor's Degree	726	721	760	819
攻读硕士学位研究生	Post-graduate Studying for Master's Degree	1573	1567	1568	1543
招收研究生数	New Students Enrollment	775	760	777	779
攻读博士学位研究生	Post-graduate Studying for Doctor's Degree	200	212	220	229
攻读硕士学位研究生	Post-graduate Studying for Master's Degree	575	548	557	550
毕业研究生数	Number of Graduates	604	652	646	650
攻读博士学位研究生	Post-graduate Studying for Doctor's Degree	194	196	174	160
攻读硕士学位研究生	Post-graduate Studying for Master's Degree	410	456	472	490

主要统计指标解释

科技活动 指在自然科学、农业科学、医药科学、工程与技术科学、人文与社会科学领域(简称科学技术领域)中，与科技知识的产生、发展、传播和应用密切相关的有组织的活动。可分为研究与试验发展(R&D)、研究与试验发展成果应用及相关的科技服务三类活动。该定义是联合国教科文组织考虑成员国特别是发展中国家开展科技统计工作的需要，而对科技活动所作的统计界定。

科技活动人员 指直接从事科技活动、以及专门从事科技活动管理和为科技活动提供直接服务，累计的实际工作时间占全年制度工作时间10%及以上的人员。(1)直接从事科技活动的人员包括：在独立核算的科学研究与技术开发机构、高等学校、各类企业及其他事业单位内设的研究室、实验室、技术开发中心及中试车间(基地)等机构中从事科技活动的研究人员、工程技术人员、技术工人及其它人员；虽不在上述机构工作，但编入科技活动项目(课题)组的人员；科技信息与文献机构中的专业技术人员；从事论文设计的研究生等。(2)专门从事科技活动管理和为科技活动提供直接服务的人员，包括：独立核算的科学研究与技术开发机构、科技信息与文献机构、高等学校、各类企业及其他事业单位主管科技工作的负责人，专门从事科技活动的计划、行政、人事、财务、物资供应、设备维护、图书资料管理等工作的各类人员，但不包括保卫、医疗保健人员、司机、食堂人员、茶炉工、水暖工、清洁工等为科技活动提供间接服务的人员。该指标用来反映投入科技活动人力的规模。

科学家与工程师 指科技活动人员中具有高、中级技术职称(职务)的人员和不具有高、中级技术职称(职务)的大学本科及以上学历人员。该指标用来反映投入科技活动人力的素质。

研究与试验发展(R&D) 指在科学技术领域，为增加知识总量，以及运用这些知识去创造新的应用进行的系统的创造性的活动，包括基础研究、应用研究、试验发展三类活动。国际上通常采用 R&D 活动的规模和强度指标反映一国的科技实力和核心竞争力。

专业技术人员 指从事专业技术工作和专业技术管理工作的人员，即企事业单位中已经聘任专业技术职务从事专业技术工作和专业技术管理工作的人员，以及未聘任专业技术职务，现在专业技术岗位上工作的人员。包括工程技术人员，农业技术人员，科学研究人员，卫生技术人员，教学人员，经济人员，会计人员，统计人员，翻译人员，图书资料、档案、文博人员，新闻出版人员，律师、公证人员，广播电视播音人员，工艺美术人员，体育人员，艺术人员及企业政治思想工作人员，共十七个专业技术职务类别。用来反映科技人力资源情况。

科技活动经费筹集 指从各种渠道筹集到的计划用于科技活动的经费，包括政府资金、企业资金、事业单位资金、金融机构贷款、国外资金和其他资金等。反映各社会经济主体对促进科技进步所做的努力。

新产品 指采用新技术原理、新设计构思研制、生产的全新产品，或在结构、材质、工艺等某一方面比原有产品有明显改进，从而显著提高了产品性能或扩大了使用功能的产品。既包括政府有关部门认定并在有效期内的新产品，也包括企业自行研制开发，未经政府有关部门认定，从投产之日起一年之内的新产品。用来反映科技产出及对经济增长的直接贡献。

专利 是专利权的简称，是对发明人的发明创造经审查合格后，由专利局依据专利法授予发明人和设计人对该项发明创造享有的专有权。包括发明、实用新型和外观设计。反映拥有自主知识产权的科技和设计成果情况。

发明 指对产品、方法或者其改进所提出的新的技术方案。是国际通行的反映拥有自主知识产权技术的核心指标。

普通高等学校 指按照国家规定的设置标准和审批程序批准举办的，通过全国普通高等学校统一招生考试，招收高中毕业生为主要培养对象，实施高等教育的全日制大学、独立设置的学院和高等专科学校、高等职业学校和其他机构。

大学、独立设置的学院主要实施本科层次以上教育，高等专科学校、高等职业学校实施专科层次教育，其他机构是承担国家普通招生计划任务不计校数的机构。包括普通高等学校分校和批准筹建的普通高等学校等。

成人高等学校 指按照国家规定的设置标准和审批程序批准举办的，通过全国成人高等学校统一招生考试，招收具有高中毕业或同等学历的在职从业人员为主要培养对象，利用函授、业余、脱产等多种形式对其实施高等学历教育的学校。包括职工高等学校、农民高等学校、管理干部学院、教育学院、独立函授学院、广播电视大学、其他机构等。其他机构是承担国家成人招生计划任务不计校数的机构。

小学学龄儿童净入学率 指调查范围内已入小学学习的学龄儿童占校内外学龄儿童总数(包括弱智儿童，不包括盲聋哑儿童)的比重。计算公式为:

$$\text{小学学龄儿童净入学率}=\frac{\text{已入学的小学学龄儿童数}}{\text{校内外小学学龄儿童总数}}\times 100\%$$

Explanatory Notes on Main Statistical Indicators

Scientific and Technological Activities (S&T Activities) refer to organized activities which are closely related with the creation, development, dissemination and application of the scientific and technical knowledge in the fields of natural sciences, agricultural science, medical science, engineering and technological science, humanities and social sciences (referred to as scientific and technological fields). S&T activities can be classified in to 3 categories: research and development (R&D) activities, application of R&D results, and related S&T services. This statistical definition is made by UNICHIEF for scientific and technological activities to meet the need of carrying out statistical work in this field for its member countries in particular those developing countries.

Personnel Engaged in S&T Activities refer to personnel directly engaged in S&T activities, in the management of S&T activities, and in providing direct service to S&T activities, who spend over 10% of the total working hours in a year in S&T activities. (1) Personnel directly engaged in S&T activities include researchers, engineers, technicians and other related personnel engaged in S&T activities in independent-accounting R&D institutions, institutions of higher learning, and in research institutes, laboratories, technology development centers and central experiment workshops under enterprises and institutions. Also included are people working in S&T research project teams, professional and technical personnel working in S&T information archiving institutes, and graduate students working on the design of their thesis. (2) Personnel engaged in the management of S&T activities and in providing direct service to S&T activities include senior management people responsible for S&T activities in independent-accounting R&D institutions, S&T information archiving institutes, institutions of higher learning, and in enterprises and institutions where S&T activities are undertaken. Also included are people responsible for the planning, administration, personnel management, financial management, logistics supply, equipment maintenance, information and library management that are related with S&T activities. People providing indirect services are excluded, such as security, medical service, drivers, plumbers, cleaners and those providing catering and related service. This indicator reflects the size of personnel engaged in S&T activities.

Scientists and Engineers refer to persons engaged in S&T activities who have obtained titles of senior and middle level professional positions, and those without such position but have completed university or higher education. This indicator reflects the quality of personnel engaged in S&T activities.

Research and Development (R&D) refers to systematic and creative activities in the field of science and technology aiming at increasing the knowledge and using the knowledge for new application. R&D includes 3 categories of activities: basic research, applied research and experiments and development. The scale and intensity of R&D are widely used internationally to reflect the strength of S&T and the core competitiveness of a country in the world.

Professional and Technical Personnel refer to persons engaged in professional and technical work or in the management of professional and technical activities, i.e., people with professional or technical positions who are engaged in professional and technical work or in the management of professional and technical activities, and people without professional or technical positions but are working on professional or technical posts. They include professionals and technicians working in 17 categories of technical occupations including engineering, agriculture, scientific researches, medical service, teaching, economic research and application, accounting, statistics, translation, libraries, archives, cultural and museum service, journalism and publication, lawyers, notarization service, radio and television broadcasting, handicraft and fine arts, sports, performing art, and political workers in enterprises. This indicator reflects the condition of human resources in S&T.

Funding for S&T Activities refers to funds obtained from various sources for S&T activities, including government funds, self-raised funds by enterprises, self-raised funds by institutions, loans from financial institutions, foreign funds and other funds. This indicator reflects the efforts made by various social economic entities in promoting the development of S&T.

New Products refer to new products produced with new technology and new design, or products that represent noticeable improvement in terms of structure, material, or production process so as to improve significantly the character or function of the older versions. They include new products certified by relevant government agencies within the period of certification, as well as new products designed and produced by enterprises within a year without certification by government agencies. This indictor reflects the direct contribution of S&T output to economic growth.

Patent is an abbreviation for the patent right and refers to the exclusive right of ownership by the inventors or designers for the creation or inventions, given from the patent offices after due process of assessment and approval in accordance with the Patent Law. Patents are granted for inventions, utility models and designs. This indicator reflects the achievements of S&T and design with independent intellectual property.

Inventions refer to the new technical proposals to the products or methods or their modifications. This is universal core indicator reflecting the technologies with independent intellectual property.

Regular Institutions of Higher Learning refer to educational establishments set up according to the government evaluation and approval procedures, enrolling graduates from senior secondary schools and providing higher education courses and training for senior professionals. They include full-time universities, colleges, high professional schools, high professional vocational schools and others.

Universities and colleges are mainly providing undergraduate courses; those high professional schools and high professional vocational schools are mainly providing professional trainings; and others refer to educational establishments, which are responsible for enrolling students but not covered in the total number of schools, including: branch schools of universities and colleges, and universities and colleges that have been proved and prepared to construct.

Institutions of Higher Learning for Adults refer to educational establishments, set up in line with relevant rules approved by the government, enrolling staff and workers with senior secondary school or equivalent education, and providing higher education courses in many forms of correspondence, spare time, or full time for adults. Professionals thus trained receive a qualification equivalent to graduates studying regular courses at regular universities, colleges and professional colleges. Institutions of higher learning for adults include schools of high education for staff and workers, schools of high education for peasants, colleges for management cadres, pedagogical colleges, independent correspondence colleges, Radio and TV universities and other educational establishments. Other educational establishments are responsible for enrolling adult students but not covered in the number of schools.

Enrollment Rate of Primary School Age Children refers to the proportion of school age children enrolled at schools to the total number of school age children both in and outside schools (including retarded children, but excluding blind, deaf and mute children). The formula is:

Enrollment Rate of Primary School-age Children = (Total Primary School-age Children at Schools)/(Total Primary School age Children Both at and Outside Schools) x 100%

18 卫生和社会服务

Public Health and Social Services

资料整理：谢　涛

18-1 卫生机构数

NUMBER OF HEALTH CARE INSTITUTIONS

单位：个 (unit)

年 份 Year	总 计 Total	医 院 Hospitals	村卫生室 Village Clinics	疗养院、所 Sanatoriums	门诊部、所 Clinics	专科防治所、站 Specialized Prevention and Treatment Stations or Centers
1970	7847	16003		10	1500	104
1975	5381	1834		2	3079	39
1980	6146	1827		12	3785	52
1985	9885	1853		12	7486	67
1990	10472	2024		11	7878	70
1991	10509	2111		11	7824	74
1992	10590	2115		11	7903	73
1993	10268	2139		12	7526	73
1994	9762	2147		12	7002	84
1995	9744	2119		11	7020	84
1996	9167	2105		10	6453	82
1997	11562	2078		10	8867	86
1998	11584	2082		10	8885	88
1999	11311	2077		11	8631	85
2000	11065	2041		11	8430	83
2001	10941	1924		10	8500	73
2002	9946	555		2	7687	168
2003	9983	552		3	7690	177
2004	9285	566		2	6949	166
2005	9459	574		1	7215	120
2006	10052	575			7687	116
2007	11089	580			7585	118
2008	10832	592			7397	107
2009	10362	614			6770	88
2010	10152	603			6499	85
2011	10455	608			6838	83
2012	35423	650	24976		6668	83
2013	35633	713	24953		6679	75

注：卫生事业机构数、床位数、卫生人员数从2012年起包含村卫生室数量。
Note:The statistics of health care units, hospital beds and health care professionals started to include the village clinics since 2012.

18-1　续表 continued

单位：个 (unit)

年　份 Year	卫生防疫站 Sanitation and Antiepidemic Station	妇幼保健所、站 Maternity and Child Care Centers	药品检验所、室 Institutions of Drug Control	医学科学研究机构 Institutions of Medical Science Research	其他卫生机构 Others
1970	106	54	5	2	63
1975	99	85	83	6	154
1980	110	97	88	7	168
1985	111	96	87	7	166
1990	120	96	87	9	177
1991	122	98	87	7	175
1992	119	96	86	8	179
1993	149	96	87	8	178
1994	149	97	87	8	176
1995	151	95	85	8	171
1996	156	95	84	8	174
1997	158	96	84	8	175
1998	158	96	85	8	172
1999	156	94	83	7	167
2000	155	94	81	7	163
2001	130	91	53	7	153
2002	107	12	87		1328
2003	110	32	92		1327
2004	110	39	92		1359
2005	113	63	96		1366
2006	114	72	95		1393
2007	113	100	59	1	2533
2008	111	99		1	2525
2009	111	98		1	2680
2010	115	100		1	2952
2011	112	100		1	2713
2012	111	100		1	2834
2013	113	101		1	2998

18-2 卫生机构人员数

NUMBER OF PERSONS ENGAGED IN HEALTH CARE INSTITUTIONS

单位：万人 (10 000 persom)

年份 Year	总计 Total	卫生技术人员 Medical Technical Personel	#医生 #Doctors	中医 Chinese Traditional Medicine Doctors	西医师 Western Medicine Doctors	西医士 Wertern Medical Assistant	#护师、护士 #Nurses	每千人口医生数(人) Number of Doctors per 1000 Population (person)
1970	10.30	8.33	4.15	1.86	1.22	1.07	1.83	1.03
1975	15.05	11.85	4.91	1.74	1.63	1.55	2.05	1.11
1980	19.94	15.59	6.32	1.82	2.59	1.91	3.09	1.35
1985	23.58	18.48	7.27	2.22	3.09	1.95	3.77	1.47
1990	26.75	20.92	8.68	2.19	5.09	1.40	5.66	1.62
1991	27.51	21.55	8.79	2.18	5.11	1.50	5.97	1.62
1992	28.24	22.15	9.02	2.20	5.18	1.65	6.25	1.64
1993	28.91	22.46	9.16	2.12	5.48	1.57	6.49	1.64
1994	29.31	22.84	9.38	2.04	5.64	1.65	6.64	1.66
1995	29.55	23.20	9.58	1.98	5.79	1.76	6.83	1.68
1996	29.65	23.47	9.72	1.93	5.92	1.90	7.00	1.67
1997	30.38	23.90	9.96	1.84	6.09	1.90	7.21	1.70
1998	30.31	23.96	10.11	1.84	6.30	1.90	7.29	1.71
1999	30.40	24.05	10.31	1.81	6.58	1.85	7.41	1.74
2000	30.14	23.88	10.30	1.76	6.76	1.74	7.53	1.74
2001	29.48	23.41	10.21	1.63	6.91	1.63	7.51	1.72
2002	25.30	20.59	8.63	1.14			6.35	1.43
2003	25.62	20.83	8.72	0.94	1.73	0.13	6.38	1.45
2004	26.06	21.38	8.99				6.62	1.49
2005	26.22	21.50	8.98				6.94	1.49
2006	26.53	21.80	9.01				7.06	1.49
2007	27.80	22.70	9.20				7.69	1.52
2008	28.63	23.52	9.27				8.12	1.52
2009	29.45	24.30	9.43				8.69	1.54
2010	30.40	25.16	9.59				9.33	1.62
2011	31.30	26.00	9.60				10.00	1.67
2012	38.71	28.85	10.91				11.57	1.77
2013	41.45	31.16	11.94				12.80	1.90

注：卫生事业机构数、床位数、卫生人员数从2012年起包含村卫生室数量。
Note:The statistics of health care units, hospital beds and health care professionals started to include the village clinics since 2012.

18-3 卫生机构床位数

NUMBER OF BEDS IN HEALTH CARE INSTITUTIONS

单位：万张 (10 000 beds)

年 份 Year	总 计 Total	医 院 Hospitals	#县及县以上医院 #Hospitals Above County Level	疗养院、所 Sanatoriums	其他卫生机构 Other Health Care Institutions	每千人口医院床位数(张) Number of Hospital Beds Per 10 000 Population (bed)
1970	6.14	5.56	2.84	0.18		1.38
1975	9.90	9.02	4.33	0.02		2.05
1980	12.59	11.22	5.41	0.20		2.40
1985	14.70	11.52	6.80	0.20	2.98	2.34
1990	16.34	13.16	8.27	0.19	2.99	2.45
1991	16.52	13.43	8.50	0.21	2.88	2.47
1992	16.62	13.46	8.58	0.22	2.84	2.44
1993	16.30	13.48	8.71	0.21	2.61	2.41
1994	16.13	13.40	8.73	0.21	2.52	2.36
1995	15.78	13.08	8.58	0.20	2.50	2.29
1996	14.42	13.08	8.63	0.15	1.19	2.24
1997	15.30	13.08	8.76	0.16	2.05	2.24
1998	15.09	13.03	8.77	0.17	1.89	2.21
1999	14.90	12.91	8.76	0.16	1.83	2.07
2000	14.96	12.99	8.80	0.16	1.81	2.18
2001	14.62	12.91	8.80	0.16	0.60	2.18
2002	12.72	8.53		0.03	4.16	2.12
2003	13.59	9.39		0.04	4.16	2.26
2004	13.78	9.52		0.02	4.24	2.29
2005	13.96	9.67		0.01	4.28	2.31
2006	14.24	9.81			4.43	2.35
2007	15.06	10.36			4.70	2.48
2008	16.73	11.32			5.41	2.75
2009	18.72	12.66			6.06	2.82
2010	20.07	13.51			6.56	3.26
2011	22.40	15.20			7.20	3.89
2012	25.30	17.38			7.92	4.10
2013	28.85	20.05			8.80	4.60

18-4 各类卫生工作人员数

NUMBER OF SANITARY TECHNICAL PERSONELS OF VARIOUS TYPE

单位：人 (person)

人员分类	Type	1990	2000	2005	2009	2010	2011	2012	2013
合　计	**Total**	**267548**	**301415**	**262263**	**294539**	**303980**	**365160**	**387086**	**414538**
医院	Hospitals	182490	140720	138843	161631	169985	179093	196263	214720
中医院	Hospitals of Chinese Medicines	11386	17442	19274	20805	22352	23773	27349	30304
乡镇卫生院	Towm Hospitals	58518	54500	69626	69304	69823	67854	70143	71243
村卫生室	Village Clinics							49202	51860
疗养院、所	Sanatoriums	1271	1387	60					
门诊部、所	Clinics	44450	34020	17940	16300	15479	17500	17299	17414
专科防治所、站	Specialized Prevention & Treatment Stations or Centers	6218	7830	4352	3119	3073	3038	3203	3198
卫生防疫站	Sanitation and Antiepidemic Station	7602	10388	9149	8094	8247	8534	8399	8605
妇幼保健所、站	Maternity and Child Care Centers	4139	6874	8796	10640	11209	12506	14111	15519
药品检验所、室	Institutions of Drug Control	1098	1373						
其他卫生事业机构	Others	6376	4087						
医学科研机构	Medical Science Institutions	810	746						
高等医院院校	Institutions of Higher Education	6489	6154						
中等卫校	Secondary Health School	3762	6043						
个体开业	Run by Individuals	2843	4252						

18-5 医院业务工作开展情况
BASIC STATISTICS ON HOSPITAL BUSINESS

项 目	Item	1995	2000	2005	2010	2011	2012	2013
机构数 (个)	Number of Institutions (unit)	523	507	574	603	608	650	713
诊疗总人次数 (万人次)	Number of Clients (10 000 person-times)	5764.80	4616.20	5452.11	7710.20	8404.63	9470.38	10056.28
#门、急诊人次数(万人次)	#Number of Outpacients and Emergency (10 000 person-times)	5460.20	4396.10	5107.19	7533.44	8247.39	9236.70	9859.71
出院人数 (万人)	Number of discharged Patients (10 000 persons)	147.71	158.93	219.45	423.28	481.61	578.82	647.55
死亡 (万人)	Dead (10 000 persons)	1.56	1.59	2.28	3.13	3.23	2.33	2.93
病死率 (%)	Rate of Death from Illness (%)	1.20	1.08	1.04	0.74	0.67	0.40	0.45
病床平均周转次数 (次)	Average times of Beds Usage (time)	17.80	18.66	23.99	32.50	33.80	35.00	34.90
病床平均工作日 (日)	Average Day of Beds Usage (day)	247.50	218.79	268.24	350.40	360.10	363.40	353.30
病床使用率 (%)	Utilization Rate of Beds (%)	67.80	59.94	73.49	96.01	98.66	99.30	99.52
出院者平均住院日 (日)	Average Days for Hospitalization Discharged (day)	13.30	11.12	10.71	10.50	10.40	10.10	9.90

18-6 农村村级卫生组织情况

STATISTICS ON HEALTH CARE INSTITUTIONS AT VILLAGE LEVEL

项　　目	Item	1995	2000	2005	2010	2011	2012	2013
行政村数 (个)	Number of Villages (unit)	32661	32400	26678	26018	26025	25575	25452
村设置的医疗点数 (个)	Medical care Station Set by Villages (unit)	31817	26879	21136	24057	25146	24976	24953
#村或集体办	#Set by Villages or Collective Set	13230	14666	11207	15395	15923	15785	15410
联合办	Set with Village Doctors	7313	4640	3777	2815	2596	2576	2449
医院设点	Set by Hospital	1526	2403	2410	3348	3934	3920	4027
私人办	Set by Individual	8178	4344	2907	1833	1919	1941	2164
其他	Others	1570	826	835	666	774	754	903
乡村医生和卫生员人数 (人)	Number of Village Doctors and Medical Working Personel (person)	61324	57511	34417	41473	44040	43873	43840
#乡村医生	#Village Doctors	43288	44490	33375	40425	42810	41664	40833
卫生员	Medical Working Personel	18036	13021	1042	1048	1230	2209	3007

18-7 全省法定报告传染病的发病及死亡情况

病 名	Name of Disease	2009			2010		
		发病率(1/10万) Incidence Rate (1/100 thousand)	死亡率(1/10万) Mortality Rate (1/100 thousand)	病死率(%) Rate of Death from Illness (1/100 thousand)	发病率(1/10万) Incidence Rate (1/100 thousand)	死亡率(1/10万) Mortality Rate (1/100 thousand)	病死率(%) Rate of Death from Illness (1/100 thousand)
总 计	**Total**	**318.62**	**0.88**	**0.28**			**516.47**
#病毒性肝炎	#Viral Hepatitis	160.17	0.11	0.07			140.59
痢疾	Dysentery	22.51		0.01			21.51
伤寒副伤寒	Typhoid and Paralyhoid	0.97					0.51
艾滋病	Aids	0.51	0.36	69.86			0.62
淋病	Gonorrhea	5.25					4.72
梅毒	Syphilis	13.85					16.12
脊髓灰质炎	Poliomyelitis						
百日咳	Pertussis	0.05					0.03
白喉	Diphtheria						
流脑	Epidemic Encephalitis	0.04	0.01	18.18			0.02
猩红热	Scarlet Fever	0.34					0.38
出血热	Hemorrhage Fever	0.44	0.01	3.20			0.40
狂犬病	Hydrophobia	0.21	0.21	100.00			0.15
钩端螺旋体病	Leplospirosis	0.03		5.88			0.03
乙脑	Encephalitis B	0.22	0.01	3.94			0.20
疟疾	Malaria	1.25					0.75
肺结核	TB	90.70	0.15	0.17			84.75

LEGAL REPORT ON INFECTION DISEASE INCIDENCE AND DEATH

2011			2012			2013		
发病率 (1/10万) Incidence Rate (1/100 thousand)	死亡率 (1/10万) Mortality Rate (1/100 thousand)	病死率(%) Rate of Death from Illness (1/100 thousand)	发病率 (1/10万) Incidence Rate (1/100 thousand)	死亡率 (1/10万) Mortality Rate (1/100 thousand)	病死率(%) Rate of Death from Illness (1/100 thousand)	发病率 (1/10万) Incidence Rate (1/100 thousand)	死亡率 (1/10万) Mortality Rate (1/100 thousand)	病死率(%) Rate of Death from Illness (1/100 thousand)
491.53	**0.86**	**0.18**	**537.56**	**0.81**	**0.15**	**473.85**	**0.74**	**0.16**
139.36	0.08	0.06	130.57	0.10	0.08	125.91	0.06	0.05
19.92	0.002	0.01	14.51			11.59		
0.41			0.36			0.66		
0.78	0.41	51.79	1.48	0.44	29.43	1.77	0.47	26.44
4.22			3.65			3.57		
16.28			16.42			16.28		
0.06			0.04			0.03		
0.02	0.005	21.43	0.02			0.01		
			0.89			0.65		
0.49	0.01	2.84	0.39	0.02	4.46	0.44	0.02	4.33
0.15	0.15	100.00	0.10	0.09	98.18	0.07	0.06	94.74
0.02			0.02			0.01		
0.02			0.02			0.03		
0.29	0.004	1.20	0.22	0.002	1.33	0.23	0.00	0.76
88.11	0.15	0.17	87.67	0.10	0.12	83.14	0.11	0.13

18-8 部分城市十种主要疾病死亡构成及顺位

顺位 order	2000		2005		2010	
	死亡原因 Cause of Death	占死亡总数% Percentage of Death in Total Deaths %	死亡原因 Cause of Death	占死亡总数% Percentage of Death in Total Deaths %	死亡原因 Cause of Death	占死亡总数% Percentage of Death in Total Deaths %
1	脑血管病 Cerebrovascular Disease	28.21	恶性肿瘤 Malignant Tumor	23.58	恶性肿瘤 Malignant Tumor	22.38
2	恶性肿瘤 Malignant Tumor	21.28	脑血管病 Cerebrovascular Disease	21.29	脑血管病 Cerebrovascular Disease	17.29
3	心脏病 Heart Disease	15.07	心脏病 Heart Disease	15.60	心脏病 Heart Disease	7.99
4	呼吸系统疾病 Respiratory System Disease	11.24	呼吸系统疾病 Respiratory System Disease	9.39	呼吸系统疾病 Respiratory System Disease	7.23
5	损伤和中毒 Injury and Poisoning	7.12	损伤和中毒 Injury and Poisoning	6.56	损伤和中毒 Injury and Poisoning	6.95
6	消化系统疾病 Digestive Disease	3.48	内分泌、营养、代谢 Endocrine System, Nutritional Disease and Disease of Metabolism	3.62	内分泌，营养和代谢疾病 Endocrine System, Nutritional Disease and Disease of Metabolism	5.25
7	内分泌系统 Endocrine System	2.47	消化系统疾病 Digestive Disease	3.36	消化系统疾病 Digestive Disease	3.92
8	传染病 Communicable Disease	1.82	泌尿生殖系统 Urogenital System	1.68	传染病和寄生虫病 Communicable and parasitic Disease	3.48
9	泌尿生殖系统 Urogenital System	1.51	精神障碍 Psychonosema	1.50	精神障碍 Psychonosema	2.77
10	精神病 Mental DiSease	1.49	传染病和寄生虫病 Communicable and parasitic Disease	1.45	泌尿生殖系统 Urogenital System	2.26
	合 计 Total	**93.69**	**合 计 Total**	**88.03**	**合 计 Total**	**79.52**

STATISTICS ON TEN MAJOR DEATH-CAUSING DESEASES IN PARTIAL CITIES

2011		2012		2013	
死亡原因 Cause of Death	占死亡总数% Percentage of Death in Total Deaths %	死亡原因 Cause of Death	占死亡总数% Percentage of Death in Total Deaths %	死亡原因 Cause of Death	占死亡总数% Percentage of Death in Total Deaths %
脑血管病 Cerebrovascular Disease	23.45	脑血管病 Cerebrovascular Disease	22.76	脑血管病 Cerebrovascular Disease	22.03
心脏病 Heart Disease	18.33	心脏病 Heart Disease	19.38	心脏病 Heart Disease	19.46
肺癌 Lung Disease	8.33	肺癌 Lung Disease	8.35	急性心肌梗死 Acute myocardial infarction	8.56
急性心肌梗死 Acute myocardial infarction	7.90	急性心肌梗死 Acute myocardial infarction	7.89	肺癌 Lung Disease	8.43
慢性下呼吸道疾病 Chronic lower respiratory diseases	6.71	慢性下呼吸道疾病 Chronic lower respiratory diseases	6.30	其他冠心病 Other Coronary Heart Disease	7.00
其他冠心病 Other Coronary Heart Disease	5.95	其他冠心病 Other Coronary Heart Disease	6.87	慢性下呼吸道疾病 Chronic lower respiratory diseases	6.26
肝癌 Liver Cancer	3.91	肝癌 Liver Cancer	3.80	肝癌 Liver Cancer	3.85
糖尿病 Communicable and parasitic Disease	3.28	糖尿病 Communicable and parasitic Disease	3.14	糖尿病 Communicable and parasitic Disease	2.79
胃癌 Gastric Cancer	2.86	胃癌 Gastric Cancer	2.79	胃癌 Gastric Cancer	2.71
结肠，直肠和肛门癌 Colon, Rectum and Anal Cancer	2.19	结肠，直肠和肛门癌 Colon, Rectum and Anal Cancer	2.28	结肠，直肠和肛门癌 Colon, Rectum and Anal Cancer	2.35
合 计 Total	**82.91**	**合 计 Total**	**83.56**	**合 计 Total**	**83.44**

18-9 部分农村十种主要疾病死亡构成及顺位

顺位 Order	2000 死亡原因 Cause of Death	2000 占死亡总数% Percentage of Death in Total Deaths %	2005 死亡原因 Cause of Death	2005 占死亡总数% Percentage of Death in Total Deaths %	2010 死亡原因 Cause of Death	2010 占死亡总数% Percentage of Death in Total Deaths %
1	脑血管病 Cerebrovascular Disease	24.92	脑血管病 Cerebrovascular Disease	24.51	脑血管病 Cerebrovascular Disease	30.07
2	呼吸系统疾病 Respiratory System Disease	19.52	心脏病 Heart Disease	24.42	心脏病 Heart Disease	19.38
3	恶性肿瘤 Malignant Tumor	16.74	恶性肿瘤 Malignant Tumor	18.23	恶性肿瘤 Malignant Tumor	6.34
4	损伤和中毒 Injury and Poisoning	12.17	损伤和中毒 Injury and Poisoning	11.07	损伤和中毒 Injury and Poisoning	6.23
5	心脏病 Heart Disease	11.80	呼吸系统疾病 Respiratory System Disease	8.43	呼吸系统疾病 Respiratory System Disease	5.40
6	消化系统疾病 Digestive Disease	4.26	消化系统疾病 Digestive Disease	3.62	消化系统疾病 Digestive Disease	5.02
7	传染病 Communicable Disease	1.73	泌尿生殖系统疾病 Urogenital System	1.64	泌尿生殖系统疾病 Urogenital System	4.48
8	高血压病 High Blood Pressure	1.64	传染病和寄生虫病 Communicable and parasitic disease	1.01	传染病和寄生虫病 Communicable and Parasitic Disease	4.27
9	泌尿生殖系统疾病 Urogenital System	1.62	起源于围生期的某些情况小计 Others	0.77	内分泌，营养和代谢疾病 Endocrine System, Nutritional Disease and Disease of Metabolism	3.96
10	新生儿病 New Born Baby Disease	1.48	精神障碍 Psychonosema	0.71	起源于围生期的某些情况 Some Cases Originated in Perinatal Period	3.76
	合 计 Total	**95.88**	**合 计 Total**	**94.41**	**合计 Total**	**88.91**

STATISTICS ON TEN MAJOR DEATH-CAUSING DESEASES IN PARTIAL COUNTRIES

2011		2012		2013	
死亡原因 Cause of Death	占死亡总数% Percentage of Death in Total Deaths %	死亡原因 Cause of Death	占死亡总数% Percentage of Death in Total Deaths %	死亡原因 Cause of Death	占死亡总数% Percentage of Death in Total Deaths %
脑血管病 Cerebrovascular Disease	28.17	脑血管病 Cerebrovascular Disease	27.94	脑血管病 Cerebrovascular Disease	25.43
心脏病 Heart Disease	20.09	心脏病 Heart Disease	20.80	心脏病 Heart Disease	20.27
慢性下呼吸道疾病 Chronic lower respiratory diseases	7.24	急性心肌梗死 Acute myocardial infarction	7.64	急性心肌梗死 Acute myocardial infarction	6.92
急性心肌梗死 Acute myocardial infarction	5.37	慢性下呼吸道疾病 Chronic lower respiratory diseases	6.31	慢性下呼吸道疾病 Chronic lower respiratory diseases	6.63
肝癌 Liver Cancer	5.18	肺癌 Lung Cancer	5.40	肺癌 Lung Cancer	5.89
肺癌 Lung Cancer	5.11	其他高血压病 Other Diseases of Hypertension	4.28	肝癌 Liver Cancer	4.89
其他冠心病 Other Coronary Heart Disease	4.73	肝癌 Liver Cancer	4.70	其他高血压病 Other Diseases of Hypertension	4.66
胃癌 Gastric Cancer	4.30	胃癌 Gastric Cancer	4.17	其他冠心病 Other Coronary Heart Disease	4.36
肺原性心脏病 Pulmonary Heart Disease	4.18	肺原性心脏病 Pulmonary Heart Disease	3.84	胃癌 Gastric Cancer	4.21
其他高血压病 Other Diseases of Hypertension	3.50	其他冠心病 Other Coronary Heart Disease	3.71	肺原性心脏病 Pulmonary Heart Disease	3.40
合计 Total	**87.87**	**合计 Total**	**88.79**	**合计 Total**	**86.66**

主要统计指标解释

卫生机构 包括医疗机构、疾病预防控制中心(防疫站)、采供血机构、卫生监督及监测(检验)机构、医学科研和在职培训机构、健康教育所等。

医疗机构 包括医院、社区卫生服务中心(站)、疗养院、卫生院、门诊部、诊所(卫生所、医务室)、妇幼保健院(所、站)、专科疾病防治院(所、站)、急救中心(站)和临床检验中心。医疗机构分为非赢利性医疗机构和赢利性医疗机构。

医院 包括综合医院、中医医院、中西医结合医院、民族医院、各类专科医院和护理院。

卫生技术人员 指卫生机构中医生、护理人员 、药剂人员、检验人员等卫生技术人员。

医生 指在医疗、预防保健机构工作且取得《执业医师证书》的执业医师和执业助理医师。

Explanatory Notes on Main Statistical Indicators

Health Care Institutions include medical institutions, disease prevention and control centers (epidemic prevention stations), blood gathering and supplying institutions, health supervision and inspection (check up) institutions, medicinal scientific research and on-job training institutions, health education and so on.

Medical Organizations include hospitals, health service centers (stations) of communities, nursing homes, health centers, clinics, clinics (health stations and infirmaries), maternity and child care agencies (centers and stations), special disease prevention and curing agencies (centers and stations), first aid centers (stations) and clinical inspection centers. Medical organizations are grouped by two types: profit-making and non-profit-making medical organizations.

Hospitals include polyclinics, traditional Chinese medical hospitals, hospitals integrated with traditional Chinese therapeutics and western therapeutics, ethical hospitals, various specialties hospitals and nursing hospitals.

Medical Technical Personnel refers to doctors, assistant nurses, pharmacists, and laboratory technicians working in medical institutions.

Doctors refer to certified physicians and certified assistant physicians with certifications working in medical and health care and prevention agencies.

19 文化和体育

Culture and Sports

资料整理：谢　涛

19-1 文化事业机构、人员数

NUMBER OF CULTURAL INSTITUTIONS AND PERSONEL

单位：个、人 (unit, person)

项 目	Item	2007	2008	2009	2010	2011	2012	2013
艺术业机构	Art Performing Institution					239	295	363
#剧团	#Troupes					172	226	307
#剧场	#Theater					65	66	53
文物事业机构	Historical Relics Institutions	149	168	171	166	175	214	291
#博物馆	#Museums	96	111	114	121	125	161	170
图书馆事业机构	Library Institutions	102	104	104	107	109	111	112
群众文化事业机构	Public Culture Institutions	1342	1356	1367	1378	1378	1379	1382
群众艺术馆	Public Art Center	18	17	17	13	13	13	13
文化馆(站)	Art Center	1229	1339	1350	1365	1365	1366	1369
艺术业人员数	Number of People Engaged in Art Performing					5018	10976	10384
#剧团人员	Staff in Troupes					4580	9216	9005
#剧场人员	Staff in Theater					437	1750	1367
文物事业人员数	Number of Historical Relics Staffs	3585	3623	3915	3297	3596	4334	4713
#博物馆人员	#Number of staff in Library	1834	2076	2281	2298	2380	3078	3360
图书馆事业人员数	Number of People Engaged in Library	2243	2233	2178	2151	2149	2219	2226
群众文化事业人员数	Number of People Engaged in Public Art	4968	4786	4951	4943	5022	5044	4912
群众艺术馆人员	Number of People in Public Art Center	722	594	610	481	489	448	494
文化馆(站)人员	Number of People in Cultural Station	4246	4192	4341	4462	4533	4596	4418
#乡镇文化站	#Township Cultural Stations	2122	2013	2181	2175	2221	2256	2046

19-2 公共图书馆发展情况

DEVELOPMENT STATISTICS ON PUBLIC LIBRARIES

项　目	Item	2000	2005	2009	2010	2011	2012	2013
机构数 (个)	Number of Library (unit)	103	102	104	107	109	111	112
藏书数 (万册)	Total Collections (10 000 volumes)	1678	1923	2181	2361	2410	2521	2648
书架单层总长度 (万米)	Total Length of Bookshelves (10 000 m)	109	101	104	111	108	51	53
有效借书证数 (万个)	Valid Library card number (10 000 units)	41	72	129	104	95	138	108
图书流通情况	Number of Circulation							
公共图书馆流通人次 (万人次)	The public library circulation (10 000 person-times)	714	1145	1271	1516	1342	1516	1763
册次 (万册数)	Volume-time (10 000 volume-times)	949	927	1047	1846	1114	1386	1570
为读者服务举办各种活动	Service for Readers							
次数 (次)	Times (time)	1222	1621	2777	1790	2258	2928	3098
参加人数 (万人次)	Number of Readers Involved (10 000 person-times)	115	176	111	105	120	128	178
当年新购图书 (万册)	New Books Purchaesd in 2012 (10 000 volume-times)	36	43	68	60	82	111	138
图书费 (万元)	Purchase Expenses (10 000 yuan)	699	1296	1475	1847	2138	4210	5076

19-3 公共图书馆藏书及分类情况

STATISTICS ON BOOKS AND TYPE OF BOOKS IN PUBLIC LIBRARIES

单位：万册　　(10 000 volumes)

年份 Year	合　计 Total	#外　文 #Foreign	#古　籍 #Ancient	#图书 #New Books	其它藏量 Other Reserves
1996	1472	82	97		
1997	1533	81	97		
1998	1599	81	96		
1999	1643	81	96		
2000	1678	82	97		
2001	1709	83	98		
2002	1759	81	99		
2003	1819	83	98		
2004	1867		94		
2005	1923		97		
2006	1981		100		
2007	2037		96		
2008	2106		97		
2009	2181		96		
2010	2361		95		
2011	2410		98	1860	453
2012	2521		98	2008	415
2013	3050		99	2156	796

注：其它藏量包括报刊、视听文献、缩微制品、电子图书和其它,总藏量含电子图书

Note: Other reserves include newspapers, audiovisual documents, microform, electronic books and other materials.Contains a total electronic books

19-4 图书、报纸、期刊出版情况
STATISTICS ON PUBLICATION OF BOOKS, NEWSPAPERS AND PERIODICALS

项 目	Item	1990	2000	2005	2010	2011	2012	2013
一、图书出版种数（种）	Category of Library Books Published (kind)	2546	4529	6535	10464	11122	14256	13900
新出版 （种）	New Publications (kind)	1827	2443	3739	6328	6544	8476	8445
总印数 （千册）	Total Prints (1 000 volume)	402517	288416	345510	275330	260867	259720	262740
总印张 （千印张）	Total Number of Paper Printed (1 000 pages)	1418989	1552128	2495183	1997639	1965882	2045531	2088169
二、杂志出版种数（种）	Category of Magazines Published (kind)	254	391	407	407	407	408	408
总印数 （千册）	Total Prints (1000 volume)	73456	220280	196800	300770	301074	341410	309375
总印张 （千印张）	Total Number of Paper Printed (1 000 pages)	119523	746145	745526	1482345	1605161	1865793	1781708
三、报刊出版种数（种）	Category of Newspapers and Periodicals Published (kind)	84	164	193	130	130	130	130
总印数 （千份）	Total Prints (1 000 copies)	623820	1342282	1956980	1816720	2003780	2060760	1982020
总印张 （万印张）	Total Number of Paper Printed (10 000 pages)	44247	339434	520833	889514	889524	931133	858508

19-5 电影、艺术活动、群众文化活动、图书馆及博物馆活动情况
STATISTICS ON MOVIE, ART ACTIVITIES, PUBLIC CULTURE ACTIVITIES, LIBRARY AND MUSEUM

项　目	Item	1990	2000	2005	2010	2011	2012	2013
城市电影活动	Movie of city							
放映场次数（万场）	Times Projected (10 000 times)						95.40	128.09
观众人数（千人次）	Number of the audience (1000 person-times)						24496	33168
艺术活动	Art Activities							
年表演场次（场）	Annual Times of Performing (time)	13100	15000	16000	22850	22570	35920	37230
观众人数（千人次）	Number of Spectators (1000 person-times)	10620	21211	16939	28454	25648	30144	28801
年人均观看次数（次）	Annual Times of Watching Per Capita (time)	0.20	0.36	0.28	0.50	0.45	0.52	0.5
群众文化活动	Public Culture Activities							
举办展览个数（个）	Number of Expo Displayed (unit)	1166	2785	2653	4276	3282	3427	4045
举办训练班结业人数(万人次)	Number of Training Activities (10 000 person-times)	4.90	9.90	13.00	10.80	69.60	83.80	87.8
图书馆活动	Library Activities							
图书流通人次（千人次）	Number of Circulation (1000 person-times)	5480	7138	11453	15155	13419	15163	17628
图书流通册次（千册）	Number of Circulation (1000 volumes)	9600	9485	9267	18462	11141	13865	15701
人均年借阅册数（册）	Number of Books Borrowed Per Capita Annually (volume)	0.18	0.16	0.15	0.32	0.21	0.24	0.27
人均年借阅人数(次)	Number of People Borrowing Annually (person)	0.10	0.12	0.19	0.27	0.20	0.15	0.16
博物馆活动	Museum Activities							
现有陈列展览个数（个）	Number of Display at Present (unit)	145	210	218	686	682	937	796
参观人数（千人次）	Visitors (1000 persons)	2089	1819	2194	19212	16321	22297	23576
人均年参观次数（次）	Number of Visit Per Capia Annually (time)	0.04	0.03	0.04	0.34	0.29	0.39	0.41

19-6 艺术表演团体、群众艺术馆、文化馆经费情况
STATISTICS ON EXPENSES OF ART TROUPES, PUBLIC ART CENTERS AND CULTURE ACTIVITIES CENTERS

单位：万元 (10 000 yuan)

项 目	Item	2009	2010	2011	2012	2013
艺术表演团体	Art Troupes					
补贴团体 (个)	Subsidized Troupes (unit)	4	4	4	1	2
国家经费补贴	National Subsidy	8374	8082	8915	2868	2625
业务及其他收入	Revenue from Business and From Others	1709	5093	2154	831	462
#演出收入	#From Performing	474	559	842	243	243
总支出	Total Expenditure	9953	13504	11168	3406	3239
第三产业增加值	Value Added of Tertiary Industry	7013	7352	8636	2186	2343
经费自给率 (%)	Percentage of Self-supply Expenses (%)	16.0	37.0	19.2	24.0	14.0
群众艺术馆、文化馆(站)	Mass Art Galleries and Culture Galleries					
总支出	Total Expenditure	994	1392	2079	1985	2476
#预算	#Budget	850	1071	1320	1344	1959
#项目支出	#Project spending	104	653	759	1144	1452
修缮费	Maintainace Fees		153			
第三产业增加值	Value Added of Tertiary Industry	372	611	732	869	1207

注：本表各项指标仅指文化厅系统内的。
Note:Items in this table refer to those within culture bureau system.

19-7 文化、文物事业经费支出及基本建设情况
BASIC CONDITIONS ABOUT EXPENDITURES ON CULTURE AND HISTORICAL RELICS AND ITS CONSTRUCTION

单位：万元 (10 000 yuan)

项 目	Item	2009	2010	2011	2012	2013
文化、文物事业经费支出总计	**Total Expenditures on Culture and Historical Relics**	**198651**	**215061**	**244474**	**286344**	**333675**
文化事业	Culture	161906	170203	194222	218712	249298
艺术表演团体	Art Performing Groups	35968	39500	43000	43492	52952
艺术表演场所	Art Performing Places	5431	6244	12807	5245	9233
图书馆	Library	24833	31444	35003	34313	43633
群众文化	Public Culture	25284	26306	29273	36247	39667
中等专业学校	Secondary Vocation School	2184	2364	5533	3511	3276
干部训练	Cadre Taining					
其他文化事业	Others	68206	66719	74136	95833	100466
文物事业	Historical Relics	36745	42504	44719	67632	84377
博物馆	Museum	23628	30029	29256	38330	54176
文物事业机构	Institutions of Historical Relics	5134	6982	8567	19254	16912
其它文物事业	Others	7983	5492	6896	10048	13290
文化、文物基本建设完成投资	Investment in Culture & Historical Relics Cause Construction	56901	55110	83371	31446	83300
文化事业	Culture Cause	43374	24094	26533	21360	52887
文物事业	Historical Relics Cause	13527	31016	56838	10086	30413

19-8 广播电视从业人员基本情况(2013)
BASIC STATISTICS ON PERSONEL ENGAGED IN BROADCASTING AND TELEVISION (2013)

单位：人 (person)

		全省合计 Total of the Province	省级 Provincial Level	市州级 Municiple and Prefecture Level	县级 County Level
从业人员	Personel	38197	15974	8116	14107
其中：长期职工	#Long-term Staff and Workers	37210	15527	7970	13713
党员	Party Members(Communists)	15039	5335	3283	6421
按岗位分:	Classified by Job Division:				
管理人员	Management Personel	6608	2369	1386	2853
专业技术人员	Professional Technical Personel	20056	7840	5193	7023
编辑、记者	Editors and Reporters	5902	1163	2324	2415
播音员、主持人	Announcers and Hosts	1187	316	433	438
按学历分:	Classified by Academic Qualifications:				
研究生及以上	#Graduate and Above	862	559	254	49
本科及大专	Undergraduate and Post-secondary	24361	10515	6232	7614
高中及以下	High School and Below	12974	4900	1630	6444
按职称分:	Classified According to Occupation:				
正高	Senior	242	157	73	12
副高	Vice-senior	1283	688	516	79
中级	Medium	7447	2633	2089	2725
初级及以下	Primary and Below	18773	8599	3770	6404
按年龄分:	Classified by Age:				
35岁以下	35 and Below	14156	7374	2824	3958
36岁至50岁	36-50	18767	6846	4085	7836
50岁以上	50 and Above	5274	1754	1207	2313

19-9 广播电视传输覆盖与经济效益
STATISTICS ON BROADCASTING AND TV COVERAGE RATING AND ECONOMIC BENEFITS

项　目	Item	2005	2010	2011	2012	2013
广播覆盖率 (%)	Broadcasting Coverage Rate (%)	95.99	98.10	98.18	98.72	98.80
电视覆盖率 (%)	TV Coverage Rate (%)	96.71	98.11	98.23	98.75	98.81
有线电视用户 (万)	Cable Television Users (10 000 household)	508.13	894.07	987.75	1048.38	1045.31
中短波发射转播台/机 (座/部)	Medium and Short-Wave Transmitting Stations (set)	27/ 43	26/76	26/80	28/82	28/86
中短波发射转播台功率（千瓦）	Power of Medium and Short-Wave Transmitters (kw)	646.00	1256.00	1311.00	1331.00	1371
调频发射转播台 (座/部)	FM Transmitting Stations (set)	189/ 266	426/584	428/598	428/604	432/609
调频发射机功率 (千瓦)	Power of FM Transmitters (kw)	273.00	520.31	545.11	551.51	558.91
电视发射转播台 (座/部)	Television Transmitting Station (set)	1068/ 1399	991/1275	992/1273	991/1273	908/1191
电视发射转播台功率 (千瓦)	Power of Television Transmitters (kw)	335.62	592.22	598.12	590.43	583.88
微波线路站数/长度 (座/公里)	Length of Micro-Wave Route Per Station (set/km)	186/ 4894	121/2961.05	119/2936.05	119/2936.05	116/2906.05
创收收入 (亿元)	Revenue (100 million yuan)	21.86	48.57	57.35	63.09	73.12
固定资产原值 (亿元)	Original Price of Fixed Assets(100 million yuan)	46.91	90.43	102.08	116.90	95.31

19-10 广播电视宣传和节目制作
BROADCASTING PUBLICITY AND PROGRAM PRODUCTION

项 目	Item	2000	2005	2010	2011	2012	2013
广播电台 (座)	Broadcasting Station (unit)	13	11	11	8	6	7
电视台 (座)	TV Station (unit)	14	12	12	9	7	8
广播电视台 (座)	Radiated TV Station (unit)	65	71	71	74	76	75
广播节目套数 (套)	Number of Radio Programs (unit)	82	81	85	85	86	87
广播平均日播音时间 (小时)	Average Broadcasting Hour per Week (h)	821.70	1040.40	1225.65	1224.75	1263.00	1289.00
广播节目年制作能力 (万小时)	Annual Capacity of Radio Program Production (10 000 h)	21.18	20.59	23.54	23.63	23.07	24.29
电视节目套数 (套)	Number of TV Programs (unit)	70	113	114	114	115	117
电视平均周播出时间 (万小时)	Average TV Hour per Week (10 000 h)	0.42	1.05	1.26	1.26	1.32	1.32
电视节目年制作能力 (万小时)	Annual Capacity of TV program Production (10 000 h)	6.74	7.93	9.48	9.83	10.84	10.65
电视剧制作 (部/集)	Production of TV Series (episode)	16/ 280	11/ 208	11/314	11/315	12/424	5/151

19-11 分单位类型、分人员类型体育系统从业人员数(2013)
NUMBER OF STAFF AND WORKERS IN SPORTS COMMISSIONS(2013)

单位：人 (person)

		合计 Total	公务员 Civilian	管理人员 Administrator	专业技术人员				运动员 Athlete	工勤人员 Worker	其他 Others
					小计 Subtotal	其中：教练员 Coach	其中：科研人员 Scientific research personnel	其中：卫生技术人员 Health technical personnel			
合计	Total	5524	1016	1131	1374	852	29	14	1030	527	446
体育行政机关	Sports Administrative Authority	1193	1016							72	105
运动项目管理部门（优秀运动队）	Sports Management Department	1150		154	234	216		8	701	61	
本科院校	Undergraduate School	348			43	32			305		
体育运动学校	Sports School for athelets	444		75	321	146	4	3		47	1
少年儿童体育学校	Sports School for Kids	673		155	450	315	2	1	6	43	19
体育中学	Middle School for Athelets	32		6	22	9				4	
训练基地	Training Base	149		39	45	40		1	18	35	12
体育场馆	Stadium	892		442	175	93				203	72
体育科研机构	Sports Science Reaserch Institution	52		10	41		23			1	
其他事业单位	Other Institution	404		150	8	1				26	220
其它	Others	187		100	35			1		35	17

19-12 等级裁判员、运动员情况

NUMBER OF ATHLETES AND REFEREES IN GRADES

单位：人 (person)

项　目	Item	1990	2000	2005	2008	2009	2010	2011	2012	2013
等级裁判员合计	Number of Referees in Grades	843	1195	787	866	1467	1517	2017	1652	2308
国际裁判	International Referees							38		
国家级裁判	National Referees		29	25	12	10	11	211		
一级裁判	First Grade	357	143	115	208	492	378	299	403	377
二级裁判	Second Grade	486	1023	647	646	965	1128	1469	1249	1931
等级运动员合计	Number of Athletes in Grade	123	418	1171	1644	1507	1654	1559	1656	2331
国际运动健将	International Master of Sports		6	2	1	6	2	4	4	
运动健将	Master of Sports		36	36	57	51	21	54	54	
一级运动员	First Grade	35	10	267	188	179	194	217	265	201
二级运动员	Second Grade	88	366	866	1398	1271	1437	1284	1333	2130

19-13 体育竞赛成果情况
STATISTICS ON ACHIEVEMENT IN SPORTS COMPETITION

项 目	Item	1990	2000	2005	2008	2009	2010	2011	2012	2013
世界比赛获奖牌数（枚）	Number of Medals Won in International Games (unit)	10	13	5	19	34	12	80	64	51
金牌	Gold Medal	9	4	3	8	12	2	48	30	25
银牌	Silver Medal	1	6	2	4	10	3	19	21	9
铜牌	Bronze Medal		3		7	12	7	13	13	17
亚洲比赛获奖牌数（枚）	Number of Medals Won in Asia Games (unit)	51	5	7	5	23	13	17	24	11
金牌	Gold Medal	37	4	5		5	8	13	15	5
银牌	Silver Medal	7		2	1	9	4	4	7	4
铜牌	Bronze Medal	7	1		4	9	1		2	2
全国比赛获前六名（人）	Top Six Places in National Games (person)			155	270	315	134	524	461	356
第一名	First Place	52	35	24	31	49	21	99	82	57
第二名	Second Place	50	22	23	31	53	21	71	74	72
第三名	Third Place	40	21	27	48	51	17	90	76	82
第四名	Fourth Place	29	35	24	39	44	23	92	68	48
第五名	Fifth Place	31	29	31	32	66	30	103	86	65
第六名	Sixth Place	38	26	26	31	52	22	69	75	32

19-14 新建健身场地设施情况(2013)

	合计 Total	村级农民体育健身工程 Town-based Peasant Fitness Project	乡镇体育健身工程 County-based Fitness Project	全民健身路径工程 Citizen "Fitness Path" Project
数量 (个) Number (unit)	6051	2680	129	2551
器材件数 (件) Number of Instrument (piece)	17921			17751
场地面积 (m2) Area (m2)	3227785	1837164	197271	380115
场地长度 (m) Length (m)	65100			
投资总额(万元) Total Invenstment (10 000 Yuan)	142906	5814	1616	37057

SITUATION OF NEW-BUILT FITNESS FACILITIES

全民健身活动中心 Citizen Fitness Center	户外健身场地设施 Outdoor Fitness Facilities					其他场地设施 Other Fitness Facilities
	体育公园 Fitness Park	全民健身广场 Citizen Fitness Square	户外体育营地 Outdoor Fitness Center	社区运动场地 Community-based Fitness Square	健身步道 Fitness Path	
21	7	106	6	127	48	376
						170
172634	97400	172101	45200	188115		137785
					65100	
77571	10960	4121	247	2247	2646	626

主要统计指标解释

文化事业机构 指从事专业文化工作和为专业文化工作服务的独立建制的单位。不包括这些单位另外举办独立核算的其他机构和各部门的业余文化组织。该指标主要反映文化事业机构发展规模水平。

艺术表演团体 指从事戏曲、音乐、舞蹈、杂技等专业艺术表演，有独立帐户的单位，不包括半工半艺、半农半艺和民间职业剧团。该指标主要反映全国专业艺术表演团体发展规模水平。

艺术表演观众人数(人次) 指售票、包场演出或民族地区免费演出的艺术表演观众人次数，不包括彩排审查和内部观摩演出的观看人次数。该指标主要反映全国观看专业艺术表演团体演出的效益规模。

等级运动员 是指经考核正式批准授予运动员称号的运动员，等级称号由高到低依次为国际级运动健将、运动健将、一级运动员、二级运动员、三级运动员。

广播节目综合人口覆盖率 指根据国家广电总局制定的《广播电视人口覆盖率统计技术标准和方法》进行统计调查的，在对象区能接收到由中央、省、地区或县通过无线、有线或卫星等技术方式传播的各级广播节目的人口数占全国总人口数的百分比。

电视节目综合人口覆盖率 指根据国家广电总局制定的《广播电视人口覆盖率统计技术标准和方法》进行统计调查的，在对象区能接收到由中央、省、地区或县通过无线、有线或卫星等技术方式传播的各级电视节目的人口数占全国总人口数的百分比。

Explanatory Notes on Main Statistical Indicators

Cultural Institutions refer to units, which have their own organizational system and independent accounting system and specialize in or serve cultural development. They exclude other establishments run by these cultural institutions and amateur cultural groups established by various departments. This indicator reflects the development of cultural units.

Art Troupe refers to the troupe which is engaged in drama, opera, music, dance, acrobatics or other art performance, opens independent accounts with banks and has self-supporting accounting system; excluding the troupes which are engaged partly in industrial or agricultural activities, partly in art performance and the professional troupes organized by the people. This indicator reflects the development of national professional art troupes.

Number of Audience at Art Performance refers to the number of attendants at commercial shows, completely booked shows or free shows given in minority national areas, and does not include the number of spectators at rehearsals for examination and internal shows for study.

Certified Grade Athletes refer to those who are awarded the title of athletes through assessment. The titles rank from high to low as: international level athletes, national level athletes, first grade athletes, second grade athletes and third grade athletes.

Radio Coverage of Population refers to the percentage of population, which can receive central, provincial, city, prefecture, and county radio programs relayed by wireless, cable, satellite and other technical means, in the surveying area, to national total population, according to Statistical Standard and Method on Television and Radio Coverage of Population established by the State Administration of Broadcasting, Film and Television.

Television Coverage of Population refers to the percentage of population, which can receive central, provincial, city, prefecture, and county television programs relayed by wireless, cable, satellite and other technical means, in the surveying area, to national total population, according to Statistical Standard and Method on Television and Radio Coverage of Population established by the State Administration of Broadcasting, Film and Television.

20 公共管理及其他

Public Management and Other

资料整理：谢　涛

20-1 工会组织情况
BASIC STATISTICS ON LABOR UNION

年份 Year	工会基层组织数(个) Number of Grassroot Labor Union Organizations (unit)	全省已建工会的基层单位职工与会员人数(万人) Number of Grassroot Staff and Workers and Members of Established Labor Union in the Province(10 000 persons)				工会专职工作人员人数(万人) Number of Full-time Workers in Labor Union (10 000 persons)
		职工人数 Number of Staff and Workers	#女职工 #Women Workers	会员人数 Number of Members	#女会员 #Women Members	
1975	18872	280.22	83.18	174.72	56.24	0.87
1980	22802	387.95	139.20	299.41	94.91	1.04
1985	25286	484.68	192.32	404.58	156.62	2.76
1990	33990	559.00	227.00	498.00	198.00	3.40
1995	28461	564.34	230.90	511.11	207.49	1.81
1996	28459	584.30	238.16	527.09	213.08	2.88
1997	20151	472.60	192.65	419.72	168.89	2.68
1998	17488	445.80	183.90	400.90	163.90	2.30
1999	18976	442.97	178.21	396.90	155.03	3.18
2000	45251	532.31	197.81	475.57	176.87	2.45
2001	111309	728.94	218.68	660.82	198.25	2.45
2004	50391	755.90	276.69	721.46	262.74	2.95
2005	54893	856.07	298.78	771.95	279.94	3.09
2006	61627	904.15	314.67	856.95	296.39	3.76
2007	69886	1004.92	358.44	972.30	345.64	3.94
2008	79048	1099.78	382.72	1073.22	377.43	4.48
2009	83436	1160.45	418.82	1127.68	411.12	4.75
2010	88647	1220.52	437.50	1184.88	429.00	5.80
2011	107995	1319.08	462.18	1267.28	453.11	6.10
2012	120561	1336.09	491.49	1292.06	481.87	6.44
2013	130513	1348.45	494.94	1312.16	487.57	6.36

注：1．因文革期间工会统计中断，表中1970、1975、1978年数据根据年平均增长值推算
2．1994年工会基层组织数不包括“双停”企业数。

Notes:a)The data in 1970, 1975 and 1978 were calculated by the average growth rate because Labor Union statistics had been suspended in the period of "The Great Cultural Revolution".

b)The number of basic level Labor Union organizations in 1994 doesn't include the enterprises which stopped their production.

20−2　基层政权和村(居)委会情况

BASIC STATISTICS ON GRASSROOT REGIME AND VILLAGE COMMITTEES

单位：个　　　　(unit)

年份 Year	镇 Township	乡 Villages	街道办事处 Regional Office	居委会个数 Number of Committees	村委会个数 Number of Village Committees
1986	859	3700	178	3257	32796
1987	836	1257	186	3394	32738
1988	828	1260	215	3483	32354
1989	840	1143	298	3545	32094
1990	849	1123	293	3573	32703
1991	849	1121	307	3709	32595
1992	852	1117	297	3830	32716
1993	857	1097	214	3921	32674
1994	864	1092	218	3998	32636
1995	865	1038	236	4110	32547
1996	823	567	252	4170	32486
1997	840	552	252	4287	32393
1998	847	543	253	4364	32293
1999	850	488	271	4425	32187
2000	860	466	283	3619	32001
2001	735	228	250	3468	31191
2002	738	224	272	3265	27667
2003	735	224	273	3351	27127
2004	738	224	274	3356	26470
2005	733	217	277	3465	29534
2006	737	210	277	3545	25828
2007	734	210	279	3653	25722
2008	735	207	285	3794	25551
2009	740	204	283	3882	25517
2010	741	199	290	3983	25763
2011	742	194	297	4051	25643
2012	746	188	298	4032	25575
2013	757	175	300	4208	25452

20-3 社会福利事业、企业单位机构及人员数

BASIC STATISTICS ON NUMBER OF SOCIAL WELFARE ENTERPRISES AND PERSONS ENGAGED

单位：个 (unit)

项 目	Item	机构数 Number of Institutions					
		2000	2005	2010	2011	2012	2013
全省合计	**Total of the Province**	**4027**	**4358**	**6149**	**6807**	**8251**	**12000**
一、事业单位	Institution	2949	3425	5395	6084	7545	11375
(一)收养性事业单位	Adoptive Institutions	2459	2755	2520	2528	2545	2213
1.优抚休(疗)养院	Special Care Nursing Home	121	99	97	97	102	105
2.社会福利收养院	Welfare Homes	2338	2656	2423	2431	2443	2108
(二)非收养性事业单位	Non-Adoptive Institutions	490	670	2875	3556	5000	9162
1.烈士纪念建筑物管理单位	Managing Organizations on Martyrs Memorials	39	45	46	51	52	55
2.军队离退休干部管理机构	Managing Organizations on Veterans	90	97	106	107	106	108
3.军供站	Military Supply Station	8	8	9	9	9	9
4.社区服务机构	Community Service Centre	175	278	2315	2887	4330	8466
5.救助管理站	Home for Beggers and Vagrants			63	81	87	86
6.未成年人救助保护中心	Protection Centre for Street Children			13	81	78	66
7.殡葬事业单位	Funeral Units	105	131	132	136	147	172
#殡仪馆	#Funeral Home	78	81	83	82	84	88
8.福利彩票发行单位	Lottery Tickets Issuing Units	50	54	52	53	54	54
9.婚姻登记服务单位	Marriage Registration Service Center			97	108	93	99
10.救灾储备单位	Relief Unit			42	43	44	47
二、社会福利企业	Social Welfare Enterprises	1 078	933	754	723	706	625

20-3 续表 continued

单位：人 (person)

项　目	Item	人员数 Number of Persons Engaged in 2000	2005	2010	2011	2012	2013
全省合计	**Total of the Province**	**55845**	**51625**	**74891**	**76524**	**84733**	**95296**
一、事业单位	Institution	21342	25899	33401	37222	44100	56987
(一)收养性事业单位	Adoptive Institutions	14203	18132	18835	20017	19754	19871
1.优抚休(疗)养院	Special Care Nursing Home	2688	2999	2723	2700	2776	3088
2.社会福利收养院	Welfare Homes	11515	15133	16112	17317	16978	16783
(二)非收养性事业单位	Non-Adoptive Institutions	7139	7767	14566	17205	24346	37116
1.烈士纪念建筑物管理单位	Managing Organizations on Martyrs Memorials	645	699	597	618	670	695
2.军队离退休干部管理机构	Managing Organizations on Veterans	770	844	871	848	882	879
3.军供站	Military Supply Station	322	283	247	246	247	236
4.社区服务机构	Community Service Centre	2131	1940	7919	9851	16586	28863
5.救助管理站	Home for Beggers and Vagrants			553	818	805	871
6.未成年人救助保护中心	Protection Centre for Street Children			183	324	547	541
7.殡葬事业单位	Funeral Units	2661	3265	3152	3349	3440	3761
#殡仪馆	#Funeral Home	2264	2668	2552	2641	2575	2592
8.福利彩票发行单位	Lottery Tickets Issuing Units	218	201	430	492	488	536
9.婚姻登记服务单位	Marriage Registration Service Center			487	538	549	603
10.救灾储备单位	Relief Unit			127	121	132	131
二、社会福利企业	Social Welfare Enterprises	34503	25726	41490	39302	40633	38309

20-4 社会保险基本情况
BASIC CONDITIONS ABOUT SOCIAL INSURANCE

年份 year	失业保险 Unemployment Insurance		城镇职工基本养老保险 Basic Endowment Insurance for Urban and Rural Employees		工伤保险年末参保人数（万人）Participants at Year-end (10 000 persons)	年末参加生育保险人数（万人）Number of People Participated in Maternity Insurance at Year-end (10 000 persons)
	年末参保人数（万人）Participants at Year-end (10 000 persons)	全年发放失业保险金（亿元）Unemployed Relief Released (100 million yuan)	年末参保职工人数（万人）Participants at Year-end (10 000 persons)	年末参保离退休人数（万人）Retirees (10 000 persons)		
1996	392.9	0.4	353.2		177.6	137.8
1997	381.2	0.5	355.8		188.5	165.5
1998	378.2	0.5	413.1	107.4	190.0	168.8
1999	517.6	0.6	455.3	122.4	183.8	189.0
2000	459.6	1.6	465.6	130.4	185.0	191.3
2001	420.8	3.2	474.4	136.6	182.3	182.1
2002	416.1	5.4	532.7	154.5	183.2	182.7
2003	390.1	5.6	554.5	167.5	189.2	182.1
2004	391.3	4.0	586.1	194.7	187.2	179.9
2005	391.5	4.0	597.6	206.4	230.3	175.9
2006	395.5	3.7	630.2	220.5	275.5	194.5
2007	405.4	3.8	651.4	235.3	328.0	225.0
2008	422.6	3.6	671.7	252.4	350.7	315.4
2009	437.0	3.6	701.9	273.7	396.5	350.6
2010	464.5	3.9	749.1	301.3	444.5	388.7
2011	496.0	3.7	766.0	341.4	467.3	412.9
2012	501.4	3.8	801.4	367.3	505.8	444.7
2013	511.9	4.2	822.0	396.0	541.0	457.9

20-5 参加基本养老保险人数
NUMBER OF PRESONS PARTICIPATED IN BASIC ENDOEMENT INSURANCE

年份 Year	合计 Total	职工 Number of Employees	企业(含其他) Enterprises (including others)	离退休人员 Number of Retirees	企业(含其他) Enterprises (including others)
1996	353.2	353.2	353.2		
1997	355.8	355.8	355.8		
1998	520.5	413.1	413.1	107.4	107.4
1999	577.7	455.3	455.3	122.4	122.4
2000	596.0	465.6	465.6	130.4	130.4
2001	611.0	474.4	474.4	136.6	136.6
2002	687.2	532.7	481.5	154.5	147.2
2003	722.0	554.5	501.1	167.5	158.6
2004	780.8	586.1	530.6	194.7	184.5
2005	804.0	597.6	539.8	206.4	195.1
2006	850.7	630.2	570.0	220.5	207.5
2007	886.7	651.4	602.6	235.3	223.0
2008	924.1	671.7	628.7	252.4	238.7
2009	975.6	701.9	660.5	273.7	259.2
2010	1050.4	749.1	690.9	301.3	258.3
2011	1107.4	766.0	725.5	341.4	325.6
2012	1168.7	801.4	757.8	367.3	351.2
2013	1217.9	822.0	779.1	396.0	379.7

20-6 城乡各种福利院基本情况
BASIC CONDITIONS OF WELFARE HOUSES IN URBAN AND RURAL AREAS

年份 Year	单位数(个) Number of Units (unit)	职工人数(人) Number of Staff and Workers (person)	床位数(张) Number of Beds (unit)	收养人数(人) Number of People Adopted (person)
1986	3955	12373	52912	46818
1987	3655	12360	57698	49356
1988	3300	11901	57356	47448
1989	3285	11759	57022	47075
1990	3252	11854	57878	48017
1991	3130	11966	57839	47684
1992	3114	12361	61878	50885
1993	3101	12955	61389	51638
1994	3066	13280	63451	52866
1995	2977	13607	64417	53662
1996	2907	13664	65853	54987
1997	2715	14163	69970	57471
1998	2650	14392	72284	59753
1999	2603	14552	76203	63326
2000	2459	14203	77871	63901
2001	2191	14173	78119	62590
2002	2145	14414	79522	65564
2003	2123	14856	117511	103320
2004	2359	16344	156461	144042
2005	2755	18132	189486	168800
2006	2770	17705	198458	179385
2007	2616	17157	206049	188308
2008	2553	18395	210342	180286
2009	2504	18190	216211	185933
2010	2596	19571	228375	189782
2011	2690	21159	233503	190917
2012	2710	21106	240985	193466
2013	2365	21283	241671	183140

20-7 婚姻登记和离婚情况

STATISTICS ON MARRIAGE REGISTERATION AND DIVORCE

年份 Year	准予登记结婚(对) Marriage Registeration Granted (couple)	初婚(人) First Marriage (person)	再婚(人) Digamist(person)	离婚(对) Divorce (couple)	离婚率(‰) Rate of Divorce (‰)
1986	402315	785319	19311	6322	0.25
1987	417552	809808	25296	6660	0.26
1988	362654	698447	26861	7389	0.29
1989	413460	801171	25749	9203	0.35
1990	408688	790477	26899	9477	0.35
1991	424708	820092	29324	9584	0.35
1992	463279	897899	28659	10793	0.39
1993	425276	822044	28508	11937	0.43
1994	457324	884817	29831	12910	0.46
1995	482063	930832	33294	13340	0.46
1996	442532	851577	33487	14590	0.50
1997	426460	820615	32305	21260	0.72
1998	399900	763163	36637	24711	0.84
1999	376961	716175	37747	19519	0.66
2000	353781	673294	34268	21255	0.71
2001	335421	632188	38654	22077	0.74
2002	321517	605055	37979	24003	0.80
2003	329256	614244	44268	29375	0.98
2004	381472	710633	52311	46369	1.54
2005	394093	717495	70691	53394	1.77
2006	445672	822294	69050	57682	1.91
2007	485278	896768	73788	65876	2.17
2008	542251	1025496	59006	76003	2.49
2009	565400	1058851	71949	81133	2.84
2010	570810	1068715	72905	89549	3.11
2011	626912	1169771	84053	98874	3.18
2012	615861	1155365	76357	109862	3.81
2013	645767	1201344	90190	127604	4.40

20-8 残疾人基本情况

BASIC STATISTICS ON THE DISABLED

单位：万人 (10 000 persons)

年份 Year	残疾人总数 Total Number of the Disabled	听力语言残疾人数 Number of Those with Hearing and Speaking Impairment	视力残疾人数 Number of Those with Sight Impairment	智力残疾人数 Number of Those with Intelligence Weakness	肢体残疾人数 Number of Those with Physical Handicap	精神病残疾人数 Number of Those with Mental Illness	综合残疾人数 Number of Disabled with 2 or More Handincaps
1975	284.46	103.64	54.88	45.40	34.47	5.69	40.38
1980	302.28	110.13	58.32	48.25	36.63	6.04	42.91
1982	309.80	112.87	59.77	49.45	37.54	6.19	43.98
1983	313.99	114.39	60.58	50.12	38.05	6.28	44.57
1984	317.35	115.62	61.23	50.65	38.46	6.34	45.05
1985	321.37	117.08	62.00	51.30	38.95	6.42	45.62
1986	325.72	118.67	62.84	51.99	39.47	6.51	46.24
1987	330.42	120.38	63.75	52.74	40.04	6.61	46.90
1988	334.58	121.90	64.55	53.40	40.55	6.69	47.49
1989	339.35	123.64	65.47	54.17	41.12	6.78	48.17
1990	351.00	127.88	67.72	56.02	42.54	7.02	49.82
1991	355.71	129.59	68.63	56.78	43.11	7.11	50.49
1992	360.06	131.18	69.47	57.47	43.63	7.20	51.11
1993	364.82	132.91	70.39	58.23	44.21	7.29	51.79
1994	369.03	134.45	71.20	58.90	44.72	7.38	52.38
1995	372.47	135.70	71.86	59.45	45.14	7.45	52.87
1996	375.89	136.95	72.52	60.00	45.55	7.51	53.36
1997	378.95	138.06	73.11	60.49	45.92	7.58	53.79
1998	381.64	139.04	73.63	60.92	46.25	7.63	54.17
1999	383.00	139.68	73.68	61.20	46.42	7.68	54.35
2000	384.36	140.32	73.73	61.48	46.59	7.73	54.53
2001	388.58	141.53	74.85	62.17	47.08	7.74	55.21
2002	389.21	143.71	77.84	59.88	47.90	5.99	53.89
2003	390.11	144.04	78.07	60.02	48.01	6.00	54.02
2004	391.05	144.39	78.21	60.16	48.13	6.02	54.14
2005	392.01	144.83	78.39	60.30	48.26	6.04	54.19
2006	379.40	88.90	62.40	34.40	105.70	30.40	55.80
2007	379.40	88.90	62.40	34.40	105.70	30.40	55.80
2008	379.40	88.90	62.40	34.40	105.70	30.40	55.80
2009	379.40	88.90	62.40	34.40	105.70	30.40	55.80
2010	379.40	88.90	62.40	34.40	105.70	30.40	55.80
2011	379.40	88.90	62.40	34.40	105.70	30.40	55.80
2012	379.40	88.90	62.40	34.40	105.70	30.40	55.80
2013	379.40	88.90	62.40	34.40	105.70	30.40	55.80

注：1.本统计表2007年——2013年根据2006年第二次全国残疾人抽样调查资料推算。
2.精神病残疾人从15岁起算。

Notes:a)The figures in this table were caculated according to the national sample survey on the disabled in 2006.
b)The Metally disabled refers to those over 15.

20-9 刑事案件发、破案情况
STATISTICS ON OCCURANCE AND CLEARING UP OF CRIMINAL CASES

指 标	Item	1995	2000	2005	2009	2010	2011	2012	2013
刑事案件发案总数 (件)	Number of Criminal Cases Occurred (case)	85876	114866	147004	195836	221735	243521	335813	279638
刑事案件破案总数 (件)	Number of Criminal Cases Cleared (case)	73831	72796	71455	90916	76401	63849	139738	118092
刑事案件破案率 (%)	Rate of Criminal Cases Cleared (%)	86.0	63.4	48.6	46.4	34.5	26.2	41.6	42.2

20-10 城市交通事故与火灾情况
BASIC STATISTICS ON TRAFFIC ACCIDENTS AND FIRE ACCIDENTS

指 标	Item	1995	2000	2005	2010	2011	2012	2013
交通事故处理发生件数 (起)	Number of Traffic Accidents (case)	8336	20148	9585	6465	6490	6007	5798
死亡人数 (人)	Deaths (person)	3401	3792	2417	1967	1909	1822	1801
受伤人数 (人)	Injuries (person)	5353	16492	10555	7684	7609	6818	6353
折合经济损失 (万元)	Losses Converted into Money (10 000 yuan)	4460	7041	4958	3294.4	4029	5391	4473
火灾发生数 (起)	Number of Fire Accsidents (case)	1393	6780	9356	9333	8262	4951	2695
死亡人数 (人)	Deaths (person)	64	54	56	17	38	11	22
受伤人数 (人)	Injuries (person)	86	106	47	7	4	10	72
折合经济损失 (万元)	Losses Converted into Money (10 000 yuan)	3221	1754	1945	3565	6014	4927	4791

20-11 审查批捕、起诉情况

STATISTICS ON EXAMINATION, ARREST AND PROSECUTION

项　目	Item	1995	2000	2005	2009	2010	2011	2012	2013
受理批捕件数　(件)	Number of Cases (case)	18870	20378	19846	22915	9120	23175	28905	27194
受理批捕人数　(人)	Number of People Arrested (person)	31122	31245	29427	34545	13391	33822	43040	37801
批准逮捕　(人)	Number of Arrests Granted (person)	25257	25114	27063	31703	12081	30633	38468	31813
不批捕人数　(人)	Number of Non-Arrest (person)	1545	4329	1522	2185	1001	2473	3725	5616
受理审查起诉件数 (件)	Number of Cases Received (case)	21240	17660	21966	26506	10028	28574	46382	36882
受理审查起诉人数 (人)	Number of Prosecution Accepted (person)	33532	25416	33410	41393	15280	43393	75876	52541
起诉人数　(人)	Prosecutor (person)	24404	22396	26926	34575	11600	35501	47348	44947
不起诉人数　(人)	Non-prosecutor (person)	43	1019	982	1048	329	1173	1343	1806

20-12 检察机关查办职务犯罪情况

STATISTICS ON CRIMES COMMITTED BY TAKING ADVANTAGE OF DUTY BY PROCURATORIAL ORGAN

项　目	Item	1995	2000	2005	2009	2010	2011	2012	2013
受理案件件数　(件)	Number of Cases Dealt (case)	10906	8343	3125	2081	1074	1733	1840	2168
立案件数　(件)	Registered Cases (case)	3640	2034	1552	1593	988	1525	1651	1935
立案人数　(人)	Registered Offenders (person)	4290	2312	1682	1868	1228	1877	2127	2374
贪污贿赂件数　(件)	Number of Corruption and Bribe Cases (case)	3081	1821	1363	1330	801	1232	1290	1508
渎职侵权件数　(件)	Number of Malversation Cases (case)	559	213	189	263	187	1515	361	427
查办大案件数　(件)	Large Cases (case)	824	882	887	1050	1039	1000	1120	1429
#5万元以上件数	#Money Involved Above 50000 yuan	685	850	839	938	936	884	911	1319
查办要案人数　(人)	Number of Offender Involved in Large Cases (person)	110	108	139	153	133	144	152	173
#厅局级人数	#Number of Offenders at Bureau Level	4	11	17	16	10	16	16	15
提起公诉人数　(人)	Number of People Prosecuted (person)	1738	1490	1265	1494	1725	1535	1871	2053

20-13 律师、公证、调解工作基本情况
BASIC STATISTICS ON LAWYERS, NOTARIZATION AND MEDIATION

项　目	Item	1995	2000	2005	2010	2011	2012	2013
一、律师工作	Lawyers							
律师事务所 (个)	Number of Lawyer Office (person)	281	350	387	466	490	512	549
专职律师	Number of Full-Time Lawyer	1593	2383	3722	5869	6602	7300	7805
兼职律师	Number of Part-Time Lawyer	297	472	165	252	278	306	334
担任法律顾问 (家)	Number of Units with Legal Advisors (unit)	12763	9727	9565	12059	12706	14046	14339
民事案件诉讼代理 (件)	Agent of Civil Cases (case)	13190	21412	27079	45403	47831	61052	63917
经济案件诉讼代理 (件)	Agent of Economic Cases (case)	18689	18931	13799				
刑事诉讼辩护及代理 (件)	Defender and Agent of Criminal Cases (case)	8836	10078	11341	17724	17964	17095	19043
非诉讼法律事务 (件)	Agent of Non-Litigious Legal Affairs (case)	35542	25142	34674	37521	37940	38011	24310
涉外及港澳台法律事务(件)	Agent of Foreign, Hogkong, Maco and Taiwan Affairs (case)	582	305	5994				
解答法律咨询 (万人次)	Agent of Legal Advisory Services (10 000 (person-times)	9.91	11.37	15.23	11.01	12.70	12.58	11.12
代写法律事务文件 (万件)	Agent of Legal Document Written on Behalf of Clients (10 000 cases)	2.38	3.44	3.49	1.59	1.61	2.09	2.3
二、公证工作	Notarization							
公证机构 (个)	Number of Notary Offices (unit)	116	117	118	116	117	117	117
公证人员 (人)	Notarial Pesonel (person)	746	769	689	643	687	739	830
#公证员	#Notaries	404	506	455	353	378	367	387
公证员助理	Assistant Notaries	144	108	62	167	309	372	244
办理公证文件 (万件)	Number of Domestic Notarized Document (10 000 cases)	25.68	36.30	31.04	32.65	32.82	33.79	28.6
#涉外公证 (件)	#Foreign Notarized Documents (case)	22915	63993	65498	79723	80818	88877	91467
三、人民调解工作	People's Mediation							
司法助理员 (人)	Judicial Assistant (person)	2652	1732	2210	1682	2623	2698	2347
人民调解委员会 (万个)	Number of People's Mediation Committees (10 000 units)	5.09	4.90	3.70	3.62	3.43	3.43	3.44
调解人员 (万人)	Number of Mediators (10 000 persons)	55.87	38.53	17.20	20.43	16.20	15.81	15.87
调解纠纷总数 (万件)	Number of Disputes Mediated (10 000 cases)	32.53	26.47	21.62	22.85	27.20	28.33	30
调解成功总数 (万件)	Number of Successful Mediation (10 000 cases)	31.36	25.77	21.13	22.14	26.33	27.60	29.33

20-14 涉外公证文书分类情况
FOREIGN-RELATED NOTARIAL DOCUMENTS BY TYPE

单位：件 (case)

分类	Item	1995	2000	2005	2008	2009	2010	2011	2012	2013
合 计	**Total**	**22915**	**63993**	**65498**	**71672**	**70482**	**79723**	**80818**	**88877**	**91467**
出生	Births	3302	9748	7243	8254	6874	11567	12956	14791	10812
学历	Academic Degree	2742	9134	10078	16682	9078	7181	6138	5367	6754
经历	Personal Experience	654	1015	806	347	289	863	875	1068	294
生存和居住	Survival and Residence	183	74	102	48	61	67	54	62	88
死亡	Death	101	83	109	139	126	103	82	106	137
收养子女	Children Adoption	331	683	539	929	707	692	591	470	269
亲属关系	Kinship	1929	3225	3962	7665	6598	6605	7811	8562	7247
婚姻状况	Marital Status	1920	4228	3691	5979	5274	5774	5464	6670	3072
继承权	Rights of Inheritance	13	14	28	52	1003	94	81	35	122
遗嘱	Testament	31	18	18	35	43	82	75	38	48
职称	Title	337	438	141	231	21	172	239	131	15
身份	Identity	49	69	150	73	58	719	697	546	82
组织资格	Qualification of Organization	46	30	16	18	44	31	12	13	14
委托书	Trust Deed	359	133	293	298	31	643	948	1184	1916
公司章程	Chapter of Company	9	22	24	21	159	39	31	38	15
副本与原本相符	Confirmation of Copy and Photo-Offset Copies to Originals	2672	11532	7861	4389	3954	12982	11230	16069	19897
证书(执照)	Operation Document	25	139	186	32	202	285	264	1035	2392
声明书	Declaration	136	384	3972	1039	33	1140	1526	1649	1255
合同(协议)	Contract(Agreement)	142	16	372	43	37	46	36	18	28
受、未受刑事处分	Criminal Record & Uncriminal Record	2267	6646	6126	7857	6470	10359	11279	12788	7770
其他	Others	5667	16362	9916	9059	14868	11943	12339	9799	24622

20-15 履行法律监督情况
SUPERVISION ON LAW ENFORCEMENT

单位：人、件 (person, case)

项 目		1995	2000	2005	2009	2010	2011	2012	2013
监督公安机关立案件数	Number of Cases Registered by Public Security		247	554	951	1088	1150	2218	3243
监督追捕人数	Number of Criminals Hunted under Supervision	272	300	204	578	903	1387	2166	3063
监督追诉人数	Number of People Being Prosecuted	132	61	78	520	1130	1309	2103	3746
刑事抗诉件数	Number of Cases Against Crimnal Prosecutions	78	192	123	124	119	187	274	357
监督刑罚执行纠错人次	Person-times of Error Correction of Execution of Punishment	3005	3546	51	345	499	319	1587	4635
民事行政监督抗诉件数	Number of Counterappeal Civil Cases	260	894	514	409	432	404	435	303

20-16 调解民间纠纷分类
CIVIL DISPUTES MEDIATION BY TYPE

项 目	Item	调解纠纷(件) Number of Disputes Mediated (case)				各种纠纷所占比重(%) Proportion (%)			
		2010	2011	2012	2013	2010	2011	2012	2013
合计	**Total**	**64546**	**134674**	**196093**	**102052**	**100.0**	**100.0**	**100.0**	**100.0**
婚姻	Marriage	23998	24025	28264	22568	37.2	17.8	14.4	22.1
继承	Rights of Inheritance	540	572	685	613	0.8	0.4	0.3	0.6
房地产开发	Real Estate Development	1140	1615	3038	1229	1.8	1.2	1.5	1.2
运输合同	Transportation Contracts	188	244	261	210	0.3	0.2	0.1	0.2
买卖合同	Selling and Purchasing Contracts	3891	5710	8856	6096	6.0	4.2	4.5	6.0
借款合同	Loans Contracts	9966	12452	22761	14684	15.4	9.2	11.6	14.4
劳动争议	Labor Disputes	2361	4562	5990	3337	3.7	3.4	3.1	3.3
人身权	Personal Rights	10398	25777	44355	13297	16.1	19.1	22.6	13.0
所有权	Right of Ownership	2262	5399	10302	3067	3.5	4.0	5.3	3.0
其他	Others	9802	54318	71581	36951	15.2	40.3	36.5	36.2

20-17　人民法院审理一审案件情况

STATISTICS ON FIRST INSTANCE CASES IN PEOPLE'S COURT

单位：件　　(case)

年 份 Year	收案 Cases Received	刑事 Criminal Cases	民商事 Civil Cases	海事海商 Maritime	行政 Administration
1985	63079	12709	40660	26	
1990	227618	29086	166960		568
1995	257312	21391	174908	456	4359
1998	252403	17763	171025	606	6368
1999	238715	19598	151191	647	6247
2000	228804	19204	146838	618	6754
2001	22162	21741	14429	745	6560
2002	211464	19548	188163	525	3753
2003	193780	18943	171282	488	3555
2004	172889	18833	150682	592	3374
2005	155478	19672	132585	745	3221
2006	156885	19914	133584	606	3387
2007	161728	21719	137328	459	2681
2008	165099	22364	140072	746	2663
2009	173032	23481	147319	710	2232
2010	179631	22963	154299	781	2369
2011	280572	25074	249792	1458	5706
2012	395414	31489	354789	1501	9136
2013	422427	31621	387593	1914	3213

注：一审案件指人民法院按照诉讼级别管辖按第一审程序审理的案件。

Note:First instance cases refer to cases in the first instance process in People's Court.

20-18 人民法院刑事一审案件收结案情况

END OF FIRST INSTANCE CASES IN PEOPLE'S COURT OF CRIMINAL LAWSUITS

单位：件 (case)

项　目	Item	收案 Cases Received				结案 Cases Closed			
		2010	2011	2012	2013	2010	2011	2012	2013
合　计	**Total**	**22963**	**25074**	**31489**	**31621**	**23209**	**24698**	**30912**	**31188**
危害公共安全罪	Crimes Harming Public Security	2863	3602	5009	5564	2894	3566	4964	5455
破坏社会主义市场经济秩序罪	Crimes Harming Socialism Market Economy Order	807	946	1319	1590	811	913	1261	1566
侵害公民人生权利民主权利罪	Crimes against Rights in Human Life and Democratic Rights	5941	6237	7011	6650	6048	6140	6919	6518
侵犯财产罪	Property Violation	8144	8506	10435	9086	8207	8405	10164	9134
妨害社会管理秩序罪	Crimes Harming Social Management Order	3937	4545	6296	7233	3957	4489	6187	7097
危害国防利益罪	Crimes Harimg National Defense Interests	7	5	10	6	7	5	9	7
贪污贿赂罪	Corruption and Bribe	1120	1093	1190	1242	1148	1050	1186	1188
渎职罪	Malversation	142	137	214	235	135	127	218	211
其他	Others	2	3	5	15	2	3	4	12
合计中含自诉案件	Self-Suing Cases	490	383	271	184	532	426	281	184

20-19 人民法院刑事案件中青少年犯罪情况

STATISTICS ON JUVENILE DELINQUENCY IN PEOPLE'S COURT OF CRIMINAL LAWSUITS

单位：人 (person)

年份 Year	刑事犯罪总数 Total Number of Criminal Cases	青少年犯罪 Juvenile Delinquency	不满18岁 Juvenile Age under 18	18-25岁 Age 18-25	青少年罪犯刑事罪犯率% Percentage of Juvenile Delinquency in Criminal Cases %
1999	20534	6836	1302	5534	33.3
2000	20076	5922	1279	4643	29.5
2001	22911	6597	1774	4823	28.8
2002	20868	5669	1901	3768	27.2
2003	20908	6207	2328	3879	29.7
2004	20429	5838	2633	3205	28.6
2005	21669	6283	2939	3344	29.0
2006	22876	6933	2945	3988	30.3
2007	17368	7459	3131	4328	43.0
2008	26682	6810	3030	3780	25.5
2009	28507	7700	2930	4770	27.0
2010	27928	7058	2287	4771	25.3
2011	29280	7263	2229	5034	24.8
2012	35419	7327	2050	5277	20.7
2013	33871	5398	1365	4033	15.90

20-20 人民法院民事一审案件收结案情况(2013)
STATISTICS ON END OF FIRST INSTANCE CASES IN PEOPLE'S COURT OF CIVIL LAWSUITS (2013)

单位：件 (case)

项目	Item	收案 Cases Received	结案 Cases Ended	调解 Mediated	判决 Judgement	驳回 Cases Rejected	撤诉 Cases Withdraw	其他 Others
合计	**Total**	**387593**	**382735**	**102052**	**78050**	**4931**	**105467**	**92235**
婚姻家庭	Marriage	49515	48969	22568	14031	142	12077	151
继承	Rights of Inheritance	1246	1213	613	311	7	276	6
知识产权	Intelligence Property Rights	5937	5634	2492	1494	5	1512	131
房地产开发	Real Estate Development	3283	3257	1229	933	23	1042	30
运输合同	Transportation Contracts	580	545	210	174	4	154	3
买卖合同	Selling and Purchasing Contracts	17430	17236	6096	3527	64	7399	150
借款合同	Loans Contracts	46715	45897	14684	8369	231	22363	250
劳动争议	Labor Disputes	10315	10041	3337	3011	130	3423	140
海事海商	Martial Commerce	1914	1985	554	964	17	442	8
人身权	Personal Right	30809	30405	13297	9242	69	7630	167
特别程序	Special Procedure	143711	143380	10843	23233	3882	14801	90621
破产	Bankruptcy	49	109		4	1	9	95
所有权及与其相关合同	Rights of Ownership and Relevant Contracts	8747	8499	3067	1550	88	3691	103
其他	Others	67342	65565	23062	11207	268	30648	380

注：结案中含上年旧存。
Note:The statistics of ended cases include statistics of last year.

20-21 人民法院行政一审案件收结案情况(2013)
STATISTICS ON END OF FIRST INSTANCE CASES IN PEOPLE'S COURT OF ADMINISTRATION (2013)

单位：件 (case)

项目	Item	收案 Cases Received	结案 Cases Ended	维持 Cases Maintained	撤消 Cases Cancled	驳回 Cases Rejected	撤诉 Cases Withdraw	单独赔偿 Sole Compensation	其他 Others
合计	**Total**	**3213**	**3128**	**285**	**226**	**434**	**1465**	**2**	**716**
土地	Land	354	343	20	30	40	136		117
公安	Public Security	398	386	49	7	40	231		59
城建	City Construction	686	679	10	49	98	387		135
交通运输	Transportation	80	79	1		6	58		14
工商	Industry and Commerce	152	157	14	8	16	85		34
环保	Environment	12	13			1	12		
林业	Forestry	107	99	14	26	20	33		6
税务	Taxes	2	2				1		1
卫生	Sanitary and Hygiene	19	19	2	3	3	4		7
其他	Others	1403	1351	175	103	210	518	2	343

注：结案中含上年旧存。
Note:The statistics of ended cases include statistics of last year.

主要统计指标解释

社会福利事业单位 指集中收养社会孤老、残、幼的机构，包括由民政部门管理的社会福利院、儿童福利院、精神病人福利院和城镇集体举办的福利院及农村集体举办的敬老院以及优抚医院和具有收养能力的社区服务中心等。该指标主要反映我国在社会福利性单位投入的水平。

社会福利事业单位收养人数 包括民政部门管理和城镇、农村集体举办的社会福利事业单位中收养的老人、少年儿童、缺乏生活自理能力的残疾人员和精神病人。该指标主要反映收养性社会福利单位的收养能力。

社会福利企业单位 指以安置城镇有一定劳动能力的盲、聋、哑和肢体残疾人员就业为目的，享受国家减免税待遇的国有或集体企业。包括福利工厂、福利商业和服务业、假肢厂和安置农场等单位。该指标主要反映我国对残疾人照顾的特殊政策。

粗离婚率 指当年离婚对数占年平均人口的比重，计算公式为:

$$粗离婚率=\frac{当年离婚对数}{年平均人口数}\times 1000‰$$

基本养老保险

1.（参保）职工人数：指报告期末按照国家法律、法规和有关政策规定参加基本养老保险并在社保经办机构已建立缴费记录档案的职工人数，包括中断缴费但未终止养老保险关系的职工人数，不包括只登记未建立缴费记录档案的人数。

2.（参保）离退休人员人数：指报告期末参加基本养老保险的离休、退休和退职人员的人数。

3.基本养老保险基金收入：指根据国家有关规定，由纳入基本养老保险范围的缴费单位和个人按国家规定的缴费基数和缴费比例缴纳的养老保险基金，以及通过其他方式取得的形成基金来源的收入。包括单位和职工个人缴纳的基本养老保险费、基本养老保险基金利息收入、上级补助收入、下级上解收入、转移收入、财政补贴和其他收入。

4.基本养老保险基金支出：指按照国家政策规定的开支范围和开支标准从养老保险基金中支付给参加基本养老保险的离休、通休、退职人员个人的养老金、丧葬抚恤补助，以及由于保险关系转移、上下级之间调剂资金等原因而发生的支出。包括离休金、退休金、退职金、各种补贴、医疗费、死亡丧葬补助费、抚恤救济费、社会保险经办机构管理费、补助下级支出、上解上级支出、转移支出、其他支出等。

5.基本养老保险基金累计结余：指截止报告期末基本养老保险基金收支相抵后的累计余额。

离休、退休、退职人员 指正式办理了离休、退休、退职手续，并享受相应的离休、退休、退职待遇的人员。

基本医疗保险

1.参保人数：指报告期末按国家有关规定参加基本医疗保险的人数。包括参加保险的职工人数和退休人员人数。

2.基金收入：指根据国家有关规定，由纳入基本医疗保险范围的缴费单位和个人，按国家规定的缴费基数和缴费比例缴纳的基金，以及通过其他方式取得的形成基金来源的款项，包括：单位缴纳的社会统筹基金收入、个人缴纳的个人账户基金收入、财政补贴收入、利息收入、其他收入。

3.基金支出：指按照国家政策规定的开支范围和开支标准从社会统筹基金中支付给参加基本医疗保险的职工和退休人员的医疗保险待遇支出，和从个人帐户基金中支付给参加基本医疗保险的职工和退休人员的医疗费用支出，以及其他支出。包括：住院医疗费用支出、门急诊医疗费用支出、个人账户基金支出、其他支出。

4.基金累计结余：指截止报告期末基本医疗保险的社会统筹和个人帐户基金累计结余金额。包括银行存款、财政专户、债券投资和其他。

失业保险

1.参保人数：指报告期末按照国家法律、法规和有关政策规定参加了失业保险的城镇企业事业单位的职工及地方政府规定参加失业保险的其他人员的人数。

2.失业保险基金收入：指按照规定从企业、事业及其他单位筹集的失业保险费及其他并入失业保险基金收入的总额。包括单位和个人缴纳的失业保险费、失业保险基金利息收入、上级补助收入、下级上解收入、转移收入、财政补贴和其他收入。

3.失业保险基金支出：指报告期内为保障失业人员和下岗职工基本生活、促进其再就业等支出的基金总额。包括失业救济金、医疗费、死亡丧葬补助费、抚恤救济费、转业训练费支出、失业保险经办机构管理费、补助下级支出、上解上级支出、转移支出和其他支出。

4.基金累计结余：指截止报告期末失业保险基金收支相抵后的累计余额。

工伤保险

1.参加保险人数：指报告期末依据国家有关规定参加工伤保险的职工人数。

2.享受保险待遇人数：指劳动者因工负伤致残、死亡或因患职业病致残，根据有关规定享受工伤保险待遇职工或供养直系亲属人数。包括伤残人数、职业病人数、因工死亡人数、供养直系亲属人数。

3.基金收入：指根据国家有关规定，由参加工伤保险的单位按国家规定的缴费基数和缴费比例缴纳的工伤保险基金，以及通过其他形式取得的形成基金来源的款项。包括：单位缴纳的社会统筹基金收入、财政补贴收入、利息收入、其他收入。

4.基金支出：指按照国家政策规定的开支范围和开支标准从工伤保险基金中支付给参加工伤保险的人员及供养直系亲属工伤保险待遇支出及其他支出。包括工伤医疗费、伤残补助金、工亡补助金、护理费、丧葬补助费、工伤预防费用、职业康复费用和其他支出。

5.基金累计结余：指截止报告期末工伤保险基金累计结余金额。包括银行存款、财政专户、债券投资和其他。

生育保险

1.参保人数：指报告期末依据有关规定参加生育保险的职工人数。

2.基金收入：指根据国家有关规定，由参加生育保险的单位按照国家规定的缴费基数和缴费比例缴纳的生育保险基金，以及通过其他方式取得的形成基金来源的款项，包括：单位缴纳的基金收入、利息收入和其他收入。

3.基金支出：指按照国家政策规定的开支范围和开支标准，从生育保险基金中支付给参加生育保险的职工，因妊娠、分娩和计划生育手术而享受的待遇及其他支出。包括：生育津贴、医疗费用支出及其他支出。

4.基金累计结余：指截止报告期末生育保险基金累计结余金额。包括银行存款、财政专户、债券投资和其他。

离休、退休、退职人员保险福利费用　指离休、退休、退职人员实际得到的生活费用总额，包括从社会保险经办机构和单位得到的费用。

1.离休金：指按规定支付给离休人员的生活费用。

2.退休金：指按规定支付给退休人员的生活费用。

3.退职生活费：指按规定支付给退职人员的生活费用。

4.医疗卫生费：指单位直接支付给离休、退休、退职人员的医疗费、住院费以及住院伙食补助等费用。

5.其他：指离休金、退休金、退职生活费和医疗卫生费以外的其他保险福利费用，如丧葬抚恤救济费、生活补贴、物价补贴、冬季取暖补贴等。

律师　指依法取得律师执业证书，担任法律顾问，民事(刑事、行政)案件代理人、刑事案件辩护人、办理非诉讼业务，解答法律询问，代写法律事务文书等，为社会提供法律服务的人员。

公证人员　指在公证处工作的人员总称，包括公证处主任、副主任、公证员、公证员助理(助理公证员)和其他从事辅助性工作的人员。

公证文书　指公证处根据当事人申请，依照事实和法律，按照法定程序制作的，具有法律效力的司法证明文书。根据公证书用途和使用地，公证书分为国内公证书、国内经济公证书、涉外民事公证书、涉外经济公证书四类。

调解员　指在人民调解委员会担负调解民间纠纷工作的人员，包括调解委员会的委员和调解小组的调解员。该指标主要反映从事人民调解工作的人员数量。

调解民间纠纷　指调解委员会按照法律规定，根据自愿原则，用说服教育的方法调解民间发生的有关民事权利和义务争执的件数，包括调解成功数和调解未成功数。该指标主要反映人民调解委员会的工作量。

立案　指人民检察院对受理的报案、控告、举报或自首及自行发现的犯罪线索、犯罪嫌疑人进行初步调查后，认为存在职务犯罪事实和应追究刑事责任，并决定作为刑事案件进行侦查的诉讼活动，是追究犯罪的开始。该指标主要反映人民检察院依法将职务犯罪线索作为刑事案件进行侦查的诉讼活动。

大案　指贪污、贿赂案数额在 5 万元以上，挪用公款案数额在 10 万元以上，集体私分、巨额财产来源不明、隐瞒境外存款案数额在 50 万元以上以及按照《人民检察院直接受理的渎职、侵权重、特大案件标准(试行)》认定的案件。该指标主要反映人民检察院立案查办的职务犯罪案件中经济损失大、社会危害严重的案件。

要案　指县、处级以上干部的犯罪案件。该指标主要反映国家工作人员中县、处级以上干部因职务犯罪被人民检察院依法立案侦查的情况。

决定逮捕　指人民检察院对直接受理、自行侦查的案件，认为需要逮捕犯罪嫌疑人时，依据法律做出的逮捕决定。该指标主要反映人民检察院对直接受理的案件行使决定逮捕权的情况。

批准逮捕　指人民检察院对公安机关、国家安全机关、监狱管理机关提出逮捕的犯罪嫌疑人进行审查，根据事实，依法做出逮捕决定。该指标主要反映人民检察院对提请逮捕机关提请逮捕犯罪嫌疑人进行审查后依法做出批准逮捕决定的情况。

决定起诉　指人民检察院对公安机关、国家安全机关、监狱管理机关和检察机关内设机构反贪污贿赂部门等移送起诉的案件进行审查，根据事实，做出提起公诉的案件。该指标主要反映人民检察院对各种刑事案件向人民法院提起公诉的情况。

申诉　指经检察机关信访部门审查处理后，移送到检察机关申诉部门的申诉案件，包括不服检察机关处理决定和不服法院刑事判决和裁定的申诉的案件。

受理劳动争议案件数　指劳动争议仲裁委员会根据国家有关规定，对劳动争议当事人的申请予以审查，符合受理条件而正式立案、准备处理的劳动争议案件数。

Explanatory Notes on Main Statistical Indicators

Social Welfare Institutions　refer to institutions taking care of old people without children, handicapped people and orphans. They include social welfare institutions run by civil affairs departments, children welfare institutions, social welfare institutions for mental patients, collective-owned old people's homes in rural areas, convalescent homes and community service centers with the capacity of receiving those people. This indicator reflects the input in social welfare institutions.

Number of People Taken in by Social Welfare Institutions　refers to the number of old people, children, totally dependent handicapped people and mental patients taken in by social welfare institutions run by civil affairs departments and those run by collective units in urban and rural areas. This indicator reflects the capacity of social welfare institutions.

Social Welfare Enterprises　are collective owned enterprises which employ the blind, deaf-mute, and other handicapped people who are able to work in cities and towns and enjoy exemption from state taxes, including welfare plants, welfare commercial services, artificial limb plants and farms, etc. This indicator reflects the preferential policies toward disabled persons.

Crude Divorce Rate　refers to proportion of divorced people to the annual average population for the reference year, the formula is:

Crude Divorce rate= number of couples divorced for the reference year/annual average population x 1000 per thousand

Basic Medical Care Insurance:

1. Number of people participating in the insurance programme refers to people participating in the basic medical care insurance programme according to related regulations by the end of reference period, including number of staff and workers and retirees participating in this insurance programme.

2. Revenue of insurance programme refer to payments made by employers and individuals participating in medical care insurance programs in accordance with the basis and proportion stipulated in state regulations, and income from other sources that become source of medical insurance fund, including income of social comprehensive funds paid by employers, income from individual accounts, government financial subsidies, interest income and other income.

3. Expenses of insurance programme refer to payment made from social comprehensive funds to those retired and resigned people covered in basic medical care insurance within the scope and standards of expenditure according to related national policies, and medical care payment made from individual accounts to staff and workers and retirees, and other expenses, including medical expenses of hospital inpatients, medical expenses for outpatients and emergency patients, payment from individual accounts and other

expenditure.

4. Balance of basic medical care insurance refer to the balance of medical care insurance of social comprehensive funds and individual accounts at the end of the reference period, including bank savings, special fiscal accounts, investment in bonds and others.

Unemployment Insurance

1. Number of people covered refers to staff and workers in urban enterprises or institutions who have participated in unemployment insurance programme in line relevant policies and regulations, and other people who have participated according to local government regulations, by the end of reference period.

2. Revenue of unemployment insurance refer to payments made by employers and individuals participating in unemployment insurance programme in accordance with relevant regulations and other income contributed to this programme, including unemployment insurance premium made by employers and individuals, interest income, subsidies from higher level agencies, income as transfer from subordinate agencies, transferred income, government financial subsidies and other income.

3. Expenses of unemployment insurance refer to total expenses during the reference period to guarantee the basic livelihood of unemployed people and laid-off staff and workers and to encourage their re-employment. Included are unemployment relief, medical fees, funeral subsidies, compensation pension, training expenses, management fees for unemployment insurance agencies, subsidies to lower level agencies, expenses as transfer to higher level agencies, transferred expenditure and other expenditure.

4. Balance of unemployment insurance refer to the balance of unemployment revenue deducting unemployment expenses at the end of the reference period.

Work Injury Insurance

1. Number of people covered refers to staff and workers who have participated in work injury insurance programme in line with relevant national regulations.

2. Number of beneficiaries refers to staff and workers and their direct dependents who can, in line with relevant regulations, benefit from work injury insurance, as a result of work injury leading to disability or death of the staff/worker, or occupational disease leading to disability. Included in this category are number of injured and disabled people, number of people with occupational diseases, number of deaths at work places, and number of direct dependents.

3. Revenue of work injury insurance refer to payments made by employers participating in work injury insurance programs in accordance with the basis and proportion stipulated in state regulations, and income from other sources that become source of work injury insurance fund, including income of social comprehensive funds paid by employers, government financial subsidies, interest income and other income.

4. Expenses of work injury insurance refer to payments made from work injury insurance funds to those who participated in the work injury insurance programme and their direct dependents within the scope and standards of expenditure according to related national policies, and other expenditure, including medical fees for work injury, injury and disability subsidies, death subsidies, nursing fees, funeral subsidies, injury prevention fees, rehabilitation fees for occupational diseases and other expenditure.

5. Balance of work injury insurance refer to the balance of the work injury funds at the end of the reference period, including bank savings, special fiscal account, investment in bonds and others.

Maternity Insurance

1. Number of people covered refers to staff and workers who have participated in maternity insurance programme according to relevant regulation at the end of the reporting period.

2. Revenue of maternity insurance refers to payments made by employers participating in maternity insurance programs in accordance with the basis and proportion stipulated in state regulations, and income from other sources that become source of maternity insurance fund, including income of funds paid by employers, interest income and other income.

3. Expenses of maternity insurance refer to payments made from maternity insurance funds to staff and workers who participated in maternity insurance programme within the scope and standards of expenditure according to related national policies, expenses paid for pregnancy, child delivery or surgeries related to family planning, and other expenditure, including allowance for child bearing, medical fees and other expenditure.

4. Balance of the maternity insurance refers to the balance of the maternity insurance funds at the end of reference period, including bank savings, special fiscal account, investment in funds and others.

Insurance and Welfare Funds for Retirees refer to the total payment for living expenses actually received by retirees, including payment received from social insurance management agencies and units.

1. Pensions for retired veteran cadres refer to living expenses paid to retired veteran cadres according to related regulations.

2. Pensions for retirement refer to living expenses paid to retired staff and workers according to related regulations.

3. Living allowances for resigned staff and workers refer to living expenses paid to resigned staff and workers according to related regulation.

4. Medical care expenses refer to medical fees, hospitalization cost and per diem subsidies during hospitalizations paid by employers directly to retirees.

5. Others refer to insurance and welfare payments other than the above-mentioned payments, including funeral subsidies, living allowances, price subsidies and heating subsidies during winter.

Lawyers are certified legal workers according to law, and who are employed by legal counseling firms to act as legal advisers, agents in criminal or civil lawsuits, or defenders in criminal lawsuits, or to handle non-litigious legal affairs, to advise on matters of law or to write legal papers for others, and provide service to the public.

Notary Personnel refers to people working for notary offices including: directors, deputy director, notaries, assistant notaries, and other people providing assistance.

Notary Documents refer to the judicatory notary documents drawn up by the request of the party and are in accordance with facts and laws and following certain legal proceedings. According to usage and locality, the notary documents are divided into following 4 types: domestic notary documents, domestic economic notary documents, foreign-related civil notary documents and foreign-related economic notary documents.

Mediators refer to workers on peoples mediation committees responsible for mediating in civil disputes and cases of slight infraction of the law. They include members of the mediation committees and mediators of mediation groups. This indicator reflects the number of people engaged in meditation.

Mediation of Civil Disputes refers to number of cases made by mediation committees in mediating in civil disputes concerning civil rights and duties through persuasion and education in accordance with the provisions of law on a voluntary basis, so as to solve disputes by helping the parties involved come to an agreement and understanding, including those unsuccessful ones. This indicator reflects the workload of the mediation committees.

Acceptance of Case refers to the decision made by the people's procuratorate office on reported cases, prosecution, impeachment, surrender, self-found criminal clues or suspects after initial investigation to confirm the act of crime and to start legal proceedings of the case as criminal case.

Large Cases refer to cases involving a corruption or bribery of over 50,000 yuan, or a misappropriation of over 100,000 yuan. Cases of collectively illegal possession of public funds, unstated sources of large properties, or disguised overseas savings deposits involving 500,000 yuan, or a case that has been defined by the "Standard on Serious and Large Cases of Misconduct and Tortious that Directly Accepted by People's Procurators Office (trial)". This indicator mainly reflects number of accepted cases of job-related criminals that caused serious economic losses or extremely harmful to the society.

Key Cases refer to cases committed by government officials with a ranking of division director or county administrator. This indicator mainly reflects the recorded and spied on cases by the people's procurators offices toward government official with a ranking of division director or county administrator.

Decision on Arrest refers to decision made by people's procurators office, in accordance with laws, to arrest the suspect(s) in the cases that are accepted and to be investigated by procurators office. This indicator mainly reflects the implementation of the decision on arrest by people's procurators office.

Approval for Arrest refers to the decision made by people's procurators office, in accordance with laws and relevant facts, to approve the arrest of the suspect(s) that is proposed by the public security departments, state security departments or authority of prisons. This indicator reflects approved arrests made by people's procurators office that are proposed by related departments.

Decision on Prosecution refers to the decision made by people's procurators office, in accordance with laws and relevant facts, to institute proceedings to the people's court against the suspect(s) of criminal cases handed over by the public security departments, state security departments or authority of prisons, or by the anti-corruption departments within the procurators office. This indicator reflects the condition of the prosecutions made by people's procurators office toward the people's court.

Appeals refer to cases transferred to the appeal departments of procurator's offices after initial review by departments dealing with complaint letters and calls of the public. Included are appeals against decisions made by procurator's offices and appeals against court rules and verdicts.

Number of Labor Dispute Cases Accepted refers to the number of cases of labor dispute submitted that, after being reviewed by the labor dispute arbitration committees in line with the relevant national regulations, are accepted and registered for treatment.

Basic Pension Insurance

1.Number of staff and workers covered refer to staff and workers participating in basic pension insurance programme in line with national laws, regulations and related policies by the end of reference period, who have already had payment records in social security management agencies, including those who interrupt payment without terminating the insurance programme. Those who have registered in the programme with no payment records are not included.

2. Number of retirees participating in basic pension insurance programme refer to number of retirees participating in basic pension insurance programme by the end of reference period.

3. Revenue of basic pension insurance refer to payments made by employers and individuals participating in pension insurance programs in accordance with the basis and proportion stipulated in state regulations, and income from other sources that become source of pension insurance fund, including the premium paid by employers and staff and works, interest income, subsidies from higher level agencies, income as transfer from subordinate agencies, transferred income, government financial subsidies and other income.

4. Expenses of basic pension insurance refer to payment made to those retired and resigned people covered in pension insurance program in terms of pension or compensation within the scope and standards of expenditure according to related national policies, and expenditure occurred due to shift of the insurance relationship or adjustment of funds among agencies, including pension for resigned people, pension for retired people, pension for people quitting jobs, various subsidies, medical fees, funeral subsidies, compensation pension, management fees for social security agencies, expenses on subsidies to lower subordinates, expenses as transfer to agencies at higher level, transferred expenditure and other expenditure.

5. Balance of basic pension insurance refers to the balance of basic pension insurance at the end of the reference period after deducting expenses from revenue.

Retired or Resigned Personnel refers to people who have formally completed formalities for their retirement or quitting work and enjoy the corresponding retirement treatments.

21 开发区主要经济指标

Major Economic Indicators of Development Zone

资料整理：陶　禹

21-1 湖北省开发区经济发展基本情况(2013)

BASIC INDICATORS OF ECONOMIC DEVELOPMENT OF DEVELOPMAENT ZONE IN HUBEI PROVINCE(2013)

指 标		Item		2012	2013	增幅(%) Percentage of Increase (%)
基本情况		**Basic condition**				
开发区批准规划面积	(平方公里)	Floor Areas Approved in Development Zone	(sq.km.)	4097.2	5106.9	24.6
开发区实际占地面积	(平方公里)	Actual Land Areas of Development Zone	(sq.km.)	1618.1	1976.6	22.2
企业个数	(个)	Number of Enterprises	(unit)	70658	84468	19.5
其中：工业企业	(个)	#Those Belong to Industrial Enterprises	(unit)	25382	29546	16.4
其中：规模以上	(个)	#Enterprises above Designated Scale	(unit)	7578	8642	14.0
高新技术企业	(个)	High and New Technological Enterprises	(unit)	1673	1919	14.7
外商投资企业	(个)	Foreign Invested Enterprises	(unit)	1621	1734	7.0
从业人员	(万人)	Population of Employment	(10 000 persons)	374.7	426.4	13.8
其中：工业企业	(万人)	#Those Belong to Industrial Enterprises	(10 000 persons)	281.2	321.6	14.3
其中：规模以上	(万人)	#Those Engaged in Enterprises above Designated Scale	(10 000 persons)	220.7	258.6	17.2
主要经济指标		**Major Economic Indicators**				
规模以上工业总产值	(亿元)	Total Output Value of Enterprises above Designated Scale	(100 million Yuan)	22812.8	27194.3	19.2
规模以上工业增加值	(亿元)	Value-added of Enterprises above Designated Scale	(100 million Yuan)	6968.5	7857.3	12.8
其中：高新技术产业	(亿元)	#Value-added of High and New Technological Enterprises	(100 million Yuan)	2007.2	2358.8	17.5
规模以上工业主营业务收入	(亿元)	Total Income From Major Business of Enterprises above Designated Scale	(100 million Yuan)	22099.5	26412.2	19.5
固定资产投资总额	(亿元)	Total Value of Investment in Fixed Assets	(100 million Yuan)	7325.7	9947.1	35.8
其中：基础设施建设投资	(亿元)	#Infrastructure Investment	(100 million Yuan)	1508.0	1922.4	27.5
施工项目个数	(个)	Number of Projects under Construction	(unit)	8315	9870	18.7
其中:亿元以上项目	(个)	#the Value of the Projects is Worth More Than 100 million Yuan	(unit)	2883	3328	15.4
新开工项目	(个)	Newly Opened Projects	(unit)	4898	5719	16.8
外商投资项目	(个)	Foreign Invested Projects	(unit)	364	469	28.8
省外内资项目	(个)	Foreign-funded Projects	(unit)	2880	3588	24.6
开发区税收总额	(亿元)	Total Tax Revenue of Development Zone	(100 million Yuan)	1071.67	1233.26	15.1
招商引资总额	(亿元)	The Total Investment	(100 million yuan)	5628.67	6540.51	16.2
其中：外商投资金额	(亿美元)	#Total Value of Foreign Investment	(100 million dollars)	48.06	56.00	16.5
出口总额	(亿美元)	Total Value of Export	(100 million dollars)	151.77	179.88	18.5

21-2 湖北省130家开发区主要指标(2013)

开发区名称	Name of Development Zone	实际开发面积(平方公里) Actual Land Areas of Development Zone (sq. km)	
		2012	2013
湖北省	**Hubei Province**	**1618.1**	**1976.6**
武汉市	**Wuhan**	**382.3**	**480.2**
武汉江岸经济开发区	Wuhan Jiang'an Economic Development Zone	3.3	3.3
武汉江汉经济开发区	Wuhan Jianghan Economic Development Zone	0.7	0.7
武汉硚口经济开发区	Wuhan Qiaokou Economic Development Zone	1.1	1.1
武汉汉阳经济开发区	Wuhan Hanyang Economic Development Zone	7.2	8.0
武汉武昌经济开发区	Wuhan Wuchang Economic Development Zone	2.3	2.3
武汉青山经济开发区	Wuhan Qingshan Economic Development Zone	5.7	6.7
武汉洪山经济开发区	Wuhan Hongshan Economic Development Zone	1.2	0.3
武汉临空港经济技术开发区	Wuhan Linkonggang Economic and Technology Development Zone	111.3	116.9
武汉汉南经济开发区	Wuhan Hannan Economic Development Zone	8.0	12.5
武汉蔡甸经济开发区	Wuhan Caidian Economic Development Zone	23.5	43.8
武汉江夏经济开发区	Wuhan Jiangxia Economic Development Zone	99.7	100.4
武汉盘龙城经济开发区	Wuhan Panlongcheng Economic Development Zone	20.0	20.0
武汉阳逻经济开发区	Wuhan Yangluo Economic Development Zone	30.9	30.9
武汉经济技术开发区	Wuhan Economic and Technology Development Zone	30.4	81.7
武汉东湖新技术产业开发区	Wuhan East Lake New Technology Industrial Development Zone	35.2	48.4
黄石市	**Huangshi**	**123.2**	**130.8**
湖北黄石港工业园区	Hubei Huangshi Port Industrial Park	1.1	1.6
湖北黄石新港工业园区	Hubei Huangshi New Port Industrial Park	9.6	11.7
湖北西塞山工业园区	Hubei Xisaishan Industrial Park	9.6	10.2
湖北下陆长乐山工业园区	Hubei Xialu Changleshan Industrial Park	11.0	11.6
黄石经济技术开发区	Huangshi Economic and Technology Development Zone	55.0	55.0
湖北阳新经济开发区	Hubei Yangxin Economic Development Zone	10.0	12.0
湖北大冶经济开发区	Hubei Daye Economic Development Zone	28.1	31.3
大冶灵成工业园	Daye Lingcheng Industrial Park	5.8	6.3
十堰市	**Shiyan**	**53.5**	**58.8**
十堰经济技术开发区	Shiyan Economic and Technology Development Zone	15.0	15.0
湖北郧县经济开发区	Hubei Yun County Economic Development Zone	15.9	17.4
湖北郧西工业园区	Hubei West Yun Industrial Park	1.5	1.5
湖北竹山经济开发区	Hubei Zhushan Economic Development Zone	8.0	10.0
湖北竹溪工业园区	Hubei Zhuxi Industrial Park	1.3	1.8
湖北房县工业园区	Hubei Fang County Industrial Park	2.2	3.5
湖北丹江口经济开发区	Hubei Danjiangkou Economic Development Zone	9.5	9.6
宜昌市	**Yichang**	**126.5**	**153.2**
湖北西陵经济开发区	Hubei Xiling Economic Development Zone	4.0	4.0
湖北伍家岗工业园区	Hubei Wujiagang Industrial Park	4.0	4.0
湖北点军工业园区	Hubei Dianjun Industrial Park	1.3	1.5
湖北夷陵经济开发区	Hubei Yiling Economic Development Zone	22.0	25.0
湖北远安工业园区	Hubei Yuan'an Industrial Park	10.0	12.3
湖北兴山经济开发区	Hubei Xingshan Economic Development Zone	1.5	2.2
湖北秭归经济开发区	Hubei Zigui Economic Development Zone	6.0	6.0
湖北长阳经济开发区	Hubei Changyang Economic Development Zone	2.0	2.8
湖北五峰工业园区	Hubei Wufeng Industrial Park	2.3	2.3
湖北五峰民族工业园	Hubei Wufeng National Industrial Park	0.4	0.7
宜昌高新技术产开发区	Yichang High-tech Industrial Development Zone	53.6	69.1
湖北宜都工业园区	Hubei Yidu Industrial Park	8.0	8.0
湖北当阳经济开发区	Hubei Dangyang Economic Development Zone	20.0	24.0
湖北枝江经济开发区	Hubei Zhijiang Economic Development Zone	18.3	20.6
枝江安福寺工业园	Zhijiang Anfu Temple Industrial Park	1.6	1.8

MAIN INDICATORS OF 130 DEVELOPMENT ZONE IN HUBEI(2013)

企业个数(个) Number of Enterprises (unit)		其中：规模以上工业企业(个) Among which, Industrial Enterprises above Designated Size (unit)		高新技术企业(个) Number of High and New Technological Enterprises (unit)		从业人员(万人) Population of Employment (10 000 persons)	
2012	2013	2012	2013	2012	2013	2012	2013
70658	**84468**	**7578**	**8642**	**1673**	**1919**	**374.72**	**426.36**
30117	**36295**	**1551**	**1590**	**634**	**726**	**105.51**	**114.92**
281	227	33	33	12	12	1.22	1.16
328	394	15	15	23	3	1.60	1.62
268	288	46	45	6	7	4.20	4.41
689	930	55	64	20	24	2.35	3.35
257	275	31	29	15	15	1.92	1.99
300	310	85	95	10	11	3.55	3.63
168	168	24	16	19	23	0.92	0.85
5069	8198	201	232	44	55	19.17	22.58
459	473	118	126	4	11	3.15	3.41
218	295	55	85	7	8	2.70	3.10
633	675	134	168		45	5.67	6.09
393	562	38	40			2.78	3.98
105	123	44	57	6	11	2.00	2.49
3650	3650	185	202	47	71	17.32	17.32
17496	21047	525	638	413	582	38.25	40.14
5242	**6087**	**398**	**454**	**118**	**143**	**22.04**	**25.11**
31	39	4	7	6	8	0.46	0.48
20	24	13	13			0.19	0.19
260	303	31	62	2	10	2.10	3.50
141	155	16	22	1	8	2.03	2.01
1856	3701	107	137	22	49	7.25	7.86
349	374	31	46	4	6	3.30	3.40
2443	1525	118	138	16	31	4.86	5.63
87	93	77	83	57	58	1.23	1.35
3428	**4136**	**402**	**529**	**66**	**73**	**13.95**	**16.85**
2502	2977	171	232	41	51	7.07	8.14
135	197	36	73	8	14	1.77	2.38
26	29	26	26			0.25	0.28
102	191	22	26	2	5	0.56	0.58
48	77	31	38	2	2	1.55	1.70
119	139	54	61	6	7	0.63	0.98
496	526	62	73	7	8	2.12	2.79
4400	**8172**	**675**	**896**	**123**	**148**	**31.31**	**36.76**
170	390	10	12	5	6	0.85	0.88
92	92	18	20	9	9	1.53	1.55
13	15	13	13	7	7	0.51	0.58
596	782	90	119	13	16	3.97	4.53
132	152	70	85	5	14	2.60	2.85
12	31	5	13	2	3	0.44	0.62
172	199	48	65	3	5	1.82	1.93
72	77	30	47	5	7	0.95	1.07
230	280	9	20	1	2	0.37	1.10
6	7		3			0.35	0.38
1712	2435	127	253	59	82	10.80	11.70
259	306	120	151	10	22	3.10	3.19
439	699	123	147	19	28	3.98	5.16
1258	4076	94	165	6	12	4.65	6.25
45	49	22	29	1	1	1.11	1.22

21-2　续表 1 continued

开发区名称	Name of Development Zone	实际开发面积(平方公里) Actual Land Areas of Development Zone (sq. km) 2012	2013
襄阳市	**Xianyang**	**148.7**	**199.0**
襄阳高新技术产业开发区	Xiangyang High-tech Industrial Development Zone	26.5	33.2
襄阳鱼梁州经济开发区	Xiangyang Yuliangzhou Economic Development Zone	2.0	2.0
襄阳经济技术开发区	Xiangyang Economic Development Zone	35.0	60.0
湖北襄城经济开发区	Hubei Xiangcheng Economic Development Zone	14.0	15.0
湖北樊城经济开发区	Hubei Fancheng Economic Development Zone	5.0	6.2
湖北襄州经济开发区	Hubei Xiangzhou Economic Development Zone	14.0	18.0
襄阳工业园	Xiangyang Industrial Park	3.0	3.0
湖北南漳经济开发区	Hubei Nanzhang Economic Development Zone	14.0	16.2
湖北谷城经济开发区	Hubei Gucheng Economic Development Zone	10.0	13.0
谷城石花经济开发区	Gucheng Shihua Economic Development Zone	5.0	8.0
湖北保康经济开发区	Hubei Baokang Economic Development Zone	8.0	9.0
湖北老河口经济开发区	Hubei Laohekou Economic Development Zone	27.0	33.0
湖北枣阳经济开发区	Hubei Zaoyang Economic Development Zone	6.0	6.0
枣阳吴店工业园	Zaoyang Wudian Industrial Park	3.0	3.0
湖北宜城经济开发区	Hubei Yicheng Economic Development Zone	9.0	11.2
鄂州市	**E'zhou**	**51.1**	**55.8**
湖北鄂州花湖经济开发区	Hubei E'Zhou Huahu Economic Development Zone	9.8	10.5
鄂州葛店经济技术开发区	E'Zhou Gedian Economic and Technology Development Zone	25.3	27.3
湖北鄂州经济开发区	Hubei E'Zhou Economic Development Zone	16.0	18.0
荆门市	**Jingmen**	**77.2**	**85.8**
湖北东宝工业园区	Hubei Dongbao Industrial Park	10.8	12.0
湖北荆门高新技术产业园区	Hubei Jingmen High-tech Industrial Development Zone	22.0	23.2
湖北荆门化工循环产业园	Hubei Jingmen Chemical Recycling Development Zone	7.0	8.0
湖北京山经济开发区	Hubei Jingshan Economic Development Zone	12.3	14.0
湖北屈家岭经济开发区	Hubei Qujialing Economic Development Zone	1.8	3.0
湖北沙洋经济开发区	Hubei Shayang Economic Development Zone	20.0	20.5
湖北钟祥经济开发区	Hubei Zhongxiang Economic Development Zone	15.0	18.0
钟祥胡集经济开发区	Zhongxiang Huji Economic Development Zone	4.4	5.2
孝感市	**Xiaogan**	**62.7**	**95.3**
孝感高新技术产业开发区	Xiaogan high-tech Industrial Development Zone	13.0	13.0
湖北孝南经济开发区	Hubei Xiaonan Economic Development Zone	15.7	17.0
湖北孝昌经济开发区	Hubei Xiaochang Economic Development Zone	10.0	10.0
湖北大悟经济开发区	Hubei Dawu Economic Development Zone	6.5	17.3
湖北云梦经济开发区	Hubei Yunmeng Economic Development Zone	20.1	20.1
湖北应城经济开发区	Hubei Yingcheng Economic Development Zone	17.0	19.0
湖北安陆经济开发区	Hubei Anlu Economic Development Zone	15.3	33.6
湖北汉川经济开发区	Hubei Hanchuan Economic Development Zone	16.6	19.2
荆州市	**Jingzhou**	**185.4**	**226.4**
湖北沙市经济开发区	Hubei Shashi Economic Development Zone	30.0	35.0
湖北荆州城南经济开发区	Jingzhou Chengnan Economic Development Zone	14.0	14.0
荆州经济技术开发区	Jingzhou Economic and Technology Development Zone	52.0	54.0
湖北公安经济开发区	Hubei Gong'an Economic Development Zone	10.6	13.8
湖北监利经济开发区	Hubei Jianli Economic Development Zone	28.7	38.4
湖北江陵经济开发区	Hubei Jiangling Economic Development Zone	10.2	14.8
湖北石首经济开发区	Hubei Shishou Economic Development Zone	18.0	22.0
湖北洪湖经济开发区	Hubei Honghu Economic Development Zone	9.4	11.4
洪湖府场经济开发区	Honghu Fuchang Economic Development Zone	5.0	12.0
湖北松滋经济开发区	Hubei Songzi Economic Development Zone	3.5	6.0
黄冈市	**Huanggang**	**161.7**	**224.6**
湖北黄冈经济开发区	Hubei Huanggang Economic Development Zone	12.4	20.3

企业个数(个) Number of Enterprises (unit)		其中：规模以上工业企业(个) Among which, Industrial Enterprises above Designated Size (unit)		高新技术企业(个) Number of High and New Technological Enterprises (unit)		从业人员(万人) Population of Employment (10 000 persons)	
2012	2013	2012	2013	2012	2013	2012	2013
8499	**9184**	**889**	**997**	**148**	**189**	**43.54**	**52.67**
5668	5909	201	262	85	117	10.92	13.50
38	38					0.10	0.10
604	653	102	120	10	27	9.51	10.23
195	212	44	55	6	6	2.20	2.50
291	326	102	108	21	23	3.42	3.78
287	465	93	118	18	25	6.76	7.35
74	86	19	23		2	0.70	0.90
95	101	68	79	2	3	2.20	2.70
793	1152	74	95	5	10	4.80	6.30
207	255	41	57	5	7	2.20	2.70
36	40	22	27	5	6	2.52	2.61
201	298	145	170	6	13	2.07	3.84
398	446	110	141	22	32	3.56	3.87
168	262	38	66	1	4	2.03	2.64
170	186	53	71	4	6	2.04	2.33
3070	**3408**	**356**	**385**	**31**	**35**	**8.68**	**10.03**
183	316	56	55	2	5	1.30	1.50
2697	2852	238	255	22	28	6.48	7.52
190	240	62	75	7	9	0.90	1.01
1044	**1209**	**408**	**466**	**66**	**72**	**17.34**	**20.07**
101	126	61	88	10	10	2.90	3.00
373	434	197	254	34	45	6.43	6.92
26	43	20	25	1	3	0.25	0.40
306	347	44	59	11	14	2.26	2.52
26	32	13	9		1	0.12	0.13
113	133	45	52	10	11	2.00	2.50
176	238	70	108	12	12	4.50	5.60
35	46	22	27	3	3	1.40	1.69
2540	**2773**	**518**	**572**	**88**	**92**	**22.25**	**25.27**
1582	1631	267	339	50	81	8.57	10.58
249	291	98	84	17	14	4.30	4.50
190	213	32	35	25	2	2.20	2.35
65	66	16	27	2	3	1.50	1.50
226	259	67	100	8	15	7.50	7.90
145	160	112	127	10	12	3.36	3.40
239	246	11	19	5	6	3.21	3.72
428	663	171	204	11	17	5.96	6.23
2557	**2940**	**650**	**716**	**69**	**75**	**33.48**	**39.54**
142	168	68	73	4	4	2.10	2.70
680	702	112	120	6	6	5.94	6.38
809	926	96	134	41	41	6.60	7.50
176	251	31	33	4	5	2.31	2.85
106	77	35	77		2	4.20	4.80
74	88	22	26			1.12	1.41
72	74	65	73	4	5	2.47	2.96
188	201	41	47	3	4	2.36	2.54
152	347	45	58	6	6	1.70	3.18
121	156	109	140	9	17	3.46	3.83
3031	**3299**	**645**	**773**	**190**	**198**	**27.20**	**30.64**
1260	1297	143	177	55	67	7.41	8.12

21-2 续表 2 continued

开发区名称	Name of Development Zone	实际开发面积(平方公里) Actual Land Areas of Development Zone (sq. km)	
		2012	2013
湖北黄州火车站经济开发区	Hubei Huangzhou Railway Station Economic Development Zone	7.0	8.0
黄州工业园	Huangzhou Industrial Park	16.5	19.0
湖北龙感湖工业园区	Hubei Longganhu Industrial Park	6.5	7.5
湖北团风经济开发区	Hubei Tuanfeng Economic Development Zone	7.6	7.8
湖北红安经济开发区	Hubei Hong'an Economic Development Zone	25.0	30.0
湖北罗田经济开发区	Hubei Luotian Economic Development Zone	8.0	8.7
湖北英山经济开发区	Hubei Yingshan Economic Development Zone	5.6	10.8
湖北浠水经济开发区	Hubei Xishui Economic Development Zone	7.0	13.0
湖北蕲春李时珍医药工业园区	Hubei Qichun Li Shizhen Pharmaceutical Industrial Park	10.0	14.0
蕲春经济开发区	Qichun Economic Development Zone	15.5	17.0
湖北黄梅经济开发区	Hubei Huangmei Economic Development Zone	19.9	20.8
湖北麻城经济开发区	Hubei Macheng Economic Development Zone	12.0	35.0
湖北武穴经济开发区	Hubei Wuxue Economic Development Zone	8.8	12.7
咸宁市	**Xianning**	**76.9**	**84.3**
湖北咸安经济开发区	Hubei Xian'an Economic Development Zone	7.0	8.6
湖北嘉鱼经济开发区	Hubei Jiayu Economic Development Zone	10.0	11.5
湖北通城经济开发区	Hubei Tongcheng Economic Development Zone	4.0	5.0
湖北崇阳工业园区	Hubei Chongyang Industrial Park	6.3	7.6
湖北通山经济开发区	Hubei Tongshan Economic Development Zone	15.0	15.0
湖北咸宁经济开发区	Hubei Xianning Economic Development Zone	16.6	16.6
湖北赤壁经济开发区	Hubei Chibi Economic Development Zone	10.0	12.0
湖北赤壁蒲纺工业园区	Hubei Chibi Puqi Textile Industrial Park	8.0	8.0
随州市	**Suizhou**	**47.0**	**50.4**
湖北随州经济开发区	Hubei Suizhou Economic Development Zone	18.0	19.0
湖北曾都经济开发区	Hubei Zengdu Economic Development Zone	17.0	18.0
湖北随县经济开发区	Hubei Sui County Economic Development Zone	4.8	4.8
湖北广水经济开发区	Hubei Guangshui Economic Development Zone	7.2	8.6
恩施自治州	**Enshi Autonomous Prefecture**	**47.6**	**52.0**
湖北恩施经济开发区	Hubei Enshi Economic Development Zone	14.7	14.7
湖北恩施州经济开发区	Hubei Enshi Prefecture Economic Development Zone	3.6	4.3
湖北利川经济开发区	Hubei Lichuan Economic Development Zone	4.0	4.1
湖北建始工业园区	Hubei Jianshi Industrial Park	2.0	2.0
湖北巴东经济开发区	Hubei Badong Economic Development Zone	7.7	8.0
湖北宣恩工业园区	Hubei Xuan'en Industrial Park	3.6	5.6
湖北咸丰工业园区	Hubei Xianfeng Industrial Park	5.0	5.8
湖北来凤经济开发区	Hubei Laifeng Economic Development Zone	5.0	5.5
湖北鹤峰经济开发区	Hubei Hefeng Economic Development Zone	2.0	2.0
仙桃市	**Xiantao**	**24.5**	**25.9**
湖北仙桃经济开发区	Hubei Xiantao Economic Development Zone	24.5	25.9
仙桃彭场工业园	Xiantao Pengchang Industrial Park	2.8	3.0
潜江市	**Qianjiang**	**22.4**	**22.4**
湖北潜江经济开发区	Hubei Qianjiang Economic Development Zone	5.0	5.0
潜江张金经济开发区	Qianjiang Zhangjin Economic Development Zone	2.4	2.4
潜江园林经济开发区	Qianjiang Yuanlin Economic Development Zone	15.0	15.0
天门市	**Tianmen**	**27.4**	**30.8**
湖北天门经济开发区	Hubei Tianmen Economic Development Zone	27.4	30.8

企业个数(个) Number of Enterprises (unit)		其中：规模以上工业企业(个) Among which, Industrial Enterprises above Designated Size (unit)		高新技术企业(个) Number of High and New Technological Enterprises (unit)		从业人员(万人) Population of Employment (10 000 persons)	
2012	2013	2012	2013	2012	2013	2012	2013
144	146	17	17	4	4	0.27	0.28
50	55	15	25	10	10	0.76	0.81
121	106	22	24	3	3	0.89	0.95
78	78	17	22	3	10	1.20	1.25
180	250	120	127	40	40	4.90	5.10
53	69	23	32	8	12	0.53	0.60
52	79	38	26	17	18	0.69	1.23
390	420	48	56	16	24	2.50	3.00
40	78	20	27	3	5	1.20	1.30
57	63	23	23	2	2	1.30	1.38
368	381	73	78	8	10	2.30	2.51
88	97	31	51	12	22	1.30	1.90
150	180	55	88	6	9	1.95	2.21
876	**986**	**406**	**474**	**41**	**50**	**10.54**	**12.91**
85	138	51	70	9	10	1.39	1.51
133	142	81	104	2	6	1.66	1.73
76	78	43	45	5	6	1.13	2.93
85	112	48	54	10	12	1.10	1.30
40	53	14	17	5	5	0.72	0.83
275	280	30	42	8	9	2.00	2.00
121	121	113	113	12	12	1.98	1.98
61	62	26	29			0.56	0.63
1344	**938**	**166**	**188**	**30**	**36**	**6.12**	**6.75**
908	454	52	61	6	12	2.90	2.90
183	221	67	73	14	18	2.10	2.50
30	31	10	13	2	3	0.17	0.19
223	232	37	41	9	10	0.95	1.16
710	**793**	**142**	**184**	**12**	**13**	**8.76**	**9.78**
330	336	32	34	1	1	2.20	2.18
20	27	3	3	1	1	1.10	1.20
38	44	14	20	1	1	0.39	0.41
26	26	11	18	3	3	0.50	0.52
112	120	9	11	1	2	0.90	0.90
38	58	14	16			0.45	1.15
78	86	19	21	3	3	0.93	1.12
46	72	22	43	1	1	1.62	1.65
22	24	18	18	1	1	0.67	0.65
1585	**1931**	**200**	**227**	**20**	**25**	**11.39**	**11.96**
1585	1931	200	227	20	25	11.39	11.96
228	230	47	50	2	2	3.83	3.85
1953	**1989**	**81**	**83**	**29**	**34**	**6.48**	**5.83**
220	217	57	54	35	33	1.62	1.58
85	117	11	14	4	4	2.01	2.11
1648	1655	13	15	3	3	2.85	2.14
262	**306**	**91**	**106**	**8**	**9**	**6.12**	**7.24**
262	306	91	106	8	9	6.12	7.24

21-2 续表 3 continued

开发区名称	Name of Development Zone	其中：规模以上工业企业(万人) Among which, Industrial Enterprises above Designated Size (10 000 persons)	
		2012	2013
湖北省	**Hubei Province**	**220.72**	**258.62**
武汉市	**Wuhan**	**58.90**	**64.66**
武汉江岸经济开发区	Wuhan Jiang'an Economic Development Zone	0.62	0.56
武汉江汉经济开发区	Wuhan Jianghan Economic Development Zone	0.26	0.27
武汉硚口经济开发区	Wuhan Qiaokou Economic Development Zone	1.50	1.50
武汉汉阳经济开发区	Wuhan Hanyang Economic Development Zone	0.92	1.64
武汉武昌经济开发区	Wuhan Wuchang Economic Development Zone	1.02	1.07
武汉青山经济开发区	Wuhan Qingshan Economic Development Zone	3.00	3.05
武汉洪山经济开发区	Wuhan Hongshan Economic Development Zone	0.32	0.29
武汉临空港经济技术开发区	Wuhan Linkonggang Economic and Technology Development Zone	5.03	5.51
武汉汉南经济开发区	Wuhan Hannan Economic Development Zone	1.36	1.47
武汉蔡甸经济开发区	Wuhan Caidian Economic Development Zone	2.20	2.30
武汉江夏经济开发区	Wuhan Jiangxia Economic Development Zone	3.42	4.02
武汉盘龙城经济开发区	Wuhan Panlongcheng Economic Development Zone	0.52	0.74
武汉阳逻经济开发区	Wuhan Yangluo Economic Development Zone	1.60	1.91
武汉经济技术开发区	Wuhan Economic and Technology Development Zone	9.99	10.32
武汉东湖新技术产业开发区	Wuhan East Lake New Technology Industrial Development Zone	28.00	30.71
黄石市	**Huangshi**	**12.23**	**14.65**
湖北黄石港工业园区	Hubei Huangshi Port Industrial Park	0.22	0.22
湖北黄石新港工业园区	Hubei Huangshi New Port Industrial Park	0.16	0.16
湖北西塞山工业园区	Hubei Xisaishan Industrial Park	1.12	1.48
湖北下陆长乐山工业园区	Hubei Xialu Changleshan Industrial Park	1.97	1.93
黄石经济技术开发区	Huangshi Economic and Technology Development Zone	1.92	2.37
湖北阳新经济开发区	Hubei Yangxin Economic Development Zone	2.70	2.80
湖北大冶经济开发区	Hubei Daye Economic Development Zone	2.68	4.10
大冶灵成工业园	Daye Lingcheng Industrial Park	1.12	1.16
十堰市	**Shiyan**	**7.21**	**8.85**
十堰经济技术开发区	Shiyan Economic and Technology Development Zone	3.55	4.16
湖北郧县经济开发区	Hubei Yun County Economic Development Zone	1.21	1.84
湖北郧西工业园区	Hubei West Yun Industrial Park	0.25	0.28
湖北竹山经济开发区	Hubei Zhushan Economic Development Zone	0.25	0.26
湖北竹溪工业园区	Hubei Zhuxi Industrial Park	0.35	0.38
湖北房县工业园区	Hubei Fang County Industrial Park	0.44	0.51
湖北丹江口经济开发区	Hubei Danjiangkou Economic Development Zone	1.16	1.42
宜昌市	**Yichang**	**20.82**	**27.77**
湖北西陵经济开发区	Hubei Xiling Economic Development Zone	0.13	0.14
湖北伍家岗工业园区	Hubei Wujiagang Industrial Park	0.45	0.50
湖北点军工业园区	Hubei Dianjun Industrial Park	0.42	0.46
湖北夷陵经济开发区	Hubei Yiling Economic Development Zone	2.70	2.82
湖北远安工业园区	Hubei Yuan'an Industrial Park	2.00	2.21
湖北兴山经济开发区	Hubei Xingshan Economic Development Zone	0.38	0.46
湖北秭归经济开发区	Hubei Zigui Economic Development Zone	1.12	1.22
湖北长阳经济开发区	Hubei Changyang Economic Development Zone	0.65	0.75
湖北五峰工业园区	Hubei Wufeng Industrial Park	0.35	0.50
湖北五峰民族工业园	Hubei Wufeng National Industrial Park		0.30
宜昌高新技术产开发区	Yichang High-tech Industrial Development Zone	6.30	9.60
湖北宜都工业园区	Hubei Yidu Industrial Park	2.28	2.36
湖北当阳经济开发区	Hubei Dangyang Economic Development Zone	3.08	4.05
湖北枝江经济开发区	Hubei Zhijiang Economic Development Zone	2.80	4.05
枝江安福寺工业园	Zhijiang Anfu Temple Industrial Park	1.01	1.14

规模以上工业增加值(亿元) Above-scale Industrial Added Value (100 million Yuan)		规模以上工业主营业务收入(亿元) Scale Industrial Core Business Revenue (100 million Yuan)		固定资产投资总额(亿元) Total Investment In Fixed Assets (100 million Yuan)		施工项目个数(个) Number of Construction Project (unit)	
2012	2013	2012	2013	2012	2013	2012	2013
6968.45	**7857.32**	**22099.48**	**26412.15**	**7325.74**	**9947.06**	**8315**	**9870**
2099.28	**2361.13**	**6887.10**	**8135.02**	**1645.51**	**2150.86**	**1175**	**1315**
13.10	11.90	15.13	19.95	10.28	12.76	9	5
10.57	13.74	35.11	42.30	7.48	6.60	5	6
29.70	30.60	93.90	95.00	15.00	18.00	9	9
52.20	61.82	159.91	208.12	101.72	80.80	33	20
37.84	44.28	175.60	182.55	5.40	5.60	3	2
29.80	33.30	113.00	120.19	18.77	24.75	25	33
6.66	6.07	24.77	23.45	5.43	4.53	7	5
207.94	284.04	473.37	559.74	272.85	345.61	207	240
21.60	31.77	84.54	109.13	22.47	43.17	17	21
113.00	139.30	193.00	352.64	101.00	138.00	48	57
109.50	136.90	360.26	466.20	189.30	353.63	82	107
23.76	30.33	84.16	101.62	24.00	36.73	52	62
84.57	109.86	271.81	383.94	163.57	172.70	59	63
596.64	683.40	1691.66	2027.90	256.18	350.00	252	287
920.00	1173.00	3458.00	4485.00	444.24	534.33	376	407
482.14	**532.99**	**1871.35**	**2320.78**	**500.06**	**705.75**	**526**	**598**
1.60	1.84	4.45	5.08	1.86	2.50	13	20
13.21	6.69	17.35	19.35	10.83	29.35	11	17
57.00	68.00	218.00	356.46	26.50	36.91	55	82
106.29	124.54	626.38	916.79	19.11	39.01	19	27
210.19	242.54	623.85	754.86	215.99	345.59	186	212
18.90	26.75	44.60	72.53	36.60	54.20	47	58
109.59	126.78	326.82	379.53	140.29	154.89	162	165
24.50	28.80	81.32	86.64	49.36	54.60	35	21
257.27	**302.05**	**812.91**	**960.45**	**277.76**	**427.92**	**478**	**597**
176.60	198.06	566.30	651.06	116.24	208.56	145	203
24.92	31.76	78.34	93.41	34.95	46.71	74	96
4.00	4.82	10.00	10.68	12.40	12.66	9	11
9.55	11.83	25.56	32.20	27.26	31.71	36	43
9.30	10.08	25.40	26.50	5.00	15.00	8	13
10.50	13.80	31.20	39.10	53.91	75.13	135	146
22.40	31.70	76.11	107.50	28.00	38.15	71	85
942.75	**1005.74**	**2805.84**	**3195.84**	**989.43**	**1296.97**	**1057**	**1269**
3.40	5.14	9.81	10.86	20.25	25.00	40	47
9.80	13.01	24.57	13.49	16.00	29.60	22	8
12.96	14.19	38.20	47.32	1.60	2.20	3	4
154.27	202.25	475.50	624.95	138.20	163.14	107	111
65.19	83.32	181.22	242.25	65.33	72.36	83	90
5.73	11.10	28.65	52.20	4.80	7.60	15	26
20.70	26.43	55.31	67.53	20.54	31.75	33	49
17.37	20.57	50.95	60.49	27.86	43.63	87	106
4.28	4.53	11.50	14.20	9.17	12.23	18	29
	0.91		3.17	8.37	10.29	13	6
459.90	495.18	1452.70	1662.00	370.00	476.00	309	387
189.35	229.11	433.72	519.60	174.00	221.15	210	234
107.13	131.01	306.13	390.50	114.91	183.11	111	151
113.50	149.70	326.80	475.50	153.90	182.00	149	146
12.25	16.65	39.94	54.19	20.07	23.69	13	16

21-2 续表 4 continued

开发区名称	Name of Development Zone	其中：规模以上工业企业(万人) Among which, Industrial Enterprises above Designated Size (10 000 persons)	
		2012	2013
襄阳市	**Xianyang**	**27.94**	**32.05**
襄阳高新技术产业开发区	Xiangyang High-tech Industrial Development Zone	8.70	10.10
襄阳鱼梁州经济开发区	Xiangyang Yuliangzhou Economic Development Zone		
襄阳经济技术开发区	Xiangyang Economic Development Zone	5.62	5.96
湖北襄城经济开发区	Hubei Xiangcheng Economic Development Zone	1.40	1.70
湖北樊城经济开发区	Hubei Fancheng Economic Development Zone	2.24	2.57
湖北襄州经济开发区	Hubei Xiangzhou Economic Development Zone	4.53	4.67
襄阳工业园	Xiangyang Industrial Park	0.30	0.41
湖北南漳经济开发区	Hubei Nanzhang Economic Development Zone	2.10	2.56
湖北谷城经济开发区	Hubei Gucheng Economic Development Zone	1.60	2.00
谷城石花经济开发区	Gucheng Shihua Economic Development Zone	1.40	1.50
湖北保康经济开发区	Hubei Baokang Economic Development Zone	2.15	2.39
湖北老河口经济开发区	Hubei Laohekou Economic Development Zone	1.73	1.82
湖北枣阳经济开发区	Hubei Zaoyang Economic Development Zone	1.56	2.03
枣阳吴店工业园	Zaoyang Wudian Industrial Park	0.74	1.02
湖北宜城经济开发区	Hubei Yicheng Economic Development Zone	1.20	1.37
鄂州市	**E'zhou**	**3.98**	**4.42**
湖北鄂州花湖经济开发区	Hubei E'Zhou Huahu Economic Development Zone	0.70	0.65
鄂州葛店经济技术开发区	E'Zhou Gedian Economic and Technology Development Zone	2.71	3.16
湖北鄂州经济开发区	Hubei E'Zhou Economic Development Zone	0.57	0.61
荆门市	**Jingmen**	**11.61**	**14.09**
湖北东宝工业园区	Hubei Dongbao Industrial Park	1.96	2.18
湖北荆门高新技术产业园区	Hubei Jingmen High-tech Industrial Development Zone	5.19	5.54
湖北荆门化工循环产业园	Hubei Jingmen Chemical Recycling Development Zone	0.21	0.31
湖北京山经济开发区	Hubei Jingshan Economic Development Zone	1.36	1.60
湖北屈家岭经济开发区	Hubei Qujialing Economic Development Zone	0.11	0.12
湖北沙洋经济开发区	Hubei Shayang Economic Development Zone	1.20	1.60
湖北钟祥经济开发区	Hubei Zhongxiang Economic Development Zone	2.20	3.40
钟祥胡集经济开发区	Zhongxiang Huji Economic Development Zone	1.08	1.26
孝感市	**Xiaogan**	**12.93**	**15.14**
孝感高新技术产业开发区	Xiaogan high-tech Industrial Development Zone	5.93	7.59
湖北孝南经济开发区	Hubei Xiaonan Economic Development Zone	1.40	1.25
湖北孝昌经济开发区	Hubei Xiaochang Economic Development Zone	1.20	1.28
湖北大悟经济开发区	Hubei Dawu Economic Development Zone	1.00	1.00
湖北云梦经济开发区	Hubei Yunmeng Economic Development Zone	2.31	2.54
湖北应城经济开发区	Hubei Yingcheng Economic Development Zone	2.44	2.51
湖北安陆经济开发区	Hubei Anlu Economic Development Zone	0.40	0.52
湖北汉川经济开发区	Hubei Hanchuan Economic Development Zone	3.87	4.14
荆州市	**Jingzhou**	**20.39**	**25.10**
湖北沙市经济开发区	Hubei Shashi Economic Development Zone	1.30	1.60
湖北荆州城南经济开发区	Jingzhou Chengnan Economic Development Zone	2.91	3.38
荆州经济技术开发区	Jingzhou Economic and Technology Development Zone	2.26	2.90
湖北公安经济开发区	Hubei Gong'an Economic Development Zone	0.88	0.98
湖北监利经济开发区	Hubei Jianli Economic Development Zone	4.00	4.80
湖北江陵经济开发区	Hubei Jiangling Economic Development Zone	0.89	1.35
湖北石首经济开发区	Hubei Shishou Economic Development Zone	2.29	2.95
湖北洪湖经济开发区	Hubei Honghu Economic Development Zone	1.04	1.12
洪湖府场经济开发区	Honghu Fuchang Economic Development Zone	1.20	1.87
湖北松滋经济开发区	Hubei Songzi Economic Development Zone	2.79	3.13
黄冈市	**Huanggang**	**14.68**	**16.76**
湖北黄冈经济开发区	Hubei Huanggang Economic Development Zone	2.93	3.46

规模以上工业增加值(亿元) Above-scale Industrial Added Value (100 million Yuan)		规模以上工业主营业务收入(亿元) Scale Industrial Core Business Revenue (100 million Yuan)		固定资产投资总额(亿元) Total Investment In Fixed Assets (100 million Yuan)		施工项目个数(个) Number of Construction Project (unit)	
2012	2013	2012	2013	2012	2013	2012	2013
1020.69	**1161.08**	**3019.22**	**3563.48**	**1001.71**	**1450.11**	**1020**	**1100**
463.60	570.70	1386.00	1793.00	363.70	550.00	321	278
				0.44	0.44		
268.05	283.90	703.01	787.78	174.78	203.12	92	94
49.00	51.20	115.00	122.20	33.21	36.30	21	19
54.00	62.00	167.00	193.00	59.28	64.00	61	72
85.97	110.56	284.56	357.47	174.78	203.12	92	94
14.50	16.30	68.50	93.75	17.60	42.27	11	18
36.38	45.10	90.23	118.90	50.72	70.80	48	51
59.20	74.20	180.40	158.99	62.84	94.32	108	115
43.60	76.00	160.40	259.98	16.21	51.00	51	51
15.92	20.55	35.86	39.46	25.46	30.58	39	31
91.75	122.90	275.30	371.40	67.30	103.67	125	145
68.98	112.20	216.00	376.90	126.47	186.00	118	207
19.50	43.20	61.50	136.25	36.68	58.00	46	43
76.40	90.52	230.69	290.00	56.37	65.10	54	60
161.26	**205.40**	**584.16**	**728.13**	**278.61**	**363.42**	**226**	**293**
14.60	22.70	54.20	79.30	32.90	52.30	38	49
133.54	162.02	478.05	575.50	217.01	273.00	172	223
13.12	20.68	51.91	73.33	28.70	38.12	16	21
356.11	**402.27**	**1264.46**	**1526.51**	**359.17**	**533.89**	**554**	**737**
57.24	63.37	176.40	229.04	119.20	141.76	294	397
178.80	210.93	571.40	717.20	205.90	261.80	316	367
6.88	8.88	26.50	37.10	6.65	9.98	7	32
52.21	63.40	165.63	225.72	49.43	71.77	84	103
3.99	3.75	12.77	14.70	5.74	0.80	12	15
13.40	18.03	47.20	63.02	31.70	55.47	45	61
84.00	117.00	286.00	392.00	35.10	96.83	55	124
23.71	31.04	81.46	113.87	23.86	33.57	31	51
351.08	**368.52**	**1089.79**	**1303.17**	**433.88**	**675.52**	**471**	**522**
220.50	242.10	642.30	794.61	251.20	412.89	259	287
18.70	33.18	61.50	118.70	92.94	130.00	93	336
10.89	12.40	33.85	37.80	9.89	23.08	45	55
4.40	7.57	11.20	23.40	4.97	11.48	7	13
53.77	69.99	201.50	274.55	87.60	132.94	119	113
83.30	90.70	315.33	365.30	24.83	37.84	344	282
19.50	24.22	51.80	70.26	46.14	53.00	70	58
95.79	118.63	350.64	477.10	112.70	157.80	82	97
334.69	**365.69**	**996.72**	**1187.39**	**524.64**	**634.16**	**660**	**877**
32.33	38.42	91.63	116.47	75.52	97.28	42	58
57.79	75.75	172.64	232.32	75.38	78.47	52	58
70.00	80.00	185.00	210.00	155.52	170.00	208	320
29.56	37.34	101.16	105.10	60.07	75.32	39	48
31.21	55.63	98.20	186.48	29.70	35.00	39	37
9.85	11.73	35.48	42.75	23.19	32.00	37	49
37.30	42.46	105.63	152.12	18.40	29.73	42	31
29.73	36.84	106.10	129.38	25.42	30.00	58	69
16.50	18.21	36.21	50.86	14.36	21.32	61	95
20.42	28.49	64.67	90.39	36.22	48.82	71	92
262.28	**296.08**	**636.79**	**822.64**	**424.28**	**563.33**	**903**	**1064**
66.43	90.40	121.13	162.43	89.45	124.37	215	256

21-2 续表 5 continued

开发区名称	Name of Development Zone	其中：规模以上工业企业(万人) Among which, Industrial Enterprises above Designated Size (10 000 persons)	
		2012	2013
湖北黄州火车站经济开发区	Hubei Huangzhou Railway Station Economic Development Zone	0.06	0.07
黄州工业园	Huangzhou Industrial Park	0.65	0.68
湖北龙感湖工业园区	Hubei Longganhu Industrial Park	0.48	0.51
湖北团风经济开发区	Hubei Tuanfeng Economic Development Zone	0.85	0.91
湖北红安经济开发区	Hubei Hong'an Economic Development Zone	2.10	2.20
湖北罗田经济开发区	Hubei Luotian Economic Development Zone	0.42	0.55
湖北英山经济开发区	Hubei Yingshan Economic Development Zone	0.57	0.76
湖北浠水经济开发区	Hubei Xishui Economic Development Zone	0.95	1.10
湖北蕲春李时珍医药工业园区	Hubei Qichun Li Shizhen Pharmaceutical Industrial Park	0.95	1.10
蕲春经济开发区	Qichun Economic Development Zone	0.80	0.84
湖北黄梅经济开发区	Hubei Huangmei Economic Development Zone	1.90	2.05
湖北麻城经济开发区	Hubei Macheng Economic Development Zone	0.66	0.90
湖北武穴经济开发区	Hubei Wuxue Economic Development Zone	1.36	1.63
咸宁市	**Xianning**	**8.58**	**11.46**
湖北咸安经济开发区	Hubei Xian'an Economic Development Zone	1.28	1.33
湖北嘉鱼经济开发区	Hubei Jiayu Economic Development Zone	1.29	1.57
湖北通城经济开发区	Hubei Tongcheng Economic Development Zone	0.85	2.50
湖北崇阳工业园区	Hubei Chongyang Industrial Park	1.01	1.06
湖北通山经济开发区	Hubei Tongshan Economic Development Zone	0.57	0.73
湖北咸宁经济开发区	Hubei Xianning Economic Development Zone	1.60	1.70
湖北赤壁经济开发区	Hubei Chibi Economic Development Zone	1.98	1.98
湖北赤壁蒲纺工业园区	Hubei Chibi Puqi Textile Industrial Park		0.59
随州市	**Suizhou**	**4.14**	**4.40**
湖北随州经济开发区	Hubei Suizhou Economic Development Zone	1.70	1.65
湖北曾都经济开发区	Hubei Zengdu Economic Development Zone	1.60	1.80
湖北随县经济开发区	Hubei Sui County Economic Development Zone	0.15	0.18
湖北广水经济开发区	Hubei Guangshui Economic Development Zone	0.69	0.77
恩施自治州	**Enshi Autonomous Prefecture**	**4.76**	**5.10**
湖北恩施经济开发区	Hubei Enshi Economic Development Zone	0.90	0.80
湖北恩施州经济开发区	Hubei Enshi Prefecture Economic Development Zone	0.10	0.10
湖北利川经济开发区	Hubei Lichuan Economic Development Zone	0.27	0.31
湖北建始工业园区	Hubei Jianshi Industrial Park	0.40	0.50
湖北巴东经济开发区	Hubei Badong Economic Development Zone	0.10	0.10
湖北宣恩工业园区	Hubei Xuan'en Industrial Park	0.36	0.52
湖北咸丰工业园区	Hubei Xianfeng Industrial Park	0.68	0.80
湖北来凤经济开发区	Hubei Laifeng Economic Development Zone	1.37	1.42
湖北鹤峰经济开发区	Hubei Hefeng Economic Development Zone	0.58	0.55
仙桃市	**Xiantao**	**5.31**	**5.54**
湖北仙桃经济开发区	Hubei Xiantao Economic Development Zone	5.31	5.54
仙桃彭场工业园	Xiantao Pengchang Industrial Park	2.82	2.86
潜江市	**Qianjiang**	**2.76**	**3.20**
湖北潜江经济开发区	Hubei Qianjiang Economic Development Zone	1.06	1.33
潜江张金经济开发区	Qianjiang Zhangjin Economic Development Zone	0.99	1.04
潜江园林经济开发区	Qianjiang Yuanlin Economic Development Zone	0.71	0.83
天门市	**Tianmen**	**4.49**	**5.43**
湖北天门经济开发区	Hubei Tianmen Economic Development Zone	4.49	5.43

规模以上工业增加值(亿元) Above-scale Industrial Added Value(100 million Yuan)		规模以上工业主营业务收入(亿元) Scale Industrial Core Business Revenue (100 million Yuan)		固定资产投资总额(亿元) Total Investment In Fixed Assets(100 million Yuan)		施工项目个数(个) Number of Construction Project (unit)	
2012	2013	2012	2013	2012	2013	2012	2013
1.80	2.20	4.30	5.60	16.20	26.80	25	27
11.45	12.31	31.80	33.52	15.23	21.84	14	18
7.00	10.90	26.43	35.70	12.90	20.00	29	34
13.38	16.60	43.52	53.79	13.93	15.41	21	17
48.50	55.20	82.00	85.00	80.00	102.60	146	175
10.93	12.57	24.10	28.95	9.70	10.50	45	53
4.81	6.68	6.47	9.65	9.74	15.35	55	61
7.50	12.50	23.50	37.00	19.13	30.50	95	125
2.50	17.70	24.80	62.90	8.90	11.50	25	33
5.10	8.20	15.80	28.61	15.30	17.10	47	51
17.10	22.10	57.10	74.10	36.93	52.80	93	95
24.15	26.31	68.85	80.11	49.99	53.47	16	16
41.63	50.33	106.99	125.28	38.10	46.69	60	79
212.48	**270.71**	**612.52**	**817.14**	**308.67**	**421.90**	**339**	**460**
22.80	31.54	67.50	98.23	25.27	48.98	33	54
61.38	73.42	188.74	252.48	67.41	105.62	77	150
26.83	33.90	71.63	76.60	21.06	26.50	26	29
15.70	19.10	45.50	58.10	17.70	23.80	48	56
8.30	12.75	25.17	42.00	7.20	11.70	23	28
20.20	24.82	88.00	90.00	94.88	116.40	85	75
46.40	62.28	94.42	160.80	65.00	74.00	28	46
10.87	12.90	31.56	38.93	3.76	4.11	13	12
115.35	**129.28**	**366.48**	**409.67**	**151.07**	**189.79**	**236**	**257**
28.77	32.40	119.88	133.29	38.20	48.14	93	95
61.00	64.80	166.00	180.90	72.70	92.00	108	125
8.28	11.81	25.00	29.29	24.77	32.37	12	15
17.30	20.27	55.60	66.19	15.40	17.28	23	22
63.23	**77.46**	**162.41**	**185.87**	**119.89**	**148.99**	**296**	**336**
27.00	33.10	71.00	68.00	55.10	66.02	130	140
0.70	0.80	2.60	2.95	8.11	11.65	13	18
5.82	7.25	14.50	18.43	5.79	7.44	12	14
5.56	6.97	9.52	15.25	4.61	7.24	15	12
2.63	4.13	7.80	10.40	17.28	15.10	38	32
2.92	3.76	8.67	10.39	7.77	13.00	17	46
5.84	8.09	15.86	23.53	8.43	9.67	34	35
5.13	6.25	12.95	17.26	8.98	13.98	26	30
7.63	7.11	19.51	19.66	3.82	4.89	11	9
142.64	**179.09**	**440.83**	**552.22**	**124.02**	**143.34**	**103**	**113**
142.64	179.09	440.83	552.22	124.02	143.34	103	113
26.30	30.04	95.17	107.93	18.00	24.45	24	16
88.54	**103.37**	**252.49**	**377.89**	**86.49**	**113.12**	**154**	**163**
36.88	45.45	104.50	167.23	25.40	39.80	47	64
40.60	44.00	125.70	163.60	12.20	16.00	38	29
11.06	13.92	22.29	47.06	48.89	57.32	69	70
78.66	**96.47**	**296.41**	**325.95**	**100.55**	**125.69**	**117**	**148**
78.66	96.47	296.41	325.95	100.55	125.69	117	148

21-2 续表 6 continued

开发区名称	Name of Development Zone	其中:亿元以上项目(个) Number of Projects above 100 million yuan (unit)	
		2012	2013
湖北省	**Hubei Province**	**2883**	**3328**
武汉市	**Wuhan**	**417**	**460**
武汉江岸经济开发区	Wuhan Jiang'an Economic Development Zone	5	4
武汉江汉经济开发区	Wuhan Jianghan Economic Development Zone	1	
武汉硚口经济开发区	Wuhan Qiaokou Economic Development Zone	6	7
武汉汉阳经济开发区	Wuhan Hanyang Economic Development Zone	20	12
武汉武昌经济开发区	Wuhan Wuchang Economic Development Zone	1	1
武汉青山经济开发区	Wuhan Qingshan Economic Development Zone	18	19
武汉洪山经济开发区	Wuhan Hongshan Economic Development Zone	1	2
武汉临空港经济技术开发区	Wuhan Linkonggang Economic and Technology Development Zone	115	157
武汉汉南经济开发区	Wuhan Hannan Economic Development Zone	11	16
武汉蔡甸经济开发区	Wuhan Caidian Economic Development Zone	28	45
武汉江夏经济开发区	Wuhan Jiangxia Economic Development Zone	55	84
武汉盘龙城经济开发区	Wuhan Panlongcheng Economic Development Zone	6	6
武汉阳逻经济开发区	Wuhan Yangluo Economic Development Zone	37	39
武汉经济技术开发区	Wuhan Economic and Technology Development Zone	23	47
武汉东湖新技术产业开发区	Wuhan East Lake New Technology Industrial Development Zone	103	111
黄石市	**Huangshi**	**186**	**220**
湖北黄石港工业园区	Hubei Huangshi Port Industrial Park	3	3
湖北黄石新港工业园区	Hubei Huangshi New Port Industrial Park	8	13
湖北西塞山工业园区	Hubei Xisaishan Industrial Park	36	57
湖北下陆长乐山工业园区	Hubei Xialu Changleshan Industrial Park	7	11
黄石经济技术开发区	Huangshi Economic and Technology Development Zone	60	95
湖北阳新经济开发区	Hubei Yangxin Economic Development Zone	22	28
湖北大冶经济开发区	Hubei Daye Economic Development Zone	43	46
大冶灵成工业园	Daye Lingcheng Industrial Park	12	14
十堰市	**Shiyan**	**156**	**210**
十堰经济技术开发区	Shiyan Economic and Technology Development Zone	62	86
湖北郧县经济开发区	Hubei Yun County Economic Development Zone	25	37
湖北郧西工业园区	Hubei West Yun Industrial Park	3	4
湖北竹山经济开发区	Hubei Zhushan Economic Development Zone	14	23
湖北竹溪工业园区	Hubei Zhuxi Industrial Park	4	5
湖北房县工业园区	Hubei Fang County Industrial Park	21	27
湖北丹江口经济开发区	Hubei Danjiangkou Economic Development Zone	27	28
宜昌市	**Yichang**	**366**	**478**
湖北西陵经济开发区	Hubei Xiling Economic Development Zone	9	13
湖北伍家岗工业园区	Hubei Wujiagang Industrial Park	5	6
湖北点军工业园区	Hubei Dianjun Industrial Park	3	3
湖北夷陵经济开发区	Hubei Yiling Economic Development Zone	59	84
湖北远安工业园区	Hubei Yuan'an Industrial Park	35	52
湖北兴山经济开发区	Hubei Xingshan Economic Development Zone	3	10
湖北秭归经济开发区	Hubei Zigui Economic Development Zone	11	17
湖北长阳经济开发区	Hubei Changyang Economic Development Zone	19	31
湖北五峰工业园区	Hubei Wufeng Industrial Park	6	7
湖北五峰民族工业园	Hubei Wufeng National Industrial Park	2	2
宜昌高新技术产开发区	Yichang High-tech Industrial Development Zone	145	219
湖北宜都工业园区	Hubei Yidu Industrial Park	16	23
湖北当阳经济开发区	Hubei Dangyang Economic Development Zone	56	103
湖北枝江经济开发区	Hubei Zhijiang Economic Development Zone	62	77
枝江安福寺工业园	Zhijiang Anfu Temple Industrial Park	6	11

新开工项目(个) Number of Newly Opened Projects (unit)		开发区税收总额(万元) Total Tax Revenue of Development (10 000 yuan)		外商投资金额(万美元) Total Value of Foreign Investment (10 000 US dollors)		出口总额(万美元) Total Value of Export (10 000 US dollors)	
2012	2013	2012	2013	2012	2013	2012	2013
4898	**5719**	**10716656.32**	**12332550.39**	**480563.91**	**560004.23**	**1517690.67**	**1798849.40**
581	**580**	**6039773.34**	**6892099.25**	**195484.65**	**221255.04**	**684720.37**	**769341.31**
7	3	42782.00	46283.00				
1		93800.00	112600.00		240.00		4352.00
7	2	94354.00	113224.00	701.00	650.00	12609.00	18408.00
12	5	236711.00	265900.00	0.70	1.36		3000.00
3	2	48640.00	50005.00	280.00	320.00	2100.00	2400.00
21	23	88200.00	95697.00	400.00	1280.00	5655.00	7797.00
6	3	35500.00	3.42			2130.00	420.00
147	163	857763.00	1040836.00	20819.00	24120.00	22454.00	27985.00
6	16	64665.00	65301.00	2891.00	3125.00	9301.00	10535.00
17	39	94991.00	108447.00	5530.00	9600.00	760.00	2000.00
45	56	301700.00	379377.00	8260.00	12000.00	10822.00	14072.60
35	45	132074.00	173787.00			3346.00	2740.00
21	26	84405.00	90047.00	9320.00	10252.00	8806.00	10900.00
68	72	2162182.00	2442512.00	51590.00	59600.00	136300.00	154132.00
197	133	2584901.00	3238654.00	94900.00	111026.00	463912.00	556694.00
386	**358**	**520247.54**	**668328.76**	**25737.06**	**29233.81**	**127700.98**	**155893.58**
7	15	2050.00	2720.00			350.00	380.00
9	10	12907.00	13785.00			200.00	200.00
25	37	72710.16	87252.19		1000.00	49087.13	40896.00
6	19	33185.30	65758.10			3303.20	41221.00
157	102	241088.00	315825.00	16968.00	20022.00	50110.00	53117.00
42	35	27000.00	31000.00	4912.00	4959.00	16986.00	20148.00
128	129	188268.00	255356.00	3700.00	4500.00	5168.00	6543.00
15	12	16319.00	19245.00			425.00	467.00
309	**338**	**209036.63**	**256693.00**	**17574.00**	**20536.00**	**39502.30**	**50964.50**
77	82	127138.00	156380.00	8554.00	9955.00	31806.00	38793.00
46	58	19883.00	27160.00	670.00	1930.00	1427.00	2610.00
6	3	2323.63	2752.00	1500.00	1000.00	100.30	211.50
23	17	10176.00	12101.00		510.00	1011.00	1310.00
2	5	1650.00	6800.00		600.00	300.00	700.00
124	131	14476.00	14483.00	2230.00	1767.00	3753.00	6220.00
31	42	33390.00	37017.00	4620.00	4774.00	1105.00	1120.00
651	**778**	**650015.39**	**749383.34**	**49014.74**	**48885.42**	**127489.50**	**139620.11**
24	35	19433.00	26648.00	1711.00	4220.00	2488.00	3493.00
4	2	11021.00	10756.00			1012.00	1933.00
	3	2496.00	2665.00				
61	57	83448.00	133450.00	4223.00	10609.00	1419.00	1532.00
52	55	67832.00	78783.00	383.00	410.00	6638.00	10260.00
6	17	23088.41	32800.00			17924.61	19500.00
18	29	36457.00	38897.00	330.00	420.00	3308.00	3820.00
59	74	16974.00	17738.00		100.00	4678.00	5480.00
6	24	7596.00	10577.00	76.90		114.00	168.00
8	3	725.00	1997.42				280.00
167	213	283475.00	338662.00	40149.30	42359.00	45029.80	48343.00
118	120	83672.00	98398.00	1571.43	2137.00	19800.00	22492.80
92	111	53649.00	58714.00	3010.00	3510.00	1462.00	2877.00
102	103	147537.00	188847.00	2680.00	2035.00	13136.20	18194.70
12	9	4442.00	5996.00	515.00		13131.00	14365.00

21-2 续表 7 continued

开发区名称	Name of Development Zone	其中:亿元以上项目(个) Number of Projects above 100 million yuan (unit)	
		2012	2013
襄阳市	**Xianyang**	**551**	**532**
襄阳高新技术产业开发区	Xiangyang High-tech Industrial Development Zone	226	224
襄阳鱼梁州经济开发区	Xiangyang Yuliangzhou Economic Development Zone		
襄阳经济技术开发区	Xiangyang Economic Development Zone	58	60
湖北襄城经济开发区	Hubei Xiangcheng Economic Development Zone	12	11
湖北樊城经济开发区	Hubei Fancheng Economic Development Zone	12	41
湖北襄州经济开发区	Hubei Xiangzhou Economic Development Zone	58	60
襄阳工业园	Xiangyang Industrial Park	6	14
湖北南漳经济开发区	Hubei Nanzhang Economic Development Zone	15	20
湖北谷城经济开发区	Hubei Gucheng Economic Development Zone	44	57
谷城石花经济开发区	Gucheng Shihua Economic Development Zone	22	25
湖北保康经济开发区	Hubei Baokang Economic Development Zone	34	28
湖北老河口经济开发区	Hubei Laohekou Economic Development Zone	44	59
湖北枣阳经济开发区	Hubei Zaoyang Economic Development Zone	48	75
枣阳吴店工业园	Zaoyang Wudian Industrial Park	17	26
湖北宜城经济开发区	Hubei Yicheng Economic Development Zone	35	40
鄂州市	**E'zhou**	**123**	**155**
湖北鄂州花湖经济开发区	Hubei E'Zhou Huahu Economic Development Zone	11	24
鄂州葛店经济技术开发区	E'Zhou Gedian Economic and Technology Development Zone	102	115
湖北鄂州经济开发区	Hubei E'Zhou Economic Development Zone	10	16
荆门市	**Jingmen**	**153**	**221**
湖北东宝工业园区	Hubei Dongbao Industrial Park	35	60
湖北荆门高新技术产业园区	Hubei Jingmen High-tech Industrial Development Zone	54	73
湖北荆门化工循环产业园	Hubei Jingmen Chemical Recycling Development Zone	6	15
湖北京山经济开发区	Hubei Jingshan Economic Development Zone	31	54
湖北屈家岭经济开发区	Hubei Qujialing Economic Development Zone	4	8
湖北沙洋经济开发区	Hubei Shayang Economic Development Zone	26	37
湖北钟祥经济开发区	Hubei Zhongxiang Economic Development Zone	23	65
钟祥胡集经济开发区	Zhongxiang Huji Economic Development Zone	12	18
孝感市	**Xiaogan**	**178**	**188**
孝感高新技术产业开发区	Xiaogan high-tech Industrial Development Zone	106	108
湖北孝南经济开发区	Hubei Xiaonan Economic Development Zone	39	47
湖北孝昌经济开发区	Hubei Xiaochang Economic Development Zone	18	30
湖北大悟经济开发区	Hubei Dawu Economic Development Zone		9
湖北云梦经济开发区	Hubei Yunmeng Economic Development Zone	46	57
湖北应城经济开发区	Hubei Yingcheng Economic Development Zone	23	27
湖北安陆经济开发区	Hubei Anlu Economic Development Zone	19	32
湖北汉川经济开发区	Hubei Hanchuan Economic Development Zone	32	38
荆州市	**Jingzhou**	**163**	**186**
湖北沙市经济开发区	Hubei Shashi Economic Development Zone	17	29
湖北荆州城南经济开发区	Jingzhou Chengnan Economic Development Zone	9	15
荆州经济技术开发区	Jingzhou Economic and Technology Development Zone	30	30
湖北公安经济开发区	Hubei Gong'an Economic Development Zone	34	44
湖北监利经济开发区	Hubei Jianli Economic Development Zone	15	17
湖北江陵经济开发区	Hubei Jiangling Economic Development Zone	11	14
湖北石首经济开发区	Hubei Shishou Economic Development Zone	13	20
湖北洪湖经济开发区	Hubei Honghu Economic Development Zone	13	15
洪湖府场经济开发区	Honghu Fuchang Economic Development Zone	2	9
湖北松滋经济开发区	Hubei Songzi Economic Development Zone	17	22
黄冈市	**Huanggang**	**235**	**262**
湖北黄冈经济开发区	Hubei Huanggang Economic Development Zone	47	58

新开工项目(个) Number of Newly Opened Projects (unit)		开发区税收总额(万元) Total Tax Revenue of Development (10 000 yuan)		外商投资金额(万美元) Total Value of Foreign Investment (10 000 US dollors)		出口总额(万美元) Total Value of Export (10 000 US dollors)	
2012	2013	2012	2013	2012	2013	2012	2013
656	**722**	**1071152.49**	**1206166.74**	**42172.36**	**40386.99**	**121238.69**	**156647.32**
185	168	621585.00	686031.00	17000.00	21530.00	55800.00	82016.00
		5256.00	3793.00				
28	31	321480.00	396287.00	6513.00	7152.00	23857.00	19157.00
9	8	78000.00	79821.00	1700.00	1830.00	1160.00	1183.00
35	49	58268.00	72835.00	958.00	1326.00	2558.00	3251.00
28	31	98166.00	153545.00	6513.00	7152.00	5175.00	9512.00
6	17	1344.36	2101.23		35000.00	1519.00	1845.00
21	16	15081.00	15973.00	1440.00	1460.00	1995.00	2132.00
86	92	42561.00	57092.00	1992.00	1250.00	5764.00	3260.00
30	19	23460.00	35896.00	15.00	61.00	962.00	2354.00
17	19	29252.00	17229.57	1500.00	1418.00	2880.00	3920.00
118	123	36143.00	49326.00	4030.00	6387.00	5630.00	19700.00
71	142	44028.00	59200.00	1859.00	2852.00	11275.00	15830.00
35	39	18210.00	29905.72			659.00	790.00
54	54	38400.00	51840.00	7566.00		10260.00	14400.00
122	**155**	**178456.00**	**194316.30**	**8444.00**	**11070.00**	**9947.00**	**12335.00**
9	20	19744.00	28801.00			1280.00	1905.00
104	121	142790.00	145097.30	6766.00	9220.00	6911.00	8730.00
9	14	15922.00	20418.00	1678.00	1850.00	1756.00	1700.00
337	**446**	**272732.45**	**305258.74**	**21636.24**	**29037.20**	**43848.41**	**56658.10**
187	269	28477.00	34954.00			814.00	1898.00
212	249	184225.00	210410.00	9508.00	11560.00	22246.00	25684.00
6	14	1228.00	5106.00			113.00	223.00
61	84	44064.00	57703.00	2119.20	5350.00	4404.00	9180.00
2	4	982.10	983.64		296.00	902.40	1156.00
19	29	18120.00	25368.00	4215.00	6100.00	6400.00	8600.00
29	57	28033.00	36405.00	5662.00	6970.00	5596.00	8038.00
8	11	28958.00	24096.00			3520.00	6500.00
242	**235**	**330956.64**	**367524.27**	**24207.73**	**23853.35**	**64175.61**	**71549.94**
85	90	230138.00	253150.00	17178.00	17209.00	25613.00	28302.00
58	293	55455.00	106000.00	1300.00	1700.00	3425.00	4200.00
25	29	8230.00	11384.20	950.00	1312.00	7725.00	3780.00
7	6	24000.00	26000.00			310.00	982.00
101	91	61193.00	66154.00	3514.00	3959.00	1338.50	3500.00
21	23	53001.00	69020.00	9008.00	10009.00	776.00	998.00
61	31	18326.00	19560.00	980.00	1000.00	2188.00	2765.90
60	73	88669.00	117276.00	4952.00	5350.00	27198.00	38877.00
398	**581**	**298584.87**	**365400.29**	**19155.00**	**44690.77**	**87180.67**	**102820.88**
34	40	19217.00	24788.00	12.11	5.40	10763.00	15217.00
18	18	34588.00	39976.00	500.00		11163.00	13031.00
142	295	108925.00	128537.00	17691.00	18668.00	40469.00	47834.00
27	27	35433.60	55722.90			6864.70	7054.60
28	8	15800.00	16100.00		27000.00	3106.00	4217.00
16	21	9311.00	8194.00			810.13	1610.00
22	18	29563.00	34472.00			10204.00	15519.00
35	40	16898.00	19818.00	835.00	924.00	2250.00	2875.00
28	44	8231.00	15191.46				
43	55	55268.00	82101.00				
478	**594**	**381963.56**	**421955.79**	**45482.83**	**62456.70**	**67803.04**	**109641.92**
68	87	135564.00	152301.00	11333.00	13971.00	16718.00	21376.00

21-2 续表 8 continued

开发区名称	Name of Development Zone	其中:亿元以上项目(个) Number of Projects above 100 million yuan (unit)	
		2012	2013
湖北黄州火车站经济开发区	Hubei Huangzhou Railway Station Economic Development Zone	10	10
黄州工业园	Huangzhou Industrial Park	10	15
湖北龙感湖工业园区	Hubei Longganhu Industrial Park	10	17
湖北团风经济开发区	Hubei Tuanfeng Economic Development Zone	11	10
湖北红安经济开发区	Hubei Hong'an Economic Development Zone	62	75
湖北罗田经济开发区	Hubei Luotian Economic Development Zone	8	10
湖北英山经济开发区	Hubei Yingshan Economic Development Zone	5	8
湖北浠水经济开发区	Hubei Xishui Economic Development Zone	7	15
湖北蕲春李时珍医药工业园区	Hubei Qichun Li Shizhen Pharmaceutical Industrial Park	2	14
蕲春经济开发区	Qichun Economic Development Zone	14	15
湖北黄梅经济开发区	Hubei Huangmei Economic Development Zone	19	23
湖北麻城经济开发区	Hubei Macheng Economic Development Zone	9	9
湖北武穴经济开发区	Hubei Wuxue Economic Development Zone	18	23
咸宁市	**Xianning**	**115**	**134**
湖北咸安经济开发区	Hubei Xian'an Economic Development Zone	8	15
湖北嘉鱼经济开发区	Hubei Jiayu Economic Development Zone	25	44
湖北通城经济开发区	Hubei Tongcheng Economic Development Zone	12	13
湖北崇阳工业园区	Hubei Chongyang Industrial Park	8	12
湖北通山经济开发区	Hubei Tongshan Economic Development Zone	3	5
湖北咸宁经济开发区	Hubei Xianning Economic Development Zone	48	46
湖北赤壁经济开发区	Hubei Chibi Economic Development Zone	8	19
湖北赤壁蒲纺工业园区	Hubei Chibi Puqi Textile Industrial Park	1	
随州市	**Suizhou**	**69**	**70**
湖北随州经济开发区	Hubei Suizhou Economic Development Zone	40	30
湖北曾都经济开发区	Hubei Zengdu Economic Development Zone	21	30
湖北随县经济开发区	Hubei Sui County Economic Development Zone	5	7
湖北广水经济开发区	Hubei Guangshui Economic Development Zone	3	3
恩施自治州	**Enshi Autonomous Prefecture**	**60**	**70**
湖北恩施经济开发区	Hubei Enshi Economic Development Zone	30	30
湖北恩施州经济开发区	Hubei Enshi Prefecture Economic Development Zone	6	9
湖北利川经济开发区	Hubei Lichuan Economic Development Zone	3	4
湖北建始工业园区	Hubei Jianshi Industrial Park	2	1
湖北巴东经济开发区	Hubei Badong Economic Development Zone	8	11
湖北宣恩工业园区	Hubei Xuan'en Industrial Park	2	5
湖北咸丰工业园区	Hubei Xianfeng Industrial Park	3	3
湖北来凤经济开发区	Hubei Laifeng Economic Development Zone	5	5
湖北鹤峰经济开发区	Hubei Hefeng Economic Development Zone	1	2
仙桃市	**Xiantao**	**57**	**66**
湖北仙桃经济开发区	Hubei Xiantao Economic Development Zone	57	66
仙桃彭场工业园	Xiantao Pengchang Industrial Park	5	6
潜江市	**Qianjiang**	**32**	**39**
湖北潜江经济开发区	Hubei Qianjiang Economic Development Zone	12	11
潜江张金经济开发区	Qianjiang Zhangjin Economic Development Zone	5	4
潜江园林经济开发区	Qianjiang Yuanlin Economic Development Zone	15	24
天门市	**Tianmen**	**22**	**35**
湖北天门经济开发区	Hubei Tianmen Economic Development Zone	22	35

新开工项目(个) Number of Newly Opened Projects (unit)		开发区税收总额(万元) Total Tax Revenue of Development (10 000 yuan)		外商投资金额(万美元) Total Value of Foreign Investment (10 000 US dollors)		出口总额(万美元) Total Value of Export (10 000 US dollors)	
2012	2013	2012	2013	2012	2013	2012	2013
13	14	3850.00	4322.00	100.00	100.00	4141.00	4355.00
11	8	7600.00	6596.90	7620.00	16470.00	1600.00	40279.00
15	18	5196.80	7501.00	630.00	448.00	766.00	1059.00
12	10	8500.00	8947.00			4200.00	742.00
97	117	120500.00	130000.00	3469.00	4822.00	1785.00	1800.00
27	29	5688.00	7678.00			3097.00	3727.00
36	45	9456.30	12185.20	3567.00	4235.00	73.90	142.60
45	67	9750.00	15000.00	10000.00	15000.00	9000.00	12000.00
15	18	21800.00	23937.00	7000.00	7060.00	13000.00	15400.00
10	12	19320.00	20641.00			1632.00	2618.00
77	90	16997.00	21601.00	260.00	269.00	1230.00	1508.00
9	9	27988.00	36950.00	746.27	746.27	930.00	979.00
35	54	34079.00	43005.00	480.00	2000.00	8424.00	8494.00
191	**306**	**216094.94**	**261728.71**	**12671.33**	**12219.87**	**19465.37**	**27773.83**
25	40	17118.00	23001.00			3650.00	4015.00
45	95	17219.00	17976.39	366.00	134.00	3800.00	7027.00
14	15	13166.00	22464.00			3923.00	4511.00
36	42	11600.00	14230.00	660.00	760.00	1600.00	1800.00
5	10	12000.00	13700.00	200.00		90.00	110.00
47	40	134900.00	174788.00	4198.00	147.00	4146.10	3154.00
6	45	32869.00	36798.00	7100.00	9200.20	1330.00	2652.28
9	11	2300.00	1390.00	70.00	2500.00	580.00	5730.00
153	**165**	**93921.00**	**97857.50**	**6128.00**	**4020.00**	**49124.00**	**61609.50**
55	56	52275.00	50110.00	1758.00	2100.00	23593.00	23389.50
72	85	31297.00	35876.50	817.00		17658.00	28072.00
8	9	2549.00	3111.00	1903.00		4073.00	6248.00
18	15	7800.00	8760.00	1650.00	1920.00	3800.00	3900.00
178	**207**	**201713.02**	**238429.30**	**39.00**	**225.00**	**7442.20**	**7565.38**
70	80	120996.00	147090.00			2220.00	2400.00
4	7	3000.00	4000.00				
8	2	51806.00	52301.00			640.00	54.00
9	10	2198.13	2980.90			840.85	754.11
17	15	6949.59	9230.00			69.95	465.80
16	34	1010.00	3482.00	39.00	100.00	181.40	282.47
26	27	5716.00	8025.40		125.00	2160.00	2180.00
17	23	6920.00	8096.00			300.00	320.00
11	9	3117.30	3224.00			1030.00	1109.00
34	**58**	**118846.07**	**142166.56**	**6862.00**	**7406.00**	**31869.00**	**36999.00**
34	58	118846.07	142166.56	6862.00	7406.00	31869.00	36999.00
15	6	14253.00	15322.00			18665.00	19554.00
131	**115**	**97462.00**	**120260.00**	**5327.00**	**4025.00**	**32221.00**	**34793.00**
36	54	28408.00	29260.00	1000.00		12060.00	12482.00
33	21	7619.00	8600.00	4327.00	4025.00	11323.00	11377.00
62	40	61435.00	82400.00			8838.00	10934.00
51	**64**	**35701.90**	**44984.39**	**628.00**	**703.00**	**3962.00**	**4635.54**
51	64	35701.90	44984.39	628.00	703.00	3962.00	4635.54

主要统计指标解释

520 户国家重点企业 指 1999 年 10 月经国务院批准确定的 520 户国家重点企业。

重组为集团的原 512 户 指经国务院批准确定的原 512 户重点企业中，经过重组，已成为某个企业集团的母公司或子公司的企业。

省级重点企业 指各省、自治区、直辖市人民政府及主管部门确定的省(自治区、直辖市)级重点企业。

现企原国家百户试点企业 指经国务院 1994 年批准确定的建立现代企业制度百户试点企业。现企原省级试点企业 指各省、自治区、直辖市人民政府及主管部门于 1994 年至 1997 年批准确定的省(自治区、直辖市)级建立现代企业制度原试点企业。

试点企业集团母公司 指国务院批准成立的国家试点企业集团的母公司(核心企业)。

国务院审批企业集团 指由国务院批准组建的国家试点企业集团。

国务院主管部门审批企业集团 指由国务院授权的部门批准组建的企业集团。

省级人民政府审批企业集团 指由各省、自治区、直辖市政府批准组建的企业集团。不包括各省、自治区、直辖市政府的主管部门批准组建的企业集团。

省级政府主管部门审批企业集团 指由省级人民政府授权的部门批准组建的企业集团。

企业景气指数 亦称企业综合生产经营景气指数，是根据企业家对本企业当前综合生产经营情况的判断及对未来的预期(选择“好”、“一般”、“不佳”)而编制的指数，用以综合反映调查总体范围内企业生产经营景气状况。企业景气指数介于 0 和 200 之间，100 为景气指数的临界值：当企业景气指数大于 100 时，表明企业生产经营状况趋于上升或改善，处于景气状态；当企业景气指数小于 100 时，表明企业生产经营状况趋于下降或恶化，处于不景气状态。

Explanatory Notes on Main Statistical Indicators

520 State Major Enterprises refer to the enterprises which were approved and defined as the 520 state major enterprises by the state council in October 1999.

Reorganized As Groups (Original 512 Units) refer to the original 512 enterprises which were permitted and defined by the state council，had become the parent companies or branch companies of certain enterprise group.

Provincial Level Major Enterprises refer the enterprises which were defined by the government of provinces，autonomous areas and manipulates direct under the central government and responsible departments as the provincial major enterprises(autonomous areas，municipalities direct under the central government).

100 Experimental Enterprises (Original State-owned) refer the 100 experimental enterprises of modern enterprises system．which were established through the permission and definition of the state council in 1994.

Experimental Enterprises (Original Provincial Units) refer to the enterprises which were establishment through the permission and definition of the government of the provinces，autonomous areas and municipalities directly under the central government and responsible departments in 1994—1997 as the original experimental enterprises of modern enterprise system under the jurisdiction of minces，autonomous areas and municipalities directly under the central government.

Parent Companies of the Experimental Enterprise Groups refer the parent companies of enterprise groups which were established through the examination and permission of the state council as the parent companies(core enterprises)of the national experimental enterprise groups.

Enterprise Groups Examined and Approved by the State Council refer to the national experimental enterprise groups which were established through the examination and permission of the state council.

Enterprise Groups Examined and Approved by the Responsible Department Of the State Council refer the enterprise groups which were established through the examination and permission of the responsible department according to the authorization of the state council.

Enterprise Groups Examined and Permitted by the Provincial Government refer to the enterprise groups which were established through the examination and permission of the government of the provinces autonomous areas and municipalities direct under the state, excluding the enterprise groups which were established through the examination and permission of responsible department of the government of the provinces, autonomous areas and municipalities directly under the central government.

Enterprise Groups Examined and Approved by the Responsible Departments of the Provincial Government refer the enterprise groups which were established through the permission of the departments authorized by the provincial government.

Index of Operating Situation of the Enterprises which is also called as the index of general operating situation. It is the index working out by entrepreneurs of these enterprises according to the current determination and future expectation(choosing good, regular and bad)of the operating condition of production and management of the enterprises to comprehensive reflect the operating situation of production and management in the scope of the investigative units. The index of operating situation of the enterprises is situated between 2--200, of which 100 is the critical value. When the index is larger than 100, it indicates that the operating condition is growing and taking a turn for the better, and at the manner of operating situation, when the index is smaller than 100, it indicates that the operating condition is decreasing and at the manner of non-operating situation.

22 “两圈”主要经济指标

Major Economic Indicators of “Twice”

资料整理：李现厂　程文懿

22-1 武汉城市圈主要经济指标(2013)

MAIN ECONOMIC INDICATORS OF WUHAN URBAN CIRCLE(2013)

指标	Item	土地面积(平方公里) Land Area (sq.km)	常住人口(万人) Total Population (year-end) (10 000 persons)	地区生产总值(亿元) Gross Regional Product(100 million yuan)	第一产业(亿元) Primary Industry (100 million million yuan)	第二产业(亿元) Secondary Industry (100 million yuan)	#工业(亿元) #Industry (100 million yuan)	第三产业(亿元) Tertiary Industry (100 million yuan)	人均地区生产总值(元) Per Capita Gross Regional Prduct (yuan/person)
合计	**Total**	**58052**	**3073.82**	**15630.00**	**1491.41**	**7766.91**	**6176.64**	**6371.68**	**50940**
武汉市	Wuhan Municipality	8494	1022.00	9051.27	335.40	4396.17	3113.30	4319.70	89000
黄石市	Huangshi Municipality	4583	244.50	1142.03	95.21	699.20	576.20	347.62	46750
鄂州市	Ezhou Municipality	1594	105.70	630.94	78.51	375.08	361.00	177.35	59791
孝感市	Xiaogan Municipality	8910	485.30	1238.93	243.13	602.31	599.48	393.49	25582
黄冈市	Huanggang Municipality	17446	625.19	1332.55	356.79	521.28	413.65	454.48	21348
咸宁市	Xianning Municipality	9861	248.50	872.11	162.90	423.09	430.17	286.12	35166
仙桃市	Xiantiao Municipality	2538	118.49	504.28	80.17	268.77	255.03	155.34	42559
潜江市	Qianjiang Municipality	2004	95.24	492.70	65.00	290.97	260.54	136.73	51787
天门市	Tianmen Municipality	2622	128.90	365.19	74.30	190.04	167.27	100.85	27792

22-1 续表 1 continued

指标	Item	就业人员(万人) Employed Persons (10 000 persons)	全社会固定资产投资(亿元) Investment in Fixed Assets (100 million yuan)	地方公共财政预算收入(亿元) Revenue of Local Governments (100 million yuan)	#各项税收(亿元) #Taxes (100 million yuan)
合计	**Total**	**1758.66**	**11894.12**	**1379.07**	**1071.06**
武汉市	Wuhan Municipality	522.24	5974.53	978.52	793.49
黄石市	Huangshi Municipality	134.20	947.69	78.36	55.09
鄂州市	Ezhou Municipality	64.85	567.19	38.43	27.90
孝感市	Xiaogan Municipality	303.40	1215.35	89.05	58.23
黄冈市	Huanggang Municipality	357.00	1365.57	79.98	53.02
咸宁市	Xianning Municipality	153.69	953.00	58.71	41.13
仙桃市	Xiantiao Municipality	89.20	306.78	21.00	16.73
潜江市	Qianjiang Municipality	55.56	303.26	20.00	14.96
天门市	Tianmen Municipality	78.52	260.75	15.02	10.52

22-1 续表 2 continued

指标	Item	地方财政支出(亿元) Expenditures of Local Governments (100 million yuan)	农村居民人均纯收入(元) Annual Per Capita Disposable Income of Rural Households (yuan)	城镇居民人均可支配收入(元) Annual Per Capita Disposable Income of Urban Households (yuan)	农林牧渔业总产值(亿元) Gross Output Value of Agriculture (100 million yuan)
合计	**Total**	**2179.15**	**9007**	**26958**	**24059.96**
武汉市	Wuhan Municipality	1122.88	12713	29821	5302.66
黄石市	Huangshi Municipality	150.79	8492	21330	1337.59
鄂州市	Ezhou Municipality	70.87	10210	20878	1384.96
孝感市	Xiaogan Municipality	227.90	9023	19819	4523.95
黄冈市	Huanggang Municipality	305.16	6966	18432	5322.20
咸宁市	Xianning Municipality	158.14	8480	18581	2647.03
仙桃市	Xiantiao Municipality	50.08	10365	19065	1362.89
潜江市	Qianjiang Municipality	46.80	10017	19187	1092.84
天门市	Tianmen Municipality	46.53	9608	17112	1085.84

22-1 续表 3 continued

指标	Item	房屋建筑竣工面积(万平方米) Floor Space Completed of Buildings (10 000 sq.m)	民用汽车拥有量(辆) Possession of Civil Vehicles (unit)	邮电业务总收入(亿元) Business Volume of Post Services(100 million yuan)	社会消费品零售总额(亿元) Total Retail Sales(100 million yuan)	进出口总额(亿美元) Imp. and Exp. Value of Commodities (USD 10 000)	出口额(亿美元) Export Value of Commodities (USD 10 000)	实际外商直接投资(万美元) Actually Foreign Direct Investments (USD 10 000)
合计	**Total**	**7484.54**	**2203879**	**282.03**	**6630.88**	**281.38**	**157.06**	**544257.60**
武汉市	Wuhan Municipality	2258.95	1320771	164.41	3878.60	217.52	119.43	404000.60
黄石市	Huangshi Municipality	437.42	120424	19.50	461.03	28.53	12.05	49000.00
鄂州市	Ezhou Municipality	493.58	97021	16.36	205.10	4.92	1.76	16202.00
孝感市	Xiaogan Municipality	1820.56	132075	25.22	602.64	10.25	7.80	27518.00
黄冈市	Huanggang Municipality	1456.91	202439	29.28	626.41	5.36	4.51	6749.00
咸宁市	Xianning Municipality	306.00	122510	14.34	320.64	3.36	2.68	24674.00
仙桃市	Xiantiao Municipality	330.20	47379	2.95	202.50	6.64	4.47	7981.00
潜江市	Qianjiang Municipality	22.13	124011	5.66	131.56	4.14	3.81	4802.00
天门市	Tianmen Municipality	358.78	37249	4.31	202.40	0.67	0.55	3331.00

粮食产量(万吨) Output of Grain (10 000 tons)	棉花产量(万吨) Output of Cotton (tons)	油料产量(万吨) Output of Oil-bearing Crops (10 000 tons)	工业企业单位数(个) Number of Enterprises (unit)	大型企业(个) Large Enterprises (unit)	中型企业(个) Medium Enterprises (unit)	小型企业(个) Small Enterprises (unit)
1078.60	**29.90**	**159.85**	**7540**	**202**	**1197**	**6141**
126.87	3.32	18.66	2289	89	316	1884
64.42	0.76	9.38	648	16	106	526
35.51	0.70	6.09	468	5	31	432
223.64	4.14	24.21	1132	25	170	937
318.98	8.62	55.39	1215	10	113	1092
104.67	0.55	10.19	801	5	117	679
80.99	2.93	13.05	358	17	124	217
52.00	3.97	11.42	355	14	124	217
71.50	4.93	11.46	274	21	96	157

入境旅游者人数(万人次) Number of International Tourists (10 000 person-times)	国际旅游外汇收入(万美元) Foreign Exchange Earnings (USD 10 000)	金融机构人民币存款(亿元) State Bank Deposits (100 million yuan)	本外币个人存款(亿元) Urban & Rural Savings Deposits (100 million yuan)	金融机构人民币贷款(亿元) State Bank Loans(100 million yuan)	普通高等学校数(所) Schools on Regular Institutions of Higher Education (unit)	普通高等学校在校学生数(万人) Enrollment on Regular Institutions of Higher Education (10 000 persons)	卫生机构床位数(张) Number of Beds in Health Care Institutions (bed)	#卫生技术人员(人) #Medical and Technical Personnel (person)
166.77	**93655.55**	**21465.00**	**9355.07**	**16792.00**	**95**	**115.8894**	**147222**	
161.37	91431.03	14916.00	5117.43	12804.00	80	96.64	66563	
0.27	190.66	1152.00	599.06	770.00	3	3.67	13220	15096
0.50	271.31	398.00	234.82	271.00	1	1.31	4410	5093
1.06	499.31	1407.00	944.69	661.00	2	4.07	16058	19391
0.90	285.77	1721.00	1199.01	655.00	4	4.83	23192	28066
1.28	500.19	778.00	449.39	443.00	2	4.20	11407	14723
1.17	380.61	380.00	271.67	148.00	1	0.77	3731	3622
0.07	26.35	372.00	256.44	132.00	1	0.33	3799	5621
0.16	70.32	341.00	282.56	114.00	1	0.07	4842	3786

22-2 鄂西生态文化旅游圈主要经济指标(2013)
MAIN ECONOMIC INDICATORS OF WUHAN URBAN CIRCLE(2013)

指标	Item	土地面积(平方公里) Land Area (sq.km)	常住人口(万人) Total Population (year-end) (10 000 persons)	地区生产总值(亿元) Gross Regional Product(100 million yuan)	第一产业(亿元) Primary Industry (100 million yuan)	第二产业(亿元) Secondary Industry (100 million yuan)	#工业(亿元) #Industry (100 million yuan)	第三产业(亿元) Tertiary Industry (100 million yuan)	人均地区生产总值(元) Per Capita Gross Regional Prduct (yuan/person)
合计	**Total**	**127909**	**2725.18**	**10483.21**	**1634.66**	**5626.00**	**5117.15**	**3222.56**	**38532**
宜昌市	Yichang Municipality	21084	409.83	2818.07	335.95	1693.77	1550.69	788.35	68846
荆州市	Jingzhou Municipality	14067	573.94	1334.93	319.09	596.20	539.84	419.64	23300
襄阳市	Xiangyang Municipality	19724	559.12	2814.02	386.45	1611.41	1470.50	816.16	50509
荆门市	Jingmen Municipality	12404	288.72	1202.61	190.30	651.93	610.98	360.38	41668
十堰市	Shiyan Municipality	23680	336.70	1080.59	143.03	547.01	498.04	390.55	32142
随州市	Suizhou Municipality	9636	218.01	661.94	124.79	320.26	281.35	216.89	30377
恩施州	Enshi Prefecture	24061	331.20	552.48	133.28	197.75	160.85	221.45	16697
神农架	Shennongjia Forest Region	3253	7.66	18.57	1.77	7.67	4.90	9.14	24265

22-2 续表 1 continued

指标	Item	就业人员(万人) Employed Persons (10 000 persons)	第一产业(万人) Primary Industry (10 000 persons)	第二产业(万人) Secondary Industry (10 000 persons)	第三产业(万人) Tertiary Industry (10 000 persons)	全社会固定资产投资(亿元) Investment in Fixed Assets (100 million yuan)	地方公共财政预算收入(亿元) Revenue of Local Governments (100 million yuan)
合计	**Total**	**1591.67**	**580.72**	**367.00**	**643.95**	**8658.71**	**685.88**
宜昌市	Yichang Municipality	223.10	70.40	67.00	85.70	2106.96	206.31
荆州市	Jingzhou Municipality	362.79	114.15	88.93	159.71	1355.60	71.95
襄阳市	Xiangyang Municipality	314.40	106.30	83.60	124.50	2086.64	191.53
荆门市	Jingmen Municipality	154.74	59.23	38.62	56.89	1014.64	59.84
十堰市	Shiyan Municipality	210.40	89.38	38.62	82.4	904.32	73.53
随州市	Suizhou Municipality	135.00	59.70	28.70	46.60	654.60	29.67
恩施州	Enshi Prefecture	185.80	78.80	20.79	86.21	510.40	50.05
神龙架	Shennongjia Forest Region	5.44	2.76	0.74	1.94	25.56	3.00

22-2 续表 2 continued

指标	Item	#各项税收(亿元) #Taxes (100 million yuan)	地方财政支出(亿元) Expenditures of Local Governments (100 million yuan)	农村居民人均纯收入(元) Annual Per Capita Disposable Income of Rural Households (yuan)	城镇居民人均可支配收入(元) Annual Per Capita Disposable Income of Urban Households (yuan)	农林牧渔业总产值(亿元) Gross Output Value of Agriculture (100 million yuan)
合计	**Total**	**509.33**	**1708.05**	**8522**	**19101**	**2848.46**
宜昌市	Yichang Municipality	152.25	364.44	9121	20934	555.63
荆州市	Jingzhou Municipality	53.39	255.92	9909	18706	578.34
襄阳市	Xiangyang Municipality	141.38	364.87	9785	19329	678.91
荆门市	Jingmen Municipality	42.06	158.79	10615	19820	337.93
十堰市	Shiyan Municipality	56.13	231.42	5226	17694	250.15
随州市	Suizhou Municipality	21.79	100.04	9490	19806	216.72
恩施州	Enshi Prefecture	40.45	216.69	5235	16639	227.22
神农架	Shennongjia Forest Region	1.88	15.88	5677	14937	3.56

粮食产量(万吨) Output of Grain (10 000 tons)	棉花产量(吨) Output of Cotton (tons)	油料产量(万吨) Output of Oil-bearing Crops (10 000 tons)	工业企业单位数(个) Number of Enterprises (unit)	大型企业(个) Large Enterprises (unit)	中型企业(个) Medium Enterprises (unit)	小型企业(个) Small Enterprises (unit)
1760.30	**280472.05**	**181.23**	**6273**	**127**	**688**	**5305**
164.53	32616.00	23.92	1233	39	179	981
386.06	138766.00	62.75	861	12	97	736
502.81	41778.00	24.97	1529	31	197	1260
267.60	47689.85	38.80	922	23	62	817
116.06	188.00	13.20	696	16	68	590
158.18	19398.20	7.37	632	5	68	554
162.86	36.00	10.17	390	1	16	360
2.20		0.05	10		1	7

22-2 续表 3 continued

指标	Item	房屋建筑竣工面积(万平方米) Floor Space Completed of Buildings (10 000 sq.m)	民用汽车拥有量(辆) Possession of Civil Vehicles (unit)	邮电业务总收入(亿元) Business Volume of Post Services(100 million yuan)	社会消费品零售总额(亿元) Total Retail Sales(100 million yuan)	进出口总额(亿美元) Imp. and Exp. Value of Commodities (USD 10 000)	出口额(亿美元) Export Value of Commodities (USD 10 000)	实际外商直接投资(万美元) Actually Foreign Direct Investments (USD 10 000)
合计	**Total**	**9412.33**	**1543915**	**170.39**	**4094.67**	**82.51**	**71.32**	**144584.00**
宜昌市	Yichang Municipality	1784.21	320768	30.51	881.93	23.50	20.17	27002.00
荆州市	Jingzhou Municipality	1083.79	220388	35.60	781.36	13.66	11.27	10824.00
襄阳市	Xiangyang Municipality	1669.67	347636	34.62	966.31	16.20	14.34	53746.00
荆门市	Jingmen Municipality	2069.97	168226	17.97	414.68	7.77	6.18	26275.00
十堰市	Shiyan Municipality	942.30	197671	18.40	491.51	4.83	4.23	15615.00
随州市	Suizhou Municipality	930.81	99630	13.26	333.86	12.67	11.27	8774.00
恩施州	Enshi Prefecture	924.17	183905	19.43	218.28	3.88	3.85	2348.00
神龙架	Shennongjia Forest Region	7.41	5691	0.60	6.75	0.01	0.01	

入境旅游者人数(万人次) Number of International Tourists (10 000 person-times)	国际旅游外汇收入(万美元) Foreign Exchange Earnings (USD 10 000)	金融机构(含外资)本外币存款余额(亿元) State Bank Deposits (100 million yuan)	金融机构本外币储蓄存款(亿元) Financial Institutions Local & Foreign Currency Deposits (100 million yuan)	金融机构(含外资)本外币贷款余额(亿元) Financial Institutions Local & Foreign Currency Balance of of Loans (100 million yuan)	普通高等学校数(所) Schools on Regular Institutions of Higher Education(unit)	普通高等学校在校学生数(万人) Enrollment on Regular Institutions of Higher Education (10 000 persons)	卫生机构床位数(张) Number of Beds in Health Care Institutions (bed)	#卫生技术人员(人) #Medical and Technical Personnel (person)
101.19	**28236.63**	**10450.00**	**6210.98**	**5866.00**	**29**	**35.25**	**137888**	**146309**
34.34	8273.10	2382.00	1203.02	1749.00	5	5.98	22797	25719
5.61	1653.85	1743.00	1182.57	798.00	8	11.35	23447	25889
4.89	2986.10	2182.00	1320.05	1245.00	5	6.46	27480	30880
2.15	523.40	1124.00	734.18	561.00	1	2.12	14524	15389
17.08	5824.11	1443.00	789.42	726.00	7	4.89	22593	23474
1.25	678.44	726.00	499.62	329.00	1	0.68	8242	9065
32.68	7415.08	809.00	466.25	449.00	2	3.77	18422	15712
3.21	882.55	41.00	15.87	9.00			383	181

主要统计指标解释

规划面积：指国土部门核定的开发区规划面积。

实际开发面积：指开发区实际开发并已完成基础设施建设的面积。

企业个数：指报告期末已在工商行政管理机关登记注册、并在开发区管理机构进行统计登记的法人单位数，包括内资企业、港澳台投资企业和外商投资企业。不含个体企业。

工业企业：包括采矿业、制造业、电力、燃气及水的生产和供应业。

规模以上工业企业：是指企业所在地在开发区内的全部年主营收入2000万元及以上的法人工业企业。即无论企业是否在开发区注册，也无论企业隶属何行政级别或部门，只要所在地在开发区的所有规模以上企业都在本制度规定的统计范围以内。反之，所在地不在开发区，尽管其在开发区注册的规模以上企业也不在本制度规定的统计范围之内。

高新技术企业：指生产高新技术产品经省科学技术厅授牌的企业。

外商投资企业：指企业注册登记类型中的中外合资、合作经营企业、外资企业和外商投资股份有限公司之和。（含港、澳、台商投资企业 ： 指企业注册登记类型中的港、澳、台资合资、合作、独资经营企业和股份有限公司之和。）

第三产业：除第一、第二产业以外的其他各业。由于第三产业包括的行业多、范围广，根据我国的实际情况，第三产业可分为两大部分；一是流通部门，二是服务部门。具体又可分为四个层次：

第一层次：流通部门，包括交通运输、仓储及邮电通信业，批发和零售贸易、餐饮业。

第二层次：为生产和生活服务的部门，包括金融、保险业，地质勘查业、水利管理业，房地产业，社会服务业，农、林、牧、渔服务业，交通运输辅助业，综合技术服务业等。

第三层次：为提高科学文化水平和居民素质服务的部门，包括教育、文化艺术及广播电影电视业，卫生、体育和社会福利业，科学研究业等。

第四层次：为社会公共需要服务的部门，包括国家机关、政党机关和社会团体以及军队、警察等。

从业人员：指报告期末在开发区企业、行政和事业单位中工作，取得工资或其他形式的劳动报酬的全部人员数。包括在岗职工，再就业的离退休人员、民办教师及在企业工作的外方人员和港澳台方人员、兼职人员、借用的外单位人员和第二职业者。不包括离开本单位但仍保留劳动关系的职工。

开发区生产总值： 即按市场价格计算的国内生产总值的简称。指开发区内所有常住单位在一定时期内生产活动的最终成果。国内生产总值有三种表现形态，即价值形态、收入形态和产品形态。

从价值形态看，它是所有常住单位在一定时期内生产的全部货物和服务价值超过同期投入的全部非固定资产货物和服务价值的差额，即所有常住单位的增加值之和；从收入形态看，它是所有常住单位在一定时期内创造并分配给常住单位和非常住单位的初次分配收入之和；从产品形态看它是最终使用的货物和服务减去进口货物和服务。在实际核算中，国内生产总值的三种表现形态表现为三种计算方法，即生产法、收入法和支出法。三种方法分别从不同的方面反映国内生产总值及其构成。

(1) 生产法是从生产的角度衡量常住单位在一定时期新创造价值的方法。即从生产的全部货物和服务总产品价值中，扣除生产过程中投入的中间货物和服务价值得到增加价值。国民经济各产业部门生产法增加值计算公式如下：

增加值＝总产出－中间投入 将国民经济各产业部门生产法增加值相加，得到生产法GDP。

总产出：指常住单位在一定时期内生产的所有货物和服务的价值，既包括新增价值，也包括转移价值。它反映常住单位生产活动的总规模。总产出按生产者价格计算。

中间投入：指常住单位在一定时期内生产过程中消耗和使用的非固定资产货物和服务的价值。中间投入也称为中间消耗，反映用于生产过程中的转移价值，一般按购买者价格计算。计入中间投入的货物和服务必须具备两个条件，一是与总产出的计算范围保持一致；二是本期一次性使用的。

(2)收入法也称为分配法。按收入法计算国内生产总值是从生产过程创造收入的角度，对常住单位的生产活动成果进行核算。按照这种计算方法，增加值由劳动者报酬、生产税净额、固定资产折旧和营业盈余四个部分组成。计算公式为：增加值=劳动者报酬+生产税净额+固定资产折旧+营业盈余。国民经济各部门的增加值之和等于国内生产总值。

(3)支出法是从最终使用的角度反映国内生产总值最终使用去向的一种方法。最终使用包括货物和服务的最终消费支出、资本形成总额、货物和服务净出口三部分，计算公式为：国内生产总值=最终消费支出+资本形成总额+货物和服务净出口。

按三种方法计算的国内生产总值反映的是同一经济总体在同一时期的生产活动成果，因此，从理论上讲，三种计算方法所得到的结果应该是一致的。但是，在实践中，由于受资料来源的口径范围的限制和计算方法的影响，要保证这三种计算方法所得的结果完全相等几乎是不可能的。

工业总产值(现价)：是以货币形式表现的，工业企业在一定时期内生产的工业最终产品或提供工业性劳务活动的总价值量。

工业总产值包括本期生产成品价值、对外加工费收入，在制品半成品期末期初差额价值三部分。

①本期生产成品价值：是指企业本期生产，并在报告期内不再进行加工，经检验、包装入库的全部工业成品(半成品)价值合计，包括企业生产的自制设备及提供给本企业在建工程、其他非工业部门和生活福利部门等单位使用的成品价值，本期生产成品价值按自备原材料生产的产品的数量乘以本期不含增值税(销项税额)的产品实际销售平均单价计算；会计核算中按成本价格转帐的自制设备和自产自用的成品，按成本价格计算生产成品价值。生产成品价值中不包括用定货者来料加工的成品(半成品)价值。

②对外加工费收入：是指企业在报告期内完成的对外承接的工业品加工(包括用定货者来料加工产品)的加工费收入和对外工业修理作业所取得的加工费收入。对外加工费收入按不含增值税(销项税额)的价格计算，可根据会计"产品销售收入"科目的有关资料取得。

对于本企业对内非工业部门提供的加工修理、设备安装的劳务收入，如果企业会计核算基础比较好，能取得这部分资料，而且这部分价值所占比重较大，应包括在对外加工费收入中。

③自制半成品在制品期末期初差额价值：是指企业报告期自制半成品、在制品期末减期初的差额价值，本指标一般可从会计核算资料中取得。如果会计产品成本核算中不计算半成品、在制品的成本，则总产值中也不包括这部分价值，反之则包括。

工业增加值：指工业企业在报告期内以货币形式表现的工业生产活动的最终成果，是企业全部生产活动的总成果扣除了在生产过程中消耗或转移的物质产品和劳务价值后的余额，是企业生产过程中新增加的价值。

计算工业增加值通常采用两种方法。一是"生产法"，二是"收入法"，目前工业统计主要采用"生产法"计算工业增加值。

"生产法"，即从工业生产过程中产品和劳务价值形成的角度入手，剔除生产环节中间投入的价值，从而得到新增价值的方法。公式为：

工业增加值=工业总产值—工业中间投入+本期应交增值税

上述公式中，本期应交增值税的企业为负数时，综合部门汇总时按零处理。

"收入法"，即从工业生产过程中创造的原始收入初次分配的角度，对工业生产活动最终成果进行核算的一种方法，其计算公式为：

工业增加值=固定资产折旧+劳动者报酬+生产税净额+营业盈余

工业中间投入：1. 定义：指企业在报告期内用于工业生产活动所一次性消耗的外购原材料、燃料、动力及其他实物产品和对外支付的服务费用。

2．计算原则：计算工业中间投入须遵循以下三条原则：(1) 必须是从企业外部购入的产品和服务的价值，不包括生产过程中回收的废料以及自制品的价值。(2) 必须是本期投入生产，并一次性消耗的产品和服务的价值，不包括固定资产转移价值：(3) 中间投入的计算口径必须与总产值的计算口径相一致：即计入工业中间投入的产品和服务价值必须已经计入了工业总产值中。

3．分类：工业中间投入按企业支付对象可以分为中间物质投入和中间劳务投入。中间物质投入是指生产过程中所消耗的外购原材料、燃料、动力以及其它实物产品和支付给物质生产部门(工业、农业、批发零售贸易业、建筑业、货物运输及邮电业)的服务费用，中间劳务投入指支付给非物质生产部门(如金融、保险、文化教育、科学研究、医疗卫生、行政管理)的服务费用。

工业中间投入按照具体内容分为直接材料、制造费用中的中间投入、管理费用中的中间投入、销售费用中的中间投入和利息支出五大项。

日常统计中计算中间投入是按第二种分类计算的。

4．计算方法：计算工业中间投入的具体方法可以分为二种。一是正算法，即将制造费用、管理费用、销售费用中属于中间投入的部分分别相加，再加上直接材料和利息支出，得出工业中间投入合计。二是倒算法，即分别用制造费用、管理费用、销售费用合计减去其中属于增加值的项目(大体包括工资、福利费、折旧、劳动保险费、职工待业保险费等)，倒算出三项费用中的中间投入，再加上直接材料和利息支出，得出工业中间投入合计。在实算操作过程中，采用倒算法计算比较简便易行。

5．资料来源：计算中间投入的资料来源，可分别根据企业“产品成本表”、“管理费用”、“财务费用”、“销售费用”明细表归纳整理填报。

高新技术增加值：增加值是指报告期内企业在生产活动中新创造的价值。

高新技术增加值指报告期省科技厅认定的高新技术企业的增加值和非高新技术企业中的高新技术产品的增加值两部分。高新技术产品指高新技术领域的产品。即满足下列条件之一的产品：①首次应用新科学原理生产的最新产品；②首次应用最新工艺生产并使产品质量、成本和劳动效率有显著改进的产品；③技术水平达到90年代国际先进水平的产品。

有两种计算方法：一是“生产法”；二是“收入法”，亦称要素分配法。计算方法为：

(1) 按生产法计算的工业增加值=工业总产值—工业中间投入+本期应交增值税；(2) 按分配法计算的工业增加值=固定资产折旧+劳动者报酬+生产税净额+营业盈余。

主营业务收入：指企业经常性的、主要业务所产生的收入。不同行业的企业主营业务收入包括的内容不同。工业企业的主营业务收入主要包括销售产品、自制半成品、提供工业性劳务等收入；商品流通企业的主营业务收入主要包括销售商品取得的收入。主营业务收入一般占企业收入的比重较大，对企业的经济效益产生较大的影响。在会计核算中单独设置“主营业务收入”科目核算经常性的、主要业务所产生的收入。

固定资产投资总额：指开发区各单位报告期内500万元以上(含500万元)项目完成的投资额（包括实际完成的建筑安装工程价值，设备、工具、器具的购置费，以及实际发生的其他费用），是以货币表示的建造和购置固定资产活动的工作量以及与此有关的费用总称。

基础设施建设投资：指报告期内开发区基础公用设施：包括供水排水、供气、供热、供电、环卫设施、排污系统、固体废弃物收集和处理系统、电信及道路、桥梁、平整土地等施工建设投资。

施工项目个数：指报告期内曾进行建筑或安装工程施工活动的建设项目个数，包括报告期内新开工项目、报告期以前开工跨入报告期继续施工的项目以及报告期施过工并在报告期内全部建成投产或停缓建的项目个数。

税收总额：指开发区全口径税收收入。包含国税收入、地税收入。主要有增值税、营业税、所得税、城市维护建设税、城镇土地使用税、房产税、印花税、资源税、土地增值税等。

招商引资总额：指报告期内除本行政区划以外的国内外投资者在开发区的投资金额之和。

外商投资金额：指外国企业和经济组织或个人(包括华侨、港澳台胞以及我国在境外注册的企业)按我国有关政策、法规，用现汇、实物、技术等在我国境内开办外商独资企业、与我国境内的企业或经济组织共同举办中外合资经营企业、合作经营企业或合作开发资源的投资(包括外商投资收益的再投资)，以及经政府有关部门批准的项目投资总额内企业从境外借入的资金。

省外境内投资额：指报告期内除湖北省以外的国内投资者（不包括港、澳、台）在开发区的投资金额。

出口总额：指实际出口的货物总金额。我国规定出口货物按离岸价格统计。

高新产品出口交货值：指企业生产的交给外贸部门或自营(委托)出口(包括销往香港、澳门、台湾)，用外汇价格结算的批量销售，在国内或在边境批量出口等的高新产品价值，还包括外商来样、来料加工、来件装配和补偿贸易等生产的产品价值。

Explanatory Notes on Main Statistical Indicators

Land Area Approved for Development Zone refers to the land area of development zone ratified for program by the state department of territory.

Floor Area of Development Zone refers to the land area of development zone that is practically exploited and occupied.

The Number of Enterprise refers to the number of impersonal entity that has registered at industrial organs and commerce administration at the end of report period and that has been counted and registered. Included in this catogary are domestic—funded enterprises, enterprises with funds from Hong kong,Macao,Taiwan and foreign—funded enterprises. Private enterprises are excluded.

Enterprises of High and New Technology refer to enterprises verified by provincial office of science and technology that produce hi-tech products.

Industrial Enterprises include mining, manufacturing, and manufacturing and supply of power, gas and water.

Industrial enterprises above designated size refer to entity industrial enterprises whose main annual turnover exceeds 5 million in the circle of development zone where enterpriese are located. That is to say,no matter enterprises has registered or not, what department enterprises belong to, all the enterprises whose location are in the development zone are counted which are above designated size. Otherwise, enterprises above designated size whose location is not in the development zone are not counted although they have registered at development zone.

Employees refer to all the workers working in enterprises in development zone,administrative unit and public institution who have got their income or payment of labour in other forms at the end of report period. Included in this category are workers on guard, re—employed laid—off workers and retirees, citizen-managed teachers; foreign workers in enterprises,workers of Hong Kong, Macao and Taiwan, part—time workers, borrowed workers from external enterprises and second—job workers. Workers having left enterprises who reserve labour relations are excluded.

Total turnover of technology, industry and trade refers to the total sum of product sales proceeds, technological gain and goods sales proceeds that are related to our products,other business gain,external—business gain in one year,and the like.

Technological turnover refers to the gain of technology transferrance, technology contract, technology advisory and service, technology share,products of pilotscale experiment and the gain of external-entrusted scientific research.

Technology contract turnover refers to the gain from contract of technology program design,design and contract of technology project.

Technology advisory and service turnover refers to the income from technical intellegence, technilcal information,technical advisory and test analysis provided availing enterprises themselves of human resources,physical resources and data system, and other kinds of technical service.

Revenue of entrusted reserch and development refers to the revenue from reserch and development of new products contracted provided to various social units.

Gross Industrial Output Value (at current price) refers to the total volum of final industrial products produced and industrial services provided in money terms during a given period .

Gross Industrial Output Value consists of 3 components: value of the finished products during the reference period, income from external processing, and value of change in semi-finished products at the end of and at the beginning of the reference period.

①value of the finished products during the reference period refers to the value of all finished(semi-finished) industrial products that are produced during the reference period without the need for further processing, checked for accepatance, packed and put into the warehouse of the enterprise, including the value of own-produced equipment and the value of products provided to the projects under construction of the enterprise, and to other non-industrial or welfare units. Value of finished products during the reference period is calculated by the quantity of products produced using own materials multiplied by the average unit prices at which products are sold(exculding value-added tax). Own-produced equipment and products for own use are value at cost prices as in the case of enterprise accounting. Value of finished products does not include the value of finished products(semi-finished products) that are produced using the materials from the clients who make the ordres.

②Income from external processing refers to income from contracted external processing of industrial products(including processing of industrial products using materials from the clients), and the income from industrial repairing work provided to other units. Income from external processing is calculated using information from the item "products sales income" in the enterprise accounting at the prices excluding value-added tax.For income from external services such as processing, repairing and installation of equipment provided to non-industrial units within the enterprise, if the accounting work of the enterprise is good enough to separate it from other records, and the share of such services is significant, it should also be included in the income from external processing.

③value of change in semi-finished products at the end of and at the beginning of the reference period refers to the value of change in semi-finished products at the end and at the beginning of the reference period, which generally can be obtained from accounting records of enterprises. If the enterprise accounting excludes the cost of semi-finished products, then it should not be inculded in the gross industrial output value,and vice versa.

High and new technology value High and new technology products refer to products in the area of high and new technology, namely any kind of products meeting following standars: ① the latest products using latest scientific principles the first time; ②the products that are produced by the latest technology and have noticeably improved the quality, cost and work efficiency; ③ products whose technical merit has reached advanced international standards of 1990s. High and new technology value refers to 2 components: the value of high and new technology enterprises designated by provincial Science and Technology Office in reference period, and value of high and new technology products of non-high-and-new technology enterprises.

Industrial value added refers to the final results of industrial production enterprises in money terms during the the reference period.

Industrial value added can be usually calculated by two approaches:the production approach,and the income approach.Industrial stastics mainly adopts the production approach to calculate the industrial value added at present.

The production approach is the approach that newly-increased value is gained by eliminating the value indulged in the production link in terms of value formation of products and labor in the process of industrial prodution. The formula is: Industrial value added= total industrial value-industrial intermediate input

+ current value added tax receivable

In this formula,when current value added tax receivale is minus, the Integration Department will treat it as zero.

The income approach is an approach that final results of industrial production activities are checked in terms of the primary distribution of original income created in the indusrial production. Here is its formula: Industrial value added= depreciation of fixed assets+remuneration of labourers+net of produce tax+ operating surplus

Industrial intermediate input:

1.Definition: It refers to the service cost for purchased raw material,gas,power and other physical products,and external-paid services consumed during the reference period for the industrial production of enterprises.

2.Calculating principles:Calculating industrial intermediate input must follow the three principles:(1)The value must be the value of goods and services that are purchased from outside,exculding the value of reclaimed waste materials in the production and that of own products.(2) The value must be the value of goods and services that are inputted into production consumed during the reference period,excluding transfer value of fixed assets.(3)The calculating units of the intermediate input must be in correspondence with that of total value, namely the value of products and service reckoned in industrial intermediate input has been reckoned in industrial value.

3.Category: Industrial intermediate input in terms of pay objectcan be classified as intermediate material input and intermediate labor input . Intermediate material input refers to the the purchased raw material, gas,power and other physical products consumed in the production, and the cost of service paid to departments of material production(industry,agriculcuture, wholesales and retail trade,construction goods transportation and post). Intermediate labor input refers to cost of service paid to departments of nonmaterial production(finance,insurance,cultural education,scientific research,medical health and administration)

Industrial intermediate input in terms of concrete content can be classified into 5 components , namely direct consumption of materials,industrial intermediate input in manufacturing cost, industrial intermediate input in management cost, industrial intermediate input in marketing cost and expenditure on interest.

Intermediate input in common calculating is calculated by the second category.

4.Calculating approaches:the calculating approaches to industrial intermediate input have two approaches. Positive calculating, namely add respectively the manufacuring cost, management cost,sales cost that belong to intermediate input, then add direct material and interest expense.The final result is reconed into the total. Negative calculating, namely manufacturing cost, management cost, sale cost that belong to value-added items(generally included are sallary, welfarism, depreciation,labor insurance, employee's job-waiting insurance,ect)is substracted respectively from the total.The result is the its intermediate input respectively. Then direct material and interest expense are added. The final result is reconed into the total. Negative calculating is easier to carry out in pratical calculating.

5.Information source: The information source in calculating intermediate input can be obtained from product Cost Table, tables of Management Cost, Financial Expense and Sales Cost.

Value added of high and new technology value added refers to the newly created value in the production in the reference period. There are two approaches to calculting, the production approach, and the income approach,also factor distribution approach. The calculation methods are: (1)industrial value added by the production approach=total industrial value-industrial intermediate input+ current value added tax receivable; (2) industrial value added by distribution approach=depreciation of fixed assets+ remuneration of labourers+net of produce tax+ operating surplus

Value added of high and new technology refers to the value added of high and new technology enterprises designated by provincial Science and Technology Office in reference period, and value added of high and new technology products of non-high-and-new technology enterprises.

Income from major business refers to the income of regular and major bussiness of enterprises. The content of the income from major business differs from enterprise to enterprise. The income from major business of industrial enterprises mainly includes the income from product sales,own semi-finished products,industrial labor; the income from major business of commodity circulation enterprises mainly includes the incoome from commodity sales.Income from major business generally takes a big share in the income of enterprise,and has a great influence on the economic benefit.The "income from major business" item is set individually to check income from regular and major business in accounting.

Total investment in fixed assets refers to the generic term for operation capacity of building up and purchasing fixed assets in money terms during the reference period and related cost. Total investment in fixed assets in reference period is calculated by actual investment(including value of actual finish constructive installation engineering,purchasing cost of equipment,tools and devices,and other actual cost)

The number of projects under construction:refers to number of projects that has carried out construction or installation engineering in reference period, including the number of newly-opened projects during reference period,projects opened before reference period and constructed over reference period,and projects that have been constructed in reference period and completed or delayed within reference period.

Total tax revenue refers to tax revenue in all units of development zone.Included in this category are national and local tax revenue.They are mainly value added tax, turnover tax, income tax, city maintenance construction tax, use tax of town land, house tax, stamp tax, resource tax, land value increment tax, ect.

Value of foreign investment refers to the investment made by the soley foreign-owned enterprises opened according to the relevant policies and regulations and by means of convertible foreign exchange, physical goods,and technology,ect ; sino-foreign joint venture run by foreign enterprises,ecnomic organizations or individuals(including overseas Chinese,fellow citizens of Hongkong,Macao and Taiwan and Sino-enterprises registered in foreign countries) with Chinese enterprises or Chinese ecnomic organizations. And capital borrow from abroad and within the total value of investment in projects approved by the relevant department of Government.

Total value of export refers to total value of pratical outward cargoes. Our country stipulates that outward cargoes are calculated on FOB basis.

23 县域经济主要指标

Economy of Cities and Counties

资料整理：舒　猛

23-1 县市主要经济指标
MAIN ECONOMIC INDICATORS OF COUNTIES

指标名称	Item	土地面积(平方公里) Land Area(Sq. km)	常住人口(万人) The Resident (10 000 persons)		#城镇人口(万人) #Urban Population (10 000 persons)		#乡村人口(万人) #Rural Population (10 000 persons)	
		2013	2012	2013	2012	2013	2012	2013
蔡甸区	Caidian District	1108	42.30	43.42	23.09	23.70	19.21	19.72
江夏区	Jiangxia District	2010	82.19	83.40	41.98	42.60	40.21	40.80
黄陂区	Huangpi District	2261	88.99	89.78	35.82	36.14	53.17	53.64
新洲区	Xinzhou District	1500	85.42	85.57	41.49	41.56	43.93	44.01
汉南区	Hannan District	288	12.43	12.68	7.26	7.41	5.17	5.27
阳新县	Yangxin County	2783	80.02	82.17	26.91	27.63	53.11	54.54
大冶市	Daye City	1566	89.81	89.96	47.66	47.74	42.15	42.22
郧县	Yun County	3863	56.10	56.17	19.61	19.63	36.49	36.54
郧西县	Yunxi County	3509	40.98	40.06	14.69	14.36	26.29	25.70
竹山县	Zhushan County	3299	41.18	41.26	14.00	14.03	27.17	27.23
竹溪县	Zhuxi County	3585	30.94	31.02	10.09	10.12	20.85	20.90
房县	Fang County	5110	39.31	36.39	13.53	12.52	25.78	23.87
丹江口市	Danjiangkou City	3121	41.61	37.69	19.28	17.46	22.33	20.23
夷陵区	Yiling District	3425	52.09	52.24	23.54	23.60	28.56	28.64
远安县	Yuanan County	1752	18.56	18.64	7.82	7.85	10.74	10.79
兴山县	Xingshan County	2328	17.02	17.05	7.02	7.03	10.01	10.02
秭归县	Zigui County	2427	36.04	36.11	12.26	12.29	23.78	23.82
长阳县	Changyang Tujia A.C.	3430	38.48	38.58	10.59	10.62	27.88	27.96
五峰县	Wufeng Tujia A.C.	2072	18.72	18.74	6.24	6.25	12.48	12.49
宜都市	Yidu City	1357	38.75	38.85	19.22	19.27	19.52	19.58
当阳市	Dangyang City	2159	46.66	46.76	21.18	21.23	25.47	25.53
枝江市	Zhijiang City	1310	49.95	45.06	24.48	22.08	25.47	22.98
襄州区	Xiangzhou District	2306	86.34	85.49	44.14	43.70	42.20	41.79
南漳县	Nanzhang County	3859	53.79	53.99	20.02	20.09	33.78	33.90
谷城县	Gucheng County	2553	50.45	50.01	20.86	20.68	29.59	29.33
保康县	Baokang County	3225	23.35	22.28	9.53	9.09	13.82	13.19
老河口市	Laohekou City	1032	47.87	48.36	22.76	22.99	25.11	25.37
枣阳市	Zaoyang City	3277	98.83	93.68	46.55	44.12	52.28	49.56
宜城市	Yicheng City	2115	51.60	51.82	22.08	22.17	29.52	29.65
梁子湖区	Liangzihu District	500	14.35	14.39	5.15	5.16	9.20	9.23
华容区	Huarong District	493	20.90	23.94	9.86	11.29	11.04	12.65
鄂城区	Echeng District	600	67.15	67.37	49.01	49.17	18.14	18.20
东宝区	Dongbao District	1645	35.40	33.11	22.85	21.37	12.55	11.74
京山县	Jingshan County	3520	57.20	50.69	28.55	25.30	28.65	25.39
沙洋县	Shayang County	2044	56.10	55.36	19.37	19.11	36.73	36.25
钟祥市	Zhongxiang City	4488	90.40	88.46	45.23	44.26	45.17	44.20
孝南区	Xiaonan District	1020	81.10	80.61	54.96	54.63	26.14	25.98
孝昌县	Xiaochang County	1217	58.10	59.35	20.23	20.67	37.87	38.68
大悟县	Dawu County	1979	61.60	61.80	24.21	24.29	37.39	37.51
云梦县	Yunmeng County	604	52.58	52.75	24.06	24.14	28.52	28.61
应城市	Yingcheng City	1103	59.45	59.71	32.35	32.49	27.10	27.22
安陆市	Anlu City	1355	57.31	57.62	26.05	26.19	31.26	31.43
汉川市	Hanchuan City	1632	93.95	91.46	46.80	45.56	47.15	45.90
荆州区	Jingzhou District	1046	56.18	56.92	41.86	42.41	14.31	14.50
江陵县	Jiangling County	981	33.41	33.97	11.10	11.29	22.30	22.68
公安县	Gongan County	2258	89.63	89.62	34.07	34.06	55.56	55.55
监利县	Jianli County	3460	108.12	105.84	36.80	36.03	71.32	69.81
石首市	Shishou City	1424	56.99	56.56	22.76	22.59	34.24	33.98
洪湖市	Honghu City	2221	82.56	84.89	30.78	31.65	51.78	53.24
松滋市	Songci City	2235	76.93	75.35	32.31	31.65	44.62	43.70
黄州区	Huangzhou District	353	36.89	36.91	27.61	27.63	9.28	9.28
团风县	Tuanfeng County	833	34.00	34.15	11.22	11.27	22.78	22.88
红安县	Hongan County	1789	60.36	60.38	21.64	21.65	38.72	38.73
罗田县	Luotian County	2129	52.67	54.68	18.90	19.62	33.77	35.06
英山县	Yingshan County	1449	35.90	35.91	12.53	12.53	23.37	23.38
浠水县	Xishui County	1949	87.57	87.65	29.77	29.80	57.80	57.85
蕲春县	Qichun County	2398	76.04	77.02	27.06	27.40	48.98	49.62
黄梅县	Huangmei County	1246	82.10	86.35	31.28	32.90	50.82	53.45
麻城市	Macheng City	1701	83.50	82.02	32.75	32.17	50.75	49.85
武穴市	Wuxue City	3599	61.50	56.12	28.30	25.83	33.20	30.29
咸安区	Xian'an District	1504	51.47	51.65	35.02	35.15	16.44	16.50
嘉鱼县	Jiayu County	1017	31.51	31.62	13.29	13.34	18.22	18.28
通城县	Tongcheng County	1141	40.73	40.85	14.72	14.76	26.01	26.09
崇阳县	Chongyang County	1968	39.52	39.74	16.60	16.69	22.92	23.05
通山县	Tongshan County	2680	36.14	36.34	12.54	12.61	23.60	23.73
赤壁市	Chibi City	1723	44.13	43.30	22.00	21.59	22.13	21.71
曾都区	Zengdu District	1425	60.31	59.37	38.90	38.29	21.41	21.08
随县	Sui Country	5673	72.35	71.42	21.74	21.46	50.61	49.96
广水市	Guangshui City	2641	70.65	76.22	29.69	32.03	40.96	44.19
恩施市	Enshi City	3972	76.31	76.45	35.41	35.48	40.90	40.97
利川市	Lichuan City	4603	65.72	65.84	22.25	22.29	43.47	43.55
建始县	Jianshi County	2666	41.40	41.47	12.34	12.36	29.06	29.11
巴东县	Badong County	3354	42.29	42.37	12.73	12.75	29.56	29.62
宣恩县	Xuanen County	2730	30.08	30.14	8.27	8.29	21.81	21.85
咸丰县	Xianfeng County	2520	30.31	30.37	10.15	10.17	20.15	20.19
来凤县	Laifeng County	1344	24.40	24.45	7.57	7.58	16.83	16.87
鹤峰县	Hefeng County	2872	20.08	20.12	6.56	6.57	13.52	13.54
仙桃市	Xiantiao City	2520	118.49	116.49	58.42	57.43	60.07	59.06
潜江市	Qianjiang City	1930	89.05	95.24	43.20	46.20	45.85	49.04
天门市	Tianmen City	2528	121.70	119.90	57.30	56.45	64.40	63.45

23-1 续表 1 continued

指标名称	Item	地区生产总值(亿元) Gross Regional Product(100 million yuan) 2012	2013	人均地区生产总值(元) Per Capita GDP (yuan) 2012	2013	固定资产投资(亿元) Investment in Fixed Assets (100 million yuan) 2012	2013	社会消费品零售总额(亿元) Total Retail Sales (100 million yuan) 2012	2013
蔡甸区	Caidian District	263.67	305.70	61908	71325	253.73	345.44	62.52	72.22
江夏区	Jiangxia District	477.24	550.44	58403	66483	397.44	500.94	104.36	119.60
黄陂区	Huangpi District	393.55	454.31	44479	50826	360.71	477.82	154.19	179.17
新洲区	Xinzhou District	384.42	444.54	45050	51996	329.11	346.89	136.10	155.97
汉南区	Hannan District	88.10	101.88	71687	81149	87.80	135.70	15.86	18.45
阳新县	Yangxin County	150.97	169.02	18643	20842	148.17	191.32	75.40	84.15
大冶市	Daye City	410.24	455.92	45724	50723	357.77	433.37	136.21	157.19
郧县	Yun County	63.51	73.62	11337	13115	89.47	109.39	42.64	49.29
郧西县	Yunxi County	46.00	53.19	11241	13127	45.13	50.61	28.88	33.26
竹山县	Zhushan County	58.13	67.13	14136	16286	81.21	95.32	28.69	32.71
竹溪县	Zhuxi County	48.76	56.18	15780	18133	52.00	52.57	20.83	23.77
房县	Fang County	52.75	60.68	13435	16033	91.48	107.12	31.27	36.15
丹江口市	Danjiangkou City	130.02	150.72	31288	38011	95.34	128.48	49.41	57.17
夷陵区	Yiling District	335.09	389.84	64482	74730	256.59	327.49	74.39	86.22
远安县	Yuanan County	130.10	152.09	70266	81769	112.14	147.95	27.00	30.89
兴山县	Xingshan County	67.41	78.08	39698	45834	18.86	27.36	19.05	21.78
秭归县	Zigui County	78.77	91.24	21907	25289	61.13	74.83	25.91	29.48
长阳县	Changyang Tujia A.C.	88.26	100.51	22995	26087	47.65	57.65	28.89	33.72
五峰县	Wufeng Tujia A.C.	44.27	50.59	23703	27008	28.01	34.95	13.10	14.88
宜都市	Yidu City	344.74	402.82	89186	103823	270.59	352.94	65.68	76.26
当阳市	Dangyang City	302.23	352.17	64937	75398	213.09	272.64	79.75	92.83
枝江市	Zhijiang City	292.77	341.95	58752	71981	214.88	290.13	79.75	92.43
襄州区	Xiangzhou District	394.60	456.05	44897	53082	289.00	300.56	107.13	124.59
南漳县	Nanzhang County	151.11	171.23	28152	31772	111.32	156.46	61.00	71.13
谷城县	Gucheng County	204.71	238.75	40548	47530	113.98	154.25	63.01	70.63
保康县	Baokang County	70.08	81.55	28811	35742	80.13	100.56	28.72	33.61
老河口市	Laohekou City	208.19	240.18	43587	49918	115.90	155.02	73.00	84.10
枣阳市	Zaoyang City	370.92	425.43	37613	44198	205.55	261.24	116.38	133.26
宜城市	Yicheng City	201.94	232.46	39218	44951	128.76	169.33	65.28	73.09
梁子湖区	Liangzihu District	45.55	52.14	31771	36279	25.91	33.41	12.72	14.68
华容区	Huarong District	171.47	191.60	82260	85459	188.62	250.01	31.06	36.50
鄂城区	Echeng District	346.12	387.20	51606	57568	235.48	283.77	137.49	156.05
东宝区	Dongbao District	208.33	234.44	59151	68440	175.84	226.46	102.59	119.52
京山县	Jingshan County	240.12	268.99	41946	49864	188.27	235.99	86.04	101.01
沙洋县	Shayang County	178.74	198.21	31816	35566	101.94	111.20	50.65	58.55
钟祥市	Zhongxiang City	297.49	332.37	32877	37165	235.40	276.72	99.12	115.97
孝南区	Xiaonan District	195.21	226.38	24048	27999	193.89	264.61	97.23	109.57
孝昌县	Xiaochang County	82.55	92.65	14194	15777	107.27	95.72	36.29	40.83
大悟县	Dawu County	92.02	104.99	15197	17015	105.58	131.90	47.93	54.40
云梦县	Yunmeng County	151.90	173.13	28914	32875	127.83	161.51	68.92	78.09
应城市	Yingcheng City	174.86	202.35	29438	33962	148.82	174.89	85.08	98.69
安陆市	Anlu City	125.33	144.79	21889	25196	122.43	154.39	67.79	78.37
汉川市	Hanchuan City	309.43	344.71	32951	37184	173.97	232.33	128.60	149.82
荆州区	Jingzhou District	176.95	195.48	31789	34568	170.11	217.61	96.77	112.35
江陵县	Jiangling County	48.65	54.96	14633	16316	30.66	43.18	24.04	27.50
公安县	Gongan County	157.62	176.37	17729	19678	138.36	168.59	84.14	98.02
监利县	Jianli County	175.37	194.87	16203	18215	112.18	126.48	82.42	95.28
石首市	Shishou City	108.90	121.91	19183	21471	93.88	117.07	67.08	76.81
洪湖市	Honghu City	144.19	163.48	17528	19526	88.50	105.15	71.52	82.04
松滋市	Songci City	153.31	179.29	19948	23548	130.83	166.98	79.55	93.00
黄州区	Huangzhou District	140.31	157.61	38085	42713	138.97	179.83	71.84	82.90
团风县	Tuanfeng County	56.54	64.35	16645	18884	46.69	56.64	18.04	20.28
红安县	Hongan County	95.97	107.67	15911	17835	94.47	117.66	38.42	44.88
罗田县	Luotian County	85.07	95.75	16175	17838	95.92	116.24	39.23	44.17
英山县	Yingshan County	63.57	71.26	17740	19847	48.51	60.82	19.95	22.72
浠水县	Xishui County	145.08	165.24	16584	18861	107.51	131.91	74.24	85.45
蕲春县	Qichun County	143.11	162.36	18870	21215	147.55	174.75	67.99	78.46
黄梅县	Huangmei County	132.72	148.83	16173	17670	118.31	150.79	72.00	83.16
麻城市	Macheng City	176.39	203.40	21060	24577	173.29	211.18	77.26	90.16
武穴市	Wuxue City	180.38	202.86	29288	34495	133.70	170.54	72.08	84.12
咸安区	Xian'an District	183.90	208.33	35783	40406	215.02	261.57	72.28	81.97
嘉鱼县	Jiayu County	153.38	174.27	48746	55210	120.18	155.44	35.53	41.54
通城县	Tongcheng County	85.10	95.09	20945	23312	74.81	96.27	36.35	41.95
崇阳县	Chongyang County	77.23	88.08	19568	22225	70.14	96.94	34.54	39.51
通山县	Tongshan County	69.69	81.21	19289	22409	86.51	110.96	32.60	36.84
赤壁市	Chibi City	244.50	284.76	55493	65140	181.39	231.82	83.58	97.04
曾都区	Zengdu District	270.16	307.28	44881	51350	196.05	252.30	122.51	142.11
随县	Sui Country	136.14	152.45	18856	21207	135.46	181.24	78.07	90.64
广水市	Guangshui City	189.22	210.98	26555	28730	160.89	195.05	72.06	81.72
恩施市	Enshi City	123.10	141.50	16151	18524	86.11	105.23	58.84	68.49
利川市	Lichuan City	73.35	82.01	11176	12467	56.77	67.83	27.39	31.48
建始县	Jianshi County	55.92	64.11	13527	15473	48.88	53.91	17.75	20.30
巴东县	Badong County	65.51	74.00	15512	17483	51.91	61.07	20.76	23.75
宣恩县	Xuanen County	40.28	45.28	13409	15038	25.19	27.52	11.74	13.37
咸丰县	Xianfeng County	48.18	54.49	15919	17961	32.75	37.87	17.04	19.75
来凤县	Laifeng County	40.89	47.09	16776	19279	31.15	40.33	14.84	17.24
鹤峰县	Hefeng County	34.97	39.51	17435	19656	29.40	31.51	14.48	16.62
仙桃市	Xiantiao City	444.20	504.28	37525	42921	241.33	306.78	176.90	202.50
潜江市	Qianjiang City	441.76	492.70	49616	53470	237.06	303.26	115.44	131.56
天门市	Tianmen City	321.22	365.19	26373	30231	210.99	260.75	176.90	202.40

23-1 续表 2 continued

指标名称	Item	财政总收入(亿元) Total Fiscal Revenue (100 million yuan) 2012	2013	地方公共财政预算收入(亿元) Revenue of Local Governments (100 million yuan) 2012	2013	#各项税收(亿元) Taxes (100 million yuan) 2012	2013	地方公共财政预算支出(亿元) Expenditures of Local Governments (100 million yuan) 2012	2013
蔡甸区	Caidian District	34.96	38.13	21.55	25.55	12.62	14.70	53.29	36.58
江夏区	Jiangxia District	46.24	55.84	43.48	38.57	31.61	24.41	86.16	57.21
黄陂区	Huangpi District	46.83	58.28	33.21	40.71	25.74	32.52	46.59	58.69
新洲区	Xinzhou District	32.47	36.76	22.89	24.66	13.97	16.45	70.73	45.19
汉南区	Hannan District	15.38	19.71	9.02	11.42	7.93	10.22	10.94	12.94
阳新县	Yangxin County	10.47	12.60	6.94	8.45	4.33	5.61	31.19	32.53
大冶市	Daye City	47.83	54.13	28.01	31.22	19.46	19.34	41.56	50.26
郧县	Yun County	9.79	8.55	6.54	4.98	2.77	3.49	27.63	29.47
郧西县	Yunxi County	3.00	3.50	2.06	2.50	1.45	1.76	11.72	23.32
竹山县	Zhushan County	4.46	5.28	3.30	3.97	2.50	2.90	20.70	26.43
竹溪县	Zhuxi County	3.77	4.26	2.68	3.21	1.88	2.27	19.64	24.00
房县	Fang County	4.55	5.42	3.33	3.99	2.54	2.89	21.66	27.09
丹江口市	Danjiangkou City	25.79	16.85	19.64	10.59	14.24	7.68	37.98	31.33
夷陵区	Yiling District	33.53	42.73	20.28	27.08	15.23	19.39	33.53	40.94
远安县	Yuanan County	9.92	12.17	7.00	9.38	5.23	6.34	14.85	18.47
兴山县	Xingshan County	7.48	9.25	4.33	6.01	3.17	4.16	14.23	15.50
秭归县	Zigui County	6.46	8.07	4.72	6.20	3.72	4.55	18.98	22.90
长阳县	Changyang Tujia A.C.	6.24	7.74	4.35	5.77	3.19	3.71	18.58	24.14
五峰县	Wufeng Tujia A.C.	2.49	3.11	1.75	2.33	1.34	1.72	15.38	22.20
宜都市	Yidu City	25.91	37.13	20.26	30.00	15.07	22.61	31.37	41.82
当阳市	Dangyang City	22.61	27.94	15.02	20.02	10.99	14.10	31.58	35.67
枝江市	Zhijiang City	21.12	27.58	14.53	20.22	10.76	15.22	28.07	31.95
襄州区	Xiangzhou District	15.79	22.62	12.51	18.32	9.13	13.55	34.51	38.78
南漳县	Nanzhang County	7.38	10.07	5.58	7.97	4.35	6.21	24.14	28.37
谷城县	Gucheng County	11.76	15.65	8.52	12.19	5.85	8.39	24.69	30.50
保康县	Baokang County	7.91	9.61	5.61	7.30	3.67	4.48	12.70	22.21
老河口市	Laohekou City	14.19	19.62	11.50	16.50	10.22	10.89	27.40	31.79
枣阳市	Zaoyang City	18.02	24.34	14.94	21.02	9.74	13.85	41.94	47.70
宜城市	Yicheng City	12.89	17.75	10.67	15.26	6.44	9.22	30.57	33.50
梁子湖区	Liangzihu District	2.57	3.01	1.81	2.40	1.38	1.85	6.01	6.74
华容区	Huarong District	5.94	6.63	3.89	4.86	7.20	3.68	12.11	9.91
鄂城区	Echeng District	16.05	18.02	11.00	13.38	15.74	10.51	44.56	18.92
东宝区	Dongbao District	13.13	14.27	9.79	8.95	8.94	7.59	12.23	13.11
京山县	Jingshan County	10.85	13.43	8.41	10.10	5.82	7.15	26.15	27.81
沙洋县	Shayang County	5.62	6.34	4.20	4.92	2.97	3.54	20.77	23.18
钟祥市	Zhongxiang City	14.95	16.63	11.09	13.03	6.86	7.97	40.62	45.76
孝南区	Xiaonan District	13.91	19.16	9.53	13.52	17.53	9.40	41.85	28.14
孝昌县	Xiaochang County	7.35	9.01	5.52	7.08	3.40	4.25	15.78	27.17
大悟县	Dawu County	8.41	10.14	5.44	6.82	3.49	4.15	12.23	30.85
云梦县	Yunmeng County	9.57	12.02	7.02	9.00	4.32	5.90	14.68	21.91
应城市	Yingcheng City	13.62	17.29	9.51	12.00	5.91	7.53	23.34	25.58
安陆市	Anlu City	7.87	10.16	5.60	7.29	4.13	5.14	21.55	22.23
汉川市	Hanchuan City	18.16	22.72	11.31	14.34	7.64	9.70	23.44	36.68
荆州区	Jingzhou District	11.48	14.50	7.86	10.75	6.13	8.28	16.72	20.02
江陵县	Jiangling County	2.33	2.81	1.50	1.87	0.91	1.20	9.42	14.44
公安县	Gongan County	9.99	11.99	6.17	7.59	4.83	5.73	11.22	33.03
监利县	Jianli County	4.28	5.67	2.82	3.69	2.43	3.21	24.42	38.97
石首市	Shishou City	5.62	7.30	3.69	4.85	2.44	3.27	18.79	21.71
洪湖市	Honghu City	5.91	7.27	4.20	5.21	2.93	3.66	17.77	31.74
松滋市	Songci City	11.73	15.08	6.40	8.50	4.63	5.99	29.21	30.64
黄州区	Huangzhou District	5.89	7.36	6.83	5.31	9.41	3.76	42.38	15.26
团风县	Tuanfeng County	4.11	4.89	3.08	3.68	2.00	2.45	15.46	17.86
红安县	Hongan County	12.40	16.12	5.61	7.88	3.57	5.34	27.65	29.65
罗田县	Luotian County	5.20	6.39	3.58	4.48	2.19	2.79	22.30	23.32
英山县	Yingshan County	2.92	3.80	2.20	2.83	1.41	1.93	12.60	18.88
浠水县	Xishui County	7.44	8.88	5.16	6.32	3.17	3.98	28.44	30.38
蕲春县	Qichun County	10.07	11.67	7.04	8.31	4.30	5.13	18.04	34.35
黄梅县	Huangmei County	8.46	9.96	6.47	7.51	3.94	4.74	19.94	31.76
麻城市	Macheng City	10.81	14.99	7.55	11.17	4.90	7.35	37.85	41.39
武穴市	Wuxue City	12.34	14.59	8.40	10.68	5.54	7.05	26.32	26.62
咸安区	Xian'an District	7.86	9.62	6.57	7.46	13.98	5.68	47.91	24.02
嘉鱼县	Jiayu County	7.75	9.41	5.69	7.28	3.91	5.18	17.53	18.57
通城县	Tongcheng County	4.88	6.41	3.63	4.70	2.26	2.95	16.68	19.01
崇阳县	Chongyang County	4.12	5.47	3.12	4.22	2.06	2.80	18.73	19.11
通山县	Tongshan County	4.85	6.36	3.56	4.82	2.58	3.31	17.29	21.29
赤壁市	Chibi City	14.97	17.11	10.80	13.12	7.31	8.96	25.40	28.35
曾都区	Zengdu District	10.38	13.72	8.64	9.33	6.53	6.79	16.69	24.31
随县	Sui Country	3.60	4.65	2.30	3.06	1.62	2.19	23.99	29.06
广水市	Guangshui City	14.01	16.60	6.43	7.41	4.45	5.41	27.15	29.45
恩施市	Enshi City	15.81	20.93	11.52	15.54	9.98	13.61	31.98	42.24
利川市	Lichuan City	12.08	13.70	6.57	7.72	4.96	5.87	29.85	35.24
建始县	Jianshi County	6.99	7.77	3.42	4.08	3.42	3.18	20.59	24.87
巴东县	Badong County	7.20	7.64	4.51	5.21	3.60	4.18	23.48	30.00
宣恩县	Xuanen County	2.60	3.14	1.81	2.19	1.51	1.84	15.03	17.46
咸丰县	Xianfeng County	4.61	5.18	2.51	3.01	3.88	2.14	18.30	21.75
来凤县	Laifeng County	5.15	6.09	2.01	2.51	1.65	2.10	15.93	16.54
鹤峰县	Hefeng County	2.52	3.10	1.66	2.02	1.30	1.70	13.60	15.19
仙桃市	Xiantiao City	27.19	32.46	17.14	21.00	13.56	16.73	47.71	50.67
潜江市	Qianjiang City	24.99	29.93	16.02	20.00	12.04	14.96	66.14	45.56
天门市	Tianmen City	15.12	19.37	11.00	15.02	7.75	10.52	41.84	48.52

23-1 续表 3 continued

指标名称	Item	外贸出口(万美元) Total Exports (USD 10 000) 2012	2013	招商引资(亿元) Invitation for Business Investment (100 million yuan) 2012	2013	城镇居民人均可支配收入(元) Annual Per Capita Disposable Income of Urban (yuan) 2012	2013	农村居民人均纯收入(元) Annual Per Capita Disposable Income of Rural Households(yuan) 2012	2013
蔡甸区	Caidian District	3596	4035	72.44	144.16	18271	20317	11054	12568
江夏区	Jiangxia District	10822	14205	87.72	149.47	17863	19846	11289	12836
黄陂区	Huangpi District	7002	7883	66.40	70.35	17174	19303	10897	12444
新洲区	Xinzhou District	15046	16552	73.89	78.21	16915	19013	10687	12140
汉南区	Hannan District	10387	11478	4.21	18.32	19159	21285	11289	12802
阳新县	Yangxin County	13900	24129	20.07	33.69	13373	14836	5551	6362
大冶市	Daye City	25100	26826	87.09	99.88	20941	23063	9443	10616
郧县	Yun County	3260	5003	23.47	30.61	11462	12902	4493	5165
郧西县	Yunxi County	490	1008	8.30	15.05	12555	13825	4318	4931
竹山县	Zhushan County	1021	1310	20.06	21.39	13236	14582	4436	5099
竹溪县	Zhuxi County	940	1394	11.95	12.35	11826	13143	4466	5105
房县	Fang County	5032	8279	26.90	32.63	14155	15521	4500	5149
丹江口市	Danjiangkou City	2148	2638	22.94	29.67	15462	17185	5213	6015
夷陵区	Yiling District	5991	7634	70.16	64.81	19353	21621	9713	11011
远安县	Yuanan County	6751	10390	45.88	53.65	17715	19806	9153	10274
兴山县	Xingshan County	21601	27711	9.04	14.55	15180	16986	5623	6271
秭归县	Zigui County	3308	3827	9.80	11.86	14518	16306	4698	5331
长阳县	Changyang Tujia A.C.	4682	5489	9.34	9.94	15387	17215	4819	5466
五峰县	Wufeng Tujia A.C.	156	402	6.03	6.43	12069	13585	4392	5001
宜都市	Yidu City	27161	32139	73.44	93.16	19431	21683	10415	11693
当阳市	Dangyang City	6205	9164	91.27	78.67	18443	20630	10445	11816
枝江市	Zhijiang City	15764	20294	98.44	70.47	17465	19572	10496	11865
襄州区	Xiangzhou District	16377	26759	110.28	144.16	15140	16690	9886	11192
南漳县	Nanzhang County	3865	5747	92.24	115.94	15525	17197	7966	8976
谷城县	Gucheng County	7608	10884	90.47	112.92	15539	17273	8182	9259
保康县	Baokang County	2998	3927	69.41	68.88	13410	14806	5538	6273
老河口市	Laohekou City	16201	21853	79.09	101.01	16267	17936	9632	10901
枣阳市	Zaoyang City	11934	16640	100.26	129.88	16982	18828	9387	10628
宜城市	Yicheng City	12314	15000	88.75	107.02	15366	16943	9639	10843
梁子湖区	Liangzihu District	87	120	1.45	6.94	17960	16806	8066	8925
华容区	Huarong District	4907	6542	74.19	95.69	19615	18991	9600	10834
鄂城区	Echeng District	10744	10962	59.21	66.10	19307	21857	9566	10781
东宝区	Dongbao District	5124	6277	88.34	106.78	19628	22015	9462	10710
京山县	Jingshan County	12089	14163	86.72	94.12	15862	17794	9454	10696
沙洋县	Shayang County	6463	8559	82.76	91.36	14706	16472	9164	10363
钟祥市	Zhongxiang City	9518	16088	89.74	110.21	14972	16799	9532	10784
孝南区	Xiaonan District	15177	17120	87.35	108.59	19336	21159	9066	10338
孝昌县	Xiaochang County	2717	3401	57.67	56.37	16490	18053	5526	6221
大悟县	Dawu County	1386	1693	44.87	26.08	16740	17900	5740	6467
云梦县	Yunmeng County	1339	3927	68.76	57.35	17792	19863	9410	10647
应城市	Yingcheng City	6132	7706	73.17	78.20	18052	20162	9523	10833
安陆市	Anlu City	4342	5256	86.43	92.31	17372	19223	7916	8956
汉川市	Hanchuan City	32153	38877	98.89	129.84	17795	19850	9020	10278
荆州区	Jingzhou District	11163	7940	69.88	76.58	18792	20811	9791	11118
江陵县	Jiangling County	1397	1623	25.80	14.40	13969	15456	7505	8542
公安县	Gongan County	6943	7101	60.87	66.56	15220	16711	8961	10193
监利县	Jianli County	3106	4777	27.34	32.12	13956	15402	8354	9521
石首市	Shishou City	10204	14891	42.50	54.16	15105	16689	8643	9840
洪湖市	Honghu City	2262	2951	46.96	55.78	14567	16002	8440	9625
松滋市	Songci City	3599	12312	72.85	71.39	15110	16722	8775	9995
黄州区	Huangzhou District	5780	8244	31.45	15.56	19257	21154	8381	9501
团风县	Tuanfeng County	727	987	14.46	7.40	14996	16598	4762	5387
红安县	Hongan County	718	1167	40.89	36.42	16542	17984	4953	5641
罗田县	Luotian County	3795	4374	14.48	11.92	16559	18037	5444	5998
英山县	Yingshan County	850	1044	8.21	5.49	16323	17638	5221	5913
浠水县	Xishui County	3464	4315	15.18	26.45	16490	18160	7128	8112
蕲春县	Qichun County	5633	6526	37.31	14.84	16372	17690	5494	6247
黄梅县	Huangmei County	1990	2895	46.40	36.24	16337	18269	7161	8135
麻城市	Macheng City	2665	3910	41.72	36.65	16691	18371	5278	6001
武穴市	Wuxue City	8472	10612	40.13	38.14	18106	19746	7880	8976
咸安区	Xian'an District	10120	6869	59.73	77.01	18218	19967	8081	9183
嘉鱼县	Jiayu County	4101	7027	73.41	71.02	18210	19971	9289	10506
通城县	Tongcheng County	4549	5355	58.31	55.30	15412	16822	7107	7988
崇阳县	Chongyang County	1459	1825	70.60	68.78	13532	14977	6491	7341
通山县	Tongshan County	339	1016	70.02	68.63	13394	14719	4898	5667
赤壁市	Chibi City	2667	7016	74.19	89.04	17676	19465	9615	10669
曾都区	Zengdu District	46200	56824	96.73	129.29	18670	21004	8971	10131
随县	Sui Country	18144	48907	69.16	67.90		18205	8672	9759
广水市	Guangshui City	5300	6940	45.25	56.64	17294	19402	8069	9105
恩施市	Enshi City	9404	10940	8.53	7.63	16993	18667	4619	5329
利川市	Lichuan City	5350	6295	9.57	15.10	12914	16070	4536	5195
建始县	Jianshi County	2273	2888	2.66	7.33	14343	15962	4527	5193
巴东县	Badong County	3977	5786	6.63	6.70	14457	15979	4552	5216
宣恩县	Xuanen County	1200	2184	2.07	6.56	14344	15974	4513	5173
咸丰县	Xianfeng County	3194	4088	7.61	10.19	14453	15892	4526	5152
来凤县	Laifeng County	1235	1710	6.37	12.27	14685	16209	4508	5153
鹤峰县	Hefeng County	3342	4583	4.51	5.30	14778	16379	4802	5521
仙桃市	Xiantiao City	35640	42384	109.93	137.14	17280	19065	9706	10365
潜江市	Qianjiang City	33471	38123	110.84	131.77	17451	19187	8785	10017
天门市	Tianmen City	5031	5499	109.47	128.36	15685	17112	8507	9608

23-1 续表 4 continued

指标名称	Item	农业总产值(亿元) Total Value of Agricultural Output (100 million yuan)		农产品加工业产值(亿元) Value of Agricultural Product Processing (100 million yuan)		常用耕地面积(千公顷) Area of Cultivated Land (1000 hectare)		粮食产量(万吨) Output of Grain (10 000 tons)	
		2012	2013	2012	2013	2012	2013	2012	2013
蔡甸区	Caidian District	45.49	57.53	178.08	194.40	24.93	24.53	13.21	13.28
江夏区	Jiangxia District	93.18	130.18	55.02	76.60	34.79	34.63	29.00	29.15
黄陂区	Huangpi District	121.16	160.49	118.67	152.30	52.83	52.54	45.62	46.06
新洲区	Xinzhou District	87.97	119.56	76.47	95.13	50.19	50.04	32.15	32.43
汉南区	Hannan District	19.57	21.52	21.19	28.57	9.85	9.85	3.35	3.40
阳新县	Yangxin County	61.36	67.07	14.16	29.47	51.89	51.74	34.75	35.33
大冶市	Daye City	55.19	60.00	111.10	139.29	35.73	35.70	27.23	28.01
郧县	Yun County	33.93	39.72	5.47	25.53	35.08	35.45	19.90	23.00
郧西县	Yunxi County	32.55	38.11	1.98	4.33	26.84	26.84	18.21	18.50
竹山县	Zhushan County	31.99	37.78	16.16	18.10	32.19	33.76	23.21	23.52
竹溪县	Zhuxi County	33.49	39.53	9.79	13.68	28.65	29.51	23.77	24.07
房县	Fang County	36.19	42.66	17.18	26.48	28.61	28.49	14.33	14.50
丹江口市	Danjiangkou City	38.58	45.52	30.91	49.11	20.71	21.11	11.65	11.90
夷陵区	Yiling District	75.41	83.42	269.12	391.74	33.52	33.66	21.20	21.62
远安县	Yuanan County	24.63	27.25	30.23	43.94	11.91	11.94	10.08	10.30
兴山县	Xingshan County	16.74	17.81	14.64	18.41	16.16	16.21	5.81	5.95
秭归县	Zigui County	29.77	32.88	36.83	44.75	23.10	23.80	8.67	8.95
长阳县	Changyang Tujia A.C.	48.46	53.49	33.61	42.41	33.65	39.65	10.22	10.61
五峰县	Wufeng Tujia A.C.	27.56	30.80	18.75	22.35	20.22	20.43	8.05	8.30
宜都市	Yidu City	58.15	64.87	112.82	220.40	15.80	15.84	11.03	11.30
当阳市	Dangyang City	105.07	115.85	189.80	214.57	53.42	54.13	51.13	52.48
枝江市	Zhijiang City	101.13	112.17	231.40	296.99	45.52	45.52	33.15	33.97
襄州区	Xiangzhou District	143.43	160.07	216.95	263.25	108.96	109.59	135.80	135.97
南漳县	Nanzhang County	62.09	68.17	92.05	97.67	41.04	41.19	44.88	44.93
谷城县	Gucheng County	50.09	54.21	164.10	103.79	28.51	28.52	27.69	27.80
保康县	Baokang County	32.28	34.69	17.47	31.35	22.64	22.93	13.73	14.10
老河口市	Laohekou City	63.27	69.13	207.51	248.53	40.44	40.45	36.95	37.18
枣阳市	Zaoyang City	146.60	156.70	281.54	327.98	110.29	111.11	136.10	136.31
宜城市	Yicheng City	76.79	84.78	214.50	264.43	62.23	62.32	69.40	69.50
梁子湖区	Liangzihu District	36.06	36.40	4.73	6.61	12.67	13.50	11.17	11.63
华容区	Huarong District	35.12	34.00	103.92	119.68	14.42	13.00	11.30	10.40
鄂城区	Echeng District	51.95	66.70	28.04	32.17	14.13	14.00	12.02	11.70
东宝区	Dongbao District	25.05	26.12	58.30	67.60	20.01	20.21	17.07	17.23
京山县	Jingshan County	82.08	87.49	291.87	367.90	69.43	69.29	70.25	71.70
沙洋县	Shayang County	88.41	94.29	150.27	182.29	78.32	78.45	80.05	81.90
钟祥市	Zhongxiang City	102.42	110.03	204.30	355.48	83.12	82.99	85.52	87.43
孝南区	Xiaonan District	47.43	52.05	78.96	130.19	31.11	34.10	21.19	21.62
孝昌县	Xiaochang County	48.22	52.20	25.26	23.95	32.20	32.63	26.44	26.67
大悟县	Dawu County	48.26	52.24	19.66	23.19	36.68	36.68	28.18	28.55
云梦县	Yunmeng County	54.24	58.64	128.34	158.33	25.32	25.42	21.59	21.73
应城市	Yingcheng City	70.35	76.70	107.53	127.05	38.21	38.19	35.31	36.20
安陆市	Anlu City	55.48	59.16	112.08	126.26	31.98	33.32	33.32	33.82
汉川市	Hanchuan City	91.91	100.16	392.67	494.99	65.20	65.16	53.40	54.62
荆州区	Jingzhou District	56.47	60.87	111.23	152.13	35.04	34.98	20.56	21.86
江陵县	Jiangling County	30.92	32.79	25.87	38.80	37.99	37.99	25.74	27.10
公安县	Gongan County	90.15	96.77	96.45	119.73	80.38	80.38	60.89	64.20
监利县	Jianli County	137.52	147.31	148.85	182.22	137.69	137.70	136.12	140.50
石首市	Shishou City	50.23	54.56	46.16	62.39	39.81	40.92	20.89	21.80
洪湖市	Honghu City	89.14	100.83	70.96	123.72	64.19	64.20	67.00	68.98
松滋市	Songci City	57.89	61.19	110.93	145.48	59.64	59.63	32.71	34.20
黄州区	Huangzhou District	18.87	19.95	62.65	71.28	10.94	10.82	5.32	5.50
团风县	Tuanfeng County	20.72	21.85	15.00	19.21	17.86	17.85	12.45	12.81
红安县	Hongan County	31.60	34.34	28.03	49.51	38.64	38.22	22.36	23.02
罗田县	Luotian County	35.21	36.80	11.90	18.41	26.15	26.25	24.88	25.47
英山县	Yingshan County	42.22	44.07	16.21	25.45	17.29	17.27	13.06	13.55
浠水县	Xishui County	82.41	85.71	53.25	71.19	44.34	44.47	50.04	50.48
蕲春县	Qichun County	61.25	64.36	80.83	100.00	40.50	40.67	50.08	51.50
黄梅县	Huangmei County	61.28	64.48	74.22	124.83	54.63	54.63	48.06	49.15
麻城市	Macheng City	78.54	82.13	26.69	45.89	53.01	53.05	53.80	54.20
武穴市	Wuxue City	66.61	70.19	58.62	91.88	35.88	36.02	30.39	31.15
咸安区	Xian'an District	37.42	42.89	144.51	191.22	35.43	35.54	18.41	18.75
嘉鱼县	Jiayu County	58.02	64.24	132.90	171.98	28.80	30.72	17.82	17.98
通城县	Tongcheng County	31.03	32.21	21.16	25.79	21.29	21.29	18.39	18.70
崇阳县	Chongyang County	34.49	38.09	14.96	18.81	23.29	23.29	19.45	19.70
通山县	Tongshan County	18.55	21.71	6.73	20.99	14.83	14.84	8.25	8.48
赤壁市	Chibi City	58.13	65.57	165.68	202.64	32.95	32.97	20.76	21.03
曾都区	Zengdu District	35.97	41.01	130.16	133.04	25.69	25.93	25.44	25.75
随县	Sui Country	90.13	100.68	109.55	128.55	78.05	78.28	89.02	91.07
广水市	Guangshui City	69.22	75.03	98.11	128.31	39.15	39.14	40.58	41.35
恩施市	Enshi City	37.99	40.80	41.24	57.95	47.25	47.14	22.30	23.10
利川市	Lichuan City	45.11	48.88	26.27	31.88	58.19	58.16	36.01	36.70
建始县	Jianshi County	27.02	29.14	4.15	11.78	33.89	34.31	22.64	23.16
巴东县	Badong County	25.12	27.34	13.51	19.19	35.98	36.32	21.84	22.21
宣恩县	Xuanen County	20.54	23.69	11.57	16.77	24.78	24.75	12.45	12.90
咸丰县	Xianfeng County	21.39	22.48	15.74	21.44	27.10	26.24	22.90	23.08
来凤县	Laifeng County	16.85	18.40	10.30	12.86	17.23	17.15	12.16	12.60
鹤峰县	Hefeng County	15.18	16.50	17.60	28.67	16.07	16.22	8.76	9.10
仙桃市	Xiantiao City	127.85	136.29	397.80	637.65	90.54	90.54	77.88	80.99
潜江市	Qianjiang City	101.34	109.28	296.97	398.69	72.08	72.10	50.04	52.00
天门市	Tianmen City	101.23	108.58	263.28	309.76	109.80	109.66	69.41	71.50

23-1 续表 4 continued

指标名称	Item	农业总产值(亿元) Total Value of Agricultural Output (100 million yuan)		农产品加工业产值(亿元) Value of Agricultural Product Processing (100 million yuan)		常用耕地面积(千公顷) Area of Cultivated Land (1000 hectare)		粮食产量(万吨) Output of Grain (10 000 tons)	
		2012	2013	2012	2013	2012	2013	2012	2013
蔡甸区	Caidian District	45.49	57.53	178.08	194.40	24.93	24.53	13.21	13.28
江夏区	Jiangxia District	93.18	130.18	55.02	76.60	34.79	34.63	29.00	29.15
黄陂区	Huangpi District	121.16	160.49	118.67	152.30	52.83	52.54	45.62	46.06
新洲区	Xinzhou District	87.97	119.56	76.47	95.13	50.19	50.04	32.15	32.43
汉南区	Hannan District	19.57	21.52	21.19	28.57	9.85	9.85	3.35	3.40
阳新县	Yangxin County	61.36	67.07	14.16	29.47	51.89	51.74	34.75	35.33
大冶市	Daye City	55.19	60.00	111.10	139.29	35.73	35.70	27.23	28.01
郧县	Yun County	33.93	39.72	5.47	25.53	35.08	35.45	19.90	23.00
郧西县	Yunxi County	32.55	38.11	1.98	4.33	26.84	26.84	18.21	18.50
竹山县	Zhushan County	31.99	37.78	16.16	18.10	32.19	33.76	23.21	23.52
竹溪县	Zhuxi County	33.49	39.53	9.79	13.68	28.65	29.51	23.77	24.07
房县	Fang County	36.19	42.66	17.18	26.48	28.61	28.49	14.33	14.50
丹江口市	Danjiangkou City	38.58	45.52	30.91	49.11	20.71	21.11	11.65	11.90
夷陵区	Yiling District	75.41	83.42	269.12	391.74	33.52	33.66	21.20	21.62
远安县	Yuanan County	24.63	27.25	30.23	43.94	11.91	11.94	10.08	10.30
兴山县	Xingshan County	16.74	17.81	14.64	18.41	16.16	16.21	5.81	5.95
秭归县	Zigui County	29.77	32.88	36.83	44.75	23.10	23.80	8.67	8.95
长阳县	Changyang Tujia A.C.	48.46	53.49	33.61	42.41	33.65	39.65	10.22	10.61
五峰县	Wufeng Tujia A.C.	27.56	30.80	18.75	22.35	20.22	20.43	8.05	8.30
宜都市	Yidu City	58.15	64.87	112.82	220.40	15.80	15.84	11.03	11.30
当阳市	Dangyang City	105.07	115.85	189.80	214.57	53.42	54.13	51.13	52.48
枝江市	Zhijiang City	101.13	112.17	231.40	296.99	45.52	45.52	33.15	33.97
襄州区	Xiangzhou District	143.43	160.07	216.95	263.25	108.96	109.59	135.80	135.97
南漳县	Nanzhang County	62.09	68.17	92.05	97.67	41.04	41.19	44.88	44.93
谷城县	Gucheng County	50.09	54.21	164.10	103.79	28.51	28.52	27.69	27.80
保康县	Baokang County	32.28	34.69	17.47	31.35	22.64	22.93	13.73	14.10
老河口市	Laohekou City	63.27	69.13	207.51	248.53	40.44	40.45	36.95	37.18
枣阳市	Zaoyang City	146.60	156.70	281.54	327.98	110.29	111.11	136.10	136.31
宜城市	Yicheng City	76.79	84.78	214.50	264.43	62.23	62.32	69.40	69.50
梁子湖区	Liangzihu District	36.06	36.40	4.73	6.61	12.67	13.50	11.17	11.63
华容区	Huarong District	35.12	34.00	103.92	119.68	14.42	13.00	11.30	10.40
鄂城区	Echeng District	51.95	66.70	28.04	32.17	14.13	14.00	12.02	11.70
东宝区	Dongbao District	25.05	26.12	58.30	67.60	20.01	20.21	17.07	17.23
京山县	Jingshan County	82.08	87.49	291.87	367.90	69.43	69.29	70.25	71.70
沙洋县	Shayang County	88.41	94.29	150.27	182.29	78.32	78.45	80.05	81.90
钟祥市	Zhongxiang City	102.42	110.03	204.30	355.48	83.12	82.99	85.52	87.43
孝南区	Xiaonan District	47.43	52.05	78.96	130.19	31.11	34.10	21.19	21.62
孝昌县	Xiaochang County	48.22	52.20	25.26	23.95	32.20	32.63	26.44	26.67
大悟县	Dawu County	48.26	52.24	19.66	23.19	36.68	36.68	28.18	28.55
云梦县	Yunmeng County	54.24	58.64	128.34	158.33	25.32	25.42	21.59	21.73
应城市	Yingcheng City	70.35	76.70	107.53	127.05	38.21	38.19	35.31	36.20
安陆市	Anlu City	55.48	59.16	112.08	126.26	31.98	33.32	33.32	33.82
汉川市	Hanchuan City	91.91	100.16	392.67	494.99	65.20	65.16	53.40	54.62
荆州区	Jingzhou District	56.47	60.87	111.23	152.13	35.04	34.98	20.56	21.86
江陵县	Jiangling County	30.92	32.79	25.87	38.80	37.99	37.99	25.74	27.10
公安县	Gongan County	90.15	96.77	96.45	119.73	80.38	80.38	60.89	64.20
监利县	Jianli County	137.52	147.31	148.85	182.22	137.69	137.70	136.12	140.50
石首市	Shishou City	50.23	54.56	46.16	62.39	39.81	40.92	20.89	21.80
洪湖市	Honghu City	89.14	100.83	70.96	123.72	64.19	64.20	67.00	68.98
松滋市	Songci City	57.89	61.19	110.93	145.48	59.64	59.63	32.71	34.20
黄州区	Huangzhou District	18.87	19.95	62.65	71.28	10.94	10.82	5.32	5.50
团风县	Tuanfeng County	20.72	21.85	15.00	19.21	17.86	17.85	12.45	12.81
红安县	Hongan County	31.60	34.34	28.03	49.51	38.64	38.22	22.36	23.02
罗田县	Luotian County	35.21	36.80	11.90	18.41	26.15	26.25	24.88	25.47
英山县	Yingshan County	42.22	44.07	16.21	25.45	17.29	17.27	13.06	13.55
浠水县	Xishui County	82.41	85.71	53.25	71.19	44.34	44.47	50.04	50.48
蕲春县	Qichun County	61.25	64.36	80.83	100.00	40.50	40.67	50.08	51.50
黄梅县	Huangmei County	61.28	64.48	74.22	124.83	54.63	54.63	48.06	49.15
麻城市	Macheng City	78.54	82.13	26.69	45.89	53.01	53.05	53.80	54.20
武穴市	Wuxue City	66.61	70.19	58.62	91.88	35.88	36.02	30.39	31.15
咸安区	Xian'an District	37.42	42.89	144.51	191.22	35.43	35.54	18.41	18.75
嘉鱼县	Jiayu County	58.02	64.24	132.90	171.98	28.80	30.72	17.82	17.98
通城县	Tongcheng County	31.03	32.21	21.16	25.79	21.29	21.29	18.39	18.70
崇阳县	Chongyang County	34.49	38.09	14.96	18.81	23.29	23.29	19.45	19.70
通山县	Tongshan County	18.55	21.71	6.73	20.99	14.83	14.84	8.25	8.48
赤壁市	Chibi City	58.13	65.57	165.68	202.64	32.95	32.97	20.76	21.03
曾都区	Zengdu District	35.97	41.01	130.16	133.04	25.69	25.93	25.44	25.75
随县	Sui Country	90.13	100.68	109.55	128.55	78.05	78.28	89.02	91.07
广水市	Guangshui City	69.22	75.03	98.11	128.31	39.15	39.14	40.58	41.35
恩施市	Enshi City	37.99	40.80	41.24	57.95	47.25	47.14	22.30	23.10
利川市	Lichuan City	45.11	48.88	26.27	31.88	58.19	58.16	36.01	36.70
建始县	Jianshi County	27.02	29.14	4.15	11.78	33.89	34.31	22.64	23.16
巴东县	Badong County	25.12	27.34	13.51	19.19	35.98	36.32	21.84	22.21
宣恩县	Xuanen County	20.54	23.69	11.57	16.77	24.78	24.75	12.45	12.90
咸丰县	Xianfeng County	21.39	22.48	15.74	21.44	27.10	26.24	22.90	23.08
来凤县	Laifeng County	16.85	18.40	10.30	12.86	17.23	17.15	12.16	12.60
鹤峰县	Hefeng County	15.18	16.50	17.60	28.67	16.07	16.22	8.76	9.10
仙桃市	Xiantiao City	127.85	136.29	397.80	637.65	90.54	90.54	77.88	80.99
潜江市	Qianjiang City	101.34	109.28	296.97	398.69	72.08	72.10	50.04	52.00
天门市	Tianmen City	101.23	108.58	263.28	309.76	109.80	109.66	69.41	71.50

23-1 续表 5 continued

指标名称	Item	棉花产量(吨) Output of Cotton Cotton (ton)		油料产量(万吨) Output of Oil-bearing Crops(10 000 tons)		猪肉产量(万吨) Output of Pork (10 000 tons)		水产品产量(吨) Output of Aquatic Products(ton)	
		2012	2013	2012	2013	2012	2013	2012	2013
蔡甸区	Caidian District	4178	6418	1.06	1.34	1.55	1.50	61764	66087
江夏区	Jiangxia District	85	138	4.05	4.14	7.51	7.81	85889	91073
黄陂区	Huangpi District	3600	3510	6.19	6.35	7.51	7.61	91695	98146
新洲区	Xinzhou District	7532	14502	4.83	5.79	3.01	3.31	102667	108267
汉南区	Hannan District	4812	5615	0.18	0.17	2.33	1.99	23073	25015
阳新县	Yangxin County	3615	3650	4.37	4.81	3.77	3.91	120035	124803
大冶市	Daye City	3321	3520	3.89	4.32	4.25	4.40	67963	72788
郧县	Yun County	73	88	1.46	1.98	4.04	4.58	3151	3313
郧西县	Yunxi County	22	22	1.50	1.61	1.98	2.00	467	493
竹山县	Zhushan County			4.09	4.23	1.84	1.86	1236	2107
竹溪县	Zhuxi County			2.40	2.54	2.06	2.07	268	295
房县	Fang County	50	44	1.61	1.70	2.03	2.04	1304	1372
丹江口市	Danjiangkou City	44	34	0.94	1.06	1.89	1.91	55149	57227
夷陵区	Yiling District		9	2.57	2.80	7.50	7.97	9220	9516
远安县	Yuanan County			1.30	1.37	2.40	2.44	2454	2583
兴山县	Xingshan County			0.74	0.82	2.35	2.72	215	239
秭归县	Zigui County			1.53	1.55	3.90	4.60	710	428
长阳县	Changyang Tujia A.C.			1.43	1.43	5.59	5.82	21594	21647
五峰县	Wufeng Tujia A.C.			0.57	0.57	3.29	2.91	83	82
宜都市	Yidu City	24	34	1.96	2.10	5.46	5.69	13849	15017
当阳市	Dangyang City	9707	8100	6.87	7.52	8.69	8.81	56025	61100
枝江市	Zhijiang City	25062	24473	5.47	5.42	8.41	8.56	72997	76375
襄州区	Xiangzhou District	14281	14282	7.97	8.16	10.44	10.65	43900	43881
南漳县	Nanzhang County	399	552	0.97	0.94	7.50	7.52	7742	8589
谷城县	Gucheng County	6		1.40	1.44	4.89	4.90	9406	9675
保康县	Baokang County			0.97	1.05	2.10	2.42	970	1281
老河口市	Laohekou City	6193	6034	2.64	2.58	5.01	5.08	38774	38822
枣阳市	Zaoyang City	8730	8922	0.80	1.28	8.00	8.02	41977	35300
宜城市	Yicheng City	10080	9783	7.18	7.35	6.01	6.23	30928	31513
梁子湖区	Liangzihu District	695	657	1.97	1.77	2.12	2.38	142930	138000
华容区	Huarong District	3637	2412	2.00	1.80	2.23	2.65	113470	135000
鄂城区	Echeng District	3018	3881	1.99	2.51	4.15	4.19	140100	154000
东宝区	Dongbao District	1930	1024	2.69	2.84	3.70	3.65	30080	31503
京山县	Jingshan County	16402	13590	4.52	5.08	8.60	8.97	74545	82345
沙洋县	Shayang County	10918	10762	13.02	13.56	7.72	7.04	186548	195135
钟祥市	Zhongxiang City	17651	20238	12.41	13.19	9.33	9.56	150005	160020
孝南区	Xiaonan District	6482	6698	2.65	3.07	2.24	2.30	64119	68012
孝昌县	Xiaochang County	1701	1681	3.12	3.89	2.87	3.45	17589	18021
大悟县	Dawu County	309	337	5.60	5.61	3.21	3.46	25279	25880
云梦县	Yunmeng County	3541	3537	1.89	2.12	3.39	3.47	45988	48850
应城市	Yingcheng City	5252	4470	2.98	3.37	3.53	3.61	64405	66810
安陆市	Anlu City	1030	1065	1.89	2.02	7.81	7.91	26564	27202
汉川市	Hanchuan City	26192	23444	4.07	3.99	4.58	5.25	147636	160000
荆州区	Jingzhou District	14609	14549	5.77	5.86	2.72	2.82	119558	125575
江陵县	Jiangling County	10870	10382	7.02	7.37	2.56	2.65	30364	31905
公安县	Gongan County	44392	40273	10.08	12.67	6.37	6.57	133138	140005
监利县	Jianli County	32021	25004	12.00	12.63	7.66	7.98	264947	279008
石首市	Shishou City	19405	18426	6.17	7.05	3.90	4.59	123724	129304
洪湖市	Honghu City	10411	9957	8.42	8.60	2.78	3.07	398127	427669
松滋市	Songci City	17292	15581	6.87	7.62	9.37	9.62	30125	31679
黄州区	Huangzhou District	11984	9818	0.68	0.61	0.62	0.63	47517	50034
团风县	Tuanfeng County	5774	6046	2.14	2.36	0.72	0.72	26858	28334
红安县	Hongan County	4705	1772	10.34	10.08	1.69	3.75	7711	8041
罗田县	Luotian County	330	348	2.55	2.85	1.57	1.73	7850	8180
英山县	Yingshan County	262	181	1.59	1.63	1.57	1.57	8220	8646
浠水县	Xishui County	12923	12225	7.23	7.64	6.38	6.39	94342	95120
蕲春县	Qichun County	7763	8003	4.90	5.37	4.02	4.03	73223	78894
黄梅县	Huangmei County	22830	21420	6.01	6.47	4.81	4.82	92410	97629
麻城市	Macheng City	12898	12320	10.05	10.42	6.72	6.73	23792	25404
武穴市	Wuxue City	12024	13041	7.06	7.91	6.60	6.60	56560	61484
咸安区	Xian'an District	197	228	4.22	4.38	3.01	3.83	28569	30105
嘉鱼县	Jiayu County	2075	1844	0.97	1.05	1.50	1.53	76436	80157
通城县	Tongcheng County	270	284	0.42	0.49	5.55	5.79	10920	11300
崇阳县	Chongyang County	543	806	0.92	1.11	4.50	4.84	11169	12067
通山县	Tongshan County			0.46	0.51	1.48	1.52	12087	13044
赤壁市	Chibi City	2125	2332	2.50	2.66	2.23	2.35	76435	80155
曾都区	Zengdu District	3255	3785	0.63	0.82	5.03	5.23	12801	13519
随县	Sui Country	8272	8519	2.24	2.40	7.35	7.66	35671	39366
广水市	Guangshui City	6574	7094	3.84	4.14	4.91	5.11	30159	32737
恩施市	Enshi City	44	25	1.60	1.77	7.80	8.16	549	589
利川市	Lichuan City			1.18	1.38	6.32	6.46	2558	2722
建始县	Jianshi County			1.50	1.62	5.65	5.96	299	403
巴东县	Badong County		11	1.95	2.06	6.46	6.59	1078	1071
宣恩县	Xuanen County			0.57	0.61	3.82	4.48	435	378
咸丰县	Xianfeng County			1.15	1.47	5.15	5.44	456	474
来凤县	Laifeng County			0.67	0.71	2.35	2.38	1343	1393
鹤峰县	Hefeng County			0.51	0.54	1.97	1.98	122	104
仙桃市	Xiantiao City	31013	29259	12.15	13.05	9.18	8.85	309150	325535
潜江市	Qianjiang City	42954	39733	10.72	11.42	7.89	8.33	107885	113603
天门市	Tianmen City	53292	49266	11.12	11.46	7.30	7.80	120509	126770

附录 全国分省主要指标

Major Indicators by Region

资料整理：王　道

附录1-1　各地区年末常住人口

THE END OF THE TOTAL POPULATION OF ALL REGIONS

单位：万人　　　　(10 000 persons)

地　区	Region	2007	2008	2009	2010	2011	2012	2013
全　国	**National Total**	**132129**	**132802**	**133450**	**134091**	**134735**	**135404**	**136072**
北　京	Beijing	1633	1695	1755	1962	2019	2069	2115
天　津	Tianjin	1115	1176	1228	1299	1355	1413	1472
河　北	Hebei	6943	6989	7034	7194	7241	7288	7333
山　西	Shanxi	3393	3411	3427	3574	3593	3611	3630
内蒙古	Inner Mongolia	2429	2444	2458	2472	2482	2490	2498
辽　宁	Liaoning	4298	4315	4341	4375	4383	4389	4390
吉　林	Jilin	2730	2734	2740	2747	2749	2750	2751
黑龙江	Heilongjiang	3824	3825	3826	3833	3834	3834	3835
上　海	Shanghai	2064	2141	2210	2303	2347	2380	2415
江　苏	Jiangsu	7723	7762	7810	7869	7899	7920	7939
浙　江	Zhejiang	5155	5212	5276	5447	5463	5477	5498
安　徽	Anhui	6118	6135	6131	5957	5968	5988	6030
福　建	Fujian	3612	3639	3666	3693	3720	3748	3774
江　西	Jiangxi	4368	4400	4432	4462	4488	4504	4522
山　东	Shangdong	9367	9417	9470	9588	9637	9685	9733
河　南	Henan	9360	9429	9487	9405	9388	9406	9413
湖　北	**Hubei**	**5699**	**5711**	**5720**	**5728**	**5758**	**5779**	**5799**
湖　南	Hunan	6355	6380	6406	6570	6596	6639	6691
广　东	Guangdong	9660	9893	10130	10441	10505	10594	10644
广　西	Guangxi	4768	4816	4856	4610	4645	4682	4719
海　南	Hainan	845	854	864	869	877	887	895
重　庆	Chongqing	2816	2839	2859	2885	2919	2945	2970
四　川	Sichuan	8127	8138	8185	8045	8050	8076	8107
贵　州	Guizhou	3632	3596	3537	3479	3469	3484	3502
云　南	Yunnan	4514	4543	4571	4602	4631	4659	4687
西　藏	Tibet	287	292	297	301	303	308	312
陕　西	Shaanxi	3708	3718	3727	3735	3743	3753	3764
甘　肃	Gansu	2548	2551	2555	2560	2564	2578	2582
青　海	Qinghai	552	554	557	563	568	573	578
宁　夏	Ningxia	610	618	625	633	639	647	654
新　疆	Xinjiang	2095	2131	2159	2185	2209	2233	2264

注：1.全国数据包括中国人民解放军现役军人数，但不包括香港、澳门特别行政区和台湾省数据；分省数据中未包括中国人民解放军现役军人数。
2.分地区数据均为常住人口。
3.2010年数据为第六次全国人口普查初步汇总数。

Notes:a)The number of national data including military personnel, but not including Hong Kong and Macao Special Administrative Region and Taiwan Province; provincial data does not include active duty PLA.
b)The regional data are permanent population.
c)2010 years of data for the sixth national census preliminary summary number.

附录1-2 各地区按三次产业分法人单位数(2012)

REGIONS BY THE NUMBER OF UNITS THREE INDUSTRIES CORPORATE UNITS(2012)

单位：个 (unit)

地区	Region	法人单位数 Corporate Units	第一产业 Primary Industry	第二产业 Secondary Industry	#工业 #Industry	第三产业 Tertiary Industry
全 国	**National Total**	**10616530**	**440853**	**2949694**	**2558302**	**7225983**
北 京	Beijing	404907	3143	49257	36155	352507
天 津	Tianjin	207512	2939	57812	47734	146761
河 北	Hebei	387093	17972	115236	104674	253885
山 西	Shanxi	244262	34118	42458	35025	167686
内蒙古	Inner Mongolia	155136	8928	28924	24250	117284
辽 宁	Liaoning	453601	14181	123687	101915	315733
吉 林	Jilin	131947	6096	31582	26364	94269
黑龙江	Heilongjiang	189208	6102	43034	34916	140072
上 海	Shanghai	455055	3769	114914	92706	336372
江 苏	Jiangsu	1096912	26265	434107	379002	636540
浙 江	Zhejiang	865140	38278	353972	329913	472890
安 徽	Anhui	324622	14004	92767	77343	217851
福 建	Fujian	399091	19288	119832	106976	259971
江 西	Jiangxi	249278	14632	67680	58982	166966
山 东	Shangdong	906064	29760	276205	235787	600099
河 南	Henan	425276	15825	142271	129139	267180
湖 北	**Hubei**	**435964**	**15682**	**102353**	**80549**	**317929**
湖 南	Hunan	343869	14280	83973	75841	245616
广 东	Guangdong	1008447	15611	325016	298767	667820
广 西	Guangxi	274666	23041	39865	34152	211760
海 南	Hainan	49117	2964	7311	3582	38842
重 庆	Chongqing	274165	35984	56330	47371	181851
四 川	Sichuan	403208	21429	79379	68414	302400
贵 州	Guizhou	133415	10244	24783	21938	98388
云 南	Yunnan	214490	19175	34418	25815	160897
西 藏	Tibet	16664	42	1069	618	15553
陕 西	Shaanxi	255333	10266	51393	38571	193674
甘 肃	Gansu	124734	7064	20026	16822	97644
青 海	Qinghai	33425	2509	5449	4372	25467
宁 夏	Ningxia	43820	2489	8081	6579	33250
新 疆	Xinjiang	110109	4773	16510	14030	88826

附录1-3 各地区按行业分法人单位数(2012)

REGION NUMBER OF CORPORATE UNITS BY SECTOR(2012)

单位：个 (unit)

地 区	Region	法人单位数 Corporate Units	#农、林、牧、渔业 Agriculture, Forestry, Animal husbandry, Fishery	#采矿业 Mining Industry	#制造业 Manufacturing	#电力、煤气及水的生产和供应业 Electricity, Gas and Water Production and Supply	#建筑业 Construction	#交通运输、仓储及邮政业 Traffic, Transport, Storage and Postal Industry
全国总计	**National Total**	**10616530**	**440853**	**107596**	**2380759**	**69947**	**391392**	**249832**
北 京	Beijing	404907	3143	189	35495	471	13102	8098
天 津	Tianjin	207512	2939	100	47162	472	10078	9726
河 北	Hebei	387093	17972	8200	94883	1591	10562	7754
山 西	Shanxi	244262	34118	7595	26189	1241	7433	5382
内蒙古	Inner Mongolia	155136	8928	4740	18085	1425	4674	4267
辽 宁	Liaoning	453601	14181	6091	93851	1973	21772	13580
吉 林	Jilin	131947	6096	1532	23580	1252	5218	2959
黑龙江	Heilongjiang	189208	6102	2432	31205	1279	8118	4271
上 海	Shanghai	455055	3769	4	92397	305	22208	16219
江 苏	Jiangsu	1096912	26265	1076	375128	2798	55105	25751
浙 江	Zhejiang	865140	38278	1508	324348	4057	24059	15490
安 徽	Anhui	324622	14004	3096	71928	2319	15424	9761
福 建	Fujian	399091	19288	3127	97279	6570	12856	9333
江 西	Jiangxi	249278	14632	4144	50775	4063	8698	8396
山 东	Shangdong	906064	29760	5183	228076	2528	40418	21757
河 南	Henan	425276	15825	7882	119630	1627	13132	6302
湖 北	**Hubei**	**435964**	**15682**	**5384**	**71998**	**3167**	**21804**	**11904**
湖 南	Hunan	343869	14280	7685	62901	5255	8132	4965
广 东	Guangdong	1008447	15611	3235	287010	8522	26249	25569
广 西	Guangxi	274666	23041	3656	27725	2771	5713	6107
海 南	Hainan	49117	2964	264	2991	327	3729	1059
重 庆	Chongqing	274165	35984	3085	42225	2061	8959	5431
四 川	Sichuan	403208	21429	5724	56827	5863	10965	8394
贵 州	Guizhou	133415	10244	5630	14905	1403	2845	1946
云 南	Yunnan	214490	19175	5801	17663	2351	8603	4201
西 藏	Tibet	16664	42	129	394	95	451	188
陕 西	Shaanxi	255333	10266	4203	32873	1495	12822	4785
甘 肃	Gansu	124734	7064	2091	13585	1146	3204	2046
青 海	Qinghai	33425	2509	822	3157	393	1077	524
宁 夏	Ningxia	43820	2489	682	5624	273	1502	784
新 疆	Xinjiang	110109	4773	2306	10870	854	2480	2883

附录1−3　续表1 continued

单位：个 (unit)

地　区	Region	#信息传输、计算机服务和软件业 Information Transmission, Computer Services and Software	#批发和零售业 Wholesale and Retail Trade	#住宿和餐饮业 Accommodation and Catering Services	#金融业 Financial Sector	#房地产业 Real Estate	#租赁和商务服务业 Leasing and Business Services
全国总计	**National Total**	**245669**	**2630690**	**186837**	**67554**	**356717**	**813851**
北　京	Beijing	22151	121945	13252	1794	14661	77035
天　津	Tianjin	3452	64701	3118	1876	5913	21553
河　北	Hebei	5106	91157	4233	2597	11472	15638
山　西	Shanxi	3691	53059	3664	1785	6364	11201
内蒙古	Inner Mongolia	2196	38712	3449	1816	6293	8901
辽　宁	Liaoning	12119	122551	7575	3615	17678	36142
吉　林	Jilin	2207	29292	1714	1007	4498	7395
黑龙江	Heilongjiang	3387	48109	2491	1624	6918	11772
上　海	Shanghai	14029	150676	11590	1479	14202	63975
江　苏	Jiangsu	23021	303339	12019	5700	30017	81495
浙　江	Zhejiang	19949	196797	9072	3065	20423	68184
安　徽	Anhui	7572	74576	5414	3069	13254	24754
福　建	Fujian	8875	100295	6455	3535	12038	30609
江　西	Jiangxi	3182	46982	3404	2300	9260	16335
山　东	Shangdong	18621	252083	16993	6168	24972	53847
河　南	Henan	6434	67285	8671	2033	11360	16271
湖　北	**Hubei**	**9085**	**106428**	**8594**	**3238**	**17674**	**31783**
湖　南	Hunan	10525	63606	7023	1989	10734	15525
广　东	Guangdong	25038	285282	18283	4759	46107	96324
广　西	Guangxi	6952	67375	3466	1643	11034	22108
海　南	Hainan	1319	10842	1457	347	5586	5357
重　庆	Chongqing	6721	70126	10019	1525	9341	21127
四　川	Sichuan	12209	63642	8006	2585	12171	24629
贵　州	Guizhou	2425	19843	2144	1062	5658	6576
云　南	Yunnan	5021	54080	3498	2607	9013	14924
西　藏	Tibet	162	1085	326	117	108	292
陕　西	Shaanxi	5088	61041	6064	1764	10340	15511
甘　肃	Gansu	1629	24181	2299	928	3275	4798
青　海	Qinghai	481	5500	653	263	992	1337
宁　夏	Ningxia	811	11300	756	399	1299	2408
新　疆	Xinjiang	2211	24800	1135	865	4062	6045

附录1-3　续表2 continued

单位：个　(unit)

地区	Region	#科学研究、技术服务和地质勘查业 Research, Technical Service and Geological Prospecting	#水利、环境和公共设施管理业 Water, Environment and Public Facilities Management	#居民服务和其他服务业 Resident Services and Other Services	#教育 Education	#卫生、社会保障和社会福利业 Health, Social Security and Social Welfare	#文化、体育和娱乐业 Culture, Sports and Entertainment	#公共管理和社会组织 Public Management and Social Organization
全国总计	**National Total**	**324932**	**75981**	**196880**	**355072**	**206885**	**121126**	**1393957**
北京	Beijing	38136	2488	14788	8304	3084	12754	14017
天津	Tianjin	10795	1458	7457	3467	1508	1863	9874
河北	Hebei	6478	2315	5088	17885	6554	2675	74933
山西	Shanxi	5449	2369	4840	8990	5217	3398	52277
内蒙古	Inner Mongolia	4258	1878	2787	5673	4486	1900	30668
辽宁	Liaoning	16450	3665	9661	13499	11123	4880	43195
吉林	Jilin	5116	1342	2157	5251	3271	1844	26216
黑龙江	Heilongjiang	6843	1666	3707	7780	4896	2026	34582
上海	Shanghai	22603	2127	13307	5760	2983	4941	12481
江苏	Jiangsu	27367	6750	18805	17764	11288	9065	64159
浙江	Zhejiang	22256	4969	9572	17736	7144	7218	71015
安徽	Anhui	8913	2654	5033	12597	5458	3204	41592
福建	Fujian	9824	2923	5919	12618	6127	5082	46338
江西	Jiangxi	5479	2164	4751	9436	7351	2899	45027
山东	Shangdong	17830	4213	17604	21213	15981	6234	122583
河南	Henan	7005	2592	4790	23071	25235	4574	81557
湖北	**Hubei**	**15165**	**4644**	**9659**	**17743**	**11243**	**5913**	**64856**
湖南	Hunan	9677	3227	5675	14873	8263	4998	84536
广东	Guangdong	30938	5406	18981	32611	9397	9290	59835
广西	Guangxi	9959	2748	4093	17788	6644	3489	48354
海南	Hainan	1478	387	892	2358	812	832	6116
重庆	Chongqing	5409	1868	6844	8815	6409	3156	25060
四川	Sichuan	11851	3510	5066	21254	14881	6505	107697
贵州	Guizhou	3368	1258	2072	9821	4159	1765	36291
云南	Yunnan	6656	2210	3381	8203	4517	3393	39193
西藏	Tibet	187	43	110	1046	505	173	11211
陕西	Shaanxi	7580	2464	5372	12248	10492	3231	47694
甘肃	Gansu	2483	1014	1776	9225	3550	1775	38665
青海	Qinghai	962	345	370	1320	789	457	11474
宁夏	Ningxia	835	309	740	1425	830	368	10986
新疆	Xinjiang	3582	975	1583	5298	2688	1224	31475

附录1-4　地区生产总值

GROSS DOMESTIC PRODUCT

单位：亿元　　(100 million yuan)

地　区	Region	2007	2008	2009	2010	2011	2012	2013
北　京	Beijing	9846.8	11115.0	12153.0	14113.6	16251.9	17879.4	19500.6
天　津	Tianjin	5252.8	6719.0	7521.9	9224.5	11307.3	12893.9	14370.2
河　北	Hebei	13607.3	16012.0	17235.5	20394.3	24515.8	26575.0	28301.4
山　西	Shanxi	6024.5	7315.4	7358.3	9200.9	11237.6	12112.8	12602.2
内蒙古	Inner Mongolia	6423.2	8496.2	9740.3	11672.0	14359.9	15880.6	16832.4
辽　宁	Liaoning	11164.3	13668.6	15212.5	18457.3	22226.7	24846.4	27077.7
吉　林	Jilin	5284.7	6426.1	7278.8	8667.6	10568.8	11939.2	12981.5
黑龙江	Heilongjiang	7104.0	8314.4	8587.0	10368.6	12582.0	13691.6	14382.9
上　海	Shanghai	12494.0	14069.9	15046.5	17166.0	19195.7	20181.7	21602.1
江　苏	Jiangsu	26018.5	30982.0	34457.3	41425.5	49110.3	54058.2	59161.8
浙　江	Zhejiang	18753.7	21462.7	22990.4	27722.3	32318.9	34665.3	37568.5
安　徽	Anhui	7360.9	8851.7	10062.8	12359.3	15300.6	17212.1	19038.9
福　建	Fujian	9248.5	10823.0	12236.5	14737.1	17560.2	19701.8	21759.6
江　西	Jiangxi	5800.3	6971.1	7655.2	9451.3	11702.8	12948.9	14338.5
山　东	Shangdong	25776.9	30933.3	33896.7	39169.9	45361.9	50013.2	54684.3
河　南	Henan	15012.5	18018.5	19480.5	23092.4	26931.0	29599.3	32155.9
湖　北	**Hubei**	**9333.4**	**11328.9**	**12961.1**	**15967.6**	**19632.3**	**22250.5**	**24668.5**
湖　南	Hunan	9439.6	11555.0	13059.7	16038.0	19669.6	22154.2	24501.7
广　东	Guangdong	31777.0	36796.7	39482.6	46013.1	53210.3	57067.9	62164.0
广　西	Guangxi	5823.4	7021.0	7759.2	9569.9	11720.9	13035.1	14378.0
海　南	Hainan	1254.2	1503.1	1654.2	2064.5	2522.7	2855.5	3146.5
重　庆	Chongqing	4676.1	5793.7	6530.0	7925.6	10011.4	11409.6	12656.7
四　川	Sichuan	10562.4	12601.2	14151.3	17185.5	21026.7	23872.8	26260.8
贵　州	Guizhou	2884.1	3561.6	3912.7	4602.2	5701.8	6852.2	8006.8
云　南	Yunnan	4772.5	5692.1	6169.8	7224.2	8893.1	10309.5	11720.9
西　藏	Tibet	341.4	394.9	441.4	507.5	605.8	701.0	807.7
陕　西	Shaanxi	5757.3	7314.6	8169.8	10123.5	12512.3	14453.7	16045.2
甘　肃	Gansu	2702.4	3166.8	3387.6	4120.8	5020.4	5650.2	6268.0
青　海	Qinghai	797.4	1018.6	1081.3	1350.4	1670.4	1893.5	2101.1
宁　夏	Ningxia	919.1	1203.9	1353.3	1689.7	2102.2	2341.3	2565.1
新　疆	Xinjiang	3523.2	4183.2	4277.1	5437.5	6610.1	7505.3	8360.2

注：本表按当年价格计算。本表数据为国家统计局最终核实数。

Note:The table at current prices.National Bureau of Statistics data for this table is to verify the final number.

附录1-5　地区生产总值指数

INDICES OF GROSS DOMESTIC PRODUCT

（上年=100）　(last year=100)

地　区	Region	2007	2008	2009	2010	2011	2012	2013
北　京	Beijing	114.5	109.1	110.2	110.3	108.1	107.7	107.7
天　津	Tianjin	115.5	116.5	116.5	117.4	116.4	113.8	112.5
河　北	Hebei	112.8	110.1	110.0	112.2	111.3	109.6	108.2
山　西	Shanxi	115.9	108.5	105.4	113.9	113.0	110.1	108.9
内蒙古	Inner Mongolia	119.2	117.8	116.9	115.0	114.3	111.5	109.0
辽　宁	Liaoning	115.0	113.4	113.1	114.2	112.1	109.5	108.7
吉　林	Jilin	116.1	116.0	113.6	113.8	113.7	112.0	108.3
黑龙江	Heilongjiang	112.0	111.8	111.4	112.7	112.2	110.0	108.0
上　海	Shanghai	115.2	109.7	108.2	110.3	108.2	107.5	107.7
江　苏	Jiangsu	114.9	112.7	112.4	112.7	111.0	110.1	109.6
浙　江	Zhejiang	114.7	110.1	108.9	111.9	109.0	108.0	108.2
安　徽	Anhui	114.2	112.7	112.9	114.6	113.5	112.1	110.4
福　建	Fujian	115.2	113.0	112.3	113.9	112.2	111.4	111.0
江　西	Jiangxi	113.2	113.2	113.1	114.0	112.5	111.0	110.1
山　东	Shangdong	114.2	112.0	112.2	112.3	110.9	109.8	109.6
河　南	Henan	114.6	112.1	110.9	112.5	111.6	110.1	109.0
湖　北	**Hubei**	**114.6**	**113.4**	**113.5**	**114.8**	**113.8**	**111.3**	**110.1**
湖　南	Hunan	115.0	113.9	113.7	114.6	112.8	111.3	110.1
广　东	Guangdong	114.9	110.4	109.7	112.4	110.0	108.2	108.5
广　西	Guangxi	115.1	112.8	113.9	114.2	112.3	111.3	110.2
海　南	Hainan	115.8	110.3	111.7	116.0	112.0	109.1	109.9
重　庆	Chongqing	115.9	114.5	114.9	117.1	116.4	113.6	112.3
四　川	Sichuan	114.5	111.0	114.5	115.1	115.0	112.6	110.0
贵　州	Guizhou	114.8	111.3	111.4	112.8	115.0	113.6	112.5
云　南	Yunnan	112.2	110.6	112.1	112.3	113.7	113.0	112.1
西　藏	Tibet	114.0	110.1	112.4	112.3	112.7	111.8	112.1
陕　西	Shaanxi	115.8	116.4	113.6	114.6	113.9	112.9	111.0
甘　肃	Gansu	112.3	110.1	110.3	111.8	112.5	112.6	110.8
青　海	Qinghai	113.5	113.5	110.1	115.3	113.5	112.3	110.8
宁　夏	Ningxia	112.7	112.6	111.9	113.5	112.0	111.5	109.8
新　疆	Xinjiang	112.2	111.0	108.1	110.6	112.0	112.0	111.0

注：本表按不变价格计算。本表数据为国家统计局最终核实数。
Note:At constant prices, this table.National Bureau of Statistics data for this table is to verify the final number.

附录1-6　地区生产总值构成(2013)

COMPOSITION OF GROSS DOMESTIC PRODUCT(2013)

(地区生产总值=100)

(GDP=100)

地 区	Region	第一产业 Primary Industry	第二产业 Secondary Industry	工 业 Industry	建筑业 Contruction	第三产业 Tertiary Industry
北 京	Beijing	0.8	22.3	18.1	4.2	76.9
天 津	Tianjin	1.3	50.6	46.5	4.2	48.1
河 北	Hebei	12.4	52.2	46.6	5.5	35.5
山 西	Shanxi	6.1	53.9	47.9	6.0	40.0
内蒙古	Inner Mongolia	9.5	54.0	47.2	6.8	36.5
辽 宁	Liaoning	8.6	52.7	46.2	6.5	38.7
吉 林	Jilin	11.6	52.8	46.5	6.4	35.5
黑龙江	Heilongjiang	17.5	41.1	35.4	5.8	41.4
上 海	Shanghai	0.6	37.2	33.5	3.7	62.2
江 苏	Jiangsu	6.2	49.2	43.3	5.9	44.7
浙 江	Zhejiang	4.8	49.1	43.6	5.5	46.1
安 徽	Anhui	12.3	54.6	46.9	7.8	33.0
福 建	Fujian	8.9	52.0	43.5	8.5	39.1
江 西	Jiangxi	11.4	53.5	44.9	8.6	35.1
山 东	Shangdong	8.7	50.1	44.3	5.9	41.2
河 南	Henan	12.6	55.4	49.6	5.7	32.0
湖 北	**Hubei**	**12.6**	**49.3**	**42.7**	**6.6**	**38.1**
湖 南	Hunan	12.6	47.0	40.8	6.2	40.3
广 东	Guangdong	4.9	47.3	44.1	3.2	47.8
广 西	Guangxi	16.3	47.7	40.0	7.7	36.0
海 南	Hainan	24.0	27.7	17.5	10.2	48.3
重 庆	Chongqing	8.0	50.5	41.5	9.1	41.4
四 川	Sichuan	13.0	51.7	44.1	7.6	35.2
贵 州	Guizhou	12.9	40.5	33.6	7.0	46.6
云 南	Yunnan	16.2	42.0	32.1	9.9	41.8
西 藏	Tibet	10.7	36.3	7.6	28.7	53.0
陕 西	Shaanxi	9.5	55.5	46.8	8.8	34.9
甘 肃	Gansu	14.0	45.0	35.5	9.5	41.0
青 海	Qinghai	9.9	57.3	46.2	11.1	32.8
宁 夏	Ningxia	8.7	49.3	36.8	12.5	42.0
新 疆	Xinjiang	17.6	45.0	36.2	8.9	37.4

注：本表按当年价格计算。本表数据为国家统计局最终核实数。

Note:At present year price,this table.National Bureau of Statistics data for this table is to verify the final number.

附录1-7 人均地区生产总值

PER CAPITA GROSS DOMESTIC PRODUCT

单位：元 本表按当年价格计算（At current price） （yuan）

地 区	Region	2007	2008	2009	2010	2011	2012	2013
北 京	Beijing	61274	66797	70452	75943	80394	87091	93213
天 津	Tianjin	47970	58656	62574	72994	84337	93110	99607
河 北	Hebei	19662	22986	24581	28668	33571	36584	38716
山 西	Shanxi	17805	21506	21522	26283	30974	33628	34813
内蒙古	Inner Mongolia	26521	34869	39735	47347	57515	64319	67498
辽 宁	Liaoning	26057	31739	35149	42355	50299	56547	61686
吉 林	Jilin	19383	23521	26595	31599	38321	43412	47191
黑龙江	Heilongjiang	18580	21740	22447	27076	32615	35711	37509
上 海	Shanghai	62041	66932	69164	76074	82560	85033	90092
江 苏	Jiangsu	33837	40014	44253	52840	61649	68347	74607
浙 江	Zhejiang	36676	41405	43842	51711	58665	63266	68462
安 徽	Anhui	12039	14448	16408	20888	25340	28792	31684
福 建	Fujian	25582	29755	33437	40025	46972	52763	57856
江 西	Jiangxi	13322	15900	17335	21253	25884	28799	31771
山 东	Shangdong	27604	32936	35894	41106	47260	51768	56323
河 南	Henan	16012	19181	20597	24446	28981	31723	34174
湖 北	**Hubei**	**16386**	**19858**	**22677**	**27906**	**34131**	**38572**	**42613**
湖 南	Hunan	14869	18147	20428	24719	29828	33480	36763
广 东	Guangdong	33272	37638	39436	44736	50295	54095	58540
广 西	Guangxi	12277	14652	16045	20219	25315	27943	30588
海 南	Hainan	14923	17691	19254	23831	28797	32374	35317
重 庆	Chongqing	16629	20490	22920	27596	34500	39083	42795
四 川	Sichuan	12963	15495	17339	21182	26133	29579	32454
贵 州	Guizhou	7878	9855	10971	13119	16413	19566	22922
云 南	Yunnan	10609	12570	13539	15752	18957	22195	25083
西 藏	Tibet	11898	13588	15008	17027	20077	22757	26068
陕 西	Shaanxi	15546	19700	21947	27133	33142	38557	42692
甘 肃	Gansu	10614	12421	13269	16113	19517	21978	24296
青 海	Qinghai	14507	18421	19454	24115	28891	33023	36510
宁 夏	Ningxia	15142	19609	21777	26860	32392	36166	39420
新 疆	Xinjiang	16999	19797	19942	25034	29496	33621	37181

附录1-8 各地区全社会固定资产投资

REGIONAL TOTAL INVESTMENT IN FIXED ASSETS

单位：亿元 (100 million yuan)

地 区	Region	2007	2008	2009	2010	2011	2012	2013
全国总计	**National Total**	**137323.9**	**172828.4**	**224598.8**	**278121.9**	**311485.1**	**374694.7**	**447074.4**
北 京	Beijing	3907.2	3814.7	4616.9	5403.0	5578.9	6112.4	6847.1
天 津	Tianjin	2353.1	3389.8	4738.2	6278.1	7067.7	7934.8	9130.3
河 北	Hebei	6884.7	8866.6	12269.8	15083.4	16389.3	19661.3	23194.2
山 西	Shanxi	2861.5	3531.2	4943.2	6063.2	7073.1	8863.3	11031.9
内蒙古	Inner Mongolia	4372.9	5475.4	7336.8	8926.5	10365.2	11875.7	14215.5
辽 宁	Liaoning	7435.2	10019.1	12292.5	16043.0	17726.3	21836.3	25107.7
吉 林	Jilin	3651.4	5038.9	6411.6	7870.4	7441.7	9511.5	10133.5
黑龙江	Heilongjiang	2833.5	3656.0	5028.8	6812.6	7475.4	9694.7	12126.0
上 海	Shanghai	4420.4	4823.1	5043.8	5108.9	4962.1	5117.6	5647.8
江 苏	Jiangsu	12268.1	15300.6	18949.9	23184.3	26692.6	30854.2	36373.8
浙 江	Zhejiang	8420.4	9323.0	10742.3	12376.0	14185.3	17649.4	20777.1
安 徽	Anhui	5087.5	6747.0	8990.7	11542.9	12455.7	15425.8	18621.6
福 建	Fujian	4287.8	5207.7	6231.2	8199.1	9910.9	12439.9	15327.4
江 西	Jiangxi	3301.9	4745.4	6643.1	8772.3	9087.6	10774.2	12866.1
山 东	Shangdong	12537.7	15435.9	19034.5	23280.5	26749.7	31256.0	36789.1
河 南	Henan	8010.1	10490.6	13704.5	16585.9	17769.0	21450.0	26220.9
湖 北	**Hubei**	**4330.4**	**5647.0**	**7866.9**	**10262.7**	**12557.3**	**15578.3**	**19307.3**
湖 南	Hunan	4154.8	5534.0	7703.4	9663.6	11880.9	14523.2	17846.3
广 东	Guangdong	9294.3	10868.7	12933.1	15623.7	17069.2	18751.5	22307.8
广 西	Guangxi	2939.7	3756.4	5237.2	7057.6	7990.7	9808.6	11907.7
海 南	Hainan	502.4	705.4	988.3	1317.0	1657.2	2145.4	2697.4
重 庆	Chongqing	3127.7	3979.6	5214.3	6688.9	7473.4	8736.2	10429.6
四 川	Sichuan	5639.8	7127.8	11371.9	13116.7	14222.2	17040.0	20325.2
贵 州	Guizhou	1488.8	1864.5	2412.0	3104.9	4235.9	5717.8	7373.6
云 南	Yunnan	2759.0	3435.9	4526.4	5528.7	6191.0	7831.1	9968.3
西 藏	Tibet	270.3	309.9	378.3	462.7	516.3	670.5	876.0
陕 西	Shaanxi	3415.0	4614.4	6246.9	7963.7	9431.1	12044.5	14867.3
甘 肃	Gansu	1304.2	1712.8	2363.0	3158.3	3965.8	5145.0	6527.9
青 海	Qinghai	482.8	583.2	798.2	1016.9	1435.6	1883.4	2361.1
宁 夏	Ningxia	599.8	828.9	1075.9	1444.2	1644.7	2096.9	2651.1
新 疆	Xinjiang	1850.8	2260.0	2725.5	3423.2	4632.1	6158.8	7724.5
不分地区	**Irrespective of region**	**2530.8**	**3734.9**	**5779.7**	**6759.1**	**5651.3**	**6106.4**	**5493.3**

附录1-9 各地区城镇固定资产投资

REGIONAL INVESTMENT IN FIXED ASSET

单位：亿元 (100 million yuan)

地 区	Region	2007	2008	2009	2010	2011	2012	2013
全国总计	**National Total**	**117464.47**	**148738.30**	**193920.39**	**241430.89**	**302396.06**	**364854.15**	**436527.70**
北 京	Beijing	3597.29	3520.95	4149.63	4916.53	5519.84	6064.86	6797.54
天 津	Tianjin	2192.17	3175.14	4446.57	5896.52	7040.68	7913.26	9103.01
河 北	Hebei	5690.31	7463.77	10476.50	12922.66	15780.26	19104.63	22629.77
山 西	Shanxi	2600.22	3194.57	4509.56	5526.60	6837.69	8584.85	10745.35
内蒙古	Inner Mongolia	4255.00	5327.04	7143.84	8687.99	10252.97	11749.77	14070.50
辽 宁	Liaoning	6576.05	8881.95	11605.12	15106.33	17431.46	21535.37	24791.40
吉 林	Jilin	3340.19	4592.71	5958.95	7395.23	7226.65	9262.23	9880.00
黑龙江	Heilongjiang	2591.69	3354.82	4695.74	6292.67	7157.92	9375.44	11794.17
上 海	Shanghai	4045.10	4404.95	4618.91	4630.47	4959.93	5114.64	5644.13
江 苏	Jiangsu	9161.37	11609.71	14266.80	17416.47	26313.46	30473.74	35983.00
浙 江	Zhejiang	5996.93	6551.10	7454.33	8438.08	13651.65	17095.96	20189.07
安 徽	Anhui	4444.58	5948.61	7945.50	10281.29	12007.87	14943.81	18090.89
福 建	Fujian	3829.02	4601.50	5548.61	7385.78	9677.09	12182.52	15045.81
江 西	Jiangxi	2954.87	4325.38	6008.12	7856.94	8753.93	10378.37	12450.84
山 东	Shangdong	10153.56	12528.96	15439.10	18844.41	25907.38	30319.76	35875.86
河 南	Henan	6609.16	8721.19	11454.89	13934.82	16934.32	20558.61	25321.52
湖 北	**Hubei**	**3927.36**	**5148.76**	**7183.67**	**9405.63**	**12195.39**	**15148.71**	**18796.85**
湖 南	Hunan	3609.54	4879.96	6880.00	8617.98	11407.74	13966.26	17230.14
广 东	Guangdong	7368.69	8640.87	10230.05	12599.26	16599.16	18250.13	21794.98
广 西	Guangxi	2596.74	3325.95	4689.88	6383.26	7580.90	9345.18	11383.93
海 南	Hainan	472.77	668.02	942.68	1257.50	1599.14	2064.44	2625.02
重 庆	Chongqing	2937.07	3715.90	4855.11	6170.61	7366.95	8610.37	10285.29
四 川	Sichuan	5043.42	6362.08	9090.09	11061.38	13687.75	16530.31	19754.36
贵 州	Guizhou	1289.13	1609.34	2049.83	2609.36	4026.47	5504.95	7102.78
云 南	Yunnan	2443.79	3106.33	4117.51	5052.61	5932.75	7553.51	9621.83
西 藏	Tibet	230.83	271.25	327.64	404.98	516.31	670.52	876.00
陕 西	Shaanxi	3168.82	4286.42	5888.37	7569.90	9108.98	11705.83	14516.71
甘 肃	Gansu	1177.46	1510.75	2076.36	2808.55	3870.08	5040.03	6407.20
青 海	Qinghai	443.69	514.05	689.09	840.01	1365.91	1808.67	2285.30
宁 夏	Ningxia	527.69	735.71	964.16	1292.80	1589.14	2033.03	2577.79
新 疆	Xinjiang	1659.19	2025.64	2434.15	3065.13	4444.99	5857.98	7363.39
不分地区	**Irrespective of region**	**2530.77**	**3734.93**	**5779.66**	**6759.14**	**5651.29**	**6106.38**	**5493.28**

注：2010年前为城镇固定资产投资口径；2011年为固定资产投资（不含农户）。

Note: Datas of the table are urban fixed asset investment before 2011, and are investment in fixed assets in 2011.

附录1-10 各地区房地产开发企业(单位)房屋施工、竣工面积和商品房销售面积

REGIONAL REAL ESTATE DEVELOPMENT ENTERPRISES(UNITS) HOUSING CONSTRUCTION, COMPLETION AND SALES OF COMMERCIAL SPACE AREA

单位：万平方米 (10 000 sqm)

地 区	Region	房屋施工面积 Housing Construction Area		房屋竣工面积 Housing Completed Area		商品房销售面积 Sales of Commercial Area	
		2012	2013	2012	2013	2012	2013
全国总计	**National Total**	**573418**	**665572**	**99425**	**101435**	**111304**	**130551**
北 京	Beijing	13122	13887	2391	2666	1944	1903
天 津	Tianjin	9864	10892	2543	2805	1662	1847
河 北	Hebei	27578	29949	4895	4437	5145	5676
山 西	Shanxi	11714	14040	1733	2285	1498	1643
内蒙古	Inner Mongolia	16507	18624	2449	2638	2524	2738
辽 宁	Liaoning	38502	41626	6438	6152	8828	9292
吉 林	Jilin	10936	12181	1928	2254	2452	2215
黑龙江	Heilongjiang	13485	13567	3246	2933	3807	3340
上 海	Shanghai	13250	13517	2305	2254	1898	2382
江 苏	Jiangsu	45098	52574	9848	9712	9019	11455
浙 江	Zhejiang	33423	37647	4293	4692	4005	4887
安 徽	Anhui	24836	30235	3965	5180	4829	6265
福 建	Fujian	21121	26287	2233	3370	3259	4676
江 西	Jiangxi	9466	11996	1747	1790	2397	3167
山 东	Shangdong	42959	50549	7325	7509	8633	10330
河 南	Henan	29559	35979	5871	5966	5968	7310
湖 北	**Hubei**	**16820**	**21866**	**3274**	**3041**	**4038**	**5299**
湖 南	Hunan	21357	25400	4458	4594	5150	5952
广 东	Guangdong	39296	46480	6356	6273	7899	9836
广 西	Guangxi	15018	16040	2334	1713	2759	2996
海 南	Hainan	5109	6173	856	609	932	1191
重 庆	Chongqing	22009	26252	3991	3804	4522	4818
四 川	Sichuan	29866	32165	5867	5109	6456	7313
贵 州	Guizhou	13245	17357	1417	1765	2187	2972
云 南	Yunnan	14362	18261	1852	2019	3238	3309
西 藏	Tibet	47	58	9	18	23	25
陕 西	Shaanxi	15411	17241	1654	1512	2756	3046
甘 肃	Gansu	5635	6848	845	916	978	1220
青 海	Qinghai	1891	2377	416	593	263	382
宁 夏	Ningxia	5033	6043	1152	1104	804	1048
新 疆	Xinjiang	6897	9460	1736	1722	1430	2017

注：商品房销售面积包括期房。

Note:Sales of Commercial, including Forward House.

附录1-11 各地区房地产开发企业(单位)投资和商品房销售额

REGIONAL REAL ESTATE DEVELOPMENT COMPANY(UNITS) OF INVESTMENT AND COMMERCIAL HOUSING SALES

单位：亿元 (100 million yuan)

地 区	Region	房地产开发投资额 Real Estate Development Investment		商品房销售额 Commercial Housing Sales		#住 宅 #Residential	
		2012	2013	2012	2013	2012	2013
全国总计	**National Total**	**71803.8**	**86013.4**	**64455.8**	**81428.3**	**53467.2**	**67694.9**
北 京	Beijing	3153.4	3483.4	3308.6	3530.8	2455.5	2434.7
天 津	Tianjin	1260.0	1480.8	1365.5	1615.5	1210.6	1443.3
河 北	Hebei	3086.5	3445.4	2303.9	2779.7	1914.6	2329.1
山 西	Shanxi	1010.5	1308.6	579.9	728.3	513.2	625.1
内蒙古	Inner Mongolia	1291.4	1479.0	1022.8	1177.4	769.4	874.4
辽 宁	Liaoning	5455.8	6450.8	4362.8	4759.2	3611.2	3941.9
吉 林	Jilin	1310.0	1252.4	1016.9	993.0	836.8	839.7
黑龙江	Heilongjiang	1535.8	1604.8	1548.3	1582.3	1201.9	1305.9
上 海	Shanghai	2381.4	2819.6	2669.5	3911.6	2209.0	3264.0
江 苏	Jiangsu	6206.1	7241.5	6067.0	7913.7	5089.1	6777.7
浙 江	Zhejiang	5226.3	6216.2	4262.7	5396.0	3541.6	4513.9
安 徽	Anhui	3151.6	3946.2	2329.9	3182.9	1921.9	2662.0
福 建	Fujian	2824.1	3703.0	2817.7	4232.1	2293.9	3410.6
江 西	Jiangxi	969.6	1174.6	1137.3	1647.9	931.4	1396.1
山 东	Shangdong	4708.3	5444.5	4111.8	5215.1	3529.5	4461.1
河 南	Henan	3035.3	3843.8	2286.7	3074.1	1915.6	2516.3
湖 北	**Hubei**	**2539.5**	**3286.0**	**2036.2**	**2790.3**	**1689.9**	**2310.0**
湖 南	Hunan	2210.5	2628.3	2085.2	2525.6	1711.5	2115.0
广 东	Guangdong	5352.8	6489.6	6407.8	8941.1	5488.4	7476.1
广 西	Guangxi	1554.9	1614.6	1159.8	1375.8	995.8	1166.7
海 南	Hainan	886.6	1196.8	735.6	1032.7	701.7	997.0
重 庆	Chongqing	2508.4	3012.8	2297.3	2682.8	1972.4	2283.6
四 川	Sichuan	3266.4	3853.0	3517.7	4020.3	2816.5	3308.6
贵 州	Guizhou	1467.6	1942.5	900.1	1276.7	740.0	988.8
云 南	Yunnan	1782.1	2488.3	1362.8	1487.2	1077.1	1192.6
西 藏	Tibet	6.9	9.7	7.4	10.6	6.2	8.8
陕 西	Shaanxi	1835.9	2240.2	1420.7	1608.1	1215.6	1413.2
甘 肃	Gansu	561.0	724.6	349.3	474.1	301.6	418.1
青 海	Qinghai	189.7	247.6	106.5	158.8	91.1	146.3
宁 夏	Ningxia	429.2	559.0	317.6	443.7	256.2	363.6
新 疆	Xinjiang	606.1	825.7	560.5	861.0	458.1	710.7

附录1－12　各地区货物进出口总额
TOTAL IMPORT AND EXPORT REGIONS

(按经营单位所在地分)

(Location of Points by Business Units)

单位：亿美元　　(100 million US dollors)

地　区	Region	2007	2008	2009	2010	2011	2012	2013
全国总计	**National Total**	**21765.7**	**25632.6**	**22075.4**	**29740.0**	**36418.6**	**38671.2**	**41596.9**
北　京	Beijing	1930.0	2716.9	2147.3	3017.2	3895.6	4081.1	4291.3
天　津	Tianjin	714.5	804.0	638.3	821.0	1033.8	1156.3	1285.1
河　北	Hebei	255.2	384.2	296.3	420.6	536.0	505.6	549.0
山　西	Shanxi	115.8	144.0	85.7	125.8	147.4	150.4	157.9
内蒙古	Inner Mongolia	77.4	89.2	67.7	87.3	119.3	112.6	120.0
辽　宁	Liaoning	594.7	724.3	629.3	807.1	960.4	1040.9	1144.9
吉　林	Jilin	103.0	133.3	117.4	168.5	220.6	245.6	258.6
黑龙江	Heilongjiang	173.0	231.3	162.3	255.2	385.2	375.9	388.8
上　海	Shanghai	2828.5	3220.6	2777.1	3689.5	4375.5	4365.9	4412.2
江　苏	Jiangsu	3494.7	3922.7	3387.4	4658.0	5395.8	5479.6	5508.1
浙　江	Zhejiang	1768.5	2111.3	1877.3	2535.3	3093.8	3124.0	3357.9
安　徽	Anhui	159.3	201.8	156.8	242.7	313.1	392.8	455.6
福　建	Fujian	744.5	848.2	796.5	1087.8	1435.2	1559.4	1693.3
江　西	Jiangxi	94.5	136.2	127.8	216.2	314.7	334.1	367.5
山　东	Shangdong	1224.7	1584.1	1390.5	1891.6	2358.9	2455.4	2665.6
河　南	Henan	127.9	174.8	134.8	178.3	326.2	517.4	599.5
湖　北	**Hubei**	**148.7**	**207.1**	**172.5**	**259.3**	**335.9**	**319.6**	**363.8**
湖　南	Hunan	96.9	125.5	101.5	146.6	189.4	219.5	251.7
广　东	Guangdong	6341.9	6849.7	6110.9	7849.0	9134.7	9840.2	10915.9
广　西	Guangxi	92.6	132.4	142.5	177.4	233.6	294.8	328.3
海　南	Hainan	35.1	45.3	48.8	86.5	127.6	143.2	149.8
重　庆	Chongqing	74.4	95.2	77.1	124.3	292.1	532.0	687.0
四　川	Sichuan	143.8	221.1	241.7	326.9	477.2	591.4	645.7
贵　州	Guizhou	22.7	33.7	23.0	31.5	48.9	66.3	82.9
云　南	Yunnan	87.9	96.0	80.5	134.3	160.3	210.1	257.9
西　藏	Tibet	3.9	7.7	4.0	8.4	13.6	34.2	33.2
陕　西	Shaanxi	68.9	83.3	84.1	121.0	146.5	148.0	201.3
甘　肃	Gansu	55.2	61.0	38.7	74.0	87.3	89.0	102.3
青　海	Qinghai	6.1	6.9	5.9	7.9	9.2	11.6	14.0
宁　夏	Ningxia	15.8	18.8	12.0	19.6	22.9	22.2	32.2
新　疆	Xinjiang	137.2	222.2	139.5	171.3	228.2	251.7	275.6

附录1-13　各地区货物出口、进口额(2013)

TOTAL IMPORT AND EXPORT REGIONS(2013)

单位：亿美元　　　(100 million yuan)

地　区	Region	按经营单位所在地分 Location of Points by Business Units 出口额 Exports	进口额 Imports
全国总计	**National Total**	**22093.7**	**19503.2**
北　京	Beijing	631.1	3660.1
天　津	Tianjin	490.1	795.0
河　北	Hebei	309.6	239.4
山　西	Shanxi	80.0	78.0
内蒙古	Inner Mongolia	40.9	79.0
辽　宁	Liaoning	645.4	499.5
吉　林	Jilin	67.6	191.0
黑龙江	Heilongjiang	162.3	226.5
上　海	Shanghai	2041.8	2370.4
江　苏	Jiangsu	3288.1	2220.0
浙　江	Zhejiang	2487.5	870.4
安　徽	Anhui	282.5	173.0
福　建	Fujian	1064.8	628.5
江　西	Jiangxi	281.7	85.8
山　东	Shangdong	1341.9	1323.7
河　南	Henan	359.9	239.6
湖　北	**Hubei**	**228.4**	**135.4**
湖　南	Hunan	148.2	103.5
广　东	Guangdong	6363.7	4552.2
广　西	Guangxi	186.9	141.4
海　南	Hainan	37.1	112.8
重　庆	Chongqing	468.0	219.0
四　川	Sichuan	419.5	226.2
贵　州	Guizhou	68.9	14.0
云　南	Yunnan	159.4	98.5
西　藏	Tibet	32.7	0.5
陕　西	Shaanxi	102.3	99.0
甘　肃	Gansu	46.8	55.6
青　海	Qinghai	8.5	5.6
宁　夏	Ningxia	25.5	6.7
新　疆	Xinjiang	222.7	52.9

附录1-14　各地区财政收入
REGIONAL REVENUE

单位：亿元

地　区	Region	2012	2013
北　京	Beijing	3314.9	3661.1
天　津	Tianjin	1760.0	2078.3
河　北	Hebei	2084.2	2293.5
山　西	Shanxi	1516.4	1700.2
内蒙古	Inner Mongolia	2497.3	1719.5
辽　宁	Liaoning	3100.0	3341.8
吉　林	Jilin	1041.3	1157.0
黑龙江	Heilongjiang	1163.2	1277.4
上　海	Shanghai	3743.7	4109.5
江　苏	Jiangsu	5860.7	6568.5
浙　江	Zhejiang	3441.0	3797.0
安　徽	Anhui	1792.7	2075.1
福　建	Fujian	1776.2	2118.7
江　西	Jiangxi	1371.9	1620.2
山　东	Shangdong	4059.4	4560.0
河　南	Henan	2040.6	2413.1
湖　北	**Hubei**	**1823.1**	**2190.0**
湖　南	Hunan	1776.0	2023.6
广　东	Guangdong	6228.0	7075.5
广　西	Guangxi	1166.0	1316.8
海　南	Hainan	409.4	480.5
重　庆	Chongqing	1705.1	1692.9
四　川	Sichuan	2382.1	2781.1
贵　州	Guizhou	1014.1	1206.0
云　南	Yunnan	1338.0	1610.7
西　藏	Tibet	86.6	95.0
陕　西	Shaanxi	1600.7	1747.2
甘　肃	Gansu	520.9	590.2
青　海	Qinghai	186.4	368.6
宁　夏	Ningxia	264.0	528.2
新　疆	Xinjiang	909.1	1128.0

注：本表数据为地方财政本级收入。
Note:Data in this table for the local fiscal income level.

附录1-15 各地区居民消费价格指数
REGIONAL CONSUMER PRICE INDEX

(上年=100) (Previous Year = 100)

地 区	Region	2007	2008	2009	2010	2011	2012	2013
全 国	**National Total**	**104.8**	**105.9**	**99.3**	**103.3**	**105.4**	**102.6**	**102.6**
北 京	Beijing	102.4	105.1	98.5	102.4	105.6	103.3	103.3
天 津	Tianjin	104.2	105.4	99.0	103.5	104.9	102.7	103.1
河 北	Hebei	104.7	106.2	99.3	103.1	105.7	102.6	103.0
山 西	Shanxi	104.6	107.2	99.6	103.0	105.2	102.5	103.1
内蒙古	Inner Mongolia	104.6	105.7	99.7	103.2	105.6	103.1	103.2
辽 宁	Liaoning	105.1	104.6	100.0	103.0	105.2	102.8	102.4
吉 林	Jilin	104.8	105.1	100.1	103.7	105.2	102.5	102.9
黑龙江	Heilongjiang	105.4	105.6	100.2	103.9	105.8	103.2	102.2
上 海	Shanghai	103.2	105.8	99.6	103.1	105.2	102.8	102.3
江 苏	Jiangsu	104.3	105.4	99.6	103.8	105.3	102.6	102.3
浙 江	Zhejiang	104.2	105.0	98.5	103.8	105.4	102.2	102.3
安 徽	Anhui	105.3	106.2	99.1	103.1	105.6	102.3	102.4
福 建	Fujian	105.2	104.6	98.2	103.2	105.3	102.4	102.5
江 西	Jiangxi	104.8	106.0	99.3	103.0	105.2	102.7	102.5
山 东	Shangdong	104.4	105.3	100.0	102.9	105.0	102.1	102.2
河 南	Henan	105.4	107.0	99.4	103.5	105.6	102.5	102.9
湖 北	**Hubei**	**104.8**	**106.3**	**99.6**	**102.9**	**105.8**	**102.9**	**102.8**
湖 南	Hunan	105.6	106.0	99.6	103.1	105.5	102.0	102.5
广 东	Guangdong	103.7	105.6	97.7	103.1	105.3	102.8	102.5
广 西	Guangxi	106.1	107.8	97.9	103.0	105.9	103.2	102.2
海 南	Hainan	105.0	106.9	99.3	104.8	106.1	103.2	102.8
重 庆	Chongqing	104.7	105.6	98.4	103.2	105.3	102.6	102.7
四 川	Sichuan	105.9	105.1	100.8	103.2	105.3	102.5	102.8
贵 州	Guizhou	106.4	107.6	98.7	102.9	105.1	102.7	102.5
云 南	Yunnan	105.9	105.7	100.4	103.7	104.9	102.7	103.1
西 藏	Tibet	103.4	105.7	101.4	102.2	105.0	103.5	103.6
陕 西	Shaanxi	105.1	106.4	100.5	104.0	105.7	102.8	103.0
甘 肃	Gansu	105.5	108.2	101.3	104.1	105.9	102.7	103.2
青 海	Qinghai	106.6	110.1	102.6	105.4	106.1	103.1	103.9
宁 夏	Ningxia	105.4	108.5	100.7	104.1	106.3	102.0	103.4
新 疆	Xinjiang	105.5	108.1	100.7	104.3	105.9	103.8	103.9

附录1-16　各地区城镇居民家庭人均可支配收入
THE AREA OF URBAN RESIDENTS PER CAPITA DISPOSABLE INCOME OF HOUSEHOLDS

单位：元　　　　(yuan)

地　区	Region	2007	2008	2009	2010	2011	2012	2013
全国总计	**National Total**	**13785.8**	**15780.8**	**17174.7**	**19109.4**	**21809.8**	**24564.7**	**26955.1**
北　京	Beijing	21988.7	24724.9	26738.5	29072.9	32903.0	36468.8	40321.0
天　津	Tianjin	16357.4	19422.5	21402.0	24292.6	26920.9	29626.4	32293.6
河　北	Hebei	11690.5	13441.1	14718.3	16263.4	18292.2	20543.4	22580.3
山　西	Shanxi	11565.0	13119.1	13996.6	15647.7	18123.9	20411.7	22455.6
内蒙古	Inner Mongolia	12377.8	14432.6	15849.2	17698.2	20407.6	23150.3	25496.7
辽　宁	Liaoning	12300.4	14392.7	15761.4	17712.6	20466.8	23222.7	25578.2
吉　林	Jilin	11285.5	12829.5	14006.3	15411.5	17796.6	20208.0	22274.6
黑龙江	Heilongjiang	10245.3	11581.3	12566.0	13856.5	15696.2	17759.8	19597.0
上　海	Shanghai	23622.7	26674.9	28837.8	31838.1	36230.5	40188.3	43851.4
江　苏	Jiangsu	16378.0	18679.5	20551.7	22944.3	26340.7	29677.0	32537.5
浙　江	Zhejiang	20573.8	22726.7	24610.8	27359.0	30970.7	34550.3	37850.8
安　徽	Anhui	11473.6	12990.4	14085.7	15788.2	18606.1	21024.2	23114.2
福　建	Fujian	15506.1	17961.5	19576.8	21781.3	24907.4	28055.2	30816.4
江　西	Jiangxi	11451.7	12866.4	14021.5	15481.1	17494.9	19860.4	21872.7
山　东	Shangdong	14264.7	16305.4	17811.0	19945.8	22791.8	25755.2	28264.1
河　南	Henan	11477.1	13231.1	14371.6	15930.3	18194.8	20442.6	22398.0
湖　北	**Hubei**	**11485.8**	**13152.9**	**14367.5**	**16058.4**	**18373.9**	**20839.6**	**22906.4**
湖　南	Hunan	12293.5	13821.2	15084.3	16565.7	18844.1	21318.8	23414.0
广　东	Guangdong	17699.3	19732.9	21574.7	23897.8	26897.5	30226.7	33090.0
广　西	Guangxi	12200.4	14146.0	15451.5	17063.9	18854.1	21242.8	23305.4
海　南	Hainan	10996.9	12607.8	13750.9	15581.1	18369.0	20917.7	22928.9
重　庆	Chongqing	12590.8	14367.6	15748.7	17532.4	20249.7	22968.1	25216.1
四　川	Sichuan	11098.3	12633.4	13839.4	15461.2	17899.1	20307.0	22367.6
贵　州	Guizhou	10678.4	11758.8	12862.5	14142.7	16495.0	18700.5	20667.1
云　南	Yunnan	11496.1	13250.2	14423.9	16064.5	18575.6	21074.5	23235.5
西　藏	Tibet	11130.9	12481.5	13544.4	14980.5	16195.6	18028.3	20023.4
陕　西	Shaanxi	10763.3	12857.9	14128.8	15695.2	18245.2	20733.9	22858.4
甘　肃	Gansu	10012.3	10969.4	11929.8	13188.6	14988.7	17156.9	18964.8
青　海	Qinghai	10276.1	11640.4	12691.9	13855.0	15603.3	17566.3	19498.5
宁　夏	Ningxia	10859.3	12931.5	14024.7	15344.5	17578.9	19831.4	21833.3
新　疆	Xinjiang	10313.4	11432.1	12257.5	13643.8	15513.6	17920.7	19873.8

注：本表绝对数按当年价格计算。
Note:In this table are at current prices.

附录1-17 各地区农村居民家庭人均纯收入

REGIONAL PER CAPITA EGIONAL PER CAPITA INCOME OF RURAL HOUSEHOLDS

单位：元 (yuan)

地　区	Region	2007	2008	2009	2010	2011	2012	2013
全国总计	**National Total**	**4140.4**	**4760.6**	**5153.2**	**5919.0**	**6977.3**	**7916.6**	**8895.9**
北　京	Beijing	9439.6	10661.9	11668.6	13262.3	14735.7	16475.7	18337.5
天　津	Tianjin	7010.1	7910.8	8687.6	10074.9	12321.2	14025.5	15841.0
河　北	Hebei	4293.4	4795.5	5149.7	5958.0	7119.7	8081.4	9101.9
山　西	Shanxi	3665.7	4097.2	4244.1	4736.3	5601.4	6356.6	7153.5
内蒙古	Inner Mongolia	3953.1	4656.2	4937.8	5529.6	6641.6	7611.3	8595.7
辽　宁	Liaoning	4773.4	5576.5	5958.0	6907.9	8296.5	9383.7	10522.7
吉　林	Jilin	4191.3	4932.7	5265.9	6237.4	7510.0	8598.2	9621.2
黑龙江	Heilongjiang	4132.3	4855.6	5206.8	6210.7	7590.7	8603.8	9634.1
上　海	Shanghai	10144.6	11440.3	12482.9	13978.0	16053.8	17803.7	19595.0
江　苏	Jiangsu	6561.0	7356.5	8003.5	9118.2	10805.0	12202.0	13597.8
浙　江	Zhejiang	8265.2	9257.9	10007.3	11302.6	13070.7	14551.9	16106.0
安　徽	Anhui	3556.3	4202.5	4504.3	5285.2	6232.2	7160.5	8097.9
福　建	Fujian	5467.1	6196.1	6680.2	7426.9	8778.6	9967.2	11184.2
江　西	Jiangxi	4044.7	4697.2	5075.0	5788.6	6891.6	7829.4	8781.5
山　东	Shangdong	4985.3	5641.4	6118.8	6990.3	8342.1	9446.5	10619.9
河　南	Henan	3851.6	4454.2	4807.0	5523.7	6604.0	7524.9	8475.3
湖　北	**Hubei**	**3997.5**	**4656.4**	**5035.3**	**5832.3**	**6897.9**	**7851.7**	**8867.0**
湖　南	Hunan	3904.2	4512.5	4909.0	5622.0	6567.1	7440.2	8372.1
广　东	Guangdong	5624.0	6399.8	6906.9	7890.3	9371.7	10542.8	11669.3
广　西	Guangxi	3224.1	3690.3	3980.4	4543.4	5231.3	6007.5	6790.9
海　南	Hainan	3791.4	4390.0	4744.4	5275.4	6446.0	7408.0	8342.6
重　庆	Chongqing	3509.3	4126.2	4478.4	5276.7	6480.4	7383.3	8332.0
四　川	Sichuan	3546.7	4121.2	4462.1	5086.9	6128.6	7001.4	7895.3
贵　州	Guizhou	2374.0	2796.9	3005.4	3471.9	4145.4	4753.0	5434.0
云　南	Yunnan	2634.1	3102.6	3369.3	3952.0	4722.0	5416.5	6141.3
西　藏	Tibet	2788.2	3175.8	3531.7	4138.7	4904.3	5719.4	6578.2
陕　西	Shaanxi	2644.7	3136.5	3437.6	4105.0	5027.9	5762.5	6502.6
甘　肃	Gansu	2328.9	2723.8	2980.1	3424.7	3909.4	4506.7	5107.8
青　海	Qinghai	2683.8	3061.2	3346.2	3862.7	4608.5	5364.4	6196.4
宁　夏	Ningxia	3180.8	3681.4	4048.3	4674.9	5410.0	6180.3	6931.0
新　疆	Xinjiang	3183.0	3502.9	3883.1	4642.7	5442.2	6393.7	7296.5

注：本表按当年价格计算。
Note:The table at current prices.

附录1-18 各地区农林牧渔业总产值及增长速度(2013)

REGIONAL FORESTYR,ANIMAL HUSBANDDRY AND FISHERY OUTPUT VALUE GROWTH RATE(2013)

地 区	Region	农林牧渔业总产值(亿元) Forestry, Animal Husbandry Fishery (million)	#农业 #Agriculture	#林业 #Forestry	#牧业 #Livestock	#渔业 #Fishing	农林牧渔业总产值比上年增长 (%) Previous Year (%)
全国总计	**National Total**	**96995.3**	**51497.4**	**3902.4**	**28435.5**	**9634.6**	**4.0**
北 京	Beijing	421.8	170.4	75.9	154.8	12.8	2.1
天 津	Tianjin	412.4	217.2	3.1	108.6	73.2	3.8
河 北	Hebei	5832.9	3473.3	96.3	1818.2	178.7	3.3
山 西	Shanxi	1447.0	932.1	90.1	338.8	9.5	4.5
内蒙古	Inner Mongolia	2699.5	1328.1	96.1	1208.5	29.0	4.7
辽 宁	Liaoning	4349.7	1673.9	136.5	1675.4	689.3	4.1
吉 林	Jilin	2670.6	1261.7	98.1	1198.5	36.7	3.5
黑龙江	Heilongjiang	4633.3	2856.3	180.6	1430.1	82.5	4.7
上 海	Shanghai	323.5	172.3	9.6	70.0	59.9	-2.9
江 苏	Jiangsu	6158.0	3167.8	107.3	1222.2	1351.1	2.6
浙 江	Zhejiang	2837.4	1336.8	141.5	546.2	758.0	0.4
安 徽	Anhui	4009.2	2003.3	233.1	1171.4	439.1	3.4
福 建	Fujian	3282.0	1376.3	293.8	513.8	986.3	4.5
江 西	Jiangxi	2578.4	1072.8	252.7	796.4	370.2	4.5
山 东	Shangdong	8750.0	4509.9	120.3	2359.0	1397.4	3.8
河 南	Henan	7198.1	4202.3	152.3	2486.3	93.5	4.4
湖 北	**Hubei**	**5160.6**	**2678.1**	**122.0**	**1395.4**	**748.4**	**5.6**
湖 南	Hunan	5043.6	2726.8	287.7	1467.4	309.9	2.7
广 东	Guangdong	4946.8	2444.7	249.4	1106.9	975.3	2.2
广 西	Guangxi	3755.2	1868.3	287.6	1101.2	366.7	4.4
海 南	Hainan	1144.9	485.4	121.2	225.5	275.5	6.2
重 庆	Chongqing	1513.7	909.2	48.0	482.8	53.8	4.6
四 川	Sichuan	5620.3	2903.5	179.4	2267.6	177.5	3.5
贵 州	Guizhou	1663.0	997.1	69.9	482.7	38.3	6.0
云 南	Yunnan	3056.0	1639.4	293.3	962.6	70.4	7.0
西 藏	Tibet	128.0	57.9	2.7	64.2	0.2	4.0
陕 西	Shaanxi	2562.5	1714.8	67.6	643.7	17.8	4.8
甘 肃	Gansu	1517.7	1104.5	22.5	253.4	2.0	4.9
青 海	Qinghai	310.3	138.3	5.7	160.1	1.3	5.6
宁 夏	Ningxia	430.0	269.0	9.8	120.0	13.2	4.7
新 疆	Xinjiang	2538.9	1806.1	48.1	604.2	17.2	7.2

注：本表绝对数按当年价格计算，增长速度按可比价格计算。
Note:In this table are at current prices, growth rates at constant prices.

附录1-19　各地区主要农产品产量(2013)

MAJOR AGRICULTURAL PRODUCTION REGIONS(2013)

单位：万吨　　(10 000 tons)

地 区	Region	粮 食 Food	油 料 Oil feed	棉 花 Cotton	糖 料 Sugar	蔬 菜 Vegetables	水 果 Fruit
全国总计	**National Total**	**60193.8**	**3517.0**	**629.9**	**13746.1**	**73512.0**	**25093.0**
北 京	Beijing	96.1	1.0	0.02		266.9	103.8
天 津	Tianjin	174.7	0.6	4.8		455.1	54.2
河 北	Hebei	3365.0	151.1	45.7	74.2	7902.1	1863.3
山 西	Shanxi	1312.8	19.5	3.1	22.5	1198.5	711.8
内蒙古	Inner Mongolia	2773.0	158.1	0.2	181.4	1421.1	294.8
辽 宁	Liaoning	2195.6	113.6	0.1	17.1	3270.9	944.7
吉 林	Jilin	3551.0	84.0	0.6	6.2	938.1	234.7
黑龙江	Heilongjiang	6004.1	19.0		123.2	946.1	274.4
上 海	Shanghai	114.2	1.5	0.4	0.7	398.4	74.7
江 苏	Jiangsu	3423.0	150.4	20.9	9.6	5237.8	814.2
浙 江	Zhejiang	734.0	37.8	2.8	63.9	1764.3	715.7
安 徽	Anhui	3279.6	225.4	25.1	20.2	2418.0	905.1
福 建	Fujian	664.4	28.8	0.01	58.6	1729.7	744.3
江 西	Jiangxi	2116.1	119.3	13.1	64.6	1257.6	637.8
山 东	Shangdong	4528.2	349.6	62.1	0.01	9658.2	3028.8
河 南	Henan	5713.7	589.1	19.0	28.3	7112.5	2599.7
湖 北	**Hubei**	**2501.3**	**333.2**	**46.0**	**28.7**	**3578.3**	**920.5**
湖 南	Hunan	2925.7	224.4	19.8	73.7	3603.5	879.4
广 东	Guangdong	1315.9	101.0		1553.2	3144.5	1485.4
广 西	Guangxi	1521.8	57.2	0.2	8104.3	2435.6	1433.4
海 南	Hainan	190.9	10.9		440.8	524.8	439.5
重 庆	Chongqing	1148.1	53.1	0.01	10.9	1600.6	319.3
四 川	Sichuan	3387.1	290.4	1.3	57.1	3910.7	840.1
贵 州	Guizhou	1030.0	91.5	0.1	159.3	1500.4	167.7
云 南	Yunnan	1824.0	60.7	0.04	2146.3	1625.4	634.5
西 藏	Tibet	96.2	6.4			67.0	1.3
陕 西	Shaanxi	1215.8	59.5	5.8	0.2	1629.4	1764.4
甘 肃	Gansu	1138.9	69.7	7.1	24.7	1578.7	611.5
青 海	Qinghai	102.4	32.6		0.02	158.9	3.0
宁 夏	Ningxia	373.4	16.8	0.0		509.0	264.3
新 疆	Xinjiang	1377.0	60.6	351.8	476.5	1669.9	1326.9

注：水果产量含果用瓜。
Note:Fruit production with fruit with a melon.

附录1-19　续表 continued

单位：万吨 (10 000 tons)

地区	Region	肉类 Meat	#猪肉 #Pork	#牛肉 #Beef	#羊肉 #Sheep Meat	奶类 Dairy
全国总计	**National Total**	**8535.0**	**5493.0**	**673.2**	**408.1**	**3649.5**
北京	Beijing	41.8	24.6	2.1	1.2	61.5
天津	Tianjin	46.5	29.8	3.3	1.5	68.5
河北	Hebei	448.8	265.3	52.3	29.1	465.7
山西	Shanxi	83.2	61.2	5.2	6.2	87.2
内蒙古	Inner Mongolia	244.9	73.4	51.8	88.8	778.6
辽宁	Liaoning	420.1	233.6	43.2	8.1	125.7
吉林	Jilin	262.7	136.3	45.0	4.2	48.3
黑龙江	Heilongjiang	221.3	133.4	39.7	11.8	522.5
上海	Shanghai	23.8	18.3		0.6	26.5
江苏	Jiangsu	383.2	229.9	3.2	7.8	59.9
浙江	Zhejiang	174.3	138.8	1.1	1.7	18.2
安徽	Anhui	403.8	253.4	18.1	15.0	25.3
福建	Fujian	211.2	157.7	2.6	2.1	15.3
江西	Jiangxi	321.9	245.1	12.7	1.1	12.2
山东	Shangdong	774.8	392.9	67.9	33.7	281.2
河南	Henan	699.1	454.1	80.6	24.8	328.8
湖北	**Hubei**	**430.1**	**330.6**	**20.2**	**8.2**	**15.8**
湖南	Hunan	519.2	430.6	18.2	10.7	8.9
广东	Guangdong	435.2	277.8	7.0	0.9	14.1
广西	Guangxi	420.0	261.3	14.3	3.2	9.6
海南	Hainan	82.9	50.5	2.6	1.1	0.2
重庆	Chongqing	207.8	155.0	7.6	3.0	6.8
四川	Sichuan	690.4	510.8	31.1	24.5	71.1
贵州	Guizhou	199.7	163.7	14.1	3.5	5.5
云南	Yunnan	359.4	276.0	31.8	14.0	59.3
西藏	Tibet	26.8	1.5	15.9	8.6	33.0
陕西	Shaanxi	112.6	88.3	7.5	7.0	188.5
甘肃	Gansu	91.0	50.8	17.2	16.6	39.1
青海	Qinghai	31.8	9.9	10.3	10.5	28.7
宁夏	Ningxia	27.4	7.1	8.7	9.0	104.2
新疆	Xinjiang	139.4	31.3	37.8	49.7	139.2

附录1–20 各地区规模以上工业企业主要经济指标(2013)

REGIONAL-SCALE INDUSTRIAL ENTERPRISES MAIN ECONOMIC INDICATORS (2013)

单位：亿元 (100 million yuan)

地 区	Region	主营业务收入 Main Business Income	主营业务成本 Main Business Costs	主营业务税金及附加 Business Tax And Additional	销售费用 Selling expenses	利润总额 Total Profit	税金总额 Total Tax
全国总计	**National Total**	**1029149.8**	**877522.4**	**15617.7**	**25339.6**	**62831.0**	**45748.5**
北 京	Beijing	18624.8	15798.3	282.4	828.8	1254.8	804.2
天 津	Tianjin	27011.1	23208.4	318.0	635.0	1992.8	1177.3
河 北	Hebei	45766.3	40019.9	423.2	727.5	2560.9	1536.2
山 西	Shanxi	18404.7	15687.3	162.6	534.6	547.9	897.9
内蒙古	Inner Mongolia	19550.8	15732.7	272.6	477.7	1682.6	1065.0
辽 宁	Liaoning	52150.4	45093.2	856.5	1076.9	2461.6	2106.5
吉 林	Jilin	21950.7	18396.7	496.1	788.1	1230.1	1106.2
黑龙江	Heilongjiang	13569.8	10694.5	665.0	297.3	1150.2	1268.5
上 海	Shanghai	34533.5	28569.0	910.7	1263.7	2415.2	1815.9
江 苏	Jiangsu	132270.4	115111.6	1127.4	2876.6	7834.1	5112.6
浙 江	Zhejiang	61765.5	53100.9	671.3	1487.0	3385.9	2298.6
安 徽	Anhui	33079.5	28607.4	420.9	814.0	1758.8	1287.9
福 建	Fujian	32847.1	28241.1	376.9	833.3	1959.5	1293.8
江 西	Jiangxi	26700.2	23246.9	272.3	421.1	1756.7	1125.7
山 东	Shangdong	132319.0	114856.6	1483.7	2402.8	8507.7	5182.3
河 南	Henan	59454.8	51194.0	640.5	1088.7	4410.8	2077.1
湖 北	**Hubei**	**37864.5**	**32146.6**	**733.4**	**1138.6**	**2080.7**	**1680.2**
湖 南	Hunan	31616.6	25830.0	849.3	849.2	1585.1	1973.0
广 东	Guangdong	103655.0	88559.8	1144.6	3519.5	5854.9	3683.7
广 西	Guangxi	16726.0	14228.6	318.7	408.0	874.0	846.8
海 南	Hainan	1640.7	1312.8	80.9	60.8	110.8	143.7
重 庆	Chongqing	15417.1	13149.8	225.1	426.2	878.4	805.0
四 川	Sichuan	35251.8	29353.2	576.0	998.8	2168.4	1820.3
贵 州	Guizhou	6878.4	5383.6	286.6	228.9	477.3	600.4
云 南	Yunnan	9773.1	7587.1	786.7	264.0	549.1	1226.8
西 藏	Tibet	93.4	80.2	1.5	6.0	7.2	9.8
陕 西	Shaanxi	17763.0	13753.7	522.7	424.7	1973.3	1378.8
甘 肃	Gansu	8443.7	7321.0	266.4	129.9	286.7	458.7
青 海	Qinghai	2045.4	1632.6	47.4	63.9	141.3	138.3
宁 夏	Ningxia	3374.5	2879.5	68.4	69.3	139.1	168.1
新 疆	Xinjiang	8608.0	6745.8	329.8	199.0	795.4	659.3

注：本表为2010年1–11月快报数据(下表同)。

Note:This table is from January to November 2009, Express Data (the same).

附录1-20 续表 continued

单位：亿元 (100 million yuan)

地 区	Region	亏损企业亏损总额 Total Loss of Enterprises Running under Deficit	应收账款 Account Received	存货 Inventory	产成品 Finished Products	资产总计 Total Assets	负债合计 Total Liability
全国总计	**National Total**	**5732.5**	**95693.4**	**95402.4**	**32759.5**	**850625.9**	**491708.3**
北 京	Beijing	176.5	3412.9	2216.3	687.7	31398.3	16363.6
天 津	Tianjin	144.6	3090.7	2730.3	859.4	22059.4	14095.8
河 北	Hebei	275.7	2781.5	3753.7	1256.8	36040.2	21164.6
山 西	Shanxi	381.6	1991.0	2016.8	759.8	28058.3	20011.0
内蒙古	Inner Mongolia	195.3	1600.7	1553.8	587.0	23141.7	13893.7
辽 宁	Liaoning	390.3	3412.4	4320.9	1349.0	37989.3	22220.0
吉 林	Jilin	181.7	1274.5	1507.9	529.7	15257.9	8354.6
黑龙江	Heilongjiang	192.4	1179.1	1629.2	518.2	14059.2	8033.3
上 海	Shanghai	281.2	5528.1	4475.1	1364.2	33538.3	16885.8
江 苏	Jiangsu	507.9	14922.6	11189.1	4067.5	92081.7	52286.7
浙 江	Zhejiang	242.5	8790.3	7741.0	3041.0	59633.1	35787.5
安 徽	Anhui	132.5	2895.9	2780.7	977.8	25168.1	14957.1
福 建	Fujian	129.1	3320.3	3197.7	1218.7	24671.1	13489.3
江 西	Jiangxi	69.3	1141.1	1665.3	635.2	13640.1	7402.1
山 东	Shangdong	264.9	6703.0	8869.6	3170.4	78881.1	44011.5
河 南	Henan	234.2	3463.6	3577.6	1190.5	42021.9	20506.4
湖 北	**Hubei**	**145.8**	**3081.6**	**3504.5**	**1256.2**	**30131.8**	**16968.4**
湖 南	Hunan	73.1	2322.8	2251.2	713.4	19031.6	10284.8
广 东	Guangdong	393.7	13404.0	10918.4	3503.6	77943.5	44656.6
广 西	Guangxi	123.9	1206.8	1598.6	656.0	13063.4	8215.2
海 南	Hainan	18.3	176.9	254.4	96.7	2328.0	1243.4
重 庆	Chongqing	115.4	1589.0	1321.8	469.8	13135.9	8315.1
四 川	Sichuan	317.7	3325.2	3463.0	1150.7	34729.2	21804.2
贵 州	Guizhou	129.5	609.5	901.0	260.9	9703.6	6155.2
云 南	Yunnan	154.3	833.1	1985.5	498.9	15344.4	9918.3
西 藏	Tibet	13.2	14.8	17.2	4.1	548.6	186.7
陕 西	Shaanxi	121.6	1741.8	2070.0	721.8	22443.1	12581.2
甘 肃	Gansu	85.2	548.5	1669.6	440.7	10159.4	6537.5
青 海	Qinghai	45.7	197.0	310.9	107.4	4597.7	3045.7
宁 夏	Ningxia	51.7	334.4	602.2	214.3	5588.0	3717.6
新 疆	Xinjiang	143.9	800.3	1309.1	452.3	14238.0	8615.7

附录1-21 各地区主要工业产品产量(2013)
MAJOR INDUSTRIAL PRODUCTS BY REGION(2013)

地区	Region	原油(万吨) Crude Oil (10 000 tons)	天然气(万立方米) Natural gas (10 000 cu.m)	布(亿米) Cloth (100 million meters)	农用化肥(万吨) Agricultural Fertilizers (10 000 Tons)	水泥(万吨) Cement (10 000 tons)	生铁(万吨) Pig Iron (10 000 tons)	粗钢(万吨) Crude steel (10 000 tons)
全国总计	**National Total**	**20946.9**	**1170.5**	**882.7**	**7037.0**	**241613.6**	**70897.0**	**77904.1**
北京	Beijing		5.8			900.5		2.3
天津	Tianjin	3044.5	18.7	2.1	13.5	951.9	2214.2	2289.5
河北	Hebei	591.0	15.6	63.4	218.4	12676.2	17027.6	18849.6
山西	Shanxi		31.6	0.5	446.1	4984.8	4303.2	4519.6
内蒙古	Inner Mongolia		0.2		113.6	6395.7	1367.2	1978.6
辽宁	Liaoning	1001.0	7.6	3.5	77.1	6005.2	5698.0	5972.9
吉林	Jilin	620.3	23.7	0.4	48.8	3391.0	1116.2	1245.4
黑龙江	Heilongjiang	4001.0	35.0	0.1	61.5	4028.5	716.3	740.2
上海	Shanghai	7.2	2.3	1.4	2.1	750.3	1637.6	1800.6
江苏	Jiangsu	201.5	0.5	81.1	250.8	17991.9	6690.6	8469.1
浙江	Zhejiang			153.5	33.1	12462.9	1059.8	1387.0
安徽	Anhui			10.0	277.3	12131.4	2017.3	2351.5
福建	Fujian			60.4	44.1	7890.4	588.3	1624.6
江西	Jiangxi			7.8	107.3	9204.2	2012.2	2156.6
山东	Shangdong	2765.6	5.1	128.5	760.0	16217.8	6580.3	6119.8
河南	Henan	476.5	4.9	31.3	488.6	16764.4	2551.9	2736.0
湖北	**Hubei**	**80.1**	**3.1**	**79.3**	**1156.9**	**11042.5**	**2416.2**	**2887.8**
湖南	Hunan			3.5	135.5	11264.7	1739.8	1746.5
广东	Guangdong	1291.8	75.3	27.5	45.7	13394.9	1149.9	1442.9
广西	Guangxi	43.7		0.2	105.7	10707.5	1567.6	1666.6
海南	Hainan	26.5	1.7		65.9	1988.4		
重庆	Chongqing		1.7	5.4	215.4	6127.0	556.2	608.9
四川	Sichuan	22.4	214.3	17.2	473.7	13897.1	2011.4	1711.5
贵州	Guizhou		0.5	0.1	533.6	8140.5	529.9	485.2
云南	Yunnan				341.9	9009.2	1936.5	1883.9
西藏	Tibet					295.8		
陕西	Shaanxi	3688.0	371.6	5.7	100.7	8545.5	882.5	916.9
甘肃	Gansu	72.8	0.2		62.4	4412.7	897.5	953.9
青海	Qinghai	214.5	68.1		425.2	1786.3	135.1	147.6
宁夏	Ningxia	6.1		0.1	70.3	1914.3	123.0	32.2
新疆	Xinjiang	2792.5	282.9	0.4	361.8	5040.2	1370.7	1176.9

附录1-21　续表 continued

地　区	Region	钢材(万吨) Steel (10 000 tons)	汽车(万辆) Car (10 000)	家用电冰箱(万台) Household Refrigerators (10 000 units)	程控交换机(万线) PBX (10 000 lines)	移动通信手持机(万台) Mobile Handset (10 000 units)	微型计算机设备(万台) Micro-computer Equipment (10 000 units)	发电量(亿千瓦小时) generation (Billion kilowatt hours)
全国总计	**National Total**	**106762.2**	**2211.7**	**9261.0**	**3115.7**	**145561.0**	**33661.0**	**53975.9**
北　京	Beijing	219.0	200.0	83.7	759.0	18716.7	1141.1	335.8
天　津	Tianjin	6640.9	55.7	49.3	4.0	10336.3	1072.2	624.3
河　北	Hebei	22861.6	97.4		7.7			2499.4
山　西	Shanxi	4486.2				2387.6		2627.9
内蒙古	Inner Mongolia	1797.7	1.7					3520.7
辽　宁	Liaoning	6863.0	108.0	84.8	58.4	2715.0	0.2	1544.3
吉　林	Jilin	1510.1	164.7					769.5
黑龙江	Heilongjiang	631.0	10.5				3.5	834.0
上　海	Shanghai	2322.8	226.9	153.9	126.9	4384.9	8101.3	959.5
江　苏	Jiangsu	12398.0	107.2	1063.1	5.2	3019.6	7520.7	4289.4
浙　江	Zhejiang	3823.4	30.6	939.6	125.5	987.8	164.3	2939.3
安　徽	Anhui	3138.6	100.7	2973.9		1.1	671.8	1965.8
福　建	Fujian	2782.8	20.6			3841.8	1284.8	1767.7
江　西	Jiangxi	2463.8	36.8	101.5	1.2	5513.4	7.7	874.6
山　东	Shangdong	8109.1	104.4	524.4	30.9	5096.7	22.4	3510.9
河　南	Henan	4255.2	40.6	517.8		9720.7		2861.8
湖　北	**Hubei**	**3344.9**	**158.7**	**226.1**	**56.1**	**714.8**	**97.9**	**2158.2**
湖　南	Hunan	1977.9	32.1	21.0	116.8	87.5	34.7	1347.0
广　东	Guangdong	3384.5	231.6	1946.0	1821.9	73672.3	2028.7	3964.8
广　西	Guangxi	2790.7	186.9					1259.5
海　南	Hainan	27.0	10.8					230.7
重　庆	Chongqing	1269.6	184.0	320.0		3545.7	5593.5	627.4
四　川	Sichuan	2785.2	80.5	89.7		814.4	5916.2	2597.3
贵　州	Guizhou	562.6		155.3		4.7		1676.3
云　南	Yunnan	2053.9	8.0		2.1			2148.4
西　藏	Tibet							29.1
陕　西	Shaanxi	1565.2	10.5	10.9				1508.7
甘　肃	Gansu	1021.6	2.1					1195.0
青　海	Qinghai	130.8						600.3
宁　夏	Ningxia	149.8						1096.5
新　疆	Xinjiang	1395.3	1.0					1611.7

附录1−22 各地区电力消费量

REGIONAL ELECTRICITY CONSUMPTION

单位：亿千瓦时 (10 000 KW/h)

地 区	Region	2007	2008	2009	2010	2011	2012
北 京	Beijing	667.0	689.7	739.1	809.9	821.7	874.3
天 津	Tianjin	494.9	515.9	550.2	645.7	695.2	722.5
河 北	Hebei	2013.7	2095.0	2343.8	2691.5	2984.9	3077.7
山 西	Shanxi	1348.8	1314.3	1267.5	1460.0	1650.4	1765.8
内蒙古	Inner Mongolia	1160.2	1220.6	1287.9	1536.8	1864.1	2016.8
辽 宁	Liaoning	1359.5	1412.0	1488.2	1715.3	1861.5	1899.9
吉 林	Jilin	462.6	496.5	515.3	577.0	630.2	637.0
黑龙江	Heilongjiang	628.9	669.9	688.7	747.8	801.9	827.9
上 海	Shanghai	1072.4	1138.2	1153.4	1295.9	1339.6	1353.4
江 苏	Jiangsu	2952.0	3118.3	3314.0	3864.4	4281.6	4580.9
浙 江	Zhejiang	2189.4	2322.9	2471.4	2820.9	3116.9	3210.6
安 徽	Anhui	769.1	858.9	952.3	1077.9	1221.2	1361.1
福 建	Fujian	1000.3	1073.5	1134.9	1315.1	1515.9	1579.5
江 西	Jiangxi	511.1	545.9	609.2	700.5	835.1	867.7
山 东	Shangdong	2596.1	2727.0	2941.1	3298.5	3635.3	3794.6
河 南	Henan	1808.0	1970.8	2081.4	2354.0	2659.1	2747.7
湖 北	**Hubei**	**989.2**	**1058.5**	**1135.1**	**1330.4**	**1450.8**	**1507.9**
湖 南	Hunan	890.6	905.0	1010.6	1171.9	1293.4	1346.5
广 东	Guangdong	3394.0	3504.8	3609.6	4060.1	4399.0	4619.4
广 西	Guangxi	681.1	753.4	856.4	993.2	1112.2	1153.9
海 南	Hainan	113.3	121.7	133.8	159.0	185.3	210.3
重 庆	Chongqing	449.2	484.4	533.8	626.4	717.0	723.5
四 川	Sichuan	1177.5	1210.1	1324.6	1549.0	1751.4	1830.7
贵 州	Guizhou	669.1	679.2	750.3	835.4	944.1	1046.7
云 南	Yunnan	745.5	829.4	891.2	1004.1	1204.1	1315.9
西 藏	Tibet	15.0	16.0	17.7	20.4	23.8	27.8
陕 西	Shaanxi	653.7	708.0	740.1	859.2	982.5	1066.7
甘 肃	Gansu	614.7	677.8	705.5	804.4	923.4	994.6
青 海	Qinghai	285.4	313.2	337.2	465.2	560.7	602.2
宁 夏	Ningxia	439.8	439.6	463.0	546.8	724.5	741.8
新 疆	Xinjiang	413.3	479.4	547.9	662.0	839.1	1151.5

附录1-23 各地区社会消费品零售总额

REGIONAL TOTAL RETAIL SALES OF CONSUMER GOODS

单位：亿元 (100 million yuan)

地　区	Region	2007	2008	2009	2010	2011	2012	2013
全国总计	**National Total**	**93571.6**	**114830.1**	**132678.4**	**156998.4**	**183918.6**	**210307.0**	**237809.9**
北　京	Beijing	3835.2	4645.5	5309.9	6229.3	6900.3	7702.8	8375.1
天　津	Tianjin	1650.6	2078.7	2430.8	2860.2	3395.1	3921.4	4470.4
河　北	Hebei	4053.8	4991.1	5764.9	6821.8	8035.5	9254.0	10516.7
山　西	Shanxi	1953.3	2421.1	2809.0	3318.2	3903.4	4506.8	5139.3
内蒙古	Inner Mongolia	1964.0	2463.0	2855.3	3384.0	3991.7	4572.5	5114.2
辽　宁	Liaoning	4097.8	5032.4	5812.6	6887.6	8095.3	9304.2	10581.4
吉　林	Jilin	2038.3	2549.2	2957.3	3504.9	4119.8	4772.9	5426.4
黑龙江	Heilongjiang	2386.2	2928.3	3401.8	4039.2	4750.1	5491.0	6251.2
上　海	Shanghai	3873.3	4577.2	5173.2	6070.5	6814.8	7412.3	8052.0
江　苏	Jiangsu	7985.9	9905.1	11484.1	13606.8	15988.4	18331.3	20796.5
浙　江	Zhejiang	6271.3	7533.3	8622.3	10245.4	12028.0	13588.3	15225.5
安　徽	Anhui	2451.9	3045.2	3527.8	4197.7	4955.1	5736.6	6542.4
福　建	Fujian	3212.3	3866.7	4481.0	5310.0	6276.2	7256.5	8275.3
江　西	Jiangxi	1718.9	2142.0	2484.4	2956.2	3485.1	4027.2	4576.1
山　东	Shangdong	8607.5	10658.8	12363.0	14620.3	17155.5	19651.9	22294.8
河　南	Henan	4690.3	5815.4	6746.4	8004.2	9453.6	10915.6	12426.6
湖　北	**Hubei**	**4115.8**	**5109.7**	**5928.4**	**7013.9**	**8275.2**	**9562.5**	**10885.9**
湖　南	Hunan	3419.2	4222.6	4913.7	5839.5	6884.7	7921.9	9018.6
广　东	Guangdong	10731.3	12986.6	14891.8	17458.4	20297.5	22677.1	25453.9
广　西	Guangxi	1932.7	2395.8	2790.7	3312.0	3908.2	4516.6	5133.1
海　南	Hainan	370.9	463.2	537.5	639.3	759.5	870.8	992.9
重　庆	Chongqing	1711.1	2147.1	2479.0	2938.6	3487.8	4033.7	4599.8
四　川	Sichuan	4105.6	4944.8	5758.7	6810.1	8044.6	9268.6	10561.4
贵　州	Guizhou	858.2	1075.2	1247.3	1482.7	1751.6	2075.9	2366.2
云　南	Yunnan	1422.5	1764.7	2051.1	2542.4	3000.1	3511.6	4004.6
西　藏	Tibet	112.6	130.0	156.6	185.3	219.0	254.6	293.2
陕　西	Shaanxi	1837.3	2317.1	2699.7	3195.7	3790.0	4383.8	4999.5
甘　肃	Gansu	854.4	1023.6	1183.0	1394.5	1648.0	1906.5	2173.8
青　海	Qinghai	212.6	259.7	300.5	350.8	410.5	476.0	544.1
宁　夏	Ningxia	239.5	295.4	339.3	403.6	477.6	542.9	610.5
新　疆	Xinjiang	857.5	1041.5	1177.5	1375.1	1616.3	1858.6	2108.2

附录1-24 各地区客运量和旅客周转量(2013年)
REGIONAL PASSENGER TRAFFIC AND TURNOVER VOLUME OF PASSENGER TRAFFIC（2013）

地 区	Region	客运量 (万人) Passenger Traffic (10 000 Persons)	#铁路 Railway	#公路 Highway	#水运 Waterway	旅客周转量 (亿人公里) Turnover Volume of Passenger Traffic (100 million person-kms)	#铁路 Railway	#公路 Highway	#水运 Waterway
全国总计	**National Total**	**2122992**	**210597**	**1853463**	**23535**	**27572**	**10596**	**11251**	**68**
北 京	Beijing	64161	11680	52481		254.0	118.0	136.1	
天 津	Tianjin	17995	3352	14556	87	267.1	178.4	88.6	0.1
河 北	Hebei	61718	8762	52956		1163.7	867.2	296.5	
山 西	Shanxi	34899	6294	28487	118	386.6	189.8	196.6	0.1
内蒙古	Inner Mongolia	20819	4635	16184		360.5	187.1	173.4	
辽 宁	Liaoning	91735	13033	78168	534	941.7	572.7	362.4	6.5
吉 林	Jilin	34148	6629	27403	116	413.7	244.8	168.7	0.2
黑龙江	Heilongjiang	45566	10107	35102	357	473.3	256.8	216.1	0.4
上 海	Shanghai	11691	7972	3476	243	195.0	75.3	119.1	0.6
江 苏	Jiangsu	151444	13435	135555	2454	1365.3	514.0	847.3	4.0
浙 江	Zhejiang	135348	11052	121185	3111	1025.1	437.0	583.0	5.1
安 徽	Anhui	126710	7210	119433	67	1286.3	552.1	734.0	0.2
福 建	Fujian	55107	6501	46895	1711	542.7	209.2	330.6	2.8
江 西	Jiangxi	65067	6945	57915	207	930.7	622.6	307.7	0.4
山 东	Shangdong	75074	9246	64019	1809	1083.8	552.4	520.3	11.0
河 南	Henan	136237	10532	125450	255	1574.7	861.9	712.4	0.4
湖 北	**Hubei**	**91522**	**10410**	**80670**	**442**	**1052.4**	**634.1**	**415.1**	**3.2**
湖 南	Hunan	159726	9231	149015	1480	1565.1	840.3	721.9	2.9
广 东	Guangdong	153120	17658	133305	2157	1780.9	570.1	1202.5	8.4
广 西	Guangxi	49275	3275	45606	394	611.3	193.7	415.7	1.9
海 南	Hainan	13328	1389	10583	1356	112.4	25.2	85.0	2.2
重 庆	Chongqing	65183	3251	61243	689	465.4	124.9	333.3	7.3
四 川	Sichuan	134775	8240	124145	2390	912.1	310.1	599.2	2.9
贵 州	Guizhou	83436	4322	77359	1755	593.6	211.2	377.9	4.5
云 南	Yunnan	47626	3189	43392	1045	431.9	106.5	323.1	2.2
西 藏	Tibet	1455	129	1326		42.4	11.4	31.0	
陕 西	Shaanxi	70133	6123	63650	360	745.2	421.4	323.1	0.7
甘 肃	Gansu	36163	2522	33556	85	595.4	383.2	212.0	0.2
青 海	Qinghai	4790	592	4140	58	95.3	54.9	40.3	0.1
宁 夏	Ningxia	8418	594	7568	256	102.9	44.5	58.3	0.1
新 疆	Xinjiang	40926	2286	38640		544.5	224.8	319.6	
不分地区		35397				5656.8			

注：不分地区合计为民航完成数。
Note: The total passenyer traffil not classified by region lefers to thut completed by civil aviation

附录1-25 各地区货运量和货物周转量（2013）

REGIONAL FREIGHT TRAFFIC AND TURNOVER VOLUME OF FREIGHT TRAFFIC（2013）

地 区	Region	货运量 (万吨) Freight Traffic (10 000 Persons)	#铁路 Railway	#公路 Highway	#水运 Waterway	货物周转量 (亿吨公里) Turnover Volume of Freight Traffic (100 million person-kms)	#铁路 Railway	#公路 Highway	#水运 Waterway
全国总计	**National Total**	**4102495**	**396697**	**3076648**	**559738**	**168164.8**	**29173.9**	**55738.1**	**79187.5**
北 京	Beijing	25748	1097	24651		1051.1	894.9	156.2	
天 津	Tianjin	45233	8349	28206	8678	3097.4	515.9	313.7	2267.8
河 北	Hebei	198009	22469	172492	3048	11674.1	4233.6	6577.9	862.5
山 西	Shanxi	156045	73181	82834	30	3592.4	2313.7	1278.6	0.1
内蒙古	Inner Mongolia	164346	67288	97058		4462.0	2589.2	1872.7	
辽 宁	Liaoning	206868	20566	172923	13379	11970.3	1341.1	2792.0	7837.2
吉 林	Jilin	44811	6516	38063	232	1681.3	580.0	1100.0	1.3
黑龙江	Heilongjiang	61094	14561	45288	1245	1930.0	949.2	972.9	7.9
上 海	Shanghai	84305	702	43877	39726	14332.7	14.8	352.4	13965.5
江 苏	Jiangsu	181775	7157	103709	70909	9924.6	381.2	1790.4	7753.0
浙 江	Zhejiang	188679	4831	107186	76662	8951.2	272.1	1322.1	7357.0
安 徽	Anhui	396391	11566	284534	100291	12335.3	877.7	6544.0	4913.7
福 建	Fujian	96674	3636	69876	23162	3939.6	163.5	821.4	2954.7
江 西	Jiangxi	135172	5217	121279	8676	3640.1	612.7	2829.0	198.4
山 东	Shangdong	264100	22876	227746	13478	8194.2	1487.4	5494.8	1212.0
河 南	Henan	184823	12929	162040	9854	7259.8	2153.3	4488.0	618.5
湖 北	**Hubei**	**131000**	**5646**	**100945**	**24409**	**4751.8**	**914.3**	**2046.3**	**1791.3**
湖 南	Hunan	184535	5169	156269	23097	3832.3	950.3	2329.5	552.4
广 东	Guangdong	349011	9711	261273	78027	9228.6	309.7	3003.4	5915.5
广 西	Guangxi	151143	6916	124677	19550	3856.4	809.4	1857.2	1189.8
海 南	Hainan	17325	960	10290	6075	621.0	13.1	75.4	532.5
重 庆	Chongqing	87241	2475	71842	12924	2298.9	182.6	695.9	1420.4
四 川	Sichuan	167759	8970	151689	7100	2248.6	816.7	1273.1	158.8
贵 州	Guizhou	72703	6461	65100	1142	1294.6	658.3	610.6	25.6
云 南	Yunnan	104329	5146	98675	508	1361.9	428.3	922.0	11.6
西 藏	Tibet	1850	72	1778		103.4	22.0	81.5	
陕 西	Shaanxi	141579	35767	105566	246	3200.6	1514.7	1685.0	0.8
甘 肃	Gansu	51463	6381	45072	10	2362.0	1550.7	811.2	
青 海	Qinghai	13372	3784	9588		451.9	249.2	202.8	
宁 夏	Ningxia	40914	8412	32502		873.0	363.6	509.4	
新 疆	Xinjiang	66908	7288	59620		1796.8	868.2	928.5	
不分地区		87291	598		17281	21846.7	142.3		17639.1

注：不分地区合计中包括铁路行包运输、管道运输企业、民航运输企业及中远集团海外公司完成数。

Note: The freight ton-kilometers ont classified by iegion refers to raihuay baggaye freight,civil aviation,pipelines and that completed bycommpanies abroad under the China Ocan shipping(Gronp)company.

中国统计出版社最新图书简目

(仅供参考，以最后出书为准)

统计资料

综合类：中国统计年鉴　中国统计摘要　中国发展报告

国际资料类：国际统计年鉴　金砖国家联合统计手册　世界能源资源年鉴

区域资料类：中国区域经济统计年鉴　中国县域统计年鉴　中国城市统计年鉴

中国农村统计年鉴　中国地区经济监测报告

经贸与投资类：中国贸易外经统计年鉴　中国对外直接投资统计公报　中国商品交易市场统计年鉴

大中型批发零售和住宿餐饮企业统计年鉴　中国零售和餐饮连锁企业统计年鉴

住户与物价类：中国住户调查年鉴　中国价格统计年鉴　中国农产品价格调查年鉴

全国农产品成本收益资料汇编

资源与环境类：中国环境统计年鉴　中国能源统计年鉴

产业类：中国工业统计年鉴　中国建筑业统计年鉴　中国房地产统计年鉴

中国第三产业统计年鉴　中国证券期货统计年鉴

科技类：中国科技统计年鉴　中国高技术产业统计年鉴　工业企业科技活动资料

人口与就业类：中国劳动统计年鉴　中国人口和就业统计年鉴　中国人才资源统计报告

社会与文化类：中国社会统计年鉴　中国文化及相关产业统计年鉴

公共管理类：中国民政统计年鉴　中国民族统计年鉴　中国乡镇街道行政区域简册

省级综合统计年鉴系列

北京 天津 河北 山西 内蒙古　辽宁 吉林 黑龙江 上海 江苏　浙江 安徽 福建 江西 山东

河南 湖北 湖南 广东 广西 海南　重庆 四川 贵州 云南 西藏 陕西　甘肃 青海 宁夏 新疆

新疆生产建设兵团

市(县)级综合统计年鉴系列

天津滨海新区 石家庄 唐山 邯郸　太原 大同 阳泉 长治 晋城 朔州　晋中 运城 忻州 临汾 呼和浩特

鄂尔多斯 包头 沈阳 大连 长春　吉林市 四平 哈尔滨 黑龙江垦区　上海浦东新区 南京 无锡 徐州

常州 苏州 南通 连云港 淮安 盐城　扬州 镇江 泰州 宿迁 江阴 丹阳　杭州 宁波 温州 嘉兴 绍兴 金华

衢州 舟山 台州 丽水 合肥 福州　厦门 宁德 福州经济技术开发区　南昌 济南 青岛 郑州 洛阳 平顶山

三门峡 南阳 武汉 十堰 荆州 宜昌　荆门 咸宁 长沙 广州 深圳 惠州　东莞 南宁 柳州 桂林 来宾 海口

三亚 成都 贵阳 昆明 西安 兰州　庆阳 银川 乌鲁木齐 兵团一师　兵团十师

调查年鉴系列

山西 内蒙古 吉林 辽宁 上海　福建 湖北 广西 重庆 四川 云南　甘肃 宁夏 新疆 南宁 桂林

“十二五”规划教材

统计学（经济管理类专业本科适用，单薇 等）　抽样调查理论与方法（冯士雍 等）

贝叶斯统计（茆诗松 等）　统计学（黄良文 等）　试验设计（茆诗松 等）

统计学：从数据到结论（吴喜之）　医学统计学（于浩）　统计学（经济、管理类专业基础教材，张小斐）

概率论与数理统计三十三讲（魏振军）　概率论与数理统计三十三：学习指导与习题解答（魏振军）

非参数统计（吴喜之 等）　统计学：经济与管理中的数据分析（李慧云 等）

卫生管理统计学（新编医学院校基础课教材，尚磊）医院统计学（新编医学院校基础课教材，徐天和 等）

社会统计学（蒋萍 等）　现代金融投资统计分析（李腊生 等）

国民经济核算初级教程（经济类、统计类、管理类专业适用，蒋萍 等）

重点图书

新中国65年　新编英汉汉英统计大词典　中华医学统计百科全书

挑大学选专业2014—考研择校指南　挑大学选专业2014—高考志愿填报指南